# Chasing the Hunter's Dream

# Chasing the

1,001 of the World's Best

Duck Marshes, Deer Runs,

Elk Meadows, Pheasant Fields,

Bear Woods, Safaris,

and Extraordinary Hunts

# Hunter's Dream

JEFFREY ENGEL, SHEROL ENGEL, AND
JAMES A. SWAN, PH.D.

An Imprint of HarperCollinsPublishers

HarperCollins books may be purchased for educational, business, or sales promotional use. For information, please write: Special Markets Department, HarperCollins Publishers, 10 East 53rd Street, New York, NY 10022.

FIRST EDITION

*Designed by Ellen Cipriano*

All photos courtesy of the authors except photos on page 217 courtesy of Bruce Matthews; photo on page 218 courtesy of Tony Wasley; photos on page 331 courtesy of Jocelyn Landry; photos on page 332 and bottom of 334 courtesy of Richard Lavoie; photos on page 333 and top of 334 © Valerie Martel 2006; photos on top of page 365 courtesy of Pamela M. Keagy; photos on pages 411 and 413 courtesy of Stephen Bodio.

Library of Congress Cataloging-in-Publication Data is available upon request.

ISBN: 978-0-06-134382-7

07 08 09 10 11 WBS/RRD 10 9 8 7 6 5 4 3 2 1

*This book is dedicated to Herb Engel, woodsman extraordinaire, and all of the fathers and mothers, husbands and wives, aunts and uncles, mentors and friends who unselfishly share their woodsmanship skills, love, respect, enjoyment, and appreciation for nature and pass along outdoor ethics, especially that it is far more important to have a quality outdoor experience than to fill your game bag.*

# Acknowledgments

*This book has been a team effort among the authors. In addition, many, many people from all over the world helped us. Here we can only name a few, but to all we hope that the spirit of the hunt is good to you.*

*Craig Wiley, our agent, made the connection with our editor Matthew Benjamin, which made this book possible. Both have been outstanding to work with.*

*Ken Schwartz at Safari Club International put us in touch with individuals worldwide. Gary Mauser provided hard-to-find statistics on Canada, and Shirley MacInnis helped us find quality Canadian outfitters.*

*Special thanks go to Andrew Swan, who kept the computer running and its operator functioning as we processed huge volumes of data from across the globe.*

# Contents

# List of Acronyms

| | | | |
|---|---|---|---|
| ANILCA | Alaska National Interest Land Conservation Act | DI | Drummond Island |
| ANWR | Arctic National Wildlife Refuge | DNR | Department of Natural Resources |
| BATF | Bureau of Alcohol, Tobacco, and Firearms | DOW | Division of Wildlife |
| | | DWR | Division of Wildlife Resources |
| BLM | Bureau of Land Management | FACE | Federation Association de Chasseurs de Europe |
| CCOC | Central Carolina Outdoor Club | FWC | Fish and Wildlife Conservation |
| CDC | Centers for Disease Control | GOABC | Guide Outfitters Association of British Columbia |
| CIC | International Council for Game and Wildlife Conservation | GPS | Global Positioning System |
| CITES | Convention on International Trade in Endangered Species | HIP | Harvest Information Program |
| COAGS | Colorado Outdoor Adventure Guide School | HMA | Hunter Management Area |
| | | HMO | health maintenance organization |
| COHA | California Outdoor Heritage Alliance | IUCN | International Union for Conservation of Nature and Natural Resources |
| CPNM | Carrizo Plain National Monument | | |
| CRP | Conservation Reserve Program | IWMC | World Conservation Trust |
| | | LBL | Land between the Lakes |
| CWD | chronic wasting disease | LP | Lower Peninsula |
| DFG | Department of Fish and Game | MNHA | Meade Natural Heritage Association |

| | | | |
|---|---|---|---|
| MSL | mean sea level | SNRA | Sawtooth National Recreation Area |
| NBOA | New Brunswick Outfitter Association | STC | Sportsmen's Team Challenge |
| NCA | National Conservation Area | TFC | Tiger Friendly Certified |
| NDOW | Nevada Department of Wildlife | TIPs | Turn in Poachers |
| | | TSEs | transmissible spongiform encephalopathies |
| NOLS | National Outdoor Leadership School | TVA | Tennessee Valley Authority |
| NOTO | Northern Ontario Tourist Outfitters Association | UMAS | Units of Management and Sustainable Use of Wildlife |
| NPS | National Park Service | UNESCO | United Nations Educational, Scientific and Cultural Organization |
| NRA | National Rifle Association | | |
| NSCA | National Sporting Clays Association | | |
| | | UP | Upper Peninsula |
| NWTF | National Wild Turkey Federation | USDA | U.S. Department of Agriculture |
| NWR | National Wildlife Refuge | USFS | U.S. Forest Service; USDA Forest Service |
| OFAH | Ontario Federation of Hunters and Anglers | | |
| | | USFWS | U.S. Fish and Wildlife Service |
| OHEP | Ontario Hunter Education Program | USGS | U.S. Geological Survey |
| | | VAT | value-added tax |
| OSHC SA | One Shot Hunt Club South Africa | WCS | Wildlife Conservation Society |
| PH | Professional Hunter | WMA | Wildlife Management Area |
| PTDC | Pakistan Tourist Development Corporation | WMU | Wildlife Management Unit |
| | | WPA | Waterfowl Production Area |
| SCI | Safari Club International | WWF | World Wildlife Fund |

# Memories and Dreams

So, you want to go hunting?

In one language or another, people have been asking that question for millions of years, and it still sends a shot of adrenaline and gets the heart pumping a little faster as you think about going out into the woods and tracking wild game just as your ancestors did all the way back to the Paleolithic age. Lining up the crosshairs in your scope on the kill zone of that big buck you have tracked for hours is a modern version of something very old and deep in the human soul.

If you are a hunter—or want to become one—know that you are not alone. There are at least 37 million people worldwide who enjoy sport hunting, about half of whom live in the United States. See Appendix 1: Hunters and Shooters of the World.

This book is for modern hunters, and those others who may wish to join them in enjoying the passion and pleasure of hunting.

The three of us, collectively, have hunted for over 100 years. This project began with our recounting to each other our own memorable hunts and favorite hunting places, then sharing them via the *Engel's Outdoor Experience* television series, where Jeff and Sherol host the show, and James is the writer. We've even won some awards along the way for telling those stories that we're pretty proud of.

As a result of our hunting experiences and the experiences of producing a television series about hunting for half a dozen years, we decided that we wanted to pool our knowledge and create a book that would enable others to learn from our experience.

There are lots of books and magazines out on techniques and gear for hunting game animals. Yes, we could write another one of those, but frankly what seemed more in keeping with the show and our love for wild game hunting was to focus on hunting destinations. Despite the abundance of most game species, and the wealth of equipment available to the modern hunter, if you haven't got a place to hunt, then the spirit of the hunt will wane, dilute the great conservation efforts that are under way, and dim the future of this noble pursuit. If this happens, man and nature will both suffer.

In our research, we could not find any book that seemed to cover the entire range of hunting destinations, from no-cost to swank resorts in North America and around the world. So that became our target.

We began by compiling a list of the places that we have hunted—good, bad, and ugly. As we began telling our fellow hunters about what we were doing, they in turn began to swap tales and places with us. Hunters must have a storytelling gene in them, because, boy, did this snowball.

Thanks to Safari Club International, who helped get the word out, we soon found our circle of hunters growing to reach all around the world. We then sifted through the mountain of places and came up with the best hunting destinations in the world. For each state and Canadian province, we provide the basics on how to get licenses, what's there to hunt, how to report poachers, and where to go to have the greatest chance of having a quality experience. You'll find comprehensive lists and descriptions of no- or low-cost federal lands that offer hunting—National Forests, National Wildlife Refuges, Bureau of Land Management Areas, U.S. Army Corps of Engineers Flood Control Projects, national seashores, a national park or two, and Bureau of Reclamation Lands.

As we write this book, there are bills in Washington to create "No Net Loss" of hunting lands on federal lands—meaning, if you lose one acre to development of some kind, then in some other place the government must add an acre of hunting land. That's a bull's-eye idea. Support it at the federal and state levels.*

You will also find state Wildlife Management Areas and how to research and locate them, as well as information about each state's unique hunting opportunities. Some states have done an outstanding job of presenting their hunting lands in print and on the Web. Others, well, they seem to have become bogged down in complex regulations and bureaucracy. Hopefully this book will help shed light on all the hunting opportunities that are out there for little or no cost, and there are lots of them.

You will also find lists of private hunting lands ranging from mom-and-pop farms offering bird hunting to some selected guides, outfitters, and hunting locations that are plush and expensive. Regardless of their price tag, we have sought to find those private lands and services that offer quality, ethical hunting.

Every hunter has his or her favorite places to hunt, and part of the hunting ethic is to share your favorite places to hunt. But there is a caveat here: We share our favorite places and those of others with the request that you respect each place as if you were its caretaker. Follow all laws and ethics as you taste its spirit. Heed its natural limits as well as feasting on its abundance. Leave it cleaner than you found it. Treat each place with care so that others who come after us will be able to experience it

---

*No-Net-Loss laws have been passed in Arkansas, Florida, Louisiana, Maryland, Mississippi, West Virginia, and Georgia. Federal legislation has not been passed as of April 2007.

and know in their bones why we came to treat these places as special. If possible, help conservation efforts to preserve and enhance these places and the wildlife on them.

In Section A, we will offer suggestions on gear preparation, choosing your guide and outfitter, and being an ethical hunter. These tips should prepare you for a hunting adventure anywhere in North America.

Section B, the most comprehensive portion of the book, focuses on places close to home that should be relatively easy and inexpensive to get to and gives a real flavor of what is around us to hunt. In the section on "Nebraska," you'll read Joe Arterburn's tale about farmland that has been in his family for five generations, yielding its annual gifts of pheasant and deer. Other folks may have special duck blinds or deer stands on public land. You may find as you read through the many stories to come that some will ring especially true for you. We hope so. Harmony between people and nature is what hunting is all about. Joe's article speaks from the heart about reverence for a good hunting place.

At the beginning of the listing for each state, we have added statistics from the U.S. Fish and Wildlife Service about numbers of hunters in a state, whether they are resident or nonresident, what they hunt, whether they hunt on private or public lands, and their impact on the economy. These numbers should give you a feeling for crowding, popularity of hunting in general and what species live in that state, and just how important hunting is to the economy of that state. Collectively, hunters pump more than $21 billion into the nation's economy. That's something to be proud of, as well as a sign of how much money

from the Pittman-Robertson Excise taxes on hunting equipment is going into wildlife management in that state.

In Section C of the book, we focus on hunting destinations more far afield that require more time, travel, and expense. We call these "dream hunts." Around the world there are many places where the spirit of the hunt is especially strong: the Okavango Delta in Botswana and teeming herds of game; the Ardennes Forest in Belgium and its magical stag and roe deer; Katy's Prairie, Texas, where swarms of snow geese descend like a snowstorm from the clouds; a rice field blind in the Sacramento Valley of California with a huge, swirling vortex of ducks and geese approaching; and Kodiak Island, Alaska, where you hunt side by side with huge brown bears, wondering who is hunting whom and who has the right to claim that big blacktail buck you just shot.

Thanks to modern travel, distant places in North America and beyond, such as Africa, Siberia, Mongolia, South America, Iceland, China, and New Zealand, are cheaper and more easily accessed than ever before. We want to help you realize your dreams.

Hunting in distant lands involves more research and planning, and so we have assembled an anthology of stories from hunters who have ventured abroad on dream hunts to tell us what they were like and to recommend whom to hunt with and why. A satisfied customer is the best advertisement of all. Note that a number of these stories mention humanitarian and conservation efforts combined with hunting. Hunting is a teacher of compassion for man and nature. We want to encourage that ethic.

Some of our suggested destinations are not places to hunt. Hunting also has cultural and historical contexts, which is crucial to maintaining respect and understanding for hunting. Some exceptional heritage destinations allow you to walk in the footsteps of great hunters of the past—Ernest Hemingway, Robert Ruark, Nash Buckingham. Other heritage places are quiet places associated with notable figures in history—Henry Thoreau's cabin at Walden Pond, Teddy Roosevelt's Elkhorn Ranch, or the "shack" where Aldo Leopold wrote his epic *A Sand County Almanac*. Still other heritage sites are museums, businesses, and festivals that celebrate particular wildlife species and hunting seasons. We've also tossed in a few spots that are favorite hunters' hangouts—special hotels, camps, and bars. They are an important part of the heritage, too.

In Section D, we offer some wild game recipes—favorite recipes from family and friends, and others from some of the finest wild game chefs in the world. Chefs swear some of these delicacies have almost magical powers over diners.

Section E gives you expert guidance on bringing your trophy back home for the taxidermist to mount. The farther you travel, the more planning is required to ensure that your mounts can be tastefully crafted into dramatic art that will make memories come alive for generations.

As you read through the following pages, note which places seem to stir you most. We all need dreams. As Mick Jagger and the Rolling Stones sing: If you lose your dreams, you lose your mind.

While this book is about and for the modern hunter, it is ultimately about natural magic because extraordinary hunting places breed memories and dreams. Those memories and dreams are the foundation of the conservation ethic and what keeps the flame in the human soul burning.

# Getting Prepared

## CHECKLIST: PREPARING FOR A GREAT HUNT

Whether you are going for a weekend hunt just a couple of hours away, for a week in the Rockies, for a trek above the Arctic Circle, or on safari to Africa or Mongolia, being prepared is always better than being sorry that you weren't prepared. The following packing list was developed for our television show *Engel's Outdoor Experience*. You don't want to make mistakes and forget something. Sure, you don't need to take it all, but use this guide to create your own checklist.

### *Engel's Outdoor Experience Packing List*

aerial photos
air freshener—
 for bathroom use
airplane tickets
ammo
axe
backpack
back tag holder
balaclava cap
 (camouflage)
ballpoint and felt-tip
 pens
bandanna
bathroom container
beer/soda
belt shell carrier
belt shell holder
binoculars (compact)
binoculars (regular)
black electrical tape
boat
boot blankets
boot dryer
boot oil/rag
boots (felt-lined)
bota water bottle
business cards
camera
camera (compact)
camouflage face
 mask
camp slippers
car-top carrier (truck)
cash
chewing gum
cigars
collapsible dome
 blind(s)
collapsible front
 "stake" blind
compact belt pliers
 (sheath)
compass (2)
coolers (various sizes)
copies of passport,
 driver's license, credit
 cards on one 8×10
 page—leave at
 home with someone
 you can call if
 needed
credit card phone
 numbers
deck shoes
decoys
deer scent
digital alarm clock
dog first-aid kit
drinking cup
 (personal)
duck stamps
earplugs (antisnoring)
electrical converter kit
electric boot dryer
electric hair dryer
emergency survival kit
extra keys for any
 vehicle

extra liners
(for any vehicles
or boats)
extra plastic bags
extra turkey calls
eyeglass screws
fanny packs (various
sizes)
filet knife
film
first-aid kit
fishing gear
fishing license
fishing regulations
flashlight (mini)
flashlight (regular)
fleece jacket
fleece neck warmer
(gaiter)
fleece vest
floppy rain hat
folding chairs
folding hunting
knife (sheath)
folding table
fold-up saw
foot powder
gaiters (leggings)
gas charcoal grill
gloves (Gore-Tex)
gloves (thin)
Gore-Tex rain suit
Gore-Tex sox
GPS/instruction
book
granola bars
gun-cleaning kit
gun-oil rag
hand cream

handgun and
shotgun
handgun shoulder
holster
hard and soft gun
case
headphones
health insurance and
ID card
heater/fuel—for blind
hip boots/chest
waders
house keys
hunting license
hunting regulations
ice scraper
insect repellent
insoles
iPod
jogging suit (lounge
wear)
jumper cables
knee braces
knife-sharpening
tool
landowner gift
lantern/fuel
large water container
laser range finder
laundry bag
leather hiking boots
locks for hard-shell
gun case
maps
matches/butane
lighters
meat saw
medications
mesh bug suit

metal detector
moleskin/feet
money pouch/
money belt
nail scissors/clippers
open-toe sandals
orange clothing
orange cloth tape
orange trail tape
other stamps
paper towels
passport
pepper spray
personal protection
handgun
photo album
photo copy of
passport
pieces of hose (for
antler tips)
pillow
pocket water
container
portable CB radios
portable grill/stove
portable table
pull house electrical
plugs
radar cap
radio
reading material
regular water bottle
rifle and extra rifle
rifle sling
rope
rubber floor mats
rubber scope cover
(rifle)
safety belt

sausage
seal-skin gloves
seat cushion
shampoo and soap
shovel (long handle)
shovel (small folding
type)
sleeping bag
(compact)
sleeping bag (full size)
sleeping cot
small duffel bag (in
truck bag)
snake-bite kit
snake-proof boots
snow camouflage
snowshoes
sox/hand warmers
sox/pocket on top
space blanket
(compact)
space blanket
(full size)
spare eyeglasses (2)
spotlight
spotting scope
stocking hat
straps/rope for car-top
rack
sunglasses
swimsuit
tape measure
tarp for back of truck
tennis shoes
tent
Therm-a-Rest air
mattress
thermometer
toilet paper

tow rope

towels and wash cloths

traveler's checks

tree stand/lock-key/ cable

tree steps

tripod

truck hitch box

truck hitch deer rack/ rope

turn down furnace/air conditioner (home)

turn off home ice machine

turtleneck sweater

tweezers

varmint call (mouth)

video camera/ accessories

vitamins

wallet and personal checks

warm coat and vest

warm neck scarf

watch/extra watch

water cups

waterproof gun case

water purifier

weather band radio

weight scale

wind gauge/ thermometer

window mount/ tripod

wipe and dry towelettes

wool jacket

wool shirt and pants

writing paper

X-large plastic bags to cover duffel bag

## GAME CARE SUGGESTION

If you are going after big game, plan ahead of time what you will do with the meat, head, skin, and so on. An excellent book on meat handling is *Making the Most of Your Deer* by Dennis Walrod (Stackpole Books, revised and updated 2004 edition).

## MAPS

Custom maps of Wildlife Management Units (WMUs) for Arizona, Idaho, Montana, New Mexico, Oregon, Utah, Washington, and Wyoming are provided by www.mytopo.com. Colorado hunt maps are available through www.huntdata.com. Other good sources of online mapping are http://earth.google.com and www.maptech.com.

## CHOOSING YOUR GUIDE AND OUTFITTER

You'd think that we'd always get the red-carpet treatment when invited to hunt with a guide or outfitter. Hah! Outfitters and guides can make or break your hunt, and we've met some of both.

As I climbed on the horse in the early morning darkness, I told one guide/outfitter that I was a novice riding horses. He chuckled, and in total darkness we climbed half a mile in darkness on loose rocks, horses sliding on almost every step. Scared the hell out of me. I'll never go back there.

On another hunt, I arrowed a fat eight-point whitetail buck. I was ecstatic. It was the biggest buck I've ever taken with a bow. The guide/outfitter was furious. He said that I should have waited and shot a bigger one for the record books, so he could use me for publicity.

I once hit a wild pig with an arrow on a guided hunt. The pig raced into a thicket and was crashing around. The guide told me to stay back, as he would dispatch the wounded pig with his rifle. The pig emerges from the thicket and stands still, 15 yards from the guide. The guide shoots twice and totally misses the pig.

Then there was the time when in the early morning darkness a turkey guide told me to sit down under a tree while he put out the decoy. The tree turned out to be an Osage orange. Ouch!!!

We could go on.

Not all of our experiences with hunting

guides have been bad, to be sure, but there have been enough nightmares that forever make us wary of whom we agree to go out with.

In most states and Canadian provinces, it is illegal to ask for compensation as a guide if you are not licensed. And it's not inappropriate for you to ask a guide to see his or her guiding license. In some states—for example, Montana—if you go out with a nonlicensed guide and pay him or her, you can be fined as well as the guide.

Wildlife laws have become very cumbersome in some places. It's your guide's responsibility to give you a safe, legal, and enjoyable outing.

Guides need to know a lot about wildlife and hunting. Most states require that guides have first-aid training. If they don't have it, they should not be guiding.

Colorado will not let guides carry weapons or shoot game when they are guiding. This prevents the guide from shooting something for you. But what happens if a bear or a mountain lion decides that you are in its way? Ask ahead of time for local laws about guides backing up a hunter.

In Colorado it's also not legal for guides to guarantee their clients a successful hunt. Check that one out before you commit to a hunt.

In some states and Canadian provinces, to be a guide all you have to be is either 18 or 19 years of age and have no recent fish and game violations; in addition, guides pay an annual fee of $150 to $200. Research on background and qualifications can be worth its weight in gold.

Some places also require a sponsor master guide/outfitter to get started. Even better, there are some outstanding programs seeking to upgrade the standards for guides. According to Dale Drown, general manager of the Guide Outfitters Association of British Columbia (GOABC; www.goabc.org), anyone 19 or older and sponsored by a guide/outfitter can become an "assistant guide," but if you want to be a guide/outfitter in British Columbia, what is called a "master guide" in Alaska, you must also pass an examination (with at least an 80% grade) and have two years' experience as an assistant guide, mostly in British Columbia. That's more like it.

With more big game huntable species than anyplace else in North America, British Columbia has 1,000 licensed assistant guides and 235 licensed guide/outfitters.

GOABC has created its own school to upgrade guides. The GOABC Guide School is a 30-day program. A $500 fee covers all expenses. Each class has a maximum size of 12, one-half of whom are Aboriginals (Indians, Inuit, or Metis). Almost everyone who takes the class and passes is employed, Dale says. An assistant guide can make $125 to $200 a day, plus tips.

In Alaska, to hunt brown bear, Dall sheep, or mountain goat, nonresidents must be accompanied in the field by a licensed Alaska big game registered guide/outfitter or by an Alaska resident 19 years or older.

To become a Class A assistant Alaskan guide, you must have hunted in Alaska for the last three years, pay a fee for a license, and be sponsored by a guide/outfitter.

To become an Alaska guide/outfitter, you must have been an assistant guide for three years; legally hunted big game for at least five years; present letters of recommendation from eight big game hunters, at least two for each year of work as an assistant; and pass an examination.

For each state, Canadian province, or country, we have tried to provide contact information for the professional guides and outfitters associations for that region. Checking in with them is always a good way to start your search or assess a guide/outfitter you may be considering.

There are well-established outdoor skills education programs—such as Outward Bound and the National Outdoor Leadership School (NOLS)—that offer classes on wilderness skills and becoming wilderness skills instructors, but these programs do not cover hunting.

In contrast is the Colorado Outdoor Adventure Guide School (COAGS; www.guideschool.com) in Colorado Springs. Licensed by the Colorado Department of Higher Education and the Division of Private Occupational Schools, COAGS programs are also approved by the Veterans Administration (VA), and over 20 colleges and universities offer college credits to COAGS graduates.

In business since 1993, COAGS began as a western big game guide training school, then expanded into fishing and wilderness recreation. Recently COAGS launched the nation's first and only whitetail deer hunting guide training program.

COAGS classes are held in Colorado and Texas (whitetails) and run about two weeks. They cover horsemanship, orienteering, compass and Global Positioning System (GPS), survival and camp cooking, CPR, and photography, as well as big game hunting and fishing. Classes are held in the field and classroom and are open to both aspiring guides and any individuals who want to improve their backcountry skills.

It would be nice if training such as GOABC and COAGS were required for all guides. It would upgrade hunting and increase your chances of having a great time.

One good question to ask a prospective outfitter is: Are you a member of the American Association of International Professional Hunting and Fishing Consultants? Most of the outfitters listed in this book are members.

Another way to check on a guide/outfitter ahead of time is through Safari Club International (SCI), which offers a Hunt Report system for its members at www.safariclub.org/static/index.cfm?contentID=144. By contacting the Trophy Records Department at SCI, it allows you to file hunt reports and check previous reports on guides and outfitters before booking a hunt.

## SLIPS: A GUIDE TO BEING A SAFE AND ETHICAL HUNTER

A ruffed grouse explodes from a blackberry thicket and weaves through a stand of aspens and spruce trees. An eight-point buck suddenly pops into a clearing and comes to a dead stop for an instant. A woodcock rockets up through a tangled grove of willows.

Often there may be just a small window of time and space when that shot can be taken. The decision window may be short, but before a shot is fired, there is a checklist of decisions that a responsible hunter must mentally review before pulling the trigger.

Raise your trigger-finger hand. Each finger on that hand represents one of the progressive decisions that a responsible hunter must make before taking a shot.

The first finger (let's start with the thumb) stands for the letter S and the question: **Is it safe?** You always need to be aware of the ultimate trajectory of the shot in your line of fire, whether from a rifle, a shotgun, or a bow. If you can't be sure that if you miss, the shot will fall harmlessly to the land, then that shot should never be taken. Regardless of anything else, always, safety first.

The second finger, the trigger finger, stands for the letter L and reminds you of the basic question: **Is it legal?** Is your target in season? Are the species and sex legal? Does killing that animal represent breaking any laws? To answer this question, you must have studied the laws thoroughly, which is not an easy task in some states. Nonetheless, it is the responsibility of a hunter to be law-abiding.

The third finger stands for the letter I: **Does taking that shot represent a positive image of hunting?** The future of hunting, more than ever before, depends on how the nonhunting public in general sees hunters. If you have a safe shot at a legal buck at a reasonable distance, but you are being observed by a group of wildlife watchers or children, maybe you should pass it up and hunt someplace else. The point here is that most people today don't have firsthand experience with hunting. If you bag the duck or deer cleanly, that's one thing; but suppose you just wound it. Now, suddenly, you have a whole audience watch as you chase a wounded animal. Hunting is not a spectator sport unless you are hunting for a show on television. People may get the wrong idea. This is one reason

that hunting seasons should never be held at the height of tourist season.

The fourth finger stands for the letter P: **Is it practical?** You may be able to hit that bighorn sheep standing 300 yards away on the edge of a cliff, but if you do, will it drop over the edge of the cliff and into a valley where you can't retrieve it? The same is true for waterfowl. If you don't have a dog, sometimes the responsible thing to do is not to shoot a duck that will fall into heavy cover where you may not be able to find it or deep water where you cannot retrieve it.

And the fifth finger stands for the letter S: **Is it sporting?** The rules of Fair Chase were established to ensure that game have a fair chance of escaping. This is often more a matter of personal ethics than law. Shooting a duck in the water may not be sportsmanlike to some, while others assert that it does not damage the breast and it is more sporting to stalk to get into range than shoot on the wing. The same is true for shooting a turkey in the roost. Some believe turkeys should all have to be called in before shooting; others maintain it is harder to stalk close enough for a shot. In both cases, the birds are sitting still, so what's the difference? The rules of Fair Chase vary somewhat, but it is never sporting to shoot big game swimming or from an airplane. And it is not legal or Fair Chase to drive animals with airplanes. Shooting any animal that is penned is a "canned" hunt, which is unethical, and often illegal, unless this is a farmer killing an animal for market.

Ethical choices aside, if the bird or animal is hit, the shot should be lethal. Remember the hunter's prayer: "God, if I shoot, let me kill quick, clean and humanely, or miss clearly."

We don't want any slips in the field, so

remember your hunting ethics on your SLIPS hand, and you will be a model for others.

Your hand is also an invaluable guide in judging distances in the field. With your arm outstretched, hold your thumb up. At 50 yards, which is about the maximum distance you should be shooting at a game bird with a shotgun, a six-foot-tall man is about the height of your thumb. When you get to a duck blind, use your thumb to determine what is 50 yards away and refuse to shoot at anything beyond that distance.

Crowding and being cut off by other hunters are two of the most common complaints of hunters in public hunting areas. You can't take a tape measure with you into the field, but you can take your hand. Continue holding that thumb up. At 100 yards away, a six-foot-tall man will be about the height of the thumbnail. That's way too far to shoot at a bird with a lethal shot, but it's also way too close to fire in that direction: a shotgun with birdshot can carry well over 200 yards; a 12-gauge shotgun with #8 shot will carry just over 700 feet; a shell with #4 shot will carry about 900 feet—300 yards.

At the bottom of the thumbnail there is a white half crescent. When you can hold your thumb up and sight it toward a person and their height is no taller than that white crescent, that person is now out of range—about 300 yards. This distance not only helps determine your zone of fire, but it should also help determine the minimum distance you should be from setting up next to another hunter in a marsh. Admittedly, five times that distance farther away is better, but the reality of hunting in many public areas is that you will not be that distant from the next hunter.

## SO, WHAT'S THERE TO HUNT?
## LIST OF GAME SPECIES OF THE WORLD

**Somewhere, someplace, each of these species is legal game.**

| | | |
|---|---|---|
| addax | badger | bighorn sheep |
| alligator | Baikal teal | bison |
| Andean deer | band-tailed pigeon | black bear |
| aoudad sheep | banteng | black-bellied plover |
| argali | barnacle goose | black-bellied tree duck |
| armadillo | bean goose | black cock |
| axis deer | beaver | black duck |

*Continued*

| | | |
|---|---|---|
| black-headed duck | coot | gerenuk |
| blacktail deer | cottontail rabbit | godwit |
| blesbok | coturnix quail | goldeneye |
| blue grouse | coues deer | golden takin |
| blue-winged teal | cougar | gray fox |
| bobcat | coyote | gray squirrel |
| bobwhite quail | crocodile | green-winged teal |
| bontebok | crow | greylag goose |
| brant | Dall sheep | grizzly bear |
| brocket deer | dama gazelle | groundhog |
| brown bear | dik-dik | guanaco |
| bufflehead | duiker | guinea fowl |
| bushbuck | Egyptian goose | harlequin duck |
| bustard | eider | harlequin quail |
| button quail | eland | hartebeest |
| California quail | elephant | Himalayan snowcock |
| Canada goose | emperor goose | hippopotamus |
| canvasback | Eurasian dove | hog deer |
| cape buffalo | fallow deer | Hungarian partridge |
| capercaillie | fox squirrel | ibex |
| caribou | francolin | impala |
| chachalaca | fulvous whistling duck | jackrabbit |
| chamois | gadwall | jaguar |
| Chilean quail | gallinule | kangaroo |
| chital | Gambel's quail | klipspringer |
| chukar partridge | garganey duck | kudu |
| cinnamon teal | gazelle | laughing dove |
| clapper rail | gemsbok | leopard |

*Continued*

| | | |
|---|---|---|
| lion | perdiz | sable |
| Magellan goose | Pere David's deer | sable antelope |
| mallard | pheasant | sage grouse |
| maral deer | pochard | sambar deer |
| Marco Polo sheep | polar bear | sand grouse |
| marmot | prairie chicken | sandhill crane |
| masked quail | pronghorn antelope | scaled quail |
| merganser | ptarmigan | scaup |
| Mexican tree duck | pudu | scimitar-horned oryx |
| Montezuma quail | raccoon | scoter |
| moose | rail | sharp-tailed grouse |
| mouflon | red fox | shoveler |
| mountain goat | red grouse | Siberian ibex |
| mountain quail | redhead | sika deer |
| mourning dove | red lechwe | sitatunga |
| mule deer | red-legged partridge | snipe |
| muntjac deer | reindeer | snow goose |
| musk deer | rhinoceros | snowshoe hare |
| musk ox | ring-necked duck | sora rail |
| muskrat | roan | Spanish partridge |
| Nepal blue sheep | Robinson Crusoe goat | springbok |
| nilgai | rock pigeon | spruce grouse |
| nutria | Rocky Mountain elk | spur-winged goose |
| nyala | roebuck | stag |
| old squaw | Roosevelt elk | steenbok |
| opossum | Ross's goose | stone sheep |
| oryx | ruddy duck | suni |
| peccary | ruffed grouse | swan |

*Continued*

| | | |
|---|---|---|
| tahr | white-fronted goose | wolf |
| tsessebe | whitetail deer | woodcock |
| tule elk | white-winged dove | wood duck |
| Virginia rail | wigeon | wood pigeon |
| walrus | wild boar | yellow-billed pintail |
| warthog | wildebeest | zebra |
| waterbuck | wild turkey | |
| water buffalo | wisent | |

**So, go get 'em!**

# North America

# New England

## CONNECTICUT

*In 2001 there were 35,000 resident hunters and 10,000 nonresident hunters: 73% went big game hunting, 49% small game, 29% waterfowl; 49% hunted on public lands; 81% hunted on private lands. Hunters pumped $43 million into the state economy. (USFWS)*

### OVERVIEW

Between 1700 and 1900, whitetail deer were scarce in Connecticut, owing to overhunting, especially market hunting. Since the implementation of seasons and the development of many areas into suburban communities, the deer population has exploded, resulting in problems associated with car-deer collisions, damage to vegetation in farmlands and around homes, and the spread of Lyme disease, which is carried by deer ticks and named for Lyme, Connecticut, where it was first identified. Today Connecticut uses hunting as a deer population control method in some commu-

**CONNECTICUT SNAPSHOT**
**CONSTITUTION STATE**

- **General information about hunting in Connecticut:** http://dep.state.ct.us/burnatr/wildlife/fguide/fgindex.htm

- **Online licensing information:** www.depdata.ct.gov/permit/alphadep.asp?g=8

- **Deer population:** 75,771, 33rd in the United States

- **Average deer harvest:** 12,703, 40th in the United States

nities and state parks, as well as on larger wild lands.

### DESTINATIONS

An excellent list of public and private places to hunt pheasants and other big and small game in Connecticut can be found at http://dep.state.ct.us/burnatr/wildlife/fguide/phshunt.asp. Note that many places require special permits.

#### U.S. Army Corps of Engineers

The U.S. Army Corps of Engineers, New England District, manages six small reservoirs in the state that offer hunting according to state regulations and local posting: Black Rock Lake, Colebrook River Lake, Hancock Brook Lake, Mansfield Hollow Lake, Thomaston Dam, and West Thompson Lake. For details, see the state hunting guide at www.ct.gov/dep/cwp/view.asp?a=2700&q=323414&depNav_GID=1633 or the U.S. Army Corps New England District headquarters. Web site at www.nae.usace.army.mil.

*Private Hunting Clubs and Preserves*

### HARWINTON ROD & GUN, INC.
Harwinton, CT 06791-0181
Phone: 860-485-9993
www.harwintonrodandgun.com

Inexpensive membership club offering released pheasant hunting on hundreds of acres of both privately owned and leased lands, as well as hunting for a variety of small and large game including deer and wild turkey on designated club properties. Trapshooting, dog training, indoor and outdoor archery range, pistol and rifle range, plus rainbow, brook, and brown trout fishing on a two-and-one-half-acre pond. Numerous activities held during the year.

### MARKOVER HUNTING PRESERVE
Danielson, CT 06239
Phone: 860-774-4116
www.markover.com

A 300-acre private hunting preserve located in the rolling hills of northeastern Connecticut offering hunts for pheasants, chukar, and Hungarian partridge. Not a membership club. Only reservations are required. Hunting licenses are not needed. Open seven days a week, September 15–March 31. You may bring your own dog or hunt with one from Markover. No charge for using the Markover dogs when you use a guide. Six-bird maximum per gun. The lodge sleeps 10.

### MILLSTREAM PRESERVE LLC
Marlborough, CT 06447
Phone: 860-295-9974;
mobile: 860-836-5744;
fax: 860-295-0417
www.millstreampreserve.com

Pheasant, quail, Hungarian partridge, and chukar on 2,000 acres of leased farmland. Millstream also offers a 10-station tower facility for a European shoot that closely replicates a traditional English driven pheasant shoot. Also offers released flighted ducks over a 15-acre pond from September 15 to March 31. No license required.

Also offers whitetail deer, duck, turkey, goose, and coyote hunts, as well as bass and fly-fishing only for trout. Year-round dog training and a 3-D archery range.

*Migratory Waterfowl*
Waterfowl hunting along the shore and on the rivers that flow into the Atlantic is an old New England tradition. General information for the state: http://dep.state.ct.us/burnatr/wildlife/fguide/waterfwl/wfg.htm.

Some of the most popular public waterfowl hunting places are the Charles Wheeler Wildlife Management Area (WMA) in Milford and Great Island in Old Lyme.

The Stewart McKinney National Wildlife Refuge is currently closed to hunting but may reopen in the near future. For details, see www.fws.gov/refuges/profiles/index.cfm?id=53546.

# DELAWARE

*In 2001 there were 13,000 resident hunters and 3,000 nonresident hunters: 67% went big game hunting, 28% small game, 50% waterfowl; 24% hunted on public lands; 82% hunted on private lands. Hunters pumped $15 million into the state economy. (USFWS)*

## OVERVIEW

Delaware is a small state with population explosions of deer and snow geese that are causing damage to crops. Several state parks allow hunting for deer with a permit. All hunters wishing to hunt on state park lands must first register with the Delaware State Parks Hunting Program. For more details, contact the Delaware Environmental Stewardship Program, 302-739-9220, www.destateparks.com/Activities/hunting/hunting.htm.

Not many states allow hunting in parks, but actually this is important to ecological conservation due to the soaring numbers of whitetail deer in the Northeast. Without predators, deer herds can devastate habitat, severely impacting many wildlife species, as well as decreasing natural beauty and increasing the spread of Lyme disease, which is carried by deer ticks. To date, birth control for wild deer herds is expensive and not terribly effective. Hiring sharpshooters to cull excess deer is costly. Allowing approved hunters to manage a herd in a park generates revenue and provides valuable recreational opportunities.

Delaware has a reciprocity agreement with Maryland: anyone who can legally hunt snow geese in Maryland may also hunt them in Delaware by purchasing a Delaware waterfowl stamp.

Delaware also offers hunting for squirrel, rabbits, pheasants, quail, turkeys, raccoon, and opossum, plus fox hunting, which is popular with horsemen.

## DESTINATIONS

*State Lands*
There are 18 state wildlife management and conservation areas. For a map and details, see www.fw.delaware.gov/NR/rdonlyres/3918379C-2885-4B5D-8138-AF083D949805/0/STATEOVERVIEW.pdf.

*U.S. Fish and Wildlife Service*
*National Wildlife Refuges*

**BOMBAY HOOK NATIONAL WILDLIFE REFUGE**
Smyrna, DE 19977
Phone: 302-653-6872; fax: 302-653-0684
www.fws.gov/northeast/bombayhook/index.htm

Deer, turkey, small game, and waterfowl hunting are offered according to state and federal regulations with local restrictions at Bombay Hook National Wildlife Refuge (NWR).

---

**DELAWARE SNAPSHOT**
**FIRST STATE**

- **General information for the State:** www.dnrec.state.de.us/fw/hunting.htm, www.delaware.thehuntingtrail.net

- **Deer population:** 30,000, 42nd in the United States

- **Average deer harvest:** 11,079, 38th in the United States

PRIME HOOK NATIONAL
WILLIFE REFUGE
Milton, DE 19968
Phone: 302-684-8419; fax: 302-684-8504
www.fws.gov/northeast/primehook/
hunting.html

Deer, upland game, and waterfowl in accordance with state and federal regulations.

## MAINE

*In 2001 there were 123,000 resident hunters and 41,000 nonresident hunters: 95% went big game hunting, 39% small game; 19% hunted on public lands; 90% hunted on private lands. Hunters pumped $162 million into the state economy. (USFWS)*

### OVERVIEW
In Baxter State Park, rising up to its 5,268-feet summit from a carpet of dark green spruce forest sprinkled with white birch trees, Mount Katahdin, the "Greatest One," is guarded, according to Abenaki Indians, by the spirit Pomola, a spirit with the head of a bull moose, the wings of an eagle, and a human body. The Abenakis believe that Pomola presides over the weather and has helper spirits, "the storm birds," that appear as tiny birds to warn outdoorsmen of approaching storms. The storm birds are often busy in winter along the Maine coast when nor'easters blow in off the Atlantic, the frothy whitecaps adding to the already dramatic tides along the Maine coast. That makes for exciting sea duck hunting, which we explore shortly. Maine is synonymous with moose,

**MAINE SNAPSHOT**
**PINE TREE STATE**

· **Noteworthy hunting information according to region can be found online at:** www.state.me.us/ifw/hunttrap/hunt_management/index.htm

· **For regulations, see:** www.state.me.us/ifw/hunttrap/index.htm

· **Or contact:**
Maine Department of Inland Fisheries & Wildlife
284 State Street
41 State House Station
Augusta, ME 04333-0041
Phone: 207-287-8000
Email: ifw.webmaster@maine.gov

· **Deer population:** 273,500, 29th in the United States

· **Average deer harvest:** 32,809, 33rd in the United States

bear, deer, woodcock, and grouse hunting, as well as migratory waterfowl along the coast. Add to that a rapidly growing wild turkey population, with spring and fall seasons, and Maine surely deserves its reputation as one of the United States' major hunting destinations.

 ## FEATURED HUNT

### Nor'easter Eiders along the Coast of Maine

JEFF ENGEL

Duck hunting in December in Maine, along the coast of the Atlantic Ocean, sends a shiver down my back, but the shiver is not from being cold. The shiver is from the anticipation of knowing what is about to come.

Maine is one of the great recreation meccas of

the United States—or the world, for that matter. This was my first opportunity to hunt Maine for sea ducks. I knew it would be cold, but I'm from Wisconsin.

Joining me for this sea duck hunt was professional dog handler and very good friend of mine Doug Kennedy and his loyal Lab Nelson.

Doug and I truly enjoy duck hunting with our own dogs. To us, a big part of the experience of the hunt is being able to share the hunt with your dog, and we really enjoy watching splendid retrieves.

Once in Bangor, we rented a vehicle and drove directly to the Maine Coast Experience lodge Eggemoggin Reach in Brooklin, Maine. The lodge is located right on the Atlantic Ocean and faces Penobscot Bay, which is filled with small islands.

The ducks here are like nothing I've hunted back home: American eider; old squaw; and three species of scoter—the surf, white-winged, and American scoters. The scoters are primarily early to midseason birds, while the old squaw birds usually arrive around midseason. The eiders are bountiful throughout the whole season.

The lodge has a warm and comfortable atmosphere. The great room welcomes you with a fieldstone fireplace and an incredible view of the Reach. The post-and-beam lodge with a fieldstone fireplace was a welcome sight after a full day of hunting sea ducks.

After we were settled in, we were treated to some down-easter hospitality: trays heaped with fresh lobster just caught from the ocean. What a way to start a hunting trip!

Our goal was to film this hunt for our television show, and our main target was the eider, which is not only one of the largest of all North American ducks but also the most striking. The males have white backs and black bellies, while the females are predominantly brown. Easily identifying the sex is a definite bonus, as our policy is to shoot only drakes, as we do in all of our duck hunts.

We were up well before dawn the next morning, fueling up on coffee and hearty breakfast, before pulling on several layers of warm clothes. Our main boat was a 36-foot cruiser, a classic lobster boat. Behind the boat, we towed a tender boat carrying decoys. It was nice to be in the shelter of the bigger boat on the way out, believe me.

At our hunting location, we anchored the larger boat, loaded up into the tender boat, and were ferried to shore. As we were getting the camera gear settled and making a blind, our assistant guide Barry went out and set up decoys.

Since there is such a deviation of water level because of the tide, we made blinds from logs and branches that were along the shoreline, and oftentimes we would have to reposition and remake the blinds to accommodate the water level.

Penobscot Bay is dotted with islands; the tides here are more than 12 feet; and the water is extremely cold. All this has to be factored into placement of the decoys and blind. Once Barry finished putting out the decoys, the tender boat returned to the main boat, and Doug and I and camera crew settled in to enjoy the spectacular scenery of the nation's first sunrise and to await the first flight of eiders to come in off the ocean.

As we got settled in, Doug zipped up a neoprene vest around Nelson. It would make him blend in with the cover and keep him warm both in and out of the water. We did not have to wait long for the ducks. In fact, there were swarms of them.

When hunting eiders, it is important to be patient and to pay close attention to distances because these birds are as big as snow geese. With the range finder, we would determine where 40 yards would be out from our blind location to a decoy in the water, and that would be the maximum distance we would shoot.

The eider is an extremely tough duck to bring down with its thick plumage. A direct hit is required to bring the duck down cleanly. With steel shot, BBs are a good load for eiders, and some use T-shot.

As we sat back to enjoy the experience, it was simply thrilling to see these graceful and beautiful birds in flight. We flipped a coin to see who would shoot first. Soon Doug got his chance at his very first eider. After a quick double tap, a beautiful drake eider folded into the cold, gray water. Nelson was only too eager to rush from the blind and lunge into the water to retrieve the bird.

One thing Doug and I had been asking ourselves is how a dog that had never been in salt water would react to hitting the water while retrieving a duck. Nelson immediately got a mouth full of water, and we were amazed at his calm reaction. He paid absolutely no attention to the salt water.

After a flawless retrieve, we carefully examined this beautiful-looking duck. The sea foam green color of his head, the unusual beak, and the stark contrast of white and black feathers indeed make this truly a trophy bird.

The eiders would sweep into the decoys, low to the water, oftentimes in small flocks up to a dozen. We were extremely careful when the flocks would come in because we wanted to pick out drakes; if a drake and hen came in flying too close together, we simply wouldn't shoot. If a flock came flying by with the birds plastered together, again we simply would not shoot, for fear of hitting a hen.

Watching the birds in flight was so fascinating at times; we nearly forgot that we were here to hunt. The birds would come in low, over the waves, looking almost like whitecaps dancing on top of the waves in the distance.

Next it was my turn, and with good fortune, I was able to drop a great drake. Nelson proved himself once again with another long retrieve.

The action on eiders was very consistent, and it was not long before we had our bag limit of seven a day. Our camera operator was content that he had taken some wonderful footage for our first day of hunting. Those of you who watch the show on television should understand that getting the shot of a passing bird on camera is often as much or more of a challenge than hitting it with a shotgun.

That night, back at the lodge, the warm field-stone fireplace radiated a welcome heat as we sat close by, talking about the wonderful retrieves Nelson had made.

The next morning came swiftly. It was only 4:00 A.M. when we loaded up the boat for the day's hunt. We were under way quickly and eagerly looking forward to another great day of hunting. As the boat pierced the blackness of night, the only light was a bright glow of green from the radar screen onto Richard's face as he steered the boat.

Again, we were sitting on the shore with the decoys out in place before daylight. I think the last few moments before dawn breaks is one of my favorite parts of the day, waiting for the sun to wake up. On that morning the beautiful pastel colors flowing across the coast of Maine could only be described as spectacular.

The first two ducks to appear were a drake and a hen eider. They surprised us so much that they landed in our decoys. It was just fascinating to watch these two birds interact with each other and bob in the waves, looking the whole time at our decoys with almost a funny expression. After a few moments, both ducks got up, flying closely together with no chance for a shot. Somehow it just felt good to let the two ducks fly away without taking a shot at them.

The next single drake came in, and I took two shots. The duck was flying low to the water, and I could see that both patterns centered the duck. Yet the duck kept flying. As the duck flew perhaps 200 or 300 yards away, I saw it glide to the water. I knew that the duck had been hit, so I called the tender boat. With the help of Barry, the assistant guide, we motored out to where the duck had landed. Sure enough, the duck was belly up.

This is an excellent example of how after every shot it is extremely important to follow and focus on that particular duck to make sure it does not fly a couple of yards and drop.

We found a very good technique of filming for this hunt was to have one television camera hidden in the rocks on the shoreline angled toward us and then to have the videographer behind us, getting over-the-shoulder shots. This way we could combine the two tapes in the studio for a very flowing scene.

The next day we were dropped off on a point. The water became very still, and like in many hunts, there are slow times. The rest of that morning, only a few ducks flew by, but it was a great time to have some quality conversations with my hunting part-ner Doug and to enjoy the company of a good hunting dog. Just after noon, the wind began to pick up, and so did the ducks. The shooting became much more exciting.

Even though we spent very little time in the water, Doug and I found it very helpful to each wear chest waders, mainly for the warmth and for the occasional time we would go out to our knees to help retrieve a duck.

We also found that using the best-quality shotgun shells with 3- to 3½-inch length was important, as these ducks proved to be very difficult to bring down. With any marginal shots, we quickly learned to simply not take a shot.

When you combine the experience of hunting along the Atlantic Coast of Maine for sea ducks with excellent meals, all the lobster you can possibly eat, watching outstanding dog work, and having a quality outdoor experience, well, you have all the components for a truly memorable duck hunt.

To hunt eiders and other sea ducks in Maine, some popular outfitters include:

**EIDERS DOWN, INC.**
Milbridge, ME 04658
Phone: 207-546-7167
www.eidersdown.com

**PENOBSCOT BAY OUTFITTERS**
Searsport, ME 04974-3932
Phone: 207-338-1883
www.seaduck.net

**RISING SUN OUTFITTERS**
Addison, ME 04606
Phone: 207-456-7890
www.risingsunoutfitters.com/index.html

---

## DESTINATIONS

*State Wildlife Management Areas*
For a guide to Maine State Wildlife Management Areas, see www.state.me.us/ifw/wma/index.htm.

*USDA National Forests*

**WHITE MOUNTAIN NATIONAL FOREST**
Laconia, NH 03246
Phone: 603-528-8721; fax: 603-528-8783
www.fs.fed.us/r9/forests/white_mountain

White Mountain National Forest is primarily located in New Hampshire, but it does include lands in Maine. Hunting opportunities in the White Mountain National Forest vary from large game, such as whitetail deer, moose, and black bear, to small game, such as rabbits, grouse, and waterfowl. State regulations govern hunting here. Contact the Bethel office of the Androscoggin Ranger District for more information, 207-824-2134.

*U.S. Fish and Wildlife Service*
*National Wildlife Refuges*

**LAKE UMBAGOG NATIONAL WILDLIFE REFUGE**
Errol, NH 03579
Phone: 603-482-3415
www.fws.gov/northeast/lakeumbagog

Covers more than 20,500 acres along the coast of Maine and New Hampshire and over 1,000 acres in the vicinity of Umbagog Lake. Ownerships and easements protect nearly all of the Umbagog Lake shoreline in New Hampshire and significant lengths of shoreline along the Androscoggin, Magalloway, Dead Cambridge, and Rapid rivers.

The refuge is open to hunting for waterfowl, upland game birds, and big game including bear, deer, and moose. All hunters must obtain a permit to hunt on the refuge. For further hunting information, contact the refuge or see www.fws.gov/northeast/lakeumbagog/hunting_regulations.htm.

## MAINE COASTAL ISLANDS NATIONAL WILDLIFE REFUGE
Milbridge, ME 04658
Phone: 207-546-2124
www.fws.gov/northeast/mainecoastal/publicuse.html

The Maine Coastal Islands NWR contains 47 offshore islands and three coastal parcels, more than 7,400 acres total spanning more than 150 miles of Maine coastline. It includes five National Wildlife Refuges—Petit Manan, Cross Island, Franklin Island, Seal Island, and Pond Island.

Portions of the refuge are open to in-season hunting. Gouldsboro Bay and Sawyer's Marsh divisions are open to migratory game bird, waterfowl, small game, and big game hunting. Bois Bubert Island is open to whitetail deer hunting only. Twenty-two additional refuge islands are open to migratory waterfowl hunting. The Petit Manan Point Division is closed to all hunting. Check with refuge headquarters for details.

## MOOSEHORN NATIONAL WILDLIFE REFUGE
Baring, ME 04694
Phone: 207-454-7161; fax: 207-454-2550
www.fws.gov/northeast/moosehorn

One of the northernmost NWRs in the Atlantic Flyway. The Baring Division covers 17,200 acres and is located southwest of Calais, Maine. The 7,200-acre Edmunds Division sits between Dennysville and Whiting on U.S. Route 1 and borders the tidal waters of Cobscook Bay. Areas of the refuge are open to deer hunting during the Maine rifle and muzzleloader season only. Contact the office for more information.

## RACHEL CARSON NATIONAL WILDLIFE REFUGE
Wells, ME 04090
Phone: 207-646-9226
www.fws.gov/northeast/rachelcarson/hunting.html

Scattered along 50 miles of coastline in York and Cumberland counties, the Rachel Carson NWR consists of 10 divisions between Kittery and Cape Elizabeth. It will contain approximately 9,125 acres when land acquisition is complete. Habitat includes a blend of forested upland, barrier beach/dune, coastal meadows, tidal salt marsh, and the distinctive rocky coast. The refuge is open to hunting for deer, fox, coyote, and migratory birds. A refuge permit is required for all hunters. ATVs are not allowed.

*Private Hunting Clubs and Preserves*

## JOHNSON FLAT HUNTING PRESERVE
Clinton, ME 04927
Phone: 207-426-8550
www.huntfishmaine.com

Released quail and pheasant on 400 managed acres; 200 acres of natural cover in central Maine. Field and continental shoots available. Released mallards—no bag limit, season, or license required; all hunts guided. Also, hunting for deer on 650 acres of managed game land and over 400 acres of leased land throughout the area. Club-house and cabins for overnight accommodations. Membership and nonmembership options.

**LIBBY CAMPS**
Wilderness Lodge and Outfitters
Ashland, ME 04732
Phone: 207-435-8274 (Radio)
www.libbycamps.com

Located deep in the Maine woods at Millinocket Lake, 45 minutes by logging roads from Ashland, this area was a favorite for Teddy Roosevelt's and Jack Dempsey's sporting pursuits. The Libby family has owned and operated a camp in this area for over 100 years. Trophy bear, moose, deer, plus grouse and woodcock hunting. Moose hunts by permit only through an annual lottery. Success rate is close to 100%. Rustic lodge and eight log cabins. Fly-fishing for salmon and brook trout. Can also book fishing trips to Labrador.

**SETTER'S POINT**
Albany Township, ME 04217
Phone: 207-824-8824
www.setterspoint.com

Upland bird hunting for chukar, pheasant, and quail, plus clay shooting and fly-fishing, on 225 acres north of North Waterford. No season, bag limit, or hunting license required.

For additional options, see: Maine Guides Online, http://maineguides.com; Hot Spot Lodges, www.hotspotlodges.com/hunting/lodges_ME.asp; and Maine Outdoors.com, www.maineoutdoors.com/hunting.

# HERITAGE DESTINATIONS

*Hunters' Breakfasts*
If you're in Maine and going to get up early to get into the woods bright and early for deer season, why not chow down with some fellow orange shirters? Hunters' breakfasts on opening morning of deer season are tradition in many Maine communities.

Hope. The Hope Volunteer Fire Department hosts a hunters' breakfast at the Hope Elementary School on Route 235 in Hope, ME 04847, 4:00 A.M. to 8:00 A.M.: scrambled eggs, bacon, sausage, baked beans, home fries, pancakes, homemade muffins, coffee, orange juice, and hot chocolate. Cost is $7.00, which includes a free coffee-filling station for your thermos. Proceeds to benefit the Hope Volunteer Fire Department. For information, contact Ginny Ryan, 207-236-8049, gryan@15elm.com.

Wales. Hunters' breakfast, 4:00 A.M.–8:00 A.M., Wales Grange Hall Room, 322 Centre Road, Wales, ME 04280. Cost is $6.00. Hosted by Webster Lodge #164 AF & AM to support the building fund. For more information, call 207-375-8889.

Brewer. St. Teresa's Parish, 440 South Main Street, Brewer, ME 04412.

Hunters' breakfasts are also held in West Paris, Farmington, and elsewhere. A good place to get the current information on community hunters' breakfasts and other Maine hunting news is www.mainehuntingtoday.com/magazine.

*L.L. Bean Main Store—Freeport, Maine*
Founded in 1912 by Leon Leonwood Bean
and in business at this location since 1917,
open seven days a week, 365 days a year, 24
hours a day, for many years this was the epicenter of outdoor sports for the United
States—and maybe the world. Over 3 million people visit the L.L. Bean store in Freeport every year. This store is a world
touchstone for hunting heritage.

**L.L. BEAN ORIGINAL LOCATION**
Freeport, ME 04033
Phone: 800-559-0747 (Flagship Store);
877-552-3268 (Hunting & Fishing Store)
www.llbean.com/shop/retailStores/
freeportFlagshipStore/retail.html

## MASSACHUSETTS

*In 2001 there were 64,000 resident hunters
and 2,000 nonresident hunters: 88% went big
game hunting, 42% small game, 28% migratory waterfowl and doves; 65% hunted on
public lands; 73% hunted on private lands.
Hunters pumped $59 million into the state
economy. (USFWS)*

### OVERVIEW
Generations of hunters know that upstate
Massachusetts is a hot place for ruffed
grouse and woodcock, and the shoreline is
the place for waterfowl. Like many areas in
New England, the whitetail deer population
is growing in Massachusetts. In 1966, 3,404
deer were killed in the state. In 2005, the
harvest had nearly quadrupled. Martha's
Vineyard and Nantucket Island have deer

densities ranging from 40 to 50 per square
mile.

Waterfowl hunting along the coast continues to be good, as is grouse upstate. If you
plan to hunt waterfowl, each hunter must

---

**MASSACHUSETTS SNAPSHOT
BAY STATE**

- **General information:** Massachusetts Department
  of Fish and Game, www.mass.gov/dfwele

- **Buy your license online:** www.mass.gov/dfwele/
  sport/index.htm

- **List of state-supported shooting clubs and ranges:**
  www.mass.gov/dfwele/dfw/dfw_range_
  enhancement.htm

- **Deer population:** 85,000–90,000, 37th in the
  United States

- **Average deer harvest:** 11,455, 37th in the
  United States

---

have an annual Harvest Information Program (HIP) number. You can get a HIP number by calling 800-WETLAND.

## DESTINATIONS

### State Lands

Massachusetts has over 120,000 acres of Wildlife Management Areas (WMAs), most of which permit hunting. For details, see www.mass.gov/dfwele/dfw/dfw_range_enhancement.htm.

For maps of WMAs, see www.mass.gov/dfwele/dfw/dfw_wma.htm.

Most state parks and forests are open to hunting. For a list, see www.mass.gov/dcr/recreate/hunting.htm.

### U.S. Army Corps of Engineers

**BARRE FALLS DAM**
Hubbardston, MA 01452-9743
Phone: 978-928-4712
www.nae.usace.army.mil/recreati/bfd/bfdhome.htm

At Barre Falls Dam on the Ware River, there are 557 acres of wetlands, forests, open fields, and river areas. Hunting and fishing are permitted in accordance with Massachusetts' laws and regulations in the more than 22,000 acres of combined federal and state land. The area offers both large and small game including deer, bear, turkey, rabbit, and stocked pheasant. Motor vehicles may only travel on established roads.

**BIRCH HILL DAM**
Royalston, MA 01331-9515
Phone: 978-249-4467

www.nae.usace.army.mil/recreati/bhd/bhdhome.htm

Hunting permitted in accordance with Massachusetts' laws and regulations. Hunters have more than 8,000 acres of combined federal and state land on which to hunt stocked pheasant and native ruffed grouse, ducks, turkey, and whitetail deer.

**BUFFUMVILLE LAKE**
Oxford, MA 01540-0155
Phone: 508-248-5697
www.nae.usace.army.mil/recreati/bvl/bvlhome.htm

A 200-acre lake with 500 surrounding acres of land in Charlton, Massachusetts, offers hunting for deer, rabbits, and upland game birds.

**EAST BRIMFIELD LAKE**
Fiskdale, MA 01521
Phone: 508-347-3705; fax: 508-347-8732
www.nae.usace.army.mil/recreati/ebl/eblhome.htm

A 360-acre lake and surrounding lands near Old Sturbridge Village. Hunting for deer, turkey, and other small game, including stocked pheasant, is allowed in the forested wetland and upland areas of the project. Hunting and fishing are permitted in accordance with Massachusetts' fish and game laws.

**KNIGHTVILLE DAM**
Huntington, MA 01050-9742
Phone: 413-667-3430
www.nae.usace.army.mil/recreati/kvd/kvdhome.htm

Some 2,430 acres of public lands and waters including miles of rivers and streams, 250 acres of old fields, wetlands, and hundreds of acres of pine, hemlock, and hardwood forests offer prime upland game habitat. The state stocks pheasant in the fall. Hunting and fishing are permitted in accordance with posted restrictions and state laws.

## LITTLEVILLE LAKE
Huntington, MA 01050
Phone: 413-667-3656; fax: 413-667-5366
Email (Project Manager): john.f.parker@ usace.army.mil
Email (Park Ranger): thomas. m.wisnauckas@usace.army.mil

Located in the Berkshire Hills in the southwest part of the state, hunting and fishing are permitted in accordance with posted restrictions and state laws in this 1,567-acre park.

## TULLY LAKE
Royalston, MA 01368
Phone: 978-249-9150
www.nae.usace.army.mil/recreati/tul/ tulhome.htm

Tully Lake is a 1,300-acre flood control project in north-central Massachusetts. Fishing and hunting are allowed on Tully Lake property in accordance with state laws.

## WEST HILL DAM
Uxbridge, MA 01569-1209
Phone: 508-278-2511
www.nae.usace.army.mil/recreati/whd/ whdhome.htm

West Hill Dam is located within the John H. Chafee Blackstone River Valley National Heritage Corridor. Some 567 acres of white pine and red oak forest, broken here and there by rolling meadows, with red maple swamps and several bogs filling the lowlands, while three small brooks feed the river. Hunting for deer, small game, and upland birds is permitted in accordance with state laws. Pheasant are stocked.

*U.S. Fish and Wildlife Service*
*National Wildlife Refuges*

## ASSABET RIVER NATIONAL WILDLIFE REFUGE
Sudbury, MA 01776
Phone: 978-443-4661;
fax: 978-443-2898
www.fws.gov/northeast/assabetriver/ 2006-2007_ASRHuntingInfo.htm

Deer, woodcock, upland game, and spring turkey hunting are permitted on 2,230 acres. Waterfowl hunting is not allowed. There is a $20 permit fee per person. Some areas of the refuge are not open to hunting, so a map is a necessity.

## GREAT MEADOWS NATIONAL WILDLIFE REFUGE
Sudbury, MA 01776
Phone: 978-443-4661; fax: 978-443-2898
www.fws.gov/northeast/greatmeadows/ 2006-2007_GRMHuntingInfo.htm

Located 20 miles west of Boston. About 85% of the refuge's more than 3,600 acres are freshwater wetlands stretching along 12 miles of the Concord and Sudbury rivers. Archery, shotgun, and muzzleloader deer seasons; waterfowl hunting is permitted.

## OXBOW NATIONAL WILDLIFE REFUGE
Sudbury, MA 01776
Phone: 978-443-4661; fax: 978-443-2898
www.fws.gov/northeast/oxbow

On 1,667 acres offering archery deer, shotgun deer, muzzleloader deer, fall and spring turkey, woodcock, ruffed grouse, gray squirrel, cottontail rabbit, and waterfowl hunting.

## PARKER RIVER NATIONAL WILDLIFE REFUGE
Newburyport, MA 01950
Phone: 978-465-5753
www.fws.gov/northeast/parkerriver/information/hunting.html

The refuge occupies the southern three-fourths of Plum Island, an 8-mile (12.9 kilometer) barrier island, and offers outstanding waterfowl hunting.

## SILVIO O. CONTE NATIONAL WILDLIFE REFUGE
Turners Falls, MA 01376
Phone: 413-863-0209
www.fws.gov/r5soc

A 7.2 million acre, four-state (Vermont, New Hampshire, Massachusetts, and Connecticut) watershed encompassing the Connecticut River valley. Some parts of the refuge are open to hunting. Contact the refuge headquarters for details.

*U.S. National Park Service*

## CAPE COD NATIONAL SEASHORE
Wellfleet, MA 02667
Phone: 508-349-3785; fax: 508-349-9052
www.nps.gov/caco/index.htm

Cape Cod is a large peninsula extending 60 miles into the Atlantic Ocean from the coast of Massachusetts. Located on the outer portion of the Cape, Cape Cod National Seashore contains 44,600 acres of marine, estuarine, freshwater, and terrestrial ecosystems. The Seashore has offered a stocked pheasant hunting program. The program is currently under review. For updates, contact the Seashore headquarters.

*Private Hunting Clubs and Preserves*

## FULLFLIGHT GAME FARM AND HUNT CLUB
Bernardston, MA 01337
Phone: 413-648-9580
www.fullflight.com

Located in western Massachusetts, a 350-acre game preserve of upland fields and woods. Offering half-day hunts, guided or unguided, for ring-necked pheasant, chukar partridge, Hungarian (grey-legged) partridge, red-legged partridge, and European tower shoots. Hunting is available 365 days of the year.

## LADYWOODS GAME PRESERVE
Uxbridge, MA 01569
Phone: 508-278-3529
www.ladywoods.com

Located in Douglas, Massachusetts, only 25 miles south of Worcester and 30 miles north of Providence, LadyWoods Game Preserve encompasses 130 acres of typical New England cover, offering pheasant and chukar hunting, September 15 to March 31. Dogs available.

# HERITAGE DESTINATIONS

## Walden Pond, Concord, Massachusetts

From July 1845 to September 1847, philosopher and writer Henry David Thoreau lived in a one-room cabin that he had built beside Walden Pond, outside of Concord, Massachusetts. The land belonged to Ralph Waldo Emerson, who had a strong influence on Thoreau's life and work.

Thoreau's retreat led to his landmark book *Walden*, which many consider to be the birth of the conservation movement. Thoreau was a hunter and advocated hunting for children as a way to develop character and conservation spirit.

Created originally by a glacial kettle, today Walden Pond is a 61-acre lake. It is part of the Walden Pond State Reservation, a popular 2,680-acre recreation area. Fishing is allowed on the pond, as well as visiting the site of Thoreau's cabin, which is marked by a simple pile of stones. A replica of Thoreau's cabin is nearby. To keep the area in a more serene mood, such as what Thoreau knew, dogs, bicycles, flotation devices, and grills are prohibited.

*Park Directions:* Walden Pond State Reservation is located near Lincoln and Concord in the Greater Boston Area. For more details, see www.mass.gov/dcr/parks/northeast/wldn.htm.

## NEW HAMPSHIRE

*In 2001 there were 52,000 resident hunters and 26,000 nonresident hunters: 91% went big game hunting, 28% small game, 8% waterfowl; 42% hunted on public lands; 83% hunted on private lands. Hunters pumped $71 million into the state economy. (USFWS)*

### OVERVIEW

Deer, bear, turkey, grouse, woodcock, small game, and waterfowl all await the hunter in

---

**NEW HAMPSHIRE SNAPSHOT**
**GRANITE STATE**

- **General information about hunting in New Hampshire:** www.wildlife.state.nh.us/Hunting/hunting.htm and www.nhoutdoors.com/nh_hunting.htm

- **Hunting licenses may be purchased online:** www.greatlodge.com/cgi-bin/licenses/customer_options.cgi?st=NH&btype=&r=0.3994504096917808

- **List of guides and outfitters:** www.nhoutdoors.com/nh_guides.htm

- **Lists of butchers and taxidermists:** www.wildlife.state.nh.us/Hunting/hunting.htm

- **List of shooting ranges:** www.wildlife.state.nh.us/Links/fish_and_game_clubs.htm

- **Operation Game Thief:** 800-344-4262

- **Deer population:** 85,000, 38th in the United States

- **Average deer harvest:** 10,132, 39th in the United States

New Hampshire. However, the biggest prize here is moose, which are growing in numbers.

In 2005 hunters took 10,595 deer and 433 black bear. If you get drawn for a moose tag, you're in luck. In 2005 hunters harvested 408 moose, with a success rate for the nine-day season that begins the third weekend in October of 77.6%. In 2006 the success rate was 67%.

## DESTINATIONS

While 80% of the forest land in New Hampshire is privately owned, most of these lands are open to hunting.

### State Lands

The state of New Hampshire owns 117 state forests, 41 state parks, 63 other tracts, and 100 Wildlife Management Areas, most of which are open to hunting. The New Hampshire Fish and Game Department owns or has hunting rights to nearly 30,000 acres distributed over nearly 100 tracts, most of which are called Wildlife Management Areas. For details on hunting state lands, see www.wildlife.state.nh.us/Hunting/hunt_NH_state_lands.htm.

### U.S. Army Corps of Engineers

**EDWARD MACDOWELL LAKE**
Peterborough, NH 03458-1068
Phone: 603-924-3431
Email: Stephen.P.Dermody@usace.army.m
www.nae.usace.army.mil/recreati/eml/emlhome.htm

A 1,200-acre lake and surrounding lands located near Peterborough that offer hunting for deer, red fox, raccoon, pheasant, grouse, and waterfowl according to state and local laws.

**FRANKLIN FALLS DAM**
Franklin, NH 03235-2202
Phone: 603-934-2116
Email: Michael.D.Hayward@usace.army.mil
www.nae.usace.army.mil/recreati/ffd/ffdhome.htm

A 15-mile stretch of the Pemigewasset River and riverside lands. A popular area for hunting pheasant, black bear, whitetail deer, and small game according to state and local laws.

**HOPKINTON-EVERETT LAKE**
Contoocook, NH 03229-3370
Phone: 603-746-3601
Email: Alister.R.Shanks@usace.army.mil
www.nae.usace.army.mil/recreati/hel/helhome.htm

A 10,000-acre flood control project along the Contoocook River that offers hunting for big and small game according to state and local regulations.

**SURRY MOUNTAIN LAKE**
Keene, NH 03431-9802
Phone: 603-352-4130
www.nae.usace.army.mil/recreati/sml/smlhome.htm

Located six miles north of Keene, Surry Mountain Lake is a 265-acre lake on the Ashuelot River and over 1,600 acres of surrounding land. Hunting for big and small game according to state and local regulations.

**WHITE MOUNTAIN NATIONAL FOREST**
Laconia, NH 03246
Phone: 603-528-8721
Email: Mailroom_R9_White_Mountain@
fs.fed.us
www.fs.fed.us/r9/forests/white_mountain

The largest single landholding in New Hampshire, the White Mountain National Forest, over 751,000 acres, is also nearly 10% of the land area in Vermont, plus a small section in Maine. Hunting for whitetail deer, moose, black bear, and small game including rabbits, grouse, and waterfowl according to state regulations.

*U.S. Fish and Wildlife Service*
*National Wildlife Refuges*

**GREAT BAY NATIONAL**
**WILDLIFE REFUGE**
Newington, NH 03801-2903
Phone: 603-431-7511
Email: jimmie_reynolds@fws.gov
www.fws.gov/refuges/profiles/index
.cfm?id=53570

The refuge is located along the eastern shore of New Hampshire's Great Bay in the town of Newington. This is a wintering ground for black ducks. The only hunting allowed on the refuge is a special, permit-only deer hunt on a Saturday and Sunday in November. There is a lottery drawing for 20 hunters each day to hunt around the second weekend of November. If selected, hunters pay a $20 permit fee. Hunters use their regular state deer tag or Unit M antlerless tag. Hunt applications for the lottery are available around September 1 each year.

The waters of Great Bay are open to waterfowl hunting during the appropriate state season. However, the Great Bay National Wildlife Refuge is not open to waterfowl hunting. Waterfowl hunters may use the water along the shoreline but are not permitted to go up on shore (dry land) to either hunt or retrieve ducks.

*Private Hunting Clubs and Preserves*

**GREEN MOUNTAIN**
**SHOOTING PRESERVE**
Ossipee, NH 03864
Phone: 603-539-2106;
fax: 603-539-2903
Email: claybirds@greenmountain
kennels.com
www.greenmountainkennels.com

Released mallards, pheasant, quail, and Hungarian and chukar partridge on 400 acres at the base of Green Mountain in Ossipee. Field and driven hunts. Sporting clays, dog training, kennels, and membership options.

**WILDERNESS ADVENTURES**
**HUNT CLUB**
Allan or Julie Guminski
Hillsboro, NH 03244
Phone: 603-478-0099;
fax: 603-478-0104
Email: wildadvt@aol.com
www.wildernessadventureshunt.com

Released pheasant, chukar, and Hungarian partridge field and driven hunts on 400 acres, plus deer, turkey, moose, and black bear.

Also sporting clays, trout fishing, and onsite lodging. Membership options.

## RHODE ISLAND

*In 2001 there were 7,000 resident hunters and 2,000 nonresident hunters: 68% went big game hunting, 60% small game; 49% hunted on public lands; 79% hunted on private lands. Hunters pumped $5 million into the state economy. (USFWS)*

### OVERVIEW

It's not very big, but Rhode Island does offer hunting for deer, geese, doves, turkey, grouse, ducks, and woodcock. The number of licenses sold here has dropped dramatically, from 22,000 in 1991 and 26,000 in 1996 to 9,000 in 2001. Urbanization! But this also means more game to go around.

---

**RHODE ISLAND SNAPSHOT**
**OCEAN STATE**

- **General information about hunting in Rhode Island:** RI Division of Fish & Wildlife
  4808 Tower Hill Road
  Wakefield, RI 02879
  Phone: 401-789-3094
  www.state.ri.us/dem or www.dem.ri.gov/pubs/regs/regs/fishwild/hunt0607.pdf

- **To purchase licenses, see:** www.state.ri.us/dem

- **Permits for taking game for wild game dinners:** www.dem.ri.gov/programs/bpoladm/manserv/hfb/hunting/hunting.htm

- **Online community for RI hunters:** http://rihunts.com

- **Deer population:** 16,000, 43rd in the United States

- **Average deer harvest:** 2,267, 42nd in the United States

---

### DESTINATIONS

The state Department of Environmental Management Division of Fish and Wildlife maintains several hundred thousand acres of land for recreation including hunting. See maps and details at www.dem.ri.gov/maps/wma.htm.

*Federal Lands*

### BLACKSTONE RIVER VALLEY NATIONAL HERITAGE CORRIDOR

Woonsocket, RI 02895
Phone: 401-762-0250
www.nps.gov/blac

Nearly 400,000 acres along the Blackstone River located within Worcester County in central Massachusetts and Providence County in northern Rhode Island. There are several sites within the corridor that allow hunting. For details, see www.nps.gov/blac/planyourvisit/valley-sites-glocester-burrillville.htm.

*Private Hunting Clubs and Preserves*

### ADDIEVILLE EAST FARM

Mapleville, RI 02839
Phone: 401-568-3185; fax: 401-568-3009
www.addieville.com

Over 900 acres in northern Rhode Island for field and driven shoots for pheasant, chukar, quail, and Hungarian partridge, plus mallards. Lodge, sporting clays, and fly-fishing. Hunts in England can be arranged. Memberships for individuals and corporations available.

## VERMONT

*In 2001 there were 74,000 resident hunters and 26,000 nonresident hunters: 94% went big game hunting, 29% small game; 47% hunted on public lands; 81% hunted on private lands. Hunters pumped $53 million into the state economy. (USFWS)*

### OVERVIEW

There is a strong hunting tradition in Vermont, with deer and moose being the biggest draws. Census for deer shows that there are 283 for every 1,000 people in the state. The 2005 bag was 8,546 whitetails, 4,956 of which were bucks. This was down from 2004 when 11,889 deer were harvested, 7,612 of which were bucks.

Some 13,091 people applied for a moose tag, and 1,046 were lucky enough to get one. The reason for the high demand is seen in the 61% success rate, as 640 moose, 334 of which were bulls, were bagged.

The year 2005 was the best spring wild turkey season in Vermont ever: 4,649 birds were taken. Another 991 were taken in the fall. The best state Wildlife Management Unit for turkeys was J1, which is located between Royalton and Barre. (See VT Fish & Wildlife Dept. map.)

Additionally, 447 black bears were harvested in 2005.

The small game mammals are cottontails, snowshoe hare, and gray squirrel; but the major small game are upland birds—ruffed grouse and woodcock.

Waterfowl hunting is generally best on and around Lake Champlain, then in the

**VERMONT SNAPSHOT**
**GREEN MOUNTAIN STATE**

- **General information:**
  Vermont Fish & Wildlife Department
  103 South Main Street
  Waterbury, VT 05671-0501
  Phone: 802-241-3700
  Email: fwinformation@state.vt.us
  www.vtfishandwildlife.com

- **Buy your license online:** www.vtfishandwildlife.com/buylicense.cfm

- **Report a poacher:** Get a reward if your tip leads to an arrest or citation; call toll-free: 800-75 ALERT (800-752-5378)

- **Deer population:** 120,000, 36th in the United States

- **Average deer harvest:** 15,711, 35th in the United States

Northeast Kingdom, located in the northeastern region of the state, on and along Lake Memphremagog. The Connecticut River valley also offers some good shooting, and there is an early Canada goose season for the whole state.

 **FEATURED HUNT**

### Moose and Man in the Green Mountains

JAMES EHLERS*

Freedom and unity. These two virtues have long defined the spirit of the Green Mountain State—Vermont. A rugged place of fiercely independent personalities, the mountainous region bounded by water to the east and west remained a sovereign entity for over a decade after the American Revolution. After drafting the state constitution in 1777, however, Vermonters were among the first to provide for each other: abolishing slavery, granting a vote to the non-landowner, providing for public education, and guaranteeing fishing and hunting rights. This paradox, freedom and unity, is forever immortalized as the state motto. And while we have flipped a few pages on the calendar since the expression was coined in 1788, the woods of Vermont still, in many ways, permit modern man to taste freedom on the winds of the coming winter and test our loyalty to our companions in the mountains where moose did once, and now again, roam. And there is no place better to do so than Vermont's Northeast Kingdom during the October hunt for the king of those North Woods.

Vermont's Northeast Kingdom, or simply "The Kingdom," a local term coined to describe the three most northeastern counties, is home to perhaps the most moose per square mile and least number of

people within a four-hour drive of the millions inhabiting Boston. It is here, in The Kingdom, on hardwood ridges and in spruce-fir swamps, miles from any pavement, that the modern hunter and his or her companions can pursue the greatest of North American game animals. In an area of roughly 2,000 square miles and 200 ponds, moose roam the wilderness and even the few roads that transect what once were mostly timber company lands. This was not always the case, however.

Prior to the eighteenth century, moose were numerous but also highly regarded as a source of food by European settlers. Hunting and the transition of the then 95% forested landscape to one nearly denuded of trees to accommodate grazing livestock during the 1800s led to the extirpation of the moose throughout most of the state. An 1899 account of an illegal moose shooting attests to the animal's rarity. Locals referred to it as "strange animal" and "the last" of its kind in Vermont. The hunting of the rare animal had been outlawed by the state legislature three years prior. Times change, however.

As the Vermont economy evolved during the twentieth century from one based solely on agriculture to some manufacturing and eventually one dominated by tourism, the forest reclaimed the once-cleared fields. And with the return of the trees came the moose. A landscape that once stood at 25% forested is now nearly 80% wooded. The few remaining pockets of a moose population, numbering less than 25, in the Northeast Kingdom in the 1960s have given rise to a current population of 5,000 that now covers the entire state, reaching even into the streets of the state's populous city—Burlington—at times. Today, in order to keep moose in balance with their habitat, the state fish and wildlife department authorizes a permit-only hunt lasting six days, open to both licensed resident and nonresident hunters through a lottery system. There are two such six-day hunts authorized for a season. The first hunt, lasting only three days, took place in 1993 after 12 years of intense study by state wildlife biologists and foresters; 25 moose were shot that year. In 2006, the number allowed increased, and hunters shot 648 moose. A conservation success by all accounts.

Even with a permit, however, a harvest is no guarantee. The hunter success rate for 2006 was 64% for either-sex licenses and 46% for antlerless licenses—58% overall. Despite their enormous size and the perception among the uninformed public that moose are sluggish and even nonreactive to human presence, the hunted moose can seem completely invisible to the stalking hunter. The Kingdom landscape affords a 1,200-pound bull sporting five-foot antlers, an advantage unavailable even to modern man and all his intricate gadgets and conveniences. The best way to hunt a moose is still as a moose would live—minimally and as close to the land as possible—from a Kingdom camp with trusted friends, a steady rifle, an accurate compass, and intimate knowledge of the seemingly bottomless bogs, hardwood whip openings, and secure bedding areas that moose call home.

Every October next to the rumble of a firebox and under the hiss of gas lamps, hunting companions still gather around a table inside a camp that in most cities a building inspector would assuredly condemn. Not in the Kingdom. Cobbled together by hardworking men of modest means in many cases, these camps and the men that own them stand in unison with the animal they hunt—anachronisms of a simpler time but perhaps more difficult in hindsight, when food, warmth, shelter, and our ability to obtain them defined man, their families, and their friendships. A time when we were free from the conveniences of a modern world but bonded together by our reliance on one another for food, shelter, and ultimately survival. Free but unified under a leaking rook. Free but unified around the orange glow of the woodstove. Free but unified

on the track of the North Woods' most majestic animal. Free but unified as people of the Green Mountain State.

Each year a lottery is held for the moose hunt, which historically takes place during a split season occurring in October. The number of permits varies from year to year, depending on the health of the herd as determined by state biologists. Typically, permit applications are due in June. There is a $10 fee to apply. For more information on the moose lottery, permit application, and licensing, visit www.vermontandfishwildlife.com and look for the lottery link in the hunting section, or call 802-241-3700.

*James Ehlers is publisher emeritus at Elk Publishing, Inc., and past editor in chief of* Outdoors *magazine.*

## DESTINATIONS

*State Wildlife Management Areas*
The state has over 80 Wildlife Management Areas totaling 118,000 acres. A map and details can be found at www.vtfishandwildlife.com/wma_maps.cfm.

*Federal Lands*

**BALL MOUNTAIN LAKE**
Jamaica, VT 05343-9713
Phone: 802-874-4881
www.nae.usace.army.mil/recreati/bml/bmlhome.htm

The river and 75-acre lake combined with surrounding lands totaling 965 acres are open for hunting and fishing in accordance with federal and Vermont fish and wildlife laws and posted regulations.

## GREEN MOUNTAINS AND FINGER LAKES NATIONAL FOREST

USDA Forest Service
Rutland, VT 05701
Phone: 802-747-6700
www.fs.fed.us/r9/gmfl

The forest encompasses a boundary area of approximately 821,000 acres in the Green Mountains in southwestern and west-central Vermont, roughly 385,000 (or 62%) of which is federally owned. Most of the Finger Lakes National Forest is located in New York. Hunting is permitted according to state regulations and local posting.

## MISSISQUOI NATIONAL WILDLIFE REFUGE

Swanton, VT 05488
Phone: 802-868-4781
www.fws.gov/refuges/profiles/index
.cfm?id=53520

Located on the eastern shore of Lake Champlain, portions of the refuge are open to waterfowl, upland game, and deer hunting in accordance with state and federal regulations. The refuge is one of the most popular and most well known waterfowl hunting locations in the region.

*U.S Army Corps of Engineers*

## NORTH HARTLAND LAKE

North Hartland, VT 05052-0055
Phone: 802-295-2855
www.nae.usace.army.mil/recreati/nhl/
nhlhome.htm

On 1,700 acres, hunting is permitted according to state regulations and local posting.

## NORTH SPRINGFIELD LAKE

Springfield, VT 05156-2210
Phone: 802-886-2775
www.nae.usace.army.mil/recreati/nsl/
nslhome.htm

The 100-acre lake and 65-acre Stoughton Pond, plus surrounding lands that total 1,361 acres, offer excellent warm-water fishing (small boats only) and hunting according to state regulations and local posting.

## TOWNSHEND LAKE

Townshend, VT 05353-2800
Phone: 802-365-7703
www.nae.usace.army.mil/recreati/tsl/
tslhome.htm

Located in the Green Mountains, hunting and fishing are allowed throughout the reservoir in accordance with federal and state laws and regulations.

## UNION VILLAGE DAM

East Thetford, VT 05043-0098
Phone: 802-649-1606
www.nae.usace.army.mil/recreati/uvd/
uvdhome.htm

This dam on the Ompompanoosuc River creates six miles of river and surrounding lands that are open to hunting according to state regulations and local posting.

*Private Hunting Clubs and Preserves*

**THE EQUINOX RESORT & SPA**
Manchester Village, VT 05254
Phone: 866-346-ROCK or 802-362-4700;
fax: 802-362-4861
http://equinox.rockresorts.com

This Old World–feel resort, which has been in business since 1769, is one of a handful of places in the United States where you can learn falconry. And you can do it while staying in elegant surroundings—plush hotel, spa, golf course, fly-fishing, and wing-shooting instruction. Classes on falconry are offered, and you can arrange for Harris Hawks to be flown over a trained hunting dog on a private hunting preserve for partridge, quail, rabbit, or pheasant in season.

**PEACEABLE HILL FARM LLC**
Shoreham, VT 05770-9555
Phone: 802-897-5913
www.peaceablehill.com

Field and tower hunts for released pheasant on hundreds of acres on three farms in the Lake Champlain Valley. Lodge, dogs, kennels, and guides available.

*Complete List of Guides, Outfitters and Clubs in Vermont*
For a list of guides, outfitters, and clubs in Vermont, see the Vermont Outdoor Guide Association at www.voga.org/vermont_hunting_guides.htm.

# HERITAGE DESTINATIONS

*Bradford, Vermont, Annual Wild Game Supper*
An annual event that's been going on for over half a century draws almost 1,000 people. The Annual Wild Game Supper at the United Church of Christ in Bradford began over 50 years ago as a fund-raiser to help build a sidewalk. Held on the eve of the opening of deer season, it has grown over the years into an annual event with 900 tickets sold to feast on home-cooked bear, beaver, boar, buffalo, moose, rabbit, venison, pheasant, vegetables, homemade rolls, and gingerbread.

*Contact Information.* Reservations only. Reservations begin selling in mid-October. To get a reservation form, call 802-222-4670, go to the church's Web site at www.mistweb design.com/UCC.html, or email ranDallx3@ charter.net. The price is $25 for adults and $12 for children under 10.

It you can't get a ticket for the feast in Bradford, don't despair. This annual supper has started a statewide movement with wild game feasts held in churches, schools, and firehouses in communities all around the state.

*Orvis Headquarters, Manchester, Vermont*
In 1856 Charles Orvis established a fly-rod shop in Manchester, Vermont, the site where their extraordinary fly rods are still built. Today Orvis is a major manufacturer and supplier of fine sporting goods and clothing with a catalog and major operations in Roanoke, Virginia, and Hampshire, England,

employing more than 3,000 associates. See www.orvis.com/store/home_page.aspx?bhcp=1.

Orvis also runs annual wing-shooting schools based on the English Churchill Method of instinctive shooting in Manchester, Vermont; Sandanona, New York; Tallahassee, Florida; and Adairsville, Georgia. For details, call 800-235-9763 or see www.orvis.com/intro.asp?subject=1648.

# Eastern Seaboard

## GEORGIA

*In 2001 there were 417,000 resident hunters and 62,000 nonresident hunters: 82% went big game hunting, 32% small game, 21% waterfowl; 20% hunted on public lands; 90% hunted on private lands. Hunters pumped $504 million into the state economy. (USFWS)*

### OVERVIEW

Georgia has strong hunting traditions, and rightfully so. Deer, turkeys, quail, raccoons, waterfowl, and doves are classic, and alligators also are increasingly popular. The gator season runs through September. You are allowed one per year, 48 inches long or greater.

Plantation quail hunting is popular, though annual harvests are down from the 1960s when 4 million bobwhites per year was the norm. In 2005, only 21% of the 622,123 quail harvested were wild.

Deer hunting in Georgia is outstanding. During a 25-year period when the population of Georgia doubled, the whitetail herd increased fivefold. The herd now numbers over 1 million.

The limit on whitetails varies from area to area, but in general it is 12 per season (10 antlerless, 2 with antlers, 1 of which must be antlers four inches or more). Counting archery, rifle, and muzzleloader seasons, you can hunt here from September through the end of January, with dogs permitted in some areas. In 2005 sportsmen killed 127,000 bucks and 192,000 does.

---

**GEORGIA SNAPSHOT**
**PEACH STATE**

- **For general hunting and license information, contact:**
  Georgia Department of Natural Resources
  Wildlife Resource Division
  2592 Floyd Springs Road, NE
  Armuchee, GA 30105
  Phone: 706-295-6401
  http://georgiawildlife.dnr.state.ga.us

- **The state of Georgia Department of Natural Resources' "Turn in Poachers" (TIPs) phone number:** 800-241-4113

- **Deer population:** 1.3 million, 7th in the United States

- **Average deer harvest:** 432,920, 5th in the United States

## FEATURED HUNT

### Georgia Quail Diversity

SHEROL ENGEL

Hunting with well-trained dogs has always been one of a hunter's great pleasures. Add moss-covered oaks, a southern gentleman of a guide (who could write the book on quail hunting), exploding coveys of quail, and the gracious hospitality of one of the nation's finest southern hunting plantations, and you have an outdoor experience worth remembering a lifetime.

The site of our traditional southern quail hunt was the esteemed Wynfield Plantation located near Albany, Georgia. After a brief scare that the snow the day before would cause our flight to be canceled, Jeff and I, and Jeff's father Herb, departed from the Milwaukee airport on a mid-December snowy morning with the mercury clinging to only 4 degrees above zero. With a flight of only two hours, we turned the clock back to October, arriving to find temperatures a full 50 degrees warmer.

We were greeted by Gina Bowles, the wife of Wynfield manager Bill Bowles. From the outset, it was clear that Wynfield Plantation is a first-class hunting destination in every respect. Gina escorted us to the plantation where we met Bill and enjoyed a tour of the beautifully appointed main lodge. Bill also shared some advice with us about staying at Wynfield.

After settling into our spacious cabin, we headed to the plantation's full sporting clays course to warm up for tomorrow's hunt. Bill and Gina's son, also Bill, pulled targets for us.

Then it was back to the main lodge for dinner. The lodge is a place where camaraderie abounds, and friendships are renewed. The food was unbelievable. We had not even hunted yet, and we were already in love with Wynfield Plantation.

Bill Bowles picked us up the next morning in one of Wynfield's custom quail hunting vehicles. Quail hunting here is a well-managed and -thought-out affair. Bill directed our hunt, which is quite a skill in itself. Simultaneously directing the dogs and the hunter, Bill ensured the hunt was safe, careful, and thoroughly enjoyable.

Herb, Jeff, and I took turns at each point. It was not long until we had our first flush of exploding quail. Jeff got his first Georgia quail, and we took time to admire the beautiful bird.

Soon enough, another covey of quail burst open. Jeff set his sights on one and made the shot. It is necessary to do this with a covey bursting out of the bushes—you will lose focus if you pay attention to all the birds and end up with nothing. Conway, one of the pointers, held what must have seemed like eternity, waiting for us to get ready and join him in the hunt. He was rewarded with Jeff's getting another bird.

Now it was Herb's turn to zero in on one of these feathered rockets. The dogs quickly got on a few birds, and Herb did not waste any time bringing them down. The rest of the afternoon was filled with action: a long shot for Jeff; Herb gets a shot; Jeff gets a double, then another double; Herb downs another. The action continued nonstop. I, of course, had lots of fun enjoying the dogs, the sunshine, and the abundance of birds. By now, we all understood a bit more about hunting Georgia quail.

All too soon, it was time to say good-bye to the warm weather and the hospitality of Wynfield Plantation. As our plane left the ground, I thought about the challenge and enjoyment of the hunt, especially with the pleasure of my husband's and Herb's company. Quail hunting is truly a hunt for men and women of all ages.

Bill suggests that to hunt Georgia quail you need some brush pants or chaps and a shotgun you are comfortable with; that is about all. You can bring your own dog, and there are quite a few extra dog kennels provided for just that. There are also bird cleaners that clean the birds and vacuum pack them for you to take home. Even insulated coolers are provided.

For more information on quail hunting in Georgia, contact:

**BILL BOWLES**
Wynfield Plantation
Albany, GA 31708
Phone: 229-889-0193
www.wynfieldplantation.com

 # FEATURED HUNT

## Georgia Quail during the Holidays

SHEROL ENGEL

Six years after our quail hunt with Bill Bowles, we spent a memorable New Year's Eve in the piney woods of Georgia to once again try our luck at these beautiful birds. We were the guests of Frank and Connie Freshwater at the Flat Rock Preserve. Frank Freshwater is a true southern gentleman with deep roots in the red soil of the South.

Meeting and getting a chance to talk with Mike Lancaster and Chris Ricks from Flat Rock Preserve in Dublin, Georgia, was a real pleasure. We were hoping the hunting would resemble the philosophy that Mike and Chris shared. They have dogs that are well trained and well treated and land that is used wisely, with conservation and good animal habitat paramount in their efforts to provide a good place to hunt. These, in my opinion, are all-important aspects of hunting.

Today we would be hunting with English pointers and English setters. The weather was beautiful, and the dogs were ready to go. So was I! When a bird dog races across a field and suddenly freezes on point, I sometimes wonder who enjoys hunting more, the hunter or the dog. It's a heart-thumping rush when a covey of bobwhites explodes at your feet. Bobwhites are a lot quicker than the pheasant we have in the North. Frank was the first to shoot, with precise accuracy, and he was shooting a 28-gauge.

The action was fast, and our game bags were already gaining a little weight. My heart almost stopped a couple of times when either right in front of my face or directly at my side quail would pop up unexpectedly.

What a treat to exchange the ice and snow back home in Wisconsin for these fast quail in Georgia. Frank was also introducing me to some southern dialect. Can you guess what "a nerdin" is? It is the way they say "another one."

We are quail hunting in southern Georgia, and so far we are having an incredible day. Quail hunting is a longtime tradition, and although the numbers are not as good as they used to be, the sport is just as rewarding.

A dog goes on point. Jeff passes up a shot—too low. Even though your heart's pumping when you walk up on a point, it is important to always clear your line of fire and let the low birds go to keep the dogs safe. The concern for safety should always outweigh taking a shot. Almost on cue, Jeff gets rewarded with a double and stopped to admire the birds.

That afternoon was rich in camaraderie, fast action, great dog work, and a whole lot of fun, southern style. That night we traded our hunting orange for formal evening wear and joined in another

southern tradition—bringing in the New Year with style. Frank and Connie made the most gracious of hosts in their Georgia plantation–style home, with all the holiday trimmings and treats. Bringing in the New Year should always be this delightful.

The next day, we were back in our hunting attire, and we headed for "Southern Woods," another beautiful Georgia plantation, with a unique interior full of a wide array of big game mounts—and some delicious southern-style cooking. With tummies full, we went to the fields and were joined by two future hunters, Grant and Wallis Fairvalley (brother and sister), friends of Frank's family.

I participated in the passing on of the hunting tradition by offering a few shooting tips to the children. They were quick studies and anxious to head out to the field so they too could experience the thrill of these fast-flushing quail.

It took seconds for both kids to find out how easy it is to miss one of those softball-sized rockets. Soon Wallis got her first quail. You never forget your first bird, and it was wonderful to be able to share in her success and excitement. Memories like this last a lifetime.

The great dog work, the beautiful pine woods, and fine southern hospitality—a person could really get used to this style of hunting.

For information about hunting in Georgia, contact:

**VALLEY OUTDOORS—HUNTING CONSULTANT**
Frank Freshwater
Phone: 478-397-0531 or 478-825-3398
www.ValleyOutdoors.us

**FLATROCK QUAIL HUNTS**
Dublin, GA 31040
Phone: 888-820-1984
www.flatrockquailhunts.com

**SOUTHERN WOODS PLANTATION**

Sylvester, GA 31791

Phone: 229-776-0585 (Lodge); mobile: 229-347-0725

www.southernwoodsplantation.com

---

## DESTINATIONS

*State Wildlife Management Areas*

The state manages over 1 million acres of Wildlife Management Areas. DiLane Wildlife Management Area in Burke County is generally considered to be the state's best public quail hunting ground.

*U.S. Army Bases Open to Hunting*

### FORT STEWART & HUNTER ARMY AIRFIELD

Fish and Wildlife Branch—Environmental and Natural Resources Division

Fort Stewart, GA 31314-4904

Phone: 912-767-2584

www.stewart.army.mil/dpw/wildlife

On 250,000 acres of woodlands within the boundaries of Fort Stewart and Hunter Army Airfield. Deer, turkeys, feral hogs, squirrels, doves, upland gamebirds, small game, and some waterfowl, especially wood ducks. The second-largest public hunting area in the state. Whitetails are prolific and large, thanks to an aggressive land management program of prescribed burning and food plots. The deer season lasts from September through January. The season bag limit is 12. All hunters must purchase a pass: $40 per person for an annual pass or $15 for a day pass; a hunting and fishing combo, $55. The cost for E1–

E4 military is $10 annually. All hunters must pass through a checkpoint.

*U.S. Army Corp of Engineers*

### ALLATOONA LAKE

Cartersville, GA 30120-0487

Phone: 678-721-6700

http://allatoona.sam.usace.army.mil/
Land%20Management/hunting.htm

Located only 30 miles from Atlanta, Georgia, near Cartersville, Allatoona Lake is situated on the Etowah River, a tributary of the Coosa River. The lake is 12,010 acres and has 270 miles of shoreline. Hunting by permit for deer, turkeys, and small game requires a permit, which is free. Only 400 permits are issued per year. Waterfowl hunting on the lake does not require a permit. State-recognized seasons apply. Deer may only be hunted with archery. Turkeys and small game may be hunted with a shotgun with #4 shot or smaller.

### CARTERS LAKE

Oakman, GA 30732-0096

Phone: 877-334-2248

http://carters.sam.usace.army.mil/
CLhunting.htm

Approximately 6,060 acres of mountain land in Gilmer and Murray counties open for deer hunting with archery equipment only. Small game and turkeys may be hunted with firearms during open state seasons. The terrain is typical of the southern Appalachian foothills and upper Piedmont region.

Hunting is permitted on most of the public land adjacent to Carters Lake. Hunting is also allowed in campgrounds (archery only) after they are closed for the season. During the annual wheelchair hunt, no archery hunting will be permitted (wheelchair hunt dates posted in Georgia hunting regulations handbook). Hunters may gain access to remote areas of the lake by boat using Corps of Engineer boat ramps around the project.

## HARTWELL LAKE

Hartwell, GA 30643-0278
Phone: 888-893-0678
www.sas.usace.army.mil/lakes/hartwell

A large lake in the upstate region of Georgia and South Carolina on the Savannah River seven miles below the point at which the Tugaloo and Seneca rivers join to form the Savannah. Extends 49 miles up the Tugaloo and 45 miles up the Seneca—nearly 56,000 acres of water with a shoreline of 962 miles. Many areas of public land and water around Hartwell Lake are open to hunting in accordance with state hunting regulations and local restrictions. Contact office for details.

The islands on Hartwell Lake are open for hunting in accordance with state hunting regulations and seasons. In the interest of safety, big game hunters are encouraged to use archery equipment while hunting on the islands.

## LAKE SIDNEY LANIER

Buford, GA 30518
Phone: 770-945-9531
http://lanier.sam.usace.army.mil

Set in the foothills of the Georgia Blue Ridge Mountains, Lake Sidney Lanier has over 692

miles of shoreline. Waterfowl hunting is permitted in accordance with state and federal regulations. Owing to limited public land surrounding the lake and intensive residential development, no other hunting is allowed.

## RICHARD B. RUSSELL DAM AND LAKE

Elberton, GA 30635-9271
Phone: 800-944-7207
www.sas.usace.army.mil/lakes/russell

Located on the Savannah River, lying between J. Strom Thurmond Lake to the south and Hartwell Lake to the north, this area is one of the best hunting opportunities in the state. Lake Russell contains 26,650 acres of water and 540 miles of shoreline; 26,500 acres of public land surround the lake.

Richard B. Russell Project provides excellent deer, turkey, and small game hunting opportunities on public lands surrounding the lake. A state Wildlife Management Area stamp is required to hunt these areas. All developed park areas and lands adjacent to the Richard B. Russell Dam are closed to all types of hunting for safety reasons. Hunting regulations, seasons, and bag limits are set by the Georgia and South Carolina Departments of Natural Resources. For further information, contact the Operations Manager's Office at 706-213-3400 or 800-944-7207.

## WALTER F. GEORGE LAKE

Ft. Gaines, GA 31751-9722
Phone: 229-768-2516
www.sam.usace.army.mil/op/rec/wfg

A 45,000-acre lake located on the Chattahoochee River between Alabama and Georgia. Eufaula NWR is located on the northern end of the lake. There are both state- and Corps of Engineers–operated campgrounds and day-use parks. Stands of hardwood, mixed forestlands, open areas, and the lake provide habitat for waterfowl, deer, squirrels, rabbits, turkeys, and bobcats. Hunting is allowed during designated state seasons on specific Corps-managed areas, provided the hunter has a valid state hunting license and Corps of Engineers hunting permit. Deer and turkeys may be taken by bow only.

For Corps permits and more information on hunting, call 229-768-2516.

**WEST POINT LAKE**
West Point, GA 31833-9517
Phone: 706-645-2937
http://westpt.sam.usace.army.mil

Surrounded by deep forests and rolling fields, West Point Lake extends 35 miles along the Chattahoochee River on the Alabama-Georgia state line. A Wildlife Management Area of nearly 10,000 acres, located at the upper end of the lake, provides habitat for many kinds of game and nongame wildlife. Hunters with a Georgia Wildlife Management Area stamp can hunt seasonally and participate in special quota hunts. Hunting is also permitted in specific Corps-managed areas, provided the hunter has a valid state hunting license and a West Point Lake Hunting Permit and is using weapons designated for the area on a current Hunting Map.

For more information, call the LaGrange Office at 706-845-4178; or for the Georgia Department of Natural Resources (DNR), Wildlife Resource Division, call 478-825-6354. For more information about hunting at West Point Lake, contact the West Point Lake Operations Manager's Office at 706-645-2937.

*USDA National Forests*

**CHATTAHOOCHEE-OCONEE NATIONAL FORESTS**
Gainesville, GA 30501
Phone: 770-297-3000; fax: 770-297-3011
www.fs.fed.us/conf

Located in the northern region of the state, this forest is the largest tract of public hunting land in the state. The Forest Service manages wildlife habitat, and the DNR manages the animals by setting hunting seasons, bag limits, and other such rules and regulations.

*U.S. Fish and Wildlife Service*
*National Wildlife Refuges*

**BLACKBEARD ISLAND NATIONAL WILDLIFE REFUGE**
Savannah, GA 31405
Phone: 912-652-4415
www.fws.gov/blackbeardisland

Blackbeard Island is one of seven refuges administered by the Savannah Coastal Refuges Complex that extends from Pinckney Island NWR near Hilton Head Island, South Carolina, to Wolf Island NWR near Darien, Georgia. Between these lie Savannah (the largest unit in the complex), Wassaw, Tybee, Harris Neck, and Blackbeard Island refuges. Together they span a 100-mile coastline and total over 56,000 acres. The Savannah Coastal Refuges are administered from headquarters located in Savannah, Georgia. Black Island refuge's 5,618 acres include maritime forest, salt marsh, freshwater marsh, and beach habitat.

Two three-day deer hunts are scheduled in the fall and winter every year. Both hunts are nonquota archery hunts, and feral hogs may be taken, as well as deer, on each. Hunters must carry a signed hunt permit with them at all times during the hunts.

**BOND SWAMP NATIONAL
WILDLIFE REFUGE**
Round Oak, GA 31038
Phone: 478-986-5441
www.fws.gov/refuges/profiles/index
.cfm?id=41685

Located six miles south of Macon, Bond Swamp NWR currently consists of 6,500 acres of Ocmulgee River floodplain situated along the fall line separating the Piedmont and Coastal plains. Currently only deer and feral hog hunting are allowed on the refuge. Gun permits are issued by quota drawing only. Archery is by sign-in. Please contact the refuge for special seasons, regulations, and permits. A special hunt permit fee of $12.50 is required if you are drawn for a quota deer and/or hog gun hunt.

**HARRIS NECK NATIONAL
WILDLIFE REFUGE**
Townsend, GA 31331
Phone: 912-832-4608
www.fws.gov/harrisneck

One of seven refuges administered by the Savannah Coastal Refuges Complex. The refuge's 2,824 acres consist of saltwater marsh, grassland, mixed deciduous woods,

and cropland. Two managed deer hunts are conducted on the refuge each year. The first, in the fall, is a nonquota archery hunt, and the second, in the winter, is a quota shotgun hunt. Feral hogs can also be taken during both of these hunts.

**OKEFENOKEE NATIONAL
WILDLIFE REFUGE**
Folkston, GA 31537
Phone: 912-496-3331
www.fws.gov/okefenokee

Okefenokee NWR, located about 11 miles southwest of Folkston, encompasses approximately 396,000 acres with 353,000 acres designated as a National Wilderness Area. Hunting for deer, feral hogs, turkeys, and small game. For details, see www.fws.gov/okefenokee/Hunting%20Matrix.htm.

**PIEDMONT NATIONAL
WILDLIFE REFUGE**
Hillsboro, GA 31038
Phone: 478-986-5441
Email: piedmont@fws.gov
www.fws.gov/piedmont

On 35,000 acres, primarily an upland forest dominated by loblolly pine on the ridges, with hardwoods found along the creek bottoms and in scattered upland coves. Hunting is permitted on approximately 34,000 acres of the refuge. The refuge offers small game, opossum, and raccoon hunting, along with whitetail deer and turkey hunting. Whitetail deer hunting and turkey hunting are offered as quota-drawn hunts. Applications for turkey hunts are available the first week of January, while deer hunt applications are available the first week of June. All hunters must possess applicable valid state hunting licenses and a refuge special-use permit. Piedmont National Wildlife Refuge annually offers a two-day deer hunt for wheelchair-bound participants. Interested hunters should contact Piedmont NWR at 478-986-5441.

## WASSAW NATIONAL WILDLIFE REFUGE
Savannah, GA 31405
Phone: 912-652-4415
www.fws.gov/wassaw

The 10,053-acre Wassaw Island NWR is a coastal barrier island refuge that includes beaches with rolling dunes, maritime forest, and vast salt marshes. It is bordered by the Wilmington River and Wassaw Sound on the north, the Vernon River and Ossabaw Sound on the south, and the Atlantic Ocean on the east. Salt marsh and tidal creeks separate the refuge from the mainland and Skidaway Island to the west. Accessible by boat only. Two three-day deer hunts are scheduled in the fall and winter. The first is a nonquota bow hunt, and the second is a quota gun hunt (feral hogs may also be taken during both hunts).

Both Wassaw and Pine Island are open to the public during daylight hours—other upland areas are closed. There are several local marinas in the Savannah area (Skidaway Island and Isle of Hope) and a public boat ramp adjacent to the Skidaway Island bridge.

*Private Hunting Clubs and Preserves*

## BIG RED OAK PLANTATION
Gay, GA 30218-0247

Phone: 706-538-6870; fax: 706-538-0171
www.bigredoakplantation.com

Located approximately an hour's drive from either Atlanta, Columbus, or Macon, Big Red Oak Plantation offers a variety of hunting packages for bobwhite quail, pheasant, whitetail deer, and turkeys on 3,500 acres. More than 20 guides and 30 pointing bird dogs are available. Sporting clays, skeet, trap, five-stand, rifle and pistol ranges, and shooting instructions available. Home-cooked meals and a lodge with four bedrooms and three baths that can accommodate 12 guests overnight. The 25-acre lake is stocked with brim and trophy bass. Open seven days a week through seasons.

## BRUSH CREEK SPORTING CLUB
Colbert, GA 30628
Phone: 706-788-2910
www.brushcreeksportingclub.com

Amid the pine trees and rolling pastures, quail and pheasant hunts, five-stand, and sporting clays course on this working cattle and feed grass farm. Continental pheasant shoots are held periodically during the year. Open to the public and membership.

The 4,000-square foot Events Barn is available to rent for corporate or private gatherings. It can host 150-plus people at one time.

## BURNT PINE PLANTATION
Newborn, GA 30056
Phone: 706-557-0407; fax: 706-557-0409
www.burntpine.com

Burnt Pine Plantation encompasses 5,500 acres of land managed for wildlife habitat.

Located just an hour east of Atlanta, Georgia, Burnt Pine offers quail, deer, pheasant, dove, and turkey hunting and five-stand. Open to the general public and members. A new 14,000-square-foot lodge with gourmet meals and southern hospitality offers quality accommodations for groups up to 86 indoors, as well as individual hunters.

**ETOWAH VALLEY GAME PRESERVE**
Dawsonville, GA 30534
Phone: 706-265-6543
www.etowahvalleygame.com

Half- and full-day hunts for pheasant, chukar, and quail on 600 acres with 10 distinct hunting areas. British hunts, guided hunts, and self-guided hunts are all offered. Sporting clays course and trophy trout fishing. Located one hour north of Atlanta on Georgia Highway 136 just a short drive off Georgia 400.

**PINE HILL PLANTATION**
Donalsonville, GA 39845
Phone: 229-758-2464; fax: 229-758-2464
www.pinehillplantation.com

An Orvis-endorsed wing-shooting facility that provides mule-drawn wagon and horseback quail hunting in the 150-year-old tradition of the South. Stay in southern plantation lodge with southern hospitality and fine food. Located on the Georgia-Florida border northwest of Tallahassee.

**RIO PIEDRA PLANTATION**
Camilla, GA 31730

Phone: 800-538-8559; fax: 229-336-0058
www.riopiedraplantation.com

An Orvis-endorsed wing-shooting lodge located 30 minutes south of Albany, Georgia, offering elegant accommodations and food in the best traditions of the South.

**RIVERVIEW PLANTATION**
Camilla, GA 31730
Phone: 229-294-4904; fax: 229-294-9851
www.riverviewplantation.com

Located along southern Georgia's Flint River, renowned as the "Quail Capital of the World." Offering traditional bobwhite quail hunting in the plantation style—guided hunts, with Georgia native guides, and trained dogs selected from 200 in the plantation's kennel. Skeet shooting range, pro shop, and private pond stocked with rainbow trout. The specialty is corporate hunts. Forty-two single rooms in eight cottages around the main lodge are available. Only 30 hunting guests are accepted at one time. Authentic southern cuisine, plus sizable stock of beverages, including a good selection of wines with your dinner.

**SOUTHWIND PLANTATION**
Bainbridge, GA 39818
Phone: 800-456-5208; fax: 229-246-9446
www.huntsouthwind.com

An Orvis-endorsed wing-shooting lodge on the Flint River and Lake Seminole 30 miles north of Tallahassee that offers quail, duck, dove, turkey, and deer hunting. A 10,000-square-foot lodge and all amenities. The lodge recommends using over and under or side-by-side shotguns.

## WILLOWIN PLANTATION
Ocilla, GA 31774
Phone: 888-245-3977
www.willowin.com

Deer, turkey, and quail hunts, with bass- and bream-stocked ponds. Local guides and dogs available. Prefer small parties. Reasonable overnight accommodations in farmhouses on the plantation. Southern cooking at its finest. Located two hours north of Jacksonville, Florida, and three and a half hours south of Atlanta.

## WYNFIELD PLANTATION
Albany, GA 31708
Phone: 229-889-0193; fax: 229-889-1955
www.wynfieldplantation.com

The 2005 Orvis-Endorsed Wingshooting Lodge of the Year, specializing in quail hunting according to southern traditions. Elegant lodge, sporting clays, skeet, and trap. Open year-round; available for meetings. Located 12 miles west of Albany.

## MARYLAND

*In 2001 there were 115,000 resident hunters and 30,000 nonresident hunters; 87% went big game hunting, 30% small game, 32% migratory waterfowl and doves; 37% hunted on public lands; 90% hunted on private lands.*

*Hunters pumped $127 million into the state economy. (USFWS)*

### OVERVIEW
Urban sprawl and clean farming have gobbled up a lot of upland game habitat in Maryland. In the 1980s Maryland hunters bagged upward of 130,000 bobwhite quail a year here. Today the harvest is down to around 10,000 birds a year. On the bright side, deer hunting is better than ever.

The outsider may not think of Maryland as associated with deer hunting, but actually the state has a growing population of whitetails, and hunts are by far the best way to keep the herd in check.

In Deer Management Region A (Allegany, Garrett) the firearm bag limit is 2 deer—1 antlered and 1 antlerless. Deer Management Region B's whitetail deer firearm bag limit is much more liberal—2 antlered deer and 10 antlerless deer. Two antlerless deer must be taken before a second antlered deer is even pursued.

An exotic, the Japanese sika deer, is also fair game in Caroline, Dorchester, Somerset, Talbot, Wicomico, and Worcester counties. The general sika bag limit is one antlered and one antlerless.

In 2006 on the mid-November opening weekend of deer season, 17,231 deer were harvested, including 143 antlered and 147 antlerless sika deer.

About half of all deer taken by hunters during all hunting seasons occurs during the two-week firearm deer season. The top 10 counties for the 2005-2006 firearm whitetail deer harvest were Washington (5,440), Frederick (4,022), Worcester (3,125), Carroll

(2,788), Garrett (2,557), Montgomery (2,477), Baltimore (2,389), Kent (2,300), Allegany (2,299), and Charles (2,294).

Also in 2006, Bill Crutchfield Jr. took a new state record on nontypical whitetail buck with a shotgun. The buck had 26 scoreable points (13 per side) and a preliminary antler score of 268⅝ inches. If the scoring stands, that would make the buck among the top 20 all-time largest nontypical deer in the world. Crutchfield's buck weighed 150 pounds after field dressing.

## DESTINATIONS

### General Information
For guides on hunting in Maryland, see www.hotspotguides.com/hunting/hguides_MD.asp.

### State Wildlife Management Areas
A list and maps for the state's many Wildlife Management Areas, including state forests and parks, can be found at www.dnr.maryland.gov/huntersguide/public-lands.asp.

### U.S. Fish and Wildlife Service
### National Wildlife Refuges

### BLACKWATER NATIONAL WILDLIFE REFUGE
Cambridge, MD 21613
Phone: 410-228-5018 (Allen Johnston)
www.fws.gov/blackwater/hunting
.html#rules

Hunting at Blackwater for whitetail deer and sika deer is on a first-come, first-serve basis—no standby. Blackwater normally hosts a month of archery, two days of muzzleloader (usually early season), one day for a youth hunt, and four days of shotgun hunting. Take special care when hunting here: there are three endangered species in this area—the southern bald eagle, the Delmarva fox squirrel, and the Arctic peregrine falcon.

### EASTERN NECK NATIONAL WILDLIFE REFUGE
Rock Hall, MD 21661
Phone: 410-639-7056; fax: 410-639-2516
www.fws.gov/northeast/easternneck/
index.html

A 2,286-acre island located at the confluence of the Chester River and the Chesapeake Bay, about six miles south of Rock Hall. Public hunting of whitetail deer is permitted on Eastern Neck NWR on specific days that are annually designated by the refuge manager in cooperation with the Maryland Department of Natural Resources. Hunters must obtain a permit to hunt at Eastern Neck NWR. A youth turkey hunt is being developed. For details, see www.fws.gov/northeast/eastern neck/services.html#hunting.

## PATUXENT RESEARCH REFUGE AND MEADE NATURAL HERITAGE ASSOCIATION REFUGE

Laurel, MD 20708-4036
Phone: 301-497-5580
www.fws.gov/northeast/patuxent/
prrdefault.html

The 12,750-acre Patuxent Research Refuge is the nation's only National Wildlife Refuge established to support wildlife research. The refuge supports a wide diversity of wildlife in forest, meadow, and wetland habitats. Hunting for upland game, waterfowl, and whitetail deer (bow, muzzleloader, and shotgun) is managed by refuge officials and the Meade Natural Heritage Association (MNHA) through a permit system. For details, see www.fws.gov/northeast/patuxent/MNHA.html.

*U.S. National Park Service*

## ASSATEAGUE ISLAND NATIONAL SEASHORE

Berlin, MD 21811
Phone: 410-641-1441 (Maryland District Visitor Information),
410-641-3030 (National Seashore Camping), or 757-336-6577
(Virginia District Visitor Information)
www.nps.gov/asis

This famous barrier island off the coast of Maryland not only has wild horses, but it has an abundance of wild game, and it is one of the few areas administered by the U.S. National Park Service that allows, even encourages, hunting. Hunting is permitted for whitetail deer, sika deer (up to six per year),

rabbit, quail, waterfowl, dove, and fox. There are special regulations for hunting here. For details, see www.nps.gov/asis/hunting-at-assateague.htm.

One friend who has hunted here considers the time spent here during a hunt for sika deer to be among the most magical of anyplace he has hunted, even though he did not shoot one.

## CHESAPEAKE BAY GATEWAYS NETWORK

NPS—Chesapeake Bay Program
Annapolis, MD 21403
Phone: 888-BAYWAYS (Maryland Tourism Information), 888-824-5877
(Virginia Tourism Information),
or 800-YOUR-BAY (Administrative Offices)
www.nps.gov/cbpo

Chesapeake Bay is an estuary stretching from southernmost Virginia to northernmost Maryland, a distance of 180 miles. The bay, and its surrounding 64,000-square-mile watershed, is a gold mine for recreational opportunities. The Gateways Network is a system of over 120 parks, refuges, museums, historic communities, and water trails in the bay watershed. Thirteen of these facilities offer hunting opportunities. To obtain information about the various facilities offering hunting, see www.baygateways.net/byactivity.cfm.

Any sportsman who has ever explored Chesapeake Bay knows there are two very strong traditions here: one is blue crabs, served in piles with beer at special crab house restaurants, and the other is hunting waterfowl flocking to the beds of eel grass on the bay.

**CHESTNUT MANOR FARMS HUNTING**
Centreville, MD 21617
Phone: 410-310-8165 (Temple Rhodes) or
410-708-1646 (Tommy Leager)
http://chestnutmanorfarms.com

Located in Queen Anne's County, Chestnut Manor offers hunts for dove, turkey, waterfowl, deer, and upland game birds. Day lodge. Motels nearby.

**GUNPOWDER GAME FARM**
Hampstead, MD 21074
Phone: 410-239-6980 or 410-374-1434
www.gunpowdergamefarm.com

Located north of Baltimore, over 450 acres for released pheasant, quail, and chukar and wild dove hunting. Guides and dogs available.

**PINTAIL POINT**
Queenstown, MD 21658
Phone: 800-697-1777
www.pintailpoint.com

An Orvis-endorsed wing-shooting lodge, Pintail Point offers released chukar, pheasant, and Hungarian partridge, wild deer and waterfowl hunting, plus sporting clays, yacht rentals, and two elegant bed-and-breakfasts on Maryland's eastern shore. Located 45 miles from Baltimore and Washington, D.C. Suitable for corporate retreats.

**PITBOSS WATERFOWL INC.**
Capt. Jeff Coats
Bel Air, MD 21015

Phone: 410-838-7264
www.pitbosswaterfowl.com

Guided hunts on Chesapeake Bay for sea ducks (scoter, harlequin, eider, old squaw), diving ducks (redheads, canvasback, scaup), and brant.

**SCHRADER'S BRIDGETOWN MANOR**
Henderson, MD 21640-1317
Phone: 410-758-1824; fax: 410-482-7189
www.schradershunting.com

Located on over 25,000 acres of outstanding hunting lands on Maryland's Eastern Shore, Schrader's offers waterfowl, whitetail, sea duck, upland birds (pheasant, chukar, quail, and Huns), flighted mallards, dove, rabbits, and squirrel hunting, plus sporting clays and 3-D archery range and freshwater and saltwater fishing. Accommodations: Bridgetown Manor, bed-and-breakfast, lodge large enough for meetings and celebrations.

**WINGS OF CHALLENGE**
Accident, MD 21520
Phone: 301-746-8868
www.wingsofchallenge.com

Located in western Maryland, 380 acres for hunting released pheasant, Hungarian partridge, and quail, plus sporting clays and 3-D archery range. Lodging nearby.

## NEW JERSEY

*In 2001 there were 108,000 resident hunters and 27,000 nonresident hunters: 83% went* *big game hunting, 45% small game, % waterfowl uncertain; 63% hunted on public lands; 77% hunted on private lands. Hunters pumped $151 million into the state economy. (US-FWS)*

## OVERVIEW

New Jersey has more than 500,000 acres of state-owned public open space, including more than 308,000 acres in 121 Wildlife Management Areas, specifically managed for wildlife-oriented recreation as well as conservation.

Deer hunters can enjoy more than a hundred days of their sport, including seasons for bow, shotgun, and muzzleloading rifle. Multiple bag limits are the rule in most zones. The 2005–2006 deer harvest was 59,657.

Waterfowl hunting in New Jersey is among the best along the East Coast. Snow geese, brant, black ducks, mallards, buffleheads, and a variety of other waterfowl pass through New Jersey, with Barnegat Bay being the ultimate hotspot. There is a long tradition of waterfowl hunting along the New Jersey coast, which in 1836 inspired Captain Hazelton Seaman to design and build the "Barnegat Bay sneakbox" boat, nicknamed "the Devil's Coffin." Eaglewood Township proudly proclaims on its welcome sign that it's the home of the first sneakbox for duck hunting.

The low-profile sneakboxes were traditionally made by hand from white Jersey cedar, so the boats would be lightweight and durable. On contact with water, the cedar swells, sealing leaks. Jersey cedar is also great for making wooden duck decoys.

Today the 14- to 16-foot sneakboxes are covered with fiberglass. Details on the sneakbox and its use, including a short movie, can be found at www.lehsd.k12.nj.us/SEAPORT/ Jones/barnegat_bay_sneakbox.htm.

The sneakbox is especially suited to traveling through narrow creeks that lead into the marsh along the Barnegat Bay shoreline and hiding in marsh grasses—the boat becoming a floating blind.

You can access Barnegat Bay for hunting waterfowl and deer at the 43,000-acre Edwin B. Forsythe National Wildlife Refuge in Oceanville. Hunters must obtain a refuge permit, as well as required state licenses and federal waterfowl stamp. Many people today hunt waterfowl on Barnegat Bay from floating blinds.

For those who like a little elbowroom and are willing to get wet, a test of wing shooting is the rail, which is found in abundance along the marshlands of the seacoast.

"Mud hennin'" is what locals call pursuing clapper rail, or "railbirds," on the salt meadows, and there's no better place to do it

---

**NEW JERSEY SNAPSHOT
GARDEN STATE**

- **General hunting information:** www.state.nj.us/ dep/fgw/hunting.htm

- **Guides:** For a list of state approved guides, and more information on licenses and seasons, see: www.state.nj.us/dep/fgw/guidelst.htm

- **To report poachers, contact:** OPERATION GAME THIEF, 800-222-0456; rewards are paid to tips that lead to arrests from OGT tips

- **Deer population:** 160,000, 35th in the United States

- **Average deer harvest:** 67,432, 28th in the United States

than the 12,703-acre Cape May Wetlands Wildlife Management Area in southern New Jersey, which has one of the highest populations of clapper rail in the mid-Atlantic states seacoast tidal region.

Rail are long-legged marsh birds—a little like woodcocks or snipes, with longer legs and shorter beaks—that live on freshwater and saltwater wetland marshes.

You can choose one or two approaches to hunting rail.

1. Put on old clothes and tennis shoes and get wet and muddy, or don waders, and walk the marsh during the last couple of hours of rising tide—the higher the tide, the better. It's a good idea to have a wading stick along to test for sinkholes. A flushing dog is very helpful for putting up birds and retrieving them, especially if they fall in deeper water or a sinkhole.

2. You can also hunt rail from a shallow draft boat, like the Barnegat Bay sneakbox.

People will usually cook rail in a crockpot, or you can bake them with a strip of bacon wrapped around each bird.

Like all migratory waterfowl, nontoxic shot and federal and state duck stamps are required. The limit on rail is 10. Rail season runs from September 1 through November 8.

## DESTINATIONS

### State Wildlife Management Areas
Some 55,000 pheasant are released yearly on selected Wildlife Management Areas. For a list of areas, see www.state.nj.us/dep/fgw/wmaland.htm.

### U.S. National Park Service

**NEW JERSEY PINELANDS NATIONAL RESERVE**
Philadelphia, PA 19106
Phone: 215-597-1903 (Headquarters), 609-894-7300 (Visitor Information)
www.nps.gov/pine

Portions of seven southern New Jersey counties, and encompassing over 1 million acres of farms, forests, and wetlands, with about half the area under private ownership. Hunting for all legal species is permitted according to state regulations.

### U.S. Fish and Wildlife Service
### National Wildlife Refuges

**CAPE MAY NATIONAL WILDLIFE REFUGE**
Cape May Court House, NJ 08210-2078
Phone: 609-463-0994; fax: 609-463-1667
www.fws.gov/northeast/capemay/index.html

Consisting of 11,000 acres on the Cape May peninsula, the refuge offers deer and migratory waterfowl hunting under state and federal regulations. For details, see www.fws.gov/northeast/capemay/PublicAccess.html#GENERAL_HUNTING.

**EDWIN B. FORSYTHE NATIONAL WILDLIFE REFUGE**
Oceanville, NJ 08231

Phone: 609-652-1665; fax: 609-652-1474
www.fws.gov/northeast/forsythe

More than 43,000 acres on Barnegat Bay. The refuge is open for deer and migratory bird hunting. For details, see www.fws.gov/northeast/forsythe/hunting%20opportunities.html.

## SUPAWNA MEADOWS NATIONAL WILDLIFE REFUGE
Pennsville, NJ 08070
Phone: 609-463-0994
www.fws.gov/northeast/nj/spm.htm

Part of the Cape May National Wildlife Refuge Complex, waterfowl and archery, shotgun, and muzzleloader deer hunting—unlimited antlerless deer and one antlered deer—subject to state and federal regulations, seasons, and bag limits as well as specific regulations for the refuge. Please contact the Refuge Office for a map of the designated hunting areas and refuge-specific regulations. Special permit required.

## WALLKILL RIVER NATIONAL WILDLIFE REFUGE
Sussex, New Jersey 07461
Phone: 973-702-7266; fax: 973-702-7286
www.fws.gov/northeast/wallkillriver/hunting.htm

Located in Sussex County, New Jersey, and Orange County, New York, hunting is permitted for deer, wild turkeys, and migratory birds on this 3,500-acre refuge. Refuge permit required.

*Private Hunting Clubs and Preserves*

## BENT CREEK HUNTING PRESERVE
Allentown, NJ 08501
Phone: 609-259-9501
www.bentcreekpreserve.net

A 500-acre preserve for released pheasant and chukar hunting; field and European shoots; guides and dogs available. A 30-target outdoor 3-D archery range is also available.

## BUTTONWOOD GAME PRESERVE
Phillipsburg, NJ 08865
Phone: 908-454-7116
www.buttonwoodpreserve.com

A 150-acre preserve for released pheasant, chukar, and quail hunts. Guides and dogs, sporting clays, and 3-D archery range available. Membership options.

## GAME CREEK HUNTING FARMS
Woodstown, NJ 08098
Phone: 856-769-0035
www.gamecreek.com

Released pheasant, chukar, and quail field and continental hunts and spring wild turkey hunts on a number of farms within a three-mile radius of the clubhouse. Rental cabin for overnights. Membership options.

## G&R GAME FARM
New Egypt, NJ 08533
Phone: 609-758-8942 (Reservations), 609-462-4222 (Information)
www.gandargamefarm.com

Located on a 265-acre working dairy farm in Ocean County, New Jersey, G&R offers released pheasant and chukar unguided hunts and tower shoots, and wild Canada goose hunting.

**GIBERSON FARMS WILDLIFE
 PRESERVE, INC.**
Pemberton, NJ 08068
Phone: 609-726-0600
www.gibersonfarms.com

Released pheasant, quail, and chukar field hunts and tower shoots, and wild goose hunts in rural south Jersey near Mount Holly. Membership options.

# HERITAGE DESTINATIONS

If you are in the Eagleswood area, hunting or not, don't pass up a chance to visit the "Hunting Shanty" gift shop, which has an exhibit on the early guns used by local waterfowl hunters.

And if you fancy wooden decoys, a must-see place is the Barnegat Bay Decoy and Bayman's Museum in Tuckerton, a 1,330-square-foot replica of a hunting shanty where you are greeted on the porch by a wax figure of the late "master" carver Harry V. Shourds. Inside are early versions of Barnegat Bay duck boats and over 100 hand-carved classic wooden decoys. The museum is open from 10:00 A.M. to 4:30 P.M., Wednesday through Sunday and closed Monday and Tuesday. Admission is $2.00, and children under 12 are free. Group and student rates are available upon request.

**BARNEGAT BAY DECOY AND
BAYMAN'S MUSEUM**
Tuckerton, NJ 08087
Phone: 609-296-8868
www.oceancountygov.com/decoy/
default.htm

## NEW YORK

*In 2001 there were 635,000 resident hunters and 79,000 nonresident hunters: 93% went big game hunting, 38% small game, 14% waterfowl; 35% hunted on public lands; 89% hunted on private lands. Hunters pumped $822 million into the state economy. (USFWS)*

### OVERVIEW
About 85% of the state is private property and that is where most hunting occurs. Whitetail deer and ruffed grouse are the most popular species, with the Adirondack Mountains being considered one of the most beautiful places to hunt in the United States.

New York hunters harvest about 150,000 ruffed grouse and 100,000 pheasant a year.

---

**NEW YORK SNAPSHOT
EMPIRE STATE**

- **General information:** New York State Department of Environmental Conservation, www.dec.state.ny.us/website/dfwmr/wildlife/worhunt.html

- **State hunting licenses can be purchased online at:** https://nyfgisales.vansis.wcom.com/fgnyia/html/welcome.jsp

- **Deer population:** 810,000, 16th in the United States

- **Average deer harvest:** 271,651, 10th in the United States

---

Wild turkey hunters bag about 25,000 gobblers in the spring and another 10,000 to 15,000 in the fall. In 2005, 89,000 bucks and 61,200 antlerless deer were bagged.

## DESTINATIONS

*State Wildlife Management Areas*
More than 85 state Wildlife Management Areas that offer hunting and encompass 200,000 acres are scattered around the state. For details, see:

**DIVISION OF FISH, WILDLIFE AND MARINE RESOURCES**
New York State Department of Environmental Conservation
Albany, NY 12233-4754
Phone: 518-474-2121
www.dec.ny.gov

*U.S. Fish and Wildlife Service*
*National Wildlife Refuges*

**IROQUOIS NATIONAL WILDLIFE REFUGE**
Basom, NY 14013-9730
Phone: 585-948-5445
www.fws.gov/northeast/iroquois

Located midway between Buffalo and Rochester, 10,818 acres of freshwater marshes and hardwood swamps bounded by woods, forests, pastures, and wet meadows, offering deer, small game, turkey, and waterfowl hunting. For details, see www.fws.gov/northeast/iroquois/PublicAccess.html.

**MONTEZUMA NATIONAL WILDLIFE REFUGE**
Seneca Falls, New York 13148

Phone: 315-568-5987
www.fws.gov/r5mnwr

Located at the north end of Cayuga Lake, in the heart of the Finger Lakes Region between Rochester and Syracuse. Some 8,000 acres offering waterfowl and deer hunting under special regulations. For details, see www.fws.gov/r5mnwr/2006-MNWRHUNT REGULATIONS.pdf.

*U.S. National Park Service*

**FIRE ISLAND NATIONAL SEASHORE**
Patchogue, NY 11772
Phone: 631-289-4810
www.nps.gov/fiis

Located only an hour's drive from Manhattan on a coastal island accessible by boat or bridge, Fire Island National Seashore provides limited opportunities for waterfowl hunting. You must first obtain a hunting permit from the Seashore. To get one you must have a valid New York State hunting license, a signed "duck stamp" (for hunters age 16 and older), a valid state driving license, and a confirmation number from the Migratory Bird Harvest Information Program (HIP).

*Private Hunting Clubs and Preserves*

**BASSWOOD LODGE AND HUNTING PRESERVE**
Ogdensburg, New York 13669
Phone: 315-379-1528
www.basswoodhunting.com

"Released," not planted, mallard and pheasant hunts and turkey and deer hunting for members. Three lodges, trapshooting, kennels, clubhouse, plus wild boar, elk, fallow deer, and buffalo hunting options. Located in northern New York State, near Lake Ontario.

## PHEASANT HOLLOW GUN DOGS AND HUNTING CLUB LLC

Bloomfield, NY 14469
Phone: 585-657-7765
www.pheasanthollow.com

Over 1,000 acres on the west side of the Finger Lakes area for released pheasant and chukar hunts. Members have exclusive access to 600-plus acres of cornfields, wheat fields, soybean fields, and woods to hunt wild turkey, deer, and geese.

## RINGNECK HUNTING PRESERVE AND GAME FARM

Darien Center, NY 14040
Phone: 585-547-3749
www.ringneckhunting.com

Located 30 miles east of Buffalo, released pheasant, chukar, and bobwhite quail. Guides and dogs available. Accommodations for up to six.

## SHAWANGUNK FISH & GAME ASSOCIATION

Middletown, NY 10940
Phone: 845-355-7431
www.shawangunkfishngame.org

An over 100-year-old membership club offering released pheasant, chukar, and quail; deer, turkey, waterfowl, and small game hunting; trap range, 3-D shoots, hunter safety classes, fishing (trout, bass, channel catfish, and pan

fish), and much more. Clubhouse membership results in access to many properties.

## TMT HUNTING PRESERVE AND SPORTING CLAYS

Staatsburg, NY 12580
Phone: 845-266–5108
www.tmthuntingpreserve.com

On 290 acres, located 70 miles north of New York City, offering released pheasant and chukar in fields or woods (to simulate grouse) and mallards. Sporting clays and clubhouse.

## WHALEBACK FARM HUNTING PRESERVE AND SPORTING CLAYS

Canandaigua, New York 14424
Phone: 585-385-9725 (Office), 585-554-3967 (Farm); fax: 585-586-1828
www.whalebackfarm.com

On 650 acres contiguous with 10,000 acres of public Game Management Land in the western Finger Lakes region, offering released field and continental hunts for pheasant, quail, chukar, and Hungarian partridge, plus hunts for turkey and deer, sporting clays, dog training, horseback riding, cross-country skiing, and fishing. Camping and clubhouse.

## WILDLIFE OUTDOOR ENTERPRISES

Big Flats, NY 14814-0418
Phone: 607-562-7414; fax: 607-562-7271
www.wildlifeproperties.net

Organization that seeks to match hunters with their desires for leased lands, as well as Steuben Hunting Lodge in Steuben County for quality whitetail deer hunts and lodging.

# NORTH CAROLINA

*In 2001 there were 272,000 resident hunters and 23,000 nonresident hunters: 76% went big game hunting, 42% small game, 35% migratory waterfowl and dove; 30% hunted on public lands; 85% hunted on private lands. Hunters pumped $438 million into the state economy. (USFWS)*

## OVERVIEW

North Carolina is a hunter-friendly state with an abundance of game and a lot of beautiful, mountainous country that meets the ocean. The deer herd is estimated at 1.1 million, and the bag limit is two a day, six per season, four of which must be antlerless. Hunters harvest about 120,000 to 140,000 whitetails a year here.

There are an estimated 11,000 black bears in North Carolina, which has a number of bear sanctuaries spread around the state.

Three turkey seasons are offered: fall,

---

**NORTH CAROLINA SNAPSHOT
TAR HEEL STATE**

- **General information:** www.wildlife.state.nc.us

- **Special permits:** North Carolina offers a number of special permit hunts, such as 5,000 permits to hunt tundra swans; for details, see www.ncwildlife.org/fs_index_04_hunting.htm; this is a no hunting on Sunday state

- **Deer hunting information:** www.ncdeerman.com/2005Stats.htm

- **Deer population:** 1.1 million, 9th in the United States

- **Average deer harvest:** 149,718, 20th in the United States

---

winter, and spring. And if you like hunting rabbits or squirrels, the season bag limit is 75.

## DESTINATIONS

### State Lands

North Carolina is aggressively seeking to provide more hunting opportunities on public lands. The state manages a number of state game lands dove fields—www.wildlife.state.nc.us/fs_index_04_hunting.htm—as well as other lands open to hunting. Call 919-707-0060 for a book of maps or see www.ncwildlife.org/fs_index_04_hunting.htm. Descriptions of game lands: www.wildlife.state.nc.us/pg01_License/pg1b_descriptions.pdf. Descriptions of hunting destinations on public and private lands: www.visitnc.com/tools_search_results.asp#top.

### Federal Lands

**USDA NATIONAL FORESTS IN NORTH CAROLINA**
Asheville, NC 28802
Phone: 828-257-4200
www.cs.unca.edu/nfsnc

In North Carolina there are four national forests (Nantahala, Uwharrie, Pisgah, and Croatan) covering 1.2 million acres, from the mountains to the Atlantic Ocean. All allow hunting according to state regulations.

### U.S. Fish and Wildlife Service
### National Wildlife Refuges

There are 11 U.S. Fish and Wildlife Service National Wildlife Refuges in North Carolina that allow certain kinds of hunting. For details, see www.fws.gov/northcarolina/hunt.html or contact them directly:

**ALLIGATOR RIVER NATIONAL WILDLIFE REFUGE**
Manteo, NC 27954
Phone: 252-473-1131; fax: 252-473-1668
www.fws.gov/alligatorriver

**BACK BAY NATIONAL WILDLIFE REFUGE***
Virginia Beach, VA 23456-4325
Phone: 757-721-2412
www.fws.gov/backbay

**CEDAR ISLAND NATIONAL WILDLIFE REFUGE**
Carteret County, NC
Phone: 252-926-4021 (c/o Mattamuskeet National Wildlife Refuge)
www.fws.gov/cedarisland

**CURRITUCK NATIONAL WILDLIFE REFUGE**
Corolla, NC 27927
Phone: 252-429-3100 (c/o Mackay Island National Wildlife Refuge)
www.fws.gov/mackayisland/currituck

**GREAT DISMAL SWAMP†**
Suffolk, VA 23434
Phone: 757-986-3705
www.fws.gov/northeast/greatdismalswamp

**MACKAY ISLAND NATIONAL WILDLIFE REFUGE**
Knotts Island, NC 27950
Phone: 252-429-3100
www.fws.gov/mackayisland

**MATTAMUSKEET NATIONAL WILDLIFE REFUGE**
Swan Quarter, NC 27885
Phone: 252-926-4021; fax: 252-926-1743
www.fws.gov/mattamuskeet

**PEE DEE NATIONAL WILDLIFE REFUGE**
Wadesboro, NC 28170
Phone: 704-694-4424; fax: 704-694-6570
www.fws.gov/peedee

**POCOSIN LAKES NATIONAL WILDLIFE REFUGE**
Columbia, NC 27925
Phone: 252-796-3004
www.fws.gov/pocosinlakes

**ROANOKE RIVER NATIONAL WILDLIFE REFUGE**
Windsor, NC 27983
Phone: 252-794-3808
www.fws.gov/roanokeriver

**SWAN QUARTER NATIONAL WILDLIFE REFUGE**
Swan Quarter, NC 27885
Phone: 252-926-4021 (c/o Mattamuskeet National Wildlife Refuge)
www.fws.gov/swanquarter

*Private Hunting Clubs and Preserves*
A complete list of hunting preserves for upland birds and foxes can be found at

---

*Although the address for Back Bay National Wildlife Refuge is Virginia, the refuge is actually located in both North Carolina and Virginia.
†Located in both North Carolina and Virginia.

www.ncwildlife.org/fs_index_04_hunting
.htm. The following are a few selected destinations:

**ADAMS CREEK HUNTING LODGE**
Havelock, NC 28532
Phone: 252-447-6808
www.adamscreekgunsports.com

Ducks—puddle, divers, and sea—plus deer
are featured here on the Intracoastal Waterway near the Neuse River. The lodge is an
1870s restored farmhouse with southern-
style meals. Sporting clays and five-stand.

**C. PIERCE FARMS SHOOTING PRESERVE**
Ahoskie, NC 27910
Phone: 252-332-5360
www.cpiercefarms.com

Released pheasant, chukar, and quail for field
and tower shoots. Guides and dogs available.
Deer hunting also available.

**DEWITT'S GAME FARM, LLC**
Ellerbe, NC 28338
Phone: 910-652-2926;
fax: 910-652-5814
www.dgfbirds.com

Released quail, pheasant, and chukar for
field and tower shoots; guided duck hunts for
released mallards. Sporting clays. Pro shop.
Corporate outings.

**DRAKE LANDING AT ANDREWS FARMS**
Fuquay Varina, NC 27526
Phone: 919-552-9455 or 919-669-8482
www.huntdrakelanding.com

A 1,250-acre preserve in an agricultural
community located 20 miles south of Ra-
leigh and 55 miles northeast of Pinehurst.
Specialty is released mallards, but field
and tower shoots for pheasant and quail
also offered. Guides, dogs, and lodging
available.

**FEATHER CREEK FARMS HUNTING
PRESERVE, LLC**
Greenville, NC 27834
Phone: 252-752-3381;
fax: 252-752-2379
www.feathercreekfarms.com

Released and wild ducks, released upland
birds (chukar, quail, and pheasant—field
and tower shoots), turkey, goose, and deer
hunts. Located in east-central North Carolina.

**THE FORK FARM**
Norwood, NC 28128
Phone: 704-438-0079
www.theforkfarm.com

Located 40 miles east of Charlotte on 1,300
acres, dove, duck, quail, pheasant, and deer
hunting, plus sporting clays. Lodge, pro shop,
overnight accommodations.

**SHADY KNOLL GAMEBIRD FARM &
SHOOTING PRESERVE**
Asheboro, NC 27203-8109
Phone: 336-879-3663
www.shadyknollbirds.com

Located in central North Carolina 30 minutes from Greensboro, Shady Knoll offers

quail and pheasant half-day hunts. Guides and dogs available. Membership option.

**TOBACCO STICK HUNTING PRESERVE**
Biscoe, NC 27209
Phone: 910-974-7100 or 910-428-1732;
fax: 910-974-3866
www.tobaccostick.com

Mallard, quail, pheasant, and chukar hunts, rustic lodging, and home-cooked meals. Guides and dogs available.

**WINTERGREEN HUNTING PRESERVE**
Bladenboro, NC 28320
Phone: 910-648-6171
www.wintergreenhuntingpreserve.com

Quail, pheasant (field and continental), and duck hunts offered on a 500-acre farm.

*Land Management Club*
The Central Carolina Outdoor Club, Inc. (CCOC) is the exclusive Charlotte-area franchise of the American Wildlife Association, a national network of sportsmen's clubs that provides year-round access to private land leases for hunting and fishing in North and South Carolina.

This is a membership club. For more information, contact:

**CENTRAL CAROLINA OUTDOOR CLUB, INC.**
Attention: Dan Hartman
Matthews, NC 28104
Phone: 704-321-2603
www.centralcarolinaoutdoorclub.com

# PENNSYLVANIA

*In 2001 there were 858,000 resident hunters and 142,000 nonresident hunters: 96% went big game hunting, 37% small game, 9% migratory waterfowl and doves; 48% hunted on public lands; 75% hunted on private lands. Hunters pumped $941 million into the state economy. (USFWS)*

## OVERVIEW
With its deer, bears, elk, waterfowl, pheasant, turkeys, and ruffed grouse, plus groundhogs and coyotes, Pennsylvania traditionally has more hunters in the field than any other state except for Texas, and they could use more. The state's deer herd is at an all-time high, resulting in more deer-auto crashes than any other state.

Hunters bag an average of 3,000 black bears, 200,000 pheasant, and over 400,000 whitetails a year in Pennsylvania, where there are 17 deer for every 1,000 people.

To create more hunting opportunities, the Pennsylvania Game Commission releases

---

**PENNSYLVANIA SNAPSHOT**
**KEYSTONE STATE**

- **General information:** www.pgc.state.pa.us/pgc/cwp/browse.asp?a=460&bc=0&c=69880&pgcNav=|
- **Information on annual Field Forecast for hunting on wildlife units around the state:** www.pgc.state.pa.us/pgc/cwp/view.sp?a=463&q=169662
- **Deer population:** 1.6 million, 3rd in the United States
- **Average deer harvest:** 476,470, 3rd in the United States

100,000 mature pheasant into various state wildlife areas every year, and it offers sportsmen's organizations with approved propagation facilities free day-old pheasant chicks to raise for release.

Pennsylvania also offers an annual Field Forecast for hunting on wildlife units around the state, which appears online at www .pgc.state.pa.us/pgc/cwp/view.asp?a=463& q=169662.

## DESTINATIONS

### State Lands

There are 63 state game lands. See www .pgc.state.pa.us/pgc/cwp/browse.asp?a=480

### U.S. Army Corps of Engineers

The Baltimore and Pittsburgh Districts of the Army Corps of Engineers maintain over 20 dams and flood control projects in Pennsylvania that offer hunting opportunities according to state regulations and local rules. For details, see:

**U.S. ARMY CORPS OF ENGINEERS, BALTIMORE DISTRICT**
Baltimore, MD 21203-1715
Phone: 410-962-7608
www.nab.usace.army.mil/whoweare

**U.S. ARMY CORPS OF ENGINEERS, PITTSBURGH DISTRICT**
Pittsburgh, PA 15222-4186
Phone: 412-395-7500; fax: 412-644-2811
www.lrp.usace.army.mil/index.html

### USDA National Forests

**ALLEGHENY NATIONAL FOREST**
Warren, PA 16365
Phone: 814-723-5150
www.fs.fed.us/r9/forests/allegheny

Located in the northwest portion of the state, including 87 miles of the Allegheny River. There are over 100 undeveloped islands, including seven wilderness islands, in this stretch of river. Hickory Creek Wilderness, Allegheny Islands Wilderness, and Allegheny National Recreation Areas also lie within the forest boundaries. Hunting is permitted according to state regulations. For details, see www.fs.fed.us/r9/forests/allegheny/ recreation/hunting.

### U.S. National Park Service

**DELAWARE WATER GAP NATIONAL RECREATION AREA**
Bushkill, PA 18324-9999
Phone: 570-588-2452 (Visitor Information Recording)
www.nps.gov/dewa

This park preserves 40 miles of the middle Delaware River and almost 70,000 acres of land along the river's New Jersey and Pennsylvania shores. Hunting is permitted in most parts of the recreation area. All applicable state and additional park-specific federal regulations must be followed. The laws of the state to which they belong govern islands in the river. For regulations and a list of closures, see www.nps.gov/dewa/planyourvisit/ hunting.htm.

**ERIE NATIONAL WILDLIFE REFUGE**
Guys Mills, PA 16327
Phone: 814-789-3585; fax: 814-789-2909
www.fws.gov/northeast/erie/r5ernwr_
visitors.html#hunting or www.fws.gov/
northeast/erie/erie_nwr_hunting.pdf

Rabbit, squirrel, grouse, woodchuck, pheasant, quail, raccoon, fox, skunk, coyote, woodcock, migratory waterfowl, whitetail deer, dove, wild turkey, and bear hunting is permitted according to state and local refuge regulations.

*Private Hunting Clubs and Preserves*

**HILLENDALE HUNTING CLUB**
Tyrone, PA 16686
Phone: 814-684-5015; fax: 814-684-8869
www.hillendalehuntingclub.com

Over 400 acres for field and European-style pheasant and chukar, plus released mallards, sporting clays, and fly-fishing in the Sinking Valley of central Pennsylvania. Clubhouse and overnight accommodations.

**KNAPPING KNAPP FARM INC.**
Titusville, PA 16354
Phone: 814-827-1092
www.theknappfarm.com

Over 1,000 acres offering hunting for pheasant, chukar, Hungarian partridge, quail, wild turkeys, and deer, with historic farmhouse bed-and-breakfast located in west-central Pennsylvania.

**NATURAL SURROUNDINGS PRESERVE INC.**
Gilbert, PA 18331
Phone: 570-977-5375 or 570-350-7962
www.nspinc.org

Melanistic mutant, blueback, buff, and Mongolian pheasant, chukar partridge, and quail hunts. All hunts must be reserved. Located near Brodheadsville.

**POWDERBOURNE**
East Greenville, PA 18041
Phone: 215-679-9860 or 215-679-3554;
fax: 215-679-0558
www.powderbourne.com

Sporting clays, skeet, five-stand, hunting for pheasant and chukar on 450 acres, plus an established restaurant located in east Greenville, Pennsylvania.

**STONE CREEK GAME BIRDS**
Avella, PA 15312
Phone: 724-947-3574
www.stonecreekgamebirds.com

A 144-acre beef cattle farm with areas set aside for field and tower/European–style hunting for pheasant, quail and chukar. Located about 45 miles southwest of Pittsburgh in Washington County.

**WARRIORS MARK SHOOTING PRESERVE**
Ginter, PA 16651
Phone: 814-378-8380; fax: 814-378-8381
www.warriorsmark.com

Over 1,400 acres in the Appalachians for field hunts for pheasant, quail, and chukar, as well as driven pheasant hunts, sporting clays, gundogs and puppies, dog training, 3-D archery, pro shop, and meeting rooms.

## SOUTH CAROLINA

*In 2001 there were 221,000 resident hunters and 44,000 nonresident hunters: 82% went big game hunting, 38% small game, 27% migratory waterfowl and doves; 20% hunted on public lands; 92% hunted on private lands. Hunters pumped $305 million into the state economy. (USFWS)*

### OVERVIEW

South Carolina is arguably the wild turkey capital of the United States, with the headquarters of the National Wildlife Turkey Federation located in Edgefield, although the whitetail deer remains the number-one game animal of the state. In 2005 a total of 123,503 bucks and 120,542 does were harvested for a statewide total of 244,045 deer.

When a hunter thinks of South Carolina, one automatically thinks of quail, but there is a bit of a shocker here. In 2005 hunt-ers bagged about 100,000 quail in South Carolina, which is about one-tenth of the average annual bag of the 1980s. Habitat is the key here to bringing back the quail tradition of South Carolina.

Otherwise, South Carolina is rich with game—hogs, waterfowl, doves, squirrels, and rabbits are also popular.

### DESTINATIONS

*U.S. Army Corps of Engineers*

**J. STROM THURMOND LAKE**
Clarks Hill, SC 29821-9701
Phone: 800-533-3478
www.sas.usace.army.mil/lakes/thurmond

The largest Corps of Engineers lake east of the Mississippi River, the lake encompasses 1,200 miles of shoreline, 70,000 acres of water, and 80,000 acres of land. About 55,000 acres are suitable for hunting according to all state regulations. For more details, see www.sas.usace.army.mil/lakes/thurmond/hunt.htm.

*USDA National Forests*

**FRANCIS MARION–SUMTER NATIONAL FORESTS**
Columbia, SC 29210
Phone: 803-561-4000
www.fs.fed.us/r8/fms

The Francis Marion and Sumter National Forests encompass about 612,500 acres, including the southern Appalachian Mountains at a 3,300-foot elevation, the rolling terrain in the middle of the state, and the

---

**SOUTH CAROLINA SNAPSHOT**
**PALMETTO STATE**

- **General information:** www.dnr.sc.gov/hunting.html

- **To report a poacher:** Operation Game Thief, 800-922-5431; earn up to $500 for a tip that leads to an arrest

- **Deer population:** 800,000, 17th in the United States

- **Average deer harvest:** 289,631, 8th in the United States

flat, sea-level plains near the Intracoastal Waterway and the Atlantic Ocean. Over half a million acres are open to hunting of all legal species. For details, see www.fs.fed.us/r8/fms/forest/recreation/hunting.shtml.

*U.S. Fish and Wildlife Service*
*National Wildlife Refuges*

## ACE BASIN NATIONAL WILDLIFE REFUGE
Hollywood, SC 29449
Phone: 843-889-3084
www.fws.gov/acebasin

The ACE Basin National Wildlife Refuge helps protect the largest undeveloped estuary along the Atlantic Coast and includes 12,000 acres of the 350,000-acre basin. Deer and waterfowl hunting are allowed on the refuge. For details, see www.fws.gov/acebasin/hunt.html.

## CAPE ROMAIN NATIONAL WILDLIFE REFUGE
Awendaw, SC 29429
Phone: 843-928-3264
www.fws.gov/caperomain

Cape Romain's 64,000 acres encompass a 20-mile segment of the Atlantic coast and include barrier islands, salt marshes, coastal waterways, fresh and brackish water impoundments, and maritime forest. Deer and rail hunting are permitted. For details, see www.fws.gov/southeast/pubs/caperomain_hnt.pdf.

## CAROLINA SANDHILLS NATIONAL WILDLIFE REFUGE
McBee, SC 29101

Phone: 843-335-8401
Email: fw4rwcarolinasandhills@fws.gov
www.fws.gov/carolinasandhills

Deer, raccoon, and turkey hunts according to special seasons and state regulations. For details, see www.dnr.sc.gov/hunting/huntapp/sandhillsnwrhunts.html.

## PINCKNEY ISLAND NATIONAL WILDLIFE REFUGE
Savannah, GA 31405
Phone: 912-652-4415
www.fws.gov/pinckneyisland

Located on 4,053 acres, approximately 2,700 acres are salt marsh and tidal creeks. Each year the refuge holds a one-day quota deer hunt to ensure that population numbers remain in balance with the surrounding habitat.

## SANTEE NATIONAL WILDLIFE REFUGE
Summerton, SC 29148
Phone: 803-478-2217
www.fws.gov/refuges/profiles/index.cfm?id=42570

Stretching for 18 miles along the northern shore of Lake Marion, the refuge protects 15,095 acres in four different units. Portions of the Pine Island and Cuddo units are open each fall for hunting of whitetail deer using primitive weapons. Limited hunting of doves, gray squirrels, raccoons, and opossums is available each fall on the Cuddo Unit. Permits and special regulations apply.

## SAVANNAH NATIONAL WILDLIFE REFUGE
Savannah, GA 31405

Phone: 912-652-4415
www.recreation.gov/detail.jsp?ID=1603

The refuge administers deer, feral hog, squirrel, and turkey hunts during the fall and winter. A brochure containing all hunting and fishing regulations as well as all necessary permits for the current year is printed each year around July 1. Hunters are required to carry a signed copy of this brochure on all refuge hunts. Annual regulations and permit application can be found on the refuge Web site.

*Private Hunting Clubs and Preserves*

## BACKWOODS QUAIL CLUB
Georgetown, SC 29440
Phone: 843-546-1466
www.backwoodsquailclub.com

Located less than 30 minutes from historic Georgetown, deer, turkey, quail, and pheasant tower shooting, plus sporting clays, overnight accommodations, meals, and bar service available.

## BRAYS ISLAND PLANTATION
Sheldon, SC 29941
Phone: 866-320-1201
or 843-846-3170;
fax: 843-466-1151
www.braysisland.com

A 5,500-acre plantation is just an hour from Charleston and Savannah with 325 home sites and 3,500 acres set aside as a nature and hunting preserve. Deer, dove, quail, chukar, pheasant, turkey, and duck hunting, sporting clays, skeet, trap, golf, and fishing.

## BROXTON BRIDGE PLANTATION
Ehrhardt, SC 29081
Phone: 800-437-HUNT, 803-267-3882,
or 843-866-2218 (Lodge)
www.broxtonbridge.com

Deer, duck, quail, pheasant, and chukar field hunts and tower shoots, plus sporting clays, pistol and rifle range, bass fishing, and trail rides on 7,000 acres with private airstrip, bed-and-breakfast, and banquet hall. Has been in the family since the 1700s.

## HARRIS SPRINGS
## SPORTSMAN'S PRESERVE
Waterloo, SC 29384
Phone: 864-677-3448; fax: 864-677-3918
www.harrissprings.com

An Orvis-endorsed wing-shooting lodge on 300 acres in the gently rolling Piedmont hills of South Carolina, offering wild turkey, deer, duck, pheasant, chukar, and quail hunting. Guides, dogs, and overnight accommodations available.

## MOREE'S SPORTSMAN'S PRESERVE
Society Hill, SC 29593
Phone: 843-378-4831 (Clubhouse)
or 843-206-4094 (After 6:00 P.M.)
www.moreespreserve.com

Quail, pheasant, chukar, duck, deer, and turkey hunting, plus sporting clays, golf, and catfish fishing on 1,200 acres. Clubhouse and overnight accommodations nearby.

## RIVER BEND SPORTSMAN'S RESORT
Fingerville, SC 29338
Phone: 800-516-960; fax: 864-592-3556
www.rvrbend.com

Located in north-central South Carolina, offering quail, pheasant, and chukar field hunts and tower shoots. Overnight accommodations, lodge, pro shop, sporting clays, skeet, paintball, and shooting instruction. Memberships, guides, and dogs available.

# HERITAGE DESTINATIONS

*Wild Turkey Center*
With more than 30,000 square feet, the Wild Turkey Center includes the Winchester Wild Turkey Museum, an Outdoor Education Center, a 3,000-square-foot conference center, The Turkey Shoppe (the NWTF's gift shop), and a large warehouse.

**NATIONAL WILD TURKEY FEDERATION**
Edgefield, SC 29824-0530
Phone: 800-THE-NWTF
www.nwtf.org

## VIRGINIA

*In 2001 there were 279,000 resident hunters and 75,000 nonresident hunters: 91% went big game hunting, 36% small game, 12% migratory waterfowl and doves; 32% hunted on public lands; 87% hunted on private lands. Hunters pumped $321 million into the state economy. (USFWS)*

### OVERVIEW
More than 1.5 million acres of U.S. Forest Service land, 34 state Wildlife Management Areas (WMAs) managed by the Virginia Department of Game and Inland Fisheries, several state forests and state parks, Federal Wildlife Refuges, and military areas are open to hunting, plus hundreds of thousands of acres on private lands.

Virginia offers hunting for bears, elk, turkeys, waterfowl, upland game birds, and small mammals, but ultimately this is deer country. There are about 161 deer for every 1,000 people in the state. Hunters harvest over 200,000 whitetails a year. The bag limit is one to two a day, five to six per season, according to the area, with no more than half being antlered. Antlerless deer tags are unlimited.

---

**VIRGINIA SNAPSHOT**
**OLD DOMINION STATE**

- **Special feature:** Virginia has recently installed an online service that helps hunters locate the best places to hunt various species of game—see www.findgame.org

- **General information:** www.dgif.state.va.us/hunting/index.cfm

- **Report a poacher:** Call 800-237-5712 or email WildCrime@dgif.virginia.gov

- **Purchase licenses online:** http://secure01.virginiainteractive.org/horf; an annual "Sportsman's License" for residents 16 years and older costs $102 and includes resident hunting license, resident bear-deer-turkey license, archery license, muzzleloader license, fishing license, and trout license; that's quite a bargain, but the Resident Lifetime License to hunt (annual bear, deer, and turkey license and all applicable licenses, stamps, or permits are required in addition to this license) begins at $255 for ages 16 to 44) and goes down to $15 for hunters 65 or older

- **Deer population:** 1 million, 10th in the United States

- **Average deer harvest:** 214,637, 13th in the United States

Deer season extends more than three months from early archery season through early muzzleloader, rifle, late archery, and late muzzleloader seasons. Two to three bucks a year. Antlerless tags are unlimited on private lands.

Urban Archery Seasons for deer are open in a number of towns and communities around the state. For details, see www.dgif .state.va.us/hunting/urban-archery.asp.

Turkeys are also popular. In spring, about 60,000 hunters take after gobblers with a 25% success rate. There is also a fall season.

In 2007 Virginia opened a spring squirrel season in June for the first time.

## DESTINATIONS

The state manages 36 Wildlife Management Units totaling 200,000 acres that offer hunting. There are also state forests, state parks national forest, National Wildlife Refuges, and military lands that are open to hunting. A complete list is available online at www .dgif.state.va.us/hunting/regulations/public lands.asp.

*USDA National Forests*

### GEORGE WASHINGTON AND JEFFERSON NATIONAL FORESTS

Roanoke, VA 24091
Phone: 540-265-5100
www.fs.fed.us/r8/gwj

Nearly 2 million acres spread across the western part of Virginia and the eastern part of West Virginia, the forests are the largest publicly owned land base for recreation in the eastern United States. Hunting permitted according to state regulations and local posting. For details, see www.fs. fed.us/r8/gwj/recreation/hunting/index. shtml.

*U.S. Fish and Wildlife Service*
*National Wildlife Refuges*

### BACK BAY NATIONAL WILDLIFE REFUGE

Virginia Beach, VA 23456-4325
Phone: 757-721-2412
www.fws.gov/backbay/hunting.htm

Deer and feral hog hunting on a 9,000-acre refuge, which is a thin strip of Barrier Island along the coast, primarily marshland. The limit is two deer per day in season, and there is no limit or season on feral hogs.

### CHINCOTEAGUE NATIONAL WILDLIFE REFUGE

Chincoteague Island, VA 23336
Phone: 757-336-6122; fax: 757-336-5273
www.fws.gov/northeast/chinco/
hunting06-07.htm

More than 14,000 acres of beach, dunes, marsh, and maritime forest. Most of the refuge is located on the Virginia end of Assateague Island; but 418 acres are on the Maryland side of the island. The refuge's boundaries also extend south and encompass all or part of the barrier islands: Assawoman, Metompkin, and Cedar.

Whitetail deer hunting is offered on Wallops Island National Wildlife Refuge as well as migratory bird hunting on Assawoman and Metompkin Island Divisions and Wildcat Marsh and Morris Island. Contact refuge for details.

**EASTERN SHORE OF VIRGINIA**
**NATIONAL WILDLIFE REFUGE**
Cape Charles, VA 23310
Phone: 757-331-2760
www.fws.gov/northeast/easternshore

Lying at the tip of the Delmarva Peninsula between the ocean and Chesapeake Bay, this 1,127-acre refuge offers archery and gun hunts for whitetail deer. For details, see www.fws.gov/northeast/easternshore/ Visitor%20Activities/Hunt%20Info.htm.

**GREAT DISMAL SWAMP NATIONAL**
**WILDLIFE REFUGE**
Suffolk, VA 23439-0349
Phone: 757-986-3705
www.fws.gov/northeast/greatdismalswamp

Over 111,000 acres of forested wetlands in southeast Virginia, with Lake Drummond, a 3,100-acre lake, at the center. Deer and bear hunting permitted according to state and local refuge regulations. For details, see www .fws.gov/northeast/greatdismalswamp/ 2006huntannouncement12-20-06.htm.

**JAMES RIVER NATIONAL**
**WILDLIFE REFUGE**
Prince George, VA 23831
Phone: 804-333-1470
www.fws.gov/refuges/profiles/index .cfm?id=51621

On 4,200 acres of forested habitat along the James River. An annual hunting program for whitetail deer during October and November. Bow, muzzleloader, and shotgun hunting opportunities available on a registration basis.

Season dates vary annually; call the refuge headquarters in late summer for exact dates.

**MASON NECK NATIONAL**
**WILDLIFE REFUGE**
Lorton, VA 22079
Phone: 703-490-4979
www.fws.gov/refuges/profiles/index .cfm?id=51610

Situated along the Potomac River on the Mason Neck peninsula, 2,277 acres of oak-hickory forest, freshwater marshes, and 4.4 miles of shoreline. The refuge conducts a whitetail deer hunt each fall. Hunt participants selected by lottery. Lottery application occurs in August. Contact the refuge office for specific information.

**RAPPAHANNOCK RIVER VALLEY**
**NATIONAL WILDLIFE REFUGE**
Warsaw, VA 22572
Phone: 804-333-1470
www.fws.gov/northeast/rappahannock/ hunting.html

Deer hunting with archery, shotgun, and muzzleloaders in season.

*Private Hunting Clubs and Preserves*
A complete list of all shooting preserves in Virginia can be found at www.dgif.state .va.us/hunting/shootingpreserves/index.asp ?location=Accomack.

**ORAPAX PLANTATION**
Goochland, VA 23063
Phone: 804-556-2261 or 866-556-0022
www.orapax.com

Located on 700 acres in Goochland County, 30 minutes west of Richmond. Half-day field hunts and European hunts for quail and pheasant. Guides and dogs available.

**ORION ESTATE HUNTING PRESERVE**
Lovingston, VA 22949
Phone: 434-263-6622
www.optimaadventures.com/orionestate
.html

Located on the James River in the rolling hills near Lovingston, released pheasant and chukar and wild bobwhite quail. Luxurious accommodations and meals, guides and dogs available. Corporate retreats a specialty. A number of major corporations have hunted here.

**PRIMLAND RESORT AND**
**HUNTING PRESERVE**
Meadows of Dan, VA 24120
1-276-251-8012 or (Toll-Free): 1-877 960 7746 (Fax) 1-800-318-9365
http://www.primland.com/

14,000-acre resort offering golf, fishing and hunting. An Orvis-endorsed wingshooting destination, offering field and European-style hunts for released pheasant, chukar, quail and mallards, and hunts for wild turkeys and deer in season. Also trail rides and sporting clays, elegant lodging and meals. Many different packages offered.

# HERITAGE DESTINATIONS

*National Firearms Museum*
A historical collection of firearms reflecting the nation's history from its birth to the present. A number of special displays, such as guns of presidents, guns used in movies, and special paints and sculptures, as well as regular exhibits. An extensive library is on-site.

**NATIONAL FIREARMS MUSEUM**
Fairfax, VA 22030
Phone: 703-267-1600
www.nationalfirearmsmuseum.org

# Gulf Coast

## ALABAMA

*In 2001 there were 307,000 resident hunters and 116,000 nonresident hunters: 93% went big game hunting, 26% small game, 23% migratory waterfowl; 13% hunted on public lands; 93% hunted on private lands. Hunters pumped $664 million into the state's economy. (USFWS)*

### OVERVIEW

In Alabama the annual harvest of bobwhite quail runs from 100,000, and wild turkeys, migratory ducks, doves, and wild boars are abundant. However, the whitetail deer is the most popular game species in Alabama.

There are an estimated 1.75 million whitetails in the state, and they can be hunted with gun, bow, crossbow, muzzleloader, and even spear; in some areas, dogs are legal. It is legal to plant food plots for deer, but baiting is not legal.

Archery hunters enjoy a 108-day season, one of the longest in the United States. The limit is one buck and one doe per day.

For public land deer hunts, the Quality Deer Management Association recommends Barbour Wildlife Management Area and Lowndes Wildlife Management Area, both of which are in the Montgomery area.

Bears, mountain lions, and ruffed grouse are protected, but in 2006 the state held its first alligator season.

# FEATURED HUNT

## Rabbit Hunting in Alabama

JEFF ENGEL

While North America has many majestic game animals including deer, elk, antelope, and bears, the whitetail deer is number-one in popularity. Second on the list is the cottontail rabbit, which is available to everyone for little or no cost.

Cottontails can run 20 miles an hour through thick cover, and out in the open they can zigzag and dodge at any moment. Plus, they make excellent table fare, and they are extremely prolific.

I hadn't hunted rabbits for many years, but a good friend and frequent visitor on our show, Dr. Martin Coffman, called and invited me to go on a rabbit hunt in Alabama. Martin is a very experienced veterinarian, and one of his true passions is hunting cottontail rabbits with beagles. One February weekend I flew down to Alabama from Wisconsin to join him with my camera crew to film a segment and enjoy some rabbit hunting adventures.

Martin had collected a group of six of his friends and about a dozen beagles. I soon began to see why this sport is so popular. Just like wing shooting with dogs, listening to and watching the dogs work the rabbit is a huge part of the fun.

Beagles are a very old breed. The Greeks described beaglelike dogs in 400 B.C. The Romans are thought to have brought beagles from England. They were imported into the United States in 1876, and they became extremely popular. Along with hunting, a beagle can make a good housedog and is great with children.

The area we were in, in south Alabama, was very swamplike and comprised open fields and water-based woods. The cottontails we were hunting weighed two to three pounds. There is also another local variety of rabbit called the swamp rabbit, or "cane cutters." These rabbits are bigger, weighing from three to five pounds, and darker colored and are found in swampier areas.

The dogs would run freely in front of us as we walked the field edges. Once the lead beagle got into the trail of a rabbit, the other dogs, with their distinctive voices, would chime in. The call "Tally

ho!"—a carryover from England, I soon learned—remains the call when the dog handlers let everyone know that a rabbit has been sighted.

I am a tremendous fan of sporting dogs, and I spend a great deal of time in fields with pointers and Labradors, but this is the first time I truly experienced what it was like to hunt with a well-trained pack of beagles. I was amazed at how exciting this experience actually was.

For this hunt I decided to use a Thompson Contender .410 pistol. I love challenges, and using this gun means that I only get one shot at fairly close range. Better make it good, or there's no rabbit stew tonight.

We were hunting on land managed to maximize deer habitat—open fields for food interspersed with thick forest and brush for cover. Both deer and rabbits thrive in these conditions, and rabbit trails and tunnels were everywhere. As the dogs started to run the rabbits, I began to recognize the yelp of various dogs. Each one had a signature voice. Their excitement was infectious.

At regular intervals, the dogs would get hot. Once the dogs would jump a rabbit, the rabbit would oftentimes make a large figure eight or semicircle, and the rabbit would often come back to within 50 yards of where it was originally jumped. I also learned that sometimes rabbits can get pretty tricky, dodging one way, then another, jumping into blackberry thickets, then into dense woods, so that openings for shots often were minimal.

Usually, before long, a distance shot would ring out from one of our fellow hunters. But more than one rabbit escaped. Even with a pack of beagles, there was no sure thing to bagging one of those speedy bunnies.

For most of the morning, I was a learner, with no close shots open, but the music of the dogs was beautiful. With two goals in mind—hunting rabbits and filming a show—in a lull I told the cameraman

that we should shoot a break to acknowledge our sponsors. Standing there with the microphone, looking at the cameraman and with the camera beginning to roll, suddenly the dogs jumped a rabbit just a few feet behind me, and off they exploded into the bushes. Why does it always seem to happen this way?

Finally, the distant howl of the dogs seemed to be closing on my direction. I waited with anticipation. Would this be my turn? Sure enough, the howl from the pack of dogs was swelling as the pack of dogs was getting closer and closer.

I slowly took my .410 pistol out from my shoulder holster, and with the muzzle raised to the sky, I waited silently and motionless beside a thicket where I hoped the rabbit might pass through. Soon I saw the blur of a rabbit coming right toward my direction, weaving its way through a network of runways.

As the rabbit ran past about 20 yards in front of me, I quickly brought the pistol down, swung on the rabbit, gave it a little bit of a lead, and took a shot. To my surprise and almost amazement, I hit the rabbit with the pint-sized load of shot. A few moments later, a pack of dogs burst out of the bushes, howling with extra excitement at what I had just taken. This was truly a thrilling hunt, much more so than I had originally thought it would be. And to take a rabbit this way made it a real trophy.

At the end of the day, we gathered up all of the dogs and met at the vehicles to compare notes and swap stories. There was a tremendous sense of camaraderie as we all gave the dogs a great deal of attention and showed appreciation for their extremely hard work. The beagles had run on and off for seven hours without quitting. The stamina that they showed was tremendous.

As I helped put the last beagle into its cage, I thought about how much fun this hunt had been. The camaraderie, the action, and of course the dogs had made this a very enjoyable and exciting outdoor experience. And it had taken me out of the snowy north woods, which in February is always welcome.

## DESTINATIONS

### State Wildlife Management Areas

There are 34 state-managed Wildlife Management Areas with 626,500 acres, plus national forest lands as well as private lands. For more information on hunting regulations in Alabama, see www.westalabamahunting trail.com/hunting-regulations.html. For a list of lodges, guides, and outfitters, see www.outdooralabama.com/links/guides.cfm.

### USDA National Forests

National forests in Alabama encompass approximately 667,000 acres of public land stretching across 17 counties. Hunting is allowed in most areas, with state regulations. For maps and more information, contact:

**USDA FOREST SERVICE NATIONAL FORESTS IN ALABAMA**
Montgomery, AL 36107
Phone: 334-832-4470; fax: 334-241-8111
www.fs.fed.us/r8/alabama

### U.S. Fish and Wildlife Service National Wildlife Refuges

**CHOCTAW NATIONAL WILDLIFE REFUGE**
Jackson, AL 36545
Phone: 251-246-3583; fax: 251-246-5414
www.fws.gov/choctaw

Rabbits, squirrels, archery whitetail deer, raccoons, feral hogs, coyotes, and nutrias may be taken in accordance with special refuge seasons. Shotguns must use nontoxic shot. Located approximately 80 miles north of Mobile, Choctaw National Wildlife Refuge contains 4,218 acres plus 236 acres in perpetual conservation easements in eight parcels in Monroe, Sumter, and Conecuh counties.

**EUFAULA NATIONAL WILDLIFE REFUGE**
Eufaula, AL 36027-8187
Phone: 334-687-4065; fax: 334-687-5906
www.fws.gov/eufaula

Located five miles north of Eufaula, Alabama, on U.S. Highway 431, then one and a half miles on 165 North, the refuge occupies the upper portion of the Walter F. George Reservoir (Lake Eufaula). Archery deer, youth firearm deer, doves, squirrels, rabbits, and waterfowl. A refuge permit is required for all hunts.

**WHEELER NATIONAL WILDLIFE REFUGE**
Decatur, AL 35603
Phone: 256-353-7243; fax: 256-340-9728
www.fws.gov/wheeler

Hunting is permitted on 18,000 acres of Wheeler NWR. Dogs can be used on rabbit, raccoon, quail, and opossum hunts. Deer (either sex) and feral hogs may be hunted with archery and muzzleloaders in season. Shotgun ammunition must be nontoxic shot.

### Private Hunting Clubs and Preserves

**RHODES HUNTING PRESERVE**
Bay Minette, AL 36507-8362
Phone: 251-937-7580; fax: 251-580-8767
www.rhodesquailfarm.com

Guided and unguided quail hunts, lodge and kennel, plus the option to combine with a deer hunt. The special here is a three-day, two-night quail and deer hunt that offers the chance to harvest two deer (one buck, six points or better, plus a mature doe of at least 60 pounds) and 48 quail during the three days. Two adult party minimum. Reservations encouraged. Quail season runs October 1 to March 31. Deer hunting ends January 31.

**SELWOOD FARM & HUNTING PRESERVE, INC.**
Alpine, AL 35014-5431
Phone: 256-362-3961; fax: 256-362-3856
www.selwoodfarm.com

Selwood Farm has offered quality foods for over 50 years. Since 1984, the farm has also offered a 1,000-acre quail and pheasant hunting preserve, five-stand and 100-target sporting clays course, a luxurious country house for overnights, and gourmet food. Selwood's plantation–style Country House can also accommodate groups up to 150 for special occasions. Selwood's is open to anyone, and there is also a membership option. Season: October through March.

**TAYLOR CREEK SHOOTING PRESERVE**
Theodore, AL 36582
Phone: 251-973-2480
www.taylorcreekshooting.com

Located just south of Mobile, Taylor Creek Shooting Preserve offers full- and half-day guided and self-guided quail and pheasant hunts and 10-stand fully automated sporting clays course. For groups of 20 or more, Taylor Creek offers Continental-style pheasant

hunts with 200 released birds. Dogs available for guided hunts include pointers, English setters, and Llewellin setters.

Lodging and restaurants are nearby. Refreshments served with full-day hunts.

**YELLOW CREEK RANCH, LLC**
Gallion, AL 36742
Phone: 877-822-4667
www.yellowcreekranch.com

Yellow Creek Ranch is located at 2977 County Road 2, within five miles of Demopolis, Alabama. It offers deer, duck, pheasant, and quail hunting for members. Facilities include four bedrooms, two baths, satellite television, full kitchen, laundry, and dining area. Can accommodate 8 to 10 hunters comfortably.

# HERITAGE DESTINATIONS

*Mann Wildlife Learning Museum at the Montgomery Zoo*
This 28,000-square-foot wildlife museum is dedicated to conservation through education. Beautiful life-size natural exhibits of deer, moose, elk, grizzly and polar bears, foxes, wolves, skunks, bobcats, freshwater and saltwater game fish, waterfowl, and much more wildlife from North America. The large mammals in the museum were taken under fair chase with bow and arrow, and all are from well-managed stable or surplus populations. The edible meat, bones, and other parts from the animals were used. This museum is largely the work of George P. Mann, a true hunter-conservationist.

MANN LEARNING MUSEUM
Montgomery, AL 36110
Phone: 334-240-4900
Email: mannmuseum@mindspring.com
www.mannmuseum.com

## FLORIDA

*In 2001 there were 191,000 resident hunters and 35,000 nonresident hunters: 83% went big game hunting, 34% small game, 28% waterfowl; 46% hunted on public lands; 62% hunted on private lands. Hunters pumped $394 million into the state economy. (USFWS)*

### OVERVIEW

The primary game species in Florida are waterfowl, deer, wild pigs, doves, woodcocks, cottontail rabbits, alligators, bobcats, wild turkeys, quail, gray squirrels, rail, and coots. Bears, fox squirrels, key deer, and panthers are protected.

Fish and Wildlife Commission (FWC) is the lead manager or landowner on about 1.1 million acres of public lands in Florida's Wildlife Management Area (WMA) system. Nearly 4.4 million acres of the WMA system are open for public hunting. There is more

---

**FLORIDA SNAPSHOT**
**SUNSHINE STATE**

· **General information about hunting in Florida from the Florida Fish and Wildlife Commission:** http://myfwc.com/hunting

· **To report a poaching or pollution violation:** Call the 24-hour Wildlife Alert hotline at 888-404-FWCC (888-404-3922); you can find more information by visiting http://myfwc.com/law/alert

· **You may purchase your license over the phone:** Call 888-HUNT-FLORIDA or 888-FISH-FLORIDA, you may also purchase via the Internet at http://myfwc.com/hunting

· **Deer population:** 820,000, 15th in the United States

· **Average deer harvest:** 113,246, 22nd in the United States

---

public land in Florida than in any state east of the Mississippi.

Florida has three national forests comprising over 1.25 million acres. The Apalachicola and Osceola National Forests are in the northern half of the state, while the Ocala National Forest is located in central Florida. Representing 3% of Florida's land base, these forests provide the largest supply of public forest recreation opportunities in the state. Deer, quail, doves, wild turkeys, and feral hogs are the most popular species.

Lack of controlled fires, exotic Bahai grasses, and the decline of row cropping have had negative impacts on quail hunting in the national forests. In the 1970s Floridians harvested 1.9 million quail per season, while today the harvest on public lands is down to around 200,000.

 ## FEATURED HUNT

### Southern-Style Duck Quest

JEFF ENGEL

Duck hunting in Florida? In January? I had never even thought about it until I received an invitation from duck hunting guide Todd Jones.

As host of our television series *Engel's Outdoor Experience*, I am always looking for interesting and unusual shooting opportunities, so when Todd gave me a call and invited me to hunt both Florida and Mississippi for ducks from a layout boat, well, I just couldn't resist.

I left the Milwaukee airport during a major snowstorm in January and headed down to Florida, where it was a very comfortable 72 degrees. On this

hunt, I was joined by Mark Rongers, who is founder and president of The Mighty Layout Boys Boat Company. Todd Jones would be our guide, and we would hunt specifically for redhead ducks. Mark and I would be side by side in one of his stable two-man layout boats, and Todd would run our main boat, which would be anchored a distance away from where we set up our boat.

Historically, the layout boat rig has been very popular among big water hunting rigs in the Great Lakes and Chesapeake Bay. The layout boat is simply a watercraft with an extremely low profile that helps conceal the duck hunter in open water. (See "Michigan" for more details.)

We launched our boat well before sunrise, and Todd took us to an area along the edge of a large bay where the water depth was only waist deep. After taking our layout boat off our main boat, we quickly set out 150 decoys in singular lines parallel to each other. After that Mark and I got into one of the two-man layout boats, and Todd took the main boat to a hidden bay while we hunted. As we lay in the boat, we watched an amazing sunrise. The big ball of orange looked like an hourglass as it came up from the horizon.

There was very little wind this day, and the ducks just were not flying. In fact, the only birds we saw were some low-flying pelicans. As we lay on our backs in the layout boat we felt a warm, gentle breeze, and with that, along with the gently rocking boat, I found it difficult not to drift off occasionally.

Mark looked off in the distance and said, "Look Jeff, there's a bufflehead, and it's a drake!" Even though our main species were mature drake redheads, Mark took the opportunity presented by this beautiful bufflehead and made a very successful shot. As in all of our waterfowl hunts, we practice voluntary restraint. We make it a serious practice to only shoot drake ducks, to help increase the survival rate of the hens and to be a part of a growing sports-man's ethic.

I also find that by practicing voluntary restraint we improve our identification skills, and it takes us to a new level of the waterfowl experience. I believe it is only practical common sense that the more hens that fly north, the greater the number of ducks to be produced, and even more ducks to then fly back south again. I also find that this improves the quality of our overall duck hunting experience.

There are several techniques that enable me to identify drakes more easily. One is making sure the decoys are set up close to the blind so the ducks will come in for a look and be closer for easier identifica-tion. I also prefer having the sun to my back so that the ducks are more sunlit, to help identify the drakes. In addition, the drakes generally follow a hen, so if a pair of ducks comes in, I will give my at-tention to the back or following duck to see if it is the drake. Also, the drakes tend to be generally larger than the hens. I strongly believe in shooting only drake ducks while duck hunting, and I get a great deal of satisfaction in passing up shots where the ducks are too close or too clustered together. It just makes my outdoor experience of duck hunting that much more enjoyable.

The next morning Mark and I were back in the ocean, laying flat on our backs in one of Todd's lay-out boats. This particular morning was also very calm, with almost no ducks flying. Eventually, a sin-gle drake bluebill came streaking by our decoys, and I was fortunate to take him with one shot. Un-fortunately, our primary species of redheads did not seem to be anywhere in the area. For the rest of the day, we laid flat on our backs, scanning the horizon, with no more shots taken.

That evening, Mark had to head out, and Todd and I drove west to the state of Mississippi and were joined by Robert Brodie. Robert is an outdoor writer with a great deal of experience writing about the

Mississippi Gulf Coast. The next morning, our desti-nation was a submerged island out in the Gulf. In the predawn light, we set out about 150 decoys and slid the layout boat from the main boat into the water. Robert then left Todd and me in the layout boat to watch another sizzling sunrise. Like Florida, the weather was too nice, and the ducks just weren't flying. Before long, Robert arrived with a pickup boat and said, "Since the redheads aren't flying, let's try fishing for some redhead fish."

We collected our decoys and took our main boat to some hidden bays. In full chest waders and camouflage, we did some casting for redfish. It felt very unusual to be fishing in full camo and made me laugh at the thought. The fishing for redfish turned out to be better than hunting for redheads, and each of us caught a five- to seven-pound redfish.

That afternoon we headed back out into the ocean to the submerged island and once again set out the decoys. The increased wind was the differ-ence we needed to get the redheads flying. Before long, we had several flocks of redheads come in with their wings cupped into our decoys. It was easy to identify the drakes and the hens. The drakes have a rust/crimsoned-colored head, with a black

chest and the remainder of the body a brilliant white.

The daily limit for redheads was two ducks, and we were very fortunate that enough waves of ducks came in that each of us was able to collect two drakes. We'd all taken a few shots and shared some great moments. It was a good day on the water.

For information about hunting in Florida and Mississippi, contact:

**BACK BAY ADVENTURES**
Capt. Todd Jones
Panama City, FL 32401
Phone: 850-722-6642
www.backbayadventures.com

---

**DESTINATIONS**

*USDA National Forests*

**OSCEOLA NATIONAL FORESTS**
Tallahassee, FL 32303

Phone: 850-523-8500
www.fs.fed.us/r8/florida

*Apalachicola National Forest.* During general gun hunting season (usually mid-November through mid-February), camping is only allowed at designated hunt camps and the five developed campgrounds. Portable restrooms and trash cans are provided at most hunt camps, and campers may stay the entire season in one hunt camp (from 14 days prior to opening day to the last day of general gun hunting season). Individual permits for dog pens may be purchased from your local Forest Service Office. No fee in hunt camps. Fees apply to developed campgrounds.

*Ocala National Forest.* This is a Wildlife Management Area in which hunting activities are managed by the Florida Fish and Wildlife Conservation Commission. A $26.50 Wildlife Management Area Permit is required for all hunters (except those indicated as exempt) to hunt in this area. A Quota Hunt Permit may also be required during certain time periods or certain game. For specific regulations that pertain only to the Ocala Wildlife Management Area, a unique brochure can be obtained at Forest Service Ranger Stations, or the Web site, which also identifies specific hunting units and regulations.

*Osceola National Forest.* Hunting is very popular in the Osceola National Forest. General gun season runs from mid-November to early January, and during that time all camping is restricted to designated hunt camps and Ocean Pond Campground. A total of nine hunt camps are located in the forest and are open year-round to the public. Two of the hunt camps have toilet and water facilities year-round and toilets are provided at the remaining seven camps during the hunting season.

The Forest is a wildlife management area, in which state regulations apply. A $26.50 Wildlife Management Area Permit is required for all hunters (except those indicated as exempt) to hunt in this area. A Quota Hunt Permit may also be required during certain time periods or for certain game species. For specific regulations that pertain only to the Osceola Wildlife Management Area, a unique brochure is published annually and can be obtained at ranger stations or the forest Web site.

*U.S. Fish and Wildlife Service*
*National Wildlife Refuges*

## ARTHUR R. MARSHALL LOXAHATCHEE NATIONAL WILDLIFE REFUGE

Boynton Beach, FL 33437
Phone: 561-732-3684
www.fws.gov/loxahatchee/home/default.asp

Waterfowl hunting on Wednesday through Sunday by permit only during state seasons. All hunters must possess an annual hunting permit, which can be obtained online through the refuge Web site. The refuge is located seven miles west of the city of Boynton Beach in Palm Beach County, Florida.

## CHASSAHOWITZKA NATIONAL WILDLIFE REFUGE

Crystal River, FL 34429
Phone: 352-563-2088
www.fws.gov/chassahowitzka

The Chassahowitzka NWR is composed of over 31,000 acres of saltwater bays, estuaries, and brackish marshes at the mouth of the Chassahowitzka River, located approximately 65 miles north of St. Petersburg, Florida. This is home for a population of whooping cranes. Waterfowl hunting permitted on Wednesdays, Saturdays, and Sundays.

## LAKE WOODRUFF NATIONAL WILDLIFE REFUGE

Deleon Springs, FL 32130
Phone: 386-985-4673
www.fws.gov/lakewoodruff

Lake Woodruff NWR contains 21,574 acres of freshwater marshes; 5,800 acres of cypress and mixed hardwood swamps; 2,400 acres of uplands; and more than 1,000 acres of lakes, streams, and canals. Deer and feral hog hunting with archery and muzzleloaders. Check refuge Web site for special seasons and details. Each hunter must complete a hunter survey at the end of each day's hunt.

## LOWER SUWANNEE NATIONAL WILDLIFE REFUGE

Chiefland, FL 32626
Phone: 352-493-0238
www.fws.gov/lowersuwannee

Lower Suwannee NWR is located along the southern edge of the Big Bend region of Florida's west coast, approximately 50 miles southwest of Gainesville. This 54,000-acre refuge is one of the largest undeveloped river delta–estuarine systems in the United States. Hunting of big game, small game, and waterfowl is permitted during designated seasons.

Deer, turkeys, and feral hogs are the most-sought-after species. Hunting license and stamps are required in accordance with state regulations. A hunt permit is also required. Special quota hunts for youth hunters, deer, and feral hogs are offered. Check with the Refuge Headquarters and www.fws.gov/lowersuwannee/hunting.html for additional hunt information.

**MERRITT ISLAND NATIONAL WILDLIFE REFUGE**
Titusville, FL 32782
Phone: 321-861-0667
www.fws.gov/merrittisland

Merritt Island NWR headquarters is located five miles east of U.S. 1 in Titusville, Florida. The refuge is an overlay of the John F. Kennedy Space Center. Approximately one-half of the refuge's 140,000 acres consist of brack-

ish estuaries and marshes. The remaining lands consist of coastal dunes, scrub oaks, pine forests and flatwoods, and palm and oak hammocks. Waterfowl hunting allowed on Wednesdays, Saturdays, and Sundays during the state season. Permit required. See www.fws.gov/merrittisland/waterfowlhunting/index.html for details.

**ST. MARKS NATIONAL WILDLIFE REFUGE**
St. Marks, FL 32355
Phone: 850-925-6121
www.fws.gov/saintmarks

St. Marks NWR, located 25 miles south of Tallahassee along the Gulf Coast of Florida, is a well-known oasis of salt marshes, freshwater swamps, pine forests, and lakes that provides a haven for wildlife and people. Deer, turkey, waterfowl, feral hog, and small game hunting. Deer hunting with archery and firearms is by permit. For details, see www.fws.gov/saintmarks/huntinginfo.html.

## ST. VINCENT NATIONAL WILDLIFE REFUGE
Apalachicola, FL 32320
Phone: 850-653-8808
www.fws.gov/refuges/profiles/index.cfm?id=41650

St. Vincent NWR, in Franklin County, Florida, is an undeveloped barrier island just offshore from the mouth of the Apalachicola River, in the Gulf of Mexico. Portions of the refuge are open to hunting whitetail deer, feral pigs, and sambar deer. Permits and special regulations apply. Contact the refuge headquarters for specific information.

## TEN THOUSAND ISLANDS NATIONAL WILDLIFE REFUGE
Naples, FL 34114
Phone: 239-353-8442
www.fws.gov/southeast/TenThousandIsland

Ten Thousand Islands NWR is located in Collier County on the southwest coast of Florida. This 35,000-acre refuge is part of the largest expanse of mangrove forest in North America. Waterfowl hunting by permit is offered November through January. See state regulations for details.

*U.S. Army Corps of Engineers*

## LAKE OKEECHOBEE/ OKEECHOBEE WATERWAY
Clewiston, FL 33440-5399

Phone: 863-983-8101
www.saj.usace.army.mil/sfoo/index.html

Lake Okeechobee is Florida's largest lake and the second-largest freshwater lake in the United States. Eight Corps recreation areas are located along the 152-mile waterway, which offers excellent boating, bass fishing, biking, wildlife viewing, and waterfowl hunting. The lake and waterway are located in south Florida between the towns of Ft. Myers and Ft. Pierce. The project office is located approximately 65 miles east of Ft. Myers and 65 miles west of West Palm Beach.

*Private Hunting Clubs and Preserves*

## BIENVILLE PLANTATION
White Springs, FL 32096
Phone: 386-397-1989; fax: 386-397-1988
www.bienville.com

An Orvis-endorsed lodge offering quail hunting (October–March), guided bass fishing, duck hunting (in season), alligator hunting (April–November, mostly at night), skeet, trap, and five-stand. There is fine dining and well-appointed lodging in the White-Tail Lodge; also five guest lodges with five bedrooms with two double beds and a private bath in each. Small groups can be accommodated.

## GILCHRIST CLUB
Trenton, FL 32693
Phone: 352-463-7070; fax: 352-463-7757
www.gilchristclub.com

Quail, turkey, deer, hog, and alligator hunting, with luxurious lodging in executive lodges along the shore of 125-acre Suwannee Lake, plus full dining room and meeting space up to 30.

## HARD LABOR CREEK PLANTATION
Chipley, FL 32428
Phone: 850-638-4316; fax: 850-638-0758
www.floridaquail.com

Traditional southern quail hunting, deer hunting, and bass fishing. Native and release bobwhite quail, the season running from October 1 through April 1. First-class three-bedroom, three-bath chalet with a large kitchen, dining room, two sitting rooms, and a recreation room with a pool table, plus two fireplaces, wet bar, satellite television, and telephone.

## HUNTING IN FLORIDA.COM
Polk City, FL 33868
Phone: 863-984-2225;
mobile: 863-206-3469
www.huntinginflorida.com

Deer, Osceola turkey, duck, dove, hog, quail, pheasant, and tower shoots available in central Florida, less than 45 minutes from Tampa and Orlando. All hunts are conducted on 20,000 acres of private lands owned or leased for exclusive hunts. Comfortable lodging, outfitting, and taxidermy services available.

## J & R OUTFITTERS
Indiantown, FL 34956-9717
Phone: 772-597-4757; fax: 772-597-4754
www.jroutfitters.com

Two and a half hours from Disney World, 4,000-plus acres of hunting grounds with a variety of beautiful scenery, ranging from age-old cabbage and oak hammocks to open prairies. A wide variety of native and exotic game. Native—deer, wild hogs, quail, wild turkeys, ducks, doves, snipes, and wild boars. Also released pheasant and pigeons with tower shooting. Trapshooting and skeet shooting, plus rifle range. Private three-bedroom, two-bath guesthouse on the ranch.

## QUAIL CREEK PLANTATION
Okeechobee, FL 34972
Phone: 863-763-2529; fax: 863-763-1414
www.quailcreekplantation.com

Quail, native turkey, and tower pheasant shoots, plus bass fishing on a private pond. The sporting clays course is the site of the 2006 Florida Sporting Clays State Championship. Accommodations: three cozy one-bedroom cabins and one camp house with four bedrooms and delicious southern-style meals.

## SILVER LAKE PRESERVE
Okeechobee, FL 34974
Phone: 863-763-3041; fax: 863-441-1364
www.silverlakepreserve.com

Quail, alligator, hog, and turkey hunting near Lake Okeechobee. The lodge has four bedrooms, each with a private bath, plus one additional. Central heat and air conditioning, Direct TV, hardwood floors, and a large and modern kitchen. The lodge can accommodate a group of up to 10 guests.

## TREASURE COAST HUNTING AND FISHING CLUB
Palm City, FL 34990

Phone: 772-219-8212; fax: 772-219-0003
www.treasurecoasthunt.com/index.html

This is a private membership club that offers bobwhite hunts for nonmembers. Other game for members-only includes native turkey, wild pigs, and released pheasant and chukar. Also sport and deep-sea fishing.

*State Hunting Organization*
See the Future of Hunting in Florida, Inc., Web site at www.thefutureofhunting.org.

# LOUISIANA

*In 2001 there were 295,000 resident hunters and 38,000 nonresident hunters: 64% went big game hunting, 42% small game, 44% migratory waterfowl and doves; 30% hunted on public lands; 81% hunted on private lands. Hunters pumped $446 million into the state economy. (USFWS)*

## OVERVIEW

The license plates for Louisiana carry the motto "Sportsman's Paradise" and rightfully so, for this is the land of massive live oak trees, fertile bayous, Spanish moss, and plentiful deer, waterfowl, doves, turkeys, squirrels, and other big game species including wild hogs, black bears, and alligators, and let's not forget nutrias, South American rodents, which are gobbling up marsh grasses with a vengeance.

Since Hurricane Katrina, New Orleans and Louisiana have done a tremendous job of recovery, but many of the National Wildlife Refuges along the Gulf Coast are cur-

rently closed because of hurricane damage. For details, see www.fws.gov/southeast/pubs/SWLcomplex_hunt.pdf.

Whitetail deer are abundant. Deer hunters can take one antlered and one antlerless deer daily, with a total season bag limit of six deer—three antlered and three antlerless. Over 200,000 deer are harvested in Louisiana every year.

Bobwhite quail, on the other hand, are in trouble. In 2005 hunters bagged about 5,000 bobwhites, which is considerably less than the 400,000 per year that was the norm back in the 1970s and 1980s. A number of upland game habitat improvement programs are in process, and hunting preserves with released birds are helping offset the decline of the natural population.

All those oak trees dripping with Spanish moss translate into squirrels. Louisiana

---

### LOUISIANA SNAPSHOT
### PELICAN STATE

- **General information:** Louisiana Department of Wildlife and Fisheries, www.wlf.state.la.us/hunting

- **To recruit new hunters:** Louisiana runs an annual "Discover Louisiana Hunting" program for currently unlicensed residents and nonresidents over the age of 16 to participate in a free weekend hunt for quail, rabbits, squirrels, and deer on one of the state's more than 60 WMAs; this is a once-in-a-lifetime event; if you wish to continue hunting, you will then have to take the Hunter Education class and purchase a license; for details, see www.discoverlouisianahunting.com

- **Report a poacher or a polluter:** The Operation Game Thief toll-free 24-hour phone number is 800-442-2511; tips that lead to arrests result in financial rewards based on the scale of the violation

- **Deer population:** 1 million, 10th in the United States

- **Average deer harvest:** 240,660, 11th in the United States

has an estimated 12 million squirrels. And the rich vegetation of bottomlands translates into rabbit heaven with approximately 15 million rabbits in the state.

Over 4 million acres of coastal marshes and nearly 1 million acres of flooded agricultural lands make Louisiana a waterfowl mecca.

## FEATURED HUNT

### Gators in Cajun Country

JAMES SWAN

The name "alligator" is derived from the Spanish *el lagarto*, which means "big lizard." Once an endangered species, today there are millions of

American alligators all along the Gulf Coast and Florida, up into the Carolinas. Under the Spanish moss–draped cypress trees of the bayous of Louisiana, you can find some really big gators. The largest American alligator ever taken was harvested on Marsh Island. It was 19 feet 2 inches long and weighed at least a ton.

To get a real feel of being out in the wilds of the bayou, nothing beats a traditional Cajun alligator hunt. The Lousiana season for wild gators starts on the first Wednesday of September and runs for 30 days. There is no minimum size. You can take them with hook and line, bow and arrow (with a minimum 200-pound test line attached), or firearm.

An alligator hunter must possess alligator CITES (Convention on International Trade in Endangered Species) tags. These tags are issued by the Louisiana Department of Wildlife and Fisheries. A nonresident hunter can take only three gators in a season. People not possessing property or having permission to hunt alligators on private property can harvest gators while accompanied by a guide who has CITES tags. Alligator Sport Hunter Licenses cost $25 for Louisiana residents and $150 for non-residents.

There are a number of good guides and outfitters, but what especially caught our fancy was gator huntin' Cajun style. The Cajuns were officially recognized as a national ethnic group by the U.S. government in 1980, over 200 years after their mixed French and Indian blood ancestors migrated to the southern Mississippi River area from Nova Scotia during the French and Indian War. Arriving in bayou country, the Cajuns took root, becoming adept at hunting, fishing, and trapping for their livelihood.

In Florida, you can hunt gators at night with a bow and fishing arrow and lights. In Louisiana, that's not legal. According to Drake Q. Dawson, the Cajun style of gator huntin' that's legal in Louisiana goes something like this:

You scout the marshes, looking for slides used by big gators. When you find a slide, you cut a willow pole about 20 feet long and 3 to 4 inches around.

Then you tie a rope (proven 2000# nylon) to a nearby large tree branch, then tie the rope to the bottom of the pole and drive it into the mud maybe 12 to 14 feet.

At the end of the pole, you cut a slit to hang the rope. The rope with the hook is 50 feet long. Now you tie the same rope again to the top of the pole so it works like a fishing pole, wearing out a big gator. If all this is not done properly, the gator will break the rig or bend the hook and get away. Now you tie the hook on the end of the line and hang it 2 to 4 feet above the water. The higher the hook, the bigger the gator.

For bait, people will use road-kill deer, nutrias, big carp, mullet, gars, or animal parts from a slaughter-house. The more old and rotten the bait, the better.

Big alligators are nocturnal and cannot be hunted at night in Louisiana. It is illegal to even have a gun and a spotlight in the same boat at night.

The baits are run early in the morning. When you find a gator on the hook, you pull him to two to three feet away, then dispatch him with a gun with a shot to the head. There are two guides for each hunter to make this happen as safely as possible.

It is also legal to shoot gators with a bow or gun as they float during daylight hours. Large ga-tors, though, Drake says, are seldom taken this way.

To hunt the "big lizards" Cajun style, contact Drake of Safari Unlimited. The guides are all local, with last names such as Breaux, Landry, Billet, and Thibidoux, and speak a local French Cajun dialect, as well as English.

While you're in Cajun country, you can also catch big alligator gars, snapping turtles, crabs, cat-fish, crawdads, and shrimp, then put all of them in a big pot of spicy jambalaya or gumbo, to eat while lively Cajun music is making your toes tap.

The cost for four nights/three days is $3,400.

The hunt includes all food, beverages, spirits (within reason), accommodations, airport pickup, profes-sional guides, trophy prep, and 20 pounds of vacuum-packed choice meat. There is an additional trophy fee for alligators 9 feet 1 inch or bigger. Tips for guides are extra.

Contact for booking:

**SAFARI UNLIMITED—DRAKE Q. DAWSON**
New Bloomfield, MO 65063
Phone: 866-491-3668
www.tonanzios.com/gatorhunt.shtml

## DESTINATIONS

*General Information*
A good Web site with Louisiana hunting and fishing information is www.thejump .net. For current hunting information in the state, see www.louisianasportsman.com /hunting.php.

*State Wildlife Management Areas*
The state offers 61 WMAs covering hun-dreds of thousands of acres. For a complete list with details, see www.wlf.state.la.us/ hunting/wmas/wmas.

*U.S. Army Corps of Engineers*

**ATCHAFALAYA BASIN FLOODWAY SYSTEM**
Port Barre, LA 70577
Phone: 337-585-0853
Email: howard.d.goldman@mvn02.usace .army.mil
www.mvn.usace.army.mil/recreation/ Recreation_Sites_Atchafalaya.asp

A scenic semiwilderness area of hardwood forests, cypress stands, marshes, and bayous that encompass 595,000 acres of the largest contiguous tract of bottomland hardwoods in the United States. See state regulations.

**BONNET CARRE SPILLWAY**
Norco, LA 70079
Phone: 985-764-0126
www.mvn.usace.army.mil/recreation/
Recreation_Sites_Bonnet_Carre.asp

Located on over 7,000 acres along the Mississippi River near the town of Norco, this area offers still-hunting-only for deer, plus small game, hogs, and waterfowl (morning hunts only.) Two boat launching ramps and a primitive campground. Special regulations apply—see www.mvn.usace.army.mil/recreation/docs/PostedRestrictions2006-2007.pdf—and special seasons as well—see www.mvn.usace.army.mil/recreation/docs/2006-2007BCSSeasonDates(2).pdf.

*USDA National Forests*

**KISATCHIE NATIONAL FOREST**
Pineville, LA 71360-2009
Phone: 318-473-7160
www.fs.fed.us/r8/kisatchie

The only national forest in Louisiana, it is spread across seven parishes and divided into five Ranger Districts that total over 604,000 acres of public lands. Hunting for all legal species is permitted. Camping is permitted. There are two National Wildlife Refuges within the forest—Catahoula and Red Dirt. For details on hunting in the forest and on these two refuges, see www.fs.fed.us/r8/kisatchie/hunting/index.html.

*U.S. Fish and Wildlife Service National Wildlife Refuges*

**ATCHAFALAYA NATIONAL WILDLIFE REFUGE**
Krotz Springs, LA 70750
Phone: 985-534-2235
www.fws.gov/atchafalaya

Located about 30 miles west of Baton Rouge and 1 mile east of Krotz Springs, Louisiana, the refuge encompasses nearly one-half million acres of hardwood swamps, lakes, and bayous, including the largest bottomland hardwood swamp in the country.

Hunting of migratory game birds, small game, and big game and sport fishing are permitted. Consult the state of Louisiana Department of Wildlife and Fisheries "Sherburne Wildlife Management Area" for hunting regulations.

**BAYOU COCODRIE NATIONAL WILDLIFE REFUGE**
Ferriday, LA 71334
Phone: 318-336-7119
www.fws.gov/bayoucocodrie

Slightly over 11,000 acres, the refuge is located 3.5 miles south of Ferriday, 10 miles southwest of Vidalia, and 50 miles northeast of Alexandria, Louisiana. Deer, feral hog, rabbit, squirrel, and woodcock hunting are permitted. See www.fws.gov/southeast/pubs/cochnt.pdf for details. Hunters must purchase and have in their possession a special refuge hunting permit, in addition to appropriate state and federal licenses and stamps.

## BAYOU TECHE NATIONAL WILDLIFE REFUGE
Franklin, LA 70538
Phone: 337-828-0092
www.fws.gov/bayouteche

Bayou Teche NWR is located in St. Mary Parish in southeast Louisiana. The 9,028-acre refuge is composed of wet bottomland hardwood laced with bayous and canals. Open to hunting from October to January. Hunting (archery and gun deer, squirrel and rabbit, and waterfowl) and fishing on the refuge are encouraged and free. Public users must carry a signed Public Use Permit, which is free and can be found on the front of the refuge's Hunting Brochure: www.fws.gov/southeast/pubs/bayouteche_hnt.pdf. Hunters must obtain lottery hunting permits prior to hunting.

## BIG BRANCH MARSH NATIONAL WILDLIFE REFUGE
Lacombe, LA 70445
Phone: 985-882-2000; fax: 985-882-9133
Email: southeast@fws.gov
www.fws.gov/bigbranchmarsh

Big Branch Marsh NWR is composed of 15,000 acres of coastal marsh and pine-forested wetlands along Lake Pontchartrain. Hunting for waterfowl, deer, hogs, and small game is permitted. For details, see www.fws.gov/southeast/pubs/bighnt.pdf. All hunters are required to carry a refuge permit and to report all species harvested.

## BOGUE CHITTO NATIONAL WILDLIFE REFUGE
Lacombe, LA 70445
Phone: 985-882-2000; fax: 985-882-9133
www.fws.gov/boguechitto

Bogue Chitto NWR encompasses 36,000 acres of the Pearl River Basin bottomland hardwood swampland. Located northeast of Slidell, Louisiana, about 45 miles north of New Orleans. Hunting of deer, feral hogs, turkeys, squirrels, rabbits, opossums, raccoons, woodcocks, and waterfowl is permitted within seasons. A refuge permit is required for all hunters. See www.fws.gov/southeast/pubs/bcthnt.pdf.

## CATAHOULA NATIONAL WILDLIFE REFUGE
Rhinehart, LA 71363-0201
Phone: 318-992-5261; fax: 318-992-6023
www.fws.gov/catahoula

Catahoula NWR is located in east-central Louisiana, 12 miles east of Jena. The refuge contains 25,162 acres divided into two units. The 6,671-acre Headquarters Unit borders 9 miles of the northeast shore of Catahoula Lake, a 26,000-acre natural wetland renowned for its large concentrations of migratory waterfowl.

The refuge is open to squirrel hunting (rabbit, raccoon, hog incidental) from the first day of the state squirrel season through October 31 and from the end of the waterfowl hunting season through the end of the state squirrel season. The refuge archery deer season runs from October 1 through January 31. Either sex (firearm) deer and muzzleloader hunts; check refuge brochure for dates. A free refuge permit must be acquired prior to hunting on the refuge.

## D'ARBONNE NATIONAL WILDLIFE REFUGE

Farmerville, LA 71363-0201
Phone: 318-726-4400; fax: 318-726-4667
Email: northarefuges@fws.gov
www.fws.gov/darbonne

Eight miles long and averaging four miles wide, the refuge consists of over 11,000 acres of bottomland hardwood forest, 3,000 acres of upland forest, 1,000 acres of moist soil habitat, and 2,000 acres of permanent water. D'Arbonne NWR is located in Ouachita and Union parishes on either side of Bayou D'Arbonne near its confluence with the Ouachita River. About 75% of the refuge is subject to annual flooding from December through May. Deer, waterfowl, turkey, and small game hunting permitted. There are four boat launching ramps on the refuge. A signed refuge permit is required of all hunters.

## DELTA NATIONAL WILDLIFE REFUGE

Venice, LA 70577
Phone: 985-534-2269
www.fws.gov/delta

Located 10 miles south of Venice, Louisiana, along the Mississippi River. The 48,000-acre refuge provides sanctuary and habitat to wintering waterfowl. Waterfowl counts in excess of 400,000 ducks and geese present on the refuge during peak population periods have been recorded. Deer, rabbits, and waterfowl are hunted here. A refuge permit is required. See www.fws.gov/southeast/pubs/dlthnt.pdf.

## LAKE OPHELIA NATIONAL WILDLIFE REFUGE

Marksville, LA 71351
Phone: 318-253-4238; fax: 318-253-7139
Email: lakeophelia@fws.gov
www.fws.gov/lakeophelia

A 17,500-acre refuge in Avoyelles Parish, central Louisiana, named for Lake Ophelia, a 350-acre permanently flooded swale. Major habitat types found on the refuge include 8,400 acres bottomland forest, 4,200 acres reforestation, 3,400 acres cropland, 500 acres of managed moist soil wetlands, and 1,000 acres of lakes and bayous.

Deer, dove, hog, coyote, small game, and turkey hunting. A hunting/fishing and ATV-use permit is required of all hunters and anglers 16 years old and older. Permits sell for $15 and are valid for an entire year March 1 through February 28. Permits may be purchased at the refuge headquarters or by mail. See www.fws.gov/southeast/pubs/lophnt.pdf.

## MANDALAY NATIONAL WILDLIFE REFUGE

Houma, LA 70360
Phone: 985-853-1078; fax: 985-853-1079
www.fws.gov/southeast/mandalay

A 4,212-acre freshwater marsh and cypress-tupelo swamp refuge located in Terrebonne Parish in southeast Louisiana, 60 miles southwest of New Orleans. Accessible only by boat. Archery deer and feral hogs and lottery waterfowl hunts were permitted in 2006–2007. To apply for a Lottery Waterfowl Hunt permit you must submit a completed Mandalay NWR Lottery Hunt

Application form and a clear photocopy of applicant's valid hunter education card. Application form available at the refuge headquarters and on the refuge Web site.

**TENSAS RIVER NATIONAL
WILDLIFE REFUGE**
Tallulah, LA 71282-9740
Phone: 318-574-2664
www.fws.gov/tensasriver

Located seven miles west of Tallulah, the Tensas River NWR in northeast Louisiana is one of the largest continuous blocks of bottomland hardwoods remaining in the nation. The refuge contains 64,012 acres and is located in Madison, Tensas, and Franklin parishes.

Hunting of squirrels, rabbits, deer, and waterfowl is permitted refuge-wide. Refuge permits are required. See www.fws.gov/southeast/pubs/tnrhnt.pdf.

**UPPER OUACHITA NATIONAL
WILDLIFE REFUGE**
Farmerville, LA 71241
Phone: 318-726-4400
www.fws.gov/upperouachita

Located in Union and Morehouse parishes, the refuge is 18 miles long and up to 10 miles wide. It consists of over 14,500 acres of bottomland hardwood forest, 5,000 acres of upland forest, 3,000 acres of shrub/wooded swamp, 16,000 acres of reforested farmland, and 2,000 acres of open water. About 80% of the refuge is subject to annual flooding from December through May. For additional information, contact the refuge office for a current hunting and fishing brochure. Also see www.fws.gov/southeast/pubs/drbhnt.pdf.

Signed refuge permits must be carried by all hunters.

*Private Hunting Clubs and Preserves*

**GOLDEN RANCH PLANTATION**
Gheens, LA 70355
Phone: 985-532-5221; fax: 985-532-6993
www.goldenranch.com

Established over 130 years ago as a sugar cane operation, this 50,000-acre plantation is only 45 minutes from the New Orleans airport. It has a privately owned freshwater marsh and offers deer, duck, quail, and alligator hunts. Also a popular retreat location.

**GROSSE SAVANNE HUNTING LODGE**
Lake Charles, LA 70607
Phone: 337-598-2357; fax: 337-598-5359
www.grossesavanne.com

An Orvis-endorsed wing-shooting lodge located in the marshes of southwest Louisiana, Grosse Savanne Hunting Lodge's waterfowl hunts on 50,000 private acres are world famous. The lodge also offers alligator hunts for big lizards 8 to 12 feet long, plus saltwater fishing and trophy-size bass. The plantation-style lodge can accommodate up to 18 guests with private bath and Jacuzzi, plus Cajun and Creole meals.

**SHALLOW LAKE HUNTING PRESERVE**
Eunice, LA 70535
Phone: 337-224-5128
www.shallowlake.net

Hunting at a southern pace—half-day hunts for quail, pheasant, and chukar for up to eight hunters (four per group maximum) and only one hunt per day. After the hunt you are treated to a home-cooked meal. Also hunts out of a blind for wild hogs.

## MISSISSIPPI

*In 2001 there were 245,000 resident hunters and 111,000 nonresident hunters: 83% went big game hunting, 48% small game, 22% migratory waterfowl and doves; 25% hunted on public lands; 92% hunted on private lands. Hunters pumped $360 million into the state economy. (USFWS)*

### OVERVIEW

There are over 800,000 acres of game habitat open for public hunting in 38 Wildlife Management Areas in Mississippi, where the bag limit on antlered buck deer is one buck per day, not to exceed three per license year, and the bag limit on antlerless deer is one per day, not to exceed three per license year—except that two additional antlerless deer per year may be taken with archery.

---

**MISSISSIPPI SNAPSHOT**
**MAGNOLIA STATE**

- **General information:**
  Mississippi Department of Wildlife, Fisheries and Parks
  1505 Eastover Drive
  Jackson, MS 39211-6374
  Phone: 601-432-2400
  www.mdwfp.com/level1/hunting.asp

- **Deer population:** 1.5–1.75 million, 6th in the United States

- **Average deer harvest:** 306,662, 7th in the United States

---

The annual harvest of bobwhite quail is around 80,000, with the northern part of the state having the best overall cover.

---

 **FEATURED HUNT**

---

### Beaver Dam Lake

JAMES SWAN

Some places seem to have a strong spirit that magnetically attracts people and moves them to do special things. The Mississippi Delta is one of those places. The Spanish moss hanging from old oak trees sprouting up out of the rich, black soil has given us cotton, gospel and blues music, and some exquisite hunting prose by writers including Archibald Rutledge and Nash Buckingham.

The Spanish adventurer Hernando De Soto explored the Mississippi Delta in 1541 and came upon what is today Tunica, Mississippi. The name "tunica" comes from a local Chickasaw Indian word, which translates as "the people."

Tunica today is the casino capital of the South. This is a far cry from the quaint slow-paced country town where in the early 1900s the noted writer and conservationist Nash Buckingham, author of *De Shootingest Gent'Man and Other Tales*, would pass through on his way to his hallowed Beaver Dam Ducking Club, tucked among the willow thickets and pecan and cypress trees on the shores of Beaver Dam Lake.

Tunica has changed quite a bit since those days, but you can still catch breakfast at his favorite hangout, the Blue and White Café, and you can follow in Buckingham's footsteps as he hunted with his favorite shotgun, a Parker double-12 nicknamed "Bo Whoop," on Beaver Dam Lake, which remains one of the nation's premier waterfowl grounds.

Buckingham had a gift for writing dialect and capturing the mood and culture of the times with a poetic quality to descriptions. As a flock of geese is approaching him in the twilight, he describes his feeling thus: "Something inside of me as old as life itself and younger than youth zigzags from spine to hair roots."

By all accounts, if you hunt Beaver Dam Lake, you will likely find swarms of birds, almost like in Nash's days. Guide/outfitter Mike Boyd, who has access to almost all the property around the lake, says that you can shoot the lake every day of the season, and it still provides plenty of ducks and geese.

The lake has changed since the days when Buckingham was here, in part due to beavers and siltation from farming, but Buckingham's blinds— "Handworker," "Hog Stand," "Teal Hole," and others— are still there.

A tornado toppled a tree on the first Ducking Club clubhouse, and a fire burned down the second, but the last clubhouse, the landing and duck shed from the old club, and the house where caretaker Horace Miller and his wife lived are all still there.

If you are in this area, either to hunt Beaver Dam Lake or just passing through, any hunter will enjoy a visit to the Ducks Unlimited national office in Memphis, Tennessee, where there is a splendid diorama honoring Nash Buckingham.

Fair warning: Mike Boyd says that if you want to hunt Beaver Dam Lake, you need to make reservations as far in advance as possible, as he typically fills up the blinds just about every day of the season.

To hunt Beaver Dam Lake, contact:

## BEAVER DAM HUNTING SERVICES
Mike Boyd, Outfitter
Phone: 662-357-0279; mobile: 662-363-6288
Email: mlboyd55@yahoo.com
Ducks Unlimited National Headquarters in Memphis, Tennessee, is open for tours from 8:00 A.M. to 5:00 P.M., Monday through Friday.

## DUCKS UNLIMITED, INC.
One Waterfowl Way
Memphis, TN 38120
Phone: 800-45DUCKS or 901-758-3825
www.ducks.org

## DESTINATIONS

*General Information*
For hunting guides to Mississippi, see www .hotspotguides.com/hunting/hguides_MS .asp.

*U.S. Army Corps of Engineers*

**ARKABUTLA LAKE**
Coldwater, MS 38618
Phone: 662-562-6261; fax: 662-562-8972
www.mvk.usace.army.mil/Lakes/ arkabutlalake/main .php?page=mainContent

One of four flood damage reduction reservoirs in north Mississippi. Located less than 30 minutes south of the Tennessee state line, Arkabutla Lake is the nearest U.S. Army Corps of Engineers project to the Memphis metropolitan area. The project includes 57,250 total acres of land and water. There are 37,700 acres of land at the project that are open to the public for hunting according to state regulations. A special deer hunt for people with disabilities is held here every year. Check the Mississippi District headquarters for information on hunting on Corps projects in Mississippi.

**NATIONAL FORESTS IN MISSISSIPPI**
USDA Forest Service
100 West Capitol Street, Suite 1141
Jackson, MS 39269
Phone: 601-965-4391
www.fs.fed.us/r8/mississippi

Encompassing over 1 million acres of unspoiled timberland, moss-draped oaks and stately pines frame each path in Mississippi's six national forests. The six forests—the Bienville, the Delta, the De Soto, the Homochitto, the Holly Springs, and the Tombigbee National Forests—are dispersed over the entire state. Hunting is allowed according to state regulations and specifics for the refuge. For details, see www.mdwfp.com.

Delta National Forest is reported to be a special place to find big whitetail bucks, in part because the state has changed the legal minimum to four points with a 15-inch spread. In other areas, the minimum spread is only 12 inches.

*U.S. Fish and Wildlife Service*
*National Wildlife Refuges*

**DAHOMEY NATIONAL**
**WILDLIFE REFUGE**
Boyle, MS 38730
Phone: 662-742-9331; fax: 662-742-3378
www.fws.gov/dahomey

A 9,691-acre refuge located in Bolivar County on Highway 446, 8 miles west of Boyle and about 15 miles southwest of Cleveland. Hunting for deer, waterfowl, turkeys, and feral hogs. Refuge permit required. See Web site for details. Youth hunts and special handicapped facilities.

**HILLSIDE NATIONAL**
**WILDLIFE REFUGE**
Cruger, MS 38924
Phone: 662-235-4989
www.fws.gov/hillside

Hillside NWR occupies over 15,500 acres along the eastern edge of the Mississippi/Yazoo River Alluvial Plain in Holmes and Yazoo counties. Offers excellent hunting for whitetail deer, squirrels, rabbits, raccoons, and waterfowl. An annual refuge permit is required to hunt here. For details, see www.fws.gov/southeast/pubs/TR_complex_hunt.pdf.

**MATHEWS BRAKE NATIONAL**
**WILDLIFE REFUGE**
Cruger, MS 38924
Phone: 662-235-4989
www.fws.gov/mathewsbrake

Mathews Brake NWR encompasses 2,418 acres in west-central Mississippi that offer excellent whitetail deer, squirrel, rabbit, raccoon, and waterfowl hunting opportunities. It is one of seven National Wildlife Refuges in the Theodore Roosevelt NWR Complex. An annual refuge permit is required to hunt here. For details, see www.fws.gov/southeast/pubs/TR_complex_hunt.pdf.

**MORGAN BRAKE NATIONAL**
**WILDLIFE REFUGE**
Cruger, MS 38924
Phone: 662-235-4989
www.fws.gov/morganbrake

Morgan Brake NWR encompasses 7,381 acres in west-central Mississippi. It is situated on the extreme eastern edge of the Mississippi/Yazoo River Alluvial Plain between U.S. Highway 49 and the adjacent loess hills in Holmes County. The refuge offers excellent whitetail deer, squirrel, rabbit, raccoon, and waterfowl hunting opportunities. It is one of seven National Wildlife Refuges in the Theodore Roosevelt NWR Complex. An annual refuge permit is required to hunt here. For details, see www.fws.gov/south east/pubs/TR_complex_hunt.pdf.

## NOXUBEE NATIONAL WILDLIFE REFUGE
Brooksville, MS 39739
Phone: 662-323-5548
www.fws.gov/noxubee

Noxubee National Wildlife Refuge is located within three counties (Noxubee, Oktibbeha, and Winston) of east-central Mississippi and consists of approximately 48,000 acres. Some 44,000 acres of the refuge are woodlands and occupied by a variety of upland species. Hunting of certain species is permitted in designated areas in accordance with applicable state, federal, and refuge regulations. For details, see www.fws.gov/noxubee/nox hunt.htm.

## PANTHER SWAMP NATIONAL WILDLIFE REFUGE
Yazoo City, MS 39194
Phone: 662-746-5060
www.fws.gov/pantherswamp

With over 38,500 acres, Panther Swamp NWR contains one of the few remaining large tracts of mature bottomland hardwoods in the delta of Mississippi. Flooding on an annual basis. The refuge has a number of bayous that slowly drain floodwaters, leaving shallow swamps and oxbow lakes that support stands of tupelo gum, cypress, buttonbush, and other species tolerant of extremely wet habitats. Fall hunting for squirrels, rabbits, deer, raccoons, ducks, and bobwhite quail and a spring turkey season in accordance with applicable state and federal regulations, including a required refuge permit. For details, see www.fws.gov/noxubee/nox hunt.htm.

## ST. CATHERINE CREEK NATIONAL WILDLIFE REFUGE
Sibley, MS 39165
Phone: 601-442-6696
www.fws.gov/saintcatherinecreek

Hunting for deer, hogs, upland game, and waterfowl is permitted according to state and federal regulations. For details, see www.fws.gov/saintcatherinecreek/huntfish.html.

## TALLAHATCHIE NATIONAL WILDLIFE REFUGE
Grenada, MS 38902
Phone: 662-226-8286
www.fws.gov/southeast/tallahatchie

The Tallahatchie National Wildlife Refuge consists of 4,083 acres in Grenada and Tallahatchie counties. Hunting for deer, hogs, upland game, turkeys, beaver, nutrias, raccoons, opossums, and waterfowl. A refuge permit is required for hunting. For hunting details, see www.fws.gov/southeast/pubs/tal lahatchie_hnt.pdf.

## MALLARD MANOR LODGE

Drew, MS 38737

Phone: 866-813-6573 or 662-658-1100

www.mallardmanor.com

In the Mississippi Delta, duck, goose, quail, rabbit, and dove hunts. Elegant lodge, southern dining, sporting clays, and corporate retreat facilities. Offers a Christian-based youth camp for teaching outdoor skills. For details, see www.mallardmanor.com/ministries.htm.

## POLLARD QUAIL FARM AND SHOOTING PRESERVE

Mathiston, MS 39752

Phone: 662-263-4881 or 662-263-5803

www.pollardquail.com

Family-owned released quail farm and shooting preserve in north-central Mississippi, raises specially conditioned flight birds ideal for the hunting preserve. Extended season: October 1–April 30. No limits. Fee based on number of birds released. Mississippi state license required.

# TEXAS

*In 2001 there were 1.1 million resident hunters and 100,000 nonresident hunters: 74% went big game hunting, 31% small game, 42% migratory waterfowl and doves; 16% hunted on public lands; 90% hunted on private lands. Hunters pumped $1.5 billion into the state economy. (USFWS)*

## OVERVIEW

Okay, Texans like to brag a little, and when it comes to hunting, they have some real things to brag about. In 2005 Texans harvested 1.9 million bobwhite quail and 450,000 scaled quail, making it the number-one quail hunting state. It's also the number-one state in doves harvested per year.

Then there's deer. Almost 4 million of them in Texas, or about 234 deer for every 1,000 people.

Then add in snow goose shooting at Katy Prairie, home to close to a million geese in the rice fields, hundreds of hunting ranches and farms, and refuges filled with waterfowl.

Texas also can boast about having one of the most unusual game birds in the United States—the chachalaca—a tropical and subtropical crow-sized grayish bird with a reddish throat, about 18 inches long with a 26-inch wingspan, found only in the southern part of the state. Chachalacas live near water and are often quite noisy.

---

**TEXAS SNAPSHOT**
**LONE STAR STATE**

- **General information:**
  Texas Parks and Wildlife Department
  4200 Smith School Road
  Austin, TX 78744
  Phone: 800-792-1112 or 512-389-4800 (Austin)
  www.tpwd.state.tx.us/huntwild

- **Buy licenses online:** https://txfgisales.vansis
  .wcom.com/fgtxisa/ApplicationAccessDispatcher

- **To report a poacher at Operation Game Thief:** See
  www.ogttx.com or call 800-792-GAME; rewards
  are given for tips that lead to arrests

- **Deer population:** 4,700,718, 1st in the United
  States

- **Average deer harvest:** 426,335, 6th in the United
  States

A list of native huntable species in the Lone Star State includes big game (whitetail deer, mule deer, desert bighorn sheep, antelope, gray or cat squirrels, red or fox squirrels, collared peccaries or javelinas, wild boars), game birds (bobwhite quail, chachalacas, Gambel's quail, lesser prairie chickens, migratory game birds, pheasant, scaled quail [blue], turkeys), plus doves, ducks, geese, snipes, woodcocks, and gallinules—and for good measure, add in armadillos, bobcats, coyotes, flying squirrels, frogs, ground squirrels, cougars, porcupines, prairie dogs, rabbits, and turtles.

Alligators are also legal. You are allowed one per year, and it can only be taken from private property.

Then let's not forget exotics. In some places in Texas, there are more species of exotic game animals than you can find in the zoo.

Little wonder that there are more licensed hunters in Texas than any other state!

 **HUNTING TIP**

## Snow Goose Decoys—Scotch Style

JAMES SWAN

Texas offers some of the best snow goose hunting in the world. Having clouds of snows, blues, and Ross geese wing over is exciting, but getting them down into range can be a challenge. Hunting snow and blue geese, especially, calls for lots of decoys—over a 1,000 is best. If hunters have to foot the bill for themselves, at $7 to $15 a decoy, a flock becomes a major investment. To save money, some folks use the "Scotch" approach to making decoys.

Some old-timers used to make Canada goose decoys from old tires. About a quarter of a tire is big enough for a body. Whitewalls are best. Just dab some gray paint on the front half of the whitewall, and you've got a body. Sticks or pieces of plywood cut to shape and painted black and white can be stuck into the ground at one end to make a head. Don't laugh. They work.

People make spreads of snow goose decoys from old orange crates and one-gallon or larger white plastic jugs. Another no-cost option is recycled white plastic mailing envelopes made into windsocks. Don't laugh until you've tried it.

You can purchase plastic silhouette decoys imprinted with photographic representations of wild birds. The "Scotch" approach is to use scrap plywood, cutting silhouettes with a jigsaw. The challenge is how to attach a stake to make them stand up. Plastic decoys bend, which allow a stake to be inserted through slits in the sides of the decoy. Wooden silhouettes are harder to stake because you want them as thin as possible to reduce weight, and that means there is little or nothing to attach a screw eye to. One solution is to cut two pairs of small holes on the body of the silhouette, one at the top and the other at the bottom. Then you make loops with heavy monofilament line, big enough to insert a stake.

The cheapest stakes are bamboo plant stakes you buy at your local nursery. They are green, so you may want to paint them, but they are a lot cheaper than dowels, last for years, and are lightweight.

Thanks to modern technology, you can buy windsocks made from the plastic building material Tyvek for about $3 each, including plastic heads that attach to the stake. They hold up well.

Last Look decoys shells are color perfect and made from plastic sheeting that you assemble into a shell with a household stapler. Last Look decoys cost about the same as windsocks, assemble very easily, are lightweight, and stack with stakes like a charm. See www.lastlookdecoy.com.

You can buy a hundred Texas Rag decoys for about $30. The bodies are made from thin white plastic and come in a roll with preprinted wings. You tear off squares of cloth and fold and use staples or duct tape to make windsocks.

Texas Rags are very lightweight and easy to make. However, if you are not careful, the fabric can rip as you tear them from the roll. Patch the tears with duct tape. You can also buy plastic heads for rags at a reasonable price or make your own from plywood.

And as a final touch, a few white tethered inflatable balloons, kites, or strings of flags—if the wind is up—will help give action to your spread.

Callers, learn to make as much noise as you can and stay concealed. When a flock of a thousand snows decide to land in your spread at the same time, you'll know why hunting can be a spiritual experience.

If you are drawn to the rice fields of Texas, Katy's Prairie is an excellent place to hunt for clouds of snow geese. One of the most respected outfitters is Bay Prairie Outfitters, located in Midfield, Texas, about 80 miles southwest of Houston. Bay Prairie can accommodate up to 60 hunters per night in a lodge and cabins with restaurant. For details, see www.texas-goose-hunting.com.

---

## DESTINATIONS

Texas offers 1,135,245 acres of public hunting lands contained within 78 units in 66 counties. You must have a permit, which costs $48, to visit a state Wildlife Management Unit. For maps and details, see www.tpwd.state.tx.us/huntwild/hunt/public/lands.

### U.S. Army Corps of Engineers

The U.S. Army Corps of Engineers manages 27 projects in Texas that offer hunting according to state regulations, with special conditions for each site. For details, contact:

**U.S. ARMY CORPS OF ENGINEERS—FORT WORTH DISTRICT**
Fort Worth, TX 76102
Phone: 817-886-1326
www.swf.usace.army.mil

### USDA National Forests

**NATIONAL FORESTS IN TEXAS**
Lufkin, TX 75901
Phone: 409-639-8501
www.fs.fed.us/texas

Located in east Texas, the national forests in Texas are composed of the Angelina, Davy Crockett, Sabine, and Sam Houston National

Forests and the Caddo-Lyndon B. Johnson National Grasslands in northeast Texas. There are 25 developed recreation areas, five scenic areas, five wilderness areas, a canoe trail, off-road vehicle trails, 52 miles of horse trails, and four hiking trails, totaling 185 miles. Hunting is permitted according to state regulations.

*U.S. Fish and Wildlife Service*
*National Wildlife Refuges*

## ANAHUAC NATIONAL WILDLIFE REFUGE

Anahuac, TX 77514
Phone: 361-286-3559
www.fws.gov/southwest/refuges/texas/
anahuac/index.html

A 34,000-acre refuge located on the upper Texas Gulf Coast where rainfall is 51 inches a year. Only 40% of the refuge is open to hunting. Offers some of the best waterfowl hunting in southeast Texas. For details, see www.fws.gov/southwest/refuges/texas/
anahuac/hunting.html.

## ARANSAS NATIONAL WILDLIFE REFUGE

Austewell, TX 77950
Phone: 361-286-3559
www.fws.gov/southwest/refuges/texas/
aransas

A 59,000-acre refuge that sprawls mostly across the Blackjack Peninsula, Matagorda Island, Myrtle Foester Whitmire, Tatton, and Lamar units. Archery and rifle hunts for whitetail and feral hogs; also mourning doves and waterfowl on Matagorda Island unit. For details, see www.fws.gov/southwest/refuges/texas/aransas/hunting.html.

This is the wintering ground for the whooping crane.

## BALCONES CANYONLANDS NATIONAL WILDLIFE REFUGE

Austin, TX 78758
Phone: 512-339-9432
www.fws.gov/southwest/refuges/texas/
balcones/index.htm

Located 30 minutes from Austin, hunting for doves, deer, feral hogs, and turkeys. A refuge permit is required. For details, see www.fws.gov/southwest/refuges/texas/
balcones/thingstodo.html.

## BIG BOGGY NATIONAL WILDLIFE REFUGE

Brazoria, TX 77422
Phone: 979-849-5118
www.fws.gov/southwest/refuges/texas/
texasmidcoast/index.htm

A 5,000-acre salt marsh refuge on Matagorda Bay. Open to waterfowl hunting. No permit required. For details, see www.fws .gov/southwest/refuges/texas/texasmidcoast/
huntfish_bb.htm.

## BRAZORIA NATIONAL WILDLIFE REFUGE

Angelton, TX 77515
Phone: 979-849-7771
www.fws.gov/southwest/refuges/texas/
texasmidcoast/brazoria.htm

Located on the Texas Gulf near Houston, waterfowl hunting according to state and federal regulations at the Christmas Point area. No special permit or fees required. For details, see www.fws.gov/southwest/refuges/texas/texasmidcoast/huntfish_br.htm.

## HAGERMAN NATIONAL WILDLIFE REFUGE
Sherman, TX 75092-5817
Phone: 903-786-2826
www.fws.gov/southwest/refuges/texas/hagerman/index.html

Hagerman NWR lies on the Big Mineral Arm of Lake Texoma, on the Red River between Oklahoma and Texas. Consists of 3,000 acres of marsh and 8,000 acres of uplands. Limited hunting of deer, doves, quail, squirrels, and rabbits is offered. All state and federal regulations apply. For details, see www.fws.gov/southwest/refuges/texas/hagerman/hunt.html.

## LAGUNA ATASCOSA NATIONAL WILDLIFE REFUGE
Rio Hondo, TX 78583
Phone: 956-748-3607
www.fws.gov/southwest/refuges/texas/laguna.html

The largest protected area of natural habitat left in the Lower Rio Grande Valley, the refuge contains 45,187 acres of habitat that mixes north and south species to increase animal species diversity. Whitetail deer hunts may be held in late fall or winter. Contact the refuge at 956-748-3607 or email r2rw_la@fws.gov in early summer for application dates and procedures.

## LOWER RIO GRANDE VALLEY NATIONAL WILDLIFE REFUGE
Alamo, TX 78516
Phone: 956-784-7500
www.fws.gov/southwest/refuges/texas/lrgv.html

Eleven different biological communities, from the Chihuahuan thorn forest to tidal wetland, mingle here. Deer, feral hog, and dove hunting. Contact refuge for details.

## MCFADDIN NATIONAL WILDLIFE REFUGE
Sabine Pass, TX 77655
Phone: 409-971-2909
www.fws.gov/southwest/refuges/texas/mcfaddin/index.html

On 55,000 acres of fresh to salt marsh with some wooded uplands and prairie ridges. Waterfowl hunting offered. Hunting is free in some areas; in other areas, there is a $10 charge per blind. For details, see www.fws.gov/southwest/refuges/texas/mcfaddin/Recreational%20Opportunities.html.

## SAN BERNARD NATIONAL WILDLIFE REFUGE
Angelton, TX 77515
Phone: 979-849-7771
www.fws.gov/southwest/refuges/texas/texasmidcoast/index.htm

A coastal marsh NWR that is very heavily used by snow geese. Waterfowl hunting is permitted. For details, see www.fws.gov/southwest/refuges/texas/texasmidcoast/huntfish_sb.htm.

**TRINITY RIVER NATIONAL WILDLIFE REFUGE**
Liberty, TX 77575
Phone: 936-336-9786; fax: 936-336-9847
www.fws.gov/southwest/refuges/texas/
trinityriver

Trinity River National Wildlife Refuge totals 17,500 acres of the bottomland hardwood forest ecosystem along the Trinity River located in southeastern Texas. Deer, feral hog, duck, squirrel, and rabbit hunting. For details, see www.fws.gov/southwest/refuges/texas/trinity river/hunting.html.

*U.S. National Park Service*

**AMISTAD NATIONAL RECREATION AREA**
Del Rio, TX 78840-9350
Phone: 830-775-7491(General Information) or 830-774-7491 ext. 206 (Hunting Permits)
www.nps.gov/amis

Reservoir located in southwest Texas at the confluence of the Rio Grande, Devils, and Pecos rivers. *Archery only* for deer, javelinas, mouflon sheep, and aoudad sheep; shotgun with birdshot may be used for rabbits, doves, quail, and ducks. Annual hunting permit required. For details, see www.nps.gov/amis/planyourvisit/hunting.htm.

**BIG THICKET NATIONAL PRESERVE**
Beaumont, TX 77701-4724
Phone: 409-246-2337(Visitor Information) or 409-839-2689 (Headquarters)
www.nps.gov/bith

Nine land units and six water corridors encompassing more than 97,000 acres, located seven miles north of Kountze, Texas. Rich diversity of habitat makes for plentiful wildlife here. Hunting for all legal species is according to state regulations. Extended feral hog season. Free permit required. For details, call 409-951-6831 or see www.nps.gov/archive/bith/huntfish.htm.

*Private Hunting Clubs and Preserves*
Texas has more shooting and hunting preserves than any other state. We've tried to select some of the most notable.

**DOS ANGELES RANCH**
Brackettville, TX 78832
Phone: 830-774-3097
www.dosangelesranch.com

An Orvis-endorsed wing-shooting lodge specializing in quail hunts on 12,400 acres in south Texas near Del Rio. Hunting for whitetail, exotics, and turkeys offered. Lodge with fly-fishing, sporting clays, and outstanding food.

**GREYSTONE CASTLE SPORTING CLUB**
Mingus, TX 76463
Phone: 800-399-3006 or 254-672-5927; fax: 254-672-5971
www.greystonecastle.com

An Orvis-endorsed wing-shooting lodge in central Texas offering released quail, pheasant, chukar, mallards, and Hungarian partridge; wild turkeys and doves; and hunts for trophy whitetail deer as well as elk, sika deer, red stag, oryx, fallow deer, and black buck on 4,000 acres west of Fort Worth. Lodge resembles a European castle and offers elegant food and many amenities.

## INDIAN HEAD RANCH
Del Rio, TX 78840
Phone: 830-775-6481; fax: 830-774-1528
www.indianheadranch.com

Rated one of the top-three exotic game ranches in Texas. Over 25 species on over 10,000 fence-free acres. Elegant lodge and guesthouses.

## MARIPOSA RANCH
Falfurrias, TX 78355
Phone: 361-325-5752; fax: 361-325-5827
www.mariposaranch.net

South of San Antonio and Corpus Christi, 45,000 acres lying between the King and Kenedy ranches. Mariposa specializes in wild quail hunting and award-winning dogs and dog training. It also offers hunts for whitetail, doves, turkeys, and nilgais, as well as sporting clays.

## ROUGH CREEK LODGE
Glen Rose, TX 76043
Phone: 800-864-4705 or 254-965-3700
www.roughcreek.com

Located 90 minutes southwest of Dallas–Fort Worth, this 11,000-acre widely acclaimed resort in the foothills of the Texas hill country offers guided hunts for bobwhites, chukar, pheasant, turkeys, deer, and exotics, plus five-stand, wobble trap and sporting clays, falconry, and much more.

Luxurious lodge and award-winning food. On the Condé Nast Traveler Gold List of the World's Best Places to Stay.

## SANDY OAK RANCH
Devine, TX 78016
Phone: 830-663-5005 or 210-415-4401; fax: 830-663-3050
www.sandyoaksranch.com

An Orvis-endorsed wing-shooting lodge located 35 miles south of San Antonio in the Sarita-Wilco sands, known for quail habitat. Wild quail and dove hunting, sporting clays, and two unusual wing-shooting sports—helice and Zzbird, which uses plastic "windmill" targets. Also gun fitting and instruction, fly-fishing, and ocean fishing, as well as luxurious cabins and food.

# HERITAGE DESTINATIONS

## Texas Wild
More people—130 million—visit zoos each year than attend football and baseball games. Almost always, when you read the interpretive signs in zoos, or listen to the guides, you are given stories about conservation of endangered species. If you hear anything about hunters, it's usually that animals are endangered because of hunting. In reality, almost always poachers are the problem, not legal hunters.

The new Texas Wild exhibit at the Fort Worth, Texas, Zoo tells it like it is. Hunters are good guys and essential to conservation. And the message is told creatively with style.

The Fort Worth Zoo is the oldest continuing zoo in Texas and the home of more than 6,000 native and exotic animals. Eleven years ago, Mrs. Ramona Bass, a member of the zoo's advisory board, was driving her four-year-old daughter home from preschool when the girl announced that we were all going to die from pollution and all the animals were going extinct because of man's actions. The overall negative message her daughter was getting at school upset Mrs. Bass.

Ramona Bass decided that people need to understand the real relationship between people and wild animals. More than a decade of work culminated last summer when the Fort Worth Zoo opened its $40 million Texas Wild exhibit.

One enters Texas Wild through a full-scale, turn-of-the-century frontier town street called Texas Town. Six surrounding exhibits on eight acres illustrate not only the different ecosystems of Texas—Hill Country, High Plains and Prairie, Piney Woods and Swamps, Gulf Coast, Brush Country, and Mountains and Deserts—but also man's imprint on the state. The viewing shelter for the High Plains and Prairies exhibit resembles an old farmhouse damaged by a tornado. In the Texas Gulf Coast exhibit, interactive displays are found in a bait shop. Nearby in an aviary, roseate spoonbills perch atop a partially sunken shrimp boat.

A theater show blends cartoons and animatronics to show weather effects. In the Farm Play Barn, children can try their hand at a cow-milking simulator and shoveling cow dung (plastic balls) into a garden bed to make vegetables grow. The cow eats the vegetables and continues the cycle of life. In the underwater viewing area of the river otter exhibit, children can climb into a glass bubble and be right beside the otters. Next door children crawl into one end of a hollow log while a black bear enters the other end. Only a pair of grates separates the two beings.

Texas Wild pushes the envelope in interpretation by also interpreting man, including hunters. One exhibit describes President Teddy Roosevelt, an avid hunter and outdoorsman, as one of the nation's first environmentalists. Other exhibits describe how hunting- and fishing-related funds contribute over $100 million a year to wildlife conservation efforts in Texas, while hiking and camping contribute nothing. Another exhibit explains why hunting deer helps keep them from overpopulating and running out of food or habitat. A computer game in the exhibit shows how ranchers can sometimes make more money by selling deer hunting leases than by grazing cattle on their land.

In the Piney Woods display, an alligator-skin handbag makes the point that the once-endangered American alligator is now so abundant that alligator farming is acceptable. Another series of interpretive panels describes the evolution of man's appetite, from the caveman's pursuit of wild game for food to the modern-day purchase of turkeys from the local butcher.

If you log on to the Texas Wild Web site and check out the advisory board, you will see that members represent a number of universities and are prominent officers of major environmental organizations: National Audubon Society, Conservation Fund, National Geographic Society, World Wildlife Fund,

# Appalachia

*In 2001 there were 303,000 resident hunters and 128,000 nonresident hunters: 75% went big game hunting, 34% hunting small game, 40% migratory waterfowl, 5% other animals; 36% hunted on public lands; 90% hunted on private lands. Hunters pumped $517 million into the state's economy. (USFWS)*

## OVERVIEW

The Ozark Mountains come together with the Mississippi River to create the world's most famous waterfowl hunting in timber,

---

**ARKANSAS SNAPSHOT
LAND OF OPPORTUNITY**

- **General information:** Arkansas Game and Fish Commission, www.agfc.com
- **Toll-free Report Poaching Hotline:** 800-482-9262
- **Deer population:** 750,000, 19th in the United States
- **Average deer harvest:** 153,035, 19th in the United States

---

especially for mallards. Stuttgart, Arkansas, for many, is the mallard hunting capital of the world.

And that's not all. Deer, turkey, quail, and squirrel hunting in Arkansas is also outstanding, and there are many public places to hunt.

## DESTINATIONS

### U.S. Army Corps of Engineers

For general information about U.S. Army Corps land in Arkansas, see www.swl.usace.army.mil/parks/index.html.

### ARKANSAS POST FIELD OFFICE

Tichnor, AR 72166

Phone: 870-548-2291

www.swl.usace.army.mil/parks/arkpost/index.htm

The Pine Bluff Project includes the portion of the McClellan-Kerr Arkansas River Navigation System from the mouth of the White River to Murray Lock and Dam. About 10,000 acres are open for public hunting downstream from Pendleton Bridge at navigation mile 22.5 on the Arkansas River. These areas are regulated as a part of the Trusten Holder Wildlife Management Area. Hunting opportunities are available for waterfowl, deer, turkeys, squirrels, rabbits, doves, quail, and other in-season game.

## BEAVER LAKE
Rogers, AR 72756-2439
Phone: 501-636-1210
www.swl.usace.army.mil/parks/beaver

Beaver Lake is located high in the Ozark Mountains of northwest Arkansas, the origin of the White River. Beaver Lake has some 487 miles of natural shoreline with towering limestone bluffs, natural caves, and a wide variety of trees and flowering shrubs. Deer, rabbits, turkeys, and squirrels are popular game animals. Arkansas state regulations apply for seasons and limits.

## BLUE MOUNTAIN LAKE FIELD OFFICE
Havana, AR 72842
Phone: 479-947-2372
www.swl.usace.army.mil/parks/bluemtn

Blue Mountain Lake is located in the shadow of Mt. Magazine, Arkansas' highest mountain. In-season hunting for all game species is permitted except in the parks, administration area, and dam area. In addition, the Blue Mountain Wildlife Demonstration Area on the west end of the lake is a first-class bird dog field trial facility. Everyone may use the facilities to train their dogs.

## BULL SHOALS LAKE
Mountain Home, AR 72653
Phone: 870-425-2700
www.swl.usace.army.mil/parks/bullshoals/index.html

Hunting for whitetail deer, eastern wild turkeys, and squirrels is outstanding; and opportunities for ducks, geese, and doves are good. Numerous boat ramps and parking areas provide access to large parcels of little-used public land.

Hunting is prohibited in developed parks. Wildlife Management Areas may have special rules. Consult the state hunting regulations. All other public land around Bull Shoals Lake is open for hunting. Normal state and federal regulations apply.

## CLEARWATER LAKE*
Piedmont, MO 63957
Phone: 573-223-7777
www.swl.usace.army.mil/parks/clearwater/index.htm

The U.S. Army Corps of Engineers manages 16,100 acres of land around Clearwater Lake, which is in the Little Rock District. Hunting is permitted on project lands. Deer, quail, squirrels, rabbits, turkeys, and doves. Many people travel to this area every year to hunt the ample supply of deer. Hunting is not permitted within the recreation areas. Also, camping is available during the hunting season.

---

*Clearwater Lake bridges the States of Arkansas and Missouri.

**DEQUEEN LAKE**
DeQueen, AR 71832
Phone: 870-584-4161
www.swl.usace.army.mil/parks/dequeen/
index.htm

Some 8,700 acres of land surrounding De-Queen Lake in the Little Rock District, with 32 miles of shoreline. Except for developed recreation areas and lands in the vicinity of the dam and other project structures, all project lands are open to the public for hunting. Principal game species include bob-white quail, mourning dove, turkey, fox squirrel, gray squirrel, cottontail rabbit, and deer.

**DIERKS LAKE**
Dierks, AR 71833
Phone: 870-286-2346
www.swl.usace.army.mil/parks/dierks/
index.htm

Approximately 33 miles of shoreline surrounding Dierks Lake. All project lands except the developed public-use areas, land around the dam, and other project structures are open to public hunting in accordance with state regulations. About 593 acres of land in the upper reaches of the project are included in the Howard County Game Management Area. Whitetail deer, bobwhite quail, mourning doves, gray and fox squirrels, cottontail rabbits, and waterfowl. For the most part, access is by the public-use area roads and privately owned timber access roads that are open to the public. Some areas are accessible only by boat.

**GILLHAM LAKE**
DeQueen, AR 71832
Phone: 870-584-4161
www.swl.usace.army.mil/parks/gillham/
index.htm

Approximately 8,600 acres of land surrounding Gillham Lake, which has 36 miles of shoreline. All project lands except the developed public-use areas and land around the dam and other project structures are open to public hunting. Principal game species found in the area are whitetail deer, bobwhite quail, turkeys, mourning doves, gray and fox squirrels, and cottontail rabbits. For the most part, the public-use area roads and timber roads that are open to the public afford direct access. Some of the more remote areas are accessible only by boat.

**GREERS FERRY LAKE**
Heber Springs, AR 72543
Phone: 501-362-2416
www.swl.usace.army.mil/parks/
greersferry/index.htm

Approximately 9,000 acres of land lying above the conservation pool is leased to the state as the Greers Ferry Lake Wildlife Management Area. Hunting for whitetail deer, eastern wild turkeys, rabbits, and squirrels is good to excellent. Deer hunting is restricted to archery tackle only. No rifles (including muzzleloading rifles) or handguns may be used to harvest any game species. Hunting is prohibited in developed parks and Sugar Loaf Mountain. Maps and other information available via the Project Office.

**LAKE DARDANELLE**
Russellville, AR 72801
Phone: 479-968-5008
www.swl.usace.army.mil/parks/dardanelle/
index.htm

Nearly 40,000 acres of waters associated with Lake Dardanelle and Winthrop Rockefeller Lake, rimmed by choice wildlife, picnic, and camping areas.

Located near the Ozark and Ouachita National Forests, the area has an abundance of wildlife. In-season hunting for deer, turkeys, waterfowl, and other small game. Canada goose hunting is excellent around the lake.

**MILLWOOD LAKE**
Ashdown, AR 71822
Phone: 870-898-3343
www.swl.usace.army.mil/parks/millwood/
index.htm

Approximately 6,500 acres of land surrounding Millwood Lake. Waterfowl is very popular. Other species found in good numbers are whitetail deer, bobwhite quail, doves, squirrels, rabbits, raccoons, armadillos, opossums, foxes, minks, and beavers. Hunting is not allowed within 300 yards of any developed recreation area or structure, including dams and levees. Duck blinds are permitted but must be temporary and removed within one week at the end of the season. No permit is required. Public hunting maps showing Corps-managed areas open for hunting are available from the local or state Corps offices.

**NIMROD LAKE**
Plainview, AR 72857
Phone: 479-272-4324
www.swl.usace.army.mil/parks/nimrod/
index.htm

Nimrod Lake includes the Lloyd Millwood Waterfowl Management Area. This area has a 2,400-acre "green tree" reservoir that is flooded annually for waterfowl. Whitetail deer, eastern wild turkeys, bobwhite quail, squirrels, rabbits, foxes, mink, black bears, doves, and waterfowl. Seasonal hunting is permitted throughout the lake except in or near recreation areas. Check with the state for specific hunting or trapping regulations.

Nimrod Lake also has designated a mobility-impaired hunting area, open only to hunters who possess a mobility-impaired hunting card obtained through the Arkansas Game and Fish Commission. There are four ground blinds, which are wheelchair accessible. For more information, contact the Nimrod–Blue Mountain Project Office.

**NORFORK LAKE**
Mountain Home, AR 72653
Phone: 870-425-2700
www.swl.usace.army.mil/parks/norfork/
index.htm

The public land around Norfork Lake provides good opportunities for whitetail deer, wild turkeys, squirrels, rabbits, and quail. Migratory birds and waterfowl such as doves, ducks, and geese are also found here. Hunting is prohibited in developed parks. Park boundaries are marked with orange bands around trees and signs located along roadways. Wildlife Management Areas may have special rules. Consult state hunting regulations.

**OZARK LAKE**
Ozark, AR 72949-9752
Phone: 479-667-2129
www.swl.usace.army.mil/parks/ozark/
index.htm

Ozark Lake is a major unit in the multiple-purpose plan of development of the Arkansas River and tributaries, known as the McClellan-Kerr Arkansas River Navigation System. The lake covers 10,600 acres of water area at mean sea level (MSL) elevation 372.0 feet. A land area of 6,349 acres surrounds the lake and extends around the shoreline for a distance of 173 miles. The public land surrounding Ozark Lake yields deer, quail, squirrels, rabbits, doves, wild turkeys, ducks, and geese in abundance for open state hunting seasons. Hunting in accordance with state laws.

**PINE BLUFF**
Pine Bluff, AR 71611
Phone: 870-534-0451
www.swl.usace.army.mil/parks/pinebluff/
index.htm

This area contains over 7,000 acres of riverfront forestland. The Arkansas River floodwaters offer some of the richest duck hunts in the world, and turkey hunting is also exceptional here. All other game species are legal.

There is an annual Nonambulatory Hunt for whitetail deer at Jardis Point, located at Dumas, Arkansas. Each applicant must provide a doctor's letter to verify qualification and level of disability. Applications can be obtained from the U.S. Army Corps of Engineers Arkansas Post Field Office, 35 Wild Goose Lane, Tichnor, AR 72166, 870-548-2291.

**TABLE ROCK LAKE**
Branson, MO 65616-8980
Phone: 417-334-4101; fax: 417-334-4169
www.swl.usace.army.mil/parks/tablerock/
index.htm

Table Rock Lake is 800 miles of shoreline from Branson, MO, to Eureka, AR, created by a dam on the White River. Hunting for all game species is permitted on the waters and on the surrounding government-owned lands of the projects and is subject to all applicable federal, state, and local laws and regulations. Permanent tree stands or steps of any type that penetrate the bark of a tree are prohibited on Corps of Engineers property. Portable stands with the owner's name and address permanently affixed are permitted. Stands are to be hung no earlier than one week before the opening and remain no longer than one week after the close of archery season.

*USDA National Forests*

**OUACHITA NATIONAL FOREST—USDA FOREST SERVICE**
Hot Springs, AR 71902
Phone: 501-321-5202; fax: 501-321-5353
www.fs.fed.us/r8/ouachita

The forest covers 1.8 million acres in central Arkansas and southeastern Oklahoma. A list of campgrounds for Ouachita, Ozark, and St. Francis National Forests can be found at www.arkansas.com/outdoors/camping/default/type/U.S.+Forest+Service.

## OZARK–ST. FRANCIS NATIONAL FORESTS

Russellville, AR 72801

Phone: 479-964-7200

www.fs.fed.us/oonf/ozark

The Ozark–St. Francis National Forests are really two separate forests. The Ozark National Forest covers 1.2 million acres, mostly in the Ozark Mountains of northern Arkansas. The St. Francis National Forest covers 22,600 acres in eastern Arkansas, one of the smallest and most diverse forests in the country.

*U.S. Fish and Wildlife Service*
*National Wildlife Refuges*

## BALD KNOB NATIONAL WILDLIFE REFUGE

Augusta, AR 72006

Phone: 870-347-2614; fax: 870-347-2908

www.fws.gov/southeast/BaldKnob

Located south of the town of Bald Knob in White County, the refuge encompasses approximately 15,000 acres of forested wetlands and croplands situated along the Little Red River and adjacent to the Henry Gray/ Hurricane Lake State Wildlife Management Area. Waterfowl, small game, raccoons, opossums, deer, and turkeys. Refuge permits are required of all hunters for all hunts. For more details, see www.fws.gov/southeast/ pubs/bldhnt.pdf.

## BIG LAKE NATIONAL WILDLIFE REFUGE

Manila, AR 72442

Phone: 870-564-2429; fax: 870-564-2573

www.fws.gov/biglake

Located in Mississippi County, 18 miles west of the Mississippi River and 2 miles east of Manila. On 11,038 total acres with swamp, 5,250 acres; open water, 2,600 acres; bottomland hardwoods, 2,100 acres; marsh, 300 acres; moist soil plants, 250 acres; and cropland, 32 acres. Refuge permit required for all hunts. Waterfowl, squirrels, rabbits, deer, raccoons, and opossums.

## CACHE RIVER NATIONAL WILDLIFE REFUGE

Augusta, AR 72006

Phone: 870-347-2614; fax: 870-347-2908

www.fws.gov/southeast/pubs/chehnt.pdf

Located in the 10-year floodplain of the Cache River from its confluence with the White River near Clarendon, Arkansas, to Grubbs, Arkansas, approximately 70 miles. Approximately 62,000 acres. Large concentrations of wintering waterfowl. Habitat includes 33,000 acres of bottomland forest and associated sloughs and oxbow lakes, 4,300 acres of croplands, and 7,500 acres of reforested areas.

Waterfowl, deer, turkey, quail, squirrel, rabbit, raccoon, and opossum hunting according to Arkansas seasons. Refuge permits required for all hunts. For specific regulations, see www.fws.gov/southeast/pubs/chehnt.pdf.

This is the area where the ivory-billed woodpecker has been sighted, so keep your eyes peeled for big black-and-white birds with red heads.

## FELSENTHAL NATIONAL WILDLIFE REFUGE

Crossett, AR 41635

Phone: 870-364-3167

www.fws.gov/felsenthal

Located in southeast Arkansas, approximately eight miles west of Crossett, a 65,000-acre refuge with an intricate system of rivers, creeks, sloughs, buttonbush swamps, and lakes throughout a vast bottomland hardwood forest that gradually rises to an upland forest community. Hunting permitted for waterfowl, squirrels, rabbits, quail, deer, feral hogs, and turkeys, with trapping for beavers and nutrias. See www.fws.gov/southeast/pubs/felsenthal_huntmap.pdf for details on seasons and permits.

**OVERFLOW NATIONAL
WILDLIFE REFUGE**
Parkdale, AR 71661
Phone: 870-473-2869 or 870-364-3167
Email: felsenthal@fws.gov

Located in southeast Arkansas in Ashley County, this 13,000-acre-plus wetland complex consists of seasonally flooded bottomland hardwood forests, impoundments, and croplands. During the winter, a 4,000-acre reservoir is created when the bottomland hardwood forests are allowed to flood. Waterfowl seasons and limits are consistent with state and federal regulations. Also see hunting regulations brochure for waterfowl sanctuary areas closed to public entry and other pertinent waterfowl hunting regulations.

Muzzleloader quota deer hunts are also held every year. Check Felsenthal NWR Web site for details.

**WAPANOCCA NATIONAL
WILDLIFE REFUGE**
Turrell, AR 72384
Phone: 870-343-2595

www.fws.gov/refuges/profiles/index
.cfm?id=43650

Located 20 miles northwest of Memphis, Tennessee, in Crittenden County, the refuge is located 4 miles west of the Mississippi River and protected from the river by a levee. It originally was the site of the Wapanocca Outing Club, which was one of the oldest and most prestigious hunting clubs. Hunting for squirrels, rabbits, raccoons, and deer (archery, permit drawing) in season.

**WHITE RIVER NATIONAL
WILDLIFE REFUGE**
DeWitt, AR 72042
Phone: 870-946-1468
www.fws.gov/whiteriver

The refuge lies in the floodplain of the White River near where it meets the mighty Mississippi River. Long and narrow, 3 to 10 miles wide and almost 90 miles long, this is one of the largest remaining bottomland hardwood forests in the Mississippi River Valley. The refuge is open for hunting of whitetail deer, turkeys, small game, and waterfowl in designated areas.

*Private Waterfowl Clubs*

**BLACK MALLARD OUTFITTERS**
Giffithville, AR 72076
Phone: 501-323-4637
or 866-DUK-HUNT
www.blackmallardoutfitters.com/
Shootinggrounds.html

A classic cedar lodge overlooking the Raft Creek bottomlands, wintering home of a large population of waterfowl. The farm plantings are managed to provide optimum food for ducks and geese. Choice of heated blinds, layout shooting, or traditional Arkansas-style hunting in green timber, plus fishing and skeet shooting.

*Upland Game Bird Hunting Preserves*

**BEAVER LAKE QUAIL PRESERVE**
Garfield, AR 72732-9698
Phone: 479-359-2473; fax: 479-359-3941
www.beaverlakequailpreserve.com

Located on the shores of Beaver Lake, the preserve offers full- and half-day non-guided and guided hunts for quail, pheasant, and chukar, plus whitetail hunting. Home-style meals and rustic cabin with private bedrooms and shared shower and bathroom.

**CADDO GAME BIRDS HUNTING PRESERVE**
Norman, AR 71960
Phone: 870-334-2500; fax: 870-334-2422
www.caddogamebirds.com

A hatchery and producer of quail and pheasant, Caddo Game Birds Hunting Preserve is located in the beautiful Ouachita Mountains of Arkansas, along the beautiful Caddo River and close to Hot Springs National Park. The preserve offers guided or non-guided hunts and packaged hunts. The preserve opens October 1.

**LEGACY RANCH**
Foreman, AR 71836
Phone: 866-798-6031;

mobile: 903-278-5000
www.ashleyoutfitters.com

An Orvis-endorsed wing-shooting lodge offering pheasant, quail, and chukar field hunts, European-style pheasant shoots, mallards, and big game—elk, deer, wild hogs, and bison. Borders the Red River in southwest Arkansas. Fishing and elegant lodge and cuisine.

**WINGS AND RINGS GAMEBIRDS, INC.**
Mount Vernon, AR 72111
Phone: 501-849-2763; fax: 501-849-2552
www.wingsandringsgamebirds.com

Half-day hunts for quail, pheasant, and chukar, plus skeet and archery target range with 25 full-bodied setups. Season runs October to March.

## KENTUCKY

*In 2001 there were 269,000 resident hunters and 54,000 nonresident hunters: 82% went big game hunting, 47% small game, 18% waterfowl and doves; 24% hunted on public lands; 90% hunted on private lands. Hunters pumped $373 million into the state economy. (USFWS)*

**OVERVIEW**
Kentucky, the land where Daniel Boone recorded his hunting success by carving "D. Boon Kilt a Bar, 1803" into the trunk of a tree, has a long and strong hunting tradition reaching back to the various Indian tribes that used the state as their hunting grounds.

Kentucky has an abundance of the normal selection of wild game of midwestern states, but what's new is its elk herd. Elk had originally been found in the bluegrass state, but they disappeared 150 years ago.

Kentucky began restoring elk in the southeastern part of the state in the winter of 1997–1998. Over the next several years, some 1,500 animals were trucked in from Arizona, New Mexico, Oregon, Kansas, Utah, and North Dakota. Today, the Kentucky herd has 5,700 free-ranging elk in the southeastern part of the state, the largest herd east of the Mississippi River. The state's goal is an elk herd of about 10,000 within the southeastern zone.

In 2006, a total of 200 elk permits were issued by random computer drawing. Two additional bull permits were awarded to conservation organizations to auction off the permits to raise money for wildlife conservation in Kentucky. Contact the state department of fish and wildlife for details on the elk hunt.

## DESTINATIONS

### State Wildlife Management Areas

Kentucky has a number of state Wildlife Management Areas. A list of over 100 can be found at http://fw.ky.gov/kfwis/wmaguide .asp?lid=600&NavPath=C151C154.

### U.S. Army Corps of Engineers

The U.S. Army Corps of Engineers offers hunting on a number of its projects in Kentucky. Contact district offices or the Kentucky Department of Fish and Wildlife for details.

**HUNTINGTON DISTRICT***
Huntington, WV 25701
Phone: 304-529-5453
www.lrh.usace.army.mil

This district includes Dewey, Fishtrap, Grayson, Paintsville, and Yatesville lakes.

**LOUISVILLE DISTRICT**
Louisville, KY 40202
Phone: 502-582-5736
www.lrl.usace.army.mil/rrl/default.htm

This district includes Barren, Buckhorn, Carr Fork, Cave Run, Green River, Nolin River, Rough River, and Taylorsville lakes.

**NASHVILLE DISTRICT†**
Nashville, TN 37202-1070
Phone: 615-736-7161 or 615-736-5181
www.orn.usace.army.mil

This district includes Barkley, Cumberland, Dale Hollow, Laurel, and Martins Fork lakes.

### U.S. Army Bases Open to Hunting

Hunting is permitted on a number of the U.S. Army bases in Kentucky. Contact the

---

*The lakes in Huntington District border both Kentucky and West Virginia.
†The lakes in Nashville District border both Kentucky and Tennessee.

individual bases or the state of Kentucky Fish and Wildlife Department for details.

**FORT CAMPBELL**
**MILITARY RESERVATION**
Outdoor Recreation Branch—Hunting and Fishing Unit
Fort Campbell, KY 42223
Phone: 270-798-2175
www.campbell.army.mil/newinternet/main.asp

Fort Campbell lies on the Kentucky–Tennessee border between Hopkinsville, Kentucky, and Clarksville, Tennessee, about 60 miles northwest of Nashville.

**FORT KNOX MILITARY RESERVATION**
Hunt Control Office
Fort Knox, KY 40121-5000
Phone: 502-624-2712
www.knox.army.mil

Fort Knox is located just 35 miles from Louisville. It encompasses 109,000 acres in four Kentucky counties.

*USDA National Forests*

**DANIEL BOONE NATIONAL FOREST**
Winchester, KY 40391
Phone: 859-745-3100; fax: 859-744-1568
www.fs.fed.us/r8/boone

The forest covers over 706,000 acres of mostly rugged lands on the eastern side of the state. Steep forested ridges, narrow ravines, and over 3,400 miles of sandstone cliffs. Most of the forest is open to the public for hunting free of charge. Whitetail deer, wild turkeys, ruffed grouse, quail, woodcocks, squirrels, rabbits, foxes, raccoons, waterfowl, elk, and more are found in the forest and can be hunted according to regulations set by the state Department of Fisheries and Wildlife. For details, see www.fs.fed.us/r8/boone/recreation/hunting.shtml or contact Kentucky Department of Fish and Wildlife Resources, Frankfort, KY 40601, 502-564-4336.

**LAND BETWEEN THE LAKES**
**NATIONAL RECREATION AREA**
Golden Pond, KY 42211
Phone: 270-924-2065
www.lbl.org/Home.html

Thousands of acres and over 300 miles of undeveloped shoreline, Land between the Lakes (LBL) offers an impressive variety of hunting opportunities and more than 230 days a year of in-season hunting. Whitetail deer and wild turkey populations are legendary. LBL offers annual spring quota and nonquota hunts for turkeys and fall archery and quota gun hunts for deer. Hunters can also enjoy a variety of camping choices, from developed campgrounds to the rustic adventure of camping LBL's backcountry.

All hunters must have an LBL Hunter Use Permit and applicable state licenses. Call 270-924-2065 for more detailed information.

*U.S. National Park Service*

**BIG SOUTH FORK NATIONAL**
**RECREATION AREA**
Oneida, TN 37841
Phone: 606-376-5073
www.nps.gov/biso

Straddling Kentucky and Tennessee, Big South Fork is one of the few National Park Service units that allows hunting. Popular big game species are whitetail deer, turkeys, and wild boars. The area is also rich in small game species including squirrels, raccoons, rabbits, and game birds. There are additional regulations that apply to hunting in Big South Fork. Apart from these, for those hunting in Tennessee, the Tennessee regulations apply; for those hunting in Kentucky, the Kentucky regulations apply. For more details, see www .nps.gov/biso/planyourvisit/hunting.htm.

*U.S. Fish and Wildlife Service*
*National Wildlife Refuges*

**CLARKS RIVER NATIONAL WILDLIFE REFUGE**
Benton, KY 42025
Phone: 270-527-5770
www.fws.gov/southeast/clarksriver

On 8,500 acres of bottomland hardwood forest in western Kentucky between Benton and Paducah on the east fork of the Clarks River. Waterfowl, dove, quail, woodcock, squirrel, rabbit, raccoon, opossum, deer, and turkey hunting are permitted. Hunters must obtain and carry a special refuge permit in addition to state and federal regulations. For details, see www.fws.gov/southeast/clarksriver and www.fws.gov/southeast/pubs/clarks-map.pdf.

**OHIO RIVER ISLANDS NATIONAL WILDLIFE REFUGE**
Parkersburg, WV 26182-1811
Phone: 304-422-0752
www.fws.gov/refuges/profiles/index .cfm?id=51660

The refuge consists of 22 islands and three mainland tracts scattered along nearly 400 miles of the Ohio River. Most of the refuge's 3,300 acres of land and underwater habitat are located in West Virginia; however, Pennsylvania and Kentucky each have two refuge islands. Most refuge property is open to hunting, with special refuge regulations in effect. Opportunities include archery deer, waterfowl, dove, and rabbit and squirrel hunting. Appropriate state licenses are required, and all hunters must carry the refuge's current hunt brochure, which serves as a permit to hunt. Hunt brochures are free and are available by contacting the refuge.

**REELFOOT NATIONAL WILDLIFE REFUGE***
Union City, TN 38261
Phone: 731-538-2481
www.fws.gov/reelfoot

On 10,428 acres in southwestern Kentucky originally established as a refuge for migratory waterfowl. Limited hunting opportunities for whitetail deer, raccoons, squirrels, and turkeys are available on the refuge. Contact the refuge for current regulations and seasons. Waterfowl hunting is prohibited on the refuge.

*Private Hunting Clubs and Preserves*

**BOILING SPRINGS LODGE HUNTING PRESERVE**
Munfordville, KY 42765
Phone: 270-528-5652
www.boilingspringslodge.com

---

*Located in both Kentucky and Tennessee.

Boiling Springs Lodge and Hunting Preserve offers hunts for quail, chukar, pheasant, deer, and eastern wild turkeys. Overnight lodging and camping and home-cooked meals.

## DEER CREEK LODGE
Sebree, KY 42455
Phone: 888-875-3000
www.deercreeklodge.net

An Orvis-endorsed wing-shooting lodge offering trophy whitetails, upland game birds, waterfowl, wild turkeys, and a variety of small game species flourishing on 14,000 pristine acres. This private club has been featured on numerous television shows.

A 10,000-foot rustic elegant lodge, gourmet food, private baths, Jacuzzi, all overlooking a trophy bass lake. Gundog training and consulting available.

## MOORE'S HUNTING PRESERVE
Calvert City, KY 42029
Phone: 270-898-8176
www.mooreshuntingpreserve.com

Quail, pheasant, and chukar hunting in western Kentucky near Calvert City and the Tennessee River and only a few miles from Kentucky Lake. Clubhouse with seating for 50; kitchen for corporate or private hunts. Special room rates for accommodations at Inn by the Lake in Gilbertsville.

## TRADEWATER OUTFITTERS AND BARE BOTTOM LODGE
Providence, KY 42450
Phone: 270-836-7998 or 270-388-2532
www.tradewateroutfitters.com/upland_game.html

A 1,500-acre hunting preserve in Crittenden County offering whitetail deer, quail, pheasant, turkey, chukar, and mallard duck hunting. Two 1,000-square-foot bunkhouses that sleep up to eight available for hunting and corporate events and meetings. Also crappie and bass fishing on Kentucky and Barkley Lakes.

## WILD WING LODGE AND KENNEL
Sturgis, KY 42459
Phone: 270-965-0026;
fax: 270-639-6101
www.wildwingkennel.com

A western Kentucky lodge with carefully developed 3,000-acre habitat of food plots, woodlots, and water improvements to enhance hunting for bobwhite quail, pheasant, chukar, deer, and wild turkeys. Rustic lodge, home-cooked meals, and bar.

## TENNESSEE

*In 2001 there were 288,000 resident hunters and 71,000 nonresident hunters: 73% went big game hunting, 44% small game, 28% migratory waterfowl and doves; 32% hunted on public lands; 95% hunted on private lands. Hunters pumped $589 million into the state economy. (USFWS)*

### OVERVIEW
The state is divided into four regions, which influences seasons and limits. Aside from quail, which are at all-time lows, perhaps what can best be said about hunting in Tennessee is that it keeps getting better.

In the 1960s hunters took fewer than 10,000 deer. In 2004 there were about 185 whitetails per 1,000 people in the Volunteer State, which translated into 179,542 deer harvested. Crossbows can be used in archery season, and three antlered bucks a year are allowed in most areas. In some areas, you can take three antlerless deer a day.

In 1973, Tennessee hunters harvested fewer than 50 black bears. Today the annual harvest is around 300.

In 1985 very few turkeys were bagged here. In 2005 the annual spring harvest was almost 34,000.

Looking toward the future, 167 elk have been released in Tennessee, and they are starting to reproduce.

## DESTINATIONS

### State Wildlife Management Areas
There are 93 state Wildlife Management Areas. Maps can be found at www.state .tn.us/twra/gis/wmamain.html.

### U.S. Army Corps of Engineers
The U.S. Army Corps of Engineers operates a number of reservoirs throughout the state that offer hunting opportunities. For more information about the Nashville District or the U.S. Army Corps of Engineers, contact:

**PUBLIC AFFAIRS OFFICER**
CELRN-PA
Nashville, TN 37202-1070
Phone: 615-736-7161
Email: Chief.Public-Affairs@lrn02.usace .army.mil
www.lrn.usace.army.mil

### USDA National Forests

**CHEROKEE NATIONAL FOREST**
Cleveland, TN 37320
Phone: 423-476-9700
Email: Mailroom_R8_Cherokee@fs.fed.us
www.fs.fed.us/r8/cherokee

Tennessee's only national forest, the Cherokee covers nearly 630,000 acres in 10 east Tennessee counties. Hunting for all legal species according to state regulations.

**CHICKASAW NATIONAL
WILDLIFE REFUGE**
Ripley, TN 38063
Phone: 731-635-7621
Email: chickasaw@fws.gov
www.fws.gov/chickasaw

The refuge lies in the Lower Mississippi River floodplain along the Chickasaw Bluff in western Tennessee. Eight miles of the western boundary abut the Mississippi River along the only stretch without a mainline levee in the Lower Mississippi River Valley. The refuge encompasses 23,809 acres including the largest block of bottomland hardwood forest in the state. Hunting for turkeys, deer, doves, woodcocks, small game, and coyotes according to state and refuge regulations. For details, see www.fws.gov/southeast/pubs/chkuse.pdf.

**CROSS CREEKS NATIONAL WILDLIFE REFUGE**
Dover, TN 37058
Phone: 931-232-7477; fax: 931-232-5958
Email: crosscreeks@fws.gov
www.fws.gov/crosscreeks

Nearly 9,000 acres—a blend of woodlands, wetlands, and croplands—in Stewart County located about four miles east of Dover. Hunting for deer, turkeys, doves, squirrels, Canada geese, and coyotes. For details, see www.fws.gov/southeast/pubs/crkhnt.pdf.

**HATCHIE NATIONAL WILDLIFE REFUGE**
Brownsville, TN 38012
Phone: 731-772-0501
Email: hatchie@fws.gov
www.fws.gov/southeast/pubs/htchnt.pdf

Hatchie NWR includes 11,556 acres along the scenic Hatchie River and is located about four miles south of Brownsville, Tennessee. Hunting for deer, turkeys, doves, small game, and waterfowl. For details, see www.fws.gov/southeast/pubs/htchnt.pdf.

**LAKE ISOM NATIONAL WILDLIFE REFUGE**
Union City, TN 38261
Phone: 731-538-2481

Email: reelfoot@fws.gov
www.fws.gov/reelfoot/fact.html

On 1,850 acres located 15 miles southwest of Union. Archery deer and raccoon hunting. For details, see refuge Web site.

**TENNESSEE NATIONAL WILDLIFE REFUGE**
Paris, TN 38242
Phone: 731-642-2091
www.fws.gov/tennesseerefuge

Encompassing over 51,000 acres of forests, wetlands, and open water along 65 miles of the Tennessee River, the refuge is located on Kentucky Lake in northwest Tennessee. Squirrel, raccoon, deer, turkey, Canada goose, and coyote hunting. For refuge hunting regulations, see www.fws.gov/southeast/pubs/tnshnt.pdf.

*U.S. National Park Service*

**BIG SOUTH FORK NATIONAL RIVER & RECREATION AREA**
Oneida, TN 37841
Phone: 423-569-9778 (Headquarters), 423-286-7275 or 606-376-5073 (Visitor Information)
Email: BISO_Information@nps.gov
www.nps.gov/biso

The free-flowing Big South Fork of the Cumberland River and its tributaries pass through 90 miles of scenic gorges and valleys. Offers hunting for deer, turkeys, wild boars, squirrels, raccoons, rabbits, and upland game birds. For details, see www.nps.gov/biso/planyourvisit/hunting.htm.

**OBED WILD AND SCENIC RIVER**
Wartburg, TN 37887
Phone: 423-346-6294
Email: OBRI_Information@nps.gov
www.nps.gov/obed

The Obed Wild and Scenic River is located in Morgan and Cumberland counties in east Tennessee on the Cumberland Plateau. The park includes parts of the Obed River, Clear Creek, Daddy's Creek, and the Emory River. Over 45 miles of creeks and rivers are included. Hunting is permitted in certain locations for all species legal in Tennessee. Please see a park ranger or stop in at the Obed Visitor Center to get information on the permissible hunting locations within the park.

*Tennessee Valley Authority*
Hunting is permitted on a number of the Tennessee Valley Authority (TVA) reservoirs and power plants in Tennessee. For details, see www.tva.gov/sites/sites_ie2.htm or contact:

**TENNESSEE VALLEY AUTHORITY**
Knoxville, TN 37902-1499
Phone: 865-632-2101

*Private Hunting Clubs and Preserves*

**BURNT OAK HUNTING PRESERVE**
Woodlawn, TN 37191
Phone: 931-920-2656
www.burntoakhunting.com

Quail and pheasant hunting on 375 acres along the Cumberland River, minutes from Clarksville and Ft. Campbell.

**CARYONAH HUNTING LODGE**
Crossville, TN 38571
Phone: 931-277-3113
www.caryonah.com

Located 80 miles west of Knoxville, the specialty at Caryonah Lodge is wild boar hunting. Lodging, food, and fishing nearby.

**CEDAR ROCK**
Shelbyville, TN 37160
Phone: 931-684-9814
www.huntcedarrock.com

Quail, pheasant, and chukar hunts on 389 acres in middle Tennessee near the Duck River. Clubhouse, guides, and dogs available. Corporate packages.

**QUAIL VALLEY HUNT CLUB**
Petersburg, TN 37144
Phone: 931-685-4628; fax: 931-684-1940
www.quailvalleyhuntclub.com

Quail, chukar, and pheasant field and European-style hunts. Several lodge options. Dogs and dog training. Wobble trap to practice. Membership options.

## WEST VIRGINIA

*In 2001 there were 229,000 resident hunters and 55,000 nonresident hunters: 95% went big game hunting, 43% small game, 25% hunted on public lands; 92% hunted on private lands. Hunters pumped $270 million into the state's economy. (USFWS)*

## OVERVIEW

One reason why 95% of the hunters in West Virginia hunt big game is deer—lots of them—over 800,000. This works out to 500 whitetails for every 1,000 people in West Virginia and an annual harvest of about 100,000 bucks and 120,000 antlerless deer.

Because the deer herd is growing, deer-car accidents also are growing. A growing number of West Virginia communities are opting for urban archery programs to control deer numbers. For details, see www.wvdnr .gov/Hunting/DeerUrbanHuntFactSheet .shtm.

Squirrels, ruffed grouse, woodcocks, and raccoons are other popular species in this heavily forested state.

In 1989, 2,000 wild turkeys were released in West Virginia. Today there are over 140,000 in all 55 counties. The total spring and fall kill for 2003 was 14,376.

Hunters bagged 1,705 black bears in West Virginia in 2006, which is a state record. Bears were bagged in 38 of the state's 55 counties.

---

### WEST VIRGINIA SNAPSHOT
### MOUNTAIN STATE

- **General information on West Virginia state hunting regulations:** www.wvdnr.gov/hunting/ hunting.shtm
- **Purchase your license online:** www.wvhunt.com/ wizard/hflw000.asp
- **Deer population:** 800,000, 17th in the United States
- **Average deer harvest:** 210,278, 14th in the United States

---

## DESTINATIONS

*State Wildlife Management Areas*

West Virginia has a large number of Wildlife Management Areas that are open to hunting. For maps and details of WMAs and other public and private lands open to hunting, see www.wvdnr.gov/Hunting/WMAMap.shtm.

*U.S. Army Corps of Engineers*

The U.S. Army Corps of Engineers has nine units in West Virginia that offer hunting—Beech Fork Lake, Bluestone Lake, Burnsville Lake, East Lynn Lake, R.D. Bailey Lake, Stonewall Jackson Lake, Summersville Lake, Sutton Lake, and Tygart Lake. They fall under the jurisdiction of the Huntington District, which may be contacted for details at:

**PUBLIC AFFAIRS, U.S. ARMY CORPS OF ENGINEERS**
Huntington, WV 25701
Phone: 304-399-5353
www.lrh.usace.army.mil/_kd/go .cfm?destination=Page&Pge_ID=1001

*USDA National Forests*

**MONONGAHELA NATIONAL FOREST**
Elkins, WV 26241-3962
Phone: 304-636-1800
www.fs.fed.us/r9/mnf

Over 919,000 acres in 10 counties in the hills of West Virginia offering hunting for all legal game species according to state regulations and local posting. See state regulations. The most popular species sought are black bears, wild turkeys, deer, gray and fox squirrels, rabbits, snowshoe hare, woodcocks, and grouse. Limited waterfowl habitat.

*U.S. Fish and Wildlife Service*
*National Wildlife Refuges*

## CANAAN VALLEY NATIONAL WILDLIFE REFUGE
Davis, WV 26260
Phone: 304-866-3858; fax: 304-866-3852
www.fws.gov/canaanvalley/
CVNWR%20hunting.htm

A 16,000-acre refuge offering hunting for deer, black bears, wild turkeys, ruffed grouse, mourning doves, waterfowl, coots, rail, gallinules, snipes, woodcocks, rabbits, hare, squirrels, red foxes, gray foxes, raccoon bobcats, woodchucks, coyotes, opossums, and skunks. The specialty here is the woodcock. They breed locally as well as stopping over on their annual migration. Hunt permits are available weekdays only, except selected Saturdays. To get your permit, send your name, address, and phone number to the refuge by phone (304-866-3858), fax (304-866-3852), or email (fw5rw_cvnwr@fws.gov). You may also stop by the office weekdays, 8:00 A.M.–3:00 P.M., to request a permit.

## OHIO RIVER ISLANDS NATIONAL WILDLIFE REFUGE
Parkersburg, WV 26102
Phone: 304-422-0752; fax: 304-422-0754
www.fws.gov/northeast/ohioriverislands/
public_use.html

Hunting for archery deer, waterfowl, doves, rabbits, and squirrels, the refuge extends along 362 miles of the upper Ohio River with 22 scattered islands and three mainland properties.

*U.S. National Park Service*

## BLUESTONE NATIONAL SCENIC RIVER
Glen Jean, WV 25846-0246
Phone: 304-465-0508
www.nps.gov/blue

This park preserves relatively unspoiled land in southern West Virginia along over 10 miles of the Bluestone River. Approximately 70% of the Bluestone National Scenic River lands are open to hunting according to state regulations and local posting. See www.nps.gov/blue/planyourvisit/hunting.htm.

*Private Hunting Clubs and Preserves*

## GREENBRIER SPORTING CLUB
White Sulphur Springs, WV 24986
Phone: 304-536-7763 or 888-741-8989
www.wvexplorer.com/Recreation/
Hunting/default.htm

For more than 200 years, this plush member-owned equity resort in the Alleghenies has been a retreat for leaders from all walks of life. An Orvis-endorsed wing-shooting lodge, aside from golf, falconry, river rafting, fox hunting, sporting clays, and fishing, there is a 5,000-acre hunting preserve for quail, pheasant, chukar, and turkeys 26 miles away. Lodge, accommodations, meals, guides, and dogs available.

**THE FALCONRY & RAPTOR
EDUCATION FOUNDATION**
White Sulphur Springs, WV 24986
Phone: 304-536-9245
www.falconryacademy.com/index.html

Offers classes on falconry. Or go out with a
falconer to hunt small game and pheasant with
Harris hawks near White Sulfur Springs.

**MOUNTAIN STATE GUIDES
AND OUTFITTERS**
Elkins, WV 26241
Phone: 304-630-2011
www.mtstgo.com

Offering hunts for deer, turkeys, pheasant,
quail, and chukar in the Appalachian Mountains. Guides and dogs.

**QUAIL HOLLOW HUNTS**
Berkeley Springs, WV 25411
Phone: 304-258-0584
www.quailhollowhunts.com

Located eight miles south of Berkeley Springs,
300-plus acres for hunting released pheasant, quail, and chukar, and wild doves.
Guides and dogs available.

# Midwest

*In 2001 there were 246,000 resident hunters and 64,000 nonresident hunters: 79% went big game hunting, 32% small game, 19% migratory waterfowl and doves; 20% hunted on public lands; 87% hunted on private lands. Hunters pumped $451 million into the state economy. (USFWS)*

## OVERVIEW

The rolling hills and fields and fertile soil of Illinois yield farms interspersed with wood-lots and crisscrossed with rivers and lakes that serve as a nourishing foundation for wildlife, especially monster whitetail deer, turkeys, quail, doves, squirrels, rabbits, Hungarian partridge, and pheasant. Then add in the Mississippi River system to the west, the Great Lakes to the east, and you see why wild geese and ducks are so abundant here. The low percentage of hunters using public land in the stats above is explained by the fact that Illinois is the nation's 4th most populous state, 24th largest in size, but it ranks 48th in the amount of public lands. The folks

---

**ILLINOIS SNAPSHOT**
**PRAIRIE STATE**

- **General information for hunting in Illinois:** http://dnr.state.il.us/admin/systems/index.htm

- **State hunting licenses can be purchased online at:** www.link2gov.com/il/dnr

- **Deer population:** 750,000–800,000, 16th in the United States

- **Average deer harvest:** 160,367, 19th in the United States

in Illinois make up for this with an extraordinary number of hunting clubs.

## FEATURED HUNT

### Time & Whitetails Heal All Wounds

PATT DORSEY*

A southern Illinois landscape of undulating hills and freshwater lakes is more than a wonderful woodland and wetland habitat for waterfowl, shorebirds, turkeys, deer, and other wildlife. It is also a must-visit hunting destination.

One exceptional place with quite a story is the 8,600-acre Peabody Recreational Lands property, near Marissa.

Huge-bodied, healthy whitetail deer materialize from even the smallest stands of cover. (Quality habitat management and aggressive doe harvests produce several Boone & Crockett and Pope & Young bucks each year.) Long-bearded tom turkeys strut in pirouettes. Ducks blacken the sky in swarms, scattering into small bunches of chuckling diners. Delicate warbler nests hang deceptively strong between cattail stems.

People are far from the only hunters. They share this place with red-tailed hawks, northern harriers, and bald eagles. River otters occasionally feast on crayfish and crappie in more than 1,000 acres of lakes, while bobcats steal through brush to prey on unsuspecting cottontails and mice.

Some might find irony here. For over 50 years, this beautiful and bountiful land was mined for coal. Some might find Newton's third law at work. Newton's third law is most familiar stated this way: "For every action there is an equal but opposite reaction." On the ground in Marissa, Illinois, Newton's law is re-

flected in a modern coal mining paradigm—a paradigm that begins with every U.S. citizen's affinity for hot water, lighting, refrigeration, and the like.

Since coal produces over half the electricity in the United States, this translates to a large hole in the ground . . . somewhere. At Marissa, rich interior coal reserves were surface—or strip—mined for over 50 years. The topography of southern Illinois is relatively flat, and the copious coal seams are shallow. By underground mining, companies can extract less than 60% of a coal seam; by strip mining, they can extract 90% to 95%, making practical economic sense.

Strip mining is not an unburdened boon to coal companies, however. It comes with a unique set of reclamation issues. State and federal laws require mined land reclamation, and Illinois has some of the toughest laws, mandating topsoil replacement, for example. But in 1954, more than 20 years before any state or federal reclamation requirements, Peabody Energy, the owner/operator at Marissa, launched "Operation Green Earth." This innovative program was aimed at planting trees and other vegetation and reintroducing fish and wildlife onto mined lands. In 10 years the company reclaimed nearly 50,000 mined acres. To date they can boast tens of thousands of acres, more than 70 million trees, and more than 30 major awards for stewardship projects.

Peabody's mission, "When the mining is complete, we will leave the land in a condition equal to or better than we found it," is a determined one, which goes beyond Operation Green Earth. Today they use new-fangled technology, ecological science, and old-fashioned farming techniques to restore soil productivity, control erosion, and improve water quality.

Pragmatically, Peabody is the largest landowner in Illinois. In terms of acreage alone, the potential wildlife benefit is enormous. Large parcels of unfragmented habitat are critical to many species, including prairie birds that require vast grasslands, such as upland sandpipers, and forest birds, such as hooded warblers. Further, because strip mining is only temporary and shopping centers, subdivisions, reservoirs, and highways are permanent, conversion of mined land to wildlife habitat may hold more hope than other conservation measures. (Nationally, Illinois ranks 49th in the amount of intact natural land.)

Peabody Recreational Lands offers trophy class deer hunting, world-class duck hunting, and first-class turkey hunting, coupled with five-star accommodations. A new, 7,600-square-foot lodge has magnificent views of the surrounding lakes and woodlands. Peabody Recreational Lands' staff and guides treat guests like family, creating a fun, cozy atmosphere for unmatched, safe, ethical hunting opportunities.

Peabody Recreational Lands at Marissa is an easy drive from Saint Louis' Lambert International Airport. To learn more, contact Wilbur Engelhardt, general manager for Peabody Recreational Lands, at 866-PRL-INFO or visit Peabody's Web site at www .peabodyenergy.com/Stewardship/Recreational Lands-Waterside.asp.

No matter the reason or the season, guests should bring a shotgun and plan to visit the new 1,600-acre World Shooting Recreational Complex, just a few miles away in Sparta. Open to recreational shooters and campers, this ultramodern complex features 120 trap fields extending along a 3.5-mile shooting line and 250 acres of water for warm-water fishing. Open trap shooting is available from 10:00 A.M. to 6:00 P.M. daily for $5 per 25-target round. Camping facilities include 746 RV campsites and 260 additional campsites with electrical service. Campsite fees are $20 per day.

For more information on the World Shooting Recreational Complex, visit Illinois Department of Natural Resources' Web site at www.dnr.state.il.us.

Time does not heal all wounds, but healing takes time. Healing is an active process, not a passive one. Activity and time created something very special in the Illinois coal belt.

*Patt Dorsey is a Colorado Division of Wildlife Area manager.*

## DESTINATIONS

*U.S. Army Corps of Engineers*

**LAKE SHELBYVILLE**
Shelbyville, IL 62565-9804
Phone: 217-774-3951
www.mvs.usace.army.mil/Shelbyville

Approximately 12,000 of the 23,000 land acres at Lake Shelbyville are forested, with oak and hickory the dominant species. The remaining land acres are open or brush covered. Game species available for hunting include doves, quail, rabbits, pheasant, whitetail deer, gray and fox squirrels, wild turkeys, foxes, coyotes, raccoons, woodcocks, and waterfowl. The Illinois DNR manages the Shelbyville Wildlife Area, located in two units, the Kaskaskia Unit and the West Okaw Unit. Both are located at the northern end of the lake. Some 1,500 campsites are located around the lake.

**U.S. ARMY ENGINEER DISTRICT, ROCK ISLAND**
Rock Island, IL 61299
Phone: 309-794-4200; fax: 309-794-5793
www.mvr.usace.army.mil

The Rock Island District covers more than 78,000 square miles and includes 314 miles of the Mississippi River from Guttenberg, Iowa, to Saverton, Missouri, and 268 miles of the Illinois Waterway from Lake Street in downtown Chicago to the LaGrange Lock and Dam, southwest of Beardstown, Illinois. Hunting is permitted within the district and is regulated by the state of Illinois and wildlife refuges within the district: Savanna District, Upper Mississippi National Wildlife and Fish Refuge, and the Mark Twain National Wildlife Refuge Complex.

*USDA National Forests*

**HOOSIER NATIONAL FOREST\***
Bedford, IN 47421
Phone: 812-275-5987; fax: 812-279-3423
www.fs.fed.us/r9/hoosier

A 200,000-acre forest in the rolling hills of the southern part of the state offering hunting according to state regulations. For more details, see www.fs.fed.us/r9/hoosier/recreation/hunting_fishing.htm.

**MIDEWIN NATIONAL
TALLGRASS PRAIRIE**
Wilmington, IL 60481
Phone: 815-423-6370; fax: 815-423-6376
www.fs.fed.us/mntp

Currently, deer may be hunted at Midewin during the archery, shotgun, and muzzle loading-only seasons, and turkeys may be hunted during the spring season. No other game or nongame species may be taken at Midewin.

There is currently no limit on archery

---

*Located in both Illinois and Indiana.

deer hunters. Firearm deer permits and turkey permits are drawn by lottery by the Illinois Department of Natural Resources, and the numbers can change from year to year.

State hunting regulations with the additions specified in the Special Hunt Area Rules. There is no special fee, but hunters are required to register for a seasonal hunting pass. Hunting passes are available at the Midewin Welcome Center. There are no overnight camping facilities. Nearby public campgrounds are available at Kankakee River State Park and Des Plaines Fish & Wildlife Area.

**SHAWNEE NATIONAL FOREST**
Harrisburg, IL 62946
Phone: 618-253-7114 or 800-MY-WOODS
800-699-6637; fax: 618-253-1060
www.fs.fed.us/r9/forests/shawnee

About one-third of the acreage (277,506 acres) within the forest and existing purchase unit boundaries is National Forest System land. This is the single largest publicly owned body of land in the state. It is within a day's drive (350 miles) of more than 45 million people, or 17% of the U.S. population.

State hunting laws are enforced in the Shawnee National Forest. Construction of or use of permanent deer stands is not permitted on national forest land.

*U.S. Fish and Wildlife National Wildlife Refuges*

**CHAUTAUQUA NATIONAL
WILDLIFE REFUGE**
Havana, IL 62644
Phone: 309-535-2290; fax: 309-535-3023
www.fws.gov/midwest/illinoisriver/chaq
.html

On 4,480 acres of bottomland forest, flood-plain wetlands, and backwater lake habitat along the Illinois River. Hunting waterfowl is permitted in accordance with Illinois and refuge regulations in the Liverpool Lake Public Hunting Area of the refuge (located outside of the main dike). This area is accessible by boat from the Illinois River. Public boat launching sites are located in Havana and Liverpool. Access for hunting waterfowl is allowed one hour before sunrise in the hunting area. Blinds must be constructed from existing dead vegetation or standing willows. All blinds are considered public property and are available on a first-come, first-served basis daily. Portable blinds are permitted. All hunting aids such as blinds and decoys must be removed at the end of each day's hunt.

## CRAB ORCHARD NATIONAL WILDLIFE REFUGE

Marion, IL 62959
Phone: 618-997-3344
www.fws.gov/midwest/craborchard

Located west of Marion, Illinois, on the northern edge of the Ozark foothills, this is one of the largest refuges in the Great Lakes/Big Rivers Region. The 43,890-acre refuge includes three man-made lakes totaling 8,700 surface acres and hardwood and pine forests, croplands, grasslands, wetlands, rolling hills, and rugged terrain with slopes of 24%. The 4,050-acre Crab Orchard Wilderness, the first wilderness area in the state of Illinois, is within the refuge. Waterfowl, upland game, turkey, and deer hunting are allowed on the refuge according to state regulations. It is illegal to drive or screw any metal objects into a tree or to hunt from a tree in which a metal object has been driven or screwed.

## CYPRESS CREEK NATIONAL WILDLIFE REFUGE

Ullin, IL 62992
Phone: 618-634-2231
www.fws.gov/midwest/cypresscreek

Located in southernmost Illinois within the Cache River watershed. Currently, the refuge protects 15,000 acres, remnants of cypress-tupelo swamps, oak barrens, and vast stands of bottomland forests. The refuge and surrounding Cache River wetlands are considered Illinois' bayou. This is the largest wetland complex in the state. The area supports waterfowl, deer, turkeys, squirrels, rabbits, and other game species that are huntable according to state regulations.

## EMIQUON NATIONAL WILDLIFE REFUGE

Havana, IL 62644
Phone: 309-535-2290; fax: 309-535-3023
www.fws.gov/midwest/illinoisriver/emq.html

Hunting waterfowl is permitted on the 11,122-acre refuge in accordance with Illinois and refuge regulations in the Liverpool Lake Public Hunting Area of the refuge (located outside of the main dike). This area is accessible by boat from the Illinois River. Public boat launching sites are located in Havana and Liverpool. Access for hunting waterfowl is allowed one hour before sunrise in the hunting area. All blinds are considered public property and are available on a first-come, first-served basis daily. Portable blinds are permitted.

**MARK TWAIN NATIONAL WILDLIFE REFUGE COMPLEX**
Quincy, IL 62301
Phone: 217-224-8580
Email: durinda_hulett@fws.gov
www.fws.gov/midwest/MarkTwain

This NWR includes 45,000 acres scattered along 345 miles of the Mississippi River and short distances up the Illinois and Iowa rivers. In 2000, Mark Twain NWR was split into five separate National Wildlife Refuges: Port Louisa NWR, Great River NWR, Clarence Cannon NWR, Two Rivers NWR, and Middle Mississippi River NWR. Deer, wild turkey, upland game, and waterfowl hunting are allowed on many of the refuges. Check with the refuge headquarters for details, as each refuge has its own special regulations.

*Private Hunting Clubs and Preserves*

**BIG OAK HUNTING PARADISE, INC.**
Lincoln, IL 62656
Phone: 217-732-4238
www.big-oak.com

Located in Lincoln, Illinois, deer, turkey, quail, pheasant, chukar, and dove hunting on two hunting areas with over 420 acres of preserve hunting and additional acreage for native wildlife hunting. Home-cooked meals. The Lincoln bunkhouse can house and feed 20 hunters and includes a lounge for resting and visiting. Members and nonmembers welcome.

**ERIENNA HUNT CLUB**
Morris, IL 60450
Phone: 815-955-9498
www.eriennahuntclub.com

A public club catering to small groups and business outings on 350 acres of land, offering half-day packages for pheasant and chukar, plus trapshooting and tower shooting.

**GREEN ACRES SPORTSMAN'S CLUB**
Roberts, IL 60962
Phone: 217-395-2588
www.huntgreenacres.com

Located in central Illinois, the 1,020-acre Green Acres Sportsman's Club offers pheasant, Hungarian partridge, red-legged partridge, bobwhite quail, chukar partridge, waterfowl, and wild turkey hunts. Also, in season, cottontail rabbit, woodcock, snipe, rail, and mourning dove hunts. European-style driven hunts are also available. Clubhouse, sporting clays, and dog training. This is a membership club.

**HARPOLE'S HEARTLAND LODGE**
Nebo, IL 62355
Phone: 800-717-HUNT (800-717-4868);
fax: 217-734-2559
www.heartlandlodge.com

An Orvis-endorsed wing-shooting lodge on 7,500 acres—bed-and-breakfast, corporate retreat, and hunting lodge located in serene Pike County. Offering wild quail, released pheasant, chukar, and Hungarian partridge, wild turkey, and whitetail deer hunting, plus sporting clays. Hosts an annual charity fund-raising hunt with St. Louis Cardinals ballplayers.

**HILLTOP MEADOWS HUNT CLUB**
Fulton, IL 61252

Phone: 815-535-1056; fax: 309-887-9378
www.hilltopmeadowshuntclub.com

A private club on 350 rolling acres of prairie grasslands, food plots, and wooded areas in Whiteside County in northwestern Illinois. Half-day and full-day hunts for released pheasant, chukar, Hungarian partridge, and quail, plus doves, deer, and wild turkeys, with shooting range and clay target shooting. Clubhouse with kitchen and overnight accommodations.

**HOPEWELL VIEWS PRESERVE**
Rockport, IL 62370
Phone: 217-734-9234
www.hopewellviewshunting.com

Located in Pike County on over 2,500 acres of prime Conservation Reserve Program (CRP) land and woodlands for hunting released pheasant, chukar, and bobwhite quail for conventional and continental shoots; whitetail deer; wild turkeys; and waterfowl. Guides, dogs, sporting clays, and a lodge that accommodates up to 20 people for overnights. Member and nonmember options.

**HOUTEKIER'S FOR THE BIRDS**
**HUNTING PRESERVE**
Illinois City, IL 61259
Phone: 309-791-0178
www.huntforthebirds.com

A 30-minute drive from Quad City, pheasant hunts September through March, with guides and dogs available. Open to the public; nonresident Illinois hunting preserve licenses for $7.

**LICK SKILLET HUNT CLUB**
Armington, IL 61721
Phone: 309-392-2616
www.lickskillethuntclub.com

Located in Tazwell County in the high prairie country where Sugar Creek tributaries join with the Illinois River. Half-day and full-day hunts for released pheasant, red-legged partridge, and quail and wild birds, with guides or not. Also wild doves and dog training. Memberships come with discounts and more options.

**MACEDONIA GAME PRESERVE**
Macedonia, IL 62860
Phone: 618-728-4328
www.macedoniagamepreserve.com

Located in southern Illinois, over 100 acres of natural and planted cover offer great conditions for released mallard, pheasant, quail, chukar, and turkey guided and nonguided hunts. Continental bird hunts may be scheduled, and they have links to nearby goose hunting clubs for combos. Guided and nonguided archery and shotgun hunts also available for large whitetails. Sandwiches and snacks available at the clubhouse. Motel accommodations available nearby. A special preserve license can be purchased for nonresident hunters.

**OTTER CREEK HUNTING CLUB**
Jerseyville, IL 62052-9530
Phone: 618-376-7601
www.ottercreekhunting.com

Located 50 miles from St. Louis, Otter Creek Hunting Club offers archery, shotgun, and muzzleloader hunts for whitetail deer, wild turkeys, and released pheasant, quail, and chukar. Two sporting clays courses, lighted five-stand, trap.

Individual and corporate memberships.

## PHEASANT VALLEY SPORTSMEN'S CLUB

Bunker Hill, IL 62014-3011
Phone: 618-585-3956 or 877-585-4868
Email: pvhc@madisontelco.com
www.pheasant-valley.com

Full- and half-day hunts for released pheasant, chukar, and quail, September 1 through April 15. Dogs and handlers and airport pickup available. Clubhouse for group functions. Also, 10-station tournament-quality sporting clays course; pistol and rifle range from 25 yards to 600 yards—training facility for Sportsmen's Team Challenge (STC) national champions, equipped for STC-Bianchi-Cowboy and Glock matches. Cowboy action-shooting team. Open to members and nonmembers. Located 45 minutes northeast of St. Louis, Missouri and one hour south of Springfield, Illinois.

## RICHMOND HUNTING CLUB

Richmond, IL 60071
Phone: 815-678-3271
www.richmond-huntclub.com

Individual and corporate memberships for pheasant, mallard, chukar, quail, Hungarian partridge, and wild turkey hunting, plus 10-station sporting clays, on 880 acres in northeastern Illinois—just a short drive from Milwaukee and Chicago.

Pro shop with rentals, clubhouse, restaurant, and bar. Fishing for bass, bluegills, crappies, northern pike, walleye, and catfish for members only.

## SMOKIN' GUN HUNTING LODGE

Hamilton, IL 62341
Phone: 888-766-5460
www.smkgun.com

Membership club with pheasant, turkey, five-stand, skeet and trap (with silo-tower shoot option), wild turkey, and deer hunts.

New lodge, seating 150; with six sleeping rooms, 21 beds. Home-cooked meals. Just two miles from the Mississippi River where Missouri, Iowa, and Illinois join. Host for Pheasants Unlimited contests (www.phu hunt.com).

A list of many more places to hunt in southern Illinois, including many offering duck, goose, and deer hunting, may be found at www .adventureillinois.com/hunting.htm.

## INDIANA

*In 2001 there were 269,000 resident hunters and 31,000 nonresident hunters: 74% went big game hunting, 55% small game, 10% waterfowl and doves; 29% hunted on public lands; 89% hunted on private lands. Hunters pumped $231 million into the state economy. (USFWS)*

### OVERVIEW

Deer, geese, and upland birds are the most popular species for most of the state, with waterfowl hunting along the Lake Michigan shoreline. Hunters take about 20,000 wild pheasant, with counties in the northeastern part of the state along the Michigan border being the most productive.

In a typical season hunters harvest about 50,000 wild bobwhite quail, with counties in the southwest and west-central region along the Illinois border being the most productive.

## DESTINATIONS

### General Outfitter Information

See the Indiana Outfitters Web site at www.indianaoutfitters.com.

### State Lands

*Fish and Wildlife Areas.* For locations and maps, see www.in.gov/dnr/fishwild/publications/maps.htm.

*Reserved Hunts.* Reserved hunts are offered for deer reduction in state parks, wildlife refuges, and military installations. For details, see www.in.gov/dnr/fishwild/huntguide1/HATG_0607/HATG0607_Reserved-Hunts.pdf.

*Reserved Dove Hunts.* Reserved dove hunts are offered in wildlife areas throughout the state. For details, see www.in.gov/dnr/fishwild/huntguide1/HATG_0607/HATG0607_Reserved-Hunts.pdf.

### U.S. Army Corps of Engineers

**U.S. ARMY CORPS OF
ENGINEERS, LOUISVILLE**
Louisville, KY 40202
Phone: 502-315-6770; fax: 502-315-6771
www.lrl.usace.army.mil

The U.S. Army Corps of Engineers Louisville District manages nine reservoirs in Indiana, which offer some hunting opportunities. For details, consult state of Indiana regulations or email the Army Corps district at lrl-pagemaster-pa@lrl02.usace.army.mil.

### USDA National Forests

**HOOSIER NATIONAL FOREST**
Bedford, IN 47421
Phone: 812-275-5987; fax: 812-279-3423
www.fs.fed.us/r9/hoosier

Located in the rolling hills of southern Indiana and with the Ohio River to the south, this forest is within a day's drive of Cincinnati, Louisville, Chicago, Evansville, and Indianapolis. The Hoosier National Forest boundary encompasses 644,163 acres, with over 192,000 acres of public land and most of the remaining in private ownership.

All Indiana hunting laws are enforced on national forest land. An array of hunting experiences can be found, from remote walk-in areas to easily accessible lands near roads. Private land is interspersed with public land,

and you must obtain written permission from private landowners to hunt or fish on their property.

For a brochure on the three National Wildlife Refuges in Indiana, see www.fws.gov/midwest/patokariver/documents/IndianaRefuges06.pdf.

## BIG OAKS NATIONAL WILDLIFE REFUGE
Madison, IN 47250
Phone: 812-273-0783
www.fws.gov/midwest/bigoaks

Big Oaks National Wildlife Refuge consists of approximately 50,000 acres within Jefferson, Ripley, and Jennings counties in southeastern Indiana. The refuge contains the largest unregimented forested block in southeastern Indiana and some of the largest grassland areas found within the region.

Large safety buffer areas separate the air force bombing range from public-use areas of the refuge. Big Oaks NWR offers opportunities to hunt deer, turkeys, and squirrels on over 25,000 acres of the refuge. For details, see www.fws.gov/midwest/bigoaks/bonwrhunting.htm.

## MUSCATATUCK NATIONAL WILDLIFE REFUGE
Seymour, IN 47274
Phone: 812-522-4352; fax: 812-522-6826
www.fws.gov/midwest/muscatatuck

Muscatatuck NWR is located in south-central Indiana. The refuge takes its name from the Muscatatuck River, which forms the southern boundary. The refuge is 7,802 acres, 60% of which are converted farmlands; 1,500 acres of lakes, ponds, moist soil, and green tree units have been restored on the refuge. Hunting for rabbits, quail, and deer is permitted in certain parts of the refuge at particular times. See Web site and state regulations.

## PATOKA RIVER NATIONAL WILDLIFE REFUGE
Oakland City, IN 47660
Phone: 812-749-3199; fax: 812-749-3059
www.fws.gov/midwest/patokariver

Patoka River NWR is located in southwest Indiana within the Wabash River Basin. The refuge is strategically located to provide important resting, feeding, and nesting habitat for migratory waterfowl. The refuge currently contains 5,813 acres. Its proposed boundary stretches for 20 miles as the crow flies in an east-west direction along the lower third reach of the 162-mile-long Patoka River. It includes 30 miles of river channel, 19 miles of cut-off river oxbows, and 12,700 acres of existing wetland habitat. Hunting is permitted on the refuge. See Indiana state regulations for details.

*Migratory Waterfowl*

## SHADOWLAND FISHING AND HUNTING CHARTER
Chesterton, IN 46304
Phone: 219-926-8280
www.shadowland.com/hunting.html

Located in the Michigan City, Indiana, area, offers guided hunts for ducks on Lake Michigan, plus trout and salmon fishing and sporting clays to warm up.

*Private Hunting Clubs and Preserves*

### DAWN TO DUSK HUNT CLUB
Valparaiso, IN 46385
Phone: 219-763-3362
www.dawn-to-dusk.com

Located 45 minutes from Soldiers Field, Dawn to Dusk Hunt Club offers hunts for released pheasant, chukar, and quail September 1 through April 15. Dove and goose hunts in season. Guides, dogs, clubhouse, and rental equipment available. Can make arrangements for lodging. Some 20 acres of sunflowers and buckwheat are planted for dove hunts. Members and nonmembers welcome. Corporate memberships available. Reservations required.

### FLATROCK HUNTING PRESERVE
Rushville, IN 46173
Phone: 765-629-2354
www.flatrockhunting.com

Released pheasant, chukar, and quail on rolling uplands of the scenic and historic Big Flatrock River in Rush County, Indiana. Season runs from October 1 to March 13. Open seven days a week.

### HILLSIDE SHOOTING SPORTS
Roanoke, IN 46783
Phone: 260-672-3715, 260-672-2213, or 260-410-6388
www.hillsideshootingsports.net

Hillside Shooting Sports is located just out-side the small town of Roanoke in the northeast part of Indiana. The range is positioned on 350 acres of rolling hills and beautiful farmland. Hillside offers pheasant and chukar hunts by appointment only, a casual lodge, five-stand, trap field, and guides, dogs, and dog training. The hunting season opens September 1 and continues through March 31. Memberships available.

### MAPLE LANE HUNTING PRESERVE
Lakeville, IN 46536
Phone: 574-299-8388;
pager: 574-258-2120;
mobile: 574-250-2977
www.maplelanehuntingpreserve.com

Located in northeast Indiana, just south of South Bend, 130 acres of wetlands and upland habitat for released Manchurian pheasant, Chinese pheasant, chukar, Hungarian partridge, and quail hunting. Also available are 10- to 20-person European-style hunts, doves, and clay targets. All reservations must be made in advance. Business specials include lunch.

### PRESNELL PLANTATION LLC
Morgantown, IN 46160
Phone: 317-752-0168 or 866-295-4390;
fax: 317-882-8614
www.presnellplantation.com

The immediate 500-acre property includes six lakes and two wetlands, food plots, and considerable cover for quail and pheasant hunts, youth pheasant hunts, and wild turkeys, plus thousands of wooded acres in multiple locations for whitetails. Fully guided goose and duck hunts on numerous properties in central and southern Indiana. Several cabins available for retreats.

**ROYAL FLUSH ENTERPRISES**
Rosedale, IN 47874
Phone: 765-548-2548
www.royalflushent.com

Dove, quail, pheasant, chukar, and wild turkey hunting on nearly 1,500 acres of diverse farmland in southwest Parke County, Indiana. Seasons: dove—federal migratory regulated, usually September 1–October 15; upland—quail, pheasant, and chukar, September 1–April 1; wild turkey—state regulated, usually late April through mid-May. Lodge and clay range. Hunts by appointment only. No membership fees. Near Turkey Run State Park.

**SUGAR CREEK HUNTING PRESERVE AND SPORTING CLAYS**
Mitchell, IN 47446
Phone: 812-849-2296 or 812-849-5020
www.indianahuntingpreserve.com

Located 90 miles south of Indianapolis and 50 miles northwest of Louisville, Kentucky, on 750 acres, Sugar Creek offers pheasant, chukar, and quail field hunts, with European-style hunts several times a year. Combination trap and skeet fields; five-stand; 10 field, 20 station sporting clays course. New lodge. Reservations available seven days a week from September 1 through April 30.

**SUMMIT LAKE HUNTING PRESERVE**
Akron, IN 46910
Phone: 574-893-4880
www.summitlakehunting.com

Located three miles east of Akron, Indiana, pheasant, chukar, and bobwhite quail hunts with professional guides and dogs available. Fishing on private lake and primitive camping also available.

**ULTIMATE ADVENTURE OUTDOORS, LLC**
Hamilton, IN 46742
Phone: 317-578-9517, 317-797-4429, or 260-488-4991
www.uoahunt.com

This is a private membership club with thousands of acres of prime hunting sources in Steuben and Dekalb counties, offering deer, waterfowl, pheasant, and quail hunts. A 2,500-square-foot lodge, with full basement for overnights.

The lodge is located in Hamilton, two and a quarter hours from Indianapolis, one hour from Fort Wayne, and two hours from South Bend.

## IOWA

*In 2001 there were 195,000 resident hunters and 48,000 nonresident hunters: 57% went big game hunting, 62% small game, 23% waterfowl and doves; 38% hunted on public lands; 85% hunted on private lands. Hunters pumped $167 million into the state economy. (USFWS)*

**OVERVIEW**
Hunting is popular in Iowa. The Iowa Department of Natural Resources reports that Iowa hunters make 3.5 million visits a year

to Iowa's 340 public hunting areas. Deer and pheasant are the most popular draws, but plenty of opportunities exist to pursue waterfowl and other small game.

Iowa has lost nearly 90% of its original wetlands (99% of its prairie potholes), but there is an active wetlands restoration in place that seeks to turn that around.

Iowa tends to be number two in pheasant production in the United States, after South Dakota, even though the state has lost 30% of its upland game habitat from 15 years ago. In the last decade, Iowa hunters have averaged harvesting slightly fewer than 1 million roosters per year.

Bobwhite quail populations are generally highest along the Missouri border in the southeast part of the state.

In 1936 it was estimated that there were somewhere between 500 and 700 whitetail deer in the state. Today the herd is estimated to be at least 360,000, and they grow 'em big out here, thanks to all that corn.

## DESTINATIONS

### State Wildlife Management Areas

The Iowa DNR manages 340 wildlife areas that total more than 270,000 acres and contain a variety of habitat types including wetland, grassland, timber, and agricultural crops. A list of all these areas can be found online at www.iowadnr.com/wildlife/wmamaps/pubhunt.html.

The boundaries of DNR wildlife areas are posted every one-eighth mile with green-and-white "Public Hunting Area" signs. These areas provide all users equal access to public lands but include few, if any, public-use facilities such as restrooms, drinking water, hiking trails, and other conveniences. Lands adjacent to public wildlife areas are privately owned and require landowner permission for access.

Brown-and-white signs, displaying a duck or duck and fish, are posted along these roads and will direct you to the nearest parking lot. Although hunting and trapping are the primary recreational activities available on these areas, bird-watching, hiking, mushrooming, and nature study are allowed.

### U.S. Army Corps of Engineers

**CORALVILLE LAKE**
Iowa City, IA 52240-7820
Phone: 319-338-3543 ext. 6300
www.mvr.usace.army.mil/coralville/default.htm

---

**IOWA SNAPSHOT**
**HAWKEYE STATE**

- **General information:** Iowa Department of Natural Resources
Wallace State Office Building
Des Moines, IA 50319-0034
www.iowadnr.com/law/regs.html

- **Licenses may be purchased by phone or online:** Phone: 800-367-1188; www.wildlifelicense.com/ia/start.php

- **TIP (Turn-in-Poachers) Hotline:** 800-532-2020; Nontoxic shot is required to hunt all game animals (except deer and turkeys) on selected public hunting areas in north-central and northwest Iowa; see the current hunting regulations booklet for a list of areas where nontoxic shot is required

- **Deer population:** 370,000, 23rd in the United States

- **Average deer harvest:** 153,713, 26th in the United States

This is a reservoir area on the Iowa River. Hunting for all legal species in Iowa governed by state regulations.

**LAKE RED ROCK**
Knoxville, IA 50138
Phone: 641-828-7522 or 641-628-8690
www.mvr.usace.army.mil/RedRock/ recreation/hunting.htm

Iowa's largest lake located just 10 minutes from Pella. State game laws apply to all of Lake Red Rock's huntable areas. For hunting map, contact the project office.

**MISSISSIPPI RIVER POOLS 11–22 (10 L&D)**
Pleasant Valley, IA 52767-0534
Phone: 309-794-4524
www.mvr.usace.army.mil/missriver

The U.S. Army Corps manages 23 developed recreation sites along 314 miles of the Mississippi River between Petosi, Wisconsin, and Saverton, Missouri.

*U.S. Fish and Wildlife Service*
*National Wildlife Refuges*

**DESOTO NATIONAL WILDLIFE REFUGE**
Missouri Valley, IA 51555-7033
Phone: 712-642-4121
www.fws.gov/midwest/desoto

DeSoto NWR is composed of 7,823 acres and lies in the Missouri River Valley floodplain on a former meander of the Missouri River. The refuge offers hunts for gun and archery whitetail deer, pheasant, and wild turkeys. For special regulations, see www.fws.gov/midwest/desoto/hunting.htm.

**DRIFTLESS AREA NATIONAL WILDLIFE REFUGE**
McGregor, IA 52157
Phone: 563-873-3423
www.fws.gov/refuges/profiles/index .cfm?id=32596

On 775 acres consisting of nine units in four counties in northeastern Iowa. Two units are open to upland game and whitetail deer hunting in accordance with state regulations. Nontoxic shot must be used for upland game. Deer hunting is restricted to archery and muzzleloader use only. Stands must be removed at the end of each day's hunt. Certain areas are posted closed to all entry.

**NEAL SMITH NATIONAL WILDLIFE REFUGE**
Prairie City, IA 50228
Phone: 515-994-3400
www.fws.gov/refuges/profiles/index .cfm?id=33670

The Neal Smith NWR was created to reconstruct tallgrass prairie and restore oak savanna on 8,654 acres of the Walnut Creek watershed. The refuge is located 18 miles east of Des Moines, Iowa, on State Highway 163. Portions are open to hunting of upland game birds, whitetail deer, and small game. Special regulations apply. Contact the refuge headquarters for details.

**PORT LOUISA NATIONAL WILDLIFE REFUGE**
Wapello, IA 52653
Phone: 319-523-6982
www.fws.gov/midwest/portlouisa

The refuge comprises over 8,373 acres, divided into four separate divisions: Big Timber, Louisa, Keithsburg, and Horseshoe Bend. Three divisions—Big Timber, Louisa, and Keithsburg—are located in the floodplain of the Mississippi River, while Horseshoe Bend is in the Iowa River floodplain. Port Louisa NWR offers opportunities for deer, migratory bird, and upland game hunting. For details, see www.fws.gov/midwest/portlouisa/hunting.html.

## UNION SLOUGH NATIONAL WILDLIFE REFUGE

Titonka, IA 50480
Phone: 515-928-2523
www.fws.gov/refuges/profiles/index.cfm?id=33580

Located two and a half hours southwest of Minneapolis. Corn and soybeans that provide feeding habitat surround this 3,334-acre refuge. The refuge is on the eastern edge of the tallgrass prairie region of the Northern Great Plains. It is a major producer of wood ducks. Limited hunting for upland game, waterfowl, and big game on certain areas of the refuge. Contact the refuge headquarters for current regulations.

*Private Hunting Clubs and Preserves*

## CHASE THE ADVENTURE HUNT AND GUN CLUB

Decorah, IA 52101
Phone: 563-532-9821
http://chasetheadventure.com

On 800 acres of woods and fields with six ponds. Released pheasant, quail, and chukar hunts from September 1 to March 31 and year-round dog training. Sporting clays, skeet, and trap. A 113-year-old barn has been converted into a lodge, with five bedrooms and a bar. Open to nonmembers and members.

## CROOKED CREEK SHOOTING PRESERVE

Washington, IA 52353
Phone: 319-653-9123;
fax: 319-653-4477
www.crookedcreekshooting.com

Located approximately five miles south of Washington, Iowa, on 1,500-plus acres of quality grassland, wetlands, and timberland. Pheasant, quail, chukar, waterfowl, and small game hunts, with deer and turkey hunts by reservation only. Likes to help youth hunters get started. No charge for hunters under 17. Ponds stocked with catfish, bluegills, crappies, and large-mouth bass. Bed-and-breakfast lodge with kitchen and a clubhouse.

## CZECH ADVENTURES

Clutier, IA 52217
Phone: 319-330-6543
www.iowa-hunting.com

On 1,000-plus acres of prime upland game bird hunting land. Half-day and full-day guided or nonguided hunts for pheasant and quail in central-eastern Iowa's Tama County. The "Buck Patch Lodge" is a rustic farmhouse that has eight beds, a living room, oil heater, stove, shower/bath, microwave, fridge/freezer, and outdoor kennels.

## FAETH'S FOWL PLAY

Ft. Madison, IA 52727

Phone: 800-469-2792 or 319-372-2792

www.faethsfowlplay.com

Pheasant, quail, and chukar, full-day and half-day hunts; dogs and guides available. Preserve season: September 1–March 31. For those with trouble walking, in-field transportation with ATVs.

## HIGHLAND HIDEAWAY HUNTING

Riverside, IA 52327

Phone: 319-648-5065

www.highlandhunting.com

Over 1,100 acres for pheasant, quail, and chukar hunting. Sporting clays and six-station clays.

## IOWA PHEASANTS 'N MORE HUNTING LODGE

Belle Plaine, IA 52208

Phone: 319-444-3912

www.iowa-hunt.com

On 3,000-plus acres of CRP agricultural land, wetlands, and ponds in the Iowa River corridor for wild pheasant and waterfowl; released pheasant and quail on 400-acre preserve; spring turkey; deer with archery, shotgun, or muzzleloader. Several packages available with lodging included. Located approximately 90 miles northeast of Des Moines.

## LAKE PRAIRIE HUNTING PRESERVE

Pella, IA 50219

Phone: 641-628-2572

www.lakeprairie.com

Located in south-central Iowa, 45 miles east of Des Moines, Lake Prairie has over 1,500 licensed acres of prime hunting grounds. Released pheasant, quail, and chukar. Lodge available for meetings. Individual and corporate memberships get reduced prices, but open to all. Call a minimum of 24 hours in advance to book a hunt.

## OAK VIEW II HUNTING CLUB

Runnells, IA 50237

Phone: 515-966-2095

www.oakview2huntingclub.com

Membership club with 600-plus acres of prime hunting ground for pheasant, chukar, and quail. Season runs September 1 through March 31.

## OAKWOOD SPORTING RESORT

Sigourney, IA 52591

Phone: 800-432-3290

www.oakwd.com

An 800-acre licensed hunting preserve with a full September 1 through March 31 season. Oakwood releases hens and cocks but only shoots roosters. Lodging and fishing also available.

## OUTDOORSMAN HUNTING CLUB

Webb, IA 51366

Phone: 712-838-4892 or 605-351-1811

www.outdoorsmanhuntingclub.com

A membership hunting club on over 1,000 acres bordering the Little Sioux River in northwest Iowa, offering pheasant, quail, and chukar hunts.

**SAFARI IOWA HUNTING RESORT**
Parnell, IA 52325
Phone: 800-307-8504
www.safari-iowa.com

Pheasant, ducks, chukar, quail, and Hungarian partridge on thousands of acres of rolling farmland. Comfortable lodging, dogs, and guides available.

A complete list of upland game bird preserves for Iowa can be found online at www.iowa dnr.com/wildlife/pdfs/iapreserves.pdf.

## MICHIGAN

*In 2001 there were 705,000 resident hunters and 48,000 nonresident hunters: 90% went big game hunting, 29% small game, 7% migratory waterfowl; 33% hunted on public lands; 79% hunted on private lands. Hunters pumped $490 million into the state economy. (USFWS)*

### OVERVIEW

Michigan, the state that looks like two hands—a right hand held palm up and facing you and, above it, a left hand on its side with the thumb sticking almost straight up—is truly a hunter's paradise. Here one finds an enormous diversity of environments, from the rocky shoreline of the Keewanau Peninsula and the copper-rich Porcupine Mountains of the Upper Peninsula; to the vast oak-pine and birch woodlands of the "fingers" of the lower peninsula; to the rich billiard-table flat agricultural lands of "the thumb," which gradually transition into rolling hills and rich farmlands

in the "wrist" of the Lower Peninsula, bordering Ohio and Indiana. The "thumb" of the Lower Peninsula is flat, prime agricultural land that holds some outstanding pheasant hunting, although most is on private lands.

Aside from the Great Lakes, the largest body of freshwater in the world, the landscape is dotted everywhere with thousands of rivers and lakes. Waterfowl hunting is virtually everywhere in the state. There is a growing elk season, black bears are common in the north, and wild hogs have become fair game. By far, however, the most popular game is Michigan's whitetail deer herd, currently estimated at 1.6 million and growing.

Nearly 750,000 hunters are in the woods for the Michigan deer seasons—archery, rifle, and muzzleloader—that run from October through the end of December. In 2005, hunters harvested 415,000 deer, and the Department of Natural Resources wildlife biologists say that they wish they had taken more.

There are vast areas of state and national forests to hunt deer, woodcocks, and grouse, as well as private ranches and farms.

---

**MICHIGAN SNAPSHOT**
**WOLVERINE STATE**

- **General Michigan hunting information:**
  Michigan Department of Natural Resources
  Mason Building, Fourth Floor
  Post Office Box 30444
  Lansing, MI 48909
  Phone: 517-373-6705
  www.michigan.gov/dnr/0,1607,7-153-10369-
  126209–,00.html

- **Deer population:** 1.6–1.7 million, 3rd in the United States

- **Average deer harvest:** 485,924, 2nd in the United States

In the Lower Peninsula, towns like Grayling, West Branch, Mio, Mesick, and Alpena explode into a sea of orange clothing in November.

 **FEATURED HUNT**

## Drummond Island in the UP

JAMES SWAN

The doe was about 45 yards away, standing broadside. The arrow streaked toward her, as if in slow motion, and struck her midbody about two inches behind the foreleg—a perfect shot. As the shaft disappeared, a "thunk" could be heard. She bolted off toward the dark spruce and birch woods, as if nothing had happened.

First times are always special. Intellectually I knew that the arrow had struck her in exactly the right place for a heart-lung shot that should prove fatal, but I was only 13, and this was the first time.

Besides, we had traveled over 300 miles, including two car ferries, to get to Drummond Island. Coupled with the unusual grassland vegetation all around us, I felt like I was in Africa hunting the Serengeti.

"Good shot," my father said, standing nearby, "but we've got to wait 15 minutes to make sure that she bleeds to death and dies quietly. Better for her— you don't want to chase her in that thicket, and the meat will be better, too. A deer that dies with a lot of adrenaline in her blood tastes more gamy."

It was the longest 15 minutes of my life.

"Okay," he said finally.

I ran to the spot where she had been standing, her clean, fresh tracks very visible in the thin, rocky soil. There were spots of bright red blood on the grass almost immediately as I followed the trail.

Fifty yards later, she was quietly lying on her side.

My father reached down and touched the stream of blood coming from where the arrow had entered and smeared it on my cheeks. "Congratulations," he said, with a big smile on his face.

The heart and liver pie we had that night, made from the vitals of the doe, stands in my mind as one of the best meals I have ever eaten.

Before a bridge was constructed to link Michigan's Upper and Lower Peninsulas, a car ferry spanned the 5-mile straits of Mackinaw. In the good old days, on the eve of rifle deer season, which is the last two weeks in November, the line of cars waiting for the ferry could be 10 miles long or longer. The reason: the big bucks are supposed to be in the Upper Peninsula, or UP.

Today, you can drive the span in minutes and enter the UP, with its strong Finnish cultural roots (UP residents are nicknamed "Upers") and thousands of square miles of state and national forests.

The UP is a sportsman's paradise, and the green gemstone of the UP is Drummond Island (DI), which sits at the southern end of the St. Mary's River that joins Lake Superior to Lake Huron. Drummond Island is the largest U.S.-owned island in the Great Lakes—133 square miles of forested landscape with 150 miles of scenic shoreline, 56 neighboring islands, and 34 inland lakes. (See satellite map at www.drummondislandchamber.com/images/DITAsmall.jpg.)

There are only 1,200 year-round residents, and two-thirds of the island's 87,000 acres is state forest land, so access to hunting lands is not a problem, and that's only part of the reason why DI is such an extraordinary setting.

At one time the deer herd on Drummond Island got up to 6,000, but they were overbrowsing the place, and there was a real starvation problem in bad winters. So the DNR issued a lot of doe tags and stopped allowing the shooting of spike bucks. The result, according to Rick Johnson at Johnson's Sporting Goods, is that the DI herd is down to 2,000 or a little lower, but they are big. *Really big.* Every year they hold a Big Buck Contest at Johnson's. They keep getting bigger.

On DI there are a wide variety of accommodations, from plush resorts to camping. And thanks to the island's strong Finnish heritage, lots of saunas are available to get the aches out of your body.

If you bag a big buck, don't forget to enter it in the Big Buck Contest at Johnson's Sporting Goods. After you bag a buck and have more time, snowshoe hare, grouse, and duck hunting is outstanding, and don't forget to bring a fishing rod. Walleyes, salmon, northern pike, and huge yellow perch are plentiful. The yellow-belly perch get to be up to 15 inches long.

You can fly a private plane to the island, but Drummond Island is accessed by car ferry from Detour. The one-mile run to the island is made every hour (except between 1:00 A.M. and 6:00 A.M.) for $25 per car.

St. Florence Catholic Church has sponsored a Hunter's Dinner on the weekend before or during the rifle deer season for the last 40 years. The homemade pies served are legendary.

There are some special regulations for Drummond Island deer hunting. For details, see www.michigan.gov/dnr/0,1607,7-153-10363_10856_10905-29585-,00.html.

Contacts:

**DRUMMOND ISLAND CHAMBER OF COMMERCE**
Drummond Island, MI 49726
Phone: 906-493-5245 or 800-737-8666
www.drummondislandchamber.com

**JOHNSON'S SPORT SHOP**
Drummond Island, MI 49726
Phone: 906-493-6300; fax: 906-493-6563

## Waterfowl on Lake Erie

JAMES SWAN

Hundreds of thousands of ducks and geese funnel along the Detroit River and into Lake Erie every fall. Dabblers come first. Blue-winged teal pass through on the "first breath of fall" cool winds of September.

They are followed by mallards, wigeon, and orange-legged black ducks that are on hand for the duck season opener. According to the local old-timers, divers, led by "the bluebills" (scaup) show

up every year like clockwork on October 20. Shortly afterward come the redheads and canvasbacks, making this fertile, shallow water area a mecca for ducks until Lake Erie and the Detroit River freeze over. Just before the ice comes, red-legged black ducks with silvery underwings arrive like a breath of winter.

Much of the marshlands of Lake Erie are in private ownership, but since 1945 hunters have enjoyed excellent duck hunting in the 2000-plus-acre marshes of Pointe Mouillee State Game Area, in Brownstown, Michigan, just north of Monroe.

When the waterfowl season starts around October 1, there are two daily drawings for half-day hunts in the marsh. No reservations. First-come, first-served. Each party gets one area to hunt solely for themselves.

There also is pheasant hunting at Pointe Mouillee. After the first day of the season, the best results come from working the dense cattail marsh cover, where you may also jump ducks.

### POINTE MOUILLE STATE GAME AREA
Brownstown, MI 48173
Phone: 734-379-9692

However, the demand for hunting this area far exceeds blind spaces in the marsh, and so hunters turn to the shallow open waters of Lake Erie. This means lots of decoys and finding the most effective hunting method for those "rafts" of divers that begin arriving in mid-October.

If the birds have just arrived, hunters with boat blinds can sometimes do well hunkering down in their boat with decoys spread close by. But by far the most effective method of hunting here is to use either sneak boats or layout boats. A sneak boat is a dull gray double-pointed, shallow draft, canoelike boat with a canvas "bonnet" around the opening to keep out water when the waves kick up. Sneak boats can run up to 18 feet long to accommodate two hunters and decoys. They are propelled by an outboard motor mounted on an outrigger in the stern.

The typical setup is to find an area offshore where the birds seem to be feeding. When you find the place, you set out 100 or more diving duck decoys.

Then you motor upwind about 250 yards, anchor, and tilt the motor up out of the water. In the front of the boat you install a portable blind, about three feet high and six feet long made from thin plywood and painted dull gray with a slit on each side to see through. Both hunters now sit as low as possible in the boat and wait.

When ducks land in the decoys, you release the anchor, which is attached to a buoy, and raise up the blind, which conceals the boat and hunters and acts as a sail to get you down on the birds faster. The hunter in the front mans the blind. The person in back steers with a canoe paddle.

When you are in range, the front hunter drops the blind, and the ducks flush. Because the wind is at your back, and these are diving ducks, the birds will start out coming straight toward you. Sometimes only the front hunter shoots. Other times the hunter in the stern will also shoot when birds are perpendicular to the boat.

A layout boat on Lake Erie is a dull-gray, double-pointed pumpkinseed-shaped boat that is anchored in the middle of a large set of decoys. The hunter lays down in a "coffin" in the center that is actually below water level. Diving ducks will come flying in low, and the hunter does not sit up to shoot until they are close. This is very exciting, and a little dangerous, especially if the lake is kicking up, which, of course, is when the ducks are flying best. Hunters are usually solo in these boats, but some people do make doubles.

When the layout hunter connects, a motorboat

anchored several hundred yards away comes to pick up the downed birds.

You can buy sneak boats and layout boats or make them yourself from plywood covered with canvas or fiberglass. (For plans, see www.whiskey riverboatshop.com/boat_designs.htm.)

---

## DESTINATIONS

*General Information*
A very comprehensive list of public and private hunting lands in Michigan can be found at www.michigan.gov/dnr/0,1607,7-153-10363 _10913—,00.html.

*U.S. Fish and Wildlife Service*
*National Wildlife Refuges*

**KIRTLAND'S WARBLER NATIONAL WILDLIFE REFUGE**
c/o Seney National Wildlife Refuge
Seney, MI 49883
Phone: 906-586-9851 (Refuge)
or 906-586-9851(Kirtland)
www.fws.gov/refuges/profiles/index
.cfm?id=31513

Located throughout eight counties in the northern Lower Peninsula (LP) of Michigan, this is the only known nesting area of one of the world's rarest birds, the Kirtland's warbler, which nests only on the ground under mid-age jack pines. To preserve such a specialized habitat, periodic controlled burning is conducted, which also helps provide food for deer. Hunting for all legal species is permitted during state seasons that do not coincide with the nesting period of the Kirtland's warbler.

**SENEY NATIONAL WILDLIFE REFUGE**
Seney, MI 49883
Phone: 906-586-9851
www.fws.gov/midwest/seney

Seney NWR protects 95,212 acres of Upper Peninsula marshes, fens, and bogs; coniferous and northern hardwood forests; upland barrens and meadows; and a 25,000-acre wilderness area. The refuge protects a wide variety of wildlife including moose and gray wolves. Hunting is permitted in the refuge according to state regulations. Deer, bears, ruffed grouse, and snowshoe hare are popular game species. For details, see www.fws.gov/midwest/seney/Hunting.htm.

Seney NWR also manages satellite refuges—Huron NWR, Harbor Island NWR, Kirtland's Warbler Wildlife Management Area, Michigan Islands NWR, and Whitefish Point NWR. See refuge Web site for details on hunting.

**SHIAWASSEE NATIONAL WILDLIFE REFUGE**
Saginaw, MI 48601
Phone: 989-777-5930

www.fws.gov/midwest/shiawassee/ShiawasseeNWRHunting.htm

The Shiawassee NWR, known locally as the "Shiawassee Flats," spans 9,427 acres of bottomland-hardwood forests, rivers, marshes, managed pools, fields, and croplands just south of the city of Saginaw in the Lower Peninsula. Deer and geese are hunted here, with local permits required as well as following state regulations. For details, see www.fws.gov/midwest/shiawassee/ShiawasseeNWRHunting.htm.

*U.S. National Park Service*

**PICTURED ROCKS NATIONAL LAKESHORE**
Munising, MI 49862-0040
Phone: 906-387-3700 (Visitor Information) or 906-387-2607 (Park Headquarters); fax: 906-387-4025
www.nps.gov/piro/planyourvisit/hunting.htm

Pictured Rocks National Lakeshore is located on the south shore of Lake Superior in Michigan's Upper Peninsula, stretching more than 40 miles between the communities of Munising (west) and Grand Marais (east). Hunting for deer, grouse, woodcocks, bears, and snowshoe hare is allowed according to Michigan state regulations and federal migratory bird regulations. Certain areas of the lakeshore are closed to hunting for public safety. Check with refuge headquarters for maps.

**SLEEPING BEAR DUNES NATIONAL LAKESHORE**
Empire, MI 49630-9797

Phone: 231-326-5134 (Headquarters) or 231-326-5134 (Visitor Information) www.nps.gov/slbe/planyourvisit/hunting.htm

A 35-mile stretch of Lake Michigan's eastern coastline near Traverse City, as well as North and South Manitou Islands. Acreage: 56,993 federal; 14,194 nonfederal. The majority of Sleeping Bear Dunes National Lakeshore is open to hunting according to state regulations. However, most high-visitor-use areas and facilities are closed. An entrance permit is required.

A special deer hunt is held on North Manitou Island. The bag limit is two deer, only one of which may have antlers three inches or more in length. Deer taken legally on North Manitou Island do not count against a hunter's regular deer season bag limit on the mainland. See www.nps.gov/slbe/planyourvisit/nmihunting.htm.

*Private Hunting Clubs and Preserves*

### BEAR CREEK HUNT CLUB

Clayton, MI 49235
Phone: 734-429-7202
www.bearcreekhuntclub.com

Chukar, Hungarian partridge, and pheasant (roosters only) are released into natural cover on this southeast Michigan preserve. Field hunts, European-style tower hunts, and South Dakota–style driven hunts for groups of 7 to 10 hunters. Rustic clubhouse. Open to the general public; memberships available.

### BUCKFALLS RANCH

Millersburg, MI 49759
Phone: 989-733-5043
www.buckfallsranch.com

Elegant 1,300-acre ranch located one hour from Alpena and Pellston in the northern LP. Owned by major league baseball stars Kirk Gibson and David Wells. Offers trophy whitetail hunting.

### CHERRY CREEK FARM

Mio, MI 48647
Phone: 989-848-5411 (Lodge)
or 313-278-5888 (Office);
fax: 989-848-2431
www.cherrycreekfarm.com

Located in Mio, Michigan, one of the famous Michigan hunting towns in the LP. On 500-plus acres, whitetail deer, pheasant, turkey, and upland bird hunting and trout fishing are offered at Cherry Creek Farm. Cabins and lodge located on a fishing pond.

### COLONIAL FARMS

Chelsea, MI 48118
Phone: 734-475-9921;
mobile: 734-347-2374;
fax: 734-475-9921
www.ColonialFarmsLLC.com

Located in Chelsea, southeast LP, breeding and training award-winning German short-haired pointers, plus 100 acres for reserved four-hour hunts for pheasant, chukar, quail, and Hungarian partridge for your dog training and hunting.

**FARMLAND PHEASANT HUNTERS, INC.**
Brown City, MI 48416
Phone: 810-346-3672; fax: 810-346-2604
www.farmlandpheasant.com

Over 5,000 acres on 30 different farms, with an average of 120 acres on each. One party to a farm per day, all-day. Pheasant, quail, and chukar. Membership club.

**GRAND RIVER GAMEBIRDS HUNTING PRESERVE**
Onondaga, MI 49264
Phone/fax: 517-569-2098
www.grandrivergamebirds.com

Lower Peninsula hunting preserve offering hunts for pheasant, quail, Hungarian partridge, and chukar. Just a 20-minute drive from Jackson or Lansing.

**HAYMARSH HUNT CLUB**
Morley, MI 49336
Phone: 989-352-7050 (Tim Somerville) or 989-352-6727 (Bud Gummer);
fax: 989-352-5680
www.haymarsh.com

Open field and European tower-style hunting for Tennessee red quail, pheasant (August through April), chukar, and Hungarian partridge on 1,400 acres. Each hunting area is about 40 acres. Sporting clays, guides, and dogs available. Located near Big Rapids in the LP.

**HORIZAN ADVENTURES**
Ida, MI 48140
Phone: 866-467-4926
www.horizanadventures.com

Ring-necked pheasant, chukar partridge, Hungarian partridge, quail, Tennessee red quail, black mutated pheasant, and wild strain ringnecks. Located in southeast Michigan, minutes away from the new Cabela's superstore in Dundee. Also hunts for ducks and doves and deep-sea fishing in Mexico.

**HUNTERS CREEK CLUB**
Metamora, MI 48455
Phone: 810-664-4307; fax: 810-664-2951
www.hunterscreekclub.com

Located one hour north of Detroit, offering pheasant, Hungarian and chukar partridge, and mallard hunting on over 1,000 acres of land cultivated exclusively for upland hunting for over four decades. Also sporting clays, skeet, and trap; fishing; and dog training. Members and guests only.

**JANKS PHEASANT FARM**
Mayville, MI 48744
Phone:989-843-6576 or 877-383-0544
www.geocities.com/jankspheasantfarm

Ring-necked and melanistic mutant (black) pheasant in fields cultivated exclusively for wildlife habitat. Half-day hunts by reservation only. Guided hunts and dog rental available. No membership fee. Located in Oakland County, north of Detroit.

**RINGNECK RANCH, LLC**
Hanover, MI 49241-9763
Phone: 517-524-8294
www.theringneckranch.com

Located in southwest Jackson County, Michigan, the ranch offers a rural farm setting with fields planted specifically for hunting wild ring-necked pheasant, Hungarian partridge, and chukar. European-style tower hunts or half- or full-day traditional field hunts through gently rolling fields, meadows, and wood lots with the Kalamazoo River running through the west edge of the property. Open to the public with no membership fee.

**ROOSTER RANCH HUNT CLUB**
Ubly, MI 48475
Phone: 989-658-2332
www.roosterranchhuntclub.com

Located in the tip of Michigan's "thumb," seven parcels of land, 800-plus acres, prime game-bird habitat for field and European-style hunts for ring-necked and black pheasant and chukar, plus fall duck hunts, dog training, and trout fishing. A 4,000-square-foot clubhouse and two lodges.

**SEXY PHEASANT GAME BIRD HUNTING**
Dundee, MI 48131-9632
Phone: 734-216-2278
www.pheasantpreserve.com

Located in Dundee, Michigan, just four miles from Cabela's superstore, 957 acres of prime hunting habitat for ring-necked pheasant, bobwhite quail, Tennessee red quail, chukar partridge, green mutant pheasant, white pheasant, and Hungarian partridge. Dogs available.

**SUGAR SPRINGS SPORTING CLAYS AND HUNTING PRESERVE, INC.**
Gladwin, MI 48624
Phone: 989-426-2645; fax: 989-426-1608
www.sshpinc.com

Located on 440 acres in central LP, field and European-style tower hunts for pheasant, chukar, quail, Hungarian partridge, and mallards. Groups of one to six hunters are assigned a minimum of 120 acres where birds are released. Chest-high native grasses and small pines provide natural conditions for hunters and dogs. Over 30 stations for shooting sporting clays. Dogs and guns may be rented. Memberships available.

**THUNDERING ASPENS HUNTING SERVICE**
Mesick, MI 49668
Phone: 231-885-2420
www.michigan.org/travel/detail
.asp?m=4;5&p=B9901

Located 110 miles north of Grand Rapids, 800 acres for quail, grouse, woodcock, pheasant, chukar, Hungarian partridge, turkey, and waterfowl hunts. Half- and full-day packages with lodging on site for 1 to 25 guns. Also offering sporting clays and a fishing guide service.

**TLC RANCH BIRD HUNTING PRESERVE AND BED & BREAKFAST**
Millersburg, MI 49759
Phone: 989-733-5443
www.tlcbirdpreserve.com

Located in the top of the Lower Peninsula near Alpena and Cheboygan, 150 acres for pheasant, chukar, quail, and grouse. Guided and nonguided hunts year-round with on-site lodging. Field and European-style hunts available. Deer hunting opportunities also available. No membership required.

**WILD WINGS GAME FARM**
Gaylord, MI 49734
Phone: 231-584-3350; fax: 231-584-3351
www.wildwingsgamefarm.com

Pheasant and chukar hunts on 120 acres
located about 10 miles west of Gaylord, in
the northern half of Michigan's LP. They
raise their own birds locally in large, wide-
open areas, to keep them as wild as possible.

**WYCAMP LAKE CLUB**
Harbor Springs, MI 49740
Phone: 231-537-4830 or 231-526-6651
www.wycamplakeclub.com

Located in the extreme northwest corner of
Michigan's Lower Peninsula between Mackinaw City and Petoskey near Lake Michigan
on over 1,000 acres of fields and streams—
old homestead orchards, oak and aspen
uplands, and cedar and pine lowlands.
European-style pheasant drives and field
hunts for pheasant, chukar, and quail. Sporting clays course. Membership comes with
benefits including use of duck blinds, trout
fishing, and use of dock.

Listings of more Michigan wing-shooting
hunting preserves can be found at www
.michiganhuntingpreserves.com/preserves
.htm and www.gamebirdhunts.com/ushunting/
Michigan.asp.

# HERITAGE DESTINATIONS

*Marshlands Museum and Nature Center*
If you do make it to Pointe Mouillee, at the
nearby Lake Erie Metropark, there is a wonderful Marshlands Museum and Nature
Center that includes an exhibit of the history of duck hunting on Lake Erie, including
vintage boats, decoys, punt guns, and James's
grandfather's century-old leather waders.

**LAKE ERIE METROPARK—**
**MARSHLANDS MUSEUM**
**AND NATURE CENTER**
Brownstown, MI 48173
Phone: 734-379-5020
www.metroparks.com/parks/pk_lake_
erie.php

*Pointe Mouillee Waterfowl Festival and*
*Michigan Duck Hunter's Tournament*
Every September since 1947 there has been
an annual Pointe Mouillee Waterfowl Festival and Duck Hunters Tournament. As many
as 30,000 people flock to Pointe Mouillee for
this festive event. Seminars; raffles; contests
like duck calling, working dogs, and punt
boat racing; plus decoy carving, wildlife art,
kids BB gun, and archery shooting. One highlight of the event is the demonstration of a
punt gun, a large cannonlike gun that was
mounted on the front of a duck boat and used
by market hunters before it was declared illegal.

The event is free of charge, and money
raised goes to help Pointe Mouillee State
Game Area.

POINTE MOUILLEE
WATERFOWL FESTIVAL
Rockwood, MI 48173
Phone: 734-379-4292
www.miwaterfowlfest.org

*Spike Keg O'Nails*

**SPIKE'S KEG O' NAILS**
Grayling, MI 49738
Email: Manager@Spikes-Grayling.com

If you are heading north, or hunting in the area around Grayling, which is the epicenter of deer hunting in the Lower Peninsula, the legendary hunters' hangout is Spike's Keg O' Nails restaurant/tavern. Spike's first opened on the day after Prohibition ended in 1933, and has been a roaring success since, with its burgers beyond comparison. During rifle deer season, there is often a line going around the block waiting to get in.

# MINNESOTA

*In 2001 there were 568,000 resident hunters and 29,000 nonresident hunters: 83% went big game hunting, 42% small game, 31% migratory waterfowl; 44% hunted on public lands; 81% hunted on private lands. Hunters pumped $483 million into the state economy. (USFWS)*

## OVERVIEW

Minnesota blends the pine forests and lakes of the north with the prairies to the west and hardwood forests of the south and east to make for a wide diversity of habitats that support many species of game including moose,

---

> **MINNESOTA SNAPSHOT**
> **GOPHER STATE**
>
> • **General information:** DNR Central Office hours: 8:00 A.M.–4:30 P.M., Monday–Friday, closed holidays; see www.dnr.state.mn.us/hunting/index.html
> DNR Information Center
> 500 Lafayette Road
> St. Paul, MN 55155-4040
> Phone: 651-296-6157 or 888-646-6367; 651-296-5484 or 800-657-3929
>
> • **Deer population:** 1.2 million, 8th in the United States
>
> • **Average deer harvest:** 239,920, 12th in the United States

elk, deer, bears, turkeys, prairie chickens, grouse, rabbits, hare, doves, pheasant, and waterfowl.

In 2005, Minnesota pheasant hunters had the best pheasant harvest in 40 years—586,000 roosters.

Each year around 500,000 Minnesota hunters harvest roughly 200,000 whitetail deer. The average weight is about 175 pounds for a buck, but the state record is 500 pounds.

## DESTINATIONS

Minnesota has over 1,300 state-managed Wildlife Management Units, 3 million acres of state forests, eight National Wildlife Refuges open to hunting, national forests, and millions more acres of private and public lands for hunting.

For an excellent guide to these myriad of hunting lands, see www.dnr.state.mn.us/hunting/tips/locations.html.

*General Information*
For general information, see http://hunting society.org/Minn.html and www.hotspot guides.com/hunting/hguides_MN.asp.

## ST. PAUL DISTRICT—U.S. ARMY CORPS OF ENGINEERS
St. Paul, MN 55101-1638
Phone: 651-290-5200
www.mvp.usace.army.mil/recreation/
default.asp?pageid=146

The St. Paul District of the Army Corps of Engineers manages a number of properties along the Mississippi River drainage, most of which offer some hunting opportunities according to state regulations. Direct questions to the district's recreation manager Frank Star, 651-290-5328.

*USDA National Forests*

## CHIPPEWA NATIONAL FOREST
Cass Lake, MN 56633
Phone: 218-335-8600
www.fs.fed.us/r9/forests/chippewa

Located in northern Minnesota, the Chippewa National Forest encompasses about 1.6 million acres; the USDA Forest Service manages about 665,000 of those acres. Aspen, birch, pines, balsam fir, and maples blanket the rolling uplands of the forest. There are over 700 lakes, 920 miles of rivers and streams, and 150,000 acres of wetlands. Hunting is permitted throughout the forest following state regulations. Some 88 miles of nonmotorized hunter walking trails have been created in the forest. For details, see www.fs.fed.us/r9/forests/chippewa/recreation/hunting/index.php.

## SUPERIOR NATIONAL FOREST
Duluth, MN 55808
Phone: 218-626-4300
www.fs.fed.us/r9/forests/superior

Located in northeastern Minnesota's arrowhead region, the Superior National Forest comprises 3 million acres and spans 150 miles along the U.S.-Canadian border, including the Boundary Waters Canoe Area Wilderness. Hunting opportunities include whitetail deer, moose, black bears, grouse, and snowshoe hare. For details, see www.fs.fed.us/r9/forests/superior/recreation/hunting.

*U.S. Fish and Wildlife Service*
*National Wildlife Refuges*

## AGASSIZ NATIONAL WILDLIFE REFUGE
Middle River, MN 56737
Phone: 218-449-4115
www.fws.gov/midwest/agassiz

On 61,500 acres in the aspen parkland region of northwest Minnesota in eastern Marshall County. This area is a transition zone where coniferous forests, tallgrass prairie, and the prairie pothole region of the Red River Valley meet. Deer hunting is allowed in accordance with Minnesota's deer firearm season regulations and special refuge regulations. A handicap-accessible stand is available upon request.

## BIG STONE NATIONAL WILDLIFE REFUGE
Odessa, MN 56276
Phone: 320-273-2191
www.fws.gov/midwest/bigstone

Straddling the headwaters of the Minnesota River in extreme west-central Minnesota, the 11,521-acre Big Stone NWR is within the heart of the tallgrass prairie's historic range. The refuge offers public hunting opportunities consistent with state-designated seasons and regulations for gray partridge, cottontail rabbits, jackrabbits, gray and fox squirrels, pheasant, turkeys, and deer. The refuge serves as a sanctuary area for migratory birds and is closed to all types of migratory bird hunting, including waterfowl, snipe, and woodcock.

**DETROIT LAKES WETLAND
MANAGEMENT DISTRICT**
Detroit Lakes, MN 56501-7959
Phone: 218-847-4431
www.fws.gov/refuges/profiles/index
.cfm?id=32586

Detroit Lakes Wetland Management District is located in northwest Minnesota and includes the counties of Becker, Clay, Mahnomen, Norman, and Polk—an area of approximately 6,000 square miles. Waterfowl production areas are open to public hunting, consistent with state regulations unless otherwise posted. Deer hunting and waterfowl hunting are the primary public uses of Waterfowl Production Areas (WPAs) in the Detroit Lakes District. Upland game-bird hunting opportunities are limited.

**FERGUS FALLS WETLAND
MANAGEMENT DISTRICT**
Fergus Falls, MN 56537-7627
Phone: 218-739-2291
www.fws.gov/midwest/fergusfallswetland

The Fergus Falls Wetland Management District includes the counties of Douglas, Grant, Otter Tail, Wadena, and Wilkin. The district manages 215 Waterfowl Production Areas (WPAs) totaling 43,962 acres and 1,101 acres of perpetual easements protecting 21,909 acres of wetlands on private land. Waterfowl Production Areas are public lands and—except where posted "Closed"—are open to hunting. The Prairie Wetlands Learning Center (Townsend WPA), district office, and maintenance shop lands are permanently closed to hunting, and several other WPAs are temporarily closed. The district Web site lists those WPAs that are closed.

**LITCHFIELD WETLAND
MANAGEMENT DISTRICT**
Litchfield, MN 55355
Phone: 320-693-2849
www.fws.gov/refuges/profiles/index
.cfm?id=32588

Located on the eastern edge of the Prairie Pothole Region in central Minnesota just a little south of the famous mythological Lake Wobegone where "all the women are strong, all the men are good looking, and all the children are above average." The district contains more than 33,000 acres of service-owned land and 8,000 acres of wetland easements. District lands include over 150 Waterfowl Production Areas (WPAs) scattered throughout seven counties. Waterfowl Production Areas are open to hunting and in accordance with state regulations and seasons. Waterfowl, pheasant, and deer hunting success is fair early in the season but drops off rapidly owing to heavy hunting pressure.

## MINNESOTA VALLEY NATIONAL WILDLIFE REFUGE

Bloomington, MN 55425
Phone: 952-854-5900
www.fws.gov/midwest/minnesotavalley

Minnesota Valley NWR is located within the urban and suburban areas of Minneapolis and St. Paul. The refuge is composed of eight linear units totaling approximately 12,500 acres, spanning 34 miles of the Minnesota River. It is a green belt of large marsh areas bordered by office buildings, highways, residential areas, and grain terminals. Hunting for deer, small game, turkeys, and waterfowl is permitted and popular in various parts of the refuge. For details, see www.fws.gov/midwest/minnesotavalley/hunting.html.

## MORRIS WETLAND MANAGEMENT DISTRICT

Morris, MN 56267
Phone: 320-589-1001
www.fws.gov/midwest/morris

The Morris Wetland Management District includes 244 Waterfowl Production Areas encompassing over 50,000 acres scattered throughout Big Stone, Chippewa, Lac Qui Parle, Pope, Stevens, Swift, Traverse, and Yellow Medicine counties in western Minnesota. Hunting and trapping (except where posted "Closed") are open and subject to all applicable state and federal laws. Small game hunters using shotguns are required to use and possess only approved nontoxic shot during the hunting season.

## RICE LAKE NATIONAL WILDLIFE REFUGE

McGregor, MN 55760
Phone: 218-768-2402
www.fws.gov/midwest/ricelake/hunting.htm

The 18,064-acre Rice Lake National Wildlife Refuge is located in the forest and bog area of northern Minnesota. Archery deer, small game, woodcock, and snipe hunting are permitted in accordance with state seasons and dates in the units designated as "open to public hunting." The Wildlife Drive and hiking trails are closed to hunting.

## RYDELL NATIONAL WILDLIFE REFUGE

Erskine, MN 56535
Phone: 218-687-2229
www.fws.gov/refuges/profiles/index.cfm?id=32583

Rydell NWR is located in the Prairie Pothole Region of northwestern Minnesota, between the flat Red River Valley Floodplain to the west and the rolling hardwood forest and lake regions to the east.

The refuge hosts an annual deer hunt for people with disabilities in October; 20 hunters can be accommodated. To receive an application, contact the Options Resource Center for Independent Living in East Grand Forks, Minnesota, 218-773-6100.

A youth deer hunt is held each year during the regular firearms deer season for youths aged 12 to 15 with a valid hunter's education certificate; 20 youths can be accommodated, and a nonhunting mentor must accompany each. For more information, contact the refuge.

## SHERBURNE NATIONAL WILDLIFE REFUGE

Zimmerman, MN 55398
Phone: 763-389-3323
www.fws.gov/midwest/sherburne

Situated approximately 50 miles northwest of the Minneapolis/St. Paul metropolitan area and 30 miles southeast of St. Cloud, the 30,700-acre refuge is located in the St. Francis River Valley. Sherburne NWR provides hunting opportunities for small game, migratory birds, and whitetail deer in accordance with all applicable federal and Minnesota state laws and subject to special refuge regulations. The refuge is not open to the state special goose hunt, special deer muzzleloader, predator, bear, crow, raccoon, or turkey hunting.

## TAMARAC NATIONAL WILDLIFE REFUGE

Rochert, MN 56578
Phone: 218-847-2641
www.fws.gov/midwest/tamarac

Tamarac NWR covers 42,724 acres and lies in the glacial lake country of northwestern Minnesota in Becker County, 18 miles northeast of Detroit Lake and 55 miles east of Fargo, North Dakota. Small game, waterfowl, and big game hunting opportunities are available on much of the refuge during state seasons. For details, see www.fws.gov/midwest/tamarac/hunting.html.

## UPPER MISSISSIPPI RIVER NATIONAL WILDLIFE & FISH REFUGE

Winona, MN 55987
Phone: 507-452-4232
www.fws.gov/midwest/UpperMississippiRiver

The refuge begins at the confluence of the Chippewa River near Wabasha, Minnesota, and ends near Rock Island, Illinois. The 240,000-acre refuge covers 261 miles of the river valley from Wabasha, Minnesota, to Rock Island, Illinois, and is the longest in the United States excluding Alaska. The refuge is open to deer and waterfowl hunting, in accordance with state regulations. Deer and waterfowl are very common on the refuge.

## WINDOM WETLAND MANAGEMENT DISTRICT

Windom, MN 56101
Phone: 507-831-2220
www.fws.gov/midwest/windom

The Windom Wetland Management District acquires and manages Waterfowl Production Areas, enforces wetland easements, and provides conservation assistance to landowners in 12 southwestern Minnesota counties.

Hunters enjoy a wide variety of opportunities to hunt on WPAs in the district. The most popular game species are pheasant, waterfowl, and deer. For details, see www.fws.gov/midwest/windom/hunting.html.

### Private Hunting Clubs and Preserves

Licenses are not required for released bird hunts in Minnesota.

## CARIBOU GUN CLUB HUNTING PRESERVE

Le Sueur, MN 56058
Phone: 507-665-3796
www.caribougunclub.com

A membership club, located four miles south of Le Sueur, Minnesota, Caribou Gun Club offers 28 fields on over 700 acres of corn, wheat stubble, alfalfa, grain sorghum, brush, and grassy areas, plus 200 acres of switch grass for pheasant, chukar, and quail hunts. A separate field is assigned for each hunting group. Also, trap, skeet, and sporting clays, flyer rings, five-stand, and a rifle range. Hosts major shooting events. Clubhouse with full kitchen accommodations.

**ELK LAKE HERITAGE PRESERVE**
Hoffman, MN 56339
Phone: 320-986-2200; fax: 320-986-6275
www.elklakepreserve.com

Located 20 miles west of Alexandria, offering field pheasant and chukar hunts, fishing, and sporting clay course, with main lodge overlooking scenic Torstenson Lake. Individual and group memberships available.

**HUNTS POINT SPORTSMAN'S CLUB**
Pequot Lakes, MN 56472
Phone: 218-568-8445; fax: 218-568-8450
www.huntspointclub.com

A 600-acre club offering field and European-style tower hunts for pheasant, quail, chukar, and Hungarian partridge, located in the Brainerd Lakes area. Deer hunting also. Hunting dog training and sporting clays. Lodge and accommodations for groups up to six.

**LONG LAKE LODGE**
Evansville, MN 56326
Phone: 320-524-2755 or 877-261-3573
www.longlakelodge.net

Located in Douglas County just west of I-94, pheasant, quail, and chukar field hunts, sporting clay, and five-stand. A 6,600-square-foot, three-level Main Lodge with clubhouse on the first floor; accommodations on second level (accessible by elevator) with four bedrooms, sauna, hot tub, deck area, meeting room, and a great room with a large stone fireplace. Ranch house nearby can accommodate more. Holds Prevent Child Abuse benefit shoot annually.

**MAJOR AVENUE HUNT CLUB**
Glencoe, MN 55336
Phone: 320-864-6025
www.majoravehunt.com

Some 350 acres for upland hunts and 160 acres of marsh and open water for waterfowl. Located 50 miles west of the Twin Cities. Guided hunts for pheasant, chukar, and quail. Member and nonmember options. Clubhouse and dog training.

**MILLE LACS HUNTING LODGE**
Onamia, MN 56359
Phone: 320-532-3384
www.millelacslodge.com

Located five miles from Mille Lacs Lake, the third-largest lake in Minnesota and one of the finest walleye lakes in the entire United States. Hundreds of acres for pheasant and chukar field hunts, sporting clays, pro shop, and meals. Memberships available.

**PHEASANT VIEW HUNT FARM**
Goodhue, MN 55027
Phone: 651-923-5499;
mobile: 651-380-2315
www.pheasantview.com

Pheasant, chukar, and quail field hunts—guided or nonguided. Membership and nonmembership options. Corporate groups welcome. Located 35 minutes from Rochester, Minnesota.

**PINE SHADOWS, INC.**
Brainerd, MN 56401
Phone: 218-829-4736
www.pineshadows.com

An Orvis-endorsed dog training program (specializes in springer spaniels) that organizes South Dakota field pheasant hunts on 10,000 acres near Aberdeen, South Dakota.

**RICE CREEK HUNTING
AND RECREATION**
Little Falls, MN 56345
Phone: 320-745-2232
www.ricecreekhunting.com

Located an hour and a half north of the Twin Cities, a 1,700-acre hunting preserve offering pheasant, chukar, waterfowl, and turkey hunts. Can also arrange deer and elk hunts. Clubhouse, conference, and lodging available.

**SAND PINE PHEASANTS AND
FAMILY RECREATION**
Avon, MN 56310
Phone: 320-363-4790
www.sandpinepheasants.com

Pheasant, chukar, and quail field hunts. Guided hunts available. Lodge for groups.

**TRAXLER'S HUNTING PRESERVE
AND RESTAURANT**
Le Center, MN 56057

Phone: 507-357-6940
www.traxlers.com

Located one hour south of the Twin Cities, an 850-acre hunting preserve with clubhouse, sporting clays, cabins, and wild game restaurant featuring alligator, New Zealand red deer, wild boar, game birds, waterfowl, and exotic fish, as well as more conventional entrees.

**UDOVICH GUIDE SERVICE**
Greaney, MN 55771
Phone: 218-787-2375
www.udovichguideservice.com

Located in northern Minnesota near Orr, 685 acres for pheasant hunts, plus deer and black bear hunts that can be arranged. Guides and dogs available.

**VIKING VALLEY HUNT CLUB**
Ashby, MN 56309
Phone: 218-747-2121 (Office)
or 218-747-2537 (Lodge)
www.vikingvalleyhuntclub.com

Hunting for released pheasant, chukar, and quail, plus wild duck, goose, and turkey hunts. Sporting clays. Membership club. Located near Pelican Lake.

**WILD WINGS OF ONEKA**
Hugo, MN 55038
Phone: 651-439-4287; fax: 651-439-6111
www.wildwingsofoneka.com

Located 15 miles northeast of St. Paul, membership club offering pheasant, chukar, turkey, and quail hunts and sporting clays.

Clubhouse on 537 acres; 14 areas—can handle up to 62 hunters at a time.

**WILLOW CREEK KENNELS
AND HUNTING**
Little Falls, MN 56345
Phone: 320-745-2331
www.willowcreekkennels.net

Released pheasant, mallard, and chukar hunts; also wild ruffed grouse hunting and dog training. Located between Brainerd and Little Falls, east of Highway 371.

**WINGS NORTH HUNTING CLUB
AND SPORTING CLAYS**
Pine City, MN 55063
Phone: 320-629-4868 or 612-202-8173
www.wingsnorth.org

Located about 55 minutes north of Twin Cities, Minnesota, Wings North has 11 different hunting areas and can accommodate up to 50 hunters, with no more than 5 hunters per unit for pheasant. Clubhouse with snack bar; sporting clays; memberships available; also dogs and guides.

## MISSOURI

*In 2001 there were 405,000 resident hunters and 84,000 nonresident hunters: 87% went big game hunting, 34% small game, 14% migratory waterfowl and doves; 20% hunted on public lands; 91% hunted on private lands. Hunters pumped $425 million into the state economy. (USFWS)*

### OVERVIEW

The beautiful Ozark Mountains, with abundant water flowing in rivers and lakes and rich farmlands, create a place for wildlife to flourish in Missouri—the state where some say there are more turkeys than people. With 93% of the state privately owned, hunting pressure is high on public lands, and knowing the right people or paying user fees is critical to enjoying the pleasures of the hunt here.

If you're a Missouri resident and own land five acres or larger, you do not need a permit to hunt small game, although seasons, methods, and limits still apply. If you want to hunt deer or turkeys on your land, you do need a no-cost resident landowner permit.

The northern third of the state is generally the best pheasant and quail land, with an annual average statewide harvest of around 30,000 roosters and half a million bobwhite quail.

That said, Missouri is famous for its deer and turkey hunting. The mix of cover and food is ideal for high population numbers. In recent years, nearly half a million archers

---

**MISSOURI SNAPSHOT
SHOW-ME STATE**

- **General information:**
Missouri Department of Conservation—
Administrative Office
Post Office Box 180 (zip 65102)
2901 West Truman Boulevard
Jefferson City, MO 65109
Phone: 573-751-4115; fax: 573-751-4467
www.mdc.mo.gov/hunt

- **Reporting a poacher—Operation Game Thief:** Dial toll-free 800-392-1111; rewards are available for information leading to the arrest of game-law violators; all information is kept in strict confidence

- **Deer population:** 1 million, 10th in the United States

- **Average deer harvest:** 275,928, 9th in the United States

and gun hunters have bagged about 300,000 whitetails a year. A number of world-record-class bucks have come from Missouri.

## DESTINATIONS

### General Information
For general information on the state of Missouri, see www.mdc.mo.gov/hunt/where.htm.

### U.S. Army Corps of Engineers

#### CLARENCE CANNON DAM AND MARK TWAIN LAKE
Monroe City, MO 63456-9359
Phone: 573-735-4097
www.mvs.usace.army.mil/MarkTwain

Approximately 45,000 acres of land and water in the Salt River Valley in northeast Missouri are available for hunting according to state and federal regulations. Species available include doves, quail, squirrels, deer, wild turkeys, rabbits, and waterfowl.

#### CLEARWATER LAKE
Piedmont, MO 63957
Phone: 573-223-7777
www.swl.usace.army.mil/parks/clearwater

Located 120 miles south of St. Louis near Piedmont, hunting in accordance with state and federal regulations is permitted on the project lands around Clearwater Lake. Game species include deer, quail, squirrels, rabbits, turkeys, and doves.

#### HARRY S. TRUMAN DAM AND RESERVOIR
Warsaw, MO 65355
Phone: 660-438-7317; fax: 660-438-7815
www.nwk.usace.army.mil/harryst/hunting.htm

The Harry S. Truman Dam and Reservoir is located within the Osage River Basin, approximately 100 miles southeast of Kansas City. The dam is 1.5 miles northwest of Warsaw, Missouri, and creates a 55,600-acre lake. Truman Lake offers opportunities for hunting whitetail deer, turkeys, squirrels, rabbits, quail, ducks, and geese. Hunters eligible to construct a waterfowl hunting blind on the lake are determined by a drawing that takes place in early September. For details, see www.nwk.usace.army.mil/harryst/hunting.htm.

### USDA National Forests

#### MARK TWAIN NATIONAL FOREST
Rolla, MO 65401
Phone: 573-364-4621
www.fs.fed.us/r9/forests/marktwain

Located in southern Missouri, the Mark Twain National Forest lies mostly within the Ozark Plateau. It is the only national forest in the state, encompassing 1,487,009 acres. Hunting is permitted according to Missouri Department of Conservation regulations. For details, see www.fs.fed.us/r9/forests/marktwain/recreation/hunting.

### U.S. Fish and Wildlife Service
### National Wildlife Refuges

#### BIG MUDDY NATIONAL WILDLIFE REFUGE
Columbia, MO 65201
Phone: 573-876-1826
www.fws.gov/midwest/bigmuddy

The present refuge of over 10,000 acres on the lower Missouri River between Kansas City and St. Louis, Missouri, has approval through Congress to acquire up to 60,000 acres of floodplains and adjacent lands. Hunting is subject to all applicable state and federal laws. Nontoxic shot must be used for all upland game hunting. For details, see www.fws.gov/midwest/bigmuddy/regulations.html.

**GREAT RIVER NATIONAL
WILDLIFE REFUGE**
Annada, MO 63330
Phone: 573-847-2333
www.fws.gov/midwest/greatriver

The Great River NWR protects approximately 11,600 acres along 120 miles of the Mississippi River, beginning 40 miles north of St. Louis. Hunting for deer, turkeys, migratory waterfowl, and upland game is permitted in certain sections of the refuge. For details, see www.fws.gov/midwest/greatriver/hunting.html.

**MINGO NATIONAL WILDLIFE REFUGE**
Puxico, MO 63960
Phone: 573-222-3589
www.fws.gov/midwest/mingo

Located in the upper end of the lower Mississippi River Valley, this 21,676- acre refuge is the only large remnant of bottomland hardwoods in the Missouri bootheel. Hunting is permitted for deer, turkeys, squirrels, and waterfowl in accordance with state and federal regulations. All hunters must register at refuge entrances. For details, see www.fws.gov/midwest/mingo/hunt.html.

**SWAN LAKE NATIONAL
WILDLIFE REFUGE**
Sumner, MO 64681
Phone: 660-856-3323
www.fws.gov/midwest/swanlake

Swan Lake National Wildlife Refuge is a 10,670-acre refuge located about 100 miles north of Kansas City. Hunting is permitted for geese from blinds and for deer with primitive weapons only. For details, see refuge Web site.

*U.S. National Park Service*

**OZARK NATIONAL SCENIC RIVERWAYS**
Van Buren, MO 63965
Phone: 573-323-4236 (Headquarters)
www.nps.gov/ozar

Ozark National Scenic Riverways protects 134 miles of the Current and Jacks Fork rivers in the Ozark Highlands of southeastern Missouri. Hunting is permitted in most areas of the riverway according to state regulations. For details, see www.nps.gov/ozar/planyourvisit/hunting-fishing.htm.

*Private Hunting Clubs and Preserves*

**B & C GAME FARM**
Brookfield, MO 64628
Phone: 660-258-5200 or 660-258-HUNT
www.bcgamefarm.com

Located on over 2,000 acres in Linn County for released quail, pheasant, and chukar field or continental hunts, plus wild turkey and deer hunting. Overnight accommodations, clubhouse, dog rentals, and guides available.

**BIRD FEVER HUNTING PRESERVE**
Richmond, MO 64085
Phone: 816-776-8023
www.birdfeverhunting.com

Located three miles north of Richmond, which is northeast of Kansas City, over 1,500 acres developed for hunting quail, pheasant, and chukar (field and Continental-style), plus wild turkey and deer hunts. Hunting lodge, 12-station sporting clays, and trap range.

**CEDAR CREST HUNTING PRESERVE**
Robertsville, MO 63072
Phone: 636-257-2355; fax: 636-257-3060
www.cchuntclub.com

Field and Continental-style hunts for pheasant, chukar, and quail on a 1,000-acre farm along the Meramec River. Guides and dogs available.

**HARDING GAMEBIRD FARM**
Ridgeway, MO 64481
Phone: 660-872-6746 or 660-872-6870
www.hardinggamebirds.com

Released pheasant, chukar, and quail on 1,000 acres; wild turkeys and deer on 2,000 acres in northwest Missouri.

**HEGGEMEIER GAME FARM
AND KENNELS**
Higbee, MO 65257
Phone: 660-456-7592
www.heggemeiergamefarmandkennel.com

Over 2,000 acres of prime habitat for hunting for released pheasant, chukar, quail, and Hungarian partridge, plus wild quail, pheas-ant, deer, turkeys, squirrels, woodcocks, snow and Canada geese, ducks, and doves. Lodging, guides, and dogs, plus sporting clays. Memberships available but not necessary.

**MOSER'S PHEASANT CREEK L.L.C.**
Franklin, MO 65250
Phone: 660-848-2621
www.hunt-pheasants.com

Located northeast of Kansas City three miles north of New Franklin, 500 acres for blue-backed pheasant and 120-acre wetland for resident mallards. Lodging in 1860s remodeled farmhouse. A 2,000-square-foot lodge.

**PIN OAK HILL GAME
MANAGEMENT AREA**
Bogard, MO 64622
Phone: 660-745-3030
www.pinoakhill.com

Released pheasant, quail, and chukar field and European-driven hunts (megahunts, too), wild quail hunts, sporting clays, plus turkey and deer hunts with guides, meals, and lodging. Located in northern Missouri 90 miles northeast of Kansas City.

**QUAIL COUNTRY HUNTING RESORT**
Lowry City, MO 64763
Phone: 417-644-2999
www.quailcountryhuntingresort.com

Located approximately an hour and a half south of Kansas City and an hour and a half north of Springfield, a 600-acre hunting preserve offering field and European-style quail and pheasant hunting. Guides and dogs available.

**RUNNING SPRING FARM**
Everton, MO 65646-0105
Phone: 417-535-2190
www.runningspringfarm.com

Located 30 miles northwest of Springfield, Missouri, a 360-acre club offering field and European-style hunts for chukar, pheasant, and quail. Trapshooting, archery and rifle ranges, and three-stand sporting clays. Overnight lodging at The Inn at Running Spring Farm, with continental breakfast included, plus other meals optional.

**TROPHY COUNTRY**
Huntsville, MO 65259
Phone: 660-277-4447; fax: 660-277-4443
www.trophycountry.com

Located on the East Fork of the Chariton River, a 6,200-acre ranch with a 2,200-acre upland bird hunting area offering released quail, pheasant, and chukar, plus hunting for wild doves, waterfowl, turkeys, coyotes, and deer. A year-round resort with fishing, mushroom hunting, gym, and many other activities. Lodging and a 10,000-square-foot building for meetings.

**TWIN LAKES SPORTING CLUB**
Mexico, MO 65265-6810
Phone: 573-581-1877
www.twinlakessportingclub.com

Located in central Missouri, released pheasant, chukar, and quail on 1,280 acres of a 1,400-acre grain-crop farm about 30 miles northeast of Columbia, Missouri. Also offers dove, turkey, deer, and wild quail hunts, sporting clays, fishing, and meeting facilities for large groups. Facilities include a 2,800-square-foot log cabin beside a lake, banquet hall, and 2,600-foot grass airstrip.

# HERITAGE DESTINATIONS

*American National Fish and Wildlife Museum: Wonders of Wildlife Where: Springfield, Missouri*
Located next to the huge store and headquarters of Bass Pro Shops Outdoor World, Wonders of Wildlife is housed in a 92,000-square-foot tastefully designed three-story wooden structure.

The tour begins with exhibits that describe who really funds wildlife management—hunters and fishermen—and the growing numbers of unendangered wildlife species conserved primarily by sportsmen's groups and their dollars. What a refreshing change of reality!

Then you slip through a tunnel and emerge into a wild canyon in the Ozarks with free-ranging wild turkeys, ducks, quail, and songbirds, all living in and around streams and ponds and more than 3 million handcrafted leaves on trees and bushes. Live barred owls and turkey vultures stare at you from just a few feet away as a melody of animal calls fills the air.

After passing over and through a rushing stream filled with trout and bass, you encounter otters and beavers eye to eye through massive panels of clear acrylic six inches thick. If the beavers retreat into their lodge, a television monitor lets you watch them.

The Hunting Conservationist Hall explains "Why I hunt" from the perspective of

12 different people, from the Osage Indian to the early settlers and the modern sportsman, as well as the place of hunting in wildlife management.

Then you meet wildlife predators—live bears, coyotes, wolves, alligators, and mountain lions—and you learn about living with them, as well as hunting them.

On individual television screens the "Heroes of Conservation Library" introduces you to Aldo Leopold, Teddy Roosevelt, George Bird Grinnell, and John James Audubon. As you approach the screens, the characters come to life and tell their stories. At the end of this room, there is a screen/mirror asking, "Will the next hero of wildlife be you?"

You get a "bass-eye-view" as you walk through a monster bass, 10 feet tall and 32 feet long, as if he has eaten you. At a video simulator, you pick up a rod and tussle with a fish of the simulator's choice, ranging from a sunfish or bass to a monster tarpon or sailfish.

A 225,000-gallon saltwater tank holds six different species of sharks, several rays, mackerel, tarpon, sea bass, bluefish, bonefish, and dorados. Next to it are special exhibits on marine life, like jellyfish. The acrylic used for this tank is nearly 14 feet tall, 26 feet across, and weighs 12 tons.

You pass through a cave with several species of bats and follow a stream from the Ozark Highlands where linker trout flourish. The stream cascades over a 19-foot waterfall and then into a lowland stream with bass, carp, catfish, and paddlefish. The museum holds 700,000 gallons of water, which circulates through 10 miles of pipes every three hours.

The last exhibit is one of the most meaningful exhibits of all: "A Difference of One."

You fill out a short questionnaire on a computer and enter it. What comes up on several screens are role models of conservation to inspire you to be an ardent conservationist.

In Wonders of Wildlife, man is a participant in the ecosystem, not just a dumb, harmful observer. Passing through this place is a positive, empowering, and even healing experience that makes you feel good about our place in the web of life. The $52 million project could not have been completed without the vision, leadership, and support of Johnny L. Morris, founder and chief executive officer of Bass Pro Shops.

**AMERICAN NATIONAL FISH AND WILDLIFE MUSEUM**
Springfield, MO 65807
Phone: 417-890-9453; fax: 417-890-9278
www.wondersofwildlife.org

## OHIO

*In 2001 there were 452,000 resident hunters and 38,000 nonresident hunters: 86% went big game hunting, 64% small game, 14% migratory waterfowl; 32% hunted on public lands; 86% hunted on private lands. Hunters pumped $636 million into the state economy. (USFWS)*

### OVERVIEW

Whitetails were once a rare sight in Ohio, but, boy, has that changed! Today there are about 600,000 deer in Ohio, and hunters bag about 210,000 per year. Ample food and habitat results in Ohio today being a producer of many Boone & Crockett and Pope & Young record-book bucks. Annual limits range from one deer in the northeast zone to three deer per year per hunter (only one antlered) in the southeast area, and many farmers want the bag limits to be higher.

This is also excellent upland bird hunting country. Ohio hunters average bagging about 200,000 pheasant and 40,000 bobwhite quail per year.

Waterfowl hunting along Lake Erie is traditionally very popular with private duck clubs—Winous Point on Sandusky Bay being legendary.

Every year the Division of Wildlife issues a Wildlife Report that provides information on the best locations to find various species. The report is available online at www.ohiodnr.com/wildlife/Hunting/Wildlife StatusReport_04/main.htm.

## DESTINATIONS

### State Wildlife Management Areas

The Ohio DNR Division of Wildlife has established more than 150 wildlife areas en-

compassing nearly 175,000 acres in 70 counties. For a complete listing of all Ohio wildlife areas, see www.ohiodnr.com/wild life/Hunting/wildlifeareas/wildare.htm.

### U.S. Army Corps of Engineers

The U.S. Army Corps of Engineers maintains 25 reservoirs for flood control in Ohio, most of which allow hunting according to state regulations. Contact the district offices for details.

**PUBLIC AFFAIRS—**
**HUNTINGTON DISTRICT**
Huntington, WV 25701
Phone: 304-399-5353
www.lrh.usace.army.mil/_kd/go
.cfm?destination=Page&Pge_ID=1001

The 45,000-square-mile Huntington District in the central and southern part of the state has designed and constructed more flood control dams, levees, and flood walls than any other Corps district in the United States. Hunting according to state and federal regulations, plus some local specific regulations, at most of the reservoirs.

**U.S. ARMY CORPS OF ENGINEERS,**
**PITTSBURGH DISTRICT**
Pittsburgh, PA 15222-4186
Phone: 412-395-7500; fax: 412-644-2811
www.lrp.usace.army.mil/what.htm#poc

The Pittsburgh District covers four reservoirs on the eastern side of the state, as well as other projects in Pennsylvania and New York. Hunting according to state and federal regulations, plus some local specific regulations, at most of the reservoirs.

*USDA National Forests*

**WAYNE NATIONAL FOREST**
Nelsonville, OH 45764
Phone: 614-592-6644
www.fs.fed.us/r9/wayne

Over 160,000 forested acres in southern Ohio, Wayne is the state's only national forest, and it produces some of the state's biggest whitetail bucks. All hunting according to state regulations is permitted. For details, see www.fs.fed .us/r9/wayne/wildlife/hunting.html.

*U.S. Fish and Wildlife Service*
*National Wildlife Refuges*

**OTTAWA NATIONAL WILDLIFE REFUGE**
Oak Harbor, OH 43449
Phone: 419-898-0014
www.fws.gov/midwest/ottawa

Located on Lake Erie, this 9,000-acre complex is composed of three refuges—Cedar Point NWR, Ottawa NWR, and West Sister Island NWR, which is Ohio's only wilderness area and is located about nine miles offshore in Lake Erie. Up to 70% of the Mississippi Flyway black ducks pass through here. In cooperation with the Ohio DNR–Division of Wildlife, controlled hunts are held for both deer and waterfowl. Hunters must apply for the hunts through the Division of Wildlife's application process in July and are assigned hunt dates and units through the same system.

*Private Hunting Clubs and Preserves*

**BULLS-EYE PHEASANT PRESERVE**
Uhrichsville, OH 44683

Phone: 740-922-5633
www.bullseyepheasant.com

Located in Tuscarawas County, released pheasant, chukar, and quail on 100 acres. Lodging nearby and meals available.

**CHERRYBEND HUNTING PRESERVE**
Wilmington, OH 45177
Phone: 937-584-4269
www.cherrybendhunting.com

Located in southwest Ohio, field and European-style pheasant hunts on a working grain farm. Memberships available.

**ELKHORN LAKE HUNT CLUB**
Bucyrus, OH 44820
Phone: 419-562-6131
www.elkhornlakehuntclub.com

Located 40 miles south of Sandusky, pheasant, chukar, and Hungarian partridge field and European hunts, plus sporting clays, five-stand, and on-site overnight lodging available.

**ELK RIDGE GAME FARM**
Bucyrus, OH 44820
Phone: 419-562-0195 (Evenings)
or 419-562-9997 (Clubhouse);
fax: 419-562-3979
www.elkridgegamefarm.com

Over 400 acres for pheasant, Hungarian partridge, and chukar on multiple properties. Guides, dogs, light lunch, and bird cards available. Large clubhouse.

## GK RIVERBOTTOM HUNT CLUB

Montpelier, OH 43543

Phone: 419-485-8717; fax: 419-485-1405

www.GKRiverbottom.com

Pheasant and chukar on over 600 acres, plus five-stand, skeet, rifle range, and 3-D archery range along the St. Joseph River between Ft. Wayne and Toledo. Clubhouse, overnight accommodations, catered meals, guides, and dogs available. Contacts with outfitters in Wyoming for big game.

## HIDDEN HAVEN SHOOTING PRESERVE & SPORTING CLAYS INC.

Sugar Grove, OH 43155-9632

Phone: 740-746-8568; fax: 740-746-8605

www.hiddenhaven.us

Released pheasant, chukar, and quail for field and European-style hunts, plus major skeet, trap, five-stand, and sporting clays club with multiple courses. Clubhouse, guides, and dogs available.

## MAD RIVER SPORTSMAN'S CLUB

Bellefontaine, OH 43311-9475

Phone: 937-593-8245; fax: 937-593-9390

www.MadRiverSportsmansClub.com

Some 300 acres in the rolling hills two miles east of Bellefontaine for field and tower shoots for pheasant, chukar, Hungarian partridge, and quail. Sponsors many sporting clays and five-stand competitions. Members only.

## MULBERRY PHEASANTRY

Camden, OH 45311

Phone: 937-787-3912

www.mulberrypheasantry.com

Pheasant, chukar, Hungarian partridge, and quail field and tower hunts. Guides and dogs available. RV and camping available.

## RUSHCREEK GAMEBIRD FARMS, LLC

Lancaster, OH 43130

Phone: 740-569-0306

www.rushcreekgamebirds.com

Field and tower shoots for pheasant, chukar, and Hungarian partridge on over 500 acres on two sites. Membership options available.

## THORN BOTTOM HUNTING

Grover Hill, OH 45849

Phone: 419-587-3555;

fax: 419-587-3556

www.thornbottom.com

Located in Washington County between Findlay and Ft. Wayne, Illinois, a 652-acre farm managed for only hunting; offers hunts for pheasant, chukar, doves, and deer. Dog training available. Breakfast/lunch catering available.

## UPLAND ACRES, LLC HUNTING PRESERVE

Defiance, OH 43512

Phone: 419-393-BIRD;

fax: 419-393-4320

www.uplandacres.com

Pheasant, quail, chukar, and Hungarian partridge field hunts next to the Flatrock Creek in Paulding County. Trap, guides, and dogs available.

# HERITAGE DESTINATIONS

*Theodore Roosevelt Game Preserve:*
*Ohio's First Public Hunting Area*

Established in 1922 and located on nearly 9,000 acres of forest in Nile Township in Scioto County in part of what was referred to as the "Little Smokies," the Theodore Roosevelt Game Preserve started Ohio's wildlife area program and provided a place to restore species including deer and turkeys. It was opened to hunting in 1935. The first deer hunt in the preserve did not take place until 1943.

For details, see www.ohiodnr.com/wild life/Hunting/deer/roosevelt.htm.

## WISCONSIN

*In 2001 there were 588,000 resident hunters and 72,000 nonresident hunters: 92% went big game hunting, 35% small game, 8% migratory waterfowl and doves; 36% hunted on public lands; 88% hunted on private lands. Hunters pumped $801 million into the state economy. (USFWS)*

## OVERVIEW

Wisconsin is not a big quail hunting state—only about 1,000 bobwhites a year are bagged. It's better for pheasant, about 200,000 of which are harvested annually, primarily between Madison and Green Bay and in Polk and St. Croix counties.

But the Badger State is first and foremost whitetail deer country. With a herd of about 1,650,000, in 1999 hunters bagged 206,207 bucks and 291,463 antlerless deer, which is 77,000 more deer bagged than in Texas, even though the Lone Star State has nearly twice as many deer.

Wisconsin is the state where chronic wasting disease (CWD) has been found in deer in the southern part of the state. CWD is of the same family of diseases as mad cow disease—transmissible spongiform encephalopathies (TSEs)—that attack the brain and lead to death. But there has never been any recorded instance where eating a CWD-infected deer led to a person contracting a brain disease. Nonetheless, since it takes years for TSEs to show up, err on the side of caution.

Most states now offer testing programs for sport-harvested deer, moose, and elk. Also, bone out the meat if you butcher your own animals. For more details, see www.dnr .state.wi.us/org/land/wildlife/whealth/issues/ CWD/index.htm.

As deer herds grow in size, the transmission of disease among animals increases—one more reason to get out there and hunt.

---

**WISCONSIN SNAPSHOT**
**BADGER STATE**

- **General information:**
  Wisconsin Department of Natural Resources
  101 South Webster Street
  Post Office Box 7921
  Madison, WI 53707-7921
  Phone: 608-266-2621
  www.dnr.state.wi.us/org/land/wildlife/hunt/ index.htm

- **Buy licenses online:** www.wildlifelicense.com/ wi/start.php

- **Deer population:** 1.6 million, 3rd in the United States

- **Average deer harvest:** 487,685, 1st in the United States

In 2006, 73,289 black bear tags were issued, with 4,370 harvested—a less than 6% success rate, which is almost half of the year 2000 when 6,598 bears were harvested.

Wisconsin hunters harvest between 100,000 and 150,000 doves a year, while turkey hunters enjoy a 23% spring hunt success and a slightly lower fall harvest success rate. Ruffed grouse is the most popular upland game bird, but stats are not available for success rates. Early Canada goose hunting here has gone from less than 1,000 a decade ago to about 14,000 birds a year these days.

## FEATURED HUNT

### Whitetail Deer Hunting in Wisconsin

JEFF ENGEL

Some of my fondest childhood memories were hunting whitetail deer with my father. I was a lucky kid to have a father who taught me whitetail-

hunting skills and spent a great deal of time with me in the woods. I remember very vividly the time when my father said to me, during a cold Wisconsin deer season, "Jeff, we've spent a lot of time together hunting deer now. You know safe gun handling; you have good woodsmanship skills. So today, Jeff, I'm going to drop you off at this point, and you can hunt by yourself. I will just walk over here about a hundred yards and look in a different direction." That meant so much to me, because I felt that I had accomplished something and that my dad thought I was mature enough, even though I was at a very young age to actually be hunting whitetail deer on my own. The responsibility that my father gave me early that Wisconsin morning was a great reflection of his ability to have faith in me and to know that I would conduct myself in a responsible manner while hunting. Ever since that time, I have been addicted to and very passionate about hunting deer. I also happen to be fortunate to live in a state that is recognized as one of the premier deer hunting states in the nation—Wisconsin.

Wisconsin's total deer hunting harvest is around 500,000. Wisconsin also has over 700,000 people that hunt deer. The archery season for deer starts in mid-September, followed by the gun season, then followed by the muzzleloader season, and then back to the archery season, which ends in early January.

Like in many areas, the bucks in Wisconsin get very active during the first or second week of November. This is also a time when archers have very good success.

Much of northern Wisconsin is considered big woods country, and the lower part of Wisconsin has many farm or small woodlot areas.

Wisconsin has a deep, rich history full of tradition when it comes to deer camps. I have had the pleasure of visiting many deer camps throughout

Wisconsin, and there seems to be a common theme among the camps. The hunters are extremely passionate about deer hunting, and they seem to study the whitetail deer throughout the year, including looking for deer sheds in early spring. The potential of harvesting a truly great buck in Wisconsin is quite good for the hunter willing to develop his woodsmanship skills. In addition, the hunter who studies the whitetail deer and their habits and movements in various areas will be more successful. The traditional deer camp will have coat hooks outside on the porch to hang all clothing so it will be as scent free as possible. Inside the cabin, in the early morning, you can almost count on having sizzling bacon with a hearty breakfast. The evening meals seem to be more of an event than a simple meal, complete with substantial bowls of chili and plates heaped with cheese and sausage.

I-94 going west out of Milwaukee is virtually back-to-back vehicles on the Friday before the hunting season opens. A good idea is to leave for your hunt on Thursday before opening. This would allow you time to enjoy the hunting experience at a more relaxed pace.

Another very interesting tradition that I found in Wisconsin is that the hunters really work closely together. When a deer is down, other members of the camp eagerly join the hunter to take the deer out of the woods and share in the celebration. Along with this, the Wisconsin whitetail venison is delicious. I know from personal experience: my wife Sherol and I will go through several deer a year.

The fall is a magical time in Wisconsin with its exploding fall colors and its wide variety of topography. Deer hunters will find that Wisconsin truly is a deer hunter's paradise.

## My First Bird!

SHEROL ENGEL

We won't talk about the last three *unsuccessful* turkey hunts (cold, wet, no birds). I had gotten my feet wet, literally, as a turkey hunter but had never bagged one.

I really thought this year would end up being a continuation of the last few—I could not understand what possessed someone to call and wait, call and wait, call and wait for that illusive wild turkey . . . Oh, what fun! Jeff kept saying that it's worth the wait just to have a turkey come in to your call. So here I

was, dressed in camouflage head to toe, crouched down in a blind, with Jeff yelping away on his mouth and slate call as a couple of decoys sat 20 yards away in the field.

To add to my nervousness and anticipation, this year I was wired for sound and shadowed by our videographer. I did not need this additional pressure. If I did things right, this footage would be part of our upcoming television show and potentially part of the DNR video Jeff was contracted to produce. (No big deal—right. SURE.)

This chilly Wisconsin springtime morning was filled with action. Early morning gobbling told us there were gobblers behind us. Fifteen minutes after opening time Jeff called in a running gobbler heading straight for the hen decoys. Motion in the window of our videographer's blind sent Mr. Gobbler flying for cover.

Responding to soft yelps and purrs, two curious jakes soon walked to our decoys. The videographer was to make a "cluck" sound when he was set to film. He frantically began "clucking." Unfortunately, he did not know that I was not going to shoot a jake. I wanted a long beard, even if it meant a sore bottom. Slowly the jakes lost interest and walked away. A scathing look was being directed my way via a frustrated videographer.

We hunted one full day (roughly 5:00 A.M. to 5:00 P.M.) much too long and hard on the derriere! It had, however, been a day filled with action and an evening (what was left of it) enjoyed with our friends and hunting partners.

Even with the previous day's activities, I really did not want to spend the next four days in that same position. So after sitting for four hours the next morning with little activity in the blind, Jeff said it was time to go "prospecting." I was relieved for the change. This is when hunting started to get fun.

All it took was a walk up some *very* steep

hills—just enough to make you feel like you were going to have a heart attack. We were panting to catch our breath when Jeff gave a few good yelps on his call. A heart-stopping response came thundering back.

Hearts thumping, we walked a little more, stopped, and called again. This time several gobblers answered, and they were close! We quickly found a substantial tree to sit under and got settled in. Another soft yelp; no answer. Oh, but then there was the sound of rustling leaves—he was coming! My heart was pounding almost out of control, but I remained quiet and still. Jeff spotted them first—there were *four* long beards! They came up the hillside silently. The rest, as they say, was history.

As the first most anxious bird separated from the rest, I aimed and shot. At 30 yards, I had a perfect shot to the neck and successfully took my first bird. Running (correction, quickly walking—should not run with a gun) up to the flopping bird, I became overwhelmed with a mixture of emotions. This was my long-awaited moment, but as I looked at the bird, I began to cry. This was not what they did in all the videos I had watched! As my husband, with great excitement, hugged and congratulated me, I felt this bizarre combination of accomplishment and sadness. There he was, a 21-pound gobbler with an 11¼-inch beard and 1-inch spurs. I smiled and cried as I looked at him.

Since the hunt, I have shared my experience with other hunters. To my amazement and relief, the feelings I had were not uncommon. There have been several male hunters that were kind enough to admit they also experienced a mixture of pride and sadness when they harvested an animal, some even admitting they had extreme emotion.

Hunting and ceremonial events have existed since the beginning of time. For me, it was not so

much the hunt but sharing it with others that has made it special.

*See Section D for a special recipe.*

## DESTINATIONS

*State Wildlife Management Areas*
All around the state, there are numerous public lands open to hunting, fishing, and trapping, including a number of state parks. For a list with details, see www.dnr.state.wi .us/org/land/wildlife/reclands/index.htm.

*U.S. Fish and Wildlife Service*
*National Wildlife Refuges*

**HORICON MARSH NATIONAL WILDLIFE REFUGE**
Mayville, WI 53050
Phone: 920-387-2658
www.fws.gov/midwest/horicon

The 21,417-acre Horicon Marsh is the largest freshwater cattail marsh in the United States. An hour's drive from Milwaukee and

Madison, this is one of the best-known waterfowl hunting locations in the States, especially for Canada geese, which may number 300,000 at a time. No special permit needed, except for Canada geese. Motors allowed. Blinds not necessary. For details, see www.dnr.state.wi.us/org/land/wildlife/reclands/horicon.

For hunting questions, see www.dnr.state.wi.us/org/land/wildlife/reclands/horicon/whattodo/hunting/FAQ.htm#03.

Horicon NWR also administers the nearby 1,000-acre Fox River NWR, which is also open to hunting.

## LEOPOLD WETLAND MANAGEMENT DISTRICT

Portage, WI 53901
Phone: 608-742-7100
www.fws.gov/midwest/leopold/

The Leopold Wetland Management District is named after Aldo Leopold. The district manages over 10,600 acres of Waterfowl Production Areas (WPAs) in 16 southeastern Wisconsin counties and 45 conservation easements, totaling 3,000 acres, in 33 eastern Wisconsin counties. These WPAs are open to hunting according to state regulations and local posting.

## NECEDAH NATIONAL WILDLIFE REFUGE

Necedah, WI 54646-7531
Phone: 608-565-2551
www.fws.gov/midwest/necedah

Located 150 miles northwest of Milwaukee, this 43,696-acre wetland is open to hunting for deer, waterfowl, turkeys, and small game according to state regulations and local posting and restrictions. For details, see www.fws.gov/midwest/Necedah/documents/NCD.pdf.

This is also the summer nesting area for a new flock of whooping cranes.

## ST. CROIX WETLAND MANAGEMENT DISTRICT
New Richmond, WI 54017
Phone: 715-246-7784
www.fws.gov/midwest/stcroix

Some 7,548 acres on 40 WPAs and 15 easements in Burnett, Washburn, Polk, Barron, St. Croix, Dunn, Pierce, and Pepin counties—the eastern edge of the prairie pothole region. Hunting is permitted according to state regulations and local posting and restrictions.

## TREMPEALEAU NATIONAL WILDLIFE REFUGE
Trempealeau, WI 54661
Phone: 608-539-2311
www.fws.gov/midwest/trempealeau

A 6,200-acre refuge along the Mississippi River in western Wisconsin. Deer and waterfowl hunting permitted according to state regulations and local posting. For details, see www.fws.gov/midwest/trempealeau/Documents/fs.pdf.

## WHITTLESEY CREEK NATIONAL WILDLIFE REFUGE
Ashland, WI 54806
Phone: 715-685-9983
www.fws.gov/midwest/ashland/whitt-crk/whit_crk.html

Located on the lower portion of Whittlesey Creek and coastal wetlands along the lakeshore of Chequamegon Bay in Lake Superior, near Ashland, Wisconsin. Deer hunting permitted. See refuge Web site or call headquarters for details.

*USDA National Forests*

## CHEQUAMEGON-NICOLET NATIONAL FOREST
Park Falls, WI 54552
Phone: 715-762-2461;
fax: 715-762-5179
www.fs.fed.us/r9/cnnf

Located between Wausau and Lake Superior in the north-central part of the state, this 850,000-acre parcel is traditionally one of the best destinations in the United States for big bucks on public lands.

*U.S. National Park Service*

## APOSTLE ISLANDS NATIONAL LAKESHORE
Bayfield, WI 54814
Phone: 715-779-3397
www.nps.gov/apis/planyourvisit/hunting.htm

Twenty-one beautiful islands in Lake Superior, accessible by boat, and 12 miles of mainland natural habitat. Long Island and the mainland unit are the most popular hunting areas, with all legal species huntable according to state regulations and local posting and regulations. During October, whitetail deer can be hunted using blackpowder weapons on Oak, Basswood, and Sand islands. Only 50 permits are issued each year. Check headquarters for details. Stockton Island has one of the most dense concentrations of black bears anyplace in the United States. Hunting is allowed there for bears.

**SAINT CROIX NATIONAL SCENIC RIVER**
Saint Croix Falls, WI 54024
Phone: 715-483-3284 (Headquarters
Recorded Message) or 715-483-3284
ext. 638 (Visitor Center Recorded
Message) www.nps.gov/sacn

The 252 miles of the Saint Croix and Name-
kagon rivers running through Minnesota and
northern Wisconsin. Hunting is permitted
along most of the riverway, according to state
regulations and local restrictions. For details,
see www.nps.gov/sacn/planyourvisit/hunting
.htm.

*Private Hunting Clubs and Preserves*
A hunting license is not required for hunting
released birds on a preserve.

**APPLE RIVER HUNTING PRESERVE**
Osceola, WI 54020
Phone: 715-248-7168
www.appleriverhunting.com

Located 50 miles from St. Paul, Minnesota,
250 acres for hunting pheasant and quail. Dog
training available. No membership needed.

**BADGERLAND PHEASANT FARM, LLC**
Westby, WI 54667
Phone: 608-634-4534
www.badgerlandpheasantfarm.com

Located in north-central Vernon County,
pheasant and chukar. Dogs available. Individual hunts or packages for discounts.

**BEST DAYS AFIELD**
Fort Atkinson, WI 53538

Phone: 920-568-9010; fax: 920-568-9009
www.bestdaysafield.com

Located 30 minutes southeast of Madison.
Released pheasant, chukar, and quail hunts,
with food and clubhouse. Membership club.

**HERITAGE HUNT CLUB**
Laona, WI 54541
Phone: 877-FEASANT or 877-332-7268.
www.heritagehuntclub.com

On 640 acres in the middle of the Nicolet
National Forest in northeast Wisconsin.
Hunts for released pheasant, quail, wild ducks,
turkeys, grouse, and geese can be arranged.
Sporting clays. Lodge with kitchen facilities.
Daily fee or membership.

**HILLSIDE SPRINGS HUNT CLUB**
Edgerton, WI 53534
Phone: 608-884 7272 or 866-884-7272;
fax: 608-884-7373
www.hillsidesprings.com

Offering pheasant, chukar, and quail hunting on over 400 acres along the banks of the
Yahara and Rock rivers in southern Wisconsin. Lodging available. Membership club.

**HUNTER'S PARK GAME FARM
AND SPORTING CLAYS**
Brillion, WI 54110
Phone: 920-864-7070
www.hunterspark.com

Over 500 acres with clubhouse in northeast
Wisconsin near Green Bay, offering field and
tower shoot pheasant hunts, five-stand, and

sporting clays. Memberships and corporate events.

**J & H GAME FARM**
Shiocton, WI 54170
Phone: 715-758-8134
www.jhgamefarm.com

Pheasant hunts and sporting clays on over 700 acres, with a 2,700-square-foot clubhouse, home-cooked food, and a large pro shop. Dogs and guides available.

**LITTLE CREEK LODGE**
Little Suamico, WI 54141
Phone: 920-826-7382; fax: 920-826-2999
www.littlecreeklodge.net

Pheasant, sporting clays, five-stand, and rifle and pistol range located on 700 acres just north of Green Bay. Lodge with kitchen. Reservations required.

**MILFORD HILLS HUNT CLUB**
Johnson Creek, WI 53038
Phone: 920-699-2249
www.milfordhills.com

Located in southeast Wisconsin, an award-winning shooting lodge offering released pheasant, quail, and chukar, sporting clays, five-stand, and wobble trap. Lodge with conference room and restaurant. Special rates for members.

**PHEASANTS ON THE LEDGE**
Oakfield, WI 53065
Phone: 920-583-3662
www.Pheasantsontheledge.com

Field and tower pheasant and chukar hunts, plus sporting clays. Located 70 miles north of Madison. Membership club.

**RUSH CREEK SPORTSMEN'S CLUB**
Spring Green, WI 53588
Phone: 888-881-2219
www.rush-creek.com

Members-only club located on 3,500 acres in southwest Wisconsin's Wyoming Valley offering pheasant, chukar, quail, deer, and wild turkeys. Clubhouse; lodging; trap.

**WERN VALLEY SPORTSMEN'S CLUB**
Waukesha, WI 53189
Phone: 262-968-2400
www.wernvalley.com

Membership club located in southeast Wisconsin half an hour from Milwaukee with 600-acre preserve offering hunting for pheasant, chukar, and Hungarian partridge; dogs, sporting clays and trap, rifle range. Has hosted state sporting clays championship.

**WOODS AND MEADOWS HUNTING PRESERVE AND SPORTING CLAYS**
Warrens, WI 54666
Phone: 608-378-4223
www.woodsandmeadow.com

Located in Jackson County in western Wisconsin, chukar, pheasant, and Hungarian partridge hunts. Very reasonable overnight accommodations. Hosted 2007 state sporting clays shoot. No membership.

 **HERITAGE DESTINATIONS**

*Aldo Leopold's Shack, Baraboo, Wisconsin*
Aldo Leopold, scientist-philosopher-hunter, is the founder of modern wildlife management science. His guiding principle of conservation—"the Land Ethic": "A thing is right when it tends to preserve the integrity, stability, and beauty of the biotic community"—stands as the foundation of responsible environmental actions and a major contribution to the advancement of the conservation movement.

Shortly after his death in 1949, Leopold's book *A Sand County Almanac*, which presents the Land Ethic and other nuggets of ecological wisdom, was published. Initially, it met with little fanfare. *A Sand County Almanac* is written as a journal of a year's cycle of nature at the Leopold family's retreat "The Shack," a converted chicken coop cabin along the banks of the Wisconsin River in Baraboo, Wisconsin.

"A prophet is without honor in his own time" is an old saying. Leopold was a visionary whose thinking took time to grow. Reissued in 1973, in the wake of Earth Day 1970, *A Sand County Almanac* sold 273,000 copies and has gone on to sell over 2 million copies and be reprinted in nine languages, becoming "the bible" for conservationists around the world.

You can visit Leopold's shack and the 150-acre forest that he and his family planted around that building. This is hallowed ground for hunters.

Nearby is a new educational center that honors Leopold's legacy. The Aldo Leopold Foundation also offers educational programs for children and adults and a number of other exceptional resources.

**ALDO LEOPOLD FOUNDATION, INC.**
Baraboo, WI 53913-0077
Phone: 608-355-0279; fax: 608-356-7309
www.aldoleopold.org

*Service of the Hunt, Wisconsin Rapids, Wisconsin*
Each year the English Lutheran Church in Wisconsin Rapids in the central part of the state celebrates "Service of the Hunt" on the eve of the nine-day rifle deer hunting season. Hunters are encouraged to wear hunting clothes to church.

**FIRST ENGLISH LUTHERAN CHURCH**
Wisconsin Rapids, WI 54494
Phone: 715-423-2840
Email: fel@felwr.org

# Great Plains

## KANSAS

*In 2001 there were 189,000 resident hunters and 103,000 nonresident hunters: 55% went big game hunting, 72% small game, 27% waterfowl and doves; 33% hunted on public lands; 91% hunted on private lands. Hunters pumped $236 million into the state economy. (USFWS)*

### OVERVIEW

In Kansas the rich fertile farmlands of the Midwest meet with the high prairie of the West. Thus, one finds whitetail deer, quail, turkeys, upland game, and waterfowl in the east, and mule deer, antelope, and prairie chickens in the west. Kansas also offers an elk hunt that is growing in popularity and size every year.

The whitetails grow big out here, but above all else, this is prime upland game bird hunting territory. Kansas's hunters normally bag at least 750,000 pheasant and over a million bobwhite quail per year.

---

**KANSAS SNAPSHOT
SUNFLOWER STATE**

- **General hunting information for Kansas:**
  Kansas Department of Wildlife & Parks
  Operations Office
  512 SE 25th Avenue
  Pratt, KS 67124
  Phone: 620-672-5911
  www.kdwp.state.ks.us/news/hunting/
  about_kansas_hunting

- **Guide to outfitters in Kansas:** An excellent guide is offered by the Kansas Outfitters Association at www.kansasoutfittersassociation.com

- **Deer population:** 275,000, 28th in the United States

- **Average deer harvest:** 88,323, 25th in the United States

---

 **FEATURED HUNT**

---

### Buffalo Hunting on the Prairie on Horseback while Living in a Teepee or Dugout

JAMES SWAN

When the *Mayflower* landed, there were at least 60 million buffalo in North America.

The herd stretched coast to coast and from James Bay south into Mexico. By 1900, there were less than 1,500 alive and less than 100 in the wild.

Yes, buffalo were hunted to near extinction. What a tragic page in American history. What is almost never said, though, is that their slaughter was encouraged by the U.S. government as part of a planned military strategy to force Indians onto reservations by taking away their natural food supply. President Ulysses S. Grant vetoed legislation that would have stopped the slaughter, and the army gave away free guns and ammunition to market hunters, who were the primary hunters of the buffalo.

Today there are more than 232,000 bison in private herds in the United States. Another 20,000 bison are in herds on public lands. And another 150,000 bison are being raised in Canada, where there is a wild herd of wood buffalo (northern subspecies) of several thousand that lives in northern Alberta.

Hunters can be proud that the restoration of the buffalo was initiated by a group of conservation-minded hunters—especially William Hornaday and Theodore Roosevelt—who formed the American Bison Society in 1905. They persuaded Congress to establish the National Bison Range in Montana, which has served as a principal source of breeding stock for many parks, refuges, zoos, and private ranches.

The Academy Award–winning movie *Dances with Wolves* features a buffalo hunt, as well as showing the carnage of unregulated market hunting. It also shows Lt. John Dunbar (Kevin Costner) living in a sod hut and a teepee.

Thanks to Lee Hawes and his family, you can have a hunting experience like that in *Dances with Wolves* on the Kansas prairie on their 1,500-acre ranch. In an email to the author, Hawes describes the hunt as:

*The buffalo harvest that most people are familiar with occurred in this area. Most historical accounts refer to the*

*area between the Arkansas River and the big hills south of the Mulberry creek as the Slaughter Pen. This area is approximately 25 miles southeast of Dodge City Kansas.*

*My great-grandfather settled here and started this ranch in 1884. He lived in a dugout for a number of years until a house could be built. He raised horses for the U.S. Calvary remount program and cattle that were driven to railheads and shipped to Kansas City by train. Prior to establishing the ranch here, he sailed around the world numerous times as a cabin boy. He then went to Texas, learned the cowboy trade, and made many cattle drives from Texas to Dodge City. He worked on ranches in Texas, including Charles Goodnight's, where he learned the cowboy trade. He was later a buffalo hunter and a personal friend of Brick Bond and Bat Masterson. My grandfather and father were both cattlemen; I have been raised a cattleman and rancher.*

*The area surrounding our ranch has been plowed up and farmed. We are an island of grass surrounded by a sea of farms. This is the only place in the entire world that you can hunt buffalo where the heart of the harvest took place. We brought the buffalo back to the ranch a number of years ago. Now it's like they never left. When you hunt here, it's not just harvesting an animal; it's knowing you can be part of something bigger than yourself. It's knowing that where you belly crawled up on a herd of buffalo, the old-timers did also. It's knowing that you have been able to do something, take part in something where it actually took place. We look forward to hunting with you and just want you to know that you are not coming just for a hunt, but an adventure. We are providing more than meals and hunting opportunity. We are giving you a chance to share in history.*

When you arrive at the Hawes Ranch, you decide if you want to live in a teepee or a prairie dugout house. You go out on horseback to scout and find the herd. You can use your own rifle, but they do supply replicas of the rifles used by buffalo hunters more than a century ago—Sharps and Remington Rolling Block in 50-70 and 50-90 caliber—that use black-powder cartridges.

Prices for a three-day hunt range from $985 for a yearling to $1,800 for a dry cow, to $3,750 for a trophy bull that will yield about 500 pounds of wrapped meat. They also offer hunts for whitetail deer and exotics.

Contact:
**HAWES RANCH OUTFITTERS**
Ford, KS 67842
Phone: 620-369-2204
www.hawes.org/hunt

## DESTINATIONS

### General Information
An excellent guide to hunting locations in Kansas can be found at www.kdwp.state.ks.us/news/hunting/where_to_hunt_in_kansas.

### U.S. Army Corps of Engineers
The U.S. Army Crops of Engineers manages 38 reservoirs in Kansas, many of which offer hunting. For a list of the reservoirs and the recreational activities they offer, see www.swt.usace.army.mil/recreat/recreat.htm.

### U.S. Fish and Wildlife Service
### National Wildlife Refuges

**FLINT HILLS NATIONAL WILDLIFE REFUGE**
Hartford, KS 66854
Phone: 620-392-5553
http://flinthills.fws.gov

Part of the John Redmond Reservoir flood control project, the refuge is 18,463 acres upstream of the reservoir, most of which is in the floodplain of the Neosho River. Prairie grasslands, bottomland hardwood timber, shallow wetlands, and croplands are managed to provide food and habitat for migratory birds and resident wildlife. Waterfowl, deer, and turkey hunting according to Kansas state regulations.

**KIRWIN NATIONAL WILDLIFE REFUGE**
Kirwin, KS 67644
Phone: 785-543-6673
www.fws.gov/kirwin

On 10,778 acres in the rolling hills and narrow valley of the North Fork of the Solomon River in north-central Kansas where the tall-grass prairies of the east meet the short-grass plains of the west. Waterfowl, doves, pheasant, quail, turkeys, prairie chickens, snipes, coots, cottontail rabbits, fox squirrels, and deer (archery only). Hunting of cottontail rabbits and fox squirrels is allowed only during pheasant season.

More details on hunting at Kirwin NWR can be found at www.fws.gov/kirwin/hunting_at_the_refuge.htm.

**MARAIS DES CYGNES NATIONAL WILDLIFE REFUGE**
Pleasanton, KS 66075
Phone: 913-352-8956
http://maraisdescygnes.fws.gov

A 7,500-acre refuge established to protect the largest contiguous tract of bottomland hardwood forest in Kansas. Located 39 miles south of Kansas City. Predominant species hunted are quail, turkeys, and white-tail deer. Squirrels and rabbits are hunted to a lesser extent. Waterfowl hunting is generally limited to small farm ponds, mine ponds, and the Marais des Cygnes River. However, during flood events, as much as 2,000 additional acres of flooded timber and old fields may become available for hunting.

Deer and spring turkey hunting are open only to those possessing a valid Refuge Access Permit. These permits are limited in number and are distributed through an application and drawing process. To apply, call or write the office.

**QUIVIRA NATIONAL WILDLIFE REFUGE**
Stafford, KS 67578
Phone: 620-486-2393
www.fws.gov/quivira

A refuge of 22,135 acres originally established to provide feeding and wintering habitat for waterfowl on the Central Flyway. Hunting for waterfowl, quail, pheasant, doves, snipes, rail, squirrels, and rabbits is permit-ted on Quivira NWR. For details, see www.fws.gov/quivira.

*Private Hunting Clubs and Preserves*

**BARREL SPRINGS HUNT CLUB**
Tribune, KS 67876
Phone: 620-376-2701; fax: 620-376-2702
www.barrelspringshunt.com

Located in western Kansas less than five hours from Denver, Colorado Springs, and Amarillo; 3,000 acres of controlled shooting and an additional 3,000 acres for hunting wild pheasant. Predator hunting and limited deer and antelope hunting available. A 24-bedroom lodge with private baths and family-style dining serving farm country meals.

**BEAVER CREEK RANCH**
Atwood, KS 67730
Phone: 785-538-2363
www.beavercreekranch.org

A 2,500-acre working ranch located just outside Atwood in Rawlins County in northwest Kansas on what was prime hunting ground for the Cheyenne and Arapaho Indians. Offers both wild and released pheasant, and quail, wild dove, turkey, and (mule and whitetail) deer hunts. Guides and dogs available. Excellent food and 600-square-feet Beaver Creek Lodge with a six-person hot tub for overnights. Transportation to and from airports also can be arranged.

**BLUESTEM HUNTING PRESERVE**
Kingman, KS 67068
Phone: 620-532-3806
www.bluestemhunting.com

Traditional Kansas guided and self-guided field hunts for pheasant, quail, and chukar on 1,000 acres of native bluestem grass and wooded creek bottom every day from October 1 through March 31. European shoots also. Accommodations for up to 16; kitchen facilities. Located approximately one hour west of the Wichita airport.

**CLAYTHORNE LODGE**
Columbus, KS 66725
Phone: 620-597-2568
www.claythorne.com

Located between Oswego and Columbus, upland and Continental-style half-day or full-day quail, chukar, and pheasant hunts, guided and unguided, with and without breakfast or lunch. Continental hunts, fishing, sporting clays, skeet and trap, with overnight accommodations, RV hookups, and meals offered. Membership options available.

**FANTASY FLYERS**
Quinter, KS 67752
Phone: 785-754-3324 or 877-754-3324
www.fantasyflyers.com

Half-day and full-day hunts for quail, pheasant, and chukar on 960 acres of prime upland bird land with free-flowing stream. Bunkhouse with kitchen facilities; 2-acre spring-fed pond for guest catch-and-release fishing.

**FLINT OAK**
Fall River, KS 67047
Phone: 620-658-4401; fax: 620-658-4806
www.flintoak.com

Given a Five-Star rating from the National Association of Shooting Ranges and located in southeast Kansas, offers field hunts and European-style driven pheasant shoots, plus dove, wild turkey, deer, and duck hunting in their seasons for members. Lodging, dining facilities, kennels, pro shop, pool and spa, game room, equestrian facilities, dog training, sporting clays, skeet, trap, five-stand, and shooting lessons offered for members and nonmembers. Can accommodate groups up to 200.

**KANSAS CREEK GAMEBIRDS, LLC**
Concordia, KS 66901
Phone: 785-335-2887 or 785-335-2381
www.kansascreekgamebirds.com

Over 4,000 acres of prime wildlife habitat in the Republican River Valley of north central Kansas, Kansas Creek offers hunting packages for native pheasant and quail, released pheasant, quail, and chukar, whitetail deer, turkeys, and ducks, with crappie fishing option, too. Accommodations and meals nearby.

**KISIWA HUNT CLUB AND**
**GUIDE SERVICE**
Halstead, KS 67056
Phone: 316-830-2755
www.bdarn.com/kansas/Hunts.html

Located three miles southwest of Halstead, Kansas, Kisiwa is open to the public and offers guided hunting for pheasant, quail, and chukar on preserve, leased, and state areas that include wooded streams, native grass, and grain fields. Hunting dogs are available at no charge. Preserve hunting: September 1–March 31; regular season hunting:

mid-November–January 31. Dressing and packaging of game as well as special packages available.

## KANSAS GUN DOGS
Halstead, KS 67056
Phone: 316-830-2755
www.kansasgundogs.com

Kansas Gun Dogs is a licensed facility dedicated to breeding and training quality gundogs. Also offered are half-day and full-day hunts for pheasant, quail, and chukar, plus Rio Grande turkeys and whitetail deer.

## LONE PINE HUNTING PRESERVE
Toronto, KS 67669
Phone: 620-637-2967
www.huntlonepine.com

Located 10 miles west of Yates Center, Kansas, Lone Pine Preserve provides upland field hunting for pheasant, quail, and chukar and European-style shoots on over 600 acres of prime habitat. On nearby 700-acre Lone Pine Extra, wild quail, turkey, and deer hunting in season. Brittany spaniels for sale.

## MUDDY CREEK GAME BIRDS
Meriden, KS 66512
Phone: 785-484-2325
www.muddycreekgamebirds.com

Self-guided and guided pheasant, bobwhite quail, and red-legged chukar hunts on over 1,000 acres located 20 minutes from Topeka and an hour west of the Kansas City airport. A 3,500-square-feet overnight lodge with kitchen facilities and hot tub can sleep up to

nine. Whitetail deer and turkey hunts can be arranged.

## PRAIRIE WINGS GAMEBINDS
Webber, KS 66970
Phone: 785-753-4871
www.kansasbirdhunting.com

Located in north-central Kansas on the border with Nebraska, guided and unguided hunts for pheasant, chukar, and quail on 5,000 acres of native habitat. Half-day and full-day hunts, with overnight lodging and meals available.

## RAVENWOOD LODGE SPORTING CLAYS AND HUNTING RESORT
Topeka, KS 66610
Phone: 800-656-2454 or 785-256-6444
www.ravenwoodlodge.com

A private hunting estate located in northeast Kansas 15 minutes southwest of Topeka offering field hunts for pheasant, chukar, and quail; European-style hunts; and hunts for wild prairie chickens, ducks, geese, turkeys, and deer. Driven hunts can be arranged. Champion English sporting clays course, tower course, five-stand, and shooting instruction are available. Clubhouse, overnight lodging in the bunkhouse, or 100-year-old Mission Creek Lodge. Can accommodate groups up to 100 for meetings and so forth.

## RINGNECK HAVEN
Pretty Prairie, KS 67570
Phone: 620-459-0121
www.ringneckhaven.com

Almost 2,000 acres of prime hunting land located in south-central Kansas near the town of Pretty Prairie, 50 miles west of Wichita. Released chukar, quail, and pheasant field and European-style hunts. Spring wild turkey in season to a limited number of hunters. Special opportunity for deer hunting, limited to only four hunters who purchase rights to hunt the entire season, which for archery runs October 1 to December 31. Accommodations available nearby.

**RINGNECK RANCH**
Tipton, KS 67485
Phone: 785-373-4835
www.ringneckranch.net

Traditional field hunts for pheasant, quail (wild or released birds options), prairie chickens, doves, deer, waterfowl, turkeys, predators, and prairie dogs. Field transportation via four-wheel-drive crew-cab hunt trucks and airport transportation available. Country-gourmet, family-style meals included (supper, breakfast, and lunch). Can accommodate up to 18 guests in modern ranch house, plus 8 more in nearby house.

**SHOW-ME BIRDS HUNTING RESORT**
Baxter Springs, KS 66713
Phone: 620-674-8863
www.showmebirds.com

Pheasant and chukar for guided field or European-style hunts on 700 acres—four stocked farms one mile apart. A 3,000-foot clubhouse, meeting room, and pro shop. Located in southeast Kansas, 90 minutes from Tulsa.

**SMOKY RIVER RENDEZVOUS**
Winona, KS 67764

Phone: 785-846-7785
www.smokyriverrend.com

Located in the Smoky Hill River area of northwest Kansas on over 4,000 acres of prime hunting grounds for pheasant. Guides and dogs available. Accommodations for up to 12 guests in the lodge, which was originally built in 1886. Three home-cooked meals a day and a full bar area.

**SPEARPOINT RANCH**
Barnard, KS 67418
Phone: 785-524-5330
www.spearpointranch.com

A working 4,000-acre cattle and grain ranch in north-central Kansas including 1,100 acres for field pheasant hunts. Packages for one or more days. Dogs available. Accommodations in a modern ranch-style house with a large fireplace, pool table, and space for relaxing. Meals are country recipes that are served family style.

**SWANSON FARMS, LLC**
Elsmore, KS 66732
Phone: 620-754-3878
www.swansonfarms.com

Guided pheasant, chukar, and quail hunts on 320-acre hunting preserve in southeast Kansas with additional hundreds of acres for turkey, coyote, and deer hunts in a multitude of packages for individuals and corporations. Full-service hunting lodge with dining facilities; bed-and-breakfast cabins at nearby Bourbon State Fishing Lake. Handicapped hunters welcome.

**T & C WILDLIFE**
Arcadia, KS 66711
Phone: 620-638-4300
www.time2hunt.com

Membership club 90 minutes south of Kansas City. Over 6,000 private acres of native grass, food plots, natural draws, wild plum thickets, dogwood, and hardwood timber with released Hungarian partridge, red-legged partridge, pheasant, and quail, wild turkeys, wild deer, doves, ducks, and geese in marsh and fields. Special: mule wagon hunts. Modern lodge overlooking Arrowhead Lake.

**WILD WINGS HUNTING**
Scott City, KS 67871
Phone: 620-872-5668;
mobile: 620-874-1547
www.wildwingshunting.com

The specialty is guided wild pheasant hunting on 5,000 acres of prime land. Also offering released quail and chukar hunting on 1,200 acres of developed upland game bird habitat. Customized packages featuring overnight lodging and home-cooked meals at a down-home bed-and-breakfast in Scott City, Kansas, Lady Di's Court. Located halfway between Pueblo and Wichita.

# HERITAGE DESTINATIONS

*Martin and Osa Johnson Safari Museum*
From 1917 through 1936, Martin and Osa Johnson filmed safaris in exotic places around the world, resulting in 25 films including *Simba* (1928), *Baboona* (1935), and *I Married Adventure* (1940) and a television series in the 1960s that launched outdoor television. Open seven days a week, this museum is an extraordinary collection of artifacts, photos, and films from those trips.

**MARTIN AND OSA JOHNSON SAFARI MUSEUM**
Chanute, KS 66720
Phone: 620-431-2730
www.safarimuseum.com

## NEBRASKA

*In 2001 there were 124,000 resident hunters and 49,000 nonresident hunters: 51% went big game hunting, 66% small game, 28% migratory waterfowl and doves; 31% hunted on public lands; 87% hunted on private lands. Hunters pumped $198 million into the state economy. (USFWS)*

**OVERVIEW**
With a nickname like the "Cornhusker State," one would anticipate that this is bird country, and it surely is. Pheasant, bobwhite quail, sharp-tailed grouse, prairie chickens, mourning doves, white-wing doves, Eurasian collared doves, turkeys, and waterfowl are here in abundance. In 2005 Nebraska hunters took 437,000 wild pheasant and 134,000 bobwhite quail. The highest quail populations tend to be in the southeastern counties, while pheasant are best in the southwest and northeast. Prairie grouse are strongest in the northwest.

This is also big deer, elk, bighorn sheep, and antelope country that traditionally turns up some of the biggest bucks in the United States, as well as being the home of Cabela's, a definite pilgrimage place for any sportsman.

According to several hunting preserve owners, the underharvested game animal here is rabbit, so bring your beagles and have a blast!

## FEATURED HUNT

### A Familiar Place

JOE ARTERBURN*

The falling snow has an icy hardness. I hear each tick, tick, tick of the white pellets bouncing off my jacket's camouflaged nylon shell. Senses acute, I ease forward, setting each foot softly on the snow, willing each step to make no noise, the snow muffling and softening the winter-dead grass and cottonwood leaves, fragrant with a moldering smell in the crisp, quiet air. I see the irregular shapes of the snow pellets against the gray sky, the dark leafless trees. In layers of wool and goose down, I am not cold. I am aware.

I am in a familiar place. Thirty-five years ago where I walk was under eight or so feet of water. Now it is a dry lake bed. Not exactly dry, because of the snow, but not a lake bed any more, either. I am hunting alone today, but in a few years I will field-dress two nice whitetails that our sons Hunter and Jack (a 4×4 and 4×5, respectively) shoot about 150 yards and 10 minutes apart on this land; and just a season after that, our youngest son, Sam, will shoot his first deer here, too, a one-antlered whitetail (a 4×0), over near where Hunter's went down.

Our farmstead, only a couple hundred yards away, is not visible from here. It's over the hill and blocked by the stand of dying hardwoods, mostly elms, I think, planted several generations ago, dying now of old age and, I suppose, lack of water. There's no farmhouse any more. Propane leaking from our heating stove exploded and blew off the roof on November 11, 1968. Mom and my sister Mary, home

and a few outbuildings. The chicken house, from the roof of which my brothers Roley and John and I—John as pilot—unsuccessfully tested our experimental wings of old bedsheets in a lathe frame, collapsed long ago, and the ice house, where they used to store ice hand-sawed from the lake, is gone too.

It is morning prime time, and I am in prime position.

The earthen dam behind me is breached, a gaping hole washed through by a big rain a few years ago—maybe eight or nine—that turned the dry riverbed far upstream into a torrent of muddy water, rushing and washing through the cottonwoods that sprouted and thrived in the rich silt of the lake bed. I remember when the cottonwoods were just saplings, and I was amused by them looking so out of place where the lake had been. Now, decades later, they are substantial trees, and the floodwater looked out of place surrounding them. The water roared in, carrying brush and debris and, for a short while, filled the old lake to its past glory. I don't know if the corrugated-steel culvert pipe—flume, we called it—through the dam was closed or if the flood simply overwhelmed the old dam. In any case, it washed out, the culvert now lying dry and askew in what was once our fishing pool below the dam.

I cut deer tracks, half covered by snow, heading northwest off the lake bed toward the bend in the shore where the lake bed makes sort of an S-curve, so about half of the lake lay east-westish, the rest north-southish. The cedars along the shoreline are big now, blocking the former view of the lake from the cabin, now a nearly flat pile of boards and flaps of black tarpaper. I think I have this right: Mom bought the cabin at a neighbor's auction and had Danny Beard, an older neighbor kid, help move it in. It wasn't really a cabin, just an old farm shed or something, maybe 10 or 12 feet wide by 15 feet or so. One room, with a cast-iron kitchen stove, door on each end, and a dusty window on the front and side

sick from high school, were in it but weren't hurt by the explosion or when the roof came back down, crushing the two-story house into a pile of broken lumber and possessions. We lived for a while in a rented farmhouse five miles away after that but ended up moving to town. The barn is still there

facing the lake. After a thorough sweeping, we hauled in an old couch, table and chairs, wooden wood box, kerosene lanterns, and, boy, did we have fun. I can't count the nights we slept in there, us kids or us kids and some of our friends from neighboring farms. Even in the winter we'd sleep there, the stove glowing with heat. Dad dumped shelled corncobs nearby, and we burned them, but a load of them didn't last as long as firewood, which we sawed, split, and stacked in the wood box.

We've been here well over 100 years. My great-grandfather helped settle this county. He must have picked this spot because the Frenchman River ran through here, feeding the lake once the dam was built. A neighbor downstream irrigated crops from a canal running out of the lake, the canal filling when he'd crank down the gate to shut off the culvert, filling the lake until water flowed down the canal. Topographical maps still show the river as a blue squiggle, the lake as a wider blue squiggle, but they're not really blue anymore and haven't been since the creek stopped running back in the late 1970s.

I'm nearly halfway through the lake, a slow, slow walk, but I haven't seen that deer yet. No deer yet. I ease through a stand of cottonwoods and stop to lean against a tree. I shrug my rifle strap higher on my shoulder and breathe deeply. Over on the far bank I can see the bottom of the upturned boat. I wouldn't notice it for the weeds growing around it, but I know it is there. Our neighbor William Cody Loux—everyone called him Code—who lived just upriver, gave us kids the boat. It was a sawed-off boat, maybe 10 or 12 feet from bow to homemade wooden stern. The rest of the boat was steel; the whole back panel was a cobbled wood plank. I never knew what became of the other half of the boat. Never asked, I guess. We flipped the boat over every spring and tarred the bottom to stop, or at least slow, leaks, but it didn't take long for water to again find its way in. When we first got it, we painted it with green house paint, but the green didn't last long, either. The boat came with solid wooden oars, and we'd row all over the lake, which, when full, covered maybe 30 acres.

Out of the trees I came and onto the grassy flat where no trees grow because this part of the lake bed had been pastured and cattle nipped off any cottonwoods that tried to grow. Good pheasant cover in here, if it's not heavily pastured, and a good place to catch deer traveling early in the morning. I wonder if my hunting knife is still up there on that low slope? I lost it belly-crawling up on some ducks one winter. I crawled more than a hundred yards over grass covered with five or six inches of fresh snow until I got to the reeds along the shoreline and then cut loose on a bunch of ducks, maybe 20 or 30, that were quacking contentedly until I arrived. That was a good knife, with a stag handle. Its loss dampened the excitement of the successful sneak. I didn't really need a knife along, but I was one of those kids who always wanted a knife on my belt so I'd be prepared for anything, no matter what I was hunting. I looked hard for a long time back along my worming track in the snow but never found the knife.

I am near the upper end of the lake bed, where it narrows to just the dry creek bed. Another half mile or so and I'll be at old Code's farmstead, the northwest quarter of Great-granddad's home section. We own it now. Dad bought it from Code and Dorothy when they moved to town. The buildings there are old too.

No deer, it looks like. Must have given me the slip; probably cut back and went behind the grain bins and that cedar shelterbelt. I don't even remember where I lost the tracks.

I guess I won't see anything today.

*Joe Arterburn is the director of Corporate Communications for Cabela's, Inc., in Sidney, Nebraska.*

## DESTINATIONS

### General Information

Nebraska has an excellent Web link that guides hunters to 24 state areas and 5 national areas that offer some of the best prairie grouse hunting in the state—the world, for that matter: www.ngpc.state.ne.us/hunting/guides/planning/grouse.asp.

### Private Hunting Clubs and Preserves

#### BEAVER VALLEY OUTDOORSMAN
Bartlett, NE 68622
Phone: 308-654-3290; fax: 308-654-3445
www.funhunting.com

Located north of Grand Island, offering a combination of wild and released pheasant and bobwhite quail on 7,000 acres of prime habitat. Sporting clays, guides, and dogs available. Also, hunts for chukar and coyotes can be arranged. Meals and lodging available.

#### BUNKER HILL HUNTING RESORT
Hastings, NE 68901
Phone: 402-463-0483
www.huntbunkerhill.com

Built on the former U.S. Navy facility 22 miles south of Grand Island, Bunker Hill has over 2,000 acres (1,000 in controlled shooting), offering upland bird, turkey, waterfowl, and deer hunting. Distinctive, historical, igloo-style bunkers used by the ammunition depot for storage have been converted into modern accommodations. Also trap, five-stand, and sporting clays.

#### BURKE FARMS HUNTING
Curtis, NE 69025
Phone: 308-367-4399
www.burkefarms.com

A 4,000-acre farm in southwest Nebraska with 2,000 acres devoted to upland bird hunting. Deer and turkey hunting on additional 2,000 acres. Lodging, guides, and dogs available.

#### GREAT NEBRASKA HUNTING
Eustis, NE 69028-9716
Phone: 308-486-4591 or 877-685-7305
www.greatnebraskahunting.com

Located 35 minutes south of Cozad, Nebraska, traditional-style hunting with stocked, not planted, pheasant and quail on 2,200 acres. Also dove, coyote, rabbit, raccoon, opossum, bobcat, turkey, and deer hunting on additional 4,000 acres. Lunch available at no extra cost.

#### HEARTLAND HUNTS
Bennet, NE 68317
Phone: 402-782-8972
www.heartlandhunts.com

Released quail and pheasant hunts, snow geese, and limited number of guaranteed deer hunts. Transportation, lodging, meals, dog training, and trapshooting range.

#### HUNTING HIDEAWAY
Mitchell, NE 69357
Phone: 308-631-6108
www.huntinghideaway.com

Wild duck, geese, and pheasant hunt packages in the Nebraska Panhandle along the

North Platte River. Can host 10 to 12 hunters at a time in a bed-and-breakfast atmosphere. Featured on several television shows.

## HUSKER HUNTS
Ord, NE 68862
Phone: 308-728-3508
www.huskerhunts.com

Located in central Nebraska on 800 acres, pheasant and quail hunts. Guides and dogs available. Lodging and home-cooked meals.

## NORTHWEST NEBRASKA
## HIGH COUNTRY
www.nebraskahighcountry.com

Group of 17 ranches and farms on the edge of the Black Hills offering many hunting opportunities for big and small game.

## OAK CREEK SPORTING CLUB
Brainard, NE 68626
Phone: 402-545-3111 or 866-625-4868
www.oak-creek-club.com

Released pheasant, quail, and chukar on over 1,000 acres. Sporting clays, rifle range, 3-D archery range, and limited stands for deer hunting. Membership club.

## PHEASANT BONANZA
Tekamah, NE 68061
Phone: 888-366-HUNT
www.pheasantbonanza.com

Pheasant, quail, and chukar, plus dove, wild turkey, deer, and duck hunting in season, on close to 10,000 acres. Large lodge, clubhouse; catering or kitchen to make your own meals. Guides and dogs, sporting clays, skeet and trap ranges. Open year-round.

## PRAIRIE HILLS HUNTING CLUB
Dannebrog, NE 68831
Phone: 308-226-2540
www.prairiehills.net

Pheasant, chukar, and quail hunting on 1,200 acres. Guides, dogs, clubhouse, bunkhouse, home-cooked meals, trap range. Memberships; nonmembers welcome.

## PRAIRIE SANDS HUNTING
Sutherland, NE 69165
Phone: 308-386-8166
www.prairiesands.com

Located in the Sandhills area, 100 miles from Cabela's headquarters, pheasant, quail, chukar, prairie chickens, and sharp-tailed grouse. Lodging, meals, guides, and dogs available. Many nearby attractions for sightseeing.

## SANDHILL SEASONS GUEST
## RANCH & HUNTS
Bartlett, NE 68622
Phone: 402-386-5457
www.sandhillseasons.com

Located in central Nebraska on a working cattle ranch. Pheasant on 930 acres of crop and rangeland. Ranch with accommodations, meals, horse riding.

## ST. JOHNS HUNTING ACRES
Clearwater, NE 68726-5209
Phone: 402-485-2616
www.stjohnshunt.com

Located in northeast Nebraska, 12 miles southwest of Clearwater off Highway 275. Field pheasant hunts on private farm. Guides and dogs available. Overnight accommodations can handle eight. Continental breakfast served.

**WILDCAT SPORTSMAN'S LODGE**
Harrisburg, NE 69345
Phone: 308-672-3687 (Wade Mueller) or
308-631-0617 (Lane Darnall)
www.wildcatsportsmanslodge.com

Chukar, pheasant, sharp-tailed grouse, turkey, coyote, dove, deer, antelope, and prairie dog hunts; sporting clays and lodge that sleeps up to six people. Located in the Wildcat Hills in the Nebraska Panhandle.

*Lodging*
Many motels and bed-and-breakfasts roll out the welcome mat for hunters in Nebraska. To find a hunter-friendly place to stay, consult www.huntthenorth.com/NELodging.html.

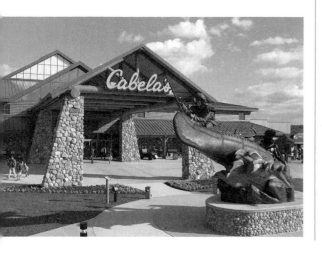

# HERITAGE DESTINATIONS

*Cabela's Headquarters in Sidney, Nebraska*
In 1961 Dick Cabela came up with a plan to sell fishing flies he purchased while at a furniture show in Chicago. When he returned home to Chappell, Nebraska, he ran a classified ad in the Casper, Wyoming, newspaper reading: "12 hand-tied flies for $1." He got one response.

Not discouraged, Cabela came up with a new plan. He rewrote the ad: "FREE Introductory offer! 5 hand-tied Flies . . . 25¢ Postage . . . Handling." And he placed it in several national outdoor magazines. Soon orders began arriving from all around the country.

A mimeographed catalog assembled on the Cabela's kitchen table began to grow in popularity, and Dick's brother joined him. In 1964 the Cabela brothers moved the business to the basement of their father's furniture store. Since then, the business has escalated to where today Cabela's catalogs are shipped to all 50 states and 120 countries. More than 120 million catalogs are mailed each year, with demand continuing to grow—the largest mail-order outdoor sports business in the world.

A visit to any Cabela's store is a sportsman's dream come true. The base camp store for Cabela's is located in Sidney, Nebraska. In addition to offering quality outdoor merchandise, the 85,000-square-foot showroom is an educational and entertainment attraction, featuring museum-quality animal displays, huge aquariums, and trophy animals interacting in realistic re-creations of their natural habitats. Enter here and you won't want to leave.

Open daily: Monday–Saturday, 8:00 A.M.–8:00 P.M.; Sunday, 10:00 A.M.–6:00 P.M.

**CABELA'S HEADQUARTERS**
Sidney, NE 69160
Phone: 308-254-7889
www.cabelas.com/cabelas/en/templates/community/aboutus/retail-detail.jsp?detailedInformationURL=/cabelas/en/content/community/aboutus/retail/retail_stores/sidney/sidney.html

## NORTH DAKOTA

*In 2001 there were 87,000 resident hunters and 52,000 nonresident hunters: 53% went big game hunting, 49% small game, 44% migratory waterfowl and doves; 35% hunted on public lands; 91% hunted on private lands. Hunters pumped $103 million into the state economy. (USFWS)*

### OVERVIEW

In 2005 North Dakota hunters harvested 809,000 pheasants, the best season in 40 years. The best populations are along the southern boundary with South Dakota, which is the pheasant capital of the United States.

If you are looking for a high-percentage deer hunt, North Dakota is definitely a place to consider. The success ratio on bucks is 70%; for does, it's 80%. The total harvest for the year is around 100,000.

This is a breeding area for many species of ducks, as well as a stopover for migratory

waterfowl. In spring, there is a snow goose hunt to help control that population, to prevent further damaging of its Arctic nesting grounds.

Add deer, bighorn sheep, antelope, moose, elk, cougars, bears, grouse, doves, ducks, geese, swans, cranes, Hungarian partridge, predators, bison, snipes, woodcocks, and lots

**NORTH DAKOTA SNAPSHOT**
**PEACE GARDEN STATE**

- **General information:**
  North Dakota Game and Fish Department
  100 North Bismarck Expressway
  Bismarck, ND 58501-5095
  Phone: 701-328-6300
  Email: ndgf@nd.gov
  http://gf.nd.gov/hunting

- **Maps of the state:** http://gf.nd.gov/info/sources .html

- **To report a game violation:** Call 800-472-2121 any time, day or night; rewards range from $100 to $1,000, depending on the crime, for tips that lead to arrests

- **Special Internet directory of lodges, guides, and services for big and small game hunting:** www .northdakotahunting.net

- **Deer population:** 243,750, 32nd in the United States

- **Average deer harvest:** 86,379, 26th in the United States

of rabbits, and you can see why there are almost as many out-of-state hunters in North Dakota as residents.

## DESTINATIONS

*USDA National Forests*

### DAKOTA PRAIRIE GRASSLANDS
Bismarck, ND 58501
Phone: 701-250-4443
www.fs.fed.us/r1/dakotaprairie

The Dakota Prairie Grasslands are composed of the Little Missouri National Grasslands, the Sheyenne National Grasslands, the Cedar River National Grasslands, and the Grand River National Grasslands—1,259,000 acres with many parcels interspersed with private lands.

*U.S. Fish and Wildlife Service*
*National Wildlife Refuges*
There are 19 USFWS NWRs offering hunting in North Dakota. Some are part of complexes.

### ARROWWOOD NATIONAL WILDLIFE REFUGE COMPLEX
Pingree, ND 58476
Phone: 701-285-3341
www.fws.gov/arrowwood

The complex manages all National Wildlife Refuge System lands in nine counties in east-central North Dakota, as well as the Chase Lake Prairie project, which includes 5.5 million acres in 11 counties. The headquarters for the complex is located near Pingree, North Dakota. Big and small game

hunting is offered on the refuges, according to state regulations and specific regulations for each refuge. Check with the main Web site and/or office for details.

### AUDUBON NATIONAL WILDLIFE REFUGE
Coleharbor, ND 58531-9419
Phone: 701-442-5474
www.fws.gov/audubon

Of 14,735 acres in west-central North Dakota, 10,421 acres is Lake Audubon itself. Deer and upland bird hunting. Deer, pheasant, grouse, and partridge hunting permitted according to state and special refuge regulations. For details, see www.fws.gov/audubon/hunt_info_2003.pdf.

### DES LACS NATIONAL WILDLIFE REFUGE
Kenmare, ND 58746
Phone: 701-385-4046
www.fws.gov/jclarksalyer/deslacs

Des Lacs NWR is a 28-mile-long river valley with three natural lakes encompassing 19,500 acres. Snow goose populations here can reach 300,000 birds. Hunting is permitted. Check with refuge for details.

### DEVILS LAKE WETLAND MANAGEMENT DISTRICT
Devils Lake, ND 58301
Phone: 701-662-8611
www.fws.gov/devilslake

The district manages over 45,000 acres of wetlands and other wildlife habitats located on approximately 201 separate Waterfowl

Production Areas (WPAs), Lake Alice National Wildlife Refuge (12,200 acres), Sullys Hill National Game Preserve (1,674 acres), Kelly Slough National Wildlife Refuge (1,867 acres), 11 easement refuges, and 154,000 acres of wetland easements. Hunting and trapping are permitted according to state seasons and federal regulations. Check with refuge headquarters for details.

**J. CLARK SALYER NATIONAL WILDLIFE REFUGE**
Upham, ND 58789
Phone: 701-768-2548
www.fws.gov/jclarksalyer

Located along the Souris River in Bottineau and McHenry counties of north-central North Dakota, the 58,700-acre refuge extends from Canada southward for approximately 45 miles. Hunting according to state seasons and federal regulations is permitted. Check with refuge for details.

**LAKE ALICE NATIONAL WILDLIFE REFUGE**
Devils Lake, ND 58301
Phone: 701-662-8611
www.fws.gov/lakealice

An 11,500-acre refuge of largely reclaimed farmlands located approximately 18 miles northwest of Devils Lake. Deer, upland game birds, migratory waterfowl, and fox hunting according to state and federal regulations. Check with refuge for annual details.

**LONG LAKE NATIONAL WILDLIFE REFUGE**
Moffit, ND 58560
Phone: 701-367-4397
www.fws.gov/longlake

A 22,300-acre refuge located near the community of Moffit in south-central North Dakota. Dove, upland game birds, waterfowl, deer, coyote, and fox hunting. Note: About 3,000 acres on the west end of the refuge are closed to waterfowl hunting. For details on seasons and open areas, see www.fws.gov/longlake/Hunting.HTM.

**LOSTWOOD NATIONAL WILDLIFE REFUGE**
Kenmare, ND 58746
Phone: 701-848-2722
http://lostwood.fws.gov

Located in the heart of the Missouri Coteau region; rolling to steep hills in midgrass prairie, dotted with more than 4,100 wetlands and small clumps of aspens. The largest contiguous block of native grassland managed by the National Wildlife Refuge System in the Prairie Pothole Region. The refuge also contains a 5,577-acre wilderness area. Deer and upland game bird hunting. Waterfowl hunting not permitted on refuge. For details, see http://lostwood.fws.gov/lnwr.htm.

**TEWAUKON NATIONAL WILDLIFE REFUGE**
Cayuga, ND 58013
Phone: 701-724-3598
www.fws.gov/tewaukon

A 8,363-acre refuge located in the Prairie Pothole Region about five miles south of Cayuga. Deer and pheasant hunting only according to state and federal regulations.

**THE HIDE-A-WAY CAMP, LLC**
Mott, ND 58646
Phone: 701-824-2821
www.dakota-web.com/hideaway

On 5,000 privately owned acres to hunt pheasant or grouse. Each party has approximately 300 to 600 acres for hunting and a different area to hunt each day. Completely furnished houses with spa and lodge for accommodations. Bison hunts can also be arranged. Located 100 miles from Bismarck and 70 miles from Dickinson.

**PUNKIN PATCH LODGE AND RANCH**
Sawyer, ND 58781
Phone: 701-624-5499; fax: 701-624-9767
http://punkinpatchranch.com

A 2,500-acre hunting preserve and lodge located east of Minot on the North Dakota prairie. Specialty: released and wild pheasant hunting and whitetail archery hunting,

plus wild turkeys, sharp-tailed grouse, Hungarian partridge, ducks, and geese. A 20-guestroom lodge, pool, private airstrip, and corporate packages.

# HERITAGE DESTINATIONS

*Theodore Roosevelt's Elkhorn Ranch*
The time that Theodore Roosevelt spent in North Dakota as a rancher and hunter had an enormous impact on his passion for conservation. No buildings remain of his Elkhorn Ranch; foundation blocks mark the outline of the 30×60-foot building. A bulletin board is next to the actual site.

To reach the site of the Elkhorn Ranch, take the dirt road going north out of the South Unit. After a drive of roughly 20 miles (32 kilometers), you will be in the vicinity of the ranch site. You must ford the river to reach the actual site. The ranch site is also accessible from the west side of the Little Missouri River. Inquire at the Visitor Center before attempting this trip. Directions via east side or west side are available at the park visitor centers.

**THEODORE ROOSEVELT**
**NATIONAL PARK**
Medora, ND 58645-0007
Phone: 701-623-4466 (South Unit Information) or 701-842-2333 (North Unit Information);
fax: 701-623-4840
www.nps.gov/archive/thro/tr_ranch.htm

## OKLAHOMA

*In 2001 there were 261,000 resident hunters and 20,000 nonresident hunters: 81% went big game hunting, 50% small game, 31% migratory waterfowl and doves; 30% hunted on public lands; 94% hunted on private lands. Hunters pumped $284 million into the state economy. (USFWS)*

### OVERVIEW

Oklahoma has lost 85% of its original bottom-land forests; nonetheless, the rolling hills and rich agricultural lands of Oklahoma produce a decent crop of pheasant; hunters bag about 100,000 ringnecks a year. But over and above that, this is quail country. In 2005 the annual bobwhite harvest was over 850,000, making it one of the best quail hunting states.

By 1900 market hunting had virtually eliminated whitetail deer from Oklahoma. Today the herd is over 500,000, and over 100,000 are harvested every year, about 40% does, and the herd is growing. Many trophy bucks come from this state.

---

**OKLAHOMA SNAPSHOT
SOONER STATE**

- **General information:** Oklahoma Department of Wildlife, www.wildlifedepartment.com/hunting.htm
- **Purchase your licenses online:** www.wildlifedepartment.com/onlinesales/onlinesalesintro.asp
- **Report a poacher to Operation Game Thief:** 800-522-8039; get cash rewards for tips
- **Deer population:** 475,000, 23rd in the United States
- **Average deer harvest:** 97,128, 24th in the United States

---

Other popular game animals include elk, wild turkeys, waterfowl, sandhill cranes, squirrels, rabbits, and light geese (snow, Ross's, and blue), which are hunted in fall and spring. This is a major staging area for waterfowl.

### DESTINATIONS

*State Wildlife Management Areas*

The state manages 64 Wildlife Management Areas. For details, see www.wildlifedepartment.com/wmastate.htm.

*U.S. Army Corps of Engineers*

**TULSA DISTRICT—U.S. ARMY CORPS**
Tulsa, OK 74128-4609
Phone: 918-669-7366 (Tulsa Welcome Center)
www.swt.usace.army.mil/recreat/recreat.htm

The Tulsa District of the U.S. Army Corps of Engineers operates 24 lake-parks that offer various forms of hunting. Hunting information for each lake may be found by checking the lake on the district Web site.

*U.S. Fish and Wildlife Service*
*National Wildlife Refuges*

**DEEP FORK NATIONAL
WILDLIFE REFUGE**
Okmulgee, OK 74447
Phone: 918-756-0815
www.fws.gov/refuges/profiles/index.cfm?id=21592

An 8,696-acre refuge in eastern Oklahoma along the Deep Fork River that currently offers rabbit, squirrel, duck, raccoon, and whitetail deer hunting during state seasons. Contact the refuge for a brochure that explains the hunting programs and regulations.

**LITTLE RIVER NATIONAL WILDLIFE REFUGE**
Broken Bow, OK 74728
Phone: 580-584-6211
www.fws.gov/southwest/refuges/oklahoma/littleriver/index.html

A 15,000-acre wetland in southeast Oklahoma offering deer, turkey, small game, and waterfowl hunting. A refuge permit is required. Special regulations for the refuge. See Web site or contact refuge headquarters for details.

**SALT PLAINS NATIONAL WILDLIFE REFUGE**
Jet, OK 73749
Phone: 580-626-4731
www.fws.gov/southwest/refuges/saltplains

A 32,030-acre refuge in northern Oklahoma that maintains a 1,200-acre area for hunting of ducks, geese, doves, quail, pheasant, and sandhill cranes according to state and federal refuge regulations, with shooting closed at noon. Deer hunting on the refuge is by permit drawing only. For details, see www.fws.gov/southwest/refuges/saltplains/hunting.html.

**SEQUOYAH NATIONAL WILDLIFE REFUGE**
Vian, OK 74962
Phone: 918-773-5252
www.fws.gov/southwest/refuges/oklahoma/sequoyah/index.html

Located in the Ozarks, the refuge permits waterfowl and upland game hunting. For details on maps and regulations, see www.fws.gov/southwest/refuges/oklahoma/sequoyah/hunting.html.

**TISHOMINGO NATIONAL WILDLIFE REFUGE**
Tishomingo, OK 73460
Phone: 580-371-2402
www.fws.gov/southwest/refuges/oklahoma/tishomingo

Located southeast of Oklahoma City and north of the Red River, a 16,464-acre refuge offering deer, turkey, feral hog, upland game, and waterfowl hunting. Refuge permits are required. For details, see www.fws.gov/southwest/refuges/oklahoma/tishomingo/hunting.html.

**WASHITA NATIONAL WILDLIFE REFUGE**
Butler, OK 73625
Phone: 580-664-2205
www.fws.gov/southwest/refuges/oklahoma/washita/hunting.htm

Located in Custer County, Oklahoma, an 8,200-acre refuge that offers hunting for geese, sandhill cranes, quail, rabbits, and deer on the refuge on Wednesdays and weekends during the season. For details, see www.fws.gov/southwest/refuges/oklahoma/washita/hunting.htm.

**WICHITA MOUNTAINS WILDLIFE REFUGE**
Indiahoma, OK 73552
Phone: 580-429-3221

www.fws.gov/southwest/refuges/
wichitamountains

The 59,020-acre refuge located on the mixed-grass prairie west of Oklahoma City and Wichita Falls offers controlled hunts for whitetail deer in November and elk in December. The hunts are managed cooperatively between the refuge and the Oklahoma Department of Wildlife Conservation. Drawings to participate in the hunt are held by the Oklahoma Department of Wildlife Conservation.

*U.S. National Park Service*

**CHICKASAW NATIONAL
RECREATION AREA**
Sculpture, OK 73086
Phone: 580-622-3161 (Headquarters) or
580-622-3165 (Visitor Information)
www.nps.gov/chic

Located on State Highway 177, just south of the town of Sulphur, Oklahoma, this refuge is subject to heavy hunting pressure. Species hunted include deer, feral hogs, doves, waterfowl, upland game, and turkeys. For details on regulations, see www.nps.gov/chic/plan yourvisit/upload/Hunting%20Map_Site %20Bulletin_FY2007.pdf.

*Private Hunting Clubs and Preserves*

**QUAIL HOLLOW GAME FARM**
Lexington, OK 73051-5614
Phone: 405-527-0730; fax: 405-527-4198
www.Quailhollowgamefarm.com

Guided field hunts for bobwhite, Gambel's, valley, and Texas blue-scale quail. Horseback

riding, trap-shooting lessons, trap range, and rifle range available.

**QUAIL RIDGE HUNTING ASSOCIATION**
Del City, OK 73115
Phone: 405-306-1578 or 405-598-9115
(Cabin); fax: 405-670-4313
www.quailridgeok.com

Located south of Shawnee and Tecumseh, guided or nonguided field and European-style quail, pheasant, and chukar hunts and wild whitetail hunts. Five-stand course. Accommodations in log cabins.

**WOODS KENNEL AND FAIRCHASE
HUNT CLUB**
Adair, OK 74330
Phone: 918-785-4593 or 888-682-4004
www.woodskennel.com

On 240 acres, guided and unguided hunts for released upland birds—quail, chukar, and pheasant. Located four miles northwest of Adair, Oklahoma. Call for driving directions. Can stay in a cabin at the preserve.

*General Outfitter Information*
For links to Oklahoma guides and outfitters, see www.worldclassoutdoors.com/oklahoma_ hunting.htm.

## SOUTH DAKOTA

*In 2001 there were 90,000 resident hunters and 119,000 nonresident hunters: 36% went big game hunting, 77% small game, 24% migratory waterfowl and doves; 44% hunted on public* *lands; 84% hunted on private lands. Hunters pumped $223 million into the state economy. (USFWS)*

## OVERVIEW

Almost 20% of the residents of South Dakota are licensed to hunt. But why are there more nonresident than resident hunters in South Dakota? Yes, there are plenty of deer, turkeys, and waterfowl in the state, but the state where the faces of the presidents watch from the side of a cliff at Mount Rushmore is the pheasant hunting capital of the world where hunters bag almost 2 million ring-necks a year, and pheasant hunting alone is worth $135 million to the state.

Pheasant are found primarily in the eastern two-thirds of the state. Deer (mostly whitetails but some mule deer), elk, and ruffed grouse are most common in the Black Hills. Quail are found in the southeast counties.

---

### SOUTH DAKOTA SNAPSHOT
### COYOTE STATE

- **General information:**
  South Dakota Game Fish and Parks
  523 East Capitol Avenue
  Pierre, SD 57501
  Phone: 605-773-3485 (Wildlife Division)
  Email: Wildinfo@state.sd.us
  www.sdgfp.info/Wildlife/hunting/Index.htm,
  http://travelsd.com/hunting

- **Buy licenses online:** www.state.sd.us/
  applications/gf82/Default.htm

- **Poachers hotline (TIPs):** 888-OVERBAG
  (683-7224)

- **Pheasant finder:** www.pheasantfinder.com/
  search.php

- **Deer population:** 170,000, 34th in the United
  States

- **Average deer harvest:** 54,269, 29th in the United
  States

---

Sharp-tailed grouse are found primarily in the western half of the state, while prairie chickens concentrate along the Missouri River, which is also the primary waterfowl flyway area. Merriam's wild turkeys, particularly found in the west, are great runners, especially on the open prairie.

Bonus species here are sandhill cranes, tundra swans, and spring light geese.

---

## FEATURED HUNT

---

### South Dakota Pheasants at Paul Nelson Farm

SHEROL ENGEL

Nothing beats flying for getting there quickly, but there's nothing like a road trip to really make you feel like you're going somewhere. After starting out in the early November morning from our home near Milwaukee, Jeff and I were through Wisconsin and had crossed the Mississippi before noon, on our way to South Dakota for a pheasant hunt with dog trainer Doug Kennedy and our cameraman. Doug had also brought along four of his well-trained Labradors. Once we crossed the South Dakota border, we really began to feel like we were entering the American West. Road signs in the shape of the old American cowboy dotted the highway.

Later that afternoon, we arrived at our destination. Paul Nelson Farm is a working farm that also offers high-quality pheasant hunting on several thousand acres. My first impression was an inviting, luxurious facility with a definite western look.

The Paul Nelson Farm is located 60 miles north of Pierre, the capital of South Dakota. They offer

high-end hunting, four-night/three-day packages, rides to and from the airport, lodging, guides, dogs, services, food, and drinks. They have a sporting clays course and shooting instructors as well. The farm can accommodate around 40 guests, and you can have the place exclusively if you book at least 25 people. Paul Nelson Farm has prime pheasant habitat. You can hunt on about 13,000 acres on which they have dug numerous ponds and wells, some as deep as 2,200 feet. They also have planted food plots that have created habitat not only for pheasant but also for many other animals, such as deer, ducks, geese, and many nongame species.

Having learned all about Paul Nelson Farm's amenities, we wanted to try out the sporting clays course before it got dark. This was loads of fun and a good way to prepare for the morning's hunt.

As the day neared its end, we took a walk outside. Just a stone's throw from the lodge, deer came to take a drink from the nearby pond. With the reflection of the pink sunset in the water, watching them drink made the world come to a peaceful stop. It was exceptional, as was visiting with our friends and the other hunters at the farm.

It had been a full day of traveling and experiences. Everyone was tired and more than ready for bed, including the dogs. We felt right at home in the comfortable and homey room that was to be our sleeping quarters for the next several days.

During the night, the temperature dropped, and it snowed a bit. Even though Paul Nelson Farm has many excellent dogs, when I bird hunt with Doug Kennedy, we always bring along some of his well-trained Labs. Doug is both a trainer and a breeder. In fact, his dog Wiz sired our own Lab, Bee. Doug has been raising and training Labradors for many years and has won numerous field awards. His training style is "soft and quiet," and it is a pleasure to observe Doug and his dogs in the field.

Our dog Bee had a shoulder injury and could

not accompany us on this trip, so Wiz was as close as we could get to having our own dog along. Quite a few hens flew up, which provided no shooting opportunity but is a good sign for the future pheasant population. It wasn't long until a few roosters were up, and we were enjoying this brisk day in the field. Even though the temperature was in the mid-20s, it was great to be out here hunting pheasants.

Watching well-trained dogs is one of the main reasons that I enjoy pheasant hunting. Wiz had done an outstanding job and was certainly enjoying himself in the field, but the other dogs were eager to have their turn. So we went back to the truck and traded Wiz for Murphy and Dolly.

Almost as soon as we started into the field, the dogs were into birds. "Rooster," Doug called loudly. Doug took the long shot with skillful accuracy, followed by a great retrieve. We were hunting

late-season pheasant, and they had become so wary that they would often flush wild as we walked the fields. We even managed to flush an occasional jackrabbit.

In the short grass at the end of the field, we spotted lots of roosters running out of the corn field into the cut field. It was comical watching them run like crazy, but they weren't dummies. They were smart enough to know they were better off running than taking flight. To counter this, the guys walked the field while I waited at the field's opposite end. I was rewarded with several nice roosters; one was a long shot, but with the aid of good dogs, I had my bird and felt a great sense of accomplishment.

Back at the truck, I noticed that one of the dogs, Murphy, had a cut on her leg. One thing Jeff and I always carry in our field first-aid kit is EMT Gel. I applied some to her cut, and she was back in business.

After a wonderful day of wing shooting, we were looking forward to another magnificent meal. Grilled steaks with whole mushrooms, potatoes, vegetables, and a superb angel food cake smothered in berries with whipped cream. The dogs enjoyed a well-deserved meal as well.

A good night's sleep was all we needed to be ready for more pheasant hunting. And in good pheasant country like this, you don't have to wait long.

*See Section D for a special recipe.*

Contact:

**PAUL NELSON FARM**

Gettysburg, SD 57442-0183

Phone: 605-765-2469; fax: 605-765-9648

www.paulnelsonfarm.com

## DESTINATIONS

*General Information*

There are nearly 5 million acres of public lands in South Dakota, with 21 federal areas allowing hunting: Black Hills National Forest, 8 National Wildlife Refuges, 6 Bureau of Reclamation sites, 1 Bureau of Land Management area, and 5 U.S. Army Corps of Engineers Projects.

An interactive public lands guide for hunting locations in South Dakota that covers all state and federal lands can be found online at www.sdgfp.info/Wildlife/Public-Lands/PubLand.htm. A South Dakota state hunting atlas can also be found at www.sdgfp.info/Publications/Atlas/Index.htm.

*Private Hunting Clubs and Preserves*

A complete list of licensed shooting preserves in South Dakota can be found at www.sdgfp .info/Wildlife/hunting/Preserves/Pheasant Sources.htm.

**BIG BEND RANCH HUNTING**
Aberdeen, SD 57401
Phone: 800-888-0435
www.bigbendranch.com

Pheasant, Hungarian partridge, and fall Canada geese and ducks within a 30-minute drive of Pierre, located on the Missouri River. Overnight lodge, meals, guides, and package deals.

**BROKEN ARROW FARMS**
Pierre, SD 57501
Phone: 605-945-2642 or 877-945-2642; fax: 605-224-1421
www.huntbrokenarrow.com

Located just outside of Pierre, 1,200 acres for pheasant, plus waterfowl and fishing options. Lodging, meals, dogs, and skeet available. All hunts guided.

**CARR FARM PHEASANT HUNTING**
St. Lawrence, SD 57373
Phone: 605-853-3330 or 605-853-2679; fax: 605-853-2894
www.carrpheasants.com

Pheasant, sharp-tailed grouse, prairie chickens, Hungarian partridge, and doves on 1,200 acres of family farm located near St. Lawrence. Lodging, kennels, dogs, guides, trapshooting, and meals.

**CIRCLE CE RANCH**
Gregory, SD 57533
Phone: 765-230-0396 or 727-772-8669
www.circlecehunting.com

Pheasant on 3,000 acres, with meals, fishing, dogs, kennels, guides, and lodging. Located in Butte Mountains area northeast of Winner.

**CIRCLE H RANCH**
Sioux Falls, SD 57108
Phone: 605-731-5050
www.circlehranch.com

Pheasant on thousands of acres of working cattle ranch. Sporting clays, trail rides, fishing, canoeing, and many more options. Lodge and meals included in packages. Corporate hunts available. Located in south-central South Dakota near Gregory.

**DAKOTA RIDGE HUNTING**
Clear Lake, SD 57226-5106
Phone: 605-874-2823
www.dakotaridgehunting.com

Pheasant on over 2,000-acre farm near Waterton and Clear Lake in eastern South Dakota. Packages include meals, lodging, round of clays, kennels, guides, and dogs.

**E CIRCLE E HUNTING FARMS**
Meckling, SD 57044
Phone: 605-624-2800; fax: 605-624-2810
www.ecirclee.com

A Cabela's-affiliated hunting farm offering pheasant with possible combinations with waterfowl, doves, and spring snow geese hunts, including corporate outings. Spacious lodge, meals, trap, and skeet range.

**K & M HUNTING**
Plankinton, SD 57368
Phone: 605-942-7516; fax: 605-942-7668
www.huntKandM.com

Located in Plankinton, close to Mitchell and near Sioux Falls, K & M offers pheasant hunting packages on over 1,000 acres with guides, dogs, accommodations, and home-cooked meals.

**OAK TREE LODGE**
Clark, SD 57225
Phone: 605-532-3335
www.Oaktreefarm.com

A Cabela's certified destination located 22 miles west of Mitchell, offering over 7,000 acres for pheasant, waterfowl, and deer hunting, plus lodging, meals, guides, dogs, pro shop, and trapshooting. Hosts the annual Clark County Pheasant Championship.

**PHEASANT HAVEN**
Sisseton, SD 57262
Phone: 605-698-7079 or 605-698-7909
www.pheasanthuntsd.com

A 1,280-acre hunting preserve located in the far northeast corner of the state offering pheasant hunts, guides, and dogs.

**REDLIN FARMS**
Summitt, SD 57266
Phone: 605-882-3313
www.redlinfarms.com

Located in Codington County north of Watertown, 4,000 acres offering hunting for traditional and preserve pheasant; also wild sharp-tailed grouse, Hungarian partridge, waterfowl, swans, turkeys, buffalos, and deer, plus summer fishing and ice fishing. Lodging, food, many amenities.

**SHATTUCK HUNTING SERVICE**
Gregory, SD 57533
Phone: 605-835-8129
www.shattuckhunting.com

Located in the southeast corner of the state near Winner, offering pheasant hunts with food and lodging, guides, and dogs.

**STUKEL'S UPLAND ADVENTURES**
Gregory, SD 57533
Phone: 605-835-8941
www.stukels.com

Located in south-central South Dakota, over 10,000 acres for pheasant, turkeys, and Hungarian partridge. Guides, dogs, lodging, food, and sporting clays offered.

**THUNDERSTIK LODGE**
Chamberlain, SD 57325
Phone: 605-734-5106 or 800-734-5168
www.thunderstiklodge.com

An Orvis-endorsed wing-shooting lodge located in central South Dakota's "Golden Triangle" offering pheasant, Hungarian partridge, and waterfowl hunts on thousands of acres of land along the Missouri River. Lodging, gourmet food, guides, and dogs. Also arranges for upland bird hunts in Argentina and Mexico, big game hunts in Canada and Alaska, and fishing in Alaska and Costa Rica.

**VALLERY HIGH PLAINS GAME RANCH**
Nisland, SD 57762
Phone: 605-257-2365
www.highplainsgameranch.com

Located north of the Black Hills, along the Belle Fourche River, hunts for pheasant, Hungarian partridge, gray partridge, and sharp-tailed grouse, plus antelope, whitetails, and turkeys. Meals, lodging, and guides. Youth hunt free with parent or guardian.

*Guides Outfitters Information*
A complete list of guides and outfitters can be found at

**SOUTH DAKOTA PROFESSIONAL GUIDES AND OUTFITTERS ASSOCIATION**
Aberdeen, SD 57401
Phone: 605-280-3169
www.angelfire.com/sd/guides

# HERITAGE DESTINATIONS

*Winner, South Dakota, Pheasant Capital of America*
In the 2000 census, Winner, South Dakota, the county seat of Tripp County in south-central South Dakota, halfway between Sioux Falls and Rapid City, had a population of 3,137 people and more pheasant than you can count. Regarding the Winner area, Mark Herwig, editor of *Pheasants Forever* magazine, said: "I've seen flocks of pheasants a half mile long and extending some 20 feet thick flying from the corn to roost in the abundant grasslands at dusk!"

The hunting takes place mostly on private ranches and Indian trust lands. For details, see www.winnersd.org/huntingguide.html.

On opening weekend of the South Dakota pheasant season, which is about October 15, people from all around the United States and the world flock to Winner, which creates a festival, including a banquet sponsored by *Pheasants Forever*, to welcome the hunters.

Winner is also a hotspot for wild turkeys (with gobblers reaching 25 pounds), antelope, and many other species of wild game.

**WINNER CHAMBER OF COMMERCE**
Winner, SD 57580
Phone: 605-842-1533;
fax: 605-842-1512
Email: thechamber@gwtc.net
www.winnersd.org

# Southwest

## ARIZONA

*In 2001 there were 119,000 resident hunters and 28,000 nonresident hunters: 55% went big game hunting, 49% small game, 42% waterfowl; 82% hunted on public lands; 32% hunted on private lands. Hunters pumped $212 million into the state economy. (USFWS)*

### OVERVIEW

There is an enormous diversity of game in Arizona as desert and mountains come together, offering very differing habitats. Big game species include antelope, javelinas, black bears, Merriam's turkeys, buffalo, mountain lions, desert bighorn sheep, mule deer, elk, and whitetail deer. Popular small game species are band-tailed pigeons, quail, blue grouse, sandhill cranes, cottontail rabbits, jackrabbits, tree squirrels, mourning doves, white-winged doves, and pheasant, plus bobcats, coyotes, foxes, skunks, and a good wintering migration of ducks and geese.

---

**ARIZONA SNAPSHOT**
**GRAND CANYON STATE**

- **General information on hunting in Arizona:** www.gf.state.az.us/h_f/hunting.shtml

- **Arizona shooting ranges:** The Arizona Fish and Game Department operates several shooting ranges to keep in shape; see www.gf.state.az.us/outdoor_recreation/shooting_sports.shtml

- **Deer population:** 85,000, 32nd in the United States

- **Average deer harvest:** 4,256, 37th in the United States

---

### DESTINATIONS

*USDA National Forests*

Hunting according to state regulations is legal on most of the 20.6 million acres of national forest lands in Arizona. National forests in the state are:

**APACHE-SITGREAVES NATIONAL FOREST**
Springerville, AZ 85938
Phone: 928-333-4301
www.fs.fed.us/r3/asnf

Located in east-central Arizona, 2 million acres with 450 miles of rivers and streams; elevations from 3,500 up to 11,500 feet. Includes the Mogollon Rim and eight cold-water lakes.

## COCONINO NATIONAL FOREST
Flagstaff, AZ 86001
Phone: 928-527-3600
www.fs.fed.us/r3/coconino/contact/index .shtml

Located in northern Arizona, 1.8 million acres with elevations to 12,643 feet.

## CORONADO NATIONAL FOREST
Tucson, AZ, USA 85701
Phone: 520-388-8300
www.fs.fed.us/r3/coronado

Located in southern Arizona, 1.7 million acres with elevations from 3,000 to 10,000 feet, including eight wilderness areas.

## KAIBAB NATIONAL FOREST
Williams, AZ 86046
Phone: 928-635-8200;
fax: 928-635-8208
www.fs.fed.us/r3/kai

Located in northwest Arizona, 1.6 million acres, with elevations from 5,500 to 10,418 feet; includes four wilderness areas. The Kaibab Plateau is the area where we learned that removal of predators for deer results in a population explosion that destroys habitat; the excess deer cause a long-term decline in the carrying capacity of the area.

## PRESCOTT NATIONAL FOREST
Prescott, AZ 86303
Phone: 928-443-8000
www.fs.fed.us/r3/prescott

Located in central Arizona, 1.25 million acres including eight wilderness areas.

**TONTO NATIONAL FOREST**
Phoenix, AZ 85006
Phone: 602-225-5200; fax: 602-225-5295
www.fs.fed.us/r3/tonto/home.shtml

Located in central Arizona, 3 million acres with elevations from 1,300 to 8,000 feet including eight wilderness areas.

For more information about the national forests of Arizona, contact:

**USDA FOREST SERVICE—**
**SOUTHWESTERN REGION**
Albuquerque, NM 87102
Phone: 505-842-3292
www.fs.fed.us/r3/about/aboutus.shtml

*U.S. Bureau of Land Management*
The Bureau of Land Management (BLM) in Arizona administers 12.2 million surface acres of public lands and another 17.5 million subsurface acres within the state. Hunting is permitted in most areas, but permits are required for some wilderness areas such as Paria Canyon–Vermilion Cliffs Wilderness Area, Coyote Buttes, and Aravaipa Canyon Wilderness Area.

**BUREAU OF LAND MANAGEMENT**
Arizona State Office
Phoenix, AZ 85004-4427
Phone: 602-417-9200
www.blm.gov/az

*Upland Game Bird Hunting Preserves*

**DESERT PHEASANT RECREATION**
Coolidge, AZ 85228
Phone: 520-723-7234 or 520-709-1019
http://pheasantrec.com

Located between Phoenix and Tucson, Desert Pheasant Recreation has operated as a shooting preserve since 1986 for field hunts of pheasant, chukar, and quail from either a desert habitat or farm fields. Memberships or day hunts. Overnight RV camping available. Driven hunts can be arranged. All hunts must be scheduled. Free dove hunts for members.

## HIGH DESERT HUNT CLUB
Mayer, AZ 86333
Phone: 928-632-7226; fax: 928-632-4418
www.highdeserthuntclub.org

On 5,000 acres, located one hour north of Phoenix near I-17 and Highway 69 on the Agua Fria River. Pheasant, chukar, and sporting clays. Reservations required.

### Safari Club International Wildlife Museum
In addition to an outstanding collection of displays of wildlife from around the globe, the museum has an active outreach program for teachers and youth group leaders. SCI also has portable "Sensory Safaris" for blind children. The children have a chance to touch elegantly mounted animals from around the world.

## SAFARI CLUB INTERNATIONAL FOUNDATION
Tucson, AZ 85745-9490
Phone: 520-620-1220
www.sci-foundation.org

# HERITAGE DESTINATIONS

### White Mountain Apache Tribe
Legendary trophy elk hunts in the spectacular White Mountains of northern Arizona on the White Mountain Apache Reservation. Black bear and trout fishing also available. Don't miss visiting historic Fort Apache while you're there.

## WHITE MOUNTAIN APACHE TRIBE
Whiteriver, AZ 85941
Phone: 877-338-9628
www.wmat.nsn.us

### Navajo Big Game Adventures—Hunt the Navajo Nation Lands
The Navajo reservation is the largest Indian reservation in the Four Corners Area, where Colorado, New Mexico, Utah, and Arizona come together. A member of the Navajo Guides Association, Navajo Big Game Adventures offers trophy desert big horn sheep, mule deer, and elk hunts on Navajo Nation Lands and works with hunters for archery, muzzleloader, and rifle hunts. Specialty: early and late mule deer hunting.

Contact:

## NAVAJO BIG GAME ADVENTURES
Navajo, NM 87328
Phone: 505-777-2630
www.wasetatrophyhunting.com

## NEW MEXICO

*In 2001 there were 105,000 resident hunters and 26,000 nonresident hunters: 86% went big game hunting, 29% small game, 26% migratory waterfowl and doves; 94% hunted on public lands; 27% hunted on private lands. Hunters pumped $153 million into the state economy. (USFWS)*

### OVERVIEW
It's hard to find a state with more diversity of game species than New Mexico. In the

"Land of Enchantment," you can shoot the grand slam of quail—bobwhite, scaled, Gambel's, and Mearns. New Mexico also offers hunting for sandhill cranes, blue grouse, and waterfowl, as well as plenty of squirrels and rabbits. But let's face it: 85% of the hunters pursue big game, and for good reason. Desert bighorn sheep, Rocky Mountain bighorn sheep, elk, antelope, bears, cougars, and deer (mule, whitetail, and coues) are all found here in abundance on millions of acres of public lands.

## FEATURED HUNT

### New Mexico Quail

CRAIG SPRINGER*

Teddy Roosevelt would be impressed. No, it's not that the sprawling and slightly undulating flat grasslands of southeastern New Mexico are encompassed in Roosevelt County. He would have loved the big sky here, the expansive open space only sliced now and again by a ribbon of a blacktop road rarely traveled, or a slim, long line of a barbwire fence separating pasture. Moreover, he'd be taken aback by the sheer number of quail—swarms of them, really—bobwhite and scaled quail that paradoxically survive a harsh and unforgiving land of little rain and lots of wind.

It's a place of legendary dust storms that push and pull dunes that offer about the only relief in the topography. Whatever it is, if it's not nailed down, it will blow away. The horizon is so distant that if you stood on a windmill, you could see so far as to see

---

**NEW MEXICO SNAPSHOT**
**LAND OF ENCHANTMENT**

- **General information:** www.wildlife.state.nm.us/recreation/hunting/index.htm
- **Guide and outfitter information:** www.wildlife.state.nm.us/enforcement/guide_outfitter/index.htm
- **Report a poacher:** 800-432-GAME; rewards up to $750 for tips that lead to arrests
- **In 2005–2006** 10,039 deer were harvested in New Mexico

the back of your head. Cattle ranchers and peanut farmers can eke out a living.

Across the landscape, you can spy here and there some of the remains, the brown hull of an old house or outbuilding of a farm or ranch that failed as it tilts eastward from incessant west winds and pulled by the gravity of time. Near the town of Pep, New Mexico, and I use the term "town" loosely, but it does have a post office, a few pump jacks pull oil and gas from the bowels of the earth. They bob methodically up and down like a big sluggish blue jay gleaning bugs off the ground.

The Hay Ranch is south of Pep, on the highway to Lovington. It's composed of 50 sections of land—that's 50 square miles—bigger than a single 36-section township in Ohio. George Hay is a third-generation Roosevelt County rancher, tall, lanky, salt-and-pepper hair, and a little hunched over from his 80-some years of ranch life. He speaks with a Texan's draw, some of the words played out a little longer than folks say elsewhere. Hay's ranch operation is less than 15 miles from the Texas state line, and many of his neighbors' ancestors were Texans by birth. Hay said that his granddad had wanderlust in Ohio—and that the young man having itchy feet had something to do with his coming to New Mexico. The ranch has been around since 1916. Winter wheat and cow pasture, that's what grow here. And, oh, yes, there's the ancillary crop: quail.

I'm walking behind Candy, a high-strung bundle of bird dog nerves, a Pudlepointer, an unusual breed of German stock. Brown and flat coated, she has enough heart for the hunt for two dogs. She's well suited for desert quail hunting. Alongside me is her owner, Bob King, who also owns the Santa Fe Guiding Company. We are walking under a skullcap dome of powdered blue graded to almost white on the horizons, broken only by a spurious bank of nim-

bus clouds miles away to the east. I silently hope to myself that it's raining over there. My 20-gauge rests over my shoulder in the wide-open shinnery oak flats. The oaks clip my brush pants at the bottom of my shins and tag my knees at their apex. They don't get much bigger than that and yet throw off a mast as big as, if not bigger than, acorns from any other large towering oak species. The shinnery oaks look misfitted, out of place, with such fat acorns, like a clumsy, gangly teenager looks in a poorly fitted tux. An ancient windmill that probably hasn't pulled water out of the ground since the Kennedy presidency has the word "Chicago" stenciled on galvanized metal. Tumbleweeds and debris pile up against the wreckage of the mill, and the metal stock tank has collapsed.

The Hay Ranch, and a gore of land along the state line southward, is the only place in New Mexico where you can potentially bump up scaled quail and bobwhite quail from the same cover. And speaking of same, an easterner might be taken aback at what bobwhite quail will use for cover in this harsh place. You won't find raspberry thickets and hedgerows and hawthorns—big knobs of grasses and forbs. Weedy draws of the eastern uplands are nonexistent here. The smallest of hummocks and swales, the bunch grasses, mesquite, and yucca provide cover the birds need from the wind, northern harriers, bird dogs, and shotgunners like us.

Candy ranges out ahead of us, quartering between yuccas and cactus and bunch grasses. King gives a trill to hold her close enough. She's intent on finding birds. "She's birdy," said King. "She's birdy," he says again, a little louder, as her quartering tightens to a zigzag. "Whoa, Candy-girl," King commands. She's locked up tight like a spring; a skinny pencil of a tail wiggles nervously. King walks in on the point, an amorphous mass of yucca, tumbleweeds, oaks, and spindly mesquite trees. You can hear a peep or two from the nervousness of the birds as they rustle the brush and leaves. Then the exploding whirr of wings in the wind—a mixed covey of bobwhites and scalies. They scatter in all directions from our ankles, getting enough lift to fly low and quick enough to make airspace now. I get a remedial lesson in the predator–prey relationship, and reeducated on why prey animals aren't so easily had by predators.

With the mass of quail getting up, even knowing it was coming, I still wasn't ready. I still get a start every time on the flush. And with so many birds to look at all at once going away from me in no

organized fashion, your attention has to get focused on a single to be a good bird hunter. In fact, in that covey of some 50-plus birds, we dropped 3. Perhaps the chaotic disorder of the flush is nature's splendid order that keeps bird hunting challenging despite a good smoothbore and a great dog.

It's no accident the Hay Ranch is flush with quail; wild birds, nature's bounty. Hay has a conservation ethic, and he is rooted to the ranch. He is motivated to do something for the birds, and "the birds" also includes a little grouse on the prairie, the lesser prairie chicken. Chicken numbers are down, to say the least; you can't hunt them. But that's something King and Hay would like to see changed. Toward that end, the two men have improved the bird habitat by fencing off small parcels of land to keep cattle and pronghorn antelope out of the protected grasses. But there's a value-added component to the small fenced-off plots—they have precious water.

"There's nothing here that water won't help," said King. "Water is the key element to habitat improvement; there's the water we wanted to put on the ground, but we're also adding food and some cover." And toward that end, King put 48 hours on a Ditch-Witch straight from an old ranch house well. He buried 11 miles of hosing to get water to the fenced-off areas. There's a dozen of them so far, and the quail and lesser prairie chickens have responded well. It's no exaggeration, with my day behind the dog, we witnessed thousands of quail, both species, and at least 100 lesser prairie chickens. These grasslands look sparse and unyielding, but the loose sands, moving continuously, have fresh tracks of birds and mammals most everywhere.

Bird numbers are naturally cyclic. They respond to the prevailing environment. The ups and downs of desert quail are well tied to moisture and in particular to when it arrives. It's no news that bobwhite numbers aren't what they used to be. Bobwhite quail were never a dominant species in southeast New Mexico, but things have been worse than what they are today. Biologist J. Stokley Ligon wrote in his 1927 report to the New Mexico State Game Commission on the status of bobwhite quail:

> The birds evidently were most numerous in the extreme southeast corner of the state and in the Canadian River Valley, near Logan. Today there is hardly more than a trace of the native birds in this habitat. Their disappearance is wholly due to the destruction of ground cover—weeds and grasses. I was able to learn of three birds having been seen in the sandhills east of Portales, near the Texas line, in April 1926, and a few have managed to exist along the lower Dry Cimarron in Union County. Much of the eastern and southern sections of the state is suitable . . . to the bob-white, but nowhere does favorable protective cover exist continuously. . . . [S]uch areas are exposed to grazing abuse.

King said he is motivated to put hunters on birds in a wild place—to let them see things that they would never see or do otherwise.

"It's wide open and uncluttered—you can walk forever," said King. "It's far different than most any other place; I feel alive out here."

Hunters are optimists, forward looking. They have to be. Conservation and hunting go together, because conservation is inherently an optimistic investment in the future. The number of chickens and quail I saw were some measure; the work on the Hay Ranch is measurably paying dividends with the private-land stewardship and sweat equity of a rancher and a guide.

**BOB KING, SANTA FE GUIDING COMPANY**
Santa Fe, NM 87508

Phone: 505-466-7964
www.santafeguidingco.com

*Outdoor enthusiast Craig Springer wrote this feature.*

---

## DESTINATIONS

One could write an entire book about public lands open to hunting in New Mexico, as there are over 20 federal lands with millions of acres that are open to hunting, much of it rugged country. This is one reason why guides and outfitters are so important. A brief look at some of the biggest areas.

*U.S. Bureau of Land Management*

**CABEZON PEAK RECREATION AREA**
Albuquerque, NM 87107
Phone: 505-761-8700
www.nm.blm.gov/recreation/albuquerque/
cabezon_peak.htm

Hunting is permitted according to state seasons and regulations.

**EL MALPAIS NATIONAL CONSERVATION AREA**
Albuquerque, NM 87107
Phone: 505-761-8700
www.nm.blm.gov/recreation/albuquerque/
el_malpais_nca.htm

A 263,000-acre area adjoining El Malpais National Monument that includes two wilderness areas and many dramatic canyons. Hunting is allowed according to state regulations.

## FORT STANTON RECREATION AREA

Roswell, NM 88201-2019

Phone: 505-627-0272

www.nm.blm.gov/recreation/roswell/fort_
stanton_acec.htm

Fort Stanton Recreation Area is composed of 24,000 acres of BLM lands within the old Fort Stanton Military Reservation in the foothills of the Sierra Blanca Mountains in southern New Mexico. Mountain streams, rolling hills, mesas, and open bottomlands. Hunting permitted according to state regulations.

## GILA LOWER BOX CANYON

Las Cruces, NM 88005-3370

Phone: 505-525-4300

www.nm.blm.gov/recreation/las_cruces/
gila_lower_box_canyon.htm

Located 20 miles north of Lordsburg, New Mexico, this area is thickly vegetated as a river runs through it. Hunting permitted according to state regulations.

## IGNACIO CHAVEZ SPECIAL
## MANAGEMENT AREA

Albuquerque, NM 87107

Phone: 505-761-8700

www.nm.blm.gov/recreation/albuquerque/
ignacio_chavez_sma.htm

Almost 50,000 acres of solitude at elevations up to 8,400 feet. Includes the Ignacio Chavez Wilderness Study Area (33,300 acres) and the Chamisa Wilderness Study Area (13,700 acres). Popular hunting area according to state regulations.

## NEGRO CANYON RECREATION AREA

Farmington, NM 87401

Phone: 505-599-8900

www.recreation.gov/detail.jsp?ID=1846

Remote area accessible only by boat from Navajo Lake. Hunting permitted according to state regulations.

## WILD RIVERS RECREATION AREA

Taos, NM 87571-5983

Phone: 505-758-8851

www.nm.blm.gov/recreation/taos/wild_
rivers_rec_area.htm

Rugged 800-feet-deep gorge of the Rio Grande and Red rivers. Hunting according to state regulations is permitted.

### USDA National Forests

General contact information for all national forest lands in New Mexico:

## USDA FOREST SERVICE—
## SOUTHWESTERN REGION

Albuquerque, NM 87102

Phone: 505-842-3292

www.fs.fed.us/r3/about/aboutus.shtml

National forests of New Mexico:

*Carson.* Northern New Mexico; 1.5 million acres; elevations from 6,000 to 13,161 feet; six wilderness areas.

*Cibola.* Central New Mexico; 1.6 million acres; elevations from 5,000 to 11,000 feet; four wilderness areas; three national grasslands (northeastern New Mexico, West Oklahoma, and Northwest Texas).

*Gila.* Southwestern New Mexico; 3.3 million acres; elevations to 11,000 feet; three wilderness areas; sixth largest forest in the continental United States.

*Lincoln.* South-central and eastern New Mexico; 1.1 million acres; elevations from 4,000 to 11,500 feet; two wilderness areas; birthplace of Smokey the Bear.

*Santa Fe.* North-central New Mexico; 1.6 million acres; elevations from 5,300 to 13,103 feet; four wilderness areas.

*U.S. Fish and Wildlife Service*
*National Wildlife Refuges*

## BITTER LAKE NATIONAL WILDLIFE REFUGE
Roswell, NM 88201
Phone: 505-622-6755
www.fws.gov/southwest/refuges/newmex/
bitterlake/index.html

Bitter Lake National Wildlife Refuge is located about 10 miles northeast of Roswell, in Chaves County. Straddling the Pecos River, waterfowl, sandhill crane, quail, dove, pheasant, and deer hunting are available at the refuge. Contact the refuge for updated hunting regulations and season dates at 505-622-6755 or by emailing steve_alvarez@fws.gov.

## BOSQUE DEL APACHE NATIONAL WILDLIFE REFUGE
Socorro, NM 87801
Phone: 505-835-1828
www.fws.gov/southwest/refuges/newmex/
bosque

This 57,191-acre refuge straddles the Rio Grande Valley in Socorro County, New Mexico. Small game and big game, including oryx, is allowed here. See hunting brochure at www.fws.gov/southwest/refuges/newmex/bosque/wildlife.html.

Every November, the Festival of the Cranes to honor the thousands of sandhill cranes that winter here—www.friendsofthe-bosque.org/crane.

## LAS VEGAS NATIONAL WILDLIFE REFUGE
Las Vegas, NM 87701
Phone: 505-425-3581
www.fws.gov/southwest/refuges/newmex/
lasvegas/index.html

Situated on a high plateau, this 8,672-acre refuge is composed of native grasslands, croplands, marshes, ponds, timbered canyons, and streams that provide habitat for over 270 species of birds. Hunting for doves and Canada geese in season.

## SAN ANDREAS NATIONAL WILDLIFE REFUGE
Las Cruces, NM 88004
Phone: 505-382-5047
www.fws.gov/southwest/refuges/newmex/
sanandres/index.html

Located approximately 30 miles northeast of Las Cruces and encompassing 57,215 acres of the southern portion of the San Andres Mountain range. The only hunting currently allowed is population reduction hunts for oryx, a species of antelope originally found in southern Africa. This animal was introduced onto White Sands Missile Range in the late 1960s, and its numbers have grown substantially, resulting in habitat destruction for species like antelope and bighorn sheep.

**SEVILLETA NATIONAL
WILDLIFE REFUGE**
Socorro, NM 87801
Phone: 505-864-4021
www.fws.gov/southwest/refuges/newmex/
sevilleta

Sevilleta NWR supports four major ecological habitats, encompasses two mountain ranges, and contains stretches of the largest river in the state. Only hunting for doves, light geese, coots, and ducks on a small portion of the refuge. For hunting regulations for the refuge, see www.fws.gov/southwest/refuges/newmex/sevilleta/hunting.html.

*Private Hunting Clubs and Preserves*

**THE LODGE AT CHAMA**
Chama, NM 87520
Phone: 505-756-2133; fax: 505-756-2519
www.ranchweb.com/chama

Elegant 36,000-acre dude ranch at 8,000 feet, one and a half hours northwest of Taos and two hours north of Santa Fe in Chama. Offers big game hunts for deer and elk, wing shooting for pheasant and chukar, and trophy trout fly-fishing.

## NEVADA

*In 2001 there were 42,000 resident hunters and 5,000 nonresident hunters: 52% went big game hunting, 23% small game, 29% migratory waterfowl and doves; 95% hunted on public lands; 28% hunted on private lands. Hunters pumped $134 million into the state economy. (USFWS)*

**OVERVIEW**
Nevada, seemingly an arid high desert sprinkled with occasional casinos and human wildlife, is actually a state rich in wildlife: mule deer, Rocky Mountain elk, three subspecies of bighorn sheep, pronghorn antelope, mountain lions, and mountain goats, plus upland game birds including chukar partridge, California and Gamble's quail, ruffed grouse, blue grouse, and doves. Cougar tags are available over the counter.

And there are surprisingly good waterfowl hunting places with water coming from snowmelt mountain streams that collects into rivers, lakes, and even marshes in the valley floors.

Hunting is popular here also because over 90% of the state is managed by the federal government and open to hunting according to state regulations.

Rising up from the sagebrush desert in western Nevada in an 80-mile-long chain just south of Elko and beginning with Secret Pass is the Ruby Mountains, named for blood-red garnets that early settlers found here.

The highest point in the Rubies is 11,387 feet Ruby Dome, which gets a fair amount of snow in the winter, as do many of the other peaks of this range. The snowfall provides sufficient water for pine and aspen trees; streams cascading down out of the hills form rivers and marshes that support a decent flight of huntable waterfowl including ducks, snipes, geese, and swans (one allowed per year).

There are only a handful of states that allow hunting for swans, but if you are looking for something *really* special, at higher elevations in the Rubies there is a popula-

tion of Himalayan snowcocks. The Himalayan snowcock is a large member of the pheasant family, gray in color with a white neck and face. The birds can reach over 28 inches long. Males and females are similar in color.

The Himalayan snowcock was originally found in the mountain ranges of southern Eurasia, from the Caucasus to the Himalayas and western China, and was introduced here from Pakistan. Over there, the popula-

tions are hanging on but not abundant. In Nevada, the birds are thriving.

Snowcocks roost up high (10,000 feet or higher) at night and then fly down in the mornings to feed on seeds, plants, and insects. During the day they gradually work their way back up to the evening roosting sites.

Snowcocks may be hunted in Elko Management Units 101, 102, and 103 and in Unit 103 of White Pine County. As you might

expect, you should be in good shape. People hunt snowcocks like chukar or sharptails.

The snowcock season runs from early September through the end of November, with the limit two birds per day. Open to nonresidents, you must have an upland game stamp and a snowcock hunting free-use per-

mit, which is available online or from the Department of Wildlife Eastern Region Office, 60 Youth Center Road, Elko, NV 89801, 775-777-2300. Permits can also be emailed to hunters from the Elko office.

---

 ## FEATURED HUNT

---

### Hunting Wild Chukar

JAKE BUSHEY*

The dogs moved along the ridge top, their noses full of chukar. Quartering into the wind, their cast became shorter and shorter as they narrowed the search and finally began to creep toward the quarry as if an invisible string was pulling them.

First Dot froze, and then Bug honored her point a short distance behind. The two little Brittanys looked like orange and white statues, with Skedaddle Mountain as a backdrop. The sight thrilled me, even though I've seen it thousands of times over the last 30 years. Suddenly the air was filled with chukar. I could see their red beaks and legs, the black bars across their chest, and gray wings beating against the air as they sailed down the canyon.

I picked out one bird and tried to get the bead of the Benelli ahead of it. I fired, was behind it, but caught up with the second shot, and the bird folded. My third shot was low, and the bird dropped a leg as it sailed around the corner with the rest of the covey. Dot grabbed the dead bird, and with a quick sprint, she avoided Bug and brought the bird to my hand.

Chukar populations in California and Nevada have exploded over the past five or six years. Weather conditions, including wet winters and springs, and dry summers when chicks hatch out, have brought populations to all-time highs.

California's season starts on the third Saturday in October and runs through the last Sunday in January, with a daily bag limit of 6 and a possession limit of 12. Nevada's season opens a week earlier and closes the last day of January. The daily bag limit is 6, with a possession limit of 18.

During the early, dry part of the season, look for chukar near water. Tracks, droppings, and feathers near a water source indicate frequent use—and a good place to start. I have watched birds sail into water from a considerable distance, water, then feed back up the hill.

After winter rains cause the hillside to "green up," look for chukar on sunny slopes or on the tops of ridges. Numerous green, tiny cigar-shaped droppings with a white tip indicate birds are using the area. On freezing mornings, droppings that are not frozen indicate that birds are nearby. When flushed, look for them just over the edge, where they can leap into the air, tip a wing into the wind, and jet out of range in seconds.

Winter snows are the great equalizer when hunting chukar. If the snow is deep enough, the birds will concentrate on the sunny slopes, cutting the area you have to cover in half. Fresh snow allows you to follow tracks to the birds and, in my opinion,

is the best chukar hunting there is. When you flush birds, watch where they fly, walk the area until you find tracks, follow the tracks, and you should get a chance at most of them.

A dog can be a tremendous advantage. Getting them in shape and getting their feet ready for the rugged, rocky slopes chukar prefer can make or brake a chukar hunt. I have seen out-of-shape dogs give up before out-of-shape chukar hunters. You'll need to carry plenty of water for you and your dogs. A water bladder for you and a bottle that can be filled for your dog each time you get near water works well.

Chukar always like to be as high as they can get after being flushed. They will run to a rallying point and "chuck, chuck, chuck" to get the covey back together. Little bowls and draws are natural areas that they will hold in and make for excellent dog work.

I headed around the hillside looking for my cripple and the rest of the covey. With the wind in our face the dogs were hunting several hundred yards ahead. They hit the scent and slowed to let me catch up and get my wind back. The dogs pointed, and when the birds flushed, I dropped the first two but missed the next one clean and quickly

reloaded. Three more flushed below me, and I was able to kill the one with three shots. The dogs found the first two birds and tracked a cripple down. I tried to steady them, but when the bird ran out of a clump of cheat grass, Bug scooped him up and brought him back. Going a short distance further they found my other cripple, and now I had five.

Working the hillside, they pointed a couple of birds I should have killed and finally pointed a single that flew straight way. I folded him at 30 yards and was done. Looking at my GPS, it said I was only 2.8 miles from the pickup and had only walked 5.9 miles, a pretty short day of chukar hunting.

I have been asked what chukar hunting means to me. It means good dogs and good shots, but more than anything else, it means goods friends and sharing this wild country with people who have the same passion I do for chasing the "Desert Ghost."

*Jake Bushey is a California Fish and Game warden.*

## DESTINATIONS

*State Wildlife Management Areas*
Nevada has over 117,000 acres of state-managed Wildlife Management Areas open to hunting. See www.ndow.org/wild/habitat/wma/index.shtm.

Nevada has 20 different federal lands open to hunting. Some of the most popular for hunting are:

*U.S. Bureau of Land Management*

### BLACK ROCK DESERT
### RECREATION AREA
Winnemucca, NV 89445
Phone: 702-623-1500
www.blm.gov/ca/surprise/highrock.html

One of the largest and flattest alkaline playas in the United States, it is 44 miles long (oriented north-south) and averages 7 miles in width. This is wilderness with no development. Chukar, sage grouse, antelope, and mule deer country, if you work for it.

*USDA National Forests*

### HUMBOLDT-TOIYABE
### NATIONAL FORESTS
Elko, NV 89801
Phone: 702-738-5171
www.fs.fed.us/r4/htnf

Located primarily in Nevada and some in northeast California, this is the largest national forest outside of Alaska, having a net acreage of approximately 6.3 million acres, including 18 designated wilderness areas. Enormous diversity of habitats here, from sagebrush-dominated rangelands to alpine forests and meadows and sparkling streams. Hunting for all species according to state laws.

*U.S. Fish and Wildlife Service*
*National Wildlife Refuges*

## DESERT NATIONAL WILDLIFE REFUGE COMPLEX

Las Vegas, NV 89124
Phone: 702-879-6110; fax: 702-879-6115
www.fws.gov/desertcomplex

The largest National Wildlife Refuge in the lower 48 states, four refuges that encompass 1.5 million acres of the Mojave Desert in southern Nevada and include six mountain ranges. Limited hunting for bighorn sheep is the special feature here.

## RUBY LAKE NATIONAL WILDLIFE REFUGE

Ruby Valley, NV 89833
Phone: 775-779-2237
www.fws.gov/pacific/refuges/field/
NV_rubylk.htm

About 65 miles southeast of Elko, and down a 17–30-mile rough, gravel road, Ruby Lake NWR lies at the southern end of the Ruby Valley in northeast Nevada at an elevation of 6,000 feet. Flanked by the rugged and scenic Ruby Mountains, the refuge is 39,928 acres of a marsh bordered by meadows, grasslands, and brush-covered uplands— one of the most remote refuges in the lower 48 states. Waterfowl hunting is permitted here.

## STILLWATER NATIONAL WILDLIFE REFUGE

Fallon, NV 89406
Phone: 775-423-5128
www.fws.gov/stillwater/stillwater.html

The Stillwater NWR Complex in western Nevada consists of Stillwater Refuge, Fallon Refuge, and Anaho Island Refuge. Together, these three refuges encompass approximately 163,000 acres of wetland and upland habitats, freshwater and brackish water marshes, cottonwood and willow riparian areas, alkali playas, salt desert shrub lands, sand dunes, and a 500-acre rocky island in a desert lake. Hunting for upland game birds and waterfowl according to state and refuge regulations. For details, see www.fws.gov/stillwater/rec2 .html.

*Private Hunting Clubs and Preserves*

## BLACK MOUNTAIN OUTFITTERS

Battle Mountain, NV 89820
Phone: 775-635-5609
www.blackmountainhunts.com

Elk, mule deer, antelope, bighorn sheep, and upland bird hunts for pheasant, chukar, Hungarian partridge, and quail. Trapshooting, lodging, food, guides, and dogs available. Membership options. Youth hunts at half price; any hunter who hunts with Black Mountain can book a youth hunt for free.

## FASCIO ENTERPRISES, INC.

Gerlach, NV 89412
Phone: 775-557-2804; fax: 775-557-2105
www.fehunt.com

A large ranch near the Black Rock Desert offering released pheasant, wild quail, chukar, dove, and waterfowl hunts, plus deer, antelope, and bighorn sheep hunts. Overnight accommodations and meals.

## WALKER RIVER RESORT
Smith Valley, NV 89430
Phone: 800-446-2573 or 775-465-2573
www.wrresort.com

Pheasant and chukar hunting on 600 acres in a high desert region along the Walker River in western Nevada, adjacent to the Sweetwater Mountains. Cottages, sporting clays, ATV riding, full resort, and other amenities.

 HERITAGE DESTINATIONS

*Grimes Point/Hidden Cave Archeological Site—Carson City, Nevada*
One of the largest and most accessible petroglyph sites in North America, Grimes Point was a hunting ground of the Shoshone Indians beginning some 8,000 years ago. Numerous stone engravings may include hunters, clans, or spirits of animals.

Directions: From Fallon, go east on U.S. 50 approximately 10 miles until you see the archaeological site sign.

## CARSON CITY BLM DISTRICT OFFICE
Carson City, NV 89701
Phone: 775-885-6000
www.americantrails.org national recreationtrails/blm/grimespoint-nv.html

## UTAH

*In 2001 there were 177,000 resident hunters and 22,000 nonresident hunters: 86% went big game hunting, 35% small game, 26% migratory waterfowl and doves; 86% hunted on public lands; 44% hunted on private lands. Hunters pumped $292 million into the state economy. (USFWS)*

### OVERVIEW
Valley quail, Gambel's quail, pheasant, chukar, wild turkeys, sage grouse, ruffed grouse, band-tailed pigeons, Hungarian partridge, blue grouse, white-tailed ptarmigan, and sharp-tail grouse all roam throughout the high desert and mountains of Utah, no doubt passing by the mule deer, antelope, mountain goats, elk, bison, moose, black bears, Rocky Mount bighorn sheep, and desert bighorn sheep that make Utah such a hunter's paradise.

A lot of Utah is arid, but where there is water, there are flocks of ducks, swans, and geese. Tundra swans are legal game here, but a hunter must first obtain a permit that requires passing an online test to ensure that you can distinguish between a tundra swan

---

**UTAH SNAPSHOT
INDUSTRY STATE**

- **General information:** www.wildlife.utah.gov/hunting

- **Map of the Division of Wildlife Resources (DWR) Wildlife Management Units:** www.wildlife.utah.gov/hunting/biggame/wmas.php

- **Listing of Utah guides and outfitters:** http://utah.com/database/guides

- **Utah deer herd:** was 289,000 in 2004; was 25,000 deer in 2005.

and a trumpeter swan. You can also hunt sandhill cranes in Utah.

## DESTINATIONS

One reason why 86% of all Utah hunters went hunting on public lands in 2001 is that there are millions of acres of public land available for hunters. There are 135 federal areas that offer various forms of hunting, and the state has more. A whole book could be written about hunting destinations in Utah. The quickest way to access information about them is the Public Lands Information Center: www.publi clands.org/explore/search_results.php.

Here we'll spotlight just a few.

*USDA National Forests*

### ASHLEY NATIONAL FOREST
Vernal, UT 84078
Phone: 435-789-1181
www.fs.fed.us/r4/ashley

Located in northeast Utah and southwest Wyoming, the Ashley National Forest is 1.3 million acres, including the High Uintas Wilderness, 460,000 acres, which is the largest wilderness in Utah.

### DIXIE NATIONAL FOREST
Cedar City, UT 84720
Phone: 435-865-3700
www.fs.fed.us/r4/dixie/index.shtml

Straddling the divide between the Great Basin and the Colorado River, this 2 million-acre national forest stretches for 170 miles across southern Utah. This is traditionally a good area for mule deer, and more elk are moving into the area.

### FISHLAKE NATIONAL FOREST
Richfield, UT 84701
Phone: 435-896-9233
www.fs.fed.us/r4/fishlake

Fishlake is the largest mountain lake in the state. Traditionally a popular hunting area.

### MANTI-LASAL NATIONAL FOREST
Price, UT 84501
Phone: 435-637-2817
www.fs.fed.us/r4/mantilasal

A 1,413,111-acre forest located in southeastern Utah offering hunting according to state regulations.

### UINTA NATIONAL FOREST
Provo, UT 84601
Phone: 801-342-5100
www.fs.fed.us/r4/uinta

The first national forest in Utah, motorized vehicles are not allowed off roads to retrieve animals. For more details on hunting in the forest, see www.fs.fed.us/r4/uinta/recreation/hunt_fish.

## WASATCH-CACHE NATIONAL FOREST
Salt Lake City, UT 84138
Phone: 801-236-3400
www.fs.fed.us/r4/wcnf

Located east and north of Salt Lake City and encompassing 1.3 million ecologically diverse acres, including seven wilderness areas, hunting according to state regulations is permitted here.

*U.S. Fish and Wildlife Service*
*National Wildlife Refuges*

## BEAR RIVER MIGRATORY BIRD REFUGE
Brigham City, UT 84302
Phone: 435-723-5887
www.fws.gov/bearriver/

Located approximately 50 miles north of Salt Lake City, hunting is permitted for ducks, geese, coots, and tundra swans according to state and federal refuge regulations. For details, see www.fws.gov/bearriver/hunting .html.

## FISH SPRINGS NATIONAL WILDLIFE REFUGE
Dugway, UT 84022
Phone: 435-831-5353; fax: 435-831-5354
www.fws.gov/fishsprings/index.htm

The refuge covers 17,992 acres with a 10,000-acre marsh system fed by five natural springs. Waterfowl hunting for ducks, geese, coots, and mergansers only. Every hunter must first register. For details, see www.fws. gov/fishsprings/HUNTING.HTM.

## OURAY NATIONAL WILDLIFE REFUGE
Randlett, UT 84063
Phone: 435-545-2522
http://ouray.fws.gov

The refuge totals 11,987 acres, including 16 miles of the Green River. Waterfowl, mule deer, and ring-necked pheasant hunting are permitted during appropriate hunting seasons according to state and refuge regulations. For details, see http://ouray.fws.gov/Hunt&Fish .htm.

*U.S. Bureau of Land Management*
The BLM manages nearly 22.9 million acres of public lands in Utah, representing about 42% of the state, located mostly in western and southeastern Utah. Hunting is permitted on BLM lands according to state regulations. See www.blm.gov/ut/st/ en.html.

*Private Lands*
Utah's Walk-in Access program, which allows hunters to hunt on land leased by the state from private landowners, opens up thousands of acres to hunters in the northern part of the state. For details, see www.wild life.utah.gov/walkinaccess.

*Private Hunting Clubs and Preserves*

## 4 MILE HUNTING CLUB
Nephi, UT 84648
Phone: 435-623-0704
www.4milehuntingclub.com

Located 80 miles south of Salt Lake City, offering field and European-style hunts for pheasant and chukar on 1,800 acres. Memberships available. Clubhouse and meals.

**HICKEN'S PHEASANT VALLEY
HUNTING PRESERVE**
Mylon, UT 84052
Phone: 435-646-3194
www.hickenschickens.com

Located southwest of Vernal and just south of Mylon, field hunts for pheasant and chukar. Memberships available. Guides, dogs, and sporting clays also available.

**LET THE GOOD TIMES FLY
HUNTING PRESERVE**
Deweyville, UT 84309
Phone: 435-257-0848
www.letthegoodtimesfly.com

On 8,400 acres in the Whites Valley for field hunts for pheasant and chukar. Guides and dogs available. Also hunting for mule deer, predators, and exotic sheep. Several membership options.

**RED RIVER OUTFITTERS**
Teasdale, UT 84773

Phone: 877-6 STREAM
or 435-425-3669 (Local)
www.rroutfitters.com

A 2,000-acre ranch along six miles of stream located near the beautiful Capitol Reef National Park in southern Utah, Red River Ranch releases 5,000 roosters a year to boost up the local ringneck population, to go with valley quail, chukar, waterfowl, and fly-fishing. Guides and dogs available. Elegant lodge and excellent food.

# HERITAGE DESTINATIONS

*Rosenbruch Wildlife Museum*
In realistic dioramas, Rosenbruch showcases over 300 species of mounted animals from all around the world in 25,000 square feet of exhibits. There is also a movie theater. Wonderful educational resource for the whole family.

**ROSENBRUCH WILDLIFE MUSEUM**
St. George, UT 84790
Phone: 435-986-6619
www.rosenbruch.org

# Rockies

## COLORADO

*In 2001 there were 159,000 resident hunters and 121,000 nonresident hunters: 84% went big game hunting, 26% small game, 19% waterfowl; 69% hunted on public lands; 57% hunted on private lands. Hunters pumped $383 million into the state economy. (USFWS)*

### OVERVIEW

Colorado has considerable deer, bears, moose, bighorn sheep, mountain lions, grouse, and rabbits, but there are more elk in Colorado than in any other state in the United States. Colorado also has millions of acres open to hunting. This is why if you happen to fly into the Denver airport in October or November, you will see more people carrying gun cases than luggage.

The mysterious mad cow–like brain disease, chronic wasting disease (CWD), was first identified in a research facility in Fort Collins. It has since spread to a dozen or more states. There is no substantiated connection between CWD and humans contracting it, but to be on the safe side, the Colorado Division of Wildlife (DOW) advises hunters not to shoot, handle, or consume any animal that appears sick. If you see or shoot an animal—deer, elk, moose—that appears sick, contact the Division of Wildlife in Fort Collins at 970-472-4300.

Even if the animal appears healthy, to be on the safe side, bone out the meat, avoid

---

**COLORADO SNAPSHOT**
**CENTENNIAL STATE**

• **General information:**
Colorado DOW Headquarters
6060 Broadway
Denver, CO 80216
Phone: 303-297-1192
http://wildlife.state.co.us/Hunting

• **Buy your hunting license online:** http://wildlife
.state.co.us/ShopDOW/AppsAndLicenses;
or by telephone, call toll-free 800-244-5613

• **Report a poacher:** Operation Game Thief,
877-265-6648

• **Deer population:** 600,900 (all species)

• **Average deer harvest:** Not available

the brain, spinal chord, bone marrow, eyes, and nerve tissues and have your animal tested by the state.

 **FEATURED HUNT**

## Elk in Wolcott, Colorado

JAMES SWAN

In Mongolia they say that every evening a giant elk comes along and steals the sun in his antlers and runs off to the west. The sun only comes back, the Mongolian legend maintains, if great hunters chase after that elk and take it back from him and put it in the eastern sky so the next day can begin.

The great hunters must have been successful last night. This hunter and his guide were perched on the crest of a rocky 1,000-foot hill, which put us at 10,000 feet elevation, as the rising sun crept up, illuminating opening day of the second weeklong elk hunting season in the White River National Forest in central Colorado. Ancient man ate the gods that he prayed to, and mornings like this are like attending a religious ceremony.

Here and there, half a mile away or more, we could see small spots of bright orange weaving in and out of the aspens in pursuit of larger spots of light tan with white butts and chocolate brown capes. Unlike the two-leggeds, the elk, although two or three times as large, moved like silent ghosts through the timber.

The sun climbed steadily higher as the great chase unfolded before us. Some elk died; many others disappeared unscathed. None came close enough to us for a shot.

As the sun rose high enough to throw light on all the valley, on the crest of an open ridge about 600 yards away, a large chocolate brown cow elk suddenly burst out into the open. Minutes before, four hunters in brilliant orange vests had been standing on that ridge, but now they were gone. The cow, obviously from her size and coloration, was a matriarch of that valley. She knew what the pumpkin people were up to. That's how she had become the matriarch.

Following the cow came a string of 29 other elk, in a line, almost like it was being choreographed. Near the back was a single bull—head held high, his white-tipped antlers gleamed in the sun. He had only one five-point antler left, and he had a limp. The missing antler and the limp could have been from errant shots, but more likely they were due to battles he had fought that fall with other bulls to keep those 29 cows as his own harem. Elk kill each other in the name of love.

The stream of elk progressed out into the middle of a sage-covered hill, then stopped. The herd began to circle up, forming a tight group. In the middle stood the bull, his gasps of white breath puffing up into the morning air. The cows were standing by their man, and all those cows, incidentally, were legal game to hunters who had cow tags.

The ideal carrying capacity for the elk herd in the White River National Forest should be 26,000 elk, but it has grown to at least 54,000. In 1999, when deep snow did fall in this area, my guide, Dan Harrison, manager of the Piney Valley Ranch, tells me that he put out 27 tons of hay for the elk one snowy January morning. In three days, it was gone.

Our hearts came to our throats. If the herd was spotted by some excited neophyte who started blazing away, it was likely that many animals would have been hit, probably wounded, not killed. The matriarch must have somehow known the coast was clear.

The old cow now split out of the herd and

headed for the edge of the mesa. She trotted 100 yards over to the edge where she could look down the steep rocky slope into the valley below; she stopped, testing the winds with her acute sense of smell. She paused, drinking in the morning air, all senses in high gear. Then she abruptly trotted back to the herd. Some elk was spoken, no doubt some in audible tones we could not hear from our distance but also in silent mental communication that skeptics deny and all people who have spent time in nature know is the primary way wild things speak to each other. As if on cue, the herd uncoiled into a line, fell in behind the matriarch, and followed her over the crest of the mesa and down the steep slope into the dense evergreen woods below.

Ten minutes later, two orange hunters appeared at the far end of the field where the elk had just been. The hunters may have seen the tracks, but all that remained was the fresh east wind, blowing through the sagebrush, and maybe even traces of the musky odor of elk lingering in the mountain air.

On that frosty morning the elk had decided not to sacrifice one of their own but instead to teach us something precious. They gave a priceless gift, something of far greater value than any rack of giant antlers: they allowed us a glimpse of their souls.

The Piney Valley Ranch is over 30,000 acres of private land, the largest ranch in Eagle County. The ranch is managed for recreational value while still proudly remaining a working ranch. The multiple-use management program allows for fishing, hunting (elk, deer, and upland birds), shooting, wildlife viewing, horseback trips, timber operations, and sheep and cattle grazing to all coexist in relative harmony.

A typical hunt is an hour's horseback ride in the A.M., some climbing, then back for lunch and rest in midday, and a ride out and climb and wait until sundown. Every day we saw at least 50 elk. Both myself and the other hunter in camp that week shot 6×6 bulls.

It helps to be comfortable riding horses. You will be at 9,000 feet elevation, so take it easy if you fly in from much lower elevation and be in shape. And practice your long shots—out to 350 yards—if you come in rifle season. Shooting sticks (or some other kind of portable rest) are highly recommended. In bow season, they tell me just about every hunter gets a chance at a bull at 20 yards or less. I can't wait.

**PINEY VALLEY RANCH**

Wolcott, CO 81655

Phone: 970-748-8458; fax: 970-748-8900

www.pineyvalley.com

 ## FEATURED HUNT

## On the Puma's Path

PATT DORSEY*

Hunting puma or mountain lion or cougar, for most hunters, is a once-in-a-lifetime experience. It is one of the few times when a predator stalks another predator and both consider the other food. Puma hunting is not for everyone, but for hunters seeking a glimpse into the world of the ghost cat, it may satisfy a primal need. More Boone and Crockett lions have been taken in Colorado than any other state.

Pumas are the world's largest small cat, offi-cially classified as a "small cat" because of their ability to purr. Their scientific name *Felis concolor* literally means "cat of one color."

Pumas are exceptional predators. They make a short stalk and quick ambush—powerful front feet grasping prey behind the shoulders with long, curved dew claws, called "ripper claws," while stout canine teeth seize the animal's head and neck.

They prey primarily on mule deer, but they can and do kill adult elk. Adaptable to food shortages, they can go days without food or prey on porcupines, beavers, rabbits, and mice. Biology is about food—a balance of calories eaten and calories burned. (Biology is also about sex: Females can reach sexual maturity at less than two years of age. Three months after a successful mating, they give birth to one to six kittens in a secreted den site, giving puma populations quick recovery abilities.)

In Colorado, hunters find pumas in areas with good ambush cover and abundant mule deer. The abundance of deer and other wildlife has brought about an abundance of pumas. While no one knows

exactly how many pumas live in the western United States, experts agree more pumas exist today than at any time since European settlement.

The Colorado DOW aided this profusion of pumas, designating it a game animal in 1965, removing its vermin status and associated bounty. Before 1965, mountain lion eradication was respectable and calculated. A carpenter's wage was $2 per day in 1881 when Colorado's state legislature placed a $10 bounty on pumas. In 1929, the stock market crashed, and Colorado increased the mountain lion bounty to $50. Five years later the state entered into an agreement with the U.S. Department of Agriculture to eradicate wolves, coyotes, bobcats, lynx, and mountain lions.

Today the state manages mountain lions for stable or increasing populations or for suppression when social issues such as livestock or human safety are concerns. Game animal status in Colorado also requires hunters to treat mountain lions as table fare, not as a mere collection of trophy parts.

A puma hunt is an extraordinary hunting experience, but it is not without controversy. Professional and public attitudes toward predators are drastically different today. In a 2005 Colorado mountain lion public opinion survey, 96% of re-

spondents agreed with the statement: "It is important to me to know that mountain lions exist, even if I never see one."

The controversy is partially a "fair chase" debate. Some pumas are taken using predator calls. Others are taken incidental to finding a "food cache" or puma kill. In Colorado, though, most are hunted with trained hounds. Herein lies part of the controversy.

From a wildlife management perspective, hunting with hounds allows a selective lion harvest, harvesting fewer females with kittens in tow. Although hunting is a tool of wildlife management, most hunters are motivated by something much deeper than wildlife management reasons.

Lion hunting with hounds sprang from a 20,000-year-long relationship between man and dogs. Most scientists agree that dogs descended from *Canis lupus,* the gray wolf. Presumably, at some time during our hunting history, a pack of human hunters found an abandoned wolf pup and picked it up. The hand-raised wolf and its superior hunting senses presented an advantage that ignited the process of dog domestication and breeding.

Most lion hunters use small packs of scent hounds. Walker, redtick, bluetick, black and tan, Plott—each breed with advantages, left to the individual houndsman's preference. Hounds bay, bark, and bawl along the trail, telling hunters if the trail has gone cold or the quarry has treed. A well-trained houndsman knows the voice of each dog and refers to the pack's ongoing communication as "music."

Shooting a lion in a tree does not mean you have hunted lions. Hunters should ensure that they get a puma hunt instead of just a puma. Good houndsmen hunt because they love "hound music" and the mysteries to which each puma trail might lead. A good puma hunt with hounds requires physical and mental hunting skills and provides

ample opportunity for the lion to escape. Fair chase mountain lion hunting means being present when the dogs are turned loose and tracking with the dogs.

Tracking any predator is not a straight line. It is a twisted journey in and out of drainages, atop ridge-lines and deep in arroyos. Hunters see more than where the lion went. They see "scratches" where toms reveal their dominance to rival toms and breed-ing females. Scratches are marks in near perpetuity, always found in weather-protected areas under rock outcrops or thick conifers. Hunters notice beds where pumas rest, watching for movement—an approach-ing meal? Hunters find shady, camouflaged food caches where kill remains are kept fresh for later feasting. Hunters begin to understand from this ex-traordinary, fellow predator how cats stalk expertly: remaining silent by stepping on rocks and bare spots where possible; vigilantly picking up and placing their feet, as opposed to dragging their toes like deer; moving along tree lines and fence lines when ventur-ing into exposed areas.

Pumas are admired as wilderness symbols and feared as livestock killers and threats to people. The future of mountain lions depends upon an appreci-ation and understanding of its "fierce, green fire" and ecological significance. For some, it is through hunting that we achieve that level of appreciation and understanding.

*Patt Dorsey is a Colorado DOW Wildlife Area manager.*

---

## DESTINATIONS

*U.S. Bureau of Land Management*

**ALPINE TRIANGLE—BLM**
Gunnison, CO 81230

Phone: 970-240-5300
www.co.blm.gov/gra/gra-rec.htm

On 600,000 acres of public land in the upper Gunnison River Basin in southwest Colorado. Ecosystems range from dry sagebrush steppes at 7,000 feet, to forests of aspen, ponderosa pine, Douglas fir, lodgepole pine, Engleman spruce, and subalpine fir, to alpine tundra meadows that reach to over 14,000 feet. Deer, elk, bears, and grouse are the most commonly hunted species.

**GUNNISON GORGE NATIONAL CONSERVATION AREA**
Uncompahgre Basin BLM Field Office
Montrose, CO 81401
Phone: 970-240-5309
www.co.blm.gov/ggnca/index.htm

The Gunnison Gorge National Conservation Area (NCA) is located about seven miles northeast of Montrose in west-central Colo-rado, just downstream from the Black Canyon of the Gunnison National Park. It encom-passes approximately 57,725 acres of public lands in Montrose and Delta counties.

Hunting is permitted in regions of this area. For details, see www.co.blm.gov/recweb/hunting.htm.

**KREMMLING RECREATION MANAGEMENT AREA—BLM**
Kremmling, CO 80459
Phone: 970-724-3437
www.co.blm.gov/kra/kraindex.htm

About 394,000 acres of BLM land in Jack-son, Grand, Larimer, Eagle, and Summit counties. The unit is largely open to hunting, with a number of game management units within the boundaries. See Colorado DOW for details and www.co.blm.gov/kra/hunting.htm.

## UPPER COLORADO RIVER RECREATION MANAGEMENT UNIT—BLM
Glenwood Springs, CO 81602
Phone: 970-247-3437
www.recreation.gov/detail.jsp;jsessionid=Fn3pgQlvXj9t8dkcBj8J3RhGKPHLqMgJBsNLCgTTZMPhlCPHpGqy!85565917?ID=1708

Follows the upper 80 miles of the Colorado River. See Colorado DOW for details on seasons and licenses.

### USDA National Forests
Most of the national forest lands are open to hunting. Hunting regulations on national forest lands are according to the Colorado DOW.

## ARAPAHO-ROOSEVELT NATIONAL FORESTS-PAWNEE NATIONAL GRASSLAND
Fort Collins, CO 80526-8119
Phone: 970-295-6700
www.fs.fed.us/r2/arnf

The forests and grassland encompasses 1.5 million acres in north-central Colorado and extend north to the Wyoming border, south of Interstate 70 to Mount Evans, west across the Continental Divide to the Williams Fork area, and includes short-grass prairie east of I-25. The Pawnee National Grassland, located approximately 30 miles east of Fort Collins, Colorado, is fairly level in elevation. The grassland is crisscrossed with eroding creek drainages, and elevations range from 4,900 feet on the prairie to 5,500 feet at the summit of the Pawnee Buttes.

## GRAND MESA-UNCOMPAHGRE-GUNNISON NATIONAL FORESTS
Delta, CO 81416
Phone: 970-874-6600
www.fs.fed.us/r2/gmug

Almost 3 million acres, the third-largest national forest in the contiguous United States. The mostly forested, mountainous lands are located on the western slope of the Colorado Rockies extending into 10 Colorado counties.

## RIO GRANDE NATIONAL FOREST
Monte Vista, CO 81144
Phone: 719-852-5941
www.fs.fed.us/r2/riogrande

The Rio Grande National Forest is 1.86 million acres located in southwestern Colorado; from 7,600-feet alpine desert to over 14,300 feet in the Sangre de Cristo Wilderness on the eastern side. Most of the forest is open to hunting.

## SAN JUAN NATIONAL FOREST
Durango, CO 81301
Phone: 970-247-4874
www.fs.fed.us/r2/sanjuan

Some 2.5 million acres stretching across five Colorado counties in the southwest corner of the state. The terrain ranges from high-desert mesas to alpine peaks, with thousands of miles of back roads and trails. The area is open to all local game species. See www.fs.fed.us/r2/sanjuan/recreation for details.

## WHITE RIVER NATIONAL FOREST
Glenwood Springs, CO 81602
Phone: 970-945-2521
www.fs.fed.us/r2/whiteriver

Located approximately two to four hours west of Denver, the forest includes eight designated wildernesses, several national trails, approximately 70 camp and picnic grounds, and over 1.5 million acres for general motorized and nonmotorized backcountry enjoyment. The elk herd in this area is roughly two times the carrying capacity. Much of the best hunting is off-road and accessible by horseback.

*U.S. Fish and Wildlife Service*
*National Wildlife Refuges*

## ALAMOSA/MONTE VISA/ BACA NATIONAL WILDLIFE REFUGE COMPLEX
Alamosa, CO 81101
Phone: 719-589-4021
www.fws.gov/alamosa

Sitting at an elevation of approximately 7,600 feet, the San Luis Valley extends over 100 miles from north to south and 50 miles from east to west, with dwarfing mountains in three directions. Only waterfowl and small game hunting are permitted on a portion of each refuge according to state regulations and special refuge regulations. Permits are only required on the first and second weekends of the first waterfowl hunting split. During the week you do not need a permit. For details, see www.fws.gov/alamosa/hunting.html.

The nearby artificially created wetlands on Monte Vista NWR's 14,804 acres provide habitat for a wide variety of waterfowl and other water birds. See Alamosa National Wildlife Complex for details.

## ARAPAHO NATIONAL WILDLIFE REFUGE
Walden, CO 80480-0457
Phone: 970-723-8202
http://arapaho.fws.gov

Arapaho NWR is situated at an elevation of 8,200 feet and located in an intermountain glacial basin in north-central Colorado. The refuge's 24,804 acres support diverse wildlife habitats, including sagebrush-grassland uplands, grassland meadows, willow riparian areas, and wetlands. Mule deer, pronghorn, elk, and moose use the refuge habitats throughout the year. Small mammals include cottontails and jackrabbits. Portions of the refuge are open to public hunting of some game species during appropriate state seasons.

## BROWNS PARK NATIONAL WILDLIFE REFUGE
Maybell, CO 81640
Phone: 970-365-3613
www.fws.gov/brownspark

The Green River runs through the heart of the 13,455-acre refuge, creating wetlands and supporting cottonwood forests. Mule deer, elk, ducks, geese, doves, cottontails, and jackrabbits are legal in certain areas.

Coyotes and prairie dogs are protected. Consult refuge Web site for details.

*Private Hunting Clubs and Preserves*

## BLACK CANYON WING AND CLAY
Delta, CO 81416-9547
Phone: 970-874-7195; fax: 970-241-9660
www.bcwandc.com/contact.htm

Located in the Four Corners Area of southwest Colorado, Black Canyon offers pheasant and chukar hunting, with sporting clays and five-stand. This is a membership club, with individual and corporate memberships available.

## BLUFFS AT VALHALLA, INC.
Byers, CO 80103
Phone: 303-822-8479 (Lodge)
www.huntthebluffs.com

Quail, pheasant, and Hungarian partridge. Memberships limited to 100 people. A 6,200-square-foot luxurious lodge with hot tub.

## COLORADO WINGSPORT
Fort Collins, CO 80524
Phone: 970-482-7574
www.pawneesports.com

A division of Pawnee Sportsmens Center, they offer hunting in the Fort Collins and Brighton vicinities with both guided and nonguided half-day hunts for pheasant, chukar partridge, and occasionally quail. Their hunting season runs September through March. Memberships are available but not required. There is a two-hunter minimum on weekend

hunts. Nonmembers are limited to two visits per season. Guided hunts (with hunting dogs) are available for additional cost.

## GUNNISON RIVER FARMS
Austin, CO 81410
Phone: 970-835-3962; fax: 970-835-4625
www.gunnisonriverfarms.com

Wild bird hunting on 1,000 acres of open fields and deep canyons for pheasant, doves, and chukar. Fully trained hunting dogs are available. Gunnison also offers tower shoots and a sporting clays course. Guests can bring their own dogs. Farm-style breakfast and dinner served. Several log cabins overlooking the Gunnison River are on the ranch for overnighters. Day hunts, overnights, memberships, and corporate retreat options. Hiking, biking, float trips, and fishing on five miles of the Gunnison River as well as 7 acres of trout ponds and 8 acres of bass ponds. A special touch: yoga classes and massage therapy are also available.

## THE HIGH LONESOME RANCH
DeBeque, CO 81630
Phone: 970-283-9420; fax: 970-283-5227
www.highlonesomelodge.com/home/index.htm

Located 30 miles east of Grand Junction, the High Lonesome Ranch and permit properties offer almost 200 square miles of land to hunt from 5,000 feet elevation to 9,200 feet. Pheasant, chukar, Hungarian partridge, and native blue grouse are found throughout the ranch. Big game hunting for elk, bears, mountain lions, turkeys, bighorn sheep, and mule deer is also available, as well as fly-fishing for brown, rainbow, cutthroat, and brook trout in private waters. Multiple lodging options are scattered around the ranch.

## HUBBARD CREEK OUTFITTERS
Hotchkiss, CO 81419
Phone: 970-872-3818
www.hubbardcreek.com/birdhunting.html

Hubbard Creek Outfitters offers guided service hunts on their own ranch and horseback pack trips for elk, mule deer, and black bears and trout fishing on Gunnison National Forest lands and on private ranches in western Colorado. They also offer fall blue grouse and spring wild turkey hunting.

## INDIAN BEND RANCH
Pueblo, CO 81003-2644
Phone: 719-544-7115; fax: 719-544-6242
www.indianbendranch.com

Small group hunting for pheasant and chukar on over 750 acres of prime cover bordering the Arkansas River. No license is required for guided upland game hunts. Clay pigeons, gun rental, ammunition, and hunting vests and hats available. Clubhouse. Overnight stays can be arranged.

## KIOWA CREEK SPORTING CLUB
Bennett, CO 80102
Phone: 303-644-4627; fax: 303-644-3633
www.kiowacreek.com

October 1 to March 31 for released pheasant, Hungarian partridge, chukar, and quail. All hunts are guided and may include one of our professionally trained dogs, or you may use your own dog. Wild goose, duck, and dove hunting available during the state seasons; prairie dog hunting as well. If you want to hunt prairie dogs, bring at least 250 rounds! Sporting clays and 3-D archery courses at the club. Also arranges for elk and antelope hunts on private lands in Wyoming and big game fishing trips to Costa Rica.

## LAYBOURN'S UPLAND GAME HUNT CLUB
Cope, CO 80812
Phone: 970-357-4379;
mobile: 970-554-1509; fax: 970-357-4389
www.laybourns.com

This is a membership club offering pheasant, chukar, and quail hunts. There is a bunkhouse on the ranch.

## LONGMEADOW HUNT CLUB
Wiggins, CO 80654
Phone: 970-483-5642;
mobile: 970-467-4868
www.longmeadowgameresort.com

A 4,000-acre hunting resort located just 75 miles northeast of Denver—the closest hunting to Denver. Longmeadow offers guided and nonguided hunts for pheasant, bobwhite quail, chukar, and doves. On-site tent, RV, and fifth-wheel campsites are available. Trapshooting is popular, and a sporting clays course is being installed.

## ROCKY MOUNTAIN ROOSTERS, INC.
Colorado Springs, CO 80907
Phone: 719-635-3257; fax: 719-630-3329
www.rmroosters.com

A private membership club offering pheasant, chukar, and quail hunting on 5,000 acres. A 6,000-square-foot clubhouse, sporting clays course, and guided or nonguided hunts. Open seven days a week, eight months of the year. All hunts by reservation only.

## ROCKY RIDGE HUNTING AND
## TRAINING KENNELS
Fort Collins, CO 80524
Phone: 970-221-4868
www.coloradopros.com/pheasant.htm

Located an hour's drive from Denver, Rocky Ridge has been providing successful hunting experiences for over 19 years. Excellent cover, strong-flying ring-necked pheasant, chukar partridge, well-trained dogs, and solitary hunting fields. Rocky Ridge also offers self-guided waterfowl hunts and fishing for rainbows, steelheads, walleyes, perch, bass, and catfish on a private 300-acre reservoir. Also offers elk and mule deer hunting at 1,800-acre Diamond Peak Ranch 55 miles northwest of Fort Collins, Colorado, and 30 miles south of Laramie, Wyoming, in the Roosevelt National Forest in Colorado.

## SCENIC MESA RANCH, LLC
Hotchkiss, CO 81419-0370
Phone: 970-872-3078; fax: 970-872-4057
www.scenicmesa.com

An Orvis-endorsed wing-shooting preserve, with 8,000 acres on the North Fork of the Gunnison River, one hour southeast of Grand Junction. Pheasant, chukar, Hungarian partridge, quail, doves, seven species of water-fowl, and a free-roaming herd of buffalo that you can hunt with modern equipment or 1870s-style Sharps rifle or Remington Rolling Block, on horseback. Also has two National Sporting Clays Association (NSCA) registered sporting clays courses. You can stay at the Gathering Lodge, three guest rooms in the Members Club House, or in teepees or remote log cabins. Fly-fishing and rafting on the Gunnison River is another option. Meals typically include buffalo, game birds, and trout taken from the ranch.

## STEEL FORK PHEASANTS, LLC
Rush, CO 80833
Phone/fax: 719-478-3051
www.SteelForkPheasants.com

On 3,000-plus acres for hunting located 38 miles east of Colorado Springs, Colorado, on Highway 94. Standard blueback and Manchurian ring-necked pheasant, bobwhite quail, chukar, and the exotic Manchurian golden pheasant. Complimentary continental breakfast; lunch is extra. Membership club. Antelope, deer, dove, and coyote hunting is also available.

## STRASBURG GAME BIRDS
## HUNTING PRESERVE
Strasburg, CO 80136
Phone: 303-622-4608
www.StrasburgGameBirds.com

Guided and nonguided half-day hunts for pheasant, chukar, and quail on 2,000 acres of ideal upland game bird habitat. No membership requirements or annual dues. Large party and corporate hunts can be arranged.

**UNCOMPAHGRE HUNT CLUB, LLC**
Delta, CO 81416
Phone: 970-874-8147 or 866-874-8147;
mobile: 970-260-8603
www.uncompahgrehuntclub.com

Club for members and nonmembers. A 40-minute drive from Grand Junction with 776 acres for wing shooting for pheasant, quail, Hungarian partridge, and chukar. Also hunting for deer, ducks, geese, and doves. Indoor and outdoor archery range.

*Land Management Club*
For information, see Colorado Outdoor Sports at www.coloradooutdoorsports.com.

# HERITAGE DESTINATIONS

*Meeker, Colorado—Sleep in the Same Room That Teddy Roosevelt Used*
In the Flat Tops Wilderness Area in the northwest part of Colorado, you will find public land access to one of the state's biggest herds of elk, as well as mule deer and grouse.

While hunting the Flat Tops or other nearby state and national forests in northwest Colorado, the place to visit or stay is Meeker, a quaint little town on the banks of the White River about two hours northeast of Grand Junction, as the raven flies, that has a long and rich history.

Visiting Meeker, there are two places where you must spend some time. One is the White River Museum, a wonderful treasure chest of antiques crammed into a series of single-story log cabins behind the Rio Blanco County Courthouse.

Summer hours are 9:00 A.M. until 5:00 P.M. all week long, May through October. During the winter the museum is open 11:00 A.M. to 3:00 P.M., Monday through Friday. Visit www.meekerchamber.com/museum .htm or call 970-878-9982 for more information.

On the opposite side of the Meeker town square is the historic Meeker Hotel. You step back in time over a hundred years when you set foot on the pine planks of the floor of the Meeker Hotel, and the greeting committee is awesome. On the knotty pine walls are the mounted heads of some of the biggest elk and deer you've ever seen, overseeing things as they have done for over 100 years.

If you were to ask one of those trophy heads, or one of the ghosts that supposedly reside in the hotel, about its history, they would tell you that Teddy Roosevelt hung his hat in the Meeker Hotel during his lion hunting expedition in 1901. Billy the Kidd also bunked here, as did Gary Cooper, Franklin Roosevelt, and a host of other notables. You can feel the presence of the past in Meeker.

**MEEKER HOTEL**
Meeker, CO 81641
Phone: 970-878-5255 (Reservations);
fax: 970-878-3412
www.themeekerhotel.com

# IDAHO

*In 2001 there were 150,000 resident hunters and 47,000 nonresident hunters: 79% went big game hunting, 38% small game, 19% waterfowl; 88% hunted on public lands; 40% hunted on private lands. Hunters pumped $231 million into the state economy. (USFWS)*

## OVERVIEW

Idaho has 83,574 square miles of outdoor recreation opportunities and a population of less than 1.4 million.

Idaho is truly a hunter's state: moose, bighorn sheep, mountain goats, mule deer, whitetails, elk, antelope, black bears, upland game, turkeys, and waterfowl.

---

**IDAHO SNAPSHOT**
**GEM STATE**

- **General information:**
  Idaho Fish and Game
  600 South Walnut
  Boise, ID 83712
  Phone: 208-334-3700; fax: 208-334-2148
  or 208-334-2114
  Idaho Relay Service: 800-377-2529 (TDD)
  fishandgame.idaho.gov/cms/hunt

- **Buy your hunting license online:** One of the best ways to plan your hunt in Idaho is to use the online Hunt Planner Web site "Idaho Hunt Planner," which is designed to provide information the hunter needs on regulations, seasons, drawing odds, harvest statistics, and hunt boundaries in one location; see http://fishandgame.idaho.gov/ifwis/huntplanner

- **Deer population:** 255,000, 25th in the United States

- **Average deer harvest:** 16,709, 30th in the United States

---

Licenses and tags are available over the counter for almost every species. The state is two-thirds public land. A new Fish and Game program—Access Yes!—is opening up more private land every year.

## DESTINATIONS

*U.S. Army Corps of Engineers*

### ALBENI FALLS DAM AND LAKE PEND OREILLE
Oldtown, ID 83822-9243
Phone: 208-437-3133
Email: gary.j.bond@usace.army.mil
www.nws.usace.army.mil/PublicMenu
Menu.cfm?sitename=albeni&pagename=home

From Spokane, Washington, 50 miles northeast on U.S. 2, Albeni Falls Dam sits on the Pend Oreille River. Behind the dam, the waters of the Pend Oreille stretch 65 miles through a glacially carved valley that separates three mountain ranges. Rimmed by mountains that rise 6,500 feet, Lake Pend Oreille is one of the largest and deepest natural lakes in the western United States. Hunting for all species. Check with headquarters for details.

Eight recreation areas around the lake are owned by the Corps of Engineers, including four developed campgrounds/day-use areas, two day-use only areas, and two primitive access areas. Albeni Cove, Priest River, Riley Creek, and Springy Point have developed campsites (no hookups) with a variety of day-use facilities. The Vista Area and Trestle Creek are day-use areas only. Morton Slough and Johnson Creek (managed by the

Idaho Department of Fish and Game) provide primitive camping and boat launch facilities.

*USDA National Forests*

## BOISE NATIONAL FOREST
Boise, ID 83709
Phone: 208-373-4100
Email: r4_boise_info@fs.fed.us
www.fs.fed.us/r4/boise

The 2.6 million–acre Boise National Forest is located north and east of the city of Boise, Idaho. Elevations range from 2,600 to 9,800 feet. The mountainous landscape developed through uplifting, faulting, and stream cutting. Major rivers: Boise and Payette rivers; South and Middle Fork drainages of the Salmon River.

Conifer forest covers most of the Boise National Forest. Shrubs and grasses grow in the nonforested areas.

The major big game species that live in the Boise Forest are mule deer, whitetail deer, elk, mountain goats, black bears, and mountain lions. Game bird species that are hunted include turkeys, blue grouse, spruce grouse, chukar partridge, gray (Hungarian) partridge, California quail, and mountain quail. Details on hunting can be found at www.fs.fed.us/r4/boise/recreation/hunting/hunt_index.shtml.

There are 70 campgrounds and picnic areas including some sites that are wheelchair accessible. Over 1,300 miles of trails are maintained. Visitors can hike and ride horseback; selected trails are open to bicycles, motorcycles, and ATVs.

## CARIBOU-TARGHEE NATIONAL FOREST AND CURLEW NATIONAL GRASSLAND
Pocatello, ID 83201
Phone: 208-523-3278
Email: Mailroom_R4_Caribou_T@fs.fed.us
www.fs.fed.us/r4/caribou-targhee/about/curlew/index.shtml

Created in 1907 by President Theodore Roosevelt, the forest now covers more than 1 million acres in southeast Idaho, with small portions in Utah and Wyoming. Game species are moose, elk, antelope, mule deer, mountain goats, black bears, whitetail deer, bighorn sheep, small animals, and game birds. Regulations vary widely, so be sure to get a copy of regulations from the local Fish and Game Office.

## CLEARWATER NATIONAL FOREST
Orofino, ID 83544
Phone: 208-476-4541
www.fs.fed.us/r1/clearwater

Located in north-central Idaho, the Clearwater National Forest comprises 1.8 million acres that range in elevation from 1,600 to nearly 9,000 feet. The forest is composed mainly of deep-forested canyons, with tumbling rivers, interspersed with high, rugged ridges. The ridges between the deep canyons have provided travel corridors across the mountains for centuries. These routes were used by the Nez Perce Indians and, in 1805–1806, the Lewis and Clark Expedition.

Clearwater has deer, elk, moose, bear, cougar, grouse hunting, and other hunting opportunities. Check with the district offices about use of ATVs.

## IDAHO PANHANDLE NATIONAL FOREST

Coeur d'Alene, ID 83814-8363

Phone: 208-765-7223

Email: Mailroom_R1_Idaho_Panhandle@
fs.fed.us

www.fs.fed.us/ipnf

Located in "the panhandle" of northern Idaho and extending into eastern Washington State and western Montana, the forest comprises about 2.5 million acres. Major big game species are mule deer, whitetail deer, elk, mountain goats, black bears, and mountain lions. Game bird species that are hunted include turkeys, blue grouse, spruce grouse, chukar partridge, gray (Hungarian) partridge, California quail, and mountain quail. Details on hunting can be found at www.fs.fed .us/r4/boise/recreation/hunting/hunt_index .shtml.

## PAYETTE NATIONAL FOREST

McCall, ID 83638

Phone: 208-634-0700

Email: Mailroom_R4_Payette@fs.fed.us

www.fs.fed.us/r4/payette

Located in west-central Idaho north of Boise, the 2.3 million–acre forest extends 100 miles west to east from Hells Canyon to the Middle Fork Salmon River. It stretches 70 miles north to south, from the Salmon River to the Weiser River. Highways 95 and 55 cross the forest and meet in New Meadows.

The major big game species that live in the Payette National Forest are mule deer, whitetail deer, elk, mountain goats, black bears, and mountain lions. Game bird species that are hunted include turkeys, blue grouse, spruce grouse, chukar partridge, gray (Hungarian) partridge, California quail, and mountain quail.

## SALMON-CHALLIS NATIONAL FOREST

Salmon, ID 83467

Phone: 208-756-5100

Email: Mailroom_R4_Salmon_Challis@
fs.fed.us

www.fs.fed.us/r4/sc

Over 4.3 million acres in east-central Idaho. Included within the boundaries of the forest are 1.3 million acres of the Frank Church–River of No Return Wilderness Area, the largest wilderness area in the continental United States. Rugged and remote, this country also contains Borah Peak, Idaho's tallest peak, the Wild and Scenic Salmon River, and the Middle Fork of the Salmon River.

The major big game species that live in this national forest are mule deer, whitetail deer, elk, mountain goats, black bears, and mountain lions. Game bird species that are hunted include turkeys, blue grouse, spruce grouse, chukar partridge, gray (Hungarian) partridge, California quail, and mountain quail.

## SAWTOOTH NATIONAL FOREST

Twin Falls, ID 83301-7976

Phone: 208-737-3200

Email: Mailroom_R4_Sawtooth@fs.fed.us

www.fs.fed.us/r4/sawtooth

Located in central Idaho lies the Sawtooth National Forest encompassing 2.1 million acres. Nearby lies the Sawtooth National Recreation Area and the Sawtooth Wilderness.

Within the boundaries of the 754,000-acre Sawtooth National Recreation Area (SNRA) are approximately 750 miles of trails, 40 peaks rising over 10,000 feet, and 300-plus high mountain lakes that add to the spectacular scenery and vistas.

The major big game species that live in this national forest are mule deer, whitetail deer, elk, mountain goats, black bears, and mountain lions. Game bird species that are hunted include turkeys, blue grouse, spruce grouse, chukar partridge, gray (Hungarian) partridge, California quail, and mountain quail.

*U.S. Bureau of Land Management*

**GREAT RIFT BACKCOUNTRY AREA**
Bureau of Land Management—Burley
Field Office
Burley, ID 83318
Phone: 208-677-6641
Email: SMaurer@plia.org
http://publiclands.org/explore/site.php?plic
state=ID&id=1926&PHPSESSID=48cd7
ea4ea3b3098530f273

The Great Rift is one of only two such features in the world. At 635 square miles, it is considered to be the largest, deepest, and most recent volcanic rift system in the continental United States. It contains undisturbed and unusual geologic features throughout the 380,000 acres of the Craters of the Moon and Wapi lava flows. Abundant wildlife, including sage grouse, mourning doves, mule deer, elk, and antelope, inhabit the area. Check with the district offices about use of ATVs.

*U.S. Fish and Wildlife Service*
*National Wildlife Refuges*

**BEAR LAKE NATIONAL WILDLIFE REFUGE**
Montpelier, ID 83254
Phone: 208-847-1757
www.fws.gov/pacific/refuges/field/ID_
Bearlk.htm

Located seven miles southwest of Montpelier, Bear Lake NWR lies in the mountain-ringed Bear Lake Valley in southeastern Idaho, north of the deep body of water that is the namesake of both the valley and the refuge. The refuge encompasses approximately 18,000 acres of the Dingle Swamp, a mosaic of bulrush-cattail marsh, open water, and flooded meadows. Waterfowl hunting is permitted here, with Idaho Fish and Game Department determining regulations.

**DEER FLAT NATIONAL WILDLIFE REFUGE**
Nampa, ID 83686
Phone: 208-467-9278; fax: 208-467-1019
www.fws.gov/deerflat

Deer Flat NWR, established in 1909, is one of the nation's oldest refuges. Located southwest of Boise, Idaho, the refuge includes the Lake Lowell sector (10,588 acres) and the Snake River Islands sector (about 800 acres). Lake Lowell is an irrigation project reservoir.

Visitors can hunt waterfowl on both the Lake Lowell and Snake River Islands sectors of the refuge. Limits and seasons are set by the Idaho Department of Fish and Game and the Oregon Department of Fish and Wildlife, as appropriate. Contact them for current hunting regulations.

Although use of permanent blinds is prohibited, portable blinds are allowed if they are removed at the end of each day. Temporary blinds may be constructed from natural vegetation less than three inches in diameter and are available on a first-come, first-served basis.

**MINIDOKA NATIONAL
WILDLIFE REFUGE**
Rupert, ID 83350
Phone: 208-436-3589
www.fws.gov/pacific/refuges/field/ID_
minidoka.htm

Minidoka NWR extends 25 miles along both shores of the Snake River, upstream from the Minidoka Dam in south-central Idaho. Over half of the refuge is open water, with small patches of marsh that attract concentrations of up to 100,000 ducks and geese during spring and fall migrations. Waterfowl and resident game bird hunting is popular. See state regulations for details.

**OXFORD SLOUGH WATERFOWL
PRODUCTION AREA**
c/o Southeast Idaho Refuge Complex
Chubbuck, ID 83202
Phone: 208-237-6615
www.fws.gov/pacific/refuges/field/ID_
oxford.htm

Oxford Slough Waterfowl Production Area is in Franklin and Bannock counties on the edge of Oxford in southeast Idaho, 10 miles northwest of Preston. This area contains 1,878 acres of marshes, meadows, and uplands and is prime for waterfowl nesting. Waterfowl hunting can be quite good here until the marsh freezes over in November. There is also limited hunting for chukar and quail. See Idaho state regulations for details.

*Private Hunting Clubs and Preserves*

**FLYING B RANCH**
Kamiah, ID 83536-9553
Phone: 800-472-1945 or 208-935-0755
(Local); fax: 208-935-0705
Email: info@flyingbranch.com
www.flyingbranch.com

Located in Lawyer Creek Canyon, this is an Orvis-endorsed wing-shooting lodge. The Flying B Ranch holds exclusive outfitter rights to over 740,000 acres of the Nez Perce and Clearwater National Forests in north-central Idaho.

Upland species commonly found on the Flying B Ranch are Hungarian partridge, chukar, pheasant, blue and ruffed grouse, and valley quail. Also mule deer, whitetails, black bears, cougars, turkeys, bobcats, elk, and moose. Some hunts can be conducted from the main lodge; others are pack hunts from backcountry camps.

Accommodations in the lodge and ranch house, plus elegant meals served with local wines. Ranch house offers a great place for retreats.

**LITTLE CANYON SHOOTING PRESERVE
AND SPORTING CLAYS**
Peck, ID 83545
Phone: 208-486-6235; fax: 208-486-6214

Email: lcs@syringa.net
www.littlecanyonshooting.com/
concept2.htm

Private ranch with an 800-acre shooting preserve offering chukar, pheasant, Hungarian partridge, and sporting clays.

**TETON RIDGE RANCH**
Tetonia, ID 83452
Phone: 208-456-2650; fax: 208-456-2218
Email: info@tetonridge.com
www.tetonridge.com

On 4,000 acres of spectacular private land surrounded by Targhee National Forest, with the Yellowstone and Grand Teton national parks within close reach. A 10,000-square-foot knotty pine lodge with cathedral ceilings and a gourmet chef.

The rustic but elegant dude ranch offers sporting clays and released bird hunting for pheasant and Hungarian partridge after September 1. Guests may bring their own hunting dogs or use the ranch's English setters.

**WESTERN WINGS BIRDS AND CLAYS**
Roberts, ID 83444
Phone: 208-228-2581; fax: 208-228-6931
Email: western@birdsandclays.com
www.westernwings.org

Western Wings offers 2,783 acres of premiere hunting habitat with chukar and pheasant. Walk-on day hunts and memberships. Membership privileges include water fowl hunting on Western Wings–controlled land (requires compliance with Idaho regulations), exclusive hunting privileges on additional 3,000-plus acres for doves and upland birds, reduced rates

on Western Wings Sporting Clay Course, antelope and elk hunting on Western Wings land (requires compliance with Idaho regulations), reduced rates on other Western Wings facilities, and areas and birds for on- and off-season dog training. Transportation from airport in Idaho Falls available; lodging and meals available.

# HERITAGE DESTINATIONS

*Snake River Birds of Prey National Conservation Area*

The 485,000-acre Snake River Birds of Prey National Conservation Area (NCA) is located along 81 miles of the Snake River in southwest Idaho. It was established in 1993 to protect a unique environment that supports one of the world's densest concentrations of nesting birds of prey. Falcons, eagles, hawks, and owls occur here in unique profusion and variety.

There is no hunting by humans here: this is the place to watch the real pros in action. Target shooting is permitted in certain marked areas.

**SNAKE RIVER BIRDS OF PREY NATIONAL CONSERVATION AREA**
Bureau of Land Management Four Rivers Field Office
Boise, ID 83705
Phone: 208-384-3300
www.birdsofprey.blm.gov/index.htm

# MONTANA

*In 2001 there were 170,000 resident hunters and 59,000 nonresident hunters: 90% went big game hunting, 23% small game, 10% migratory waterfowl and doves; 68% hunted on public lands; 58% hunted on private lands. Hunters pumped $238 million into the state economy. (USFWS)*

## OVERVIEW

Under the big blue skies of Montana, where the plains meet the Rockies, hunting is a vital part of the economy and culture.

Big game hunting is paramount here— black bears, elk, deer, mountain goats, moose, bighorn sheep, mountain lions, and antelope are abundant, plus bison—although wing- shooters bag around 150,000 pheasant, 60,000 Hungarian partridge, 70,000 sharp- tailed grouse a year, and a fair amount of waterfowl.

---

**MONTANA SNAPSHOT**
**TREASURE STATE**

- **General hunting information from Montana Fish, Game, and Parks Department:** http://fwp.mt .gov/hunting/default.html

- **Montana's toll-free hotline to report poaching and other crime: 800-TIP-MONT** (800-847-6668); tips that lead to convictions result in rewards up to $1,000

- **Deer population:** 350,000–400,000, 27th in the United States

- **Average deer harvest:** 53,749, 30th in the United States

---

In recent years the success rate of elk hunters in Montana has been almost 20%. One of the hottest public lands areas for big game is the 375,000-acre Upper Missouri Breaks National Monument in central Mon- tana. According to Stoneydale Press publisher Dale Burk, who is based in Stevensville, Mon- tana, and has killed 56 elk in his lifetime through 2006, nonresidents coming to hunt in Montana need to pay special attention to the terrain and the weather. "Blizzards out here can turn anyplace into a wilderness," he says. "When it snows or rains heavy, don't force it. When it lets up, that's the best time to hunt, because the animals have been laying low, too, and they will be out looking for food."

For more information on the Upper Mis- souri Breaks National Monument, see www. mt.blm.gov/ldo/um/index.html.

Dale Burke's Stoneydale Press, inciden- tally, is a gold mine of books and tapes about hunting in Montana: www.stoney dale.com.

# FEATURED HUNT

## Going Solo for Mule Deer in Montana

JEFF ENGEL

When hunting is really in your blood, it can make you do some unusual things. As a host of *Engel's Outdoor Experience,* I always have a camera crew following me on my hunts. After so many years of doing that, I thought I would like to experience what it was like to actually hunt alone again and try to film the entire hunt myself.

Along the drive from Wisconsin to eastern Montana, I stopped at Theodore Roosevelt National Memorial Park, which is located in southwestern North Dakota. Teddy Roosevelt first came to this area in 1883 on a hunting trip. A side trip visiting the park was well worth it. As I drove through the park, I came across an elk herd with a large 6 × 7 bull right in the middle of the herd. The elk herd said more than words could say about why we create national parks to honor great conservationists and to provide a wonderful opportunity for people to see undisturbed wild areas.

After two days of driving, I finally passed the large road sign "Welcome to Montana." With a wonderful panoramic view to the west, it is clear why the state is called "Big Sky Country." After a much-needed night's rest, I was up well before the sun.

My quest was mule deer, and they are plentiful here. The state has a deer population of about 400,000. I would be looking for only one, but one that would cooperate.

The temperature was a very moderate 30 degrees. In previous trips to Montana during the same time period, in early November, I have hunted in temperatures as high as 70 degrees and as low as minus 11 degrees. On this trip I was towing my Aluma trailer with an ATV securely fastened on it. My hunting technique would be to take the ATV to very remote areas and then from there go on foot the rest of the way.

The West is a very visual place: almost everywhere you look, you can find interesting forms and composition both natural and man-made. Just being in this rugged beautiful country is a big part of the hunt.

My hunting strategy was straightforward. I would ease up to points of land and carefully look over the edge and spend a great deal of time just glassing the countryside, looking for the mule deer. There was also about three inches of fresh snow on the ground, perfect for seeing deer.

As I walked along, I thought I was the only one

hunting in this area, but I came across a fellow hunter—a wolf spider—walking across on top of the ice. A wolf spider is a predator who prowls about looking for food, just like me. Since he is cold-blooded, I presumed the snow may have been warmer than the air above. I never knew that spiders were out in these conditions and walked on top of the snow.

As I glassed and hiked through the hills, I set the camera up so I could walk past it or walk into frame to film B-roll to be edited into the television show. Doing this makes you appreciate the kind of shots you need to tell a good story.

I was really beginning to enjoy this experiment of filming the hunt. The solitude and the stark surreal landscape seemed to be more vivid when you hunt alone. I also found myself being much more aware of my surroundings and my vulnerability.

I was looking for a buck whose antlers would exceed the ear tips. When the ears are straight out, they measure approximately 23 inches, so I was looking for a buck that exceeded the ear width. Along with hopefully harvesting a mature buck on film, I was very much looking forward to bringing home some fresh venison for Sherol. We find that we enjoy eating venison several times each week for its nutritional value as well as excellent taste, and Sherol is a supreme chef when it comes to preparing it.

I was seeing about five to eight bucks a day, but I just wasn't seeing the right one. After the third day of hunting, I slowly crested a hill, and I spotted one of the biggest mule deer bucks I have ever seen. Under normal circumstances I would not hesitate to take an immediate shot at this monster. Unfortunately, in the time it took me to position my camera and rifle, he had disappeared. But just seeing such a tremendous buck was a thrill.

My goal was to have the camera running, with the deer in focus, center framed, while I took the shot. Once I took a successful shot, I would reverse the angle for the camera and film myself shooting; then back at the studio I would combine the various shots to create a smooth, flowing scene. At that moment I began to question why I was filming the hunt

myself, but this opportunity just created an even greater challenge for me.

A few more days passed, and I continued to see a lot more deer, but I was still looking for that special deer and to be able to film him and shoot him at the same time.

Hunting without a cameraman presented its own challenges. Although I saw plenty of deer, I had to pass many up, waiting for the perfect opportunity. It seemed like there wasn't time to get my camera set up and rifle before they spotted me.

Still, the scenery was beautiful, and despite everything, I was really enjoying the solitude. I also found it extremely refreshing to be alone, to just think about woodsmanship skills and practice the many techniques my father had taught me throughout the years. That afternoon, as the sun was about to kiss the horizon, I spotted a very nice mule deer buck standing broadside about 200 yards away. The buck was unaware of my presence, and I had plenty of time to set up my camera and tripod and get my rifle into position.

Once I confirmed the camera was running, I slowly got my rifle and was able to take a shot. It was as if I had bagged two bucks, not one!

On this hunt I had an outstanding outdoor experience. I had the fortune of being able to harvest a buck while filming it myself. There just seemed to be a certain satisfaction of knowing it all came together.

Another lesson I learned from this trip: Next time I'll take a cameraman along.

For more information on hunting deer in Montana, contact:

**COTTONWOOD OUTFITTERS/JOHN WILKINSON**
Miles City, MT 59301
Phone: 406-232-4910
www.cottonwoodmt.com

 **HUNTING TIP**

## Native American Guidance for Hunters

There is a strong Native American presence in Montana, and so we asked a member of the Blackfoot to give us some advice on spiritual aspects of hunting.

There are four bands or tribes that make up the *Blackfoot Tribe*: the Blackfeet (Amskapi Pikuni), who reside in northern Montana on the Canadian border, the major populace in Browning, Montana; the Blood (Kainaiwa), residing in southern Alberta just across the border; the Piegan (Piikani Nation); and Siksika (Siksika Nation), who reside east of Calgary, Alberta. Together they form the Blackfoot Nation or the Blackfoot Confederacy.

Today there are 16,500 enrolled members in the Blackfeet Tribe alone. Some 7,000 of them still reside on the Blackfeet Reservation, where they hunt and fish on 1.5 million acres of land. Hunting on the Blackfeet Reservation has dramatically improved since the adoption of hunting laws and hunting restrictions set by the Blackfeet Fish and Game Department. These laws and hunting restrictions on some species has drastically increased the elk, whitetail deer, mule deer, moose, antelope, and bighorn sheep herds.

A significant part of the spiritual and cultural regeneration of Native people is based on the restoration of the tribal lands and the indigenous species that once occupied them.

The Blackfoot have been hunters of necessity for thousands of years. Buffalo, deer, elk, antelope, and all small game have always been primary fare for the Blackfoot. Therefore, to illustrate the extent to which hunting is central to the Blackfoot culture, in the Blackfoot language, the term for "meat" is *nita'pi waksin*, which translates as "real food." All other food is called *kistapi waksin*, which translates as "not real food."

Alvin Yellow Owl describes some of the spiritual traditions of the Blackfeet.

### "BLACKFEET HUNTING TRADITIONS"
#### BY ALVIN T. YELLOW OWL, JR.

My ancestors of the Blackfeet tribe migrated with the buffalo so that they could obtain the meat for food, hides for clothing and shelter, and the many other parts that were used for all of life. Nothing went to waste; all was used one way or another.

The buffalo meant life to my people, the Blackfeet—that's why there are so many songs sung about them and stories told about them.

The night before the hunt they would dance and sing, preparing for the next day, knowing it might be their last. Hunting buffalo was like preparing to go to war not knowing if you were going to come back or not; but if you did, you were honored. Only the best hunters went, just like the best warriors protected the camp. If you didn't come back and you lost your life to a buffalo, it was a good death that you died with honor to your people.

The day of the hunt the scouts would come back and tell everybody where the buffalo were. The hunters/warriors would paint themselves and their horses. They also smudged with sweetgrass. ["Smudging" is lighting a braid of sweetgrass, then drawing the smoke toward your heart, then to your mind, then all around you and back to your heart again, and then to your weapons.] They smudged to protect themselves and their horses for the hunt, so they would not get injured and also to have a good and successful hunt. They also smudged to protect the animals that they were about to kill, praying to make it a swift and brave death and thanking them for giving their lives so we as a people could prosper.

Another method that my people, the Blackfeet, used to hunt buffalo was to drive them off a cliff called a buffalo jump using drivelines. This was a very successful method, killing huge quantities at a time. If it weren't for the buffalo, elk, deer, and many other animals that gave their lives, we wouldn't be here now. I strongly believe that.

Everything has a spirit to guide it through life, and if you take that life, make sure you're taking it for the right reason and make an offering in its place. Giving tobacco to Mother Earth for that life is a practice that our ancestors did.

After the kills were made, the women and children

would start preparing the meat for drying and the hides for teepees and clothing and whatever else was needed. This is how life was as a Native American.

You depended on the game around you for meat and clothing, but everything we took from Mother Earth, we thanked Her for it. We thanked the wind for the cool breeze in our faces and the sun for keeping us warm and giving life to everything around it and the moon to guide us at night.

As hunters, we all dream about how it would be to hunt long ago with our ancestors, not only the native ancestors but also the European ancestors of long ago. We dream about how they prepared for the hunt and the different weapons that were used. The weapons that we still use today, including the long bow, which was the principal weapon, were made from many things in nature, each of which has its own spirit. No matter how our ancestors hunted, they all had one thing in common: to be the best provider for their families. If you didn't kill, you went hungry.

As a Native American and an avid hunter, growing up on the Blackfeet Reservation my very first memory of hunting is riding with my dad in a yellow Chevy truck in the middle of winter. We drove along a rode toward Kiowa camp a while; then this whitetail doe stepped out, and he shot it. He gutted it and took the meat, heart, and liver. He didn't leave very much. Every part of the animal has value; you come to understand this if you hunt to survive.

Then we went to my grandmother's house. He put the deer on the table, and my grandfather, Pete Yellow Owl, took a slice of raw liver and ate it. I did this, too. It was natural because that's how we did things at their house. But before we ate the liver and cooked the meat of the deer, my grandfather sang a song, burnt some sweetgrass, and thanked the deer for giving her life so that we could eat. That was also my first memory of my grandfather Pete Yellow Owl, burning sweetgrass and singing in our native tongue, thanking the deer for giving her life that night.

I am 41 years old now. I have a lovely wife of 18 years, Donna, and three children and three grandchildren. It seems like years ago since both my father and grandfather passed away—my father, when I was 9, and my grandfather, when I was 21. I still today thank Mother Earth for giving me that time to spend with my dad going hunting and fishing, even if it was a very short time. I still practice some of the native ancestors' traditions, like burning of sweetgrass before a hunt and in everyday life.

Like my ancestors, I thank Mother Earth for this good day and to make it a successful hunt and to make my friends safe and to let our arrows and our bullets fly true and make a clean good kill. And if a kill is made, we leave an offering of tobacco, thanking Mother Earth for this fine day and thanking Her for the meat She has provided us for our families.

I believe that every hunter should take the time to connect with Mother Earth and realize that what you're doing is actually taking a life from Her. Like a mother, She mourns that life but is glad to give it up to provide for her other children like you and me. But She also provides us with the wind in our hair, the sun in our faces, the cool crisp autumn mornings, the sound of a creek next to our treestands, and the birds flying over us, heading due south. Can you imagine going hunting and none of these things happening? Isn't this why most of us go hunting nowadays anyway, to enjoy the sights and sounds and connect with nature and also to teach our younger generation how to respect, enjoy, and use this great gift that is given to us?

Like my grandfather, I still burn sweetgrass and sage and still pray to Mother Earth. In today's society, my prayers are a little different, but the meaning is still the same and that is to connect to whatever you're doing at that moment and thanking Mother Earth for that time and place and the friend or family member you have to share it with. It doesn't get any better than that.

If all hunters would add a little spirituality to their hunts, this would make them better hunters. It would get them more in tune with nature and the surroundings. Not only looking but also listening more to everything seen and heard. It makes one a more respectful hunter and more respectful of nature.

We all have to do our part as hunters. As hunters, our hunting grounds are shrinking in this world, so the land that we have left we need to respect and take care of so the animals can thrive and prosper. Like a grandmother, the earth is getting older, and as children we are the only ones who can take care of her. So it's our turn now to take care of our Grandmother Earth, including having respect for her grandchildren, the animals that we hunt. These animals allow us to take their lives so that a son and dad, daughter and mother, and old friends can spend that time with each other, making memories that will last a lifetime.

You can buy smudging herbs directly from the Blackfeet Nation through their Web site at www.blackfeetnationstore.com/herbs.html.

For hunting information and guides on the Blackfeet Reservation, contact:

**BLACKFEET FISH AND GAME DEPARTMENT**
Browning, MT 59417
Phone: 406-338-7207

## DESTINATIONS

### General Information

Nearly one-third of Montana, over 30 million acres, is public land. There are 16 million acres of national forests, 8 million acres of BLM lands, 300,000 acres of land and water managed by the Bureau of Reclamation, and 10 National Wildlife Refuges. Fortunately, there is a current listing of all the public lands in Montana at www.recreation.gov/recFacilitySearch.do. This Web search also includes a number of cabins in national forests that can be rented out for hunts.

Maps (http://fwp.mt.gov/hunting/planahunt) and details on public and privateaccess (http://fwp.mt.gov/hunting/hunteraccess/public.html) may also be found online.

Lists of Montana guides and outfitters may be found at www.montanahuntingguides.com, http://huntfind.com/hunting_guides/montana_hunting.html, http://biggameoutfittersdirectory.com, and www.biggamehunt.net/directory/guides_United_States_Montana.html.

You can also check the guides and outfitters out through the Montana Outfitters and Guides Association at http://hunting

.about.com/gi/dynamic/offsite.htm?zi=1/XJ/
Ya&sdn=hunting&cdn=sports&tm=7&f=10
&tt=14&bt=1&bts=1&zu=http%3A//www
.moga-montana.org.

*Special Wing-shooting Opportunities*

**EAGLE NEST LODGE**
Hardin, MT 59034
Phone: 866-258-3474; fax: 406-665-3712
www.eaglenestlodge.com

Built along the banks of the fabled Bighorn River, more than 40,000 acres for upland hunting for wild pheasant, Hungarian partridge, and sharp-tailed grouse, plus world-class fly-fishing, spacious lodge, extraordinary cuisine, and a pro shop. Eagle Nest Lodge is endorsed for both wing shooting and fly-fishing by Orvis.

**FORRESTER'S BIG HORN**
**RIVER RESORT**
Fort Smith, MT 59035
Phone: 800-665-3799
www.forrestersbighorn.com

An Orvis-endorsed wing-shooting, fly-fishing, and outfitting resort on three miles of the Bighorn River offering wing shooting for wild pheasant, Hungarian partridge, sharp-tailed grouse, and chukar. Stay in luxurious lodge or cabins; outstanding food. Many of the guides are from the Crow tribe.

A complete guide to wing shooting in Montana by Chuck Johnson and Ben O. Williams is available from Wilderness Adventure Press:www.wildadv.com/store/index

.php? main_page=product_info&products _id=101.

## HERITAGE DESTINATIONS

*Ulm Pishkun State Park*
Hunting buffalo with primitive archery equipment is not easy, and it is dangerous. One of the most effective methods of early Indian hunting for buffalo was to have a swift runner, a "buffalo caller," drape a buffalo robe over himself and mingle with a herd. The buffalo caller, with the help of other hunters making noises, would seek to drive a herd of one-ton bison toward the cliff edge. The buffalo caller would then run out of the herd toward the cliff and leap off it, landing safely on a ledge a few feet below, where he could crawl into a crevice for safety.

Following his lead, and driven by other hunters, some of the herd would seek to follow the buffalo caller, plunging over the cliff and falling 50 feet to the rocks below, where other hunters with spears and bows would finish them off.

One indication of how many buffalo were killed here is that between 1945 and 1957 up to 150 tons of phosphorus-rich bones were quarried from this site to use for fertilizer and making munitions

"Pishkun" originates from a Blackfeet Indian word that means "deep blood kettle." For over 600 years, roughly A.D. 1000 to A.D. 1700, Indians stampeded herds of buffalo over a mile-long 50 feet-high cliff along the

Missouri River at this place. It is one of the largest prehistoric buffalo killing grounds in North America.

The pishkun method of buffalo hunting waned as horses were introduced, enabling Indian hunters to ride up beside buffalo to shoot arrows, and then bullets, from very close range.

Today there is a 6,000-square-foot museum on the site, and many special events take place during the year, including Native American art, dancing, traditional games and singing, and demonstrations of traditional hide tanning. In September of each year the park holds an atlatl spear-throwing contest.

Location: 10 miles south of Great Falls on I-15 at Ulm Exit, then 3.5 miles northwest on Ulm-Vaughn Road. Day-use area only.

**ULM PISHKUN STATE PARK**
Ulm, MT 59485
Phone: 406-866-2217
http://fwp.mt.gov/lands/site_282807.aspx

## WYOMING

*In 2001 there were 65,000 resident hunters and 68,000 nonresident hunters: 82% went big game hunting, 25% small game, 7% migratory waterfowl; 65% hunted on public lands; 25% hunted on private lands. Hunters pumped $123 million into the state economy. (USFWS)*

### OVERVIEW
There are 9 million acres of national forests alone in Wyoming—that's more acreage than in some small states. Wildlife is abundant here, making this state truly a hunter's paradise.

---

**WYOMING SNAPSHOT**
**EQUALITY STATE**

- **General information:**
Wyoming Game and Fish Department
5400 Bishop Boulevard
Cheyenne, WY 82006
Phone: 307-777-4600
http://gf.state.wy.us/HuntNetTest/frmhun
page.aspx

- **Online license application:** https://gf.state.wy.us/
elsapplication/ELSWelcome.aspx

- **Stop poaching tip line:** Rewards are paid when
your tip leads to an arrest or citation; call 800-
442-4331 or 307-777-4330 or see http://gf.state.
wy.us/wildlife/enforcement/stoppoaching/
submittip.aspx

- **Deer population:** 54,000 (includes other species),
41st in the United States

- **Average deer harvest:** 10,062, 40th in the United
States

---

There are 44 federal lands in Wyoming that offer hunting opportunities. We have tried to select out some of the best.

Guides and outfitters are more common in Wyoming than almost any other state. To find guides and outfitters, contact:

**WYOMING BOARD OF OUTFITTERS**
Cheyenne, WY 82002
Phone: 307-635-1589 or 800-264-0981
http://outfitters.state.wy.us

The big game animals are whitetail and mule deer, elk, bighorn sheep, antelope, mountain goats, moose, mountain lions, black bears, and bison. Merriam's turkeys, sage grouse, blue and ruffed grouse, sharp-tailed grouse, pheasant, and waterfowl are the wing-shooter's quest.

Since 1939, Lander, Wyoming, has hosted the nation's most unique celebrity big game hunt, the One Shot Antelope Hunt.

Only 24 lucky hunters—politicians, actors, musicians, athletes—get invited every year. Each gets only one shot to kill an antelope. To help their accuracy, the bullets are blessed by the Shoshone tribe.

The event is held as a fund-raiser to benefit the Water for Wildlife Program—see www.waterforwildlife.com—which over the years has created over 300 watering facilities in the high desert, benefiting all species of wildlife. It has also led to an African one-shot hunt, which is described in the section on South Africa.

## HUNTING TIP

### Protecting an Antelope Cape

If you are lucky enough to bag an antelope and want to have a head or shoulder mount of the head, antelope hair is not firmly attached to the skin. Don't drag a fallen animal. Cape out the skin you want to save as soon as possible and remove all meat and fat from the underside of the skin. Salt the hide quickly, using feed salt such as Morton Kiln-Dried Mill Run Salt, which is available in 50-pound bags from feed stores. It may take 20 pounds to protect the cape.

### DESTINATIONS

#### General Information

The Wyoming Private Lands Public Wildlife Access Walk-in Areas Program and Hunter Management Areas (HMAs) together offer 1,180,000 private acres for hunting and other outdoor sports. For the Walk-in Areas Program, the state leases hunting rights from private landowners, whose lands are open to walk-in access during seasons and only for specified species. Details can be found at http://gf.state.wy.us/wildlife/access/plpw/huntingwalk/hunting.asp.

There are 31 Hunter Management Areas, which provide access on private lands, or a combination of private and public lands, with written permission required. It is possible to acquire this permission for 26 of the areas online at http://gf.state.wy.us/wildlife/access/plpw/management/hunter_mgmt.asp. You can also obtain permission in person at Hunter Management Areas Check Stations.

To receive permission for areas through the mail: photocopy hunting license and vehicle ID information—make, year, color, model number, and license plate number. Specify which HMA you are requesting permission for. Mail information along with a 10 × 13-inch self-addressed, stamped (63¢) envelope to: Wyoming Game and Fish Department, Access Permission—(HMA name), 3030 Energy Lane, Casper, WY 82604.

#### U.S. Bureau of Land Management

The BLM manages 24 areas in Wyoming that offer hunting according to state regulations and local postings. There are 10 offices spread around the state. For maps and details, see www.blm.gov/wy/st/en.html.

#### USDA National Forests

There are four major national forests in Wyoming that all offer hunting according to state regulations and local postings.

**BIGHORN NATIONAL FOREST**
Sheridan, WY 82801
Phone: 307-674-2600
www.fs.fed.us/r2/bighorn

The forest encompasses 1.1 million acres in the Big Horn Mountains of north-central Wyoming.

**BRIDGER-TETON NATIONAL FOREST**
Jackson, WY 83001
Phone: 307-739-5500
www.fs.fed.us/btnf

Located in western Wyoming, the 3.4 million acres of the Bridger-Teton National Forest make it the second-largest national forest outside of Alaska. Included are more than 1.2 million acres of wilderness.

**MEDICINE BOW-ROUTT NATIONAL FOREST AND THUNDER BASIN NATIONAL GRASSLAND**
Laramie, WY 82070-6535
Phone: 307-745-2300
www.fs.fed.us/r2/mbr

Encompasses nearly 3 million acres from the north and eastern borders of Wyoming. In the far eastern part of this range one finds some of the best opportunities for sage grouse, sharp-tailed grouse, and antelope.

**SHOSHONE NATIONAL FOREST**
Cody, WY 82414
Phone: 307-527-6241
www.fs.fed.us/r2/shoshone

A 2.4-million acre national forest located in the Wind River and Absaroka Mountain ranges of northwestern Wyoming. The forest is especially good elk and bighorn sheep country.

*U.S. Fish and Wildlife Service*
*National Wildlife Refuges*
Wyoming has seven National Wildlife Refuges—Banford, Cokeville Meadows, Hutton, Mortenson, National Elk, Pathfinder, and Seedskadee. Details on each may be found at http://mountain-prairie.fws.gov/refuges/wy.

**NATIONAL ELK REFUGE**
Jackson, WY 83001
Phone: 307-733-9212
www.fws.gov/nationalelkrefuge

Located in Jackson Hole, Wyoming, the refuge's nearly 25,000 acres provide a winter home for one of the largest wintering concentrations of elk, with nearly 7,500 animals annually. The refuge is open to elk hunting only from mid-October through early December. Hunters must have a valid state elk license, a Hunter Education card, a Wyoming Conservation Stamp, an Elk Management Stamp, and a refuge access permit. For details, see www.fws.gov/nationalelkrefuge/NERHuntingRegs.htm.

*Hunting Clubs, Resorts, and Preserves*

**BALD MOUNTAIN OUTFITTERS**
Pinedale, WY 82941
Phone: 307-367-6539
www.baldmountainoutfitters.com

Featured on a number of television shows, Bald Mountain Outfitters offers guided hunts for elk, mule deer, Shiras moose, antelope, black bears, and bighorn sheep in the Pinedale area and the Bridger Wilderness, and whitetail deer, wild turkeys, and antelope in the Black Hills of northeastern Wyoming. A dude ranch and cabins are available at the Hidden Heart Ranch—www.hiddenheartranch.com.

**CANYON RANCH**
Big Horn, WY 82833
Phone: 307-674-6239; fax: 307-672-2264
www.canyonranchbighorn.com

An Orvis-endorsed fly-fishing lodge and guest ranch located 15 miles from Sheridan, offering spring hunts for Merriam's wild turkeys on the ranch.

**RON DUBE'S WILDERNESS ADVENTURES**
Wapiti, WY 82450
Phone: 307-527-7815; fax: 527-6084
www.huntinfo.com/dube

Guided hunts for elk and bighorn sheep with one of the most respected guides in the area, with option to stay in a teepee and learn about Native American culture.

## HERITAGE DESTINATIONS

*Buffalo Bill Museum and Historical Center, Cody, Wyoming*
William F. "Buffalo Bill" Cody was born near LeClaire, Iowa, in February 1846. At the age of 12, he worked for a wagon train to Fort Laramie. A year later he tried his hand in the Colorado gold rush. By age 15, he was a Pony Express rider.

Cody served as a scout for the Union's 7th Kansas Cavalry during the last years of the Civil War. In 1867, Cody began hunting

buffalo for Kansas Pacific work crews, earning his moniker "Buffalo Bill" and his reputation as an expert shot. The next year, Cody was employed by the U.S. Army as a civilian scout and guide for the Fifth Cavalry. His experience and skills as a plainsman made him an invaluable tracker and fighter. In 1872, Cody received the Congressional Medal of Honor for valor in action during the Indian Wars, one of only four civilian scouts to receive this honor.

Under the protection of the army, Buffalo Bill Cody guided visiting dignitaries—such as the Grand Duke Alexis of Russia—on lavish hunting expeditions as publicity stunts, with the blessings of General Philip Sheridan.

In 1872, Cody was persuaded by writer Ned Buntline to take to the stage, portraying himself. The show led to the formation of Cody's own troupe in 1873, which included real-life western heroes "Wild Bill" Hickok and Texas Jack Omohundro.

For the next few years, Cody alternated his time between serving as a scout for the Fifth Cavalry during the Plains Indian resistance and show business.

In 1883, Cody created Buffalo Bill's Wild West Show, which ran for 30 years throughout the United States and Europe, making Cody an international celebrity and launching the career of sharpshooter Annie Oakley.

In the town named for him, Cody, Wyoming, you will find the Buffalo Bill Historical Center, a large modern complex of art and history that includes the Buffalo Bill Museum, the Whitney Gallery of Western Art, the Plains Indian Museum, the Cody Firearms Museum, and the Draper Museum of Natural History. This is a must for anyone interested in firearms and the colorful history of the American West—a great place to visit midday during a hunt for sage grouse or antelope, which are very abundant nearby.

**BUFFALO BILL HISTORICAL CENTER**
Cody, WY 82414
Phone: 307-587-4771
www.bbhc.org/home/index_flash.cfm

# Pacific Coast

*In 2001 there were 261,000 resident hunters and 12,000 nonresident hunters: 47% went big game hunting, 40% small game, 42% waterfowl; 45% hunted on public lands; 65% hunted on private lands. Hunters pumped $315 million into the state economy. (USFWS)*

## OVERVIEW

Over the last 20 years, there has been a decline in California hunting license sales, from 690,000 per year to less than 300,000, but this does not tell the whole story. This is the only state where you can take three species of elk—Rocky Mountain, Roosevelt, and tule. Wild boars and turkeys are so plentiful in some areas that they are causing considerable crop damage. California pheasant hunters bag about 150,000 wild birds a year, primarily in the rice fields of the Central Valley; and more than 700,000 California, Mountain, and Gambel's quail are harvested per year. California is also second only to Texas in the number of doves harvested per year—over a million—and first in band-tailed pigeons and second in jack snipes.

Sixty percent of all the ducks and geese of the Pacific Flyway winter in California's Central Valley. California duck hunters' average annual bag is the best in the United States—28—that's twice the bag of Arkansas, Saskatchewan, Texas, Florida, Louisiana,

---

**CALIFORNIA SNAPSHOT
GOLDEN STATE**

- **General information:**
  California Department of Fish and
  Game—Wildlife Branch
  1812 Ninth Street
  Sacramento, CA 95814
  Phone: 916-445-3406
  www.dfg.ca.gov/wmd

- **License information:**
  Department of Fish and Game—License
  and Revenue Branch
  1740 North Market Boulevard
  Sacramento, CA 95834
  Phone: 916-928-5805, fax: 916-419-7587
  www.dfg.ca.gov/licensing/index.html

- **CALTIP hotline to help stop pollution and
  poaching:** 1-888-DFG-CALTIP (1-888-334-2258)
  Rewards up to $1,000 have been paid for tips
  that lead to arrests and citations.

and North Dakota; three times that of South Dakota; and nearly five times higher than Wisconsin.

The chief problem for California hunters is that the deer herd has shrunk from 2 million blacktails and mule deer in the l970s to 600,000—primarily due to loss of habitat. According to deer biologist Ken Mayer, Zone B, which includes the Mendocino National Forest, is the blacktail "deer factory" for the state, but you have to be willing to go far from the roads to find the big ones. For details, see www.fs.fed.us/r5/mendocino.

For bowhunters, California offers what is quite possibly the earliest archery deer season in the United States. Along the coast, Zone A opens right after the 4th of July and ends the end of July. These tags never sell out.

 **FEATURED HUNT**

### Extreme Deer Hunting

JERRY KARNOW*

I planned for months for my mule deer hunt in the San Bernardino Mountains north of Palm Springs in southern California. First, I secured a deer tag for deer hunt Zone D-14. Although the area historically had a poor success rate for deer hunters, the 1,500 available tags usually sell out. The juncture where the San Bernardino Mountains meet the Sonoran Desert looks barren, and one would think there were no deer, but it is actually rich in wildlife. And, fortunately, I knew more about the area than most, as I'm a California Fish and Game warden, and I used to patrol the region.

Not only are there trophy deer; black bears are abundant, and trophy-sized desert bighorn sheep roam the higher elevations. Also, with the transition from desert to chaparral to mountains with pine trees, the area has populations of three different species of quail: Gambel's quail, California valley quail, and mountain quail.

Adding to the diversity of wildlife is a high concentration of rattlesnakes—sidewinder, red diamond, specked, and western. Perhaps it is the abundance of snakes that discourages some hunters to venture into this area.

It was late October 2006, and the warm, dry Santa Ana winds of southern California had kicked in. A raging wildland arson fire driven by these heavy winds had recently taken out thousands of acres and homes and was still out of control in some of the steep mountainous regions of southern California. Five brave firefighters had lost their lives protecting homes.

I got a hold of my hunting partner, Steve, who was a California Department of Forestry captain in that area. To my relief, Steve was out of town. The five firefighters killed were identified as employees from the U.S. Forest Service—the worst loss suffered by their agency.

As in all hunts, I researched the conditions of the landscape and wildlife populations. The tragic fire was not in the plans, and I knew that just months before a wildfire consumed thousands of acres of the area we planned to hunt. Yet the earlier fire might result in new growth, which would be food for the deer.

This hunt is not a typical deer hunt, and if several factors are not in place, it can be difficult to connect with deer. But if the conditions are right and we hike into the depths of the roughest mountains, we have always connected with fabulous heavy antlered deer and witness tremendous wildlife. Three subspecies of deer roam the area: California mule deer, southern mule deer, and burro deer.

Steve and I met in the town of Banning and began by organizing our food and gear. It was the most critical part of our hunt. With careful planning and several years of trial and error, we tried to find the lightest gear possible: very light compact sleeping bags, one change of clothes, tiny stoves, light rifles, light rain gear, light food, and light efficient backpacks that can withstand packing out an entire deer. The food and water was planned to the meal for five days.

There is no water where we hunt. It all had to be packed in. Five days' worth of water to drink and to use to mix with freeze-dried food meant heavy packs and that water is worth gold. As we headed out on our journey, the anticipation of the hunt increased but also the realization of the grueling climb of several thousand feet in elevation loaded with heavy packs with all that water.

If you aren't in shape, forget this hunt. You park your vehicle and start the hike near the desert floor just north of Palm Springs. There are no trails to follow, other than game trails and a small portion of the Pacific Crest Trail—just ridgelines and landmarks we recognized over the years. It is slow going climbing sometimes along sheer cliff, using hands to traverse loose rock, and many hours hiking steep ridgelines. Two deer I had taken in the area in the past I shot in very steep terrain; both tumbled hundreds of feet down a canyon. One of those bucks was a very respectable heavy antlered 20-inch wide 4×3 with tall eye guards (nine-point buck in eastern standards). I wonder what year I will no longer be able to hunt the area as I get older?

We reached our parking spot and were on foot within minutes. The weather was fairly warm, and we ran across a beautiful Sonoran gopher snake and a long-nosed snake. It was November! We started in the late afternoon and hiked by flashlight for another two hours after dark. After about five hours of hiking, we made camp—simply laying our sleeping bags in the dirt and eating cheese, crackers, a can of sardines, and a Power Bar.

We were at the base of some steeper terrain and knew it would take another five hours to get to where we wanted to make base camp. It was all uphill from here.

We slept for about six hours, listening to coyotes howling close by throughout the night. Before light, we stuffed our bags, ate hard-boiled eggs and a Power Bar, and were off up a steep ridge. As the sun rose, we peeked to the west into several canyons with the sun at our backs. There are no roads, no houses, and humans rarely visit the area. Yet it is all public lands managed by the U.S. Forest Service and the BLM.

Typically you do not find deer signs at first. After about five hours of hiking, you begin to find signs. We were delighted to see groups of deer emerging as the sun first hit the ridges. Our excitement mounted as we realized the deer once again would be here.

Ten years prior, Steve and I had hunted the area and hiked out after dark, losing sight of our way out. We came upon a dry waterfall area, and as we worked our way down the rock embankment, Steve slipped and destroyed his rifle scope. He did not get hurt; but I'll have to say, Redfield Scopes stand by their product—they shipped Steve a brand-new scope! We learned a lesson on safety that trip.

We chose to hunt this first week of November, as the weather usually changes to cooler temperatures, and the season ended on the 12th. It also meant the deer start to rut. As we glassed the canyons, we spotted two bucks and about 18 does. One buck was a respectable forked-horn clearly in rut chasing a doe. We pressed on to get into the country where we wanted to drop our gear and start seriously hunting. Those packs were heavy. We were prepared to hunt to the last day of the season—that meant we had about four full days of hunting. Steve and I vowed we would not kill a buck in this country unless it was a heavy antlered 3×3 or a nice 4×4.

As we got closer to the "hunting grounds," we could see the edge of the fire line: burned black chaparral and green vegetation. The area was seemingly endless square miles of steep mountainous badlands with scattered areas of lush timber stands at the top of most ranges. Steve and I looked to the north and talked about the California state record-book desert bighorn sheep that was taken recently only a few miles from where we were standing and wondered if we would see any on this trip.

We came across a tent. It was closed up, and as we got nearer, we could smell rotting flesh, like a dead animal. It was strange enough that someone would be this far in—but also the smell. We thought the worst, and as trained emergency persons, we took off our packs and investigated. The tent had been there for some time, and we expected to find a dead body inside. We carefully opened the tent. To our relief, no dead guy. Inside was some rotting meat, several sleeping bags, flashlights, booze, and canned food. There were two large bright spotlights inside as well. It was all heavy stuff, and it made me wonder if it was a poachers' camp. About 10 years prior, I had arrested two guys that were poaching deer and bear in the same general area. They had backpacked in and would stay for long periods of time, leaving similar gear for weeks.

We closed up the tent and moved on. It would be about another hour of hiking until we made our own base camp. To this point we had consumed a fair amount of water. We knew we would use up water packing uphill the several miles with heavy packs. Between the two of us, we had packed in five gallons for five days. In this country, water is the key to how successful you can be. Five gallons was pushing it. In past years, we had hiked in a month before hunting season and packed in a few stash gallons of water. This trip we packed it all in.

As we climbed the last major ascent, we contacted the burn area. The area was absolutely torched by such high-intensity heat that the granite rock was black and brittle, causing our footing to be compromised. At the top of that mountain, though, the coolest thing happened. We came upon a "helispot," as firefighters call them—a location where a helicopter-landing zone was established to drop off firefighters and supplies to fight the wildland fire this past summer. An unopened one-pint bottled water was lying right in the helispot! It was like finding a gold nugget.

We finally made our base camp where we would stash our gear and sleep for the next three or four nights. We did not have much stuff other than just the essentials, so we really didn't have much of a camp spread. We laid out our sleeping bags; organized our daypacks, food, water, and hunting gear; and headed out to start glassing the very remote areas for deer.

During the rest of the day, we saw a few more does and no more bucks. We returned to our base at dark. We were camped in an area that we could hunt immediately from. We planned to be able to hunt at first light several mornings and to dark several evenings during the prime hours the deer moved about.

Each night I used my two tiny folding stoves I packed in and boiled water in superlightweight titanium kettles. The stoves weighed very little and did not use any liquid fuel. I was merely using inexpensive Esbit folding stoves that hold solid white Esbit fuel cubes that supposedly burn for 12 to 15 minutes at 1,400 degrees Fahrenheit. They were just enough to do the job. After boiling the water, being extremely careful not to spill any, I poured it into different freeze-dried meals that were absolutely fabulous. At night, as we slept, several owls serenaded us. Several times it was so loud it would wake us up, usually adding to some eerie dream.

On the second day in we started at first light glassing an area we had always seen bucks. Immediately we spotted several deer in three different groups. Of those deer, we spotted a buck that looked like a heavy antlered 3×3. We focused on him.

We slowly worked our way down the ridgeline in hopes of catching the buck as he passed over our ridge or finding him feeding in one of the small canyons. I glassed him with binocs and my spotting scope. The landscape was open and deserty, but there were many crevices and smaller canyons. Continuing working our way down, we lost sight of him to get into position. We never saw that buck again. He disappeared like a ghost.

Day three we hunted hard in a different area and in the burn area. We concentrated on one canyon where several years ago we saw a grand 5×5 buck. We saw a few does, but that was all.

On day four, we decided to split up and hunt ranges we had never hunted about an hour hike away. We had our small two-way radios to keep in contact. Steve staked out above a heavily used saddle that had awesome game trails. I ventured further to the north to glass some new territory.

After about two hours of following some heavily used game trails and glassing every nook in canyons and finger ridges, I spotted a 2×2 buck bedded in the open across a canyon about 500 yards away.

I slowly worked my way closer. I even took a photo of him through my spotting scope. I got within about 300 yards of the buck until I would lose sight of him owing to the rough terrain. I looked for other deer and didn't see any. I was only about a third of a mile from Steve and told him about the deer. I told him it was not big enough and was passing him up. I jumped up and down to see if I could get the buck to move and move up other deer; but he never moved. He didn't have a clue.

After about another hour I was further down the canyon. There were deer trails and deer signs everywhere. I moved very slowly. I spotted another 2×2 buck that was also bedded down in the open. It had considerably larger, heavier antlers. This got my blood rushing a little. It's a different deer! I moved in closer and got directly across from him, about 200 yards away. I set up my spotting scope and took a photo. Way cool, and that deer didn't have a clue I was there. I continued glassing with my binoculars and the scope. Then I saw the buck I wanted.

It was almost surreal. As I looked through my binoculars at the 2×2, I caught the antlers of another buck about 15 feet to the right at the base of

a mountain mahogany bush. He was bedded, lying down with his chin literally touching the ground, and he was looking right at me. He was clearly a 4×4 with eye guards, tall, and heavy antlered. He didn't appear to be spooked, so I put my spotting scope on him.

I positioned my rifle on my daypack as a secure rest and put him in my Leupold crosshairs. There was a significant wind blowing down canyon, which helped keep the deer from hearing me or scenting me. But the larger, older deer saw me. He was keeping his eyes on me as I looked at him. He was about 200 yards away, but I did not have a rangefinder to know for sure. I was shooting a Ruger M77 .243 caliber rifle—a fairly light caliber for the larger deer in open country, with a wind. The canyon was steep, and if the deer tumbled, it would travel a long way. A bedded shot would be perfect. After plenty of time to relax, I settled on shot placement and squeezed the trigger. I missed the first shot, and the buck stood up. My second shot hit him in the neck, and he went down and down toward the draw of the canyon until I lost sight of him. The 2×2 buck mounted the doe in the commotion.

I told Steve I got a 4×4 down and my location. He headed my way. I hiked into the draw and across to the other side of the canyon until I located my buck—a large-bodied 4×4 with decent eye guards and a 19-inch-wide antler spread. I savored the moment while I happily filled out my D-14 tag.

We took many photos and then began to butcher the deer. My method of processing a deer in the field is to do it while the deer lies on the ground. The deer is skinned on one side, and the deer meat is removed. It is then flipped over on its hide while the other side is processed. Back straps, tenderloins, heart, and neck roast went into ziplocks and a pillowcase and were put in the small daypack. The four quarters were each hung by cord and immediately cooled down and glazed over. The cliché "now the work begins" has new meaning in this country and especially as deep in the Badlands as we were. We packed the entire deer back to camp, carrying the four quarters slung over our backs as twos strapped together by cord, and I held the deer head and antlers.

As luck would have it, a storm was finally coming in, and it started to rain. It was good for hunting, but now we would have to contend with staying dry. It ended up dropping some rain but not enough for concern. Back at camp, we completely deboned the deer off the legs and packaged the meat in separate pillowcases. We slept well after a hot meal from the tiny stoves.

Day five, we pulled camp in the dark. I put the entire deer in my backpack. Half of the deer meat had to be strapped outside the back, but the Badlands pack was made for that. We had just enough water for the rest of the pack out. We planned to hunt on our way out for Steve's deer and just pack out slowly. We did see more deer on the way out but no bucks.

By the time we made it back to the truck, we were out of water and wiped out. Definitely extreme deer hunting at its finest!

*Jerry Karnow is a California Fish and Game warden and the legislative liaison for the California Fish and Game Wardens Association.*

## DESTINATIONS

### General Information

By far the best way to get a handle on hunting destinations in California is the California Department of Fish and Game (DFG) quarterly magazine *Tracks, Wingbeats*, a 30-page full-color magazine that describes all public hunting destinations in the state. It is available to all hunters free of charge and is mailed to subscribers. A subscription is established by calling 916-653-6420, faxing 916-653-1856, or emailing publications@dfg.ca.gov.

A list of places for waterfowl hunting on public lands in California can be found at www.calwaterfowl.org/Hunting_2.htm. The following are some of the best.

### GRAY LODGE WILDLIFE AREA
Gridley, CA 95948
Phone: 530-846-7500
www.dfg.ca.gov/lands/wa/region2/graylodge/index.html

A 9,100-acre refuge in the Sacramento Valley, 90 miles north of Sacramento. Upward of 1 million waterfowl winter here. This is a Zone A, with daily fees and reservation system. Pheasant hunting also good here.

### GRIZZLY ISLAND WILDLIFE AREA
Suisun City, CA 94585-9539
Phone: 707-425-3828
www.suisunwildlife.org/grizzly.html

With 84,000 acres of land, bays, and sloughs, the Suisun Marsh is the largest contiguous estuarine marsh in the entire United States. The Grizzly Island Complex occupies about 15,300 acres of the marsh. This is a Zone A for waterfowl, pheasant, rabbits, plus tule elk and wild boars. Daily access fee and reservation system. Waterfowl hunting is best on opening day and then in December–January. The Joice Island Unit has the best success. It opens late and is by reservation only. Tule elk and wild boar hunting requires special permits.

## MENDOTA WILDLIFE AREA
Mendota, CA 93640
Phone: 559-655-4645
www.dfg.ca.gov/lands/wa/region4/
mendota.html

On 11,900 acres located three miles south of Mendota in Fresno County. Waterfowl and pheasant hunting. A Zone A area, with daily fees and reservations system.

*U.S. Bureau of Land Management*
The BLM manages 15.2 million acres in California, roughly 15% of the state. Hunting is open on nearly all of these lands. The general office contact is:

## BUREAU OF LAND MANAGEMENT— CALIFORNIA STATE OFFICE
Sacramento, CA 95825-1886
Phone: 916-978-4400; fax: 916-978-4416
www.blm.gov/ca/st/en.html

## ALTURAS FIELD UNIT
Alturas, CA 96101
Phone: 530-233-4666
www.blm.gov/ca/alturas/recreation.html

A half-million acres in four northeast counties, ranging from evergreen forests to rocky lava flows to high desert plains. Outstanding hunting for antelope, mule deer, chukar, and grouse, according to habitat.

## BLACK ROCK DESERT—HIGH ROCK CANYON—EMIGRANT TRAILS NATIONAL CONSERVATION AREA
Cedarville, CA 96104
Phone: 916-279-6101
www.blm.gov/ca/surprise/highrock.html

Almost 1.5 million acres, from the Warner Mountains east into the high desert of northwestern Nevada. Antelope, chukar, rabbits, and sage grouse in the desert. In higher areas with forest, mule deer and blue grouse.

## CARRIZO PLAIN NATIONAL MONUMENT—BAKERSFIELD FIELD OFFICE
Bakersfield, CA 93308
Phone: 661-391-6000; fax: 661-391-6040
www.blm.gov/ca/bakersfield/huntingcpna
.html

Located 100 miles from Los Angeles, a vast open grassland, rimmed by steep mountains, rings Soda Lake. California quail, chukar, rabbits, deer, tule elk, wild pigs, coyotes, and California ground squirrels. Antelope ground squirrels, kit foxes, and burrowing owls, all protected species, live here. Some areas are off limits to hunting, and there is a substantial amount of private land within the CPNM.

## CLEAR CREEK MANAGEMENT AREA— HOLLISTER FIELD OFFICE
Hollister, CA 95023

Phone: 831-630-5000; fax: 831-630-5055
www.blm.gov/ca/hollister/recreation.html

Approximately 315,000 acres of public land located in central California bounded by the Pacific Ocean on the west and the San Joaquin Valley to the east. Upland game birds, small game, deer, wild pigs, and varmint hunting. An information packet that includes maps and resource area information costs $4. Call 831-630-5000.

## COW MOUNTAIN RECREATION AREA
Ukiah, CA 95482
Phone: 707-468-4000
www.blm.gov/ca/ukiah/cowmtn.html

A 52,000-acre area of steep, chaparral-covered slopes with scattered stands of fir, pine, and oak. Elevations from 800 to 4,000 feet. Blacktail deer, bears, wild turkeys, and other upland species. Five campgrounds are available.

## FOLSOM MANAGEMENT AREA
Folsom, CA 95630
Phone: 916-985-4474
www.blm.gov/ca/folsom/recreation.html

More than 230,000 acres of public land scattered throughout 14 central California counties of the Sierras. Hunting is allowed on all public lands with the exception of the Cosumnes River Preserve in Sacramento County, the Dave Moore Nature Area in El Dorado County, and along the lower Merced River in Mariposa County. Deer, black bears, gray squirrels, black-tailed jackrabbits, valley quail, mourning doves, and wild turkeys. No huntable populations of feral pigs or chukar partridges.

## NEEDLES RECREATION AREA
Needles, CA 92363
Phone: 760-326-7000
www.blm.gov/ca/needles/camp.html

Southern California's east boundary adjacent to the Colorado River—over 3 million acres of desert with elevations ranging from a low of 500 feet above sea level to well over 7,000 feet at Kingston Peak. Mule deer, chukar, quail, sage grouse, and bighorn sheep are found here.

*USDA National Forests*

## ANGELES NATIONAL FOREST
Arcadia, CA 91006
Phone: 626-574-1613
www.fs.fed.us/r5/angeles

Located just north of Los Angeles, 694,187 acres including almost the entire San Gabriel Mountain range. Hunting permitted except for the San Dimas Experimental Forest. The archery deer season in Los Angeles County is the longest in the state—late September to early December. Also a popular area for hunting valley quail.

## EL DORADO NATIONAL FOREST
Placerville, CA 95667
Phone: 916-622-5062
www.fs.fed.us/r5/eldorado

Located in Alpine, Amador, El Dorado, and Placer counties in the central Sierra Nevada. Hunting for all species according to state regulations. Especially known for wild turkeys and deer. Numerous campgrounds and three cabins available for rental.

## INYO NATIONAL FOREST
Bishop, CA 93514
Phone: 760-873-2400
www.fs.fed.us/r5/inyo

Extending 165 miles along the California/Nevada border between Los Angeles and Reno, 1.9 million acres of lakes, meadows, winding streams, rugged Sierras, and the arid Great Basin Mountains. A number of campgrounds in the area. Prime sage grouse, chukar, and antelope country in high desert. Mule deer, mountain quail, and blue grouse become the prevalent species at higher altitude.

## KLAMATH NATIONAL FOREST
Yreka, CA 96097
Phone: 530-842-6131
www.fs.fed.us/r5/klamath

On 1.7 million acres located in Siskiyou County, California, and Jackson County, Oregon; includes five wilderness areas, which are roadless, and 28 campgrounds. This is prime deer country, with some elk, quail, grouse, and ptarmigan at higher elevations.

## LASSEN NATIONAL FOREST
Susanville, CA 96130
Phone: 530-257-2151
www.fs.fed.us/r5/lassen

Some 1,875 square miles within seven northeast counties where the sagebrush of the high desert and forests meet. Most of the forest is open to hunting. Blacktail deer, mule deer, antelope, turkeys, waterfowl, wild pigs, and black bears. Numerous campgrounds. A major deer hunting area.

## LOS PADRES NATIONAL FOREST
Goleta, CA 93117
Phone: 805-683-6711
www.fs.fed.us/r5/lospadres/contactus/
index.html

Nearly 2 million acres of the Coastal Range stretching almost 220 miles from the Carmel Valley area to the western edge of Los Angeles County. Hunting of all legal species, especially deer and wild pigs. Some campgrounds and picnic areas, but much is remote and roadless.

## MODOC NATIONAL FOREST
Alturas, CA 96101
Phone: 530-233-5811
www.fs.fed.us/r5/modoc

A very popular hunting area in the northeast region for mule deer and antelope; also for ducks and geese early in the season on the numerous wetlands and reservoirs throughout the forest. After the creeks and reservoirs freeze, hunting is usually limited to geese. Hunting is not permitted within two state game refuges: one in the northwest section of the district and one in the southern section.

## PLUMAS NATIONAL FOREST
Quincy, CA 95971
Phone: 530-283-2050
www.fs.fed.us/r5/plumas

Located in northern California between the Sierra Nevada and the Cascade Ranges, over a million acres filled with hundreds of high alpine lakes and thousands of miles of streams. Deer, mountain quail, and grouse hunting, as well as excellent fishing and many campsites.

## SAN BERNADINO NATIONAL FOREST

San Bernardino, CA 92408
Phone: 909-382-2600
www.fs.fed.us/r5/sanbernardino

Located about 60 miles east of Los Angeles in the San Gabriel, San Bernadino, San Jacinto, and Santa Rosa mountains. Mule deer, mountain and valley quail, and turkeys. Waterfowl on Baldwin Lake in Big Bear and Lake Hemet in San Jacinto. Band-tailed pigeons, cottontail rabbits, jackrabbits, and black bears. Numerous campgrounds. A high fire danger area. Be careful.

## SEQUOIA NATIONAL FOREST

Porterville, CA 93257
Phone: 559-784-1500
www.fs.fed.us/r5/sequoia

Hunting according to state regulations is allowed on Forest Service land inside Sequoia National Forest and Giant Sequoia National Monument. This is deer, bear, mountain quail, and grouse hunting territory.

## SIERRA NATIONAL FOREST

Clovis, CA 93611
Phone: 559-297-0706
www.fs.fed.us/r5/sierra

Located east of Fresno and west of the Sierra Nevada Crest between Yosemite and Sequoia-Kings Canyon national parks. The forest varies from brushy front country to dense forests and barren alpine peaks and valleys. Deer, bear, mountain quail, and grouse hunting; some turkey hunting at lower levels.

## SIX RIVERS NATIONAL FOREST

Eureka, CA 95501-3834
Phone: 707-442-1721
www.fs.fed.us/r5/sixrivers

East of Eureka in northwest California, stretching south from the Oregon border about 140 miles. Many camping units throughout the forest. Hunting primarily for blacktail deer, black bears, blue grouse, and valley and mountain quail.

## STANISLAUS NATIONAL FOREST

Sonora, CA 95370
Phone: 209-532-3671
www.fs.fed.us/r5/stanislaus

Nearly 900,000 acres of central California. Hunting is primarily for blacktail deer, black bears, blue grouse, and valley and mountain quail. There are a number of campgrounds in the forest.

## TAHOE NATIONAL FOREST

Nevada City, CA 95959
Phone: 530-265-4531
www.fs.fed.us/r5/tahoe

A vast territory, from the foothills on the western slope to the high peaks of the Sierras. Mule deer, blue grouse, bears, and mountain quail.

There are over 50 National Wildlife Refuges in California and Nevada. Most offer hunting for waterfowl and pheasant on Wednesdays, Saturdays, and Sundays by advanced reservations available from the California DFG, then waiting lines as early hunters leave. For details, see www.fws.gov/cno/refuges/default.cfm. Here we will highlight some of the best, which offer quite possibly the best waterfowl hunting in the United States.

## KERN NATIONAL WILDLIFE REFUGE
Delano, CA 93215
Phone: 661-725-2767
www.fws.gov/refuges/profiles/index
.cfm?id=11610

Located in the southern portion of the San Joaquin Valley, 20 miles west of Delano, on the southern margin of what was once the largest freshwater wetland complex in the western Unites States. On 10,618 acres of natural valley grasslands and developed marsh.

## KLAMATH BASIN NATIONAL WILDLIFE REFUGES
Tulelake, CA 96134
Phone: 530-667-2231; fax: 530-667-8337
www.fws.gov/klamathbasinrefuges/
hunt.html

A large, extremely popular area for waterfowl along the California-Oregon border, with a large lake, marshes, and croplands surrounding. Pheasant hunting can also be quite good. The season begins first in this part of the state, so opening day is crowded. Birds are common here until the marshes freeze, then goose hunting is still good. Nearby Tule Lake NWR is usually better for geese.

## SACRAMENTO NATIONAL WILDLIFE REFUGE COMPLEX
Willows, CA 95988
Phone: 530-934-2801 or 530-934-7774
(24-hour Information); fax: 530-934-7814
www.fws.gov/sacramentovalleyrefuges

A complex of five national wildlife refuges—Colusa, Delevan, Sacramento, Sacramento River, and Sutter—and three state wildlife management areas located approximately 90 miles north of Sacramento and adjacent to I-5. The five federal refuges offer some of the best waterfowl hunting on public lands in the United States. There is also a large population of pheasant. The nearby Gray Lodge State Game Area and Little Dry Creek Unit of Butte Sink WMA area also offer outstanding waterfowl and pheasant hunting.

## SALTON SEA STATE RECREATION AREA
North Shore, CA 92254
Phone: 760-393-3052
www.recreation.gov/detail.jsp?ID=40

Located in the southeast part of the state, Salton Sea is the largest body of water in the state of California. This is home to a very large population of wintering waterfowl, as well as a popular sport fishery.

*Waterfowl Hunting on Private Lands*
Some 400,000 to 600,000 acres of the Sacramento Valley are planted in rice. The fields are harvested just before the birds arrive in

the fall, leaving fields with six inches to one foot of water, rice stubble, and about 300 pounds of rice grains per acre. On those private lands, you usually will have to pay a fee to use a blind or go with a guide. For guides and current conditions in the Sacramento Valley, contact Kittles Outdoor and Sport Company, 1004 Market Street, Colusa, CA 95932, 530-458-4868, or see www.kittlesoutdoor.com.

An extensive list of waterfowl clubs in California can be found at www.norcalduck clubs.com/wtfwl.html.

### Private Hunting Clubs and Preserves

There are 46 clubs and preserves licensed for upland bird hunting in California. For a complete online directory, see www.dfg.ca.gov/licensing/pdffiles/LGBC_Flyer_List.pdf. The following are some of our favorites.

### BIRDS LANDING HUNTING PRESERVE AND SPORTING CLAYS

Birds Landing, CA 94512

Phone: 707-374-5092; fax: 707-374-2814
www.birdslanding.net

Pheasant and chukar and competition sporting clays course located within easy access of Sacramento, San Francisco, and San Jose. Approximately 1,200 acres of prime pheasant habitat adjacent to the Suisun Marsh. Pro shop. Rental dogs are available. Restaurant serves breakfast and lunch.

### BLACK POINT SPORTS CLUB

Petaluma, CA 94954
Phone: 707-763-0076; fax: 707-313-0186
www.blackpointsportsclub.com

Pheasant and chukar hunting just 30 minutes north of San Francisco on the shore of San Francisco Bay. Black Point also offers sporting clays, meeting facilities, and dog training. This is a membership club. Contact for details.

## CAMANCHE HILLS
## HUNTING PRESERVE
Ione, CA 95640
Phone: 209-763-5270
www.camhills.com

Located at the base of the western foothills of the Sierras just 15 minutes from Ione, California, 30 minutes from Stockton, California. Pheasant and chukar in large fields with natural cover. Camanche Hills is one of the very few clubs in California that has a flighted mallard program for duck hunting.

## COSUMNES RIVER RANCH
Plymouth, CA 95669
Phone: 530-677-9580 ext. 105 (Daytime)
or 209-245-4905 (Evenings)
www.riverranch.us

Only 45 minutes from downtown Sacramento in the Sierra Foothills of Amador and El Dorado counties. Wild and released California valley quail, dove, Rio Grande turkey, and blacktail deer hunting in meadows and oak woodlands along seven miles of river frontage on a 3,500-acre ranch. Two remote sites can be rented. Gourmet meals can also be arranged.

## FOUR WINDS PHEASANT CLUB
Redondo Beach, CA 90278 (not location of the club)
Phone/fax: 310-370-2238
www.pheasantclub.com

Day hunts for released pheasant, quail, chukar, and Pharaoh quail in private and assigned wheat and barley fields. Within easy driving distance of Los Angeles. Dogs and guides available. For members, dove and rabbit hunting in season; coyote and ground squirrel hunting all year around.

## GAINES RANCH DUCK CLUBS
Durham, CA 95938
Phone: 530-518-8626; fax: 530-882-5333
www.gainesranch.net

Located in Richvale, several properties offering both upland game and waterfowl hunting. At the Afton Ranch Licensed Game Bird Club they offer hunting for pheasant, quail, and chukar. They also offer four-man seasonal waterfowl blinds and guided hunts on flooded rice fields.

## HASTINGS ISLAND
## HUNTING PRESERVE
Rio Vista, CA 94571-1604
Phone: 707-678-3325; fax: 707-678-1604
Email: clubmail@hihp.com

Located 50 miles east of San Francisco in the Sacramento River Delta country. Over 4,700 acres for pheasant and chukar hunting. Dogs available.

## HIGH DESERT HUNT CLUB
Gorman, CA 93243
Phone: 888-425-HUNT;
fax: 949-863-0633
www.highdeserthunt.com

Located 60 miles from Los Angeles in the upper west side of the Antelope Valley, pheasant, chukar, and quail. Each hunting party gets a large area all to their own with diverse habitats. There also are wild California valley quail and doves, plus exceptional bird dogs and guides. Continental breakfast and full lunch are served. Pro shop and overnight lodging in private cabins.

**LAKEVIEW FARMS, INC., HUNTING & FISHING PRESERVES**
Rocklin, CA 95765
Phone: 530-633-9112 or 916-645-9117
www.lakeviewfarmsinc.com

Some 1,600 acres on four separate preserves with rice stubble, sudan grass, and natural habitats. Pheasant, chukar, wild turkey, waterfowl, and quail hunting, 14-station sporting clays course, dog training, and fishing. The late-season Canada goose hunting is noteworthy. Membership club.

**RAAHAUGE'S PHEASANT CLUB**
Norco, CA 92860
Phone: 951-738-9212; fax: 951-738-8835
http://rpclub.com/index.html

Pheasant and chukar on 400 acres; also nearby large shooting range and waterfowl blinds. Open Tuesday through Sunday, located within 45 minutes of Los Angeles, Orange, Riverside, and San Bernardino counties. Package options ranging from single day hunts to memberships and corporate memberships.

**RS BAR RANCH**
Paicines, CA 95043
www.rsbarranch.com

The former 19,000-acre Rock Springs Ranch lying just east of Monterey and near Pinna-

cles National Monument—an Orvis-endorsed wing-shooting lodge offering hunting for released chukar and pheasants, blacktail deer, wild boar, and valley quail—has recently changed ownership. Twelve guest rooms with fireplace, spa, and all amenities. The new owners plan to continue the ranch's tradition of excellence. Check their Web site for updates.

**TEJON RANCH**
Lebec, CA 93243 (Contact Location)
Phone: 661-248-3000 (Main Phone)
www.hunttejon.com

The largest contiguous expanse of land under single ownership in California. Located along I-5, approximately 60 miles north of Los Angeles. Guided hunting for elk, deer, wild boars, and wild turkeys. The ranch can set its own bag limits and seasons, to some extent. The scenery is spectacular. Lead ammo is banned here to protect condors.

**TURK STATION LODGE**
Coalinga, CA 93210
Phone: 559-935-1902;
fax: 559-935-1966
www.turkstationlodge.com

Located halfway between San Francisco and Los Angeles just off I-5. Released pheasant, bobwhite quail, and chukar partridge. Valley quail and doves in season. Each species of game bird is hunted in a different habitat. Wild boar and exotic goats and sheep hunting on two wild and beautiful ranch properties nearby.

# HUNTING TIP

## Beating the Access Problem

Wilderness Unlimited is a membership club that offers members hunting, fishing, and camping access on over 100 private farms and ranches in California and two dozen more in Oregon.

Their Sacramento Valley duck club, with an old-fashioned funky bunkhouse, fabulous food, and access to numerous blinds all around the Sacramento Refuge Complex, has soul. Wilderness Unlimited also offers buffalo hunts on an 8,000-acre ranch in southern Oregon. To contact Wilderness Unlimited, see: www.wildernessunlimited.com.

Wilderness Unlimited is the biggest and most diversified private outdoor sports land management organization in the western states—but not the only one: The Golden Ram Sportsmen's Club has leases on 16 ranches with 90,000 acres in California. For information, see www.goldenramhunting.com.

## OREGON

*In 2001 there were 234,000 resident hunters and 15,000 nonresident hunters: 91% went big game hunting, 24% small game, 17% waterfowl; 78% hunted on public lands; 38% hunted on private lands. Hunters pumped $365 million into the state economy. (USFWS)*

### OVERVIEW

Oregon has an amazing diversity of landscapes, from the rugged Coastal Mountains to the rich agricultural Willamette Valley, the fertile lands along the Columbia River, the snow-capped North Cascade Mountains, the arid high desert to the east, the forested Willowa Mountains of the northeast, and the waterfowl paradise of Klamath Lake in the southeast corner.

The result of this is a wide diversity of wildlife. The coastal range has Roosevelt elk and blacktail deer, with a small population of Columbia whitetail deer in the north. The blacktails go up into the Cascades but stop on the western slopes; mule deer, bighorn sheep, and antelope populate the drier mountain and high desert. Some of the biggest mule deer around are found in the Whitehorse and Trout Creek districts, where permits are in high demand.

In the Willowa Mountains of the northeast, there are Rocky Mountain elk, mountain goats, and Idaho whitetails.

The black bear population for the state is between 25,000 and 30,000, and the cougar population runs from 3,000 to 5,000. Both appear where food is available.

Oregon hunters harvest some 200,000 chukar per year in the eastern sagebrush

---

**OREGON SNAPSHOT**
**BEAVER STATE**

- **General information:**
  Oregon Department of Fish and Wildlife
  3406 Cherry Avenue NE
  Salem, OR 97303
  Phone: 503-947-6000 or
  800-720-ODFW (800-720-6339)
  www.dfw.state.or.us/resources/hunting/
  big_game

- **Deer population:** 647,600 (includes other species), 22nd in the United States

- **Average deer harvest:** 1,153, 43rd in the United States

desert. The bag of mountain and valley quail combined is around 100,000 per year.

The ring-necked pheasant is not a native species to North America. In 1881 it was first introduced into the United States in the Willamette Valley in Oregon by Judge Owen Denny, an American diplomat posted in China, who imported 200 ring-necked pheasant from Asia. Today Oregon hunters bag about 60,000 ringnecks a year, mostly in the Willamette Valley, a fertile agricultural area running from Eugene to Portland.

On both the northern border along the Columbia River and the southeast corner, around Klamath Lake, Oregon has extraordinary waterfowl hunting.

Two special programs of note: There are some special deer hunting areas that are reserved for traditional archery equipment only. And Oregon has a "Master Hunter" program. People who take additional Hunter Education classes and workshops beyond the basic course qualify for special hunts.

## FEATURED HUNT

## Canada Geese along the Columbia River

ERIK PETERSON*

Seven different subspecies of Canada geese winter in Oregon. From small cackling geese, with their high-pitched cackle and size not much bigger than a mallard, to the huge great basin honkers, there's tremendous diversity.

The early arrivals tend to show up along the Columbia River of northwest Oregon beginning in October. Cackling Canada geese are joined by Taverner's or "Tav's," lesser Canada's, Vancouver Canada geese, Western or Great Basin Canada geese, Aleutian Canada geese, and the semiprotected Dusky Canada geese. Throw in an occasional snow goose and white-fronted goose, and you have quite a goose variety pack.

Several of these goose populations are thriving and causing problems for agriculture. Yet one subspecies, the Dusky, is declining (due primarily to changes in its nesting habitat in the Copper River Delta from the 1964 Alaska earthquake, not human activities). Consequently, the hunting objective is to control the numbers of most of the Canada goose subspecies but minimize harvest of the Dusky.

To gain the privilege to hunt in the Northwest Permit Zone that the Dusky frequents, a hunter must pass an Oregon Department of Fish and Wildlife goose ID test to obtain a Northwest Permit Zone Goose ID card. The 40-question test can be taken online at www.dfw.state.or.us/resources/hunting/waterfowl. Assuming you pass, it takes a week or two to process before you get your goose card in the mail.

Goose shoot days in the Northwest Permit Zone are limited to Wednesday, Saturday, and Sunday. All geese harvested must be presented at a goose Check Station, where their breast color and culmen length are measured to determine if a Dusky was harvested. Taking of a single Dusky results in surrender of the hunter's goose card for the remainder of the season. Once the quota of Duskies for each of the three hunt periods has been met in a particular area, the season is closed to goose hunting until the next hunt period.

All formalities aside, the challenge and sport in the blind in northwest Oregon becomes identifying the various goose subspecies and letting the "dark ones," or Duskies, land unharassed. (Having a flock of Duskies walking the edge of your decoys does add a nice bit of lifelike movement to your spread.)

What is in most circumstances a fool 'em until they have their feet down situation gets a bit spicier on this hunt. Adding to the challenge, Dusky Canada geese tend to stay together and mix with their cousins at times.

Should you get the chance to hunt geese on the lower Columbia River, at a place like Sauvie Island (a few miles downstream from Portland), and you're overwhelmed by the sound of thousands of geese, you're in good historic company. The Lewis and Clark Expedition 200 years ago was said to have left Sauvie Island early, as they could not get adequate rest because of the continual noise of the waterfowl on the island.

If the intricacies of a lower Columbia River goose hunt seem a bit daunting, there's distinctly different game upriver. Western Canada geese by the thousands invade the central Oregon wheat country every fall. From early November to the end of January (unless it gets really cold, forcing the birds to head south), this is honker heaven. Resting on local rivers and lakes, these birds generally feed in the morning and again in the afternoon. This behavior presents an opportunity to draw them into your decoys on three occasions, twice as they go out to feed and at midday as they make their way back to the water to rest.

A fair-sized spread of honker decoys and folks who are good on a call increase your odds of success a great deal. But nothing beats being in the right spot that the geese want to be in. If you're in the right blind on the right day, it's nothing short of spectacular.

While the average size of a Western or Great Basin goose is in the 10-pound range, honkers approaching 20 pounds are not unheard of. Keep in mind, if you're used to hunting smaller geese, these big honkers look a lot closer than they really are

when they're coming in, so be patient and let them almost sit on top of you. They're big, strong birds, so you want to make sure they're well in range before you open up on them.

You'll note, at various locations in north-central Oregon, the presence of old rock blinds on the edges of some wheat fields. While clearing the fields of rock, farmers put the pickings to good use by providing a hiding place for goose hunting each fall. (Instead of a traditional rock pile, the pieces of basalt were formed into a donut shape, providing concealment for hunters in the center.) Climb into one, and you'll get a sense of a hunt from another time. Before the comforts of a sunken pit blind, or the portable camo sophistication of modern layout blinds, they used what they had. Hunters of a bygone era fooled geese by appearing to be rock piles, and they were quite successful. Today, both goose hunters and the geese they hunt have become increasingly sophisticated.

If the sound of honking geese stirs you, check your November or December calendar. The geese *will* be there. Will you?

Wilderness Unlimited is a private hunting and fishing club that leases ranches for the use of its members throughout Oregon and California. The Oregon Wilderness Unlimited office is located on one of the club's waterfowl properties on Sauvie Island. Contact:

**WILDERNESS UNLIMITED**
Hayward, CA 94545
Phone: 510-785-4868
Email: info@wildernessunlimited.com
www.wildernessunlimited.com

*Erik Peterson is the Oregon land manager for Wilderness Unlimited.*

## DESTINATIONS

A list of state-managed big game hunting units and maps can be found online at www.dfw.state.or.us/resources/hunting/big_game/units/index.asp.

### U.S. Bureau of Land Management

The BLM manages millions of acres of lands open to hunting according to state regulations in Oregon. For more details, contact:

**OREGON STATE OFFICE—BUREAU OF LAND MANAGEMENT**
Portland, OR 97204
Phone: 503-808-6002
www.blm.gov/or/index.php

### USDA National Forests

**DESCHUTES AND OCHOCO NATIONAL FOREST AND CROOKED RIVER NATIONAL GRASSLAND**
Prineville, OR 97754
Phone: 541-416-6500
www.fs.fed.us/r6/centraloregon/index.shtml

Located in central Oregon, the forest is part of the old Blue Mountain Forest Reserve that was established in 1906 by President Theodore Roosevelt. Hunting according to state regulations for all species.

**MALHEUR NATIONAL FOREST**
John Day, OR 97845
Phone: 541-575-3000
www.fs.fed.us/r6/malheur

In the Blue Mountains of eastern Oregon lies the 1.46 million-acre Malheur National Forest. Hunting for small game, upland birds, mule deer, rocky mountain elk, pronghorn antelope, cougars, bears, and bighorn sheep on Wildlife Management Units. A list of the major units that are located in the forest can be found at www.fs.fed.us/r6/malheur/recreation/hunt.shtml.

**ROGUE RIVER–SISKIYOU NATIONAL FOREST**
Medford, OR 97501-0209
Phone: 541-858-2200
www.fs.fed.us/r6/rogue-siskiyou

Surrounding much of the Rogue Valley in southwestern Oregon, this 630,000-acre forest offers hunting according to state regulations for all species.

**SIUSLAW NATIONAL FOREST**
Corvallis, OR 97333
Phone: 541-750-7000
www.fs.fed.us/r6/siuslaw

Located in the rugged coastal range of Oregon, this forest is open to all hunting according to state regulations. It is a prime area for blacktail deer, Roosevelt elk, and grouse.

**UMATILLA NATIONAL FOREST**
Pendleton, OR 97801
Phone: 541-278-3716
www.fs.fed.us/r6/uma

On 1.4 million acres in the Blue Mountains in the northeast corner of the state, straddling the Oregon-Washington border. Hunting for all species according to state regulations.

## WALLOWA-WHITMAN
## NATIONAL FOREST
Baker City, OR 97814
Phone: 541-523-1405 (TDD)
or 541-523-6391
www.fs.fed.us/r6/w-w

Located in the northeast corner of the state and containing Hells Canyon, 2.3 million acres ranging in elevation from 875 feet in Hells Canyon to 9,845 feet in the Eagle Cap Wilderness. Hunting according to state regulations. A prime area for elk, mountain goats, mule deer, and whitetail deer, as well as grouse in the timber and chukar in the desert.

## WILLAMETTE NATIONAL FOREST
Eugene, OR 97440
Phone: 541-225-6300
www.fs.fed.us/r6/willamette

The forest stretches for 110 miles along the western slopes of the Cascades. The forest is 1.6 million acres and extends from the Mt. Jefferson area east of Salem to the Calapooya Mountains northeast of Roseburg. Hunting according to state regulations. This is a prime area for blacktail deer and Roosevelt elk.

*U.S. Fish and Wildlife Service*
*National Wildlife Refuges*

## BANDON MARSH NATIONAL
## WILDLIFE REFUGE
Newport, OR 97365
Phone: 541-867-4550
www.fws.gov/oregoncoast/bandonmarsh

Located along the southern Oregon coast near the mouth of the Coquille River and the city of Bandon. The southern one-third of the Bandon Marsh Unit is closed to hunting because it falls within the city limits of Bandon. All state waterfowl regulations apply.

## BEAR VALLEY NATIONAL
## WILDLIFE REFUGE
Tulelake, CA 96134
Phone: 530-667-2231
www.fws.gov/klamathbasinrefuges/
bearvalley/bearvalley.html

The 4,200-acre Bear Valley Refuge in the Klamath Basin is open to walk-in deer hunting before November 1.

## HART MOUNTAIN NATIONAL
## ANTELOPE REFUGE
Lakeview, OR 97630-0107
Phone: 541-947-3315
www.fws.gov/sheldonhartmtn/Hart/
index.html

Hunting is permitted in accordance with state and federal regulations. A very limited number of tags are offered for deer, pronghorn, and bighorn sheep hunts in the late summer and fall. Chukar may be hunted in limited areas of the refuge. No hunting is allowed within three miles of refuge headquarters.

## KLAMATH MARSH NATIONAL
## WILDLIFE REFUGE
Chiloquin, OR 97624-9616
Phone: 541-783-3380
www.fws.gov/klamathbasinrefuges/
klamathmarsh/klamathmarsh.html

The refuge primarily consists of over 40,000 acres of wet meadows and open water wetlands along Klamath Lake in the southeast part of the state. This is one of the best waterfowl hunting areas in the United States. For details, see www.fws.gov/klamathbasin refuges/kmhunt.html.

**MALHEUR NATIONAL
WILDLIFE REFUGE**
Princeton, OR 97721-9502
Phone: 541-493-2612
www.fws.gov/malheur

The refuge spans an area 40 miles long and 39 miles wide, including over 187,000 acres in the southeast part of the state. Pheasant, quail, chukar, Hungarian partridge, and rabbit hunting are permitted in the Malheur Lake Hunt Area and the Buena Vista Upland Game Hunt Area. Waterfowl hunting is permitted only in the Malheur Lake Hunt Area.

**MID-COLUMBIA RIVER REFUGES**
Richland, WA 99351
Phone: 509-545-8588
www.fws.gov/midcolumbiariver

Four U.S. Fish and Wildlife Service refuges located along the Columbia River—Cold Springs, McKay Creek, Toppenish, and Umatilla—offer the following hunting opportunities:

*Cold Springs.* Geese, ducks, coots, snipes, pheasant, and quail may be hunted in designated areas in accordance with state and federal regulations. Upland bird hunting is permitted only during designated waterfowl hunt days from noon until the end of state shooting hours. See www.fws.gov/mid columbiariver/Coldspringspage.htm.

*McKay Creek.* Access for waterfowl and upland bird hunting is restricted to the three parking lots accessible from the county road. Reservoir water levels are often not sufficient for waterfowl hunting until late in the season. See www.fws.gov/midcolumbiariver/McKay page.htm.

*Toppenish.* Waterfowl and upland game bird hunting. See www.fws.gov/midcolumbi ariver/Toppenpage.htm.

*Umatilla.* Regulated deer hunting is permitted on portions of the refuge, as is waterfowl and upland game bird hunting. For more information, call the Waterfowl Season Hunting Hotline at 503-922-HUNT. Also see www.fws.gov/midcolumbiariver/Umatilla page.htm.

**SHELDON-HART MOUNTAIN NATIONAL
WILDLIFE REFUGE COMPLEX**
Lakeview, OR 97630
Phone: 541-947-3315
www.fws.gov/sheldonhartmtn/index.html

More than half a million acres in the high desert of eastern Oregon–western Nevada. Hunting permitted in accordance with state and federal regulations. A limited number of tags are offered for deer, pronghorn, and bighorn sheep hunts. Tag drawings are administered through the Nevada Department of Wildlife (NDOW). Several species of upland birds may also be hunted. Hunting for sage grouse also requires a permit issued by NDOW. Waterfowl hunting permitted in the general area, but several sections are closed.

**BEAR CREEK PHEASANT FARM**
Noti, OR 97461
Phone: 541-206-4682
www.BearCreekPheasantFarm.com

Located just north of Cheshire in the heart of the Willamette Valley, this 300-acre preserve offers pheasant, chukar, and duck hunting. Guides, dogs, and dog training available.

**CANYON CREEK HUNTING PRESERVE**
Dufur, OR 97021-3226
Phone: 541-467-2306; fax: 541-467-2303
www.canyoncreek.info

Located in Dufur and Tyghe Valley, pheasant, chukar, quail, and Hungarian partridge, lodge, guides, and dogs. Members only—big game hunts for elk, bighorn sheep, deer, and varmints on 17,000 acres in Wasco County.

**ELLIS HUNTING RANCH**
Pilot Rock, OR 97868
Phone: 541-443-2381 or 800-543-9251
www.ellishuntingranch.com

Over 33,000 acres 15 miles south of Pendleton. Wild birds and preserve hunting for pheasant and chukar, plus hunts for elk, deer (including whitetails), cougars, black bears, and coyotes. Lodging and guides available.

**FARMSTEAD HUNTING PRESERVES**
Grass Valley, OR 97029

Phone: 541-333-2498 or 541-333-2364
www.huntfarmstead.com

Four separate preserves totaling 3,200 acres in north-central Oregon, just south of Grass Valley, offering pheasant, chukar, Hungarian partridge, and quail hunts, plus wild goose hunting. Reservations required.

**GABLE CREEK UPLAND GAME BIRD RANCH**
Mitchell, OR 97750
Phone: 541-462-3228
www.gablecreek.com

Hunting for released pheasant and chukar on 1,287 acres in central Oregon. Lodge, guides, and dogs available. Kids 12–16 half price with parents.

**GATEWAY VALLEY PRESERVE**
Madras, OR 97741
Phone: 541-475-6027
www.gatewayvalley.com

Located in north-central Oregon, approximately 90 minutes from Portland, a 1,282 acre preserve on a 4,000-acre working ranch/farm. Released pheasant and chukar, guides, dogs, and accommodations available. Kids under 18 hunt free with parents.

**GREAT EXPECTATIONS HUNTING PRESERVE**
Kimberly, OR 97848
Phone: 541-934-2395 or 541-934-2117; fax: 888-581-0550 (Bookings Only)
www.gehunting.com

Located in eastern Oregon, south of Pendleton, 985 acres for hunting pheasant, chukar, Hungarian partridge, and quail. Sporting clays, lodge, and meals available.

**HIGHLAND HILLS RANCH**
Condon, OR 97823
Phone: 866-478-4868 or 541-296-1296
www.highlandhillsranch.com

The Orvis Wingshooting Lodge of the Year for 2003–2004, located on 3,000 acres of wilderness canyons and meadows in north-central Oregon and offering pheasant, chukar, quail, Hungarian partridge, and trophy mule deer hunting. Lodging, guides, dogs, and corporate retreats available.

**J & B GUIDE SERVICE**
Happy Valley, OR 97086
Phone: 503-381-9466
www.jandbguideservice.com

Goose hunts for seven species of Canada geese, in southwest and northwest Oregon, plus Chinook and steelhead fishing.

**OLEX PRESERVE**
Arlington, OR 97812
Phone: 541-454-2011; fax: 541-454-2236
www.olexbirdhunting.com

Released pheasant, quail, and chukar on 1,200 acres in north-central, Oregon, near the Columbia River. Trap, guides, and dogs available.

**PHEASANT VALLEY HUNTING RANCH**
Vale, OR 97918

Phone: 541-473-3867
www.pheasantvalleyranch.com

Located in east-central, Oregon, released pheasant, chukar, and quail, plus doves and wild ducks. Guides and dogs available.

**ROE OUTFITTERS, LLC**
Klamath Falls, OR 97601
Phone: 541-884-DUCK (541-884-3825)
www.roeoutfitters.com

Guided duck, goose, mountain and valley quail, turkey, and big game hunts in the Klamath Lake area of southern Oregon. Accommodations, fishing, and river rafting also offered.

**TREO RANCHES**
Heppner, OR 97836
Phone: 888-276-6794 or 541-676-5840; fax: 541-676-5400
www.treoranches.com

Guided and nonguided hunts for pheasant and chukar in north-central Oregon. Sporting clays; lodge with overnight accommodations.

**WILD TIMES GUIDES**
Merrill, OR 97633
Phone: 888-925-WILD (888-925-9453)
www.wildtimesguides.com

Located in the Klamath Basin, guided waterfowl hunts and fly-fishing in Oregon, varmint hunts for ground squirrels in Oregon, and guided waterfowl hunts in Alberta. Featured on numerous television shows, Wild Times holds two of the six permits to guide on the 80,000-acre Lower Klamath National and Tule Lake Wildlife Refuges.

## HERITAGE DESTINATIONS

*Museum at Warm Springs*

The museum at Warm Springs is located in northeast Oregon near Kah-Nee-Tah Resort. Learn about Lewis and Clark, early hunters and trappers, and local Indian tribes. Don't forget to have the quail baked in clay at Kah-Nee-Tah Lodge.

**MUSEUM AT WARM SPRINGS**
Warm Springs, OR 97761
Phone: 541-553-3331
www.warmsprings.biz/museum

*Sherman County Museum*

A 14,280-square-foot museum with over 15,000 artifacts from earlier days along the Columbia River. A very "hands-on" museum with many exhibits about conservation and Native American culture.

**SHERMAN COUNTY MUSEUM**
Moro, OR 97039
Phone: 541-565-3232; fax: 541-565-3080
www.shermanmuseum.org

## WASHINGTON

*In 2001 there were 210,000 resident hunters and 17,000 nonresident hunters: 82% went big game hunting, 32% small game, 22% migratory waterfowl; 71% hunted on public lands; 56% hunted on private lands. Hunters pumped $350 million into the state economy. (USFWS)*

**OVERVIEW**

Like California and Oregon, Washington has tremendously diverse habitats, from the rain forest on the Olympic Peninsula with its blacktail deer and mountain goats to the snowcapped North Cascades mountain ranges with mountain goats and blue grouse, to the eastern-slope high desert sagebrush and farm-lands with quail, sharptails, and mule deer, to the pine forests in the far east on the western slope of the Rockies with whitetails and turkeys.

Yakima County is usually best for quail. Hunters bag somewhere between 100,000 to 150,00 a year for the entire state.

In 2005, the state's 135,653 deer hunters enjoyed a 29.3% success rate. The most sought-after tag for mule deer is the Desert Unit in the Columbia Basin area. In 2004 more than 4,500 hunters applied for 15 buck permits. During most years the hunters score a success rate of 90% or greater, with deer going up to 300 pounds. Right after that comes the Okanogen Highlands of north-central Washington, where one generally finds the largest mule deer herd in the Pacific Northwest.

Washington turkey hunters enjoyed a 35.7% success rate for the spring of 2005 and a 43.7% success rate for the fall hunt.

The state maintains online records of success for many species according to sea-sons and locations. For details, see http://wdfw.wa.gov/wlm/game/harvest/2005/index.htm.

For those who enjoy hunting pheasant, the Washington Department of Fish and Game releases 30,000 to 40,000 pheasant on 25 sites in western Washington (http://wdfw.wa.gov/wlm/game/water/wwapheas.

htm). For released birds on shooting preserves there is no license required and no season.

For waterfowl hunters, the Skagit Flats area in western Washington along Puget Sound is hard to beat. In December, close to 1 million dabbling ducks and 250,000 geese are in the area. The birds tend to stay on the Sound when it gets cold but move inland when it warms up.

On the Skagit Flats there is a new private lands–public access program, supported by state waterfowl stamp sales. This is a limited-entry hunt, with hunters chosen from a lottery. Hunt units have been laid out in 8- to 20-acre plots. You may hunt any waterfowl, and regular limits are the rule, but this is snow goose central. During the week for which hunters are drawn, they and their party will have exclusive use (for three hunt days) of a multi-acre tract of private farmland situated on the western third of Fir Island that is intensively used by wintering snow geese.

Birds spend the night on Skagit Bay and then migrate inland toward the Fir Island/ Hayton Snow Goose Reserve on Fir Island, settling into the reserve or the adjacent fields. Passing bald eagles, which flock in the area, can help out—as they fly by, the geese become restless and move about.

You hunt cultivated agricultural fields and must improvise your own blinds. You either use good concealment (birds get wary of obvious blinds very quickly) or dress in white coverall and lay on the ground in the middle of the decoys. A minimum of six dozen decoys is recommended.

The shooting areas are on the west side of Fir Island. Parking is regulated closely, and there are restricted zones to avoid hunting too closely to farm buildings and homes. Hunting within 100 feet of a public paved road is illegal.

The season runs from mid-October through January. Tundra and trumpeter swans are in the area, and they are not legal here. Hunters must submit a mandatory report of the number of geese harvested. The report can be found online through the Washington Department of Fish and Wildlife Web site at http://wdfw.wa.gov/wlm/wlm_survey/report _form.php. For additional information about Fir Island snow goose hunting, see http:// wdfw.wa.gov/wlm/game/water/snow_goose/ index.htm.

## DESTINATIONS

The Department of Fish and Wildlife manages a number of Wildlife Management Units around the state. For details, see http:// wdfw.wa.gov/lands/wildarea.htm.

There are 42 federal land areas in Washington that permit hunting. Some of the most popular follow.

## COLVILLE NATIONAL FOREST

Colville, WA 99114

Phone: 509-684-7000

www.fs.fed.us/r6/colville

A 1.1 million-acre national forest in the northeast part of the state bordering Canada with huntable mule deer, whitetail deer, black bears, cougars, turkeys, small game, and birds, especially grouse, according to state regulations. There are also woodland caribou, moose, wolves, bighorn sheep, and grizzly bears, which are protected species.

## GIFFORD PINCHOT NATIONAL FOREST

Vancouver, WA 98682

Phone: 360-891-5000

www.fs.fed.us/gpnf

Located in southwest Washington, the forest contains 1,372,000 acres including Mt. St. Helens and Mt. Adams. The elk herd in the Mt. St. Helens area has exceeded its carrying capacity, resulting in starvation. The Washington Department of Fish and Wildlife wants to reduce the herd size from 12,500 to 10,000 over the next few years.

## MT. BAKER–SNOQUALMIE NATIONAL FOREST

Mountlake Terrace, WA 98043

Phone: 800-627-0062

www.fs.fed.us/r6/mbs

Located along the western slopes of the Cascade Mountains from the Canadian border to the northern boundary of Mt. Rainier National Park, the forest extends over 140 miles, covering portions of Whatcom, Skagit, Snohomish, King, and Pierce counties and including Mt. Baker. Hunting according to state regulations is permitted throughout the forest, with blacktail deer and grouse being the most popular species.

## OKANOGAN NATIONAL FOREST

Okanogan, WA 98840

Phone: 509-826-3275

www.fs.fed.us/r6/oka

The 1,706,000-acre forest stretches from the Columbia River to the Canadian border on the eastern side of the Cascades. Grass and shrubs are found near the Columbia River, Ponderosa pine forests at midelevations, Douglas fir in the Cascade Mountains, and sub-Alpine and Alpine zones at elevations above 6,000 feet. Hunting allowed according to state regulations and local posting.

## OLYMPIC NATIONAL FOREST

Olympia, WA 98512-5623

Phone: 360-956-2300

www.fs.fed.us/r6/olympic

Located in the Olympic Peninsula, the Olympic National Forest is composed of over 632,000 acres and surrounds Olympic National Park. Hunting is permitted throughout the forest according to state regulations and local posting.

## WENATCHEE NATIONAL FOREST

Wenatchee, WA 98801

Phone: 509-662-4335

www.fs.fed.us/r6/wenatchee

On 2.2 million acres covering an area approximately 40 miles wide and 140 miles long, stretching from upper Lake Chelan on the north to the Yakima Indian Reservation on the south along the east side the Cascades; 40% is wilderness. Hunting permitted according to state regulations and local postings.

*U.S. Fish and Wildlife Service*
*National Wildlife Refuges*

**CONBOY LAKE NATIONAL WILDLIFE REFUGE**
Glenwood, WA 98619
Phone: 509-364-3410
http://ridgefieldrefuges.fws.gov/CLNWRHome.htm

On 6,500 acres at the base of Mount Adams in southern Washington. Waterfowl and deer hunting is permitted during the regular state hunt seasons in designated refuge public hunting areas.

**RIDGEFIELD NATIONAL WILDLIFE REFUGE**
Ridgefield, WA 98642
Phone: 360-887-4106
http://ridgefieldrefuges.fws.gov

Located on the shore of the Lower Columbia River, 10 miles downstream from Portland/Vancouver, a 5,217-acre mosaic of riverine floodplain habitat, intensively managed seasonal and permanent wetlands, and agricultural lands. The refuge allows waterfowl hunting for migratory waterfowl according to state and federal regulations.

**SADDLE MOUNTAIN NATIONAL WILDLIFE REFUGE**
Richland, WA 99352
Phone: 509-371-1801
www.fws.gov/hanfordreach

The 195,000-acre refuge is located on the site of the former Hanford Nuclear Facility. Hunting for chukar, valley quail, waterfowl, mule deer, and elk according to state regulations and others specific to the reservation. Most important, rimfire rifles are not allowed. For details, see www.fws.gov/hanfordreach/hunting.html.

**TOPPENISH NATIONAL WILDLIFE REFUGE**
Toppenish, WA 98948
Phone: 509-865-2405
www.fws.gov/midcolumbiariver

Some 1,763 acres of brushy creek bottoms, meadows, sagebrush, and croplands along Toppenish Creek in the Columbia River Valley. Hunting for waterfowl and upland game birds according to state and federal regulations.

**WILLAPA NATIONAL WILDLIFE REFUGE**
Cathlamet, WA 98612
Phone: 360-484-3482
www.fws.gov/pacific/refuges/field/WA_willapa.htm

Located on the shores of Willapa Bay near the Pacific Ocean, 13 miles north of Ilwaco, Washington, offering waterfowl, upland game, and big game with archery hunting according to state and federal regulations on 11,000 acres.

**BURBANK GUIDE SERVICE (DBA OF BURBANK ENTERPRISES, LLC)**
Burbank, WA 99323
Phone: 509-545-8000; fax: 509-546-2001
www.burbankgoose.com

Located at the confluence of the Snake and Columbia rivers in prime waterfowl hunting country, guided hunts for ducks and seven different subspecies of Canada geese from pit blinds and portable blinds on private land. Also offering hunts for released pheasant, chukar, Hungarian partridge, and wild pheasant. Can arrange trips to Argentina and Hungary.

**DRY COULEE GAME FARM, LLC**
Okanogan, WA 98840
Phone: 509-422-0350
www.gamefarmandvizsla.com

Field hunts for released chukar, pheasant, and wild Hungarian partridge and quail in the Okanogan Valley. Open year-round. No license required.

**MILLER RANCH**
Sprague, WA 99032-0249
Phone: 509-370-5535
www.millerranch.com

Located 30 miles south of Spokane, pheasant, chukar, quail, duck, geese, mule deer, and wild turkey hunts. Clubhouse, dogs, guides, sporting clays, lodging, and food available. No license required for preserve hunting.

**PHEASANT VALLEY SHOOTING PRESERVE AND SPORTING CLAYS**
LaCrosse, WA 99143
Phone: 509-549-3912
www.shootingpreserve.com

Some 4,000 acres on the Palouse River one-and-a-half hours south of Spokane, offering released pheasant, chukar, and Hungarian partridge and guided hunts for wild ducks and geese, mule deer, and whitetail deer. Sporting clays and membership options.

**R & M GAME BIRDS HUNTING PRESERVE AND SPORTING CLAYS**
Lyle, WA 98635
Phone: 509-365-3245;
fax: 509-365-HUNT
www.rmgamebirds.com

Located just west of the Klickitat River of south-central Washington, overlooking the Columbia River Gorge and Mt. Hood. Preserve hunts for pheasant and chukar, dog training, and sporting clays.

# Far West

## ALASKA

*In 2001 there were 72,000 resident hunters and 21,000 nonresident hunters: 90% went big game hunting, 19% small game, 15% water-fowl; 91% hunted on public lands; 20% hunted on private lands. Hunters pumped $217 million into the state's economy. (USFWS)*

### OVERVIEW

Alaska has 11 species of big game—bison, black bears, brown bears, caribou, deer, elk, moose, mountain goats, Dall sheep, musk oxen, and wolves—spread across an area as large as one-fifth of the lower 48 with fewer miles of roads than Rhode Island.

Add to that ducks, geese, cranes, four species of grouse (ruffed, blue, spruce, and sharp-tailed) and three species of ptarmigan (willow, rock, and white-tailed), plus snow-shoe and arctic hare. About the only major game they don't have is wild turkey, and they are working on that.

Much of this land is remote and wild,

and the terrain is very diverse, from soaring snowcapped mountains to flat tundra that stretches as far as the eye can see, to lush islands with more temperate climates due to warm ocean currents, to the forested taiga interior.

If you have not been here before, guides are highly recommended. One way to look for a guide is to consult www.alaskansportsman .com/directory/Alaska_Hunting/index.php.

A current list of all registered guides and

transporters is available for $5 from: Department of Commerce, Community & Economic Development, Division of Corporations, Business and Professional Licensing, Big Game Commercial Services, P.O. Box 110806, Juneau, AK 99811-0806, 907-465-2543.

 **FEATURED HUNT**

## Alaska Caribou Adventure

CHRIS BATIN*

The rocky spires of the Alaska Range reached up like a massive hand as the Super Cub climbed for altitude. Holding on to my seat, I peered out the window while casting an occasional nervous glance up toward pilot Art Warbelow. Looking down into the precipitous canyon, I spotted an eagle soaring above a more passive piece of terrain.

"You sure caribou are up this high?" I asked Art as the two spires passed to what seemed to be feet of the wingtips. "Even the eagles are reluctant to fly this high."

"The warm weather has pushed the caribou to the top of the ridges," he said over the whine of the engine. "You'll like the area. Why, there are some caribou right over on that ridgetop, and there's a sheep right next to them."

Art banked the Cub for a closer look. Sure enough, two small caribou bulls were near a sloping ridge, while an immature Dall sheep stood on the rocky face of the peak. The caribou shook their heads at us as we passed over them. We continued on to the area I was to hunt.

"This Steese-Fortymile caribou herd is something else," Art said as we flew down a winding river valley. "There are over 12,000 animals in the herd.

Right now, the animals are beginning to group up and migrate south to their wintering grounds, which will give you an excellent opportunity to look over several bulls and choose the best one. Best of all, I'm sure you won't have nearly the hunting pressure that you experienced last year on the Alaska Peninsula."

The Cub soon approached the landing strip, which was nothing more than a flat section of alpine ridgetop. The plane bounced down and vibrated to a stop on the shale-covered ridge. I quickly unloaded my gear. "See you in three days," Art called before shutting the window and lifting off into the mountain-studded skyline to the south.

I always experience euphoria when the plane disappears from sight, leaving me with a one-on-one challenge with the terrain and my quarry. Plans laid months ago, hours spent studying maps and planning strategies pay off with quick decisions and confidence; now it was time to put it all together.

I scanned the rugged alpine landscape. Since caribou are highly migratory, success greatly depends on choosing the right area to intercept the herds as they move through. I had a good feeling about a saddle between two peaks about three miles distant. Within minutes, I was on the trail, breaking through tangles of blueberry bushes, their winy aroma slowly cleansing the pollution and smells of civilization out of my lungs and nostrils.

I quickly found a caribou trail and followed it, only later to discover that it was in actuality a bear trail. Minutes later, I blamed my shortness of breath on my loud whistling and off-key singing that I always recommend when "trespassing" on bruin property, especially through bruin berry patches.

With the berry understory quickly disappearing in the distance, I began trudging through head-high willow and alder thickets, my legs more accustomed to the inactivity of months of fishing rather than the weight of a 75-pound pack. I cursed the branches and the sweltering heat. Sweat ran freely. My pack bit into shoulder muscles not yet toughened by miles of overland packing.

An hour later, I sat down to rest on a piece of quartz. Mixed feelings of challenge, excitement, and accomplishment ran rampant in anticipating the upcoming events. I breathed deeply as if to savor each one. If only someone could invent a pill that would produce this feeling during the rest of the year.

The saddle lies between a peak at 5,300 feet and one at 4,400 feet. It's a barren piece of ground, with a few patches of sedge and some scattered scrub bushes. With all the rain that fell the week prior to my hunt, Art said there would definitely be water nearby. I set up camp, unpacked my container, and started looking. No water to be found. I thirstily eyed a small stream about 3,000 feet below me, but the setting sun kept me from trying any such foolhardy marathon. I would need to make the hike first thing in the morning, before hunting. That would be a hike that I would not look forward to.

While scavenging handfuls of berries to satiate my need for liquids, I found a boggy section of tundra. Remembering some long-lost bit of advice from an old Boy Scout manual in my Eagle Scout days, I dug a hole in the bog. Slowly, it filled up with blackish water. An hour later, the sediment settled, and I had a delightful cup of cold spring water, located not more than 30 feet from my camp. I wasn't about to dine on freeze-dried food sans water, so I cooked up a feast to celebrate my discovery and prompt cancellation of my 6,000-feet-round-trip hike for two gallons of water.

With the blue flames of the small cookstove hissing away, I busied myself checking minor details to prepare for the hunt.

Chores finished, I sat down to eat my celebration feast when I heard a rock tumble down the rocky mountainside behind me. Thoughts of the grizzly whose real estate I earlier trespassed upon instantly came to mind. I slowly turned, rifle in hand, only to lay eyes on a small herd of caribou: 10 cows, seven calves, and two small bulls. They grazed slowly down the slope toward my tent. Smiling, I ate my supper while watching them. Television could never match this live showing of "Caribou Capers." Occasionally, one of the bulls would raise its snout and sniff in my direction. Eyes would bug glaringly at me whenever I moved about, usually followed by a few curious steps forward. As the herd moved down into the saddle and up the mountainside that loomed directly opposite my tent, I made a toast to the caribou, the wilderness area in which they lived, and the opportunity for being there.

The pre-aura of daylight painted a pinkish streak across the horizon at 4:00 A.M. Frost covered my water bucket, and the cold nipped at my face. These conditions, which would normally send me crawling back under the covers, encouraged me to get up and experience every tingling goosebump, the cold, clammy boots, and the anticipation of some fresh-brewed coffee on a ridgetop where not another human being, machine, or civilized mechanism could be seen or heard. The hunter was becoming part of the hunt.

As my swamp water boiled, I looked around. Not a caribou to be seen. A quick cup of coffee, some food bars thrown in the pack, and I was soon hiking a quick pace to a gradual sloping ridge about 500 yards west of the saddle. From the tracks in the tundra, this is where the caribou that I observed the previous night had come down.

Shadows hung heavily on the west side of the mountain. I searched every depression, every ridgetop, for a white mane that signaled a big caribou. Seeing nothing, I started to glass the timberline. I never finished. Two clicks on the hillside to my left riveted my attention. The sound was a dead giveaway: the clicking of caribou tendons. Turning slowly, I could only pick out gray images against the sunlit ridge. A splash of white against a black background grabbed my attention. Throwing up my rifle, I searched the scope for an image. Anxiety rushed through my limbs as I focused on a heavily tined caribou looking directly at me. I quickly scanned the herd and found another good bull—but not as impressive as the one in my scope. I centered the crosshairs. The distance was far: about 300 yards.

The bull started to walk away with the cows. I acted on instinct. I crouched down and scooted through the brush for about 50 yards. Yet the bull was walking too fast and would soon disappear over the ridge. I sat down, adjusted my rangefinder scope, held slightly in front of the shoulder of the walking bull, and squeezed off. The recoil of the 165-grain boat tail kicked my head back and eyes off the animal and into the sun. But I heard the bullet hit home as I pulled the rifle down to ready myself for another shot if need be. The bull took two steps, stumbled and fell.

I was soon running over the tundra and up the hill toward my trophy. The other caribou snorted and leaped into the air before taking off down the ridge. I stopped and jumped in the air, a bit of hunting success insanity taking hold. At that very moment, I was not a hunter but the hunt itself, of everything that comprises it: the behavioral tendencies of the caribou, the freedom of soul, the skill of a predator once again fulfilling an age-old desire to harvest a resource. But above all, appreciation and respect for the caribou for bringing this all about swelled within me. In silent reflection, I gave thanks.

I slowly walked up to the bull, a handsome animal with 37 tines and heavy beams. It was extremely fat and would provide many a caribou dinner during the upcoming winter. Adhering to European tradition, I cut two scrub spruce shoots: one I placed in the animal's mouth to signify its last meal, and the other I dipped in the blood and placed in the band

of my hat. This covenant between man and animal completed the hunt. Now there was work to do.

The next two days were spent quartering, prepping, and packing the caribou back to the ridgetop for pickup. Feet toughened up, and eyes were quick to spot the slightest movement. Thoughts of the hunt were mentally replayed over and over again during the pack. Ptarmigan scuttled away. I even treated an ermine I met on a ridgetop to a few handfuls of caribou scrap. I would see caribou from time to time, but the cold weather had sent most of them down toward the timberline.

I spent the last day on a ridetop watching the endless horizon of mountains change colors like a giant kaleidoscope as the sunlight spotlighted carpets of red cranberry and yellow alder through slow-moving clouds.

When the drone of Art's Super Cub in the distance forced me to head for the strip, I felt a part of me remain on the ridge. Yet I quickly captured the feeling and locked it in my mind. They'll be times when I'll gently unlock it, when work schedules keep me from going afield, or when old age wears down my physical stamina to the point of retirement. And I'll reminisce and relish the memories. But at the time I was living it to its fullest, and as I eased on my pack, I made one last toast: To caribou hunting in the Forty-Mile area. May it provide similar rewards to all those who favor a true Alaska hunting experience.

## PLANNING YOUR HUNT

If you want a truly remote hunt, away from the crowds, as well as the opportunity to save a few hundred dollars, which could pay for your caribou tag or new spotting scope, consider flying out via commercial airlines to one of the smaller cities/villages such as King Salmon, Aniak, Kenai, or Port Alsworth. Remember that although your overall cost for commercial transportation will be slightly higher, you'll save on the air charter costs from what you'd pay to fly directly to the hunting grounds from Anchorage. Also, it's been my experience that pilots based in these villages tend to have the advantage when it comes to locating herd numbers and appropriate landing areas. They fly this huge piece of real estate day after day and know the country and game movements. Also, the charter operators located on the west side of the Alaska/Aleutian ranges don't have to cope with tackling the mountain passes of Lake Clark. When inclement weather sets in, Anchorage operators may be stranded at Lake Hood for days at a time, while operators on the other side of the pass are usually flying. This fact alone is worth considering an air charter operator based in one of the villages mentioned above. Also consider an alternate herd, like the Kilbuck Mountain herd, out of Aniak. Research your options based on what you want to achieve.

## FINDING ANIMALS

If you're planning an early-to-late-August hunt, you'll need to be dropped off high . . . very high. Caribou are at all elevations at this time of year, but the big bulls prefer the cooling effects of snowpacks and windy ridges, which also helps keep the mosquito and fly pests at bay. The Bonanza Hills and Stony River country offer excellent hunting opportunities as well as the Chilikadrotna country, a favorite of mine. The western portion of the Mulchatna River headwaters is another top choice, with both good numbers of moose and caribou in the vicinity. A good opportunity here for a multispecies hunt for a party of three or more. If there are only two hunters in your group, I'd opt for the alpine drop-off for both moose and caribou. Also, avoid a float hunt if you're not experienced with floating Alaska's rivers. Try some float fishing trips first, then tackle a float hunt. Operating an inflatable loaded with meat requires experience, even on relatively calm rivers like the upper Mulchatna, where an

innocent-enough-looking sweeper, if unavoided, can result in disaster. Enough said.

Consider this: While newly hired pilots with any company—even with thousands of hours of flying experience—may not often exude the best personality in the world, realize that you're paying for air transportation to and from the area. In remote areas such as the Mulchatna, it's often difficult to shop around for another outfit with a Super Cub or Maule. So grin and bear it and let the prima donna pilot think he's hot stuff. If you have a complaint, don't unload until you're back at dockside, with all your meat and gear packed into your vehicle or duffels.

Here's another tip: Later in the season, say from mid-September on, watch for approaching storms. Several days prior, the caribou bulls will be on the move. Too many times I've seen caribou bulls move into the lower elevations a day or two prior to the arrival of a storm. Listen to the weather reports (always take a weather-band radio) and have your pilot place you accordingly. If in doubt, ask for a drop-off where several alpine valleys merge together and empty into a lowland area. Caribou will funnel out of these passes and migrate to the safety of the flats. If the weather doesn't turn bad, you can take a spike camp and hike into the alpine high country and take a nice bull.

Whatever method you decide, go with two tents, a base camp and a spike camp, for alpine hunts for three to five days. A spotting scope is a must here, as you'll see the caribou's white mane from a long distance. Many times, solitary bulls will bed down for an afternoon on a sunny mountainside, giving you the opportunity to mark its location and plan your stalk. But do so that evening or at first light, because caribou bulls are up early, feeding and walking at the same time.

You can also expect to see an occasional black bear in the hill country of the upper Mulchatna. They'll be seen in and around ridgetops and wherever you'll find berry patches. Locate berries, and you'll find black bears—simple as that.

Expect to pay anywhere from $1,200 to $1,800 or more for such a hunt, with a few of the more distant areas running as high as $3,400 per person, depending on type of aircraft used. Solitude will cost you more, whereas a drop-camp in an area with other hunters may be a third or half as much. There are enough tundra potholes, lakes, and gravel bars in Mulchatna country where one shouldn't worry about competition or be dropped off near other hunters. Insist on this. During the 20 years I've hunted this area, I've yet to see another hunter afield.

Many hunters prefer the challenge of stalking caribou while they are still in the mountains in early to late August. The mountains are ablaze with color, the weather is in the forties to seventies, and sweet blueberries abound. High alpine plateaus and mountains from 3,000 to 5,000 feet dwarf 100-year-old spruce in the valleys below. On these ridges, where it appears nothing can exist, you'll find the biggest bulls, fat and lazy from feeding on grasses and lichens all summer. Look for them on windy knolls, where they escape the constant harassment of flies and mosquitoes. You'll also find caribou cooling off on alpine snowbanks, especially on a hot day.

In many areas of Alaska, reaching these high-plain drifters in early fall requires chartering transportation. Forget the large float planes. To land on rugged mountain ridge tops or tiny alpine lakes requires the go-cart of the airplane world, the Super Cub. Don't be fooled by its size. The plane is one-person wide, and the passenger sits behind the pilot. Hunters are generally limited to 50 to 70 pounds of gear for a weeklong hunt. Balloon tires allow the aircraft to land on the rocky ridges and float on the often spongy tundra.

The herd in Mulchatna is easily accessible, has a good percentage of trophy bulls, and offers additional hunting opportunities for black bears and moose. According to air charter pilots, over 80% to 90% of their caribou hunters who fly out are successful.

The Forty-Mile herd near Tok is another popular and ruggedly beautiful area to hunt. It's possible to see at least 15 caribou per trip or, during the migration in September, as many as 100 or more.

The Central and Western Arctic and Porcupine herds have the most animals but are also more expensive to hunt. And since the Mulchatna and Peninsula herds offer such an availability of trophy bulls at a fraction of the price, there is really no reason for a hunter to consider a high Arctic trip for caribou in the next few years. The exception is a bow hunt along the Dalton Highway, targeting the Central Arctic caribou herd. A good do-it-yourself hunt for archers. But rifle hunters need to hike five miles from the Dalton, which is a very long hike over horrible tundra. Consider your physical condition and time before choosing this route.

If you still insist on hunting the Arctic (which offers unique scenery and adventure not found elsewhere), in many instances, air transportation alone will run over $1,000 per hunter. And unless you donate your meat to local villagers, expect to pay up to a dollar a pound to ship at least 200 pounds of meat, per animal, from Bettles to Fairbanks. This takes into consideration that the plane will be loaded with your gear for the flight back. If you pack extralight, the pilot will be able to fly gear and meat back in one haul, eliminating this expense.

To help combat costs, I recommend you drive the Dalton Highway to a pickup point near Bettles and have the air charter operator ferry you from this location to and from the hunting area. This saves air charter time and also eliminates the expense of having to air ship the meat to Fairbanks. Hunters have a very good chance of taking a trophy caribou if they have patience and restrain themselves from shooting the first bull they see.

Joe Jackson of Wild Kobuk River Runners (http://home.gci.net/~kobukriver) offers a good do-it-yourself float for Western Arctic caribou. Call him for assistance in planning your hunt. He's been a regular on the Alaska hunting scene for years, is a longtime Alaskan, and knows the area well. Use him rather than the outsiders who drop off in his area. You won't regret it.

"Most hunters from the Lower 48 are familiar with seeing and judging whitetail deer racks," he said. "They see a small caribou with a rack three to four times that of a whitetail, and they take their shot, only to realize later they were a bit premature in their decision, especially when a trophy bull walks by. For most, the caribou is the largest antlered animal they've seen in their life."

What are the features to look for in a trophy caribou? Look for two girthy main beams that sweep up and out over the forehead, often stretching 60 inches or more. The bull should have good brow tines or shovels, reaching far out onto the nose. Good bez tines, located off the main beam just above the brow tine, are important. And the terminal portion of the main beam should be palmated and flattened, with numerous rearward-facing tines.

Let us hunt the caribou with all the enthusiasm and challenge that it offers. But let us also respect it for what it is; a symbol of our last great wilderness on earth, the Alaska high-plains tundra. Indeed, the barren-ground caribou is a resource that we can't lose without losing ourselves in the process.

*Equipment.* Once you've been dropped off in the middle of a wilderness area, you are on your own until the plane returns. This is no place for cheap hunting gear, and forgetting an item can at least cause a grave inconvenience or, at most, imperil your health or even life.

Pack a quality freestanding tent. A four-person tent will usually house two people and gear. It should be able to withstand winds of at least 40 miles per hour, preferably more. An unleaded gas stove is a must, as is plenty of fuel. Take standard as well as emergency rations of lightweight, freeze-dried or vacuum-packed foods for main meals. Creamy soups, cheeses, beef jerky, and trail mix provide quick, high-energy snacks for lunch and at midday. Instant oatmeal breakfasts are quick and simple.

I favor a 15×45 waterproof spotting scope and Alpen 8-power binoculars, probably one of the best deals in optics going today. A lightweight, sturdy tripod is a must-have item for glassing in the almost ever-present wind.

Over the last several years, Seal Skinz have kept my feet dry and comfortable in both hunting boots and hippers. Combine polyester underwear with polar fleece outerwear and a quality rain shell. Also pack a lightweight parka, as temperatures do drop down to the low teens at night, then skyrocket to the low sixties during the day. And don't forget a hat and neoprene Glacier Gloves for wet weather, and wool gloves for general use. And believe it or not, take the suntan lotion. When the weather cooperates, glassing all day on the open tundra, even at 40 degrees, can produce a nasty sunburn.

*How to Get There.* Take a commercial airline to the base city closest to the herd that you'll be hunting. These are the cities of Kenai or King Salmon for the Alaska Peninsula or Mulchatna herds, Tok for the Forty-Mile herd, and Fairbanks Fort Yukon or Bettles for the northern Arctic herds and Porcupine herd. Charter an air taxi service to the hunting area.

*Where to Stay.* This is wilderness hunting. You need to be self-sufficient in the alpine country for anywhere from 3 to 14 days. Owing to inclement weather in September and October, add an extra 2 days on the tail end of your trip.

*Best Season.* Caribou season in Alaska opens in many units around mid-August. Caribou are still in velvet at this time, and the rack makes for a handsome trophy. Velvet is rubbed off by late August or early September, a good time to hunt across the state. The exception is the northern Brooks, where winter is starting to set in. An admonition: Avoid late September and October hunts, however, as the caribou are in full rut, and the meat is virtually unpalatable.

*Chris Batin is editor and publisher of* The Alaska Hunter *and a contributing writer for* Outdoor Life *magazine. He is considered one of the country's foremost experts on Alaska fishing and hunting. For more information on Chris Batin's books and DVDs on Alaska hunting, visit* www.AlaskaHunter.com.

## FEATURED HUNT

## Alaskan Black Bear Hunt

JEFF ENGEL

The wind spit icy pellets into my face as our small skiff churned against the endless waves and I huddled deep in my rain gear. I took solace in knowing that elsewhere cars were piling up behind traffic lights, and message lights were blinking as millions of people were engaged in the endless hustle and bustle of daily life. I was in southeast Alaska, near a town called Kate on a spot-and-stalk hunt for coastal black bear.

The solitary miles of wave-washed beaches and the feeling of isolation were profound in this very remote region. Alaska is the home of some of the largest black bears that roam the planet. It was my hope to be fortunate enough to spot one and, if all went well, harvest a mature boar (male bear) with an excellent spring coat. And as always, I

planned to share the meat with many people to celebrate the wild spirit.

If you think of black bear hunting, I bet the last thing you think of is living at sea. Yet my watery quest for Alaskan black bear had little to do with the land that these bears actually live upon. Rather, I would be staying in a boat and hunting from it for much of the time.

This Alaskan adventure began in April, which would mean I would be hunting in the spring. My guide was Scott McLeod, who owns and operates Raven Guide Service. Scott greeted us at the airport and escorted us to the *Kath Ern*, a 45-foot cabin cruiser that would serve as our home for the next several days. I know of several people who have hunted with Scott, and he came highly recommended.

I've had the pleasure of working with many different guides over the years, and I soon realized that anyone who successfully guides bear hunting in Alaska has some unusual abilities. First and foremost, he must be a mariner. After all, we would be cruising the ocean, and the water is deadly cold. During the entire trip, my very life could be dependent on Scott's knowledge of wind, tide, and the care he has put into the essential equipment that would keep us moving, warm and dry.

I would also depend heavily on Scott's knowledge of the area. We would be hunting hundreds of square miles of isolated bays, inlets, and islands. Unlike much of the Lower 48, you just can't walk out if something goes wrong.

Our routine was to spend the evening on the main boat and then take a skiff throughout the day and cruise the shoreline, hoping to spot a black bear eating sedge grass along the shore. Once a bear is spotted, the questions begin: Is it a male? Is it a mature bear? What is the wind doing? Can we find a way to get to the bear once we land? Can we get close enough for a shot?

As we would cruise the rugged shoreline we would see bears on a regular basis, but we were truly looking for an old, mature boar, and we were being very selective. We would spend a great deal of time using our binoculars and searching up and down the shoreline, looking for a black speck.

One of the enjoyable aspects of the hunt was life aboard the *Kath Ern*. The weather was always a challenge, and the *Kath Ern* was a welcoming shelter. The meals were excellent, as was the camaraderie. But I also enjoyed the more contemplative times. There is a certain soulful joy in solitude that you feel as you look skyward toward the mountains and at the never-ending wave action.

There were many aspects of this trip that were unique to Alaska, such as seeing animals like pine martins and sea otters and having eagles often soaring above our heads. As we glassed one shoreline, we even came across the remains of a crashed bush plane. A reminder that here nature is always the boss.

After several days of observing a great many bears, Scott took down his binoculars from his eyes and looked at me and said, "Jeff, I think we found your bear." On a distant shoreline, Scott pointed out a small black speck as I raised my binoculars; the speck appeared to be a black bear; in fact, it appeared to be a very large black bear.

We motored our boat about a mile downwind from the bear, found a secure place to land the boat, and prepared our long stalk toward the bear along the shoreline. Once we got to within 150 yards of the bear, Scott again confirmed this was truly a very, very large one. I cradled my arm in the crack of a large boulder as I steadied my rifle. At the sound of the shot the bear ran into the thick moss-covered woods. Scott quickly turned to me and said, "Jeff, the shot looked good. I'm sure the bear is lying just inside the woods."

Sure enough, as we approached the spot where the bear was, Scott was correct, and we found the bear right away. The bear squared well over seven feet. I was very humbled and proud to take such a magnificent black bear. At that site we skinned the bear and quartered its meat and made several trips back to the beach in preparation for taking our bear back to the main boat.

A couple of suggestions for hunting Alaskan black bear by boat: Bring along the best possible waterproof rain gear you can get. I found that by wearing a complete top-and-bottom waterproof set along with a waterproof baseball-style hat and finishing off the outfit with hip boots made for a very compatible outfit for this type of hunt. Also, since you will be living on a boat, space is always at a premium, so it is wise to bring along as little as possible but as much as you need.

I also carried along a basic survival pack in a Ziploc bag that I kept in my outer pocket of my hunting parka, just in case we would have trouble. In the Ziploc case I had a half a roll of electrical tape along with waterproof matches, those in a waterproof container of their own; and in a different waterproof container, I had cotton balls immersed in Vaseline as a fire starter. Also in the plastic bag I had two lighters, a couple of granola bars, a large plastic bag, a compass, a whistle, and a long piece of rope. I also carried on my belt a sturdy folding knife and a

Leatherman tool; in the event that something went wrong, the items that I carried would at least make a night or two bearable.

On this trip, Alaska had been good to me. It had given me a true hunting adventure, the excitement of a great hunt, and a beautiful black bear to serve as a lifetime reminder of this exceptional trip. I knew that my license fees would help to perpetuate the awesome resource I had the privilege to enjoy. I also knew that wildlife professionals, paid in part by license revenue, and guides like Scott McLeod would work not to abuse the ecosystem but to maintain it so that Alaskan hunting adventures and the wild Alaska that makes it possible will exist for generations to come.

For more information on bear hunting in Alaska, contact:

**RAVEN GUIDES—THE ALASKA COMPANY**
Scott McLeod, Guide
Sitka, AK 99835
Phone: 907-747-6405
www.alaskaravenguides.com

 **FEATURED HUNT**

## Extreme Duck Hunting in Alaska

JEFF ENGEL

The barnacle-encrusted rocks were vivid in the clear, cold seawater. After a great deal of anticipation, our boat was landed on a hidden inlet near Kodiak Island. It was December, very cold, and we were about to embark on a true duck hunt adventure in Alaska.

Today Alaska is truly a sportsman's paradise. It's a massive sprawling country where glaciers are as big as Rhode Island, and vast roadless areas can only be reached by airplane. There are more than 3,000 rivers and 3 million lakes in this largest state of the United States: Alaska is two and one-half times the size of Texas.

Our quest on this trip was to hunt sea ducks, especially the beautiful harlequin duck, a species that is relatively common here but more difficult to find in the Lower 48. The harlequin duck is one of America's most stunning and beautiful game birds, with its slate and blue plumage with white accents and chestnut-covered flanks.

On Kodiak Island inland, you can hunt the puddle ducks like mallards and wigeon that we find down south, but here the unique hunt is for sea ducks. Other ducks that we would be hunting would be Barrow's goldeneyes, common goldeneyes, and scoters.

The natives call harlequins "squeakers" because of their high-pitched squeaky calls. This time of year the harlequins congregate along the rocky coasts and shoreline of Kodiak Island. Earlier in the year the females nested along clear, turbulent freshwater and streams as far inland as Montana, Idaho, and Wyoming. The females raise a brood there. While filming a television show in the Bob Marshall wilderness during the summer, we were fly-fishing a remote creek and came across a family of harlequin ducks.

On this hunt as well as all our duck hunts, we chose to shoot only drakes. It would be a challenge, for they are fast flyers often aided by cold blasts of north wind. In addition, harlequins often fly in pairs, and small flocks cluster very closely together. Our challenge is to find a drake that is separated enough to make an effective shot.

After a full day of flying from Wisconsin, we spent the night in the city of Kodiak on Kodiak Island. Early the next morning we took a bush plane from Kodiak to the small village of Port Lions, where our hunt would begin. Soon after we left the Kodiak airport we were flying through a majestic mountain range. Even from the air it is difficult to grasp the immense size of the state of Alaska. I also find that part of the adventure of hunting in Alaska is taking a bush plane flight through breathtaking land-scapes.

Joining me on this trip were good friends Larry Raschella and Bill Gaines. Larry is a shotgun shooting champion, not to mention a true American hero who served in the Vietnam War and was decorated with a Purple Heart. Bill is the president of the California Outdoor Heritage Alliance (COHA). COHA is an umbrella sportsmen's lobbying organization created to coordinate and unite hunting, recre-ational shooting, and conservation interests in order to strengthen their political influence. The organiza-tion was created in response to rapidly mounting political and social threats to hunting, the recre-ational use of sporting firearms, and science-based wildlife management in California and beyond.

Bill and his California Outdoor Heritage Alli-ance staff work tirelessly at all levels of government where policy decisions are made that could impact our hunting and shooting rights and opportunities—including the Congress, California state legislature, state Fish and Game Commission, state and federal agencies, and regional and local jurisdictions. CO-HA's track record of defending our outdoor tradi-tions, on arguably the toughest playing field of them all, California, is unequaled.

Waiting for us on the cinder bed of the air-strip was our guide Bob May. We selected Bob be-cause of his extensive experience in hunting sea ducks on Kodiak Island. Bob took us a short dis-tance to where the three of us shared a comfort-able and warm cottage-type house, and this would be our sleeping headquarters for the next several days.

Since the sun does not get up until after 8:00 A.M., we had the luxury of beginning a duck hunt where the wake-up call was not at 3:00 A.M. As Bob picked us up in his pickup, we took a short drive to the dock where his boat would be waiting. We found a very enthusiastic black Lab riding in the bed of the pickup truck. His dog couldn't wait to get into Bob's boat and start the day of sea duck hunt-ing, nor could we.

As we traveled near small islands and inlets, we saw numerous sea otters and eagles. Once we arrived at a hidden bay, we left the big boat and used a skiff to travel a short way down the coast. We then set up in a picturesque Alaskan bay. Out in front of us we set out about a dozen decoys.

The wind started to kick up, and the ducks began to fly. We quickly made a log blind on the shore and prepared for our hunt.

Now the ducks were really flying. At first they were clustered too close together to single out a drake, or they were flying out of range. We added some more logs to our blind to make sure we were concealed a little bit better, and then the ducks started to arrive, landing in the decoys.

I was also surprised as to how tough the sea ducks here were to bring down. Sea ducks have extremely dense plumage, and it takes large shot to bring them down. Something like a #4 or #2 shot works well.

For the next couple of hours we were able to isolate and pick out several drake harlequin ducks, with some superb retrieving by Bob's black Lab Buck. Around 3:00 P.M. the decoys were picked up, and we headed back for a warm and delicious meal.

The next morning at dawn we were up and on Bob's boat, heading out to sea, again with a skiff trailing. We set up in a small hidden bay, and like the shoot from yesterday, the ducks really were plentiful. We again shot some beautiful drake harlequins along with some beautiful goldeneyes.

We did not see or hear another waterfowl hunter during our hunt. It was truly enjoyable knowing and having a feeling that we were on an extremely remote duck hunt. Bob May had done a wonderful job finding areas that were secluded and private.

That night the temperature dipped to below zero. The next morning we headed to the dock. Bob had concerns for his outboard motors and the pos-

sibility of them not working properly owing to the extreme cold. In fact, once we were onboard Bob's boat, both motors had frozen up and were not releasing a stream of water. This could be trouble. Thankfully, after a while the engines warmed up, and Bob was able to safely take us out to sea to again find a hidden, remote area for sea ducks.

After a very enjoyable morning of hunting, we again put the decoys in the skiff and headed back to the main boat. While on the boat Bob turned his weather-band radio on, and we learned that a severe storm was coming our way, very fast. The prediction was for 50-knot winds and seas in excess of 20 feet. The short-term forecast seemed desperate.

After talking to us, Bob said it would be a wise decision to head to one of his remote cabins and spend the night there and not take the risk of going back to the main lodge. Once we left the sheltered harbor, the effects of the weather became quickly evident. The weather turned dramatically for the worse. Bob took a shortcut through a bay, and his boat ended up being an ice breaker. Once we got to the open water, we found ourselves in heavy seas, and it was very apparent that the decision to spend the night in the remote cabin was a wise one.

As we headed to Bob's remote cabin, with the icy Alaskan wind in my face, I couldn't help but wonder what tomorrow would bring. Finally we ended up in a hidden bay where we anchored our boat and took a skiff to a very comfortable cabin that Bob uses in the summertime. Luckily, Bob had plenty of provisions, and there was lots of dry firewood, so we spent an extremely comfortable evening watching the storm through glass windows.

The next morning, to our delight, was wonderful. The winds had diminished and the seas were calmer. We started with a wonderful hot breakfast. We couldn't help but crack a few jokes about the contrast of the extreme cold temperature outside, about 12 degrees, and the sizzling frying bacon inside.

Although it was bitter out, a little cold was not going to keep us from the ducks. Today we would be hunting old squaws. Bob had a very interesting way of hunting these beautiful black-and-white birds with long tails. From his main boat he would let out two lines of old squaw decoys directly behind the boat. We would then simply wait in the boat and have old squaws fly by. At first I didn't think it would be possible to be sitting in a large silver, very noticeable boat, with decoys trailing behind. To my surprise, this system worked. Soon we had several flights of old squaws flying around, through, and into our decoy spread.

Both Larry, Bill, and I had some great old squaw shooting in the comfort of Bob's boat. Not only was this type of hunting enjoyable, but it was very comfortable.

On this duck hunting trip to Alaska we experienced everything from sunny days to severe storms. We were once again reminded that nature can always give you a taste of humility. In the end, the trip really wasn't about shooting ducks; it was about spending quality times with close friends, enjoying and appreciating nature and just knowing that we as Americans have the freedom to hunt in areas like this and that we have the privilege to have a true outdoor experience.

For information about hunting sea ducks on Kodiak Island, contact:

**WHALE PASS LODGE**
Bob & Denise May
Port Lions, AK 99550
Phone: 800-4-KODIAK (800-456-3425)
or 907-454-2500
www.whalepasslodge.com

---

## DESTINATIONS

### General Information
There is no lack of places to hunt in Alaska, but many are difficult to access. There are 26 state game management units. For general hunting information about seasons, licenses, permits, and so on, consult www.wildlife. alaska.gov/index.cfm?adfg=hunting.resources.

### USDA National Forests
Virtually the entire national forest system in Alaska is open to hunting. For details on hunting seasons, bag limits, and areas of the national forests, consult the Alaska hunting regulations. For general, region-wide information, contact:

**USDA FOREST SERVICE,**
**ALASKA REGION**
Juneau, AK 99802-1628
Phone: 907-586-8806; fax: 907-586-7840
www.fs.fed.us

### U.S. Bureau of Land Management
The BLM manages most federal lands not administered by the National Park Service (NPS), the U.S. Fish and Wildlife Service (USFWS), and the U.S. Forest Service (USFS)—some 87 million acres. Virtually all of this land is open to hunting. There are some federal restrictions to use of motorized vehicles in certain areas. Visit the BLM Web site at http://aurora.ak.blm.gov or obtain additional information on hunting uses of BLM-administered lands from:

**BLM ALASKA—EXTERNAL AFFAIRS**
Anchorage, AK 99513
Phone: 907-271-5555; fax: 907-272-3430

### U.S. Geological Survey Maps
U.S. Geological Survey (USGS) topographic and other maps can be obtained by mail order or over the counter in several Alaska locations. The USGS maintains a map distribution office at Alaska Pacific University in Anchorage that can provide fast service over the counter or by mail or telephone for people out of state. In Fairbanks, hunters may obtain maps at the Geophysical Institute's map office.

**U.S. GEOLOGICAL SURVEY**
Earth Science Information Center
Anchorage, AK 99508
Phone: 907-786-7011; fax: 907-786-7050

**MAP OFFICE, GEODATA CENTER**
Geophysical Institute—UAF
Fairbanks, AK 99775
Phone: 907-474-6960

### U.S. Fish and Wildlife Service
### National Wildlife Refuges

**ALASKA MARITIME NATIONAL**
**WILDLIFE REFUGE**
Homer, AK 99603

Phone: 907-235-6546; fax: 907-235-7783
http://alaska.fws.gov/nwr/akmar/index.htm

This refuge contains 4.9 million acres of remote islands in the Bering Sea. Caribou and reindeer were introduced to some of the islands during World War II and the Cold War to provide food for troops. The caribou herd on Adak Island number about 3,000. These are big animals and abundant. There is no season nor bag limit. For details, see http://alaska.fws.gov/nwr/akmar/visitors-educators/caribhunting/adak.htm.

The herd on Unimak Island, which is at the tip of Alaska Peninsula, is native. Brown bears may also be hunted here by permit. For details, see http://alaska.fws.gov/nwr/akmar/visitors-educators/caribhunting/unimak.htm.

Caribou on Cape Thompson are part of the Western Arctic caribou herd that roams over a broad area including the refuge land. Contact Alaska Department of Fish and Game for details. Reindeer on the Pribilof Islands are owned by the Native Corporations. Hunting can be arranged by acquiring permits through the Tribal Ecosystem Offices on St. Paul and St. George.

**ALASKA PENINSULA NATIONAL WILDLIFE REFUGE**
King Salmon, AK 99613
Phone: 907-246-4250
http://alaskapeninsula.fws.gov

The Alaska National Interest Land Conservation Act (ANILCA) established the 3.7 million-acre Alaska Peninsula NWR in 1980. This is a spectacular area of towering mountains, active volcanoes, broad valleys, fjords, tundra, and glacially formed lakes lying between Becharof National Wildlife Refuge to the north and Izembek NWR to the south. Brown bears, caribou, wolverines, wolves, moose, ptarmigan, and waterfowl are found here. Guide services, as well as aircraft charters and boat rentals, are available in King Salmon. There are approximately 7,000 caribou in the northern Alaska Peninsula herd.

**ARCTIC NATIONAL WILDLIFE REFUGE**
Fairbanks, AK 99701
Phone: 907-456-0250 or 800-362-4546;
fax: 907-456-0428
http://arctic.fws.gov

Yes, this is the massive controversial ANWR—spectacular wild country stretching from the shore of the Arctic Ocean to the rugged Brooks Range, possibly with huge oil and natural gas resources underground. Caribou, musk oxen, Dall sheep, moose, brown bears, black bears, waterfowl, ptarmigan, wolverines, waterfowl, and much, much more. This is a true wilderness. The Porcupine caribou herd has about 123,000. The Central Arctic herd has about 32,000. The Teshekpuk Lake caribou herd has about 29,000.

The refuge is open to the public year-round. No permit is required if you are not there for a commercial purpose. For a listing of guides authorized to hunt ANWR, see http://arctic.fws.gov/huntguide.htm.

**BECHAROF NATIONAL WILDLIFE REFUGE**
King Salmon, AK 99613
Phone: 907-246-4250
http://becharof.fws.gov

From the rugged, rocky coastline to the 4,835-foot summit of Mt. Peulik, the refuge includes everything from tundra to braided, glacier-fed rivers to saw-toothed mountain ranges. Becharof Lake is 35 miles long, 15 miles wide, and as much as 600 feet deep and is fed by two major rivers and numerous streams. It is the second biggest lake in Alaska, the largest in the entire National Wildlife Refuge System, and a salmon factory. Moose, caribou, black bears, and waterfowl; but this is home to the largest brown bear population in Alaska.

There are no visitor fees. Outfitters and guides are available in King Salmon. See www.kingsalmonguides.com, www.alaskatrophyadventures.com/hunt04.htm, and www.outdoorsdirectory.com/areas/hunting/south central/king-salmon.htm.

## INNOKO NATIONAL WILDLIFE REFUGE
McGrath, AK 99627
Phone: 907-524-3251
http://innoko.fws.gov

Located in coastal northwest Alaska, in the famed Iditarod race area, Innoko NWR supports healthy moose and waterfowl populations. Caribou, black bears, and other furbearers are also hunted in season. Approximately half of the refuge is black spruce muskeg, wet meadows, and sedge or horsetail marshes with innumerable lakes and ponds of varying size. The rest of the terrain is hills, most of which are less than 1,000 feet in elevation. The refuge covers some 3,850,000 acres, with 1,240,000 acres of designated wilderness found in the southeast.

## IZEMBEK NATIONAL WILDLIFE REFUGE
Cold Bay, AK 99571
Phone: 907-532-2445
http://izembek.fws.gov

The refuge surrounds and protects Izembek Lagoon, 150 square miles of brackish water containing one of the world's largest eelgrass beds. The state-owned tidelands within the lagoon are designated as the Izembek State Game Refuge.

The refuge's hunting opportunities, particularly for brown bears and waterfowl, are world renown. When salmon are running, brown bear densities can be as many as six bears per mile along some streams. Fall waterfowl hunting is spectacular for Canada geese, black brant, mallards, pintail, wigeon, scaup, goldeneyes, and sea ducks—harlequins, long-tailed, black scoters. Ptarmigan are abundant. The southern Alaska Peninsula caribou herd is currently at a healthy level. In the area primarily between Pavlof Bay and Port Moller Bay, a resident moose season is open in December and January.

## KANUTI NATIONAL WILDLIFE REFUGE
Fairbanks, AK 99701
Phone: 877-220-1853 or 907-456-0329; fax: 907-456-0428
http://kanuti.fws.gov

Kanuti National Wildlife Refuge (Kanuti Refuge) lies on the Arctic Circle in north-central Alaska between 66° and 67° north latitude and 151° and 153° west longitude. The refuge is located approximately 100 miles (161 kilometers) south of the Brooks Range and 150 miles northwest of Fairbanks, Alaska. This is a major waterfowl nesting and staging area. Other wildlife include moose, caribou, black bears, brown bears, beavers, wolves, and wolverines. The refuge is closed to airplane hunting for moose, and the number of permits for nonresidents is limited. For details, see http://kanuti.fws.gov/hunting.htm.

The refuge also supports 16 species of fish including several species of whitefish, northern pike, grayling, and salmon.

**KENAI NATIONAL WILDLIFE REFUGE**
Soldotna, AK 99669-2139
Phone: 907-262-7021; fax: 907-262-3599
http://kenai.fws.gov

The interior of the Kenai Peninsula can get cold in the winter, but the maritime climate created by the ocean and warm currents that flow offshore makes for more moderate temperatures in winter along the shore. Hunting season for moose, Dall sheep, and caribou begins in mid-August. Brown and black bears, mountain goats, wolves, lynx, wolverines, and waterfowl are also found here.

The majority of refuge lands are open to hunting, but there are restricted and closed areas, such as Skilak Wildlife Recreation Area, the Sterling Highway Corridor, and the headquarters/visitor center complex and adjacent trails. When planning your hunt, check with refuge staff and consult the state of Alaska hunting regulations.

**KODIAK NATIONAL WILDLIFE REFUGE**
Kodiak, AK 99615
Phone: 888-408-3514 or 907-487-2600;
fax: 907-487-2144
http://kodiak.fws.gov

The 1.9 million-acre Kodiak National Wildlife Refuge roughly encompasses the southwestern two-thirds of Kodiak Island, Uganik Island, the Red Peaks area on northwestern Afognak Island, and all of Ban Island. No place on the refuge is more than 15 miles from the Pacific Ocean.

Kodiak Island is the home of the Kodiak brown bear, *Ursus arctos middendorffi*, the largest bear in the world. The refuge is the home of about 2,300 of these giants. Hunting for Kodiak brown bears is restricted. Also popular are the abundant Sitka blacktail deer, and sea ducks. Fishing for salmon and halibut is outstanding, and let's not forget the Alaskan king crab, snow crab, and Dungeness crabs.

Permits are required from some native access parks of the refuge. Public-use cabin reservations are available by applying for a quarterly lottery, then on a first come, first served basis thereafter. Cabin reservations cost $30 per night. Contact refuge headquarters for details.

**KOYUKUK NATIONAL WILDLIFE REFUGE**
Galena, AK 99741-0287
Phone: 907-656-1231 or 800-656-1231;
fax: 907-656-1708
http://koyukuk.fws.gov

This 3.5 million-acre NWR lies within the floodplain of the Koyukuk River in a basin that extends from the Yukon River to the Purcell Mountains and the foothills of the Brooks Range. This region of wetlands is home to waterfowl, beavers, and moose; and in wooded lowlands one finds bears, wolves, lynx, and marten, as well as large salmon runs.

Subsistence and sport hunting are

allowed on refuge lands in accordance with Alaska state and federal regulations. Moose hunting is popular. A large portion of the refuge is included in the Koyukuk Controlled Use Area, which prohibits the use of aircraft for moose hunting. Caribou hunting can be good in years that caribou from the migratory Western Arctic herd, which numbers more than 450,000, move into the northernmost reaches of the refuge in winter months.

The refuge is also home to both black and grizzly bears, wolves, and smaller game including snowshoe hare, grouse, and ptarmigan, plus waterfowl.

### SELAWIK NATIONAL WILDLIFE REFUGE
Kotzebue, AK 99752
Phone: 907-442-3799 or 800-492-8848; fax: 907-442-3124
http://selawik.fws.gov

Refuge lands include part of the American portion of the Bering Land Bridge that was used by the ancestors of many of today's large mammals and early humans when traveling between Asia and the Americas some 12,000 years ago. The refuge includes approximately 24,000 lakes and wetlands that contain considerable migratory waterfowl as well as whitefish, arctic grayling, and northern pike.

The Western Arctic caribou herd, the largest in Alaska, travels through the refuge in spring and fall. Portions of the herd sometimes winter on Selawik. Moose, brown bears, wolverines, and ptarmigan are also plentiful. The refuge is used for subsistence hunting by local residents, mostly Inupiaq Eskimos and some Athabascan Indians from Huslia. Refuge access is difficult. Airplane charter services and big game guides are available.

### TETLIN NATIONAL WILDLIFE REFUGE
Tok, AK 99780
Phone: 907-883-5312; fax: 907-883-5747
http://tetlin.fws.gov

Located 94 miles northwest of the U.S.-Canada border and 205 miles southeast of Fairbanks, Alaska, the Alaskan Highway makes the Tetlin NWR one of only two road-accessible National Wildlife Refuges in Alaska. Ducks, caribou, and moose are the species most often pursued. Both black and brown bears, wolves, and the majestic white Dall sheep are also found on refuge lands. In addition to ducks and geese, small game hunters also enjoy hunting for spruce, ruffed and sharp-tailed grouse, and snowshoe hare.

### TOGIAK NATIONAL WILDLIFE REFUGE
Dillingham, AK 99627-0069
Phone: 907-842-1063; fax: 907-842-5402
http://togiak.fws.gov

With the Ahklun Mountains in the north and the cold waters of Bristol Bay to the south, the refuge lands include more than 600 miles of rugged coastline. The home of wolves, moose, brown and black bears, and wolverines, more than 150,000 caribou from two different herds are found on Togiak Refuge seasonally.

There is also good hunting for waterfowl and upland game birds. Hunting guide services are available for some species, and unguided hunting is also popular. Nonresident brown bear hunters are required to use the services of a registered guide.

### YUKON DELTA NATIONAL WILDLIFE REFUGE
Bethel, AK 99559

Phone: 907-543-3151; fax: 907-543-4413
http://yukondelta.fws.gov

Almost 70% of the refuge is below 100 feet in elevation and consists of a broad, flat delta stitched through with rivers and streams and dotted with countless lakes, sloughs, and ponds. Bordering the expanse of tundra and wetlands are 2.5 million acres of forest and shrub habitat and uplands sporting mountains more than 4,000 feet high. The refuge also includes two large islands—Nelson and Nunivak.

The drier upland habitats have brown and black bears, caribou, moose, and wolves. Offshore, Nunivak Island, Nelson Island, and occasionally other parts of the refuge have musk ox herds. There is considerable waterfowl activity in this area.

You cannot drive to the refuge. Various airlines provide regular commercial flights to and from Bethel. From Bethel, most nonlocal visitors travel into the refuge by small aircraft.

**YUKON FLATS NATIONAL**
**WILDLIFE REFUGE**
Fairbanks, AK 99701
Phone: 907-456-0440 or 800-531-0676;
fax: 907-456-0447
http://yukonflats.fws.gov

The third largest conservation area in the National Wildlife Refuge System, the 9 million-acre Yukon Flats NWR is located in eastern interior Alaska. Mixed forests dominated by spruce, birch, and aspen and a complex network of lakes, streams, and rivers characterize the area. The refuge supports the highest density of breeding ducks in Alaska and includes one of the greatest waterfowl breeding areas in North America.

Beaver, lynx, marten, mink, muskrat, and river otters thrive on the water-laced floodplain. Moose can be found throughout the refuge. Grizzly bears are found throughout the refuge in low concentrations, while the more common black bears tend to keep to the forested lowlands. Wolves can be encountered anywhere on the refuge. Dall sheep are found on the alpine tundra of the White Mountains and Hodzana Highlands.

Additional places to hunt in Alaska can be found at www.wildlife.alaska.gov/index.cfm?adfg=hunting.resources.

# HERITAGE DESTINATIONS

*Midnight Sun Shootout*
Held each summer in the Anchorage area, come and shoot and rub elbows with media celebrities, state and federal dignitaries, enjoy a great meal, and help raise funds for the shooting sports and important conservation programs in Alaska. This event raises upwards of $200,000 every year for shooting sports in Alaska, including Becoming an Outdoorswoman, Eddie Eagle Gunsafe Program, and the 4-H shooting league.

The Hunter Heritage Foundation, the Alaska Department of Fish and Game, the Alaska Fish and Wildlife Conservation Fund, Safari Club International–Alaska Chapter, and the Friends of the National Rifle Association (NRA) sponsor the event. For more information, contact:

## HUNTING HERITAGE FOUNDATION OF ALASKA

Palmer, AK 99645
Phone: 907-745-6166; fax: 907-745-6175
www.alaskaoutdoorcouncil.org/hunter_
heritage_foundation.html

### Museum of the Aleutians

The 9,400-square-foot museum in Unalaska is the only archeological exhibition in the Aleutians. Displays of various cultures and traditions including hunting customs and beliefs of Aleuts.

## MUSEUM OF THE ALEUTIANS

Unalaska, AK 99685
Phone: 907-581-5150; fax: 907-581-6682
aleutians@arctic.net
www.aleutians.org

### Stay at the Afanasi Creek Cabins of Alaska's Kenai Peninsula Pioneer Trapper/Photographer Harry Johnson

Twenty-eight-year-old blacksmith Harry Johnson traveled from Erie, Pennsylvania, to Seward, Alaska, in 1904. One of his first jobs was on the meat-hunting crew for the Alaska Central Railway, where he met photographer William McPherson and learned about glass plate photography.

Johnson tried his hand at gold mining but found that trapping and photography were his strong suits. From 1904 to 1963, he kept a photographic record of the Seward, Moose Pass, and Hope area, collecting numerous outstanding photos of people and wildlife that today are prized for historical collections.

In l921 Johnson built his cabin on Afanasi Creek in the Kenai Mountains north of Hope. He trapped the valley from the 1920s to the 1950s, except for a stint with Army Intelligence in the Aleutians during World War II, where he was considered a hero. Highly regarded for his photos and trapping, Johnson was the inspiration for the 1970s movie *Sourdough*, which was filmed at the Afanasi Creek cabin.

The cabin sits on a tributary of Resurrection Creek, 17 miles north of Hope. The main cabin is 15 × 16 feet, with some unusual carvings inspired by his Scandinavian heritage. The nearby guest cabin is 12 × 14 feet.

Thanks to the U.S. Forest Service, you can stay at Harry Johnson's cabins. For details, contact:

## CHUGACH NATIONAL FOREST— SEWARD DISTRICT

Seward, AK 99664
Phone: 907-224-4131
www.fs.fed.us/r10/chugach/pages_district/
seward.html

# HAWAII

*In 2001 there were 17,000 resident hunters and less than 1,000 nonresident hunters: 91% went big game hunting, 44% small game; 57% hunted on public lands; 64% hunted on private lands. Hunters pumped $15 million into the state's economy. (USFWS)*

## OVERVIEW

Surf, sun, beaches, palm trees. Sportsmen coming to Hawaii may think of surfing or fishing, but Hawaii also has a surprising number of hunting opportunities on private and public lands. On Kauai, Oahu, Molokai, Maui, Lanai, and Hawaii, you can hunt both big game mammals—deer, sheep, goats, and pigs—as well as two species of pheasant, chukar partridge, quail, doves, sandgrouse, and Rio Grande wild turkeys, all in your shirtsleeves. According to Mike Coelho, Hawaii Conservation Resource Enforcement officer on Lanai, you can hunt mammals year-round on private lands, so long as you have the landowner's permission. The bird season is regulated on public and private lands, but some shooting preserves do offer an extended season.

## DESTINATIONS

### General Information

*Hawaii.* Birds: ring-necked, Nepal kalij, and green pheasant; California valley, Japanese, and Gambel's quail; chukar partridge; gray, Erckel's, and black francolins; chestnut-bellied sandgrouse; mourning, barred, and spotted doves; and wild turkeys.

*Kauai.* Big game: wild pigs, wild goats, and blacktail deer.

*Lanai.* Big game: mouflon sheep and axis deer. Birds: ring-necked and green pheasant; Gambel's, California valley, and Japanese quail; chukar partridge; Erckel's and gray francolins; spotted and barred doves; wild turkeys.

*Maui.* Big game: wild pigs and wild goats. Birds: ring-necked and green pheasant; California valley and Japanese quail; chukar partridge; gray and black francolins; spotted and barred doves; and wild turkeys.

*Molokai.* Big game: wild goats and wild pigs. Birds: ring-necked and green pheasant; California valley quail and chukar partridge; gray and black francolins; spotted and barred doves; and wild turkeys.

*Oahu.* Big game: wild pigs and wild goats. Birds: ring-necked and green pheasant; California valley, Japanese, and Gambel's quail; Erckel's, gray, and black francolins; chukar partridge; and barred and spotted doves.

### Selected Hunting Destinations

**MAUI HUNTING SAFARI**
Makawao, HI 96768
Phone: 808-573-8426;
fax: 808-572-3906
www.mauihuntingsafari.com

Offering year-round hunting of free-range "Hawaiian" feral goats, "Polynesian" wild boars/pigs, and axis deer, on privately owned ranches such as Kaupo Ranch and Nu'u Mauka Ranch where Maui Hunting Safari has exclusive hunting privileges. You may use rifle, muzzleloader, or archery. With wild pigs, which are hunted with dogs, or you can hunt "Hawaiian-style" with a knife.

**PALAWAI OUTFITTERS**
Lana'i, Hawaii 96763
Phone: 866-596-GAME (866-596-4263)
www.palawai.com

A 36,900-acre ranch offering free-range axis deer and mouflon sheep year-round; also ring-necked and Hawaiian blue pheasant, chukar partridge, gray francolin, dove, Rio Grande turkey, Erckel's francolin, and quail hunting September through mid-March. Steep, rocky, and brushy terrain; warm and humid weather.

# Canada

With a total population of 33 million, less than California, most of which is concentrated in a few urban areas within 3.85 million square miles, Canada is the second-largest country by area in the world, after Russia. The United States, by contrast, is 3.7 million square miles including Alaska and has over 300 million people—10 times the population of its northern neighbor.

While close to one-third of the land in the United States is tillable, less than 5% of Canada is considered tillable for agricultural crops. Millions of square miles of lakes and rivers, mountains, spruce fir forests, muskegs, and vast prairies, most of which is on Crown land (government land), where hunting is permitted, and an abundance of wildlife make Canada an enormous resource for hunters all around the world.

Hunter license fees alone bring in almost $600 million a year to government treasuries. There are two special regulations for nonresidents:

1. Persons exporting cougars, grizzly bears, or wolves to points outside Canada must obtain a federal Export Permit issued in accordance with the Convention on International Trade in Endangered Species (CITES) of Wild Flora and Fauna.

2. Nonresident hunters coming into Canada need to take special care to ensure that their firearms pass through customs each way. To bring firearms into Canada for hunting purposes, you must

    a. be at least 18 years old and
    b. declare your firearms at your first point of entry into the country.

To do so requires filling out a Nonresident Firearm Declaration Form; the form must be confirmed by a Canadian Customs officer. Customs ask that you have these forms filled out before you get to the Customs Office. Forms can be obtained by calling 800-731-4000 or by asking your guide, who can mail them to you ahead of your departure. Background checks are randomly performed at the discretion of the Canadian Customs officer.

The fee for the declaration form is $50, which must be paid at the point of entry. You only pay this fee once in 12 months. So if you plan to make more trips to Canada in the same year, customs won't collect the declaration fee on subsequent visits. Each form has room for three firearms.

You can also borrow a gun from your outfitter, but you must always be with the outfitter when you use it.

Nonresidents may also apply for a Possession and Acquisition License for Firearms. The license is good for five years and costs $60.

For all inquiries related to Canadian firearms regulations, contact the Canadian Firearms Centre at www.cfc-ccaf.gc.ca or call 800-731-4000.

*Mapping.* Canada's premier online mapping resource The Atlas of Canada offers a wealth of information for everyone. See http://atlas.nrcan.gc.ca/site/english/index.html.

Canada is divided into 10 provinces—Alberta, British Columbia, Manitoba, New Brunswick, Newfoundland and Labrador, Nova Scotia, Ontario, Prince Edward Island, Quebec, and Saskatchewan—and 3 territories—Northwest Territories and Nunavut and Yukon Territory. We have ordered this section alphabetically.

## ALBERTA

*In 2001–2002, 191,595 big game licenses were sold (resident and nonresident), 42,432 nonresident small game licenses, and 19,527 migratory waterfowl permits.*

**OVERVIEW**

Alberta extends 746 miles (1,200 kilometers) from south to north. It is prairie in the south where it contacts Montana, and to the north there are forest and muskeg. It is one of only two provinces that is landlocked. About 3% of its 411,253 square miles is water.

More than half the 3 million residents of Alberta live in Calgary and Edmonton. There are lots of wide-open spaces here.

As a major producer of grains, the plains of Alberta are a magnet for waterfowl. For the most part, this is country where you can ask the farmer and get permission to access his lands. You can hunt on your own here, if you are willing to do some driving and have binoculars. Many people, however, opt for outfitters and guides to save time.

In 1906, a group of Calgary sportsmen introduced the ring-necked pheasant to Alberta, releasing 80 birds near Midnapore, Bragg Creek, Rosebud Creek, and Strathmore. The southern prairie of Alberta has become excellent for pheasant, Hungarian partridge, and the native sharp-tailed grouse.

Alberta is known for huge whitetails, mule deer, and moose. Chronic wasting disease (CWD) has been found here, so we encourage you to have your animal tested and bone out the meat to be on the safe side.

Wood Buffalo National Park is the home to about 2,200 wood buffalo, which are the only true free-ranging buffalo herd that escaped the market-hunting slaughter of buffalo in the 1800s.

The park is not open to hunting, but the bison range freely into the areas surrounding the park, which are huntable. Wood buffalo

are normally hunted in winter, with hunters making long snowmobile rides to catch up to the animals.

The teeming herds of caribou we see in photos are the more northern barren ground caribou. The numbers of woodland caribou, which frequent wooded areas further south, are down. A concerted effort is under way to conserve the woodland caribou, whose numbers have been declining in recent years. See www.srd.gov.ab.ca/fw/status/reports/caribou/index.html.

Alberta prohibits exporting the gall bladder and paws of black bears; however, you can export red meat, hide with claws attached, and head or skull with teeth attached.

## DESTINATIONS

For general hunting information and locations for Alberta, see www.abhunting.com.

*Selected Guides and Outfitters*

### ALBERTA ADVENTURE OUTFITTERS, LTD.

Caroline, AB T0M 0M0
Phone: 403-722-2035
www.albertaadventure.ca

Situated in northern Alberta approximately 300 miles north of Edmonton, black bear, whitetail deer, mule deer, elk, wolf, coyote, waterfowl, and varmit hunts; speciality archery moose hunts with additional whitetail and mule deer. Black bear hunt is exclusively a fly-in hunt in a 3,000-square-mile area. Excellent perch and pike fishing at main lodge.

### MAGNUM WATERFOWL OUTFITTERS

Manning, AB T0H 2M0
Phone: 800-95-GEESE;
mobile: 731-234-8640
www.magnumwaterfowl.com

Located in the Peace River Valley, five to six hours north of Edmonton, this is the first agricultural land that ducks and geese see as they move south from their summer nesting grounds. Magnum Waterfowl has an 85% repeat clientele, which speaks for itself.

# HERITAGE DESTINATIONS

*Head-Smashed-In Buffalo Jump*

Located 11.2 miles north and west of Fort Macleod, Alberta, this is one of the world's oldest and largest buffalo jump sites. This site was used for over 5,500 years by Indians who would drive herds of buffalo over a cliff and then butcher them in a camp below. This is a UNESCO (United Nations Educational, Scientific and Cultural Organization) World Heritage Site, complete with museum and Indian drumming and dancing in the summer months.

**HEAD-SMASHED-IN BUFFALO JUMP**
Fort Macleod, AB T0L 0Z0
Phone: 403-553-2731; fax: 403-553-3141
www.head-smashed-in.com

## BRITISH COLUMBIA

*In 2001–2002, 171,520 big game licenses were sold (resident and nonresident) and 8,185 migratory waterfowl permits.*

### OVERVIEW

There are 4.2 million people in British Columbia, which lies in the southwest corner of Canada, adjacent to Washington and Idaho on the south. Nearly half of the province's population lives in the Vancouver-Victoria area.

British Columbia has large areas of wild lands with considerable diversity, ranging from the coastal rain forests and mountains to the interior valleys, which can be quite hot and dry in the summer, and drier mountains to the east.

More than anything else, British Columbia is big game country; 22 of the 28 species of big game in North America are hunted here. Big game species hunted include bison, black bears, caribou, cougars, elk, grizzly bears, mountain goats, mountain sheep, mule and blacktail deer, whitetail deer, and wolves. For most people, this means hiring an outfitter and guide. If you are looking for guides and outfitters, we recommend you contact the Guide Outfitters Association of British Columbia (GOABC), which also represents guides/outfitters in the Yukon Territory, Northwest Territories, and Nunavut. They run their own guide school and have an exemplary code of ethics that is a model for similar associations anywhere.

**GUIDE OUTFITTERS ASSOCIATION OF BRITISH COLUMBIA**
Richmond, BC V6Y 4A4
Phone: 604-278-2688; fax: 604-278-3440
www.goabc.org

GOABC has recently started a Web site that allows hunters to bid on hunts in British Columbia, the Yukon Territory, Northwest Territories, and Nunavut that are offered by its outfitter members. For information, see www.mountainhunter.net. There is a $5 per month fee to participate. This is eBay for hunting!

### Advice for Hunters Planning a Hunt for Mountain Sheep or Goats

JOHN SIEVERS*

You've finally chosen an outfitter, all the references have been checked, and you've written a check as a deposit, large enough to purchase real estate in some places. So why let physical preparedness or lack of planning ruin your mountain hunt of a lifetime?

Having been involved in the guide outfitting industry in British Columbia and the Yukon for more than 25 years, I've been privileged in assisting hundreds of clients from all around the world to fulfill their mountain hunting dreams. But I've also seen many clients go home disappointed because they didn't take the time to prepare for what they thought would be an easy hunt. Hunting the high mountain ranges of the west can be extremely challenging at the best of times. Here are a few helpful suggestions that will make your high country adventure a lot more enjoyable.

Communication with your outfitter is very important prior to your hunt. Don't be reluctant to ask as many questions about your trip as you can. Try to find out what camp you will be hunting. Some of the guide territories up north are close to 10,000 square miles and vary in terrain greatly from one camp to another. It is not uncommon to travel two or three days by horse just getting to the camp where your hunt will take place. If you've booked a horse hunt, make sure that you're prepared for long days in the saddle. I've seen hunts end before they began because the client hadn't realized what was involved in this kind of hunt.

Traveling by horse can be very physically demanding if you're not used to riding. It is very important to ride as much as you can in the months and weeks prior to your hunt. Familiarize yourself with the rigging and know how to halter a horse or notice anything that does not look right as you're heading down the trail.

Another very important detail to a horse hunt is the packing and selection of gear. Plan on packing all of your gear to fit on one pack animal. What I like to do is put all of my extra clothes into an internal frame backpack, not exceeding 50 pounds, and wear a smaller daypack while in the saddle. The larger pack can easily be top packed on a packhorse, while allowing you easy access to the things you need in your daypack.

Once all the diamond ropes have been snugged tight, chances are there will not be any access to your gear until you're ready to camp that evening. I always wear my binoculars around my neck and tie my rain gear onto the saddle. Wearing a daypack while riding is less strenuous to your saddle horse than filling the saddlebags with gear. This allows me quick and easy access to all the important items in my daypack, such as ammo, snacks, water bottle, hat, and gloves. Nothing is more frustrating for a guide than having to unpack a horse to gain access to a hunter's bullets or gloves.

Also, take the time before you head off down the trail to see that your saddle has been properly adjusted to fit you. When standing in the saddle, you should be able to slide your hand freely between your groin area and the seat of your saddle. It is very important to be able to hold on when, heaven forbid, you have a rodeo going down the trail.

Another very important thing to keep in mind

is to always keep an eye on your guide and all the other horses in the string. If your guide gets off his horse to walk for a while, you should do the same. Your knees will thank you for it at the end of the day, as will the horses, and always tell your guide if you see something in the rigging that doesn't look right. It's a lot easier to make a minor adjustment to the gear than it is to stop and repack.

Well, now that you've arrived in spike camp and you have survived the trip there, it is time to start hunting. This is when all the physical training that you have done in the months leading up to your hunt come into play. Hunters should be prepared both mentally and physically before even considering a trip into our remote wilderness. With the country's most rugged mountain ranges and extreme weather patterns, ill preparedness now could mean the difference between a successful trip and disaster.

Physical conditioning is probably the most important aspect of your trip. There is not a piece of exercise equipment built that can duplicate the rigors of a day hiking the high country. The best way to prepare for a hunt is to put on your backpack and the boots you plan on hunting in and start slowly. Daily walks with a light load to start, then gradually increase the distance and weight of your pack until you are in what I like to call "sheep shape." Horses and airplanes can get you to your spike camp, but the rest is up to you. Five miles and a 50-pound pack are not uncommon for a day in the field; and let's face it, they don't call them mountain goats and mountain sheep because they live in the valley bottoms.

One of the most important things is proper selection in footwear. You've paid, in some cases, close to $30,000 for your hunt. Don't cheap out on your boots. Make sure your boots are worked in and comfortable for all-day use. I have seen a lot of hunts turn bad because of blisters or someone just didn't take care of their feet.

Your selection of clothing is also very important. Always make sure you have enough clothes in your pack for any type of weather; just because there was not a cloud in the sky when the day started, that doesn't mean you can't be in a snowstorm a couple of hours later. Even in July and August, it can snow, so you should always be prepared with your choice of clothing; also have water and some high-calorie snacks in your pack. For the opportunity at a shot at the trophy of a lifetime, many times I've chosen to spend the night on a mountainside as opposed to hiking off the mountain and back to camp.

Proper selection of gun and ammunition are also very important if you are planning a mountain hunt. Long-distance shooting is not uncommon here. I strongly recommend hunter and gun become intimately acquainted prior to the hunt. Hunting in western Canada offers hunters a variety of game, second only to the African continent. It is not uncommon to harvest a 250-pound Dall sheep and a 1,400-pound Alaska Yukon moose on the same 10-day trip. As you can see, proper selection of caliber and bullet is as crucial as is comfort in shooting the weapon of your choice.

Another detail I would like to comment about is travel arrangements. It is very important to allow enough time between connecting flights. Traveling abroad with firearms, horns, and capes always requires some preplanning. Make sure you have all the proper documentation necessary prior to travel, ensuring a swift and hassle-free airport experience. Your chosen outfitter will supply you with all the necessary documentation needed.

Another detail to take into consideration is some sort of travel insurance. I've seen the weather turn bad and all air flight be grounded for several days, leaving hunters stranded in camp. Although this is rare, it does happen; so be prepared.

Hunting the rugged mountain country of west-ern Canada is truly the experience of a lifetime. Proper preparation and planning of your trip is the key to measuring the success of any hunt. Take the time, do your homework, and I guarantee you will not be disappointed with your mountain hunt in the pristine wilderness that western Canada has to offer.

Good luck and good hunting!

**JOHN SIEVERS, GUIDE/OUTFITTER**
San Juan River Outfitters
Monte Lake, BC V0E 2NO
Phone: 250-375-2550; mobile: 604-790-0703
Email: Borrego@telus.net

*John Sievers guides fair chase stalk hunts for Shiras moose, elk, grizzly bear, black bear, mule and whitetail deer, cougar, bobcat and lynx, on Vancouver Island in SE British Columbia and mountain goat and mountain sheep on the western slopes of the Rockies.*

**DESTINATIONS**
For a general list of guides and outfitters in BC, see www.goabc.org; or call 604-278-2688.

*Selected Guides and Outfitters*

**CASSIAR STONE OUTFITTERS, LTD**
Booking Agent: Teslin River
Outdoor Adventures
100 Mile House, BC V0K 2E2
Phone/fax: 250-395-6051
Email: teslinadventures@telus.net
www.cassiarstone.com

Highly recommended for guided hunts for moose, mountain goats, mountain caribou, stone sheep, grizzly bears, black bears, wolverines, and wolves. There is outstanding fishing for grayling and trout in many of the areas they hunt. Make sure to bring along rain gear and insect repellant for black flies and mosquitoes.

**JIM SHOCKEY**
Victoria, BC V8V 4Y9
Phone: 888-826-1011
www.jimshockey.com

Probably the best-known hunter in Canada, with his own television series, several popular books, and a number of world-record trophies taken with muzzleloading rifle. Jim outfits hunts in British Columbia, Yukon Territory, Saskatchewan, and Mexico, with his own specialty being black bears and whitetails.

**THE LODGE AT GOLD RIVER**
Gold River, BC V0P 1G0
Phone: 250-283-2900
www.thelodgeatgoldriver.ca

Located on Vancouver Island, this very luxurious resort offers outstanding fishing, helicopter rides, kayaking, caving, skeet shooting, and more. Also exclusive access to the Evansdale Farm and the Mid Island Pheasant Club for hunting stocked pheasant on 1,350 acres in Campbell River, British Columbia, plus duck hunts.

*Conservation Organizations with Strong Sportsman's Focus*

**BRITISH COLUMBIA**
**WILDLIFE FEDERATION**
Burnaby, BC V5B 3A6

Phone: 604-291-9990 or 888-881-2293; fax: 604-291-9933
www.bcwf.bc.ca

The British Columbia Wildlife Federation was established in 1951 to help the government manage fish and wildlife by coordinating consultations with local sportsmen's clubs. Today the British Columbia Wildlife Federation's mission is to coordinate all the voluntary agencies, societies, clubs, and individuals interested in the sound, long-term management of British Columbia's fish, wildlife, park, and outdoor recreational resources. Their mission is also to develop and offer a comprehensive educational program to make all British Columbians aware of the value of their fish, wildlife, park, and outdoor recreational resources. The organization offers many outstanding educational programs every year and serves as a unifying voice for British Columbia wildlife conservation.

**WILD SHEEP SOCIETY OF**
**BRITISH COLUMBIA**
Abbotsford, BC V2T 6X4
Phone: 604-803-3911
www.wildsheepsociety.org

An affiliate of FNAWS (Foundation for North American Wild Sheep), the Wild Sheep Society of British Columbia is concerned with restoring, conserving, and protecting the wild sheep population of British Columbia, as well as insuring the right to hunt wild sheep according to sound conservation policies.

# MANITOBA

*In 2001–2002, 60,877 big game licenses were sold (resident and nonresident), 18,287 small game licenses, and 15,038 migratory waterfowl permits.*

## OVERVIEW

"Manitoba" is a Cree name that means "the place where the spirit (manitou) speaks." Of the 1.2 million people of Manitoba, 70% live in Winnipeg.

There are 100,000 lakes in Manitoba. Lake Winnipeg, Lake Winnipegosis, and Lake Manitoba are the three largest lakes. The three largest rivers are the Churchill River, Nelson River, and Hayes River, which all flow into the Hudson Bay.

Teeming flocks of ducks and geese in potholes and marshes on the prairies and the shores of Hudson's Bay are balanced by huge whitetail bucks awaiting you in the northern forest in Manitoba, where you can go from prairies in the west and lakes and forests in the east and south to Arctic tundra with polar bears in the north.

---

**MANITOBA SNAPSHOT**

- **General hunting information:** To find guides, contact Manitoba Lodges and Outfitters Association, www.mloa.com

- **General information about traveling in Manitoba:** www.travelmanitoba.com

- **For assistance with firearms and hunting regulations:** Contact Manitoba Wildlife Federation, www.mwf.mb.ca/hscertificate.htm

- **Deer population:** 180,000–200,000

---

Almost all flights into Manitoba pass through Winnipeg. If you have an overnight stay before you hook up with the next leg of your trip, stay at the Winnipeg Airport Hilton, for they have a shuttle service to local outfitters.

## DESTINATIONS

### JIMMY ROBINSON'S SPORTS AFIELD DUCK CLUB

St. Ambroise, MB R0H 1G0
Phone: 204-243-2649
www.sportsafieldduckclub.com

Founded in 1935 by the late Jimmy Robinson, editor of *Sports Afield* and sportsman, Robinson is the only man to be in five halls of fame: Fishing, Trapshooting, Skeet, the Minnesota Hall of Fame, and the Waterfowl Hall of Fame.

Robinson's duck club has hosted celebrities including Ernest Hemmingway, Ted Williams, Clark Gable, Bob Stack, and British royalty, who have all donned waders and trucked out into these fabled marshes. Before dawn, local Metis guides take hunters out into the marsh in heavy wooden handmade "marsh boats," one guide per two hunters, in pure wild silence. No motors allowed in the marsh. The marsh is known for diving ducks as well as puddle ducks.

The Club House, built in 1958, has hot water, electric heat, bunk beds, and chef and is located an hour's trip from the Winnipeg International Airport. Two groups per week—Sunday to Wednesday and Wednesday to Saturday—maximum 16 hunters per group.

**KASKATTAMA GOOSE LODGE**
Winnipeg, MB R3N 0K1
Phone: 204-982-9680
or 888-244-7453
www.greatwhitenorthresorts.com/
Kaska.html

Climb on a Cessna Grand Caravan in Winnipeg and fly north 650 miles to Kaskattama Goose Lodge, one of the few goose hunting lodges left on the Hudson Bay coast. Developed with loving care by Charlie and Christine Taylor, the lodge is located on Cape Tatnam near the mouth of the Kaskattama River, an area where Cree and Metis have hunted snow, blue, Ross, and Canada geese and ducks for thousands of years.

If you are lucky, you may find a traditional Indian goose decoy, made from a weather driftwood log with an axe. To make the head, they used a twisted willow root with a 90-degree angle for the head and blackened it in a fire. To make the light-colored cheek patch of a Canada goose, they would carve away the blackened root with a knife, revealing the light sapwood below. It worked very well for many generations.

Kaskattama is located near a major denning area for polar bears, so it is quite common to see mother bears and their cubs wandering the coast scavenging for food while they wait for the ice to form. Artic foxes, wolves, black bears, moose, and caribou also abound in the area around Kaska.

The season begins in late August, when it's shirtsleeve weather, and runs through the end of September.

# HERITAGE DESTINATIONS

*Oak Hammock Marsh Interpretive Centre*
Oak Hammock Marsh Interpretive Centre is a 14-square-mile Wildlife Management Area, including a section of original tallgrass prairie that attracts close to half a million waterfowl at a time. This is some of the best waterfowl hunting in all of Canada, especially for Canada geese. There is a long tradition of hunting here, as well as respect for hunters. In case a heavy fog rolls in while you're out in the marsh, there is a loud bell that sounds at the landing to help people know the way back to the dock.

To hunt the marsh, contact:

**OAK HAMMOCK OUTFITTERS**
Winnipeg Beach, MB R0C 3G0
Phone: 204-334-1490 (Winnipeg)
or 204-389-2242 (Lodge)
www.oakhammockoutfitters.com

On one side of the marsh, there is a very modern and beautifully designed interpretive center. Built with support from Ducks Unlimited, hunters will find many items in the gift shop to take back home.

**OAK HAMMOCK MARSH**
**INTERPRETIVE CENTRE**
Stonewall, MB R0C 2Z0
www.ducks.ca/OHMIC/English/indexfr
.html

## NEW BRUNSWICK

*In 2000–2001, 61,604 big game licenses were sold (resident and nonresident), 13,578 nonresident small game licenses, and 5,975 migratory waterfowl permits.*

### OVERVIEW

The maritime province of New Brunswick in the far northeast of Canada is 28,150 square miles nearly 85% of which is black spruce and fir forest. The 2006 human population was 749,168, but in that forest there are about 80,000 whitetail deer, 22,000 moose, and 16,000 black bears.

In 2005, 48,804 residents and 989 nonresidents bought deer tags. The total harvest was 6,881—a 14% overall success rate. However, for those 16,164 residents who purchased antlerless deer tags, the success rate was 49.3%.

New Brunswick has had an annual moose season for the last 30 years. Tags are highly sought after. In 2005, 54,026 residents and 1,824 nonresidents applied for

moose tags; 3,266 residents and 100 nonresidents got their moose tags. The reason for the demand becomes clear when you learn that moose hunters in 2005 had a 63% success rate. That success rate, by the way, has been going up steadily over the years, while the deer harvest rate has been going down.

In 2005, 1,978 black bears were harvested. Nonresident hunters had a 52% success rate, while resident success was 15%. This shows the value of guides.

These figures are gleaned from an outstanding analysis of hunting compiled by the New Brunswick Department of Natural Resources; see www.gnb.ca/0078/publications/BigGameReport-e.pdf#pagemode=bookmarks.

Ruffed grouse, woodcocks, geese, ducks, rabbits, and hare are other popular game species here, with sea duck hunting being especially good.

### DESTINATIONS

#### BEAR PAW HUNTING LODGE
Bathurst, NB E2A 3Z4
Phone: 506-548-5157
www.bearhuntingoutfitters.com

Located in the northern part of the province, 25 miles from Bathurst. The surrounding dense spruce forest supports a healthy bear and moose population. Bowhunts for bears is a speciality.

#### BLACK BEAR LODGE
Phone: 506-488-2244
Mill Cove, NB E4C 3E5
www.bearlodge.net

---

**NEW BRUNSWICK SNAPSHOT**

- **General hunting information in New Brunswick:** www.gnb.ca/0078/fw/HuntingOpportunities/index-e.asp

- **To find a guide, lodge, or outfitter in New Brunswick:**
  New Brunswick Outfitters Association
  5619 Route 105
  Mills Cove, NB E4C 3E5
  Phone: 506-488-2292 or 800-215-2075;
  fax: 506-488-2068
  www.nboa.nb.ca

- **Deer population:** 90,000

---

A top-rated lodge offering black bear, white-tail, moose, waterfowl, and upland bird hunts and fishing for salmon, trout, small-mouth, striped bass, pickerel, and sturgeon. Member of the New Brunswick Outfitter Association (NBOA), New Brunswick Bear Committee, and North American Hunting club.

## NEWFOUNDLAND AND LABRADOR

*In 2001–2002, 38,708 big game licenses were sold (resident and nonresident), and 16,998 migratory waterfowl permits.*

### OVERVIEW
Newfoundland is an island in the Atlantic off the northeast coast of Canada, opposite Quebec; the only authentic early Norse settlement in North America, St. Johns is the oldest English-speaking city in North America. About half a million people live in Newfoundland today.

Labrador is on the mainland, north of Quebec; it is an area the size of New Zealand with slightly less than 30,000 inhabitants, 30% of which are Inuit, Innu, or Metis.

This area is an "ecotone," where two or more different habitat types come together—in this case, the Arctic and temperate regions meet. The blending of two different habitats is associated with an abundance of wildlife packed into 150,000 square miles of wilderness. Deer are scarce or nonexistent in these northern spruce and fir forests, being replaced with caribou, as well as moose, wolves, and black bears.

Newfoundland is home to more than 10,000 woodland caribou, 100,000 moose, and 450,000 barren ground caribou. Success rates of 85% are common for big game hunters in this sportsmen's paradise, which includes more than two-thirds of the Atlantic salmon rivers in North America.

Grouse, waterfowl, and snowshoe hare are popular small game, and they are now joined by another Arctic species, ptarmigan. One unique legal game waterfowl species in Newfoundland and Labrador is the murre.

Here one finds some special regulations: Nonresidents who want to come to this province to hunt big game bear must apply for a license through one of the province's outfitting companies. They must also possess a Game Export Permit to take game out of the province and a CITES Permit to take parts of black bears out of the province. It's also illegal to hunt with crossbows. Sunday hunting is now allowed starting in late October–

---

**NEWFOUNDLAND AND LABRADOR SNAPSHOT**

- **General information:** www.env.gov.nl.ca/env/wildlife/hnttrapfish/index.htm; Regional Canadian Wildlife Service Offices—St. John's, 709-772-5585; Lewisporte, 709-535-0601; and Goose Bay, 709-896-6167

- **Newfoundland and Labrador travel information:** www.newfoundlandandlabradortourism.com/welcome.zap; Visit Newfoundland, http://visitnewfoundland.ca
Newfoundland and Labrador Outfitters Association
Post Box 149, Unit 8
23 Stentaford Avenue
Pasadena, NL AOL 1K0
Phone: 709-686-6350; fax: 709-686-2081
Email: info@nloa.ca
www.nloa.ca

early November until the close of big game season.

One note: A public health advisory has been issued advising people to avoid eating liver and kidney of moose and caribou in this region owing to levels of cadmium that exceed health standards.

## DESTINATIONS

For the nonresident, hunting in Newfoundland and Labrador really requires a guide-outfitter as many of the camps and best locations are accessible by plane or boat only. The best place to start looking for your guide is through the Newfoundland and Labrador Outfitters Association.

### NLOA

Pasadena, NL A0L 1K0
Phone: 709-686-6350
Email: info@nloa.com
www.hloa.ca

*Selected Guides and Outfitters*

### ADVENTURE NORTH*

Bedford, NS B4A 3S1
Phone: 902-835-8033
www.adnorth.com

Situated in southeast Newfoundland adjacent to the Long Range Mountains and approximately 55 miles southwest of Deer Lake on Cormack Camp. A complete wilderness camp accessible only by float plane. Moose, woodland caribou, and black bear hunting.

---

*This company books in both Newfoundland and Nova Scotia.

The hunting season begins in mid-September and ends late in October.

### OWL'S NEST LODGE

St. John's, NL A1C 6E7
Phone: 709-368-9013 (Home) or
709-722-5100 (Work); fax: 709-722-0808
www.webpage.ca/owlsnest/page1.htm

Operates 11 lodges in Newfoundland, offering moose, woodland caribou, and black bear hunts; these can be combined with partridge, grouse, duck, and goose hunting.

### RAY'S HUNTING & FISHING LODGE, LTD.

Howley, NL A0K 3E0
Phone: 709-635-3628; fax: 709-635-8169
www.rayshunting-fishing.com

Located on the shore of the largest lake in the province, Grand Lake, Ray's offers guided black bear, moose, and caribou hunts and fishing for lake trout and Atlantic salmon.

 **HERITAGE DESTINATIONS**

*Howley, Newfoundland*

In 1904 four moose were released on the island. Now the herd numbers 120,000. A statue commemorates the 100 years of successful moose relocation, as well as the $100 million a year that moose hunters contribute to the Newfoundland and Labrador economy.

## NORTHWEST TERRITORIES AND NUNAVUT

*Big game information not available; 223 migratory waterfowl permits sold in 2002.*

### OVERVIEW

The province of Northwest Territories, and the adjacent territory of Nunavut, officially established in April 1, 1999, is an immense area stretching 2,000 miles east to west from the 60th parallel to the North Pole and covering more than 1.3 million square miles—approximately half the land mass of Canada—and includes Great Bear Lake and Great Slave Lake.

The total population of the Northwest Territories was 41,861 as of 2006, most of whom live in Yellowknife.

Nunavut, which stretches from the mainland to Greenland and includes all the islands in Hudson Bay, James Bay, and Ungava Bay, is both the least populated and the largest of the Canadian provinces and territorities. It has a total population of 31,000 spread over an area

as big as western Europe—one-fifth of all land in Canada. Iqualit (ee-kha-lu-eet), population 6,000, is the capital and the largest of 26 settlements in this vast land.

The native population is mixed Inuit and Dene (Indian and Metis) and has lived here for at least 4,000 years. Many villages are accessible only by airplane. Some 85% of the population is Inuit. Native hunting seasons are different than sport hunting.

Much of this northern land is tundra, although Ellesmere Island has a mountain range with an 8,000-foot peak. The further south one goes, the more one finds taiga, with spruce and other trees interlaced with streams, ponds, and rivers, as well as rugged mountains in the northern extension of the Rockies.

This is big game country: black bears, polar bears, grizzly bears, wood bison, barren-ground caribou, Arctic Island caribou, mountain goats, moose, musk oxen, Dall's sheep, wolves, walrus, and wolverines. Small game is not as diverse as in other provinces, but hare, woodchucks, marmots, and squirrels are open year-round, and grouse and ptarmigan season runs from September 1 through April 30. In summer, a profusion of waterfowl breed all along the shores of the ocean, as well as in the many ponds and streams that lace the tundra.

You must have a hunting license to hunt small game. To hunt big game, you'll need a hunting license and wildlife tag(s) issued for each species, which must be attached to the animal immediately after the kill. Licenses and tags are issued for one year starting July 1 and ending June 30.

Licenses and tags may be purchased from most Resources, Wildlife, and Eco-

---

### NORTHWEST TERRITORIES AND NUNAVOT SNAPSHOT

- **Northwest Territories hunting information:** Department of Environment and Natural Resources, Wildlife Division and Fisheries Division, www.nwtwildlife.com/hunting 800-661-0788

- **Nunavut hunting and visiting information:** www.nunavuttourism.com/master.asp?Id=41 For a complete list of guides and outfitters, see www.explorenwt.com/adventures/sport .hunting/outfitters.asp

nomic Development offices in the territory. In Yellowknife and some of the larger communities, licenses and tags can also be purchased from outfitters. However, big game licenses and tags for big game species hunted by nonresidents can be purchased only at offices of the Northwest Territories Department of Resources, Wildlife, and Economic Development.

Trophy fees must be paid by nonresidents before a harvested animal or any part thereof is exported from the Northwest Territories. All fees are subject to a 7% goods and services tax.

If you need more details, contact:

**CANARCTIC GRAPHICS**
Box 2758
Yellowknife, NT X1A 2R1
Phone: 867-873-5924; fax: 867-920-4371

 **FEATURED HUNT**

## Canadian Polar Bear

JEROME KNAP*

The wood bison, ptarmigan, and walrus hunted in this far northern land are all truly unique hunts, but the most unique hunt of all has to be for *nannook*, the polar bear, which is the only animal that would consider man to be a food source. Some 99.9% of the diet of polar bears is other animals.

Canada is the only nation in the world offering organized polar bear hunts. Tags are allocated to each Inuit village each year based on population studies conducted by government wildlife biologists. Sport hunting tags must come from village quotas, which are based on an annual census. The world population of great white bears is 22,000, and Canada's polar bear population is estimated at 12,000 to 15,000. The government of Nunavut allows just over 500 polar bears to be hunted. In 2005, 76 of those were hunted for sport.

According to Dr. Mitch Taylor, Nunavut's polar bear biologist, the world population of polar bears is twice as large as what it was 50 years ago. Lately

we have heard a good deal about global warming and its impact on polar bears. But, at the present time, in this area the polar bear population is high and stable.

This hunt is important to the people of Nunavut. A study commissioned by the Nunavut government and Safari Club International finds that sport hunts coming to Nunavut, the majority of whom are American, spent $2.9 million in Nunavut in 2001–2002. Each bear is worth about $25,000 to the Nunavut communities.

This hunt is not for everyone. You will fly in to a remote village, where your Inuit guide meets you. You register at the local wildlife office, then spend the night in a local motel. The next day, weather permitting, you travel by chartered airplane, snowmobile, or dogsled to the hunting area. All travel in the hunting area must be done by dogsled.

Weather is a factor. When the hunting begins in late March, the temperatures can reach −35°F. By mid-May, it warms to the coldest being 20°F. The timing of the hunts depends on the weather and movements of the animals. Hunting later than May means the bear's pelt may not be prime.

In cold weather you may stay in a snow house ("igloo" is a white man's term), sleeping on foam mattresses covered with caribou skins. When it is warm, you sleep in a tent.

Historically the Inuit survived on seal, caribou, and fish through the winter. Some guides will bring along caribou and Arctic char, but you always will eat hearty meals to help with the cold.

All hunting is done via dogsled, sometimes going 15 to 20 miles out onto the ice of the Arctic Ocean, looking for bears feeding on seals. The dogs not only serve as transport, but when the dog team gets within 3 or 4 miles of the bear, the bear starts to run, and the chase is on. When the distance is about half a mile away, two to three dogs are released to corner the bear. At 200 to 300 yards, all the dogs are freed to help out. This enables the hunter to get close enough for a killing shot.

Inuit have lived here for thousands of years, evolving a lifestyle based on acute sensitivity to nature and wildlife, as well as being noted for warmth and friendliness. "Inuit time" may sometimes be slower, but an intuitive sense of where the animals are and what the weather will be is crucial to success and survival.

Canada North has been organizing polar bear hunts for over a decade. During that time, the success rate has ranged from 86% to 93%, with 80% of the bears being in the 9- to $9^1/_2$-feet-length class.

Contact:

**CANADA NORTH OUTFITTING, INC.**
Almonte, ON K0A 1A0
Phone: 613-256-4057
www.canadanorthoutfitting.bigbluesky.ca/
torngat.htm

*Jerome Knap is affiliated with Canada North Outfitting, Inc.*

# FEATURED HUNT

## Musk Ox

JAMES SWAN

You may have heard tales of hunting musk ox in winter in the Far North, –30 and colder, hours of riding on a snowmobile, and the animals all herding up to protect their young. It is also possible to hunt these extreme northern bison in August and September, when the bulls are in the rut, and the weather can be shirtsleeve comfort.

If you book with Adventure Northwest, you fly into Yellowknife, spend the night, and then fly to Kugluktuk in Nunavut, then to Holman, Northwest Territories.

Inuit guides typically begin the hunt for "Oomingmak" with a prayer for safety and success, explaining to the spirits what is about to take place. The travel to camp is by ATV and may be 10 miles or more.

You will be hunting on tundra, undulating, wet, cold land with no trees for cover. This is summer, and the sun may be up until midnight. The animals move about solo or in small groups. For archers, stalking within 30 yards for the shot is a real challenge in these conditions.

Combination caribou and musk ox hunts are also possible, and some locations offer fishing for Arctic char and grayling.

In Holman, you will find an abundance of native arts and crafts, plus the northernmost nine-hole golf course in the world.

Contact:

**ADVENTURE NORTHWEST**
Booking through: Global Sporting Safaris, Inc.
Casper, WY 82604

Phone: 888-850-HUNT (888-850-4868);
fax: 888-206-4486
www.gssafaris.com/northwest_territory_
hunting.html

## NOVA SCOTIA

*In 2001-2002, there were 23,727 small game licenses, 56,395 big game licenses, and 6,645 waterfowl permits sold in Nova Scotia.*

Home of the highest tides in the world (54 feet in the Bay of Fundy), no point in Nova Scotia is more than 33 miles from the sea. Hunting sea ducks, as one might expect, is very popular here. In 2001, 6,645 waterfowl permits were issued, nearly as many as in British Columbia, and Nova Scotia is just 21,425 square miles—with 4,625 miles of coastline.

This province is composed of a peninsula and 3,800 offshore islands that jut out into the Atlantic from northeast Quebec. The waters of the Atlantic result in a relatively mild

---

**NOVA SCOTIA SNAPSHOT**

· **General hunting information:** www.gov.ns.ca/natr/hunt/default.htm

· **To find a guide in Nova Scotia:**
Nova Scotia Guides' Association
Post Office Box 641
Liverpool, NS B0T 1K0
Phone: 902-682-2239
Email: pm.waterman@ns.sympatico.ca
www.chebucto.ns.ca/recreation/NSGA

· **To report a poacher:** 800-565-2224

· **Deer population:** 46,000

· **Average deer harvest:** 10,243

maritime climate. The province contains 3,000 lakes, and forests cover three-fourths of the surface area. This translates into whitetail deer, moose, black bears (favorite big game), grouse, pheasant, woodcocks, snowshoe rabbits, and of course, waterfowl. For a nonresident to hunt in Nova Scotia, they must have a licensed guide or be accompanied by a resident (over 19) who has obtained a Special Permit to Guide. The biggest draw is moose. There are three one-week moose seasons in the fall. Permits are issued by a drawing.

In 2005 the success rates for the three moose seasons were 90%, 83%, and 43%. As might be expected, moose permits are in high demand. For example, in the first 2005 season (which ran from September 26 to October 1), 5,732 people applied for 155 permits.

**DESTINATIONS**

**BEARS EAST ADVENTURES**
Middle Sackville, NS B4E 3K7
Phone: 902-252-2287;
mobile: 902-209-2870
www.geocities.com/bearseastadventures/
home

A small family-operated business offering quality, affordable fall bear hunts. Guide/outfitter Roger Lewis is a member of the Nova Scotia Guides Association and has served as both president and vice president of the Bowhunter Association of Nova Scotia. Base camp is on the banks of the famous St. Mary's River near Sherebrooke Villiage on Nova Scotia's eastern shore, which supports a large black bear population. Speciality is archery hunting. Many bears taken weigh over 300 pounds.

**FREE SPIRIT GUIDE SERVICE**
Tatamagouche, NS B0K 1V0
Phone/fax: 902-657-3814
www.klickns.com

Whitetail deer and black bear hunts, designed for both traditional and compound bow hunters as well as gun hunters, near the villages of Tatamagouche and Wallace, Nova Scotia, Canada.

## ONTARIO

*In 2001–2002, 307,722 big game licenses were sold (resident and nonresident), 189,322 nonresident small game licenses, and 58,458 migratory waterfowl permits.*

**OVERVIEW***
The Iroquois called it "Kanadario," which means "sparkling water." Today Ontario is the home of 12 million people, nearly half of whom live in Toronto.

Ontario is the second-largest province in Canada, with over 1 million square kilometers or 386,102 square miles. With a population of approximately 12 million, Ontario holds almost half of the country's total population. The province is bordered by Quebec to the east, Manitoba and Minnesota to the west, Michigan and New York to the south along the Great Lakes, with the famed Hudson Bay/James Bay in the north moving into the Arctic. It is 1,050 miles traveling east-west and 1,075 miles north-south. A 20-hour drive from Windsor/Detroit to the northwest border entering Manitoba helps to put driving distances in perspective.

Ontario has just over 410,000 hunters and sells approximately 675,000 licenses each year. The shared Ontario-U.S. border is almost entirely water. Indeed, water covers about one-sixth of the province; there are 400,000 lakes, and streams everywhere. The province touches four of the five Great Lakes—Superior, Huron, Erie, Ontario—and St. Clair. It's little wonder that Ontario is a very popular place to hunt waterfowl. Along the shores of James Bay and Long Point, a provincial park on a sandspit peninsula that juts 20 miles out into Lake Erie (see www.ontarioparks.com/english/long multiple.html), is considered to be among the best waterfowl hunting spots in the province. Ontario contains about 2% of the world's forests, with more than 90% being owned by the province. Forests cover two-thirds of Ontario—oak-hickory in the south, with spruce, maple, birch, and fir becoming predominant as one moves north. There are pheasant in the south, but as one moves north, this becomes prime ruffed grouse country.

The Hudson Bay lowlands and the Canadian Shield cover 90% of Ontario, which is world renowned for its moose and black bear hunting. There is no elk or caribou hunting in the province, although there are hopes to have seasons in the near future.

In some districts, you need to have a guide to hunt big game if you are a nonresident. If you bag a deer and want to take it home to the states, you need to purchase a Nonresident Export Permit, which is $35.

The number of huntable species in the province has never been better, with flourishing populations of whitetail deer, wild turkeys (eastern), and black bears reaching capacity levels. The provincial whitetail population is estimated to be between 350,000 and 400,000. The general bag is one antlered deer per year, but in some Wildlife Management Units you can take up to six antlerless deer with proper tags. A good resource for deer hunting in Ontario is www.ontariodeerhunting.ca.

Moose (eastern), timber wolves, and small game populations are also at high success numbers. Canada geese are at exceptionally high levels, with great flocks of resident geese creating opportunities through early and late season hunts. Generally, waterfowl (geese, ducks) woodcock and grouse (or as the local hunter would refer to them, partridge) are at excellent numbers.

With wild turkey being reintroduced into the province in the mid-1980s, Ontario now hosts an estimated over 80,000 birds, with a 2-bird spring limit and hopefully a hunt in the fall to open soon. Other species currently in the province, but without an open season, are elk (currently being reintroduced) and woodland caribou in the north, where only a native hunt exists owing to animal populations.

Hunters have the option of using their choice of rifle, shotgun, muzzleloader, or archery equipment. Archery in Ontario includes traditional long or recurve bows, compound bows, and crossbows, which are permitted in any open archery season for any licensed hunter.

Hunting techniques vary by game species and allow many opportunities to hunters to enjoy their favored approaches—that is, spot and stalks, drives or pushes, tree stands, over baits, with hounds or dogs (some restrictions may apply in certain areas).

Nonresident hunters must look at specific areas for regulations around open seasons especially for moose hunts where nonresidents must be booked through a licensed outfitter. Tags are generally available through outfitters for moose hunting opportunities. There are also some areas in the southern part of the province where there may not be an open big game season for nonresidents. All seasons are outlined in the Ontario Hunting Regulations Summary (visit the Ministry of Natural Resources Web site at www.mnr.gov.on.ca) and should be reviewed before any hunt is booked or scheduled.

For a nonresident to qualify to hunt in Ontario, one must show an accredited hunting certificate or a hunting license from another jurisdiction. For waterfowl, a hunter would purchase a nonresident small game license as well as a migratory bird stamp. For wild turkey, similarly one would purchase a nonresident small game license as well as a wild turkey license.

A note for wild turkey hunting enthusiasts: A mandatory Wild Turkey Education Program course and exam must be taken before a turkey license can be issued. This is a one-day course held in specific areas on specific dates throughout the province. There are plans to create an online course, but at the time of publication there is none available.

Whether you want to hunt moose in the deep forest or chase whitetail in mixed farm fields and tree cover in the south or in heavy forest in the central part of the province, call in a big tom, hunt fields for geese, or have a green head cup as he coasts into your decoys, the hunting opportunities abound in the province with enough variety to challenge and appeal to any hunter.

Handguns are not legal to use for hunting in Ontario. Crossbows are. All licensed hunters must wear an outer garment of at least 400 square inches of hunter orange above the waist during rifle seasons for deer, moose, or black bears; a blaze-orange cap also must be worn.

*Overview written by Spynos Chrysochou, Ontario Federation of Anglers and Huters.*

 **FEATURED HUNT**

### A Spiritual Encounter with a Wolf

**FATHER THEODORE VITALI***

In the spring of 1987, while hunting black bears in northern Ontario, I experienced an encounter that transformed my thinking and to a large extent my own Christian spirituality. I encountered a wolf. I had been hunting in northern Ontario with Bill Ritchie and his sons, especially Lark and Brian Ritchie, since 1980. Bill died in November 1986, and his sons Lark, Darryl, Allan, and Brian were conducting a memorial hunt in his honor. It was an extraordinary event from my perspective because I loved Bill and admired him greatly. He was a true guide in every sense of the word. He had introduced me to Native American spirituality by and through his stories and in and through the values he so obviously embraced. He was a member of the wilderness community and shared this with all his hunters but, I believe, especially with me.

About midway through the hunt (it began in or around Memorial Day), I was in a blind along a deserted logging road deep in a typical northern Ontario forest. It was dark, foggy bordering on mist, and at times raining. It was about 8:00 P.M. The bait I was hunting over was about 30 yards away from me. I sat in my blind, hunkered down under my rain gear and poncho, resting my rifle under the poncho. It had been quiet for sometime. Suddenly, I sensed something behind me. I knew from experience that a bear might circle a hunter and come to the bait from behind him. Therefore, though not really hearing anything, I slipped the safety off my rifle and very slowly turned around to see what was there. About seven or eight paces from me sauntered a large male wolf. He was looking at me as he walked past. My eyes caught his as I watched him pass by me, climb a small embankment, eye the bait, pause for what seemed a very long time, then turn and drift off into the darkness of the forest. I felt no fear at all. I felt entranced by his presence. I didn't want him to go away. I wanted to watch him and share with him this extraordinarily intimate moment. But he was gone.

After he left, I thought a lot about what I had just experienced. Perhaps the clearest experience I had was that of intimacy between the wolf and me. I felt continuity between us. I can still remember with great vividness that there were no "fences" here, nothing breaking up the continuity between him and me. I felt as though this was some kind of communion, some kind of sharing of life without barriers and without the imposition of human contraptions or artificialities. I felt a direct connection to something much more than the ordinary in that moment.

For months and now years I have reflected on this experience. This was hunting in its purest form because both the wolf and I were engaged in the same thing: predation—he for the immediacy of his physical survival, I for my spiritual survival. We were both in the wilderness, both predators, both part of the continuum of life and death that constitutes the world we live in and the life we ultimately live.

I also felt the intimacy of God incarnate in this wilderness experience. I felt God's presence as both creator and redeemer, the fullness of the Incarnation: God become man, God become creature in the ecology of creatures, the world. Somehow and for whatever reason, I felt the full power of Christ's Incarnation in the presence of the wolf. Perhaps what I ultimately felt was the humility of my humanity as an animal in the ecology of creation, an intimate participant in the life God gave me and the world. I don't know.

What I do know is that I was changed forever by and through this experience. I found myself in a way I had never found or experienced myself before. I believe I discovered who and what I was: a creature among creatures blessed by God with life in the continuum of life and death.

That year I did not get a bear. I hunted as hard as I ever hunted but saw no bears, just a wolf. But in the visitation of the wolf, I received as a hunter the greatest prize of all, the discovery of myself as a fellow creature in the world. I received the gift of knowing who and what I was and am and thus who and what I am before God. In my view, this is the ultimate value of hunting: the securing of that most intimate experience, the experience of belonging to the world as a fellow creature, that is, as God created it.

*Father Theodore Vitali is a Catholic priest and chairman of the Philosophy Department at St. Louis University.*

## DESTINATIONS

### General Information

Hunting is allowed in a number of provincial parks, and there are 34 Wildlife Management Areas and a number of Wildlife Extension Landowner Agreement Areas.

For more information, see the Ontario Hunter Education Program (OHEP), www .ohep.net; the Ontario Ministry of Natural Resources, www.mnr.gov.on.ca; and Ontario Tourism, www.ontariotravel.net.

### Private Hunting Clubs and Preserves

### BARDROCHAT PHEASANT FARM
Ian Chapman
Harriston, ON N0B 2K0
Phone: 519-338-3051 (Farm);
mobile: 519-569-0816
Email: ichapman@hotmail.com
www.bardrochat.com

Located on a century-old farm 90 miles northwest of the Toronto Airport, specializes in guided English-style driven hunts for pheasant and chukar for five to six hunters. Accommodations and restaurants are within easy driving distance.

### THE PELEE CLUB
Cincinnati, OH 45202
www.peleeclub.com

Located on Pelee Island in Lake Erie, 36 square miles of fertile farmland and scenic shoreline in the western end of Lake Erie in Ontario waters, the Pelee Club was founded in 1883 by business and professionals. The island is accessible by boat or airplane. This historic club currently has 38 members but is always looking for a few more. Four U.S. presidents have visited the club and were made honorary members. Waterfowl, quail, and pheasant hunting, world-class fishing, and an enormous heritage resides in the hallowed halls of lodge and surroundings.

## PRINCE EDWARD ISLAND

*In 2001–2002, 2,969 small game licenses and 2,416 waterfowl permits sold. No big game hunting is allowed.*

### OVERVIEW
An island located in the Gulf of Saint Lawrence north of Nova Scotia and east of New Brunswick, Prince Edward Island, Canada's smallest province with a population of 138,000, has no big game hunting but offers hunting for ruffed grouse, Hungarian par-

## QUEBEC

*In 2001–2002, 291,265 big game licenses were sold (resident and nonresident), 178,128 nonresident small game licenses, and 29,138 migratory waterfowl permits.*

tridge, waterfowl, snipe, woodcock, snowshoe hare, coyote, raccoon, and fox.

Nonresident hunters must be accompanied by either a licensed resident hunter or a registered hunting guide while hunting on Prince Edward Island. A resident can accompany up to two nonresident hunters, but they cannot accept money for this. A guide can accompany up to four nonresidents at a time. They cannot hunt while guiding but can kill injured birds.

For information on Prince Edward Island outfitters, see www.gov.pe.ca/infopei/index.php3?number=905&lang=E.

## OVERVIEW

Quebec, which the Algonquins called "Kebe," meaning "the place where the river narrows," has a population of 7.5 million people and is the largest province (Northwest Territories, Nunavut, and Yukon are "territories").

The province is divided into three regions: the Canadian Shield; St. Lawrence Lowlands, which borders on the St. Lawrence River (2,361 miles long), which links Quebec to the Atlantic Ocean; and the Appalachian Mountains. There are more than 1 million lakes and waterways in Quebec, which has more freshwater than any other province. And if it's not water, forest covers

## DESTINATIONS

**WILD GOOSE LODGE**
French River, PE C0B 1M0
Phone: 800-463-4053
www.wildgooselodge.com

A premier four-star-rated waterfowl hunting destination between Cavendish and Kensington on the North Shore. Ocean-view lodge.

half of Quebec, the most forested of any province in Canada.

This is moose country: 18,890 were harvested in 2006. But whitetail deer were even more popular—68,879 were taken in 2006. In the far north, 7,406 caribou were bagged, and the 2006 black bear harvest was 4,293.

If you are planning to hunt big game or upland game, blaze-orange clothing is required.

Ruffed grouse and spruce grouse are found in the forests, with ptarmigan in the far north. Snowshoe hare and migratory waterfowl are found throughout the province.

 **FEATURED HUNT**

## Caribou Hunting on the Ungava Peninsula, Leaf River

JAMES SWAN

The nearly treeless Arctic is a place of contrasts: barren rock and frigid water or an unbelievable cornucopia of wild fish and game. North America's version of Africa's Serengeti Plains with its teeming herds of animals is the Arctic tundra if you are there at the right time and place. And one of the best places to find the most abundant Arctic big game of all, caribou, is the Ungava Peninsula in northern Quebec, about 1,000 miles north of Montreal as the goose flies. In this barren land the Naskapi Indians believe that the god of the caribou lives on a mountain of white caribou hair.

There are 300,000 to 400,000 caribou in this herd—the largest herd of big game in the world—but they roam over 400,000 square miles, so having a good guide is important to success. And success is

important here. The goal of Alain Tardiff's Leaf River Lodge is for each hunter to bag their 2 caribou limit in a fair chase hunt, and most do. A key to finding animals is the use of boats, and each guide has his or her own.

A bonus on this hunt is the abundance of brook trout and an occasional larger lake trout that can be taken on flies in the Leaf and Whale rivers. It's not unusual to catch 50 to 60 two- to three-pound brookies in a day in these parts and have a caribou cheering section looking on.

Full guided and semiguided hunts are available, with prices varying according to the size of your party. Comfortable cabins come with bathrooms, hot showers, and fabulous food.

Caribou hunting season is August 12–September 29. In August, day temperatures may be in the fifties. By the end of September, there may be snow on the ground. Dress in layers and always bring some rain gear.

Best to book as far in advance as possible because space is limited, and this camp is very popular for obvious reasons. Contact:

**LEAF RIVER OUTFITTERS**
Saint-Henri, QC G0R 3E0
Phone: 418-882-6210 or 800-463-4868 (USA);
fax: 418-882-0140
www.leafriverlodge.com

Caribou hunting is also quite good along the Swampy River. Swampy Outfitters, located 95 miles northwest of Schefferville in the Caniapiscau River region of Quebec, has huge herds of caribou that migrate through the area and a success rate of 100% for the last several years. Fishing, bear hunting, and bird hunting are also available.

**SWAMPY RIVER OUTFITTERS**
Jay, ME 0Y239

Phone: 888-244-7824
www.bigcaribou.com

 **FEATURED HUNT**

### Greater Snow Geese on the St. Lawrence River

JAMES SWAN

The largest species of white goose (males may weigh up to seven pounds), greater snow geese on their southbound migration from their high Arctic breeding grounds have stopped along the St. Lawrence River in Quebec for thousands of years.

In the 1950s this species of snow-white birds with black wingtips and pink feet and bills numbered about only 12,000. Today the number is approaching almost 1 million, and from mid-September through early November, some 300,000 or more snow geese may be found on and around the St. Lawrence River in Quebec.

Hunting the swarms of geese is associated with the tides, and much of the hunting area is held privately. There are opportunities for both guided and nonguided hunting, both pass shooting and decoying birds to blinds. A very useful Web link to this area that provides details is http://www.goose -hunting-tips.com/outfitters-montmagny.html.

Days of open seasons change each year. Government regulations for snow geese hunting in the district may be found at www.qc.ec.gc.ca/faune/ chasse/html/district_f_info_e.html.

There are several places where you can hunt. They all offer lodging and food, sometimes retriever dogs. Prices vary. Some outfitters recommended by Jocelyn Landry at Ducks Unlimited, Canada, are:

**CROISIÈRES LACHANCE, INC.**
Berthier-sur-Mer
Contact info: François Lachance
www.fpq.com/en/outfitters.profile.asp? 12-543

## L'Ô-OIE-SIS ENR.

Cap-Saint-Ignace

Contact info: Michel Lavoie

www.oieblanche.com/contact.php

## POURVOIRIE BERTRAND VÉZINA

Isle-aux-Grues

Contact info: Mrs. Bibiane Vézina

www.fpq.com/en/outfitters.profile.asp? 12-687

## POURVOIRIE KENNEBEC

Saint-Vallier

www.fpq.com/en/outfitters.profile.asp? 12-708

## POURVOIRIE LAVOIE ENR.

Isle-aux-Grues

Contact info: Gilbert Lavoie

www.fpq.com/en/outfitters.profile.asp? 12-704

## POURVOIRIE LISETTE VÉZINA PAINCHAUD

Isle-aux-Grues

Contact info: Mrs. Lisette V. Painchaud

www.fpq.com/en/outfitters.profile.
asp?12-711

## ZEC DE L'OIE BLANCHE

Montmagny

http://pages.globetrotter.net/sacomm/
zec.htm

## DESTINATIONS

Small game hunting is permitted on Provincial lands throughout the province. Private hunting for released birds is less common.

*Upland Game Bird Preserves*

## CLUB ROUE DU ROY, INC.

Hemmingford, QC J0L 1H0

Phone: 450-247-2882 or 888-747-2882

Email: plongtin@roueduroy.com

www.roueduroy.com/Intro_en.html

Open since 1960, this is a private membership club, located near Montreal, for families and corporations, offering guided pheasant hunting for groups of four or more from May to December. The club is open every day except for Monday and Tuesday. On statutory holidays, the club is always open. From January to the end of April, the club is open only during the weekends.

The club also offers traditional skeet, Olympic skeet, modern skeet, trap, five-stand, and sporting clays, as well as fishing for rainbow trout 12 inches and up.

# HERITAGE DESTINATIONS

*Fêtes de la Saint-Hubert,*
*Cap-Saint-Ignace, Quebec*

Saint Hubert is the patron saint of hunting who is honored in festivals and special church services in many places in Europe. This tradition is carried on in Cap-Saint-Ignace, Quebec, every year on the first weekend in September at the "Fêtes de la Saint-Hubert," a special church service where hunters, wearing hunting clothing, bring their guns and their dogs into the church for a blessing. The procession, including Royal Canadian Mounted Police, enters and exits the church under an archway of guns, and the music for the service is played on hunting horns.

It is a good idea to reserve space ahead of time if you wish to be in the church for the service, as this is a very popular annual event. (Most people are bilingual, but French is the preferred local language.) Contact:

**FÊTES DE LA SAINT-HUBERT**
Cap-Saint-Ignace, QC G0R 1H0
Phone: 418-246-5390
Email: sainthubert@globetrotter.net
www.capsaintignace.ca

*Snow Goose Festival in Montmagny, Quebec*
Migrating greater snow geese have stopped along the St. Lawrence River in Quebec for thousands of years. When the clouds of white geese arrive, it is spectacular, and so the town of Montmagny has created a special annual event to celebrate the arrival of snow geese from their breeding grounds on the Arctic tundra. Annually since 1971 the "Festival de l'Oie Blanche" is held in the beginning of

October. It lasts for nearly a week. There are many different activities, as well as opportunities to hunt the geese.

**FESTIVAL DE L'OIE BLANCHE**
Montmagny, QC G5V 3S3
Phone: 418-248-3954; fax: 418-248-3959
Email: fob@cgocable.ca
www.festivaldeloie.qc.ca

*Sketch of a snow goose hunter's blind*

## SASKATCHEWAN

*In 2001–2002, there were 23,796 small game licenses and 75,238 big game licenses, and 18,387 migratory waterfowl permits sold.*

### OVERVIEW

In 2005, the province sold 13,870 nonresident hunting licenses, the majority of which went to individuals from the United States. This is roughly one-fifth of all licenses sold that year. It's estimated that Americans coming to Saskatchewan to hunt spend $50 to $60 million a year. The U.S. monetary contribution constitutes the primary economic base for many lodges, outfitters, and guides, as well as rural communities.

Saskatchewan facts: Sharp-tailed grouse is one of the most popular game birds. Saskatchewan is half forest; one-third is farmland. There are over 100,000 lakes, rivers, and marshes; the southern part is mainly flat land. Athabasca Provincial Park has sand

**SASKATCHEWAN SNAPSHOT**

- **General information:**
  Parks and Renewable Resources
  3211 Alberta Saint
  Regina, SK S4S 5W6
  Phone: 800-567-4224
  www.se.gov.sk.ca

- **Outfitters:** For a list of all outfitters in the province, see www.huntsask.ca/default.asp?page=500&pid=8&ptid=43&pzone=41&srch=qck&menu=47
  Saskatchewan Outfitters Association
  Prince Albert, SK S6W 1A2
  Phone: 306-763-5434; fax: 306-922-6044
  www.soa.ca

- **Deer population:** 380,000

dunes 98.5 feet high. The main rivers are the Assiniboine, North and South Saskatchewan, and Churchill. The Saskatchewan population of 1 million produces 28% of Canada's grain and 54% of Canada's wheat.

## DESTINATIONS

### BAIT-MASTERS HUNTING CAMP
Green Lake, SK S0M 1B0
Phone: 306-832-208
www.baitmaster.net

An elegant lodge located on Green Lake in the west-central region of Saskatchewan. Produces some of the biggest whitetails in the world. This place is known for huge bucks, as well as black bear and waterfowl hunts.

### WALTER'S WILDERNESS CAMP
Carrot River, SK S0E 0L0
Phone: 306-768-2485
www.waltershunt.com

Located in the north-central region, east of Prince Albert in the Wildcat Wilderness Area. Black bears and whitetails—over 65% success the last five years—plus upland birds and tremendous waterfowl hunting. Heated tree stands. Member of Saskatchewan Outfitters Association.

## YUKON TERRITORY

*In 2006 Yukon issued 4,595 hunting licenses; 742 were nonresident big game hunting licenses; 100 of the nonresident big game hunting licenses were issued to nonresident Canadians specially guided by Yukon residents. (This is a special provision in the regulations that allows a maximum of 100 Yukon residents to guide a friend or family member from outside the Territory primarily for moose, caribou, and black bear on a not-for-profit basis.) The remaining 642 were commercial clients of the Yukon big game outfitting industry.*

Named for the Indian word "Yu-kun-ah," meaning Great River, which is the 2,200-mile-long Yukon River, the population of the 186,272-square-mile (about the size of Nevada and Utah combined) Yukon Territory is 32,000, 70% of whom live in Whitehorse. In short, there are a lot of wide-open spaces here, and carbon dating of bones and fossils shows that people have been hunting here for 25,000 to 40,000 years.

This is big game country—65,000–70,000 moose, 10,000 black bear, 7,000 grizzly bears, 1,700 mountain goats, 22,000 mountain sheep, 150,000 caribou, and 500 wood bison. To hunt any species of big game you must buy a seal for that species, in addition to a big game license. A nonresident

---

**YUKON TERRITORY SNAPSHOT**

- **General information about hunting in the Yukon Territory:** www.environmentyukon.gov.yk.ca/hunting/hunting.html

- **Turn in poachers / polluters hotline:** 800-661-0525

- **Outfitters:**
  Yukon Outfitters' Association
  302 Steele Street B4
  Whitehorse, YT Y1A 2C5
  Phone: 867-668-4118; fax: 867-668-4120
  Email: info@yukonoutfitters.net
  www.yukonoutfitters.net

cannot hunt big game animals in the Yukon unless they are outfitted by a licensed outfitter and accompanied by a licensed big game guide. There are only 19 outfitting concessions in Yukon Territory. Each is exclusive. No other outfitter may operate in the same area. You can hunt small game such as rabbits, ground squirrels, porcupines, grouse, and ptarmigan without a guide, but you must purchase a nonresident license.

## DESTINATIONS

### BONNET PLUME OUTFITTERS
Mayo, YT Y0B 1M0
Phone: 867-633-3366
www.yukonhunting.com/bonnetPlume

Exclusive guiding rights on a 7,200-square-mile area near the Wernecke Mountains of the northern Yukon province, accessible only by air, for Dall sheep, Alaska/Yukon moose, barren ground caribou, grizzly and black bear, wolf, and wolverine hunts. All hunts—horse, foot, and boat—in the spirit of the fair chase.

### TROPHY STONE SAFARIS, LTD.
Whitehorse, YT Y1A 4A2
Phone: 867-668-6564; fax: 867-668-6563
www.yukonhunting.com

Hunt stone sheep, mountain grizzly, mountain caribou, and Alaskan/Yukon moose with highly personalized program. Base camp located 120 air miles north of Whitehorse at camp accessible only by plane or boat. Trophy Stone Safaris is the only permitted big game outfitting company in the 7,000-square-mile province Wildlife Area 14.

### WIDRIG OUTFITTERS, LTD.
Whitehorse, YT Y1A 3C8
Phone/fax: 867-393-3802
www.widrig.yk.ca

Specializing in horseback hunts for grizzly and black bears, moose, Dall sheep, wolverines, wolves, and caribou, Widrig is located in northeastern Yukon along the border of the Northwest Territories. Hunts take place in almost 4,000 square miles of completely isolated, rugged, and scenic mountains. Fishing for trout and grayling part of the package.

 # HERITAGE DESTINATIONS

*Beringia Interpretive Centre*
Imagine what it would have been like 10,000 years ago when migrants from Asia crossed the land bridge from Siberia and headed south into North America, encountering huge wooly mammoths, cave bears, bison, and sabertooth cats. The climate was cool and dry in the Yukon in those days, which encouraged rich fossil remains of those days when hunting success meant survival.

At Mile 914 on the Alaskan Highway just south of the Whitehorse Airport, you can get a feel for life in those days at the Yukon Beringia Interpretive Centre.

The exhibits will tell you a lot about life in prehistoric times, but for hunters this place is doubly special because every summer around the end of July they conduct Annual Yukon Atlatl Championships at Yukon Beringia Interpretive Centre. Registration begins on July 10. Fees: individuals: $5; families: $10. Fee includes admission to the Centre on that day.

Spear-throwers (atlatls, throwing boards) and darts are provided by the Centre, but you can bring your own equipment. Target Throwing Categories: child 6–10, youth 10–13, teen 14–16, open female, open male, family, pro class.

Interest in the use of atlatls is actually rapidly growing, as people seek to experience their roots and find a new way to challenge their hunting and target shooting skills. The World Atlatl Society has a magazine and can help you find where to buy an atlatl or get plans to make one. The "darts" are like long arrows, and people can get surprisingly accurate with them. A number of people hunt rabbits and even wild pigs with atlatls. For more information, see www.worldatlatl.org.

**YUKON BERINGIA**
**INTERPRETIVE CENTRE**
Whitehorse, YT Y1A 2C6
Phone: 867-667-8855; fax: 867-667-8854
www.beringia.com

# Dream Hunts

# Around the World

Be honest: We all have dreams of places we'd like to go and hunts we'd like to take. The purpose of this section is to inspire those dreams with some tales of very special hunts all around the world.

A dream becomes a reality through careful, practical planning. The section begins with general guidance on how to prepare for a hunt abroad.

Then we move to regions of the world where extraordinary hunting adventures await you. We have purposefully sought out some very rare and special ones that will push the boundaries of your dreams—Iceland, Chile, Mongolia, Siberia.

## THINGS TO KNOW BEFORE YOU GO ON A SAFARI

JEFF ENGEL

When you go on a safari, I've learned that you should always take measures to ensure your comfort, safety, and enjoyment because you will be in some pretty wild places where many variables cannot be controlled. Consider the following tips as a checklist to prepare for your dream hunt.

### PLAN AHEAD

To begin with, it is very important to contact the airlines ahead of time to find out exactly how many bags are permitted at check-in and exactly what the maximum weight is. Coordinate all of your frequent-flyer and sky-mile paperwork prior to your flight to make sure that these are all credited to your account.

Do not carry rollerball-type pens for high-altitude flights, as the pens have a tendency to burst or leak.

When possible fly as direct as you can, without additional legs, to make certain your guns and luggage arrive.

Take along an electrical converter kit to convert 110 to 220 volts if there is any question about any electrical items being compatible with the area you are visiting.

Make copies of all your important information: license, credit cards, insurance card, hunter education certificate, social security card, and passport; copy all of these onto a single 8×10 page you keep with you at all times. In the event you were to lose a wallet or purse, this single page with all your personal information would become invaluable. But be sure that all copies are safe and under your control at all times; in today's world of identify theft a stranger in a strange land is always perceived as a target.

Olive colors often blend in better in the bush environment than light-colored khaki clothing.

## TAKE RESPONSIBILITY FOR YOUR OWN NEEDS

When it comes to footwear, I like an extremely soft-soled ankle-high hiker type of boot. I also like to bring along all-leather boots to prevent the serious thorns from penetrating the footwear. A nylon or Cordura-sided boot won't protect you from the thorns properly.

Always check out the climate of your destination before you depart and take steps to ensure your comfort and safety. For example, people think of Africa as full of steaming, hot jungles. It is in some places, but I always take along a stocking cap, as in the evenings it can get quite cold. Additionally, early morning and late afternoon drives in a Land Cruiser while on safari can get quite cold, so it's nice to have a light pair of gloves and a hat tucked in your backpack just for times like this.

Take along a medium-size duffel bag or backpack to keep in the truck while on safari for the day. In this backpack I'll keep cameras, extra clothes, gloves, caps, candy to give away, and other items that I would use throughout the day. By keeping everything in a small bag or backpack, it's all very handy.

Make sure that when you import your rifle that you check with the country that you're hunting in because oftentimes a single hunter will not be allowed to bring two rifles of the same caliber into the country. Take along your own personal soft gun case for use while driving in the Land Cruiser. Oftentimes a quality or suitable gun case may not be available.

Avoid anything of value in your check-in luggage. It's amazing how many times bags are gone through while behind closed doors at airports.

If you change planes in Africa, the commuter flight might have your bags on the ground where you enter the airplane for the next leg. It may be your responsibility to take these bags and put them on the airplane. It is important to make sure that your luggage is transferred from one aircraft to the other.

Often sleeping accommodations in the bush do not include a heater. Take along a jogging outfit or some other kind of outfit that you could put on in the event nights would get chilly.

Often the Professional Hunter (PH) may have a rifle that you can rent. This is a very personal decision to me because although it is easier not to travel with a rifle, I have found that the times I didn't take my own rifle, the hunt just seemed to be missing something. There is just something about the feel of your own rifle in your hands and the comfort/confidence level that you have when using your own rifle. My preference is to take my own. However, it is also a very good idea to have a meet-and-greet service assist you at the airport in Africa to help facilitate the paperwork to import your rifle into their country.

If you have room in your duffel bag, include two or three rolls of toilet paper to make sure you have the type of paper you may prefer while in camp.

Many people believe that hunting during a full moon is not as good as a no-moon evening, so consider the moon phase prior to booking the dates of your hunt.

It may sound silly, but traditionally a washcloth is not provided at the safari camp, so I always bring along my own.

## MAKE THE TRACKERS/GUIDES YOUR FRIENDS

Consider how to ensure that the guides, trackers, and assistants will be on your side. Tipping is great, but that comes after the hunt is over.

For example, while driving in the back of a Land Cruiser, periodically your PH will stop for a water break or even a sandwich. Typically, the trackers are not or may not be offered water or food. I routinely drink half a bottle of water and share the rest with the trackers who have come along for the day.

Same goes for my sandwich—I typically eat half of the sandwich and share the rest of it with the tracker. Not only do I do this because I feel it is good to treat the trackers with a great deal of respect; after showing a little consideration and kindness to the trackers, it's amazing how much more attention they seem to give you.

I can vividly recall one time where we had just stopped for lunch, and I had shared my food and water with the tracker. As we were driving down the dirt road shortly thereafter, I was sitting on an elevated seat in the Land Cruiser looking toward the back of the truck. Suddenly the tracker noticed a very large over-hanging thorn branch and at the very last second grabbed my head to push it down to save me from being seriously hurt. Would he have had the same attention if I had not shared food and water with him? Probably, but then again, if they are on your side, they will look out for you in ways that will make the overall experience better in every way.

At the beginning of any safari, I ask the PH who the head tracker will be. And before the hunt starts, I offer the head tracker a gift—something like a Leatherman tool—to show my appreciation and respect.

Be sure to take along a good supply of extra baseball caps, tennis shoes, shirts, and pants, and anything that a baby could use and give these to the camp staff personnel. These items are always appreciated, and I make it a point of having at least half of my duffel bag include items to be given away to the local people.

I also always take 5 to 10 pounds of candy along on a trip. Every morning I give a big handful of candy to all of the trackers. During the morning breakfast, if there is camp staff around, I always give them a good handful of candy, too.

Find out from the PH prior to leaving what size boots the head tracker has. Then bring along a new extra pair of boots for the tracker as a gift for him. Flashlights are also very much appreciated by the trackers.

## TIPS WHEN IN THE FIELD

It's important to always let the PH or trackers walk in front of you in the bush. These people know what to look for when it comes to snakes and other dangerous things. They are accustomed to looking for these and can oftentimes save your life.

Always carry one to two flashlights on your person while in the field for the unscheduled time when darkness falls while in the bush.

Make sure that the sling of your rifle is well oiled so it does not squeak as you are walking in the bush.

Every night thoroughly check your body for ticks. Better yet, take an evening shower because the pepper ticks are extremely small and difficult to see. They have a habit of creating a very annoying itching sensation.

I always take along several one-inch orange dots with a sticky side for sighting in. So once you get to camp, you can take any cardboard box and put an orange dot on it; then place the target 100 yards away, and you have an instant target to check the zero of your rifle.

While in the field, memorize which way to turn the scope ring for lower or higher power, so when the moment of high tension happens, you immediately know which way to turn the scope for higher or lower power.

Every time you walk into your living quarters, pay special attention to the presence of snakes, especially if you have a thatched roof hut. On a recent safari, I got a phone call after returning back home, and the PH told me a 15-foot (4.5-meter) black mamba snake was shot in my hut. It was living in the thatched roof. So it is important that as you approach the inside, always be aware of the possible presence of dangerous snakes. Spitting cobras, for example, tend to seek out toilets. So routinely when a toilet is used, carefully lift up the lid to make sure there is no snake.

Prior to the hunt, ask the PH what type of drinking water is available. If the available drinking water is roof runoff water or other nonpurified water that he intends to have you drink, then certainly make sure you stop at the local store to purchase bottled water.

While driving to your hunting spots in the back of a Land Cruiser, constantly keep your eyes forward because of low-lying thorn branches that can easily scrape across your face and cause terrific harm. Also be extremely careful not to fall off the back of the Land Cruiser. I have personally seen people fall off when the driver makes a sudden turn, with devastating, bad results. So be very aware of your surroundings and pay attention to what the driver is doing.

Every morning before putting on your shoes or boots, check them for scorpions. The warmth inside the boots can attract scorpions throughout the night.

Just before you pull the trigger at game, make 100% certain that you know you can harvest that animal. Any animal that is wounded is counted, and you will pay the full price for that animal. If you have the slightest doubt about scoring an exact, correct hit, always pass on the shot, no matter how much pressure you get from people in your party.

Always carry your passport and your gun import form with you at all times while in the field.

I always take a very lightweight set of rain gear, like Frogg Toggs. This rain suit is extremely lightweight and very waterproof and can easily fit in the bottom of a duffel bag or a backpack that is stowed in the vehicle.

When traveling back home, it's a good tip to put your hiking boots in a separate plastic bag and load them in your duffel bag last. The reason for this is that when you get to the customs side back in the United States, they may ask you to take out your hiking boots so they can spray them. Having your boots in a plastic bag easily accessible in your duffel will certainly save you time.

## TRAVEL AND WILDERNESS MEDICINE

DR. KENNETH J. KURT*

The bidding for an African hunt is fast and furious. Suddenly you find yourself the last bidder. You have just purchased a hunt of a lifetime—a leopard and Cape buffalo hunt in Tanzania with a world-class outfitter! Now for the plan: to study the area where you intend to hunt.

Start your travel plan by selecting a travel clinic. Clinics can be found in most major cities, in the yellow pages or, better yet, on the Internet. Traveling abroad requires a passport and visa. Check your health insurance for coverage outside the United States. Most health maintenance organizations (HMOs) do not cover medical costs outside the United States. International SOS health insurance is reasonable, as is evacuation insurance. Research the country for political turmoil, including dangerous airports, to ensure a safe return home.

Remember, accidents while traveling are more common than all the diseases. Wear a seatbelt whenever possible.

When hunting in remote areas, preparation is critical. Wear protective clothing for a night out. If you get lost, stay put. Carry a wilderness kit that contains matches, a compass or GPS, and some protection from wind and dehydration. Remember, dehydration is the enemy.

What are the required immunizations? Yellow fever is a virus transmitted by *Aedes aegypti*, a mosquito, in tropical South America, sub-Saharan Africa, and Southeast Asia. Yellow fever vaccination must be documented in the International Certificate of Vaccination.

Hepatitis A is a virus caused by eating contaminated food and water. The vaccine is a must for most travelers. Two injections six months apart will give 10 years of protection.

Typhoid fever is caused by the bacterium *Salmonella typhi*, which causes fever and diarrhea with abdominal pain. Prevention is with either a three-day oral dose or one injection of typhoid vaccine. Adventurous eaters are at risk for both hepatitis A and typhoid. Boil, broil, and bake your food. If you cannot peel your fruit, don't eat it!

Meningococcal meningitis can be prevented by a very good vaccine. Vaccinate if endemic in the area you will be hunting. (Note: Also have your freshman college student vaccinated, as it is not uncommon in our college populations.)

Routine immunizations should be current. Diphtheria/tetanus vaccine and MMR (measles, mumps, rubella) are excellent and safe vaccines. A polio injection may be necessary in some African countries. India and Pakistan still have wild virus present. Don't forget a flu shot and pneumonia vaccine. Any protection from these diseases will help avoid problems that spoil a hunt.

For personal protection against the mosquito population, a repellant should contain 30% DEET, which may also be good for tick prevention. Wear protective clothing to deter fleas, gnats, blue flies, and mosquitoes.

Prophylaxis for malaria: you have a choice of Lariam, 250 milligrams taken once weekly for seven weeks over a two-week stay, versus Malarone daily, starting one day prior to departure. Mild side effects, like nausea, will usually pass. One of the most important items to take along is sunscreen—the sun is hot and air is dry. UV protection and sunglasses will help prevent sunburn and eye injuries.

Traveler's diarrhea affects over 50% of all travelers. Don't eat a food if you can't peel or cook it. E-coli is most commonly caused by undercooked meat. Treat minor diarrhea with Imodium AD. If there is no improvement in 48 hours, start an antibiotic such as a quinolone (Cipro or Levaquin). Doxycycline, 100 milligrams twice daily, is a good alternative. A traveler with severe diarrhea accompanied by blood and abdominal pain should start on antibiotics in combination with Imodium as soon as possible to prevent disabling dehydration. Again—dehydration is the enemy!

Water should be boiled or filtered before drinking. Consider all streams and lakes contaminated, no matter how clean they appear. Parasites that contaminate streams in the United States can cause severe diarrhea and abdominal pain.

"Beaver fever," or *Giardia* infection, from mountain streams and lakes in remote or underdeveloped areas has spoiled trips for many a hunter. *Giardia* is the most common cause of diarrhea in the United States. It responds well to metronidazole, 250 milligrams three times daily for 10 days.

If you hunt high in the mountains, you may experience being lightheaded and nauseated with some disorientation. High-altitude sickness can be prevented by gradual ascent. Starting at 5,000 to 6,000 feet, stop over night with no alcohol and plenty of water, then gradually ascend, as symptoms may be subtle. Daimox, 250 milligrams daily prior to departure, will help prevent high-altitude sickness. If allergic to sulfa, you may try nifedipine or dexamethasone. The only treatment for high-altitude sickness is to descend.

Another minor problem may be jet lag. The recipe for lesser symptoms is an overnight flight. Use headphones and Ambien or Sonata for sleep. Again, use no alcohol and drink plenty of water. Stay awake the next day, no naps. Take another Ambien that night. If fatigued, taking Provigil, 20 milligrams, may prevent excessive sleepiness. Plan, protect, and prevent for a safe and enjoyable hunt.

I would recommend a comprehensive physical and dental exam prior to departure for all major expeditions. Don't take chances. You owe it to yourself. A well-prepared hunter is a safe hunter.

Below are names and Web sites for resources of use to the international traveler. See each Web site for contact information and phone numbers.

**CENTERS FOR DISEASE**
**CONTROL (CDC)**
www.cdc.gov

**INTERNATIONAL SOS**
(international health care)
www.internationalsos.com

**MEDJET ASSISTANCE**
(medical evacuation)
www.medjetassistance.com

*Dr. Kenneth J. Kurt is located in Franklin, Wisconsin. He can be contacted at the email address NMC@drkenkurt.com.*

---

## TRAVEL INSURANCE

As much as some sportsmen, and -women, plan and anticipate every possible need for their dream hunting trips, unexpected events can—and do—happen when traveling. And while travel insurance can't ensure you spot that trophy whitetail or promise perfect weather, it can save major out-of-pocket expenses—and your life—if you need to cancel your trip or experience a medical emergency when you're far from home.

There are five things you as a sportsman should consider when purchasing travel insurance: (1) loss of your prepaid deposit(s) if you must cancel or if your trip is interrupted, (2) the potentially huge costs of an emergency medical evacuation, (3) major medical expenses or transportation while traveling (many health insurance plans provide little, if any, coverage outside the United States), (4) loss or delay of expensive hunting or fishing equipment or licenses, and (5) travel delays due to inclement weather in unfamiliar regions of the world.

Some insurance providers, such as www.sportsmanstravelinsurance.com (provided by AIG Travel Guard), offer a travel insurance plan designed exclusively for your hunting or fishing excursions. This plan includes:

• **Trip Cancellation.** Coverage for your prepaid nonrefundable expenses such as outfitters cancellation penalties and airline ticket cancellation or change fees for reasons such as inclement weather, sickness, injury, and other named unforeseen circumstances.

• **Trip Interruption.** Coverage for forfeited, nonrefundable prepaid deposits and additional transportation expenses in the event that you must return home early or the additional expenses to reach the original destination if the trip was delayed and leaves after the trip departure date for reasons such as inclement weather, sickness, injury, or other named unforeseen circumstances.

• **License Refund Coverage.** If you can't go on your out-of-state trip, you can be refunded the cost of your hunting or fishing license. With some licenses costing thousands of dollars, this is a must for outdoorsmen and -women.

• **Travel Delay.** This reimburses you for a weather-related delay of 12 hours or more for reasonable accommodations and traveling expenses such as hotel rooms and additional meals until travel is possible, up to specific predetermined limits.

• **Sportsmen's Equipment Coverage.** Nothing is more frustrating than arriving at your prepaid hunt without your equipment, owing to an airline baggage mishap. Coverage is provided for the loss, theft, or damage to your equipment and luggage, including hunting rifles, apparel, rods, reels, tackle, bows, arrows, and other gear.

• **Sportsmen's Equipment Delay Coverage.** If your baggage is delayed or misdirected for more than 24 hours, you can be reimbursed for the rental of hunting and/or fishing equipment.

• **Worldwide Medical Coverage.** Many providers have medical expense coverage anywhere in the world; they arrange and cover the cost of medical evacuation en route, if necessary. This coverage pays medical expenses within one year of any injury or sickness occurring on the trip, provided initial treatment was received during the trip.

• **Emergency Medical Transportation.** Twenty-four-hour emergency hotlines offer you emergency medical transportation if you suffer a serious illness or injury while on your hunting or fishing trip. Most travel insurance providers will arrange a medical evacuation to the nearest, adequate medical facility.

Sportsman's travel insurance even provides you with a sportsman's hotline that supplies up-to-the-minute weather, fishing, and hunting reports; local hunting regulations and locations of game registration stations; 24-hour roadside assistance services; construction and detour information if driving to destination; and locations of nearby bait, tackle, and sporting goods stores—everything to enhance the traveling sportsman's hunting experience!

However, when traveling deep into the woods, far down the streams, or high in the mountains where your typical mobile phone service does not reach, you should also consider renting a satellite phone to connect you to worldwide communication, especially in the event of a medical emergency.

Be sure to always protect yourself while traveling to any destination, whether you're going on a big game hunt in Montana or a safari in Africa. Most travel insurance companies post their policies, as well as their list of excluded travel suppliers, on the Internet. Read the policies before you buy and call the travel insurance company with any questions or "what ifs" you may have. Be aware before you leave home that if you need to make a claim, you will need to provide the travel insurance company documentation or receipts related to the claim's filed expenses. From the time you book your trip, hang on to every piece of correspondence, invoice, statement, canceled check, and receipt. A reputable insurance company will be more than happy to walk you through policies or procedures and answer any questions you may have.

## FILMING YOUR OWN HUNT

JEFF ENGEL

I've had the privilege of hosting a national, award-winning outdoor adventure/hunting television series. We have been on location in almost 30 states, most of the provinces in Canada, and five countries. The section gives many tips you can use to successfully video your own hunt. Good luck.

The first and best advice I can give is to not go it alone. You should always have someone else accompany you, so you can focus on the hunting. When you are filming a partner while hunting, it is very important to have very good communication between the camera operator and the hunter and plan out your basic shots as much as possible. As an example, if you are filming a hunting partner while turkey hunting, it is best to set the camera up on a tripod above the upper right shoulder of the hunter. (This is assuming the shooter is a right-handed shooter.) Set up close enough to each other so you can communicate effectively.

As the camera operator is filming game coming in, it is imperative that the hunter not shoot until he gets a signal from the camera operator because the perspective of the hunter sitting on the ground while hunting turkeys may be different from the camera's view. It takes a great deal of discipline, but the hunter should never take a shot at game until he gets some type of prearranged signal from the camera operator. I can give you many, many personal examples where this has been extremely frustrating.

On several occasions while filming turkey hunts throughout the country, I have had the camera operator behind me. By my perspective, the turkey was in sight, and I was ready to take a shot. However, he or she might not have the same sight picture as I did. So as anxious as I was to shoot, I could not, and would not, shoot until the videographer gave me the signal.

I can also remember many times while filming in Africa where I would have my shooting sticks up, my rifle set, and I would be ready to fire at an animal—and the camera operator was still trying to get the animal in focus. And if you only can bag one of this species, and the camera is not ready when you shoot it, you have lost the show for television.

Filming kudus has been especially diffi-

cult, as they are nervous animals, and you usually only have a moment to take a shot. So by the time I would get my rifle up on the sticks and the camera operator would get the animal in focus, the animal would be gone. This can be extremely frustrating, but we always remind ourselves that we are there to get the full hunt on tape, and we are not there just to take an animal.

We always use a tripod while filming. By using a tripod, your footage will be steadier, and zooms will be smoother. There is a place for nontripod use when you want to create a live-action feel, but knowing when to use and not use a tripod is a very important part of the creative process of filming. If you intend on panning scenery, you always want to use a tripod with a slow and smooth pan.

As far as zooms go, most professional zooms are slow, steady, and deliberate. We make it an absolute rule that the majority of our shots, zoom shots especially, are taken from a tripod.

It is also good to have a fluid-head attached to the tripod for a smoother pan. It is better to get the subject carefully framed and focused and at the right distance before pressing "record." Using the zoom on your camera can be effective when you are drawing the viewer's attention to detail or a far-off object, but be careful not to overuse the zoom. When possible, pan and practice a smooth, even zoom before pressing the record button. Zooming smoothly is a learned skill, and you should practice it when you are not recording.

We find that the most important part of filming a hunt is getting the actual shot. One of my favorite techniques is filming over the hunter's shoulder, slowly zooming into the animal, then getting as much footage of the animal as possible. Only then should the camera operator give the hunter the shoot signal.

Once the animal has been taken, we then reenact the beginning part of the stalk and everything up until the actual shot. We do this so that we can develop the story line.

Good broadcast-quality audio will make your viewing back home even more enjoyable. We use wireless microphones. If the camera operator is following two hunters, each of the hunters will have a microphone. If we are filming a turkey hunt with one hunter, the single hunter will have a wireless microphone, and we will put the second wireless microphone in the general area where we think the gobbler may come from. The microphone may be hidden near where the decoys are set up. We then use these microphones to record ambient and natural sounds.

Whether it is a sunset, sunrise, scenery, or a close-up, get the scene the way you want to see it to be filmed before you push the recording button. Then don't touch the camera until you have 12 to 15 seconds of uninterrupted footage of perfectly still recording of the subject. When editing for a show, we always press "record" and have 5 seconds of preroll footage before the action starts; again at the end of the scene we will include 5 seconds of postroll footage so back in the studio the editor has enough footage for dissolves.

It is also imperative to make sure that the red record button is pushed. This may sound simple, but on numerous occasions, during the heat of excitement, I have had camera operators forget to press the little red record button. I can vividly recall filming out West

one year when I had a gorgeous Merriam's turkey strut for several minutes out in front of me, and the camera operator gave me the signal to shoot. In my mind, this was going to be spectacular footage. After the shot, we reviewed the footage and, to our extreme disappointment, found out that the camera operator had forgotten to press the record button. He was so caught up in the emotion of having a turkey so close that he just forgot to push the button.

Another time when I was filming in Illinois, we had spent two and a half days sitting in a tree stand, where temperatures were hovering 5 to 10 degrees above zero. A buck eventually walked out along the edge of a cornfield. I gradually raised my muzzleloader. When the deer got to within about 75 yards, the camera operator whispered to me, "Take him." I was fortunate to make a good shot, and I had collected a beautiful whitetail buck on film—so I thought. After we got down from the tree stand, to my disappointment, we found that he forgot to press the red button. This made for a good laugh—sort of.

There will also be times when you wonder to yourself, Should I film that or not? We make it a general rule to always film if there is a question. We then can sort out the best footage back at the studio. It is also a lot of fun to catch bloopers while filming, so if the camera operator sees an amusing, comical event that is unrehearsed and unscripted, make sure the camera keeps rolling. Tape is relatively cheap, and this footage could be hilarious to watch.

I should add here that clowning with guns for the camera is dangerous. When actors do this, they have a squad of armorers to check and recheck all weapons, and they rehearse ahead of time.

When filming your friends while hunting, politely but firmly direct the hunters in order to get the shots you need. Your leadership will be appreciated, and the overall hunt will go more smoothly. It is also important to get different angles of the hunter walking. As an example, you may want to follow right behind the hunter with a camera at a very low angle to get his feet in motion. You may also want to reverse the angle and walk in front of the hunter, walking backwards to get the view of the hunter walking toward the camera. It is also nice to get very close up shots of feet walking on rock or through mud or water. This can give the scene a very personal feel.

Also, with all filming, pay attention to composition and use the "law of thirds," where you mentally divide the viewing screen into three horizontal and three vertical sections, creating a grid. Focal points are created where the sections intersect. By locating the main subject in one of the outer sections of the screen, if an animal is walking or flying a certain direction, you will have enough space in front of the animal to make it appear as if it is in motion. The law of thirds also helps you express your creativity through the lens of the camera.

Many cameras can be focused either automatically or manually. It is particularly important *not* to use the auto focus when shooting a subject that is behind branches or in tall grass. Use the auto function very sparingly and only when your subject is in an open area, with no objects to distract the focus.

When you are filming game that was re-

cently taken by a hunter, spend an extra few minutes cleaning up any blood from the animal and posing the animal in a very respectful manner.

Even though I host the show, and most of my time is spent standing in front of the camera, I make a point of filming "B-roll portions" of the show myself, because I enjoy it. B-roll is additional footage that is shot to intercut with the primary footage used in a television show. It is frequently used as a cutaway shot, and it enhances the overall story line. B-roll is also used to add dimension to a story and to create richer video imagery—things like animal tracks, birds, any interesting rock formations, sunrises, sunsets, and anything that would be of interest to film that would enhance the overall story line.

While filming, always get "the big picture" scenery shot to get a feel as to where you are, but don't forget to get the close-ups of things like people's eyes or your dogs' eyes to show expressions.

You will also want to label, name, and number each tape as it comes out of the camera. It is better to do this in the field rather than back at the cabin.

Whenever possible, try to have the sun behind the camera operator and always be aware or how light will affect the creativity of the scene. You also want to film using a variety of perspectives. Filming from a wide variety of angles gives viewers that are watching a feeling that they are right there in the adventure.

You also want to be sure to carry extra batteries and tape and keep them in a very convenient place for easy access. Make sure you also carry a good-quality cleaning cloth, and make it a habit to clean the lens often. I also find that carrying a folded black trash bag in my gear makes for good temporary rain cover.

Videotaping your hunt is a wonderful way of preserving your memories forever. Sharing memories and reliving those moments constitute one of the true joys of hunting.

**GENERAL FILM CHECKOFF SHEET**

Sunrise

Sunset

Sighting rifle/ shotgun day before hunt

Hunt dialog day before hunt

Truck ride to hunting area— early A.M.

Loading rifle/ shotgun—close-up

Climbing up rocks

Camera behind feet—following steps

General overall scenery

Close-up of animals, plants, insects (B-roll)

Various close-ups of deer

Interesting rock formations

Walking on distant hillside

Panoramic scenes— no people

Walking past camera

Walking up to camera, glassing walking out

Stalking deer

Safety off just before shot at deer

Shot at deer (close-up)

Approaching downed deer

Describing how to get deer back to truck

Congrats after kill

Father and son/ daughter conversations and fun throughout the trip

Using binoculars

Using spotting scope

Close-up deer tracks

Old farm/ranch/ buildings/autos/well pumps/etc.

Close-up deer and rack

Next to deer/discuss stalk

Driving out with deer in truck

Something original in every show

Different angles for B-roll (for this show or other shows)

Remember to film people, animals, scenery, and so on, from different angles, close up, and farther away.

It seems like the more fun you have while filming, the better the results are. So go out and really enjoy yourself.

# Africa

For many people, Africa is synonymous with big game hunting. Just saying the name conjures up images of Ernest Hemmingway on safari, followed by scores of porters, dangerous animals everywhere.

Even though things have changed somewhat, Africa remains the most common dream hunting destination in the world. And 24 African countries today offer hunting, which is an enormous boost to the economy. In South Africa alone, big game hunting is worth $2 billion a year. A good deal of that money supports conservation at the local and national levels.

We can share only a fraction of the extraordinary hunts that await you in Africa. Even including airfare, African hunts are often less expensive than hunts in North America.

## BOTSWANA

 DREAM HUNT

### Cape Buffalo in the Okavango Delta

JEFF ENGEL

As the tires of the Land Cruiser dug deep into the road ruts of heavy sand, we drove deeper and deeper into the African bush of the Okavango Delta in pursuit of what some people say is the most dangerous game in the world—Cape buffalo.

Our professional hunter was Jeff Rann from Rann Safaris, a winner of the Safari Club International Outfitter of the Year Award. Accompanying Sherol and I on this trip were our two good friends, well-known actor Marshall Teague and his wife Lindy.

Botswana, which is slightly smaller than Texas, is bordered by Zambia and Zimbabwe to the north and west and South Africa to the south and southeast. About 17% of Botswana's land area has been

set aside as natural parks and game reserves, and it is a land of contrasts. About 85% is the Kalahari Desert, which lies to the south. In the north there is the lush green and tremendous waterways of the Okavango Delta.

The Okavango Delta is a series of lagoons, hidden channels, and lakes covering an area of over 8,000 square miles in the middle of the Kalahari Desert. It is the largest inland delta in the world. Its mysterious waterways and peaceful and tranquil lagoons constitute one of the truly natural wonders of the world.

The water and the lush vegetation it supports make the Okavango teem with wildlife.

The flight from Atlanta to Johannesburg was a long 18 hours. After spending the night in Johannesburg, we took a flight to Maun in Botswana, where Jeff Rann met us. We loaded our safari gear into several Land Cruisers and embarked on an incredible three-and-a-half-hour drive from the modern airport and asphalt roads into thick African bush, following only a sparse two-track dirt road that forced us to occasionally ford streams and ponds. Our Land Cruisers had a snorkel muffler that stuck up above the water so you wouldn't get stuck in a place where hippos and crocodiles live.

The Okavango is the old wild Africa where free-ranging game still exist. The greeting committee was herds of elephants, as Botswana is home to some of the largest free-roaming elephant herds in the world.

One of the purposes of this trip was to film for our television series *Engel's Outdoor Experience*. As we plunged into the bush, I couldn't help think to

myself that shooting a Cape buffalo generated quite a bit of pressure and anxiety all by itself; adding the extra layer of a cameraman filming and documenting everything you do was going to make the hunt even more challenging.

Eventually we arrived at a camp that consisted of individual tents separated along the river, with a main cook tent and dining area. Each couple had their own luxury tent, and although we were deep in the African bush, this camp was extremely comfortable. This place was first class, including tablecloths and fine china and even a generator providing cool beverages.

After settling in, Marshall and I headed out to the rifle range to make sure our rifles were dead on. Our gun of choice was a .416 Rigby. We would be using 400-grain bullets. You need something like this to take down a big bull because a buffalo's thick skin and ribs are three inches thick. Fortunately our guns were right on.

After a delicious dinner in the African bush, Sherol and I settled into our tent for our first night in the Okavango Delta. As I lay in bed, I heard a lion roaring perhaps 100 yards away from our tent. Now we were in wild Africa! With my fully loaded rifle leaning against the canvas tent, less than an arm's length from the bed, I closed my eyes with a smile on my face and just enjoyed the exotic sounds of the African night.

The next morning after a great breakfast, we set out on Jeff's Land Cruiser to hunt the African Cape buffalo. Jeff knows this area well, as a number of waterways and most of the roads we traveled were made by Jeff. In fact, we traversed the land without roads much of the time. Oftentimes we had to use the front winch of the Land Cruiser to move logs out of the way. Other times I was amazed that our Land Cruiser would cross rivers where the height of the water would come over the hood of our vehicle.

We had drawn straws, and I was the first hunter up. My emotions were in overdrive, with my anticipation level extremely high.

We would cruise in the Land Cruiser, stopping often to look for tracks. On our second day of hunting, Sherol and Lindy spotted a vulture flying high overhead. This could mean some other animal had success hunting. As we approached we found fresh lion tracks in the dust in the road. Prides of lions follow Cape buffalo herds. Then the head of a lioness popped up out of the grass. More than any time in my life I felt like I was in the place where nature was in full control. We all smelled the unmistakable odor of a decaying animal. After a brief search we found him: a mature bull Cape buffalo way in the dense brush, partially eaten by lions. As Jeff and I approached the buffalo, Marshall kept watch with his rifle ready.

Jeff said to me, "This was a great old bull. I've seen him before in this area."

Jeff further explained he was never really with the herd—he was always in the back, trailing. He said this big old bull had probably been pushed out of the herd. Jeff explained that he was on his own, and the lions had killed him a couple of days ago.

For the first four days we did not come across any fresh buffalo sign but saw a wide variety of

animals. One morning we came upon two chee-tahs sitting at the base of a termite mound, look-ing for plains game to pursue. Strange birds and insects were everywhere. As our vehicle splashed through streams and swamps, hippos and croco-diles watched. I have never been some place where so many animals considered us a food source.

As the Land Cruiser bounced down the barely navigable two-track road, I happened to notice a dark object in a low-lying bush that we passed. I motioned Jeff to stop and back up. As he backed up the 20 feet or so, we came parallel with the bush, and sure enough, coiled in the center of the bush was a black mamba.

We were able to get some extraordinary video

of the black mamba, as if on cue it uncoiled and slithered down the tree and slowly made his way across the dirt road in front of us. The black mamba is one of the most deadly snakes in the world. Also one of the fastest moving.

As we drove further, we came across a pair of bat eared foxes. It seemed like that wherever you looked, there was some new and interesting wildlife.

On day five we finally saw a herd of well over 100 buffalo in the distance. My heart sank in my chest, as I knew we were about to embark on a stalk of a lifetime.

We drove the truck about a mile away and parked well downwind from the herd. The stalk of the herd time seemed to be in slow motion—time was not measured by minutes or seconds but by the number of beads of sweat rolling down the center of my back.

Jeff and his trackers did an outstanding job get-ting us close to the herd. As we came within 200 yards, I could not forget the warning from the book *Nyati, the Art of Hunting the African Buffalo*: "There is no other animal that can absorb so much lead and keep functioning for so long when it is certifiably clinically dead on his feet as a wounded Cape buffalo."

We worked closer. Cape buffalo have eyesight, hearing, and smell better than ours. This was not a time for a mistake. Many hunters have been wounded or gored to death by wounded Cape buffalo.

The herd was moving to the left. Trailing on the far side of the herd was a single lone bull, about 80 yards away, walking in a slow methodical fashion.

After Jeff confirmed he was indeed an out-standing trophy bull, I set up the shooting sticks and aimed my crosshairs on the low center part of the shoulder. My heart was pumping in overdrive. My whole life as a hunter had taken me to this mo-ment, to hunt what some say is the most dangerous game animal in the world. For a moment the huge

Cape buffalo stood broadside and looked in our direction, and I fired the first round. The shot was perfect. But even though the shot was where it was supposed to be, the bull stood there for a moment and made a 180-degree circle.

Jeff said, "You made a good shot. Take him right in the shoulder again." I instantly shot in the other shoulder; that shot was also right on. At this point the bull started to run to the left. I could not believe my eyes—I have two perfectly placed bullets from a .416 Rigby into both shoulders, and this huge Cape buffalo is continuing to run as if nothing had happened!

Jeff said calmly, "Take him again." I fired a third round. This bullet struck high in the shoulder near the vertebrae. I would like to say I had strategic bullet placement on the third shot, but in reality I was shooting at a black blob running away. To my luck the bullet hit dead center in the spine, and the bull collapsed.

As I stood there in amazement, I thought of what friends who had taken buffalo had said—there was no other animal that absorbs so much lead. They were so right. It took a total of three well-placed shots to bring this animal down.

As we approached closer, Jeff said, "I don't think he is going to get up, but just be ready. If he lifts his head up, give him another shot." And Jeff repeated calmly, "I'm pretty sure he is dead." As we approached the downed buffalo, Jeff and I and the trackers were walking in knee-deep water.

The closer I got, the more magnificent he looked. We then took many photographs beside the old bull. It was indeed a pleasure of a lifetime and an honor to harvest such a magnificent animal.

With the help of everyone, we loaded the big Cape buffalo into the back of the vehicle and drove back to camp. As we entered the camp, the staff workers came out and started jumping up and down and singing, for they knew they would have

fresh meat. As we walked into camp, the staff went into a beautiful song of celebration. I was overcome by the emotion of the whole event.

That evening the camp chef prepared back straps from my Cape buffalo. After a memorable meal, all of us sat around the campfire. I found it hard to believe that I had just taken a 43-inch Cape buffalo in this wildest of places. But the biggest trophy of all was just being there with my adrenaline pumping in overdrive, sharing the whole experience with close friends, and feeling the awe of being next to such a magnificent animal. I will never forget this incredible moment.

That night we again heard the distant roar of the lions. It had been a good day of hunting. It seemed like everything was celebrating.

The next day was Marshall's turn. We returned to the same area where I had taken my bull. Marshall's dream was to take an old bull with bosses that looked like "the craters of the moon." "Bosses" are the base of the horns as they emerge from the skull.

Extremely fresh lion tracks intermingled with those of the herd. Jeff now knew that the herd was very close. As we walked through the canopy of bush with the sun shining through the leaves, we came across the herd. We began a stalk from the downwind direction. Our hearts were in our throats

Botswana
357

as we crept to within 25 yards of the herd that was milling around in front of us. There was, indeed, one exceptional bull in the herd with truly massive bosses—exactly what Marshall was looking for.

As we patiently waited for the bull to present a shot, Jeff suddenly but very calmly whispered, "Don't move a muscle." Suddenly two huge, full-maned lions appeared to our right. They were hunting the same buffalo that we were and were well under 20 yards away. Marshall was ready with his rifle up just in case a lion were to charge. A staring match unfolded, and then in an instant, both lions bolted away from us.

We returned our attention to the Cape buffalo when suddenly a third full-maned lion appeared to our left. The lion just stood there, staring. We later measured this distance at 14 yards. Sherol and I were both videoing the whole experience, and our other photographer was behind Marshall. The lion first stared at Marshall, and then his eyes shifted directly to Jeff; then the lion's eyes noticeably turned to Sherol, and his eyes locked with Sherol's. Talk about a stare-down.

At that moment the lion could have easily charged. Directly behind the lion perhaps 10 yards were the Cape buffalo, and the lion repeatedly looked behind him and then turned his head to look at us and then turned his back to look at the Cape buffalo, then looked at us once more. What an extraordinary experience.

All the while, Marshall had his rifle at ready. The buffalo also stared and watched. As the time seemed to slow down, we all waited to see what would happen next. Fortunately the big cat eventually decided to leave the area.

The buffalo had been watching the whole affair. Since the buffalo was facing directly at us, Marshall made a perfect shot just below in the buffalo's chest. We also later measured how far Marshall's buffalo was away—24 yards.

The herd took off, raising a cloud of dust. We knew by now that we would have to track it. There was plenty of sign, but there was also danger everywhere.

Jeff said, "Good blood, you hit him right in the chest." As they found the spoor, Jeff asked Marshall, "Are you ready?" Marshall whispered back, "Believe you me, I am ready."

After a short distance of intense tracking, Jeff and his trackers found the bull. It was dead. Marshall had his bull of a lifetime and was overcome with emotion. In many of Marshall's movies, such as *Road House* with Patrick Swayze, Marshall was the tough guy. Seeing the emotion on Marshall's face, I knew he was not acting at this time. This was real, very real.

As we all approached the bull, in a very soft-spoken voice Jeff said, "Marshall, I think you got the bull you wanted."

Unable to speak as he held on to the tremendous horns of his African Cape buffalo, Marshall finally said, "I dreamed of this animal my entire life."

Sherol, Lindy, Marshall, and I gave each other tremendous bear hugs, and we were all overcome with emotion. As we returned to the camp, word quickly spread that Marshall had taken a great Cape buffalo. Again the local tribe greeted us with a rhyth-

mic song and dance. The celebration was etched into all of our minds.

That night while sitting along the campfire, we enjoyed more delicious back straps from the Cape buffalo, along with a delicious oxtail soup made from the tail of the buffalo.

It is moments like these that seem to crystallize in your mind, and these moments are never forgotten. To share this incredible experience with my wife, Marshall, Lindy, and Jeff Rann and his incredible camp staff was the most incredible hunt of our lives. Would I do this again? In a heartbeat.

*See Section D for a special recipe.*

To hunt with Jeff Rann, contact:

**777 RANCH**
Hondo, TX 78861
Phone: 830-426-3476; fax: 830-426-4821
www.777ranch.com (Texas, also an excellent hunting destination)
www.safarisouth.org (Botswana)

 **FEATURED HUNT**

## African Red Lechwe in the Okavango Delta

SHEROL ENGEL

After several days of hunting with Jeff Rann from Rann Safaris and filming Jeff and our friends and Hollywood actors Marshall and Lindy Teague—Lindy had been hunting kudu, and Marshall and Jeff had been pursuing the enormous and dangerous Cape buffalo—we had one more day left to hunt. I was drained from the experiences, but now it was finally my turn.

Under the light of the African moon, I started to anticipate my first "big game" hunt ever, which would begin at daybreak the next morning. The animal I chose to hunt was the red lechwe, a beautiful antelope that spends almost its entire life in the water, which is why this place was perfect habitat.

The Okavango Delta, deep in Botswana, is one of the world's greatest mysteries. It is water in a desert—the Kalahari Desert, which is the largest continuous stretch of sand in the world. The magnificent Okavango Delta is an expanse of waterways, floodplains, forested islands, and lagoons that covers about 7,000 square miles. It is home to a multitude of animal and bird species.

Apart from the permanent channels, the Delta is covered by shallow water, flooded grasslands, backwater swamps, ox-bow lakes, and hidden lagoons, mostly interconnected by narrow waterways. There are an estimated 50,000 islands scattered throughout the Delta. Flood levels in the Delta are highest between March and September, and we were there in the last days of May.

We headed down one of the many rivers, going downstream from our camp, heading for a very remote part of the river. The area reminded me a little of the Everglades.

The red lechwe was indigenous to the Okavango Delta and usually traveled in herds, sometimes as large as 1,000 at a time. They live in the areas where the water is about knee-deep, and they feed on the short grass; they are grazers. Jeff Rann said that he had not been in this area for over a month, and there was no way of knowing what we

might find, but he did guarantee that there would be hippos and crocodiles.

As we were scooting along in the boat, Jeff told us what he would have to do if a hippo went down in front us. He would have to race the boat right over them while they are on the bottom, to avoid hitting them. He suggested we hang on tight. He no sooner finished saying that when a flock of ducks exploded right next to the boat. We flew past quite a few more hippos and saw crocodiles floating among the reeds. The river was full of wildlife, and our hearts were pumping.

As we traveled through the channels in the swamp, Marshall kept his rifle ready, just in case a crocodile or a hippo decided that we might make a tasty meal.

We soon spotted a red lechwe far in the distance. I was ready with my .300 Winchester rifle at my side. I could jump out of the boat at a moment's notice. It was too small, Jeff said.

An hour passed as we scanned the landscape. Clouds of birds and other wild game seemed everywhere. Jeff Rann's talent for spotting game came true as he pointed out a much bigger lechwe. Definitely worth going after, he said.

We landed the boat on some higher ground, hopped out, and began to stalk, which meant wading through knee-deep crocodile-infested waters. Fortunately, there were lots of small islands that provide some dry ground—a welcome break from wading through the water.

We finally got set up on the bull, but then he slipped away, so we had to circle around. Back into the water with the hippos, crocodiles, and snakes and no hip boots. I asked myself, "Am I out of my mind!" At the same time, I was having the time of my life.

Suddenly the tracker caught a glimpse of the bull we were following. Jeff could see him, too, and he led me to a place about 180 yards away, next to an enormous termite mound, which made for great cover. I got set up on shooting sticks just as the lechwe started to run off through the water. Was he going to jump into a hole and submerge? Lechwe do that sometimes, Jeff said.

He eventually stopped. My heart was pumping so hard I could hear it in my ears. This would be my first shot at a big game animal. It took all my will to steady myself for the shot and stay calm. Jeff told me to take it right on the shoulder. I aimed, held my breath, and slowly pulled the trigger. Jeff yelled, "You hit him—good hit—alright!"

I was so excited as Jeff ran toward him—we all were. When he found the bull, I was beyond words. Jeff said it was a perfect shot right on the shoulder, and he was a beautiful red lechwe, a big old male.

We all shared hugs and the excitement of being so privileged to get this great animal. My husband Jeff asked how this lechwe compared in size to others. To my delight, Jeff Rann said that he was record-book size.

It took us quite awhile to drag the lechwe back to the boat. The sun was fading. We did not want to be out there at night. Not to mention that we were waist deep in crocodiles and hippos. I did, however, take comfort knowing that the meat from this animal would be well received by the local village people.

As we got under way, I began to relax, thinking the excitement for the day was over, when suddenly, out of nowhere, there were four hippos right in the middle of the river! Luckily for them, and us, the hippos quickly submerged, and we passed safely over them. We all were speechless. Just a reminder of who is boss out here.

This hunt, my first, for big game will stay with me for the rest of my life. Sharing it with Jeff and our friends Lindy and Marshall made it all the more memorable. My thanks to Jeff Rann and Kwezi Kennedy for a fantastic experience.

For information on hunting in Botswana, contact:

**RANN SAFARIS**
Jeff or Steve Rann
777 Ranch
Post Office Box 610
Hondo, TX 78861
Phone: 830-426-3476; fax: 830-426-4821
Email: rannsafaris@yahoo.com
www.rannsafaris.com

 **DREAM HUNT**

## After "Africa's Greatest Trophy"

BOB KEAGY*

The spiral-horned antelope are unusually difficult animals to hunt. They are very intelligent,
extremely alert, and often live in very difficult terrain. Within the spiral-horned family there are the
"big four," consisting of the elusive and rare sita-
tunga, the unbelievably beautiful bongo, the huge
but furtive Lord Derby eland, and lastly, what is
sometimes called "Africa's Greatest Trophy," the
mountain nyala, found only in Ethiopia. I had the
first three but lacked the mountain nyala, which is a
different animal than that found in the marshy lowlands farther south.

When you say "Ethiopia," people tend to think
of deserts. Yes, there are deserts in Ethiopia, but there
also is a wonderful, heavily forested mountainous region, which is where mountain nyalas live.

At the SCI convention in 2001, my wife Pam
and I met with Nassos Roussos of Ethiopian Rift Valley Safaris, as well as Nassos's 25-year old son Jason.
Upon meeting, we were impressed by the aura of
calm expertise and assurance that they projected,
as well as their evident enthusiasm for the beautiful
mountain nyala. Their U.S. booking agent Rich Elliott assured us that he would look after our licenses,
assist in air reservations, and advise us on visas, gun
import permits, and a myriad of details. In fact, we
liked Ethiopian Rift Valley Safaris enough that we
booked a 21-day mountain nyala hunt, with a 3-day
Omo Valley add-on for October–November 2003.
So much for my usual banker's caution!

We left San Francisco, bound for Frankfurt on
Lufthansa, with a lengthy following flight to Cairo,
then onward to Addis Ababa. The last leg of the
flight seemed endless, as it's four hours from Cairo
to Addis Ababa alone. Nevertheless, it eventually

ended, and we landed at the shiny new Addis Ababa Airport late on the evening of the 27th.

We were met in a timely manner by Jason Roussos and driven across sprawling Addis Ababa to the Saudi-built Addis Ababa Sheraton. This hotel simply has to be seen to be believed, but after some 30 or so hours in the air, we were pretty beat.

The next morning we began our four-hour drive to the Arsi Mountains base camp. As we drove, we got to know Jason a bit better. He would prove to be an excellent and perceptive guide, a fine and cheerful companion, a trained wildlife biologist, and (happily) an interested photographer to help Pam catch some truly stunning photos.

Shortly after midday we arrived at the tented camp that would be our base for both mountain nigali and, hunted in the same general area, Menelik's bushbuck, also indigenous only to Ethiopia.

The base camp consisted of four tents set in a stand of pine and eucalyptus trees, both originally imported in contemplation of a never-developed paper industry. Our tent was clean and neat, with roll-up canvas windows, comfortable cots, and a bath and latrine area directly behind. There was also Jason's tent, as well as the dining tent and a cook tent. A large campfire was centrally located, with inviting lawn chairs. The overall quality appeared excellent and, owing to the piney mountain environment, reminded me a good deal of a North American elk camp.

Mountain nyalas are nocturnal/diurnal, so the hunting day began at 4:15 A.M., with a quick breakfast, then driving to a point one or two miles from that day's glassing point. We would then walk silently up the mountain in the dark, using flashlights, until the first glimmer of dawn allowed us to turn off the lights. We'd soon arrive at our day's glassing point, often overlooking a salt lick, and begin to glass intently. Jason would send scouts out along all the adjacent ridgelines to check any likely areas.

We often saw small groups of females and occasionally a young nyala bull or two in the morning light, but nothing to really throw a stalk on. The light slanting down the verdant valleys, softened and diffused by gently rising morning mists, was very lovely

We were usually back to base about 11 A.M., as the animals bedded down by that point. We would have a leisurely lunch, then back out in the afternoon. The chances of stumbling on a big mountain nigali in the waning afternoon were not great, so the afternoon emphasis was on the Menelik's bushbuck.

On the sixth day, not having seen anything acceptable, we were going to try a slightly different area and left camp very early. In this area we hunted paralleling a beautiful little stream, dancing artfully over granite boulders. The trail we were on followed the stream, climbing up the steep-sided valley and its luxuriant foliage.

We were making a small turn, again paralleling the stream, when Jason urgently whispered, "Down! Down! Down!"

We instantly knelt down in the foliage while Jason and the trackers peered intently up the slope. There, peering down around a great tree, was a male mountain nyala with big horns. I couldn't tell how big, because the nyala was staring straight at me, and all I could see was the first curl.

Jason urgently whispered, "Get Ready!" And I got the shooting sticks in place. It was about a 100-yard shot, roughly 45 degrees uphill, but I would have to skim, and not hit, the edge of the tree in order to slip the .340 into the nyala's brisket and heart. The obvious challenge was to get the shot as close to the tree as possible but not touch it, lest I deflect the shot. One of the trackers put his knee under my left elbow, providing additional support. I had a good sight picture. Jason said, "Shoot." And I squeezed off the .340 Weatherby.

One of the few problems with a .340 Weatherby

is that between the recoil and muzzle blast, you lose your target for a fraction of a second.

I cranked another .340 into the chamber and caught the heart-wrenching sight of the nyala bolting along the slope, already 150 yards away. The nyala then suddenly disappeared, and Jason yelled, "He's down!" Whew!

Feeling my 59 years, I joined the jubilant crowd in the creek bottom, where the bull mountain nyala had fallen in 12 inches of ice-cold water. Jason and the trackers were beyone excited, and I didn't know how big a nyala had to be to elicit this sort of wild hoorahing and dancing about, but I had a feeling it must be really, really big.

It was. I looked at the wonderful lyre-shaped horns, and I realized that they were bigger than anything I'd ever seen. At right on 38 inches, these were among the largest taken in all of Ethiopia in many a year.

Posing for pictures wearing 10-inch tall boots in 12 inches of ice-cold water was not so trying an experience, as I would seldom have another trophy like this!

After skinning the nyala, arranging for the trackers to get a mule to pack out the meat, and hiking roughly two miles back down the trail to the Land Cruiser, we were still back at camp by noon-time. We hoped some of the monumental luck would hang around while we hunted Menelik's bushbuck, but we hiked and hiked to no avail.

Jason was in contact with Addis, and since the charter aircraft for the Omo was only available at certain times, we determined to take advantage of an aircraft availability, break camp, and go on to the Omo. We could return to Munessa for the bushbuck at a later time.

Returning to the sumptuous Sheraton, we flew the next morning to the Omo Valley in a chartered Caravan. The flight began over the farmland surrounding Addis Ababa, but soon the checkerboard pattern of the farmlands gave way to rugged mountainous country, slowly the terrain flattened, and then, below us, was the wide, flat green Omo Valley, a world heritage site. Situated on the Kenyan border, the Omo Valley looked like a set from *Out of Africa* and was simply beautiful.

The Ethiopian Rift Valley Safaris camp is a permanent one, with concrete bungalows and en suite baths, thatched roofs, well-tended walkways, a veranda overlooking the roiling, rushing Omo River, and a dining hall. The site is well shaded, and this is indeed welcome, as the Omo can be very hot.

The Omo is famed for its variety of antelope, including lesser kudu, northern Grant's gazelle, gerenuk, and tiang, as well as buffalo in some areas. Lesser kudus are usually hunted in the foothills, spotting them from ridges. They are creatures of heavy cover, but a few were in the riverine brush adjacent to the Omo camp.

We decided to cruise the brushy areas and see if we happened upon a lesser kudu. The odds weren't great, but what the heck!

We rolled along through the brush, or hiked, on old logging roads, spotting many of the beautiful rollers, bee-eaters, and go-away-birds. Jason was pleased to spot lion tracks, as lions had been hunted out by the natives for quite some time.

Lesser kudus are notoriously difficult, and when the time came, this was no different—an impossibly quick shot through a screen of thornbush. The .340 was true, however, and it was the lesser kudu bull of my fondest wishes. It was a heavy old battler, with worn-down tips, torn ears, and scars on its flanks. At 30 inches it wasn't the biggest lesser kudu in the book, but, oh boy, did it have character!

Returning to camp, we passed one of the many goat herds in the Omo, tended by little *totos*—10-year-old kids, each, however, with his fully automatic AK-47. Every male that can walk carried an AK-47, although some of the less wealthy

carried the older SKS carbines. This was somewhat unsettling, but fortunately everyone appeared very friendly.

We interspersed our Omo adventure with some great fishing in a lake near to camp. The Nile perch weren't biting, but the big, ugly African catfish were, and we soon had the bottom of the boat writhing and wriggling with dozens of indignant, struggling catfish. Jason tried to put them in a closed-off area under the seat, but there were simply too many in the boat, and putting one in allowed two others to escape to the general mass on the floor of the boat. Laughing, we kept a few for a tasty, crispy, catfish fry at dinner and gave the rest to the villagers.

Pam was clicking away happily at the wealth of animal and bird life—Bateleur eagles, rollers, kingfishers, storks, egrets, secretary birds in their myriads, beautiful sunrises and sunsets. On the road back to camp, we ran into flowering trees looking for all the world like Hawaiian plumeria, in shades of vibrant pink and yellow. More pictures!

We collected wonderful specimens of northern Grant's gazelles and Guenther's dik-diks and photographed gerenuk and endless tiangs. We were also able to get striking pictures as unseasonal rains cooled and cleaned the landscape, bringing colors into sharp contrast.

Returning to Addis Ababa after a full week in the Omo, we drove back to the Munessa concession for the elusive and notably uncooperative Menelik's bushbuck. The Menelik's bushbuck is only found in Ethiopia and is much darker than any

other bushbuck. This time Artemis smiled on us, and we got a dandy, gold-medal specimen with a snap-shot on the first afternoon.

Well . . . what could be better? The answer, in Ethiopia, is to take a few days and appreciate the history of this ancient land.

Ethiopia has a proud history of being Christian since the fall of Solomon's Temple, and it is a widely held belief that the Arc of the Covenant is jealously guarded to this day by Ethiopian monks.

Foremost among these ancient sites are Lalibella and Gondor, both famous. We chose, with the assistance of Jason, to visit Lalibella. Arrangements were made through the touring division of Ethiopian Rift Valley Safaris, including air tickets, a guide, a Land Cruiser, and hotel accommodations.

Suffice it to say that Lalibella is well worth seeing, but two days we thought to be ample. The churches are quite impressive and carved out of the living rock, but they are also very spread out for defensive purposes and are often only reached after a strenuous climb.

After Lalibella, we returned once more to the Sheraton. Changing our Lufthansa reservations to depart four days early was easily done, and we spent our last day shopping, checking the salting of the trophies, and having a last dinner with Jason.

On this trip, counting zeroing shots, I fired my trusty .340 Weatherby nine times, while Pam took over 5,000 digital images. I began to wonder who had the better of the deal, but overall it would be difficult to overstate just how well this hunt had gone. Every hunt can't be the "best." And, to be honest, this was an extremely expensive hunt, but it is hard to imagine any trip that could have been more enjoyable.

Rich Elliott, the booking agent, can be reached at ervs@shawneenet.com or 618-966-3563. His mailing address is:

**MR. RICH ELLIOTT**
Post Office Box 121A
Crossville, IL 62827

*Bob Keagy is Past-President of the GoldenGate Chapter of Safari Club International.*

## SOUTH AFRICA

 **DREAM HUNT**

### South African Horseback Hunt

JEFF ENGEL

Hunting by horseback in the African bush is truly a unique experience. On this trip we would be hunting with Ant's Nest Africa safaris, which is run by Anthony and Tessa Barber. Ant's Nest is located three hours north of Johannesburg and is located in the Waterburg region of the Northern Province, which is a malaria-free zone. Along with operating this one-of-a-kind hunting camp, Ant and Tessa's long-term plan is to reestablish the original African bush.

Anthony and many local farmers in the Waterburg area are increasingly relying on a new economic model for their livelihood. These farmers are reducing or eliminating their cattle herds and crops and letting the bush grow back to its original state. By allowing hunting on their property, it is more economically valuable than raising beef or wheat.

In this area, there are over 15 species of animals, including kudus, giraffes, zebras, leopards, wild cats, waterfowl, and many species of birds.

Anthony has spent his whole life in the South

African bush veld, and Tessa is originally from Kenya. Their love of nature is reflected in the exquisite craftsmanship and beauty of their accommodations as well as Ant's outstanding guiding skills.

A very special treat on this safari was hunting by horseback, and our specific animal that we would be going after was the blue wildebeest.

Aside from the peace and quiet and freeing yourself from roads, horseback riding in the bush has another benefit: it lets you get very close to animals. The animals typically did not seem to even notice us as we approached on horseback. After spending a good part of the morning riding, we came across a small herd of wildebeests. We dismounted the horses, and I drew my rifle from the scabbard. As the horses were led off, I set up my shooting sticks and prepared for a shot. In this situation, I would rely totally on Ant's ability to judge the size of the blue wildebeest, and I put my full concentration on the sight picture. After the shot, I was very fortunate to harvest a heavy bossed and wide-horned blue wildebeest.

At sundown at Ant's Nest, Anthony and Tess have a "sundowner." This is an event where they bring out chairs and drinks and a collapsible table, and we simply enjoy watching the sun setting below the horizon. It had been a wonderful day hunting in Africa. Although my legs were a bit saddle sore, it was a truly remarkable and enjoyable experience.

A couple tips if you go on this type of hunt. Do some riding back at home to get your body in "saddle condition." Also, it's quite helpful to practice shooting your rifle off of shooting sticks. I prefer shooting sticks made by Stoney Point.

Something I like to do during my practice sessions is to do a number of jumping jacks, enough to get my heart rate, pulse rate, and breathing up, then immediately go to the shooting sticks and take a shot. Being in this condition can help pre-

pare you for a potential shot you would have in the bush.

For information on hunting in South Africa, contact:

**ANT'S NEST**
Ant and Tessa Baber
Post Office Box 441
Vaalwater 0530 South Africa
Phone: +27 14 755 3584
www.waterberg.net

 **DREAM HUNT**

## One Shot Hunt Club South Africa

JACK HAGEN*

For many, an African safari remains as an unfulfilled dream to be realized when time and circumstances permit. To help ensure that hunters are welcome in Africa in the coming years, a group of international hunters and African outfitters has created a program for hunters to directly benefit local African communities. This group conducts its programs through two organizations—One Shot Hunt Club South Africa and the OSHC Foundation Inc.

The One Shot Hunt Club South Africa (OSHC SA) began in 2000 when several veterans of the One Shot Hunt Club of Wyoming decided that they wanted to start a similar club in South Africa. In May 2001, OSHC SA held its first three-day event at a game farm near Kimberly.

Ten teams of two shooters each competed in the event that included shooting competition, Bushman dancers, banquets, and an awards ceremony. The species hunted was springbok—an ani-

mal that is similar in both size and difficulty to hunt to the North American pronghorn.

Since that original event, competitions have been added for a one-shot bow hunt and a one-shot pistol hunt. Hunters from New Zealand, North America, and South Africa have participated in these annual events.

For the hunts, shooters are divided into teams of two hunters each. Each pair of hunters is accompanied by a PH who serves as the official timekeeper and scorer for the hunters as well as functioning as a guide. Once the hunt begins, team members alternate the right to hunt every 30 minutes. The objective for each hunter is to successfully kill a target animal with one shot. Misses or shots that wound animals and cannot be recovered without additional shots are counted as zero. An added challenge is that shooting can only be done offhand or using a natural support such as a tree or a rock. Shooting from vehicles or using nonnatural supports, such as shooting sticks, is not allowed. The only exception being that pistol shooters are allowed to use shooting sticks.

Scores for each team are based on the number of one-shot kills and the time taken by the team to complete its shots. The winning team is the one that has two one-shot kills in the shortest period of time. Fewer than half the teams have successfully killed two animals with one shot each.

Beginning in 2005, the OSHC SA moved its annual South African event to the Aventura Tshipise Resort northeast of Polokwane (formerly Pietersburg). In this new area, impalas are much more common than springboks, so the species hunted is impala.

Following the first OSHC SA event in 2001, several officers of the club had the occasion to visit a few community grade schools in the Kimberly area. The needs of the schoolchildren and the shortage of resources were dramatically obvious. Even though it was South Africa's winter, many of the children were without shoes, and many came to school hungry because their families couldn't afford to provide them with breakfast.

Wanting to return something to the country that had provided them with so many hunting opportunities over the years, the One Shot Club began a program to collect tennis shoes and funds for maize meal to be distributed to needy schoolchildren during the next year's event.

Conversations with school and government officials during the 2002 event indicated that most of the school systems had very few working computers available for teaching, textbooks were usually shared among several students, and students didn't have enough money to purchase such basic school supplies as pencils and paper.

The virtual nonexistence of computers available for teaching students was seen as a major impediment for these schools. The frustration felt by both the teachers and school officials caused by the lack of teaching computers was very evident.

Identification of these needs resulted in the club's deciding that support for needy South African schoolchildren was to be the primary mission of the club. Efforts were initiated to encourage the donations of computers and school supplies that could be given to the school systems.

Before the 2003 event, a number of organizations in the United States provided very generous donations of computers, software, textbooks, and school supplies that required 20 full pallets to ship. Federal Express further supported this effort by airfreighting the pallets of materials to Johannesburg at its own expense.

Following the 2003 event, officers of the club worked with the Educational Ministry of the Free State to maximize the utilization of computers, text-

One Shot Hunt Club

books, and school supplies within the school system. This effort eventually resulted in the creation of a computer-training center near Christiana. A local school provided the facility, the club provided the

computers, and a local resort funded the wiring and computer infrastructure.

In 2004, the club distributed another shipment that included computers, textbooks, school supplies, tennis shoes, and first-aid supplies as well as blankets and cornmeal.

In 2005, the club launched a new effort to donate programmable hearing aids to poor children with hearing impairment. As these hearing aids cost nearly $2,000 each in South Africa, few natives can afford them. This hearing aid program is continuing, thanks to the donations of additional hearing aids by a concerned individual and the support of a local hearing clinic.

Funding for the club's activities has been provided both by direct cash contributions and by donated hunts, services, and goods that are auctioned by the club. Most of the funds received by the club are used to purchase items—such as meals, blankets, and medical and school supplies—locally in Africa for distribution and to support the club's activities.

One of the newer programs of OSHC SA is to create partnerships with African outfitters and local communities to help market donated hunts. For these partnerships the outfitters donate their daily

fees, the community donates the trophy fees, and the club then sells the hunts. When a hunt is sold, all of the net receipts are transferred directly to the local community. Sales of hunts donated under this program have provided support to a village in Mozambique and to the Mpembeni Community in Zululand in South Africa.

OSHC SA's newest program is to work with its African members to arrange the distribution of 550 new wheelchairs that were donated by another charitable U.S.-based organization.

The club has registered nonprofit corporations in both South Africa and the United States. Both corporations have as their formal mission the providing of support to needy African schoolchildren and their communities.

The U.S.-registered corporation is used to receive funds, goods, or services that are donated by U.S.-based individuals and organizations. Because it is recognized by the IRS as a 501 (c) (3) organization, donations by U.S. individuals and corporations are fully tax deductible.

The South African corporation is recognized as a Section 21 corporation and serves a similar purpose for South African individuals and businesses donating funds, goods, or services. Additionally, the South African corporation provides an organization that can import donated goods duty-free—which is next to impossible for a foreign-chartered corporation.

Neither the club nor the foundation has any paid employees, and all of its officers and directors contribute both their time and travel expenses without either being paid or reimbursed.

For hunters who are planning to be in South Africa, participating in the one-shot event is a great way to contribute to the future of South Africa, meet others of similar interests, and broaden their contacts within South Africa. For those who do not wish to hunt but would like to participate in some of the activities of the event, there are options available, including tickets for attending one or both of the banquets, which include auctions of donated hunts, artwork, and many other items. Individuals and organizations who may wish to contribute to the U.S.-based foundation without participating in the activities of the annual event may do so by contacting any of the club's U.S. officers.

Anyone who is interested in participating in the activities of the club is invited to contact either the U.S. or the South African officers of the club. The addresses, telephone, fax, and email contact information for these officers are shown below. For a detailed schedule of future activities, listings of the current club and foundation directors, officers, and members, pictures from past events, newsletters, club sale and auction items, and an event registration form, see the club's Web site at www.oneshot-huntclubsa.com.

*United States:*
**HECTOR KITSCHA**
Custom Travel Ltd.
9415 West Forest Home, Suite 201
Hales Corners, WI 53130
Phone: 414-433-0089
Email: ctravel@execpc.com

*South Africa:*
**SANDY MCDONALD**
Post Office Box 11471
Bendor Park 0699 South Africa
Phone: +27 15 289-9288
Email: enquires@mcdonaldhunt.com

*\*Jack Hagen is the author of* The Zambezi Incident: An Adventure Novel. *He is on the Web at www .JackGHagen.com.*

# DREAM HUNT

## Cape Buffalo, a Most Dangerous Game

JEFF ENGEL

Of Africa's big five—the elephant, lion, leopard, rhino, and Cape buffalo—the Cape buffalo is considered by many to be the most dangerous to hunters. Found throughout East and South Africa, solitary or in herds of a thousand or more, they can charge, seemingly unprovoked, at any time, running up to 37 miles an hour with amazing vicious agility. Buffalo are grazers. They are found where there is a good supply of grass, water, and shade. I would again be hunting with Kolobe Safaris. Daniel du Toit operates a most impressive hunting camp. The accommodations are rustic thatched and natural stone chalets. After months of dialogue about Cape buffalo hunting, I was finally in Africa for the hunt.

I chose to hunt Cape buffalo with Kolobe Safaris because I knew Daniel was a competent and secure

professional hunter. It was very important for me to know that my backup rifle would be from somebody that I truly trust, perhaps even with my life.

After a prompt pickup from the Johannesburg airport, we drove north close to the Zimbabwe and Mozambique border. There Daniel had preseason scouted several herds of Cape buffalo. Several ani-

mals in the herd, Daniel told me, were true trophies.

The first morning of the hunt, I revered seeing another spectacular sunrise. The sunrises in Africa always seem dramatic, maybe because there is so much excitement in the air. For this hunt, I chose to take my favorite dangerous games caliber, a .416 Rigby. I have had tremendous luck with this particular cartridge, and I was confident in its proficiency. I had spent the previous six months shooting the rifle on shooting sticks back at home in Wisconsin, from ranges from 10 to 100 yards, and I felt very comfortable with it.

When people think of Africa, they often think of dense jungle or vast plains. Actually, Africa is extremely diverse. The area that we were hunting was brushy and relatively flat, with plenty of places for the buffalo to hide.

Daniel also explained to me that Cape buffalo live in all sorts of environments such as swamps, plains, and here in the thick, heavy bush that reminded me a bit of the scrub oak in Wisconsin.

The night before the hunt, Daniel and I watched and fed a crackling fire. This relaxed time together gave us a chance to get to know each other. Daniel explained to me that he would like to approach within 50 yards of the Cape buffalo.

The normal human reaction is to walk away from danger. We would be walking toward it. I asked Daniel what one of his favorite techniques for hunting the buffalo was. He explained, "You definitely want the wind in your face and move as slow as possible." He explained that we would be walking very slowly and glassing from time to time. He also cautioned that after the shot we would have to remain "calm and quiet." "Sometimes the herd moves out and sometimes the herd is aggressive. There is always a different scenario." These were interesting words to hear on the eve of my Cape buffalo hunt. I had a great deal of anticipation for tomorrow morning's hunt. I was ready.

Soon after we started walking in the thick bush, we found a rub, which looked very much like a whitetail rub back home. Daniel explained it was a bush where the buffalo had been rubbing their horns. He reminded me that we were hunting a one-ton animal that could kill us in the blink of an eye.

My senses were in overdrive, for I knew that in an instant we could face a charging one-ton mass of muscle and bone. If this happened, I would have one shot to stop him. Even with a shot that is "dead on," they are built like a fortress, which makes this a dangerous hunt, no matter how good you are.

As we walked along, we found a large hoof mark in the dry dirt. I said, "This is definitely not a whitetail deer track." Daniel just smiled. Cape buffalo have average eyesight and hearing but an excellent sense of smell. We constantly tested the wind, making sure it was always in our face.

We were walking into the bush, not knowing what to expect, looking for a good trophy bull that would have thick horns with a nice drop and heavy bosses that would run outward and downward well pass its ears. The ears, tip to tip, are typically 32 inches, so we were hoping to find a bull with the horns extended well beyond the ears.

We spent the entire day slowly walking through the bush, occasionally getting a glimpse at a Cape buffalo, but it appeared that all we were seeing were cows or a few small bulls. Being in the same habitat where Cape buffalo were created a sense and a feeling that I have never felt while hunting before.

As the sun began to set, Daniel suggested that we head out of the bush because it is no place to be toward evening when Cape buffalo are around. I readily agreed.

The next morning we were up early and back

"in the danger zone." After walking and glassing for several hours, we suddenly came upon a herd. We were extremely careful to be downwind because we did not want to spook this herd. A stampede is the last thing that you want to have happen.

As our early shadows fell to the ground, it seemed like the whole place was filled with mysterious shapes. Suddenly I saw an expression on Daniel's face, and he said, "There is a Cape buffalo, and he is only forty yards away!" We could not tell how many there were, but they seemed to be everywhere at this moment. We again instantly checked the wind to make sure it was in our favor. Daniel's calmness was reassuring because my pulse was off the charts. I think I had more adrenaline than blood in my veins at that moment as I prepared to take a shot.

As we studied the animals, looking for a good bull, I could not help reminding myself that these huge Cape buffalo are built like a veritable fortress—heavy horns and bones with overlapping ribs, making quartering shots more difficult.

The shot we were looking for was a broadside heart-lung shot directly into the front leg. Daniel whispered very calmly to me, "Look at the bull in the far right side of the herd." As I was looking, he smoothly and suddenly placed my shooting sticks

in front of me. I am doing everything I can to stay calm and steady myself for a shot of a lifetime.

At that moment, a smaller bull walked right in front of the bull Daniel suggested I shoot. As I stood there, a mere 20 yards away from the herd, I waited for the smaller bull to pass and immediately took my shot. As I stood such a short distance away from a huge bull Cape buffalo, I realized that I had never experienced such penetrating eyes of any animal or human being before.

The shot hit directly into the shoulder of the buffalo, and the whole herd took off in a dust storm. This is the most dangerous time of all, not knowing exactly how well the bull was hit, for sure. Bulls can stalk hunters and can come charging out of seemingly nowhere. Daniel assured my by saying it was a "very, very, good shot. It was a solid good hit on the shoulder and low."

After the shot, I quickly reloaded. As I looked at my hand, I could physically see it was trembling. I had just put a 400-grain bullet in the shoulder of this massive Cape buffalo, and it seemed like I could not reload my rifle magazine fast enough. I made sure my rifle was loaded to full capacity as we waited in silence. After about 10 minutes, we slowly started to penetrate the thick bush, and very soon we saw

our bull standing. Daniel said, "There he is. Take him." I launched one more .416 round at the buffalo. The bull barely flinched. Daniel said, "Shoot him again." Again I shot, for the third time. Then the bull disappeared. Daniel then said, "Let's get closer." I looked at him in almost disbelief, but we knew we had to follow up on the bull quickly.

As we moved forward, I again quickly loaded up my magazine and verified there was a live round in my chamber. Just then, we saw the bull standing broadside, and Daniel said, "Take him, just behind the shoulder." Before the word "shoulder" came out of Daniel's mouth, I took a shot, and the bull was down—this time for good. Daniel said, "GOOD! GOOD! He is down."

I again reloaded my rifle as we approached the downed buffalo. After a very, very cautious approach, the bull truly was down. We approached the bull's back end just to be careful, in case he would get up, but there was no movement. I touched him with the rifle barrel. He did not stir. Daniel grabbed my hand and shook it into overdrive.

I was in awe of this massive animal, both in body and in horns. The bull had a deep drop and tremendous character. He was exactly what I had in my mind's eye of a big-bossed, deep-dropped, wide-horned bull.

Daniel and I spent a great deal of time just looking at and appreciating this tremendous animal. I had never before hunted on such "high alert." My senses were at the absolute peak. I could not believe how this huge animal could absorb so many bullets from a .416. Every shot appeared to be well placed, but Daniel explained to me that these bulls could take an extreme amount of lead.

Daniel reassured me that the meat from this huge Cape buffalo would feed many village people, and the memory of this hunt is an experience that I will never forget.

For information on hunting in Africa with Kolobe Safaris, contact:

**KOLOBE SAFARIS**

Daniel du Toit, Professional Hunter and Outfitter

Minerwa, Roedtan, South Africa

Phone: +27 15 667 0533 (Main Lodge);

mobile: +27 83 280 7643 (Daniel du Toit)

www.kolobesafaris.co.za

## DREAM HUNT

### Kolobe Hunting Safari for Blue Wildebeest and Nyala

JEFF ENGEL

It was a long flight, but when I finally arrived at my final destination, Kolobe Safaris, located about 150 miles north of the Johannesburg airport, I knew that I was in hunter's heaven. I chose to return here after my Cape buffalo hunt where I was treated so well and saw so much game. This time my quest was for two very fascinating and unique animals, the blue wildebeest and the spectacular nyala.

Operated by Daniel du Toit, Kolobe Safaris is everything you can imagine when it comes to a comfortable and modern bush camp presented in a true African motif—stone walls and thatched roofs;

there are private chalets for the hunters along with complete running water and luxurious accommodations, especially for being out in the bush.

Another huge attraction to Kolobe Safaris is the wonderful food that is offered on a daily basis, as well as spending the evening circled around a campfire where stories are reminisced and plans are made for the next day's hunt, while in the distance lions roar and hyenas cackle.

The next morning we had a light breakfast and loaded up into a Land Rover with elevated seats behind the truck. It is enjoyable to ride in the

back of one of these trucks as you go through the bush and see the wide variety of wildlife—giraffes, zebras, gemsboks, bonteboks, impalas, warthogs, birds galore. There are over 900 species of birds in South Africa in all the colors of the rainbow.

Once we arrived at our location, we started out on foot, and almost immediately a warthog popped out the bushes. Seems appropriate as "Kolobe" means "warthog."

We started seeing sign of the blue wildebeest, which derives its name from the silvery blue sheen to its short-haired coat.

Daniel had done a great deal of preseason scouting and knew where a herd was located. We trekked through the bush, seeing increasingly more and more sign until, sure enough, there was a herd of blue wildebeests.

At this point, a crow-sized bird, the grey lourie, or as the locals call it, the "go-away" bird, began singing in a nearby tree. When he sees you coming, he begins squawking, "Go-away, go-away," which can tip off a herd. Fortunately he went away, and we pressed on.

As we carefully approached the herd, I readied my shooting sticks to get prepared for the shot. These animals are large, almost the size of an elk, and one thing I have learned is to truly rely and trust your Professional Hunter because I still have a hard time determining the size of an animal like the blue wildebeest as far as inches—I am so used to hunting deer.

After a very quick discussion, Daniel pointed out one specific bull on the right side of the herd. After some reassuring words, I carefully slipped the safety off my .300 Winchester magnum rifle and squeezed off a shot. The shot connected directly on the shoulder. The animal bolted away. Had it hit him?

We waited for a few minutes and approached slowly. The tracks were very identifiable; with a great blood trail, we quickly found the animal. To

both of our amazements, the bull only went about 40 yards.

I am always surprised how big and interesting these African animals look, especially when your hands are grasped around the horns. We spent some quality time paying respect to this outstanding animal. Daniel also reassured me that the meat would be used at one of our fine dinners. After radioing for some help from other trackers, we lifted the wildebeest into Daniel's Land Rover and headed back to camp, where we were greeted by a cheering throng of natives, who were eager for their share of the meat. What a wonderful way to start an African safari.

That night while sitting around the campfire, Daniel asked how I felt about driving about four hours north to try our luck for a big nyala. That night as I laid in my bed, staring at the thatched roof, I counted nyalas, not sheep, for a long time before I could slip into sleep.

The next morning Daniel's father Neil, who is a physician in South Africa, joined us for breakfast and wished us well on our hunt. The custom in Africa is to have a light breakfast, a large lunch, and a light dinner. We packed up the Land Rover and drove north, close to the Zimbabwe border. This country was very rolling with some mountain ranges bordering the horizon, reminding me of Wyoming.

The male nyala is a dark brown antelope, with white on the face and neck, vertical white stripes on the body, and tall horns that rise dramatically above its head. The female is reddish brown with clear striping. It is large, almost the size of an elk, and very wary.

As we started to walk in the bush, we soon began to see sign, then animals. The first nyala we saw was a small bull with horns maybe 12 inches, but it was great just to see their wonderful color markings up close. Their coats are sort of a slate gray. They have lateral lines down their sides, with white spots on their backsides, helping them blend into brushy thickets. Along the throat, the hair hangs down in a stately manner like a beard, and they have a wonderful white mask between the

eyes. Truly a magnificent-looking animal. And if that is not enough to make them special, they have golden yellow legs.

We walked through the bush for several hours, shapes of animals briefly flashing through the brush like ghosts. Daniel's keen eyes finally spotted a big bull nyala, but he soon disappeared into the brush. We quickly made a circle downwind, hoping to get a glimpse of him. As we approached a riverbed, we slowly walked to the edge, and sure enough, there were several nyalas walking in the dry river.

Suddenly the bull appeared less than 50 yards away. We could hardly believe our luck. There was a female nyala right behind the bull. She saw us and immediately lunged over a small bush. The bull, however, stood there for a moment. Luckily, my scope was set at its lowest power, and I slowly brought my rifle up and took a methodical and deliberate shot. Again, the bullet had reached its mark directly on the shoulder. As the bull nyala lunged forward, it was very evident he would not go very far.

After a very short walk, we found the beautiful animal. Great fortune had been with us today, and we were all extremely appreciative to harvest such a magnificent animal.

This big bull nyala was a real trophy-book animal; in fact, it was world-class, its horns measuring over 29 inches.

Teddy Roosevelt once said that "eventually all hunters become nature lovers." Every African sunset reminds me of this.

*See Section D for a special recipe.*

### KOLOBE SAFARIS

Daniel du Toit, Professional Hunter and Outfitter
Minerwa, Roedtan, South Africa
Phone: +27 15 667 0533 (Main Lodge);
mobile: +27 83 280 7643 (Daniel du Toit)
www.kolobesafaris.co.za

 ## FEATURED HUNT

## Hunting Africa with Dad

JEFF ENGEL

After 18 hours of travel, our plane was finally landing in Port Elizabeth, South Africa.

I have had the extreme fortune of hunting Africa many times and have had some memorable trips, but this trip was special, as my good friend Greg Heyerman and my father, Herb Engel, accompanied me. For both, this was their first African safari.

This would be a very special hunt for my father and me. As my first and greatest mentor, my father had taught me much about "the hunt" and about life from a very early age. He took me on my first hunt when I was just six. Now, half a century later, I would have the opportunity to give something back in the best way that I knew how.

My father chose to hunt two very challenging animals. The majestic kudu, an elk-sized antelope,

and the stately gemsbok, another large antelope with long, straight horns and a striking white face.

We arrived at camp late in the day. After spending so much time in the airplane seats, a flat, comfortable bed was a welcome change.

The next morning we met our host, Johan Dryer. I though Johan would be an excellent choice for a PH to take my father on his first African safari, as Johan is extremely patient, very knowledgeable,

and very bush-smart, and I felt his personality would blend in well with my father's.

Johan's main lodge has all the modern conveniences and a wide variety of tasty cuisine. Every dinner is prepared by a talented chef who gives you a chance to explore new foods unique to Africa.

At age six, my father taught me the difference between a mallard and a wood duck. Now, over five decades later, I was able to give something back to him, taking him to Africa and showing him the difference between a gemsbok and a kudu. The expression "full circle" comes to mind.

Early the next morning my father got his first taste of the African bush. The morning sunrise was nothing short of spectacular, as so many African sunrises seem to be. Our guide was Mike Foster, who was competent, friendly, and extremely professional. Game seemed everywhere, and we had a brief glimpse of a running gemsbok.

As the hours passed, we walked further and further into the bush, and my father was showing no signs of his 80 years. Even though I have hunted with him for my entire life and was aware of how

strong his willpower can be, I was still impressed by his walking mile after mile without a single complaint.

We would stop often to glass the distant hillsides. Kudus are generally difficult to spot in these bush areas because they blend in so well with the habitat. Eventually, we did spot a few, but they were quite far away, and it was too late in the day to begin a stalk.

The next morning we were back in the field at sunrise, greeted by wild zebras in the morning sun—only in Africa! Then it was off on foot once again. The morning temperature at first daylight was about 45°F. By 11:00 A.M., the temperature reached 75° to 80°. As we walked along, we saw a wide variety of wildlife including blesboks, impalas, and giraffes. Every time I see a giraffe, I smile, especially when they start to trot away, because it always seems like they run in slow motion.

We walked all day, once again in rough country. Although still quite determined, I could tell that the miles of hiking were beginning to take their toll on my father.

Shooting light was just starting to fade when Mike spotted several kudus across the canyon. There was an exceptional bull in the herd. From this point forward, we had to move very quickly. Fortunately, the wind was with us. And soon the bull was about 200 yards away, upwind and broadside—perfect.

After a little advice from Mike, my father got set to take his shot as I was filming the whole event for our television show. Through the view finder, I could visibly see the animal kick up his back heels at the impact. We knew my father's shot was well placed, but night was rapidly approaching. We reached the spot where the kudu had been hit. There was no blood. We began following kudu tracks, but now total darkness was upon us, and the African bush is not a good place to be in the dark.

Mike decided to use flashlights and keep looking. If we did not find the animal soon, we would have to wait until morning. After searching for about half an hour, my father was physically and

emotionally exhausted and beginning to have doubts. Out in front, Mike called out: "Over here, Herb, I have fresh blood." We stumbled over to Mike, in the dark, and were very pleased to see a significant blood trail. Soon we traced it to a magnificent bull kudu.

My father was ecstatic. Greg and I could not shake his hand enough times. This is one of those special moments in life that you will never, ever forget—like when you take your first whitetail buck.

That night at the dinner table several bottles of

wine lost their corks as we settled into the easy chairs, repeated the events of the hunt, and just stared into the fire, appreciating this wonderful moment in time.

The following morning we were back out in the bush, this time looking for a gemsbok, which has such a striking white face and horns. This time Johan Dryer himself would be the Professional Hunter for my father, as I followed with a camera. A huge part of the hunt to me is learning about culture and about the great variety of birds and plant life, and Johan is a walking encyclopedia about the local area.

After the arduous kudu hunt, my father's energy was renewed, and he was determined to continue even though his 80-year-old muscles were beginning to rebel.

After several hours of hard walking, Johan signaled that he had seen something. It turned out to be a leaping herd of impalas, something that has no counterpart in North America. It meant that we were now in gemsbok country, and Johan soon spotted a small herd.

We made sure that the wind was into our face and began a stalk. It lasted several hours through some country that would have been tough for a man half my father's age to travel through, but the occasional glimpse of a gemsbok kept him going.

Finally, we caught up with a herd. The nearest animal was about 600 yards away, much too far for a "for-sure shot." Suddenly the wind gave our scent away, and the herd was off. We would see no more gemsboks that day, and by nightfall, my father was exhausted. That night again we had a wonderful meal, complete with some delicious steaks from my father's kudu. What could be better?

The next day started off warmer than usual, and the heat was causing my father to tire much more quickly—until Johan located a nice herd of gemsboks with several large bulls. This stalk would

be one of our toughest so far. The terrain was rough and rocky. Between the hot sun and the necessity for speed in this challenging territory, it would be a true test of my father's willpower.

As we crested a small hill, we saw two nice gemsbok bulls about 200 yards away. The wind began to pick up, making the shot more difficult, but my father knew that his chance had finally come. Suddenly both bulls began to fight, shoving each other back and forth. Johan said, "Take the bull on the right when they stop." At that moment they stopped, and my father shot. My father was comfortable with the placement of the bullet, but both bulls disappeared into the brush without a trace.

Again, there was no blood, it was getting dark, and we were still unable to locate his gemsbok. After reviewing the shot on the video camera, it seemed like the shot placement was very good, but there was no blood and there was no gemsbok. Now we had no choice but to head back to camp. My father was deeply concerned about not finding his animal. He spoke very little that evening and retired to bed early, in a very somber mood.

At daybreak, we were back in the field with additional trackers. We had eight men, and we spread out across various canyons and walked up and down, searching. After about an hour, to my surprise right in front of me lay a tremendous bull gemsbok, down for the count. For some reason, I happened to be the one to stumble on his trophy. I was carrying a rifle, and I was so overjoyed to find the bull that I took a shot into the air as a signal for all to know that our search was over.

As exhausted as my father was, he could not wait to come over and see his gemsbok for himself. It was very emotional for him. First, to find out that he had made a good shot, then that the animal was down for good, and then that I had found his gemsbok. The whole hunt had just come together at that moment.

Will Rogers once said, "I have known many worries in my life, and few have come to pass." Well, today there would be no worries. I will never forget the expression on my father's face as he approached his bull.

It almost seemed poetic that after all the years

my father had spent with me as a mentor and teaching me the ways of the woods and how to be a good and ethical hunter that I would be the one to find his gemsbok.

I can truly remember that at age six when I was invited by my father to join him in a duck blind I carried a Daisy air gun, and my father had me treat the gun as if it were a loaded 12-gauge shotgun. At that moment, I became a hunter. On this, we had journeyed full circle as I got to make him a successful African hunter.

**HUNT AFRICA WITH JOHAN DRYER**
Post Office Box 519
Grahamstown 6140 South Africa
Phone: +27 46 622 3791; fax: +27 46 622 3791
www.hunt-africa.net/geninfo.html

## TANZANIA

 **DREAM HUNT**

### Old-Fashioned Walking Safaris in the Selious Game Reserve

RICHARD BONHAM*

The "safari" for many conjures up images of long lines of porters trekking through deep jungle. Well, that kind of safari is actually pretty rare in these hi-tech days, but there is at least one place where you can take an old-fashioned walking safari. These safaris are designed for the "hunting purist" who wishes not only to experience the excitement of the buffalo hunt but also to experience the ad-

venture of a porter-supported walking safari in one of the last great wilderness areas left in the world, the Selous Game Reserve in southern Tanzania. Fair chase at its best . . . and often a lot of hard work.

During the hunts, which can be on 7-, 14-, or 21-day licenses, no time is spent in a vehicle; for the most part, ground is covered that is not accessible by vehicle.

Our lightweight camp is carried by usually 30 porters; in addition, we take cooks, waiters, a skinner, and a tracker. The camp is basic but comfortable, with hot showers available and a "short drop loo."

Hunting with a retinue of porters means that we can move camp to where the game is. In a seven-day hunt we would probably move it twice. The camp is usually set up on the banks of the Rufiji River, which also gives the opportunity for some very good tiger fish fishing. Again, a challenge and a lot of fun on the fly.

The hunting begins at dawn after a light breakfast. We leave the base camp with two porters who carry a picnic lunch and water. Sometimes we may

move slowly along dry sand rivers, hoping to come upon a lone bull on the edge of a riverside thicket, or maybe walk up into the hill country, looking for the spoor of a herd that has watered and is returning to the grazing area. On picking up fresh tracks, we follow them up, never knowing where they will lead us and how long we will be on the trail. Sometimes it is all day, never to catch up; other times,

when luck is in, within minutes a tick bird will jump-start the adrenalin as it alerts us we are on them.

As we walk and track, the hunt leads us into many surprises, sometimes welcome, sometimes not. We may find ourselves surrounded by an agitated herd of cow and calf elephants, or a hippo torpedoes out of a water hole toward us. Or maybe as we rest up in the shade of a tree, sipping a cup of freshly brewed tea, a pack of wild dogs saunters by, followed by their pups as bee-eaters hover overhead.

Providing meat for the porters and ourselves is an integral part of the hunt, and if the buffalo are playing hard to get, we look for impalas, harte-beests, or wildebeests to take back to camp.

This safari is not for the trophy hunter. We walk every inch of the way, which means we do not cover the ground most vehicle-based hunts are able to do, and so we do not have the opportunity to look over as many animals. Although, having said that, we have never drawn a blank and have taken respect-able trophies in the 43- to 45-inch class. The essence is in the fair chase of a mature bull, not the trophy.

You have to be reasonably fit to undertake these safaris, as some days you may walk up to eight hours. But that first cold drink back at camp will taste an awful lot better when you do get there, tired, exhausted, maybe outwitted, but, most im-portant, happy!

*Richard Bonham, of Richard Bonham Safaris, is an outfitter who organizes and leads safaris in Kenya and Tanzania. For more information, see www.richard bonhamsafaris.com.*

## ZIMBABWE

 **DREAM HUNT**

### The Elephant Question

IVAN CARTER*

Africa is a huge place—some 11.6 million square miles. The United States, which covers 3.7 mil-lion square mile, is about three-tenths the size of Africa.

It is an enormous and very diverse continent. At the turn of the last century, there was an estimated population of 1 million-plus elephants inhabiting an area covering almost 30% of the continent south of the Sahara. Today the estimated population is a little less than half of that in an area covering less than 10% of the continent. The 10% covers areas unwanted by humans. Therefore, they are marginal habitats even for elephants.

In Zimbabwe, where 500 bull permits are available per annum, the country has an elephant population of around 85,000 breeding at a rate of 4% per year, adding 3,400 every year, half of which are cows.

The argument that hunting is a tool toward population-control holds is a footnote. What elephant hunting does do is generate a source of income for the government, making elephants become an asset that will be cared for and supported.

Again using Zimbabwe as an example, where a healthy population would be in the region of 25,000, today there exist perhaps as many as 85,000—statistics show that up to 15% of the trees in an area with more than 5 elephants per square mile are destroyed each year. Areas such as Hwange National Park in Zimbabwe, Chobe Game Reserve in Botswana, and Luangwa Valley in Zambia are all showing many signs of becoming overrun by elephants. One can ask: Why hasn't this happened in the past? The answer is simple. Owing to their ability to cover vast distances, elephants were far more mobile as a population than they are today; so they would move out of an area. Nowadays they are enclosed by the hidden fences of human habitation and farming areas. The consequences for the places where they reside are dramatic.

In the 1960s the Tsavo Game Reserve in Kenya experienced an overpopulation of elephants. Aerial photographs showed a dustbowl with tree trunks scattered like matchsticks, the elephants dying along with all the other game. Today, over 50 years later, the area is just beginning to recover.

"It's nature—let it be," cries the "green movement"; but the fact is, we cannot. In former times the elephants would have migrated out of the area to less populated regions, but they are unable to do

so today because of development and explosive human population growth.

Let's step away from hunting for a moment and look at parks like the Tsavo, Amboselli, Chobe, or Kruger. Undoubtedly these are parks where the elephant populations are huge drawing cards in attracting high-end tourists. So even without harvesting an elephant, they have a huge value, as they keep the tourist dollars flowing.

If one were to take a close look at the Chobe River, one would find a swath of destruction and erosion where the bush is almost nonexistent. Just 15 years ago this region had the reputation of having the largest variety of mammals seen on game drives. Today the selection is poor. For example, bushbuck are no longer common, their habitat having been destroyed. Sable numbers have diminished, since they are unable to make the long commute between water and food. The only species doing well is the elephant. When their numbers diminish owing to starvation, as happened in the Tsavo National Park in the 1970s, and the Chobe National Park, it's a slow 25-year recovery path. In the meanwhile, who will pay the bills? In a country where cattle play an important role in the lives of villagers, there will be enormous pressure to allow farming operations to take place in areas that no longer produce tourist dollars. Elephants will then be shot off for no profit, and poaching will blossom.

The tragedy is that there are no easy answers. Even if Zimbabwe were to commit to reducing the elephant population, to have any significant effect, numbers would have to be reduced by some 30,000. This translates to 82 elephants per day for a full year, with a conservative estimate of 41 tons of meat and hide to process daily.

Sport hunters give an elephant value, giving the government departments the resources they need to manage this asset through population control. Reducing numbers through hunting produces a healthier remaining population, a cheap protein source to an undernourished part of the population, and dollar value on the hides and ivory.

In closing, let me say that being in close proximity to wild elephants is something that leaves people in awe and moved at a very deep level. I have spent much of my life close to these magnificent animals. Hunting and viewing them is a true

privilege. If we can treat hunting elephants with the respect it deserves, and if we manage wild elephant populations correctly, they will remain in great numbers for our children's children.

*Ivan Carter was born in Zimbabwe and has been guiding since 1989. He is considered one of Africa's best guides and wildlife photographers. For more information, see http://ivancarter.com/index.html.*

# Europe

## THE ALLURE OF HUNTING IN EUROPE

 **DREAM HUNT**

### Hunting in Europe

TOM DUM*

While serving in the 10th Infantry Mountain Division in Germany (as a private first class) in 1956–1958, I became fascinated by the people and culture of Europe, as well as wildlife that were new to me as someone who grew up in Ohio. Later, I returned to Europe to hunt beginning in 1986 in Bulgaria, when it was a Communist country. Since then I have hunted in 10 countries in Europe and feel drawn to return again and again.

What has captivated me is the depth of the hunting tradition still embedded in European countries. The traditions include the wearing of green hunting clothes, the breaking of a branch from the tree the deer was feeding from and placing it in the stag's mouth, and the placing of a twig from the tree in the hunter's cap. An exceptionally memorable moment was when I was required to stand in the rain in Switzerland while a final eulogy for fallen animals was read to the accompaniment of hunting horns. My Swiss friend and hunting companion said they had been doing this for hundreds of years and expected to continue doing this for 100 more years. (A DVD of the horn music is *Hunting Fanfares and Signals* #31 0164-2-131, by Multi Sonic, which has hunting compositions from the Duke of Krumlov's hunts in 1794.) I think that in the end the traditional ceremony brings a deeper satisfaction to the hunting experience.

A look at the German hunting license requirements shows that knowledge of all the facets of this tradition is as important as knowing about guns and game. The depth of the hunting tests and a practical field exam coupled with gun-range tests certainly show a knowledge of hunting.

There is another major difference between Europe and the United States, and that is in the pricing of the hunt. In America there is one price covering everything, and if you don't get any game, that is too bad. I have been on two great pack-in elk hunts in this country, and all I got was some nice trout from fishing in the streams. In Europe, first you pay for the cost of the hunt: the guide, usually an interpreter, food, lodging, license, and transportation. Then you pay for the game according to the size of the trophy or, with small animals, the number shot.

For example, I made a chamois hunt in Slovenia and was unsuccessful. As a result, my cost was very low. I noticed that the Diana Group is now giving one price at the Safari Club Convention, but hunts are still available for under $5,000. Still, keep in mind that this varies from country to country (Spain is very high) and different game. For example, an English driven partridge hunt is not cheap.

The next benefit I found was that there are interesting things to do and see when you are not hunting. This can be a great advantage to a non-hunting spouse or friend. The typical hunt in Europe starts at dawn and then again in the late afternoon, so there is time for castle viewing or shopping. Also, the places you may be staying can be fascinating. For example, once in the Czech Republic two Italian hunters and I had the complete run of a huge castle with all its art and gun rooms.

What do you hunt? The red stag is considered the king of European animals. There are three species: the European, the Spanish and the Scottish. The other deer are the roe and the fallow deer. The wild boar has high prestige in Germany and over most of Europe. In Spain and a few related countries, there are the ibex and the chamois of the mountains. Most American small game are found in Europe. Pheasant and partridge are hunted in driven hunts. These can be very formal hunts involving lots of people—game beaters and much shooting.

The most unique European game bird is the capercaillie, the largest grouse in the world, jet black with a red topknot. It is hunted in Scandinavia, Russia, and Austria. When you hunt them in the spring, the male bird is crowing. When it stops, you stop, like children playing "freeze." The bird cannot see or hear you approaching when it is calling, so that is the only time you can approach them.

In the fall, you find capercaillie feeding near the gravel roads as they are looking for grit. Both the capercaillie and the black cock (another grouse) can be shot with both rifle and shotgun. In Sweden, after missing a black cock with my shotgun, I shot one with a rifle at 150 yards after he settled in a tall pine tree.

Generally, the old Eastern bloc countries have cheaper hunts. Hunting in Germany is tight because there are few outfitters for foreign guests. Gun problems and licenses will be handled by your outfitter. But there are several things I have learned. In Germany, you must register your gun as soon as you enter the country and also when you leave. There is no charge for this, and it can be done in 15 minutes with the customs officer at the airport. But you must take your gun to the U.S. Customs Office and get a tag for it before you get on your airplane, so there will be no question about its ownership. In England, Scotland, and Ireland, you may want to use your gamekeeper's gun, as in these countries there is more red tape.

You may also want to visit one of the many gun manufacturers centered in Europe, such as Ferlach in Austria, Suhl in Germany, Liege in Belgium or London, Sako in Finland, or the many fine shotgun makers in Italy. You can order a gun or even purchase a gun; when you get home, your local gun dealer can do the paperwork and import it. This is really not as difficult as it sounds, as there is just one form that the Bureau of Alcohol, Tobacco, and Firearms (BATF) must approve before the gun clears customs. However, currently the euro is at an all-time high, and you may not save much money. The small gun makers such as in Ferlach are open for a visit, and a letter ahead of time to the larger manufacturers such as Browning or Merkel is recommended.

How do you find European outfitters? Many of them are at the Safari Club International Convention each year. Don Causey's Hunting Report (www.hunt

ingreport.com) is a good place to find a rundown on world outfitters. The Diana Group (www.diana.dlk), which is based in Denmark, is one of the largest and oldest outfitters in Europe. They have a most beautiful catalog that will most certainly get your taste for a European hunt aroused. The Kettner Group of Cologne, Germany (jagdreisen@kettnre,de) has recently been purchased by Sigarms, and they offer hunts all over Europe and are one of the few to offer them in Germany. I have hunted with both groups and have been well pleased. I also recommend Robert Kern's The Hunting Consortium (email: hunt@huntcon.com). He has a well-known reputation, as he originally arranged hunts for our army in Germany.

Finally, I recommend James McCloskey's book on actual hunts made in Germany, *Gunning Adventurers in Germany*, and a beautiful book titled *Game and Hunting*, by Kurt G. Bluchel, on the history of European hunting, which is still available on the Internet.

*Tom Dum is a past president of the Golden Gate Chapter of Safari Club International and has written for the SCI monthly newspaper* Safari Times.

## BELGIUM

## HERITAGE DESTINATION

### Honoring Saint Hubert

JAMES SWAN

In France and Belgium, each fall special ceremonies and festivities are held to honor Saint Hubert, the patron saint of hunting. The epicenter of his venera-

tion is the town of Saint-Hubert in Belgium, not far from the Ardennes forest. The annual colorful festivities draw crowds of 10,000 or more. Elsewhere in Europe, schools are closed on Saint Hubert's Day, November 3, as churches conduct the Mass of Saint Hubert, where hunters, their dogs, and falcons are brought into the church for blessings.

The tradition of Saint Hubert offers a way to make a strong connection between hunting, religion, and ethics. Many, perhaps most, hunters, let alone the general public, have not heard of Saint Hubert, so some background.

### THE STORY OF SAINT HUBERT

Hubert, the eldest son of Bertrans, duke of Aquitaine, was born in A.D. 638. He became a prince in the House of Aquitaine in France. Hubert enjoyed the "good life" of nobility, but most of all, he loved hunting. Legend has it that one Good Friday, when he should have been in church, Hubert galloped off on horseback to hunt deer. His hounds cornered a large stag. As Hubert approached, suddenly he had a vision of a glowing crucifix appearing over the deer's head. A voice spoke to him: "Hubert, unless thou turnest to the Lord, and leadest a holy life, thou shalt quickly go to hell."

Hubert climbed down off his horse, then begged forgiveness. The voice instructed him to seek guidance from Lambert, bishop of Maastricht. Not long after seeking out the bishop, Hubert's wife died. He soon entered the Abbey of Staveleot and became a priest.

Lambert advised Hubert to make a pilgrimage to Rome in A.D. 705. During Hubert's absence, Lambert was murdered. Hubert was selected by the pope to succeed his mentor as bishop. Later Hubert built St. Peter's Cathedral in Liege, Belgium, on the spot where Lambert had died, and he in turn became the patron of the city.

Hubert applied his passion to his faith, establishing Christianity in large sections of the Ardennes forest of Belgium, stretching from Meuse to the Rhine. He preached to many of the hunters of the forest and is said to have hunted and kept dogs. Rabies was a problem for those who owned dogs, but Hubert is said not only to have been protected from the deadly disease but to have been blessed with miraculous powers to heal rabies, aided by a special white and gold silk stole that he said was given to him by the Blessed Virgin Mary. He also had a golden key, which was reputed to be a healing amulet.

Hubert died quietly on A.D. May 30, 727, with the words, "Our father, who art in heaven . . ." on his lips. In 1744 he was canonized as a saint—the patron saint of hunting and butchers.

First buried in Luttich, Hubert's body was later moved to the Andain monastery in the Ardennes, which today is known as Saint-Hubert's Abbey. The location of the abbey, and the Belgian town of Saint-Hubert, is supposed to be close to where Hubert saw the stag and had his vision with the cross between the stag's antlers.

Each November 3, Saint Hubert's Day, all across France, Luxembourg, and Belgium, thousands of people attend special masses and celebrations to honor Saint Hubert. During these festivities, special blessings are said for the safety and success of hunters and the health of their animals—dogs are blessed for protection from diseases like rabies—and special religious music written for hunting horns is performed (*Grande Mess de Saint Hubert*). In certain parts of Europe the deer hunting season is suspended on November 3 to honor Saint Hubert.

The physical center of devotion to Saint Hubert today remains the town of Saint-Hubert in Belgium, where thousands of people gather every November 3. To many European hunters, making the pilgrimage to Saint-Hubert on Saint Hubert's Day is like a Muslim making a pilgrimage to Mecca, a Jew praying at the Wailing Wall, or a Christian visiting Jerusalem at Easter.

The Ardennes forest remains a popular hunting ground for stags, roe deer, hinds, and wild boars.

**TOURIST INFORMATION OFFICE**
rue Saint Gilles, 12
B-6870 Saint-Hubert
Phone: +32 61 61 30 10; fax: +32 61 61 54 44
Email: rsi.Saint-Hubert@swing.be
www.saint-hubert-tourisme.be

## FINLAND

# HERITAGE DESTINATIONS

## The Hunting Museum of Finland

The museum celebrates a 10,000-year-old Finnish hunting tradition, from the Stone Age to the present. Clothing, weapons, methods of hunting, and anthropological relics like hunting amulets are featured. There is also a library and collection of photo archives. Open Tuesday–Friday, 9:00 A.M. to 5:00 P.M.; Saturday and Sunday, 10:00 A.M. to 6:00 P.M. Closed in January.

**THE HUNTING MUSEUM OF FINLAND**
Tehtaankatu 23 A
11910 Riihimäki, Finland
Phone: 358-19-722-293; fax: 358-19-719-378
www.metsastysmuseo.com/hunting.htm

## FRANCE

## HERITAGE DESTINATIONS

### Musee de la Chasse et de la Nature

Collections of weapons, trophy mounts, and paintings by Peter Paul Rubens, Jan Brueghel de Velours, Alexandre-François Desportes, Jean-Baptiste-Siméon Chardin, Jean-Baptiste Oudry, and others. Open afternoons; closed Mondays and holidays.

**MUSÉE DE LA CHASSE ET DE LA NATURE**
60, rue des Archives, 3rd Arrondissement
Paris, France
Phone: +33 01 53 01 92 40

## ICELAND

## DREAM HUNT

### Hunting Geese Under the Northern Lights

Hunters are used to rising in early morning blackness and waiting for the sun to wake up. Late afternoon hunts conclude with the sun setting as you return home in darkness.

Imagine yourself in a blind in the early morning, waiting for geese to come in, and the sky is illuminated by brilliant cascading, shimmering showers of green, blue, and yellow clouds, so vivid that you can see the birds flying like spirits on the wind. Or ending up your day with the path back home illuminated by shimmering waves of the aurora borealis. That's goose hunting in Iceland; and with a season that runs from August through March, you can be sure that the later you come here to hunt, the more the northern lights will be your illumination in the skies more than the sun.

Such magical sights make it easy to understand why there are many myths and legends about the northern lights being spirits or ghosts. In Scotland and Denmark, they are sometimes referred to as "the Merry Dancers." Some American Indians see the aurora borealis as bonfires created by the gods to shed light on people during long winter months.

Regardless of how you perceive them, one of the best places in the world to hunt geese is under the northern lights in Iceland.

This volcanic island in the North Atlantic is just south of the Arctic Circle. It was uninhabited when discovered by adventurous sailors from Scandinavia and Ireland in the ninth and tenth centuries A.D. It's name comes from 10% of the island being glaciated.

Iceland today is the most sparsely populated country in Europe. Almost four-fifths of the country is uninhabited. In January 2006 Iceland's total population was 300,000 people, of which around 180,000 lived in the capital Reykjavik and in nearby coastal areas.

Blessed with nutrient-rich ocean waters, the only land mammal on Iceland originally was the Arctic fox, which thrived on the abundant bird life.

In Iceland you can hunt species that you may not hunt anyplace else—reindeer; pinkfoot, greylag, and barnacle geese; sea birds—puffins and guillemots; and seals; as well as more conventional Arctic fare like ptarmigan and ducks.

There is no limit on greylag, pinkfooted, and barnacle geese. Hunters sometimes bag as many as 30 geese per person, per day.

A five-day waterfowl trip includes at least three days of hunting. This is a maritime climate. Temperatures may get down to freezing, but they will rise to 40° to even 60°F during the day. Rain gear is essential.

While in Iceland, don't forget to enjoy bathing in the natural hot springs. The island sits on top of a volcanic hotspot, which also provides geothermal power and heat for many homes and geysers for entertainment.

*Permits/Seasons.* The outfitter will need a copy of your resident country hunting license four to five weeks prior to your scheduled arrival. They will also need a document proving that you are the legal owner of the gun/guns you intend to bring to Iceland. These documents will enable the outfitter to obtain a weapon license and a hunting license for Iceland.

Goose hunting season is from August 20 until March 15. The best period is September 10 to October 20. The northern lights are out then. In early season, geese are hunted in the mountains. As the season progresses, the hunting moves down to the coast.

There are only 300 wild reindeer hunting licenses issued yearly. Most are allocated to local hunters. Only a limited number of permits are issued for foreign reindeer hunters each year. The season is from August 1 to September 15.

They also offer outstanding ptarmigan hunting. A good shot on a good day may bag 50 per day. The season is from October 15 until December.

*Travel Tip.* Icelandair (www.icelandair.com) offers very reasonable package deals, for example, starting at $724 (per person/double occupancy) for round-trip air, two nights hotel in Reykjavik, Scandinavian buffet breakfast every morning, from San Francisco. Iceland is a great place to enjoy a hunt on a trip to and from Europe. You can stop over seven days in Iceland with no additional airfare charge. For more general information, consult Iceland Tourism at www.iceland.is.

Contacts:

**ICELANDIC HUNTING CLUB**
Bjorn Birgisson, Manager
Almont 3
270 Mosfellsbaer Iceland
Mobile: +354 894 3095; fax: +364 566 6924
www.huntingiceland.com

**LAX-Á ANGLING CLUB**

Vatnsendablettur 181

203 Kopavogur, Iceland

Phone: +354 557 6100; fax: +354 557 6108

www.randburg.com/is/fishing

## NORWAY

 DREAM HUNT

## The Red Deer of the West Coast of Norway

KÅRE VIDAR PEDERSEN*

You will never, ever see the morning stars so bright as when you start the ATV and drive up the mountain at five o'clock in the morning. Down by the old farm at sea level, in the famous Nerøyf-

jorden, the deepest and most narrow fjord in Norway, the temperature is 36° or 37°F. But the higher we drive, the colder it gets, and when parking the quarter bike at the highest-placed old cabin, a northern wind is fairly cold. Ice cold, so to say!

But don't worry, you will soon enough be sweating when we have to take a two-hour hike to enter the valley where the red deer prefer to graze at this time of year. Some stags were roaring last night—I could hear them through my bedroom window—but it is still at least a week or two early before the rut will start.

Because of the extremely hot fall so far, most of the red deer prefer to stay high up in the mountains until the snow comes. The reason is partly to avoid the nasty midges and ticks that trouble the deer until their thick winter coat is almost finished growing.

Parking the quarter bike at about 2,500 feet above the sea, another stag is irritated by our presence, or maybe he suspects us to be another stag who is challenging his position. But it is too dark to discover him, even with our binoculars, and he has all the advantage he needs to spot us, so we will not waste any time on that one.

Two more hours and a lot of walking later, we stop to drop our backpacks and rest our legs, while leaning on a big rock and trying to spot some reds even higher up. We are at about 3,300-feet elevation and should be able to see at least a few deer as soon as the light is good enough.

Five minutes later, we are looking at 15 red deer grassing on the other side of the valley— mostly hinds and calves, but at least two nice 8-pointers and one really good "royal stag" with 12 points in his high, wide antlers.

The distance to the closest stag is about 550 yards, so it is necessary to do some climbing to get a clean, safe shot. It is not an easy climb, not a nice Sunday walk, but I can guarantee you that you will never, ever forget this hunt, even if you do not get a deer in the end.

This area is one of the most beautiful and spectacular places in the whole of Norway. As a matter of fact, last year this community was listed on the list of UNESCO's World Heritage Sites. You will be astonished by the dark seawater, the green valleys, and the 6,000-feet-high peaks that surround this very special fjord. During the hunt, often the peaks get a dressing with pure, white snow on the top, which makes it even more beautiful.

*Permits/Seasons.* The outfitter will need a copy of your resident country hunting license at least one month ahead of your arrival. There are no problems bringing your own gun to Norway; just make sure that you have the necessary papers with you, that can swear to the authority that this is your gun, and that you have a legal purpose to bring it with you.

The red deer season in Norway is from September 10 until November 15. Usually the deer stay high up in the mountains in the beginning; then during October, they move closer to sea level. This means that for the first weeks of the hunting season usually you have to do a lot of walking and climbing to get close to them. Later on you will be able to wait for the deer at some special places where they are feeding in the early mornings and late evenings. During the daytime there will be some driven hunts arranged, where hopefully you will be able to shoot the deer from a stand.

The population of red deer in Norway is presently about 150,000, from which something like 35,000 are shot every year. For more information, see www.testjeger.no or www.jaktogfiskeformidling.no.

**JOHNNY EKRA, PROFESSIONAL HUNTER**
Mobile: 0047 95863230

**KÅRE VIDAR PEDERSEN, PH**
Mobile: 0047 93245326

*Kåre Vidar Pedersen is a Professional Hunter and outdoor writer living in Norway.*

## HERITAGE DESTINATIONS

### Saami Museum—Samiid Vuork a-D'avivrat

The Saami Museum is full of exhibits of modern and prehistoric native culture including hunting methods. The museum has a collection of more than 4,500 items relating to reindeer herding, agriculture, fishing, handicraft, and religion from Saami areas in Norway, Sweden, Finland, and Russia.

The open-air section consists of traditional buildings from various Saami settlements and the remains of a system of hunting pits for wild reindeer. Research indicates that the system of hunting pits was used from 2,900 to 800 B.C.

By reservation, the museum allows for overnight stays in *lavvo* (teepee-like tents) and earth huts on the grounds.

The site on which the museum stands is called "Stáluguolbba," named after a Saami folktale that recounts a fight between "Stállu," a giant, and a Saami man, Beskán, in this area.

**DE SAMISKE SAMLINGER**

Postboks 143

9735 Karasjok, Norway

Phone: 78 46 99 50; fax: 78 46 99 55

Email: svd@trollnet.no

www.samimuseum.com/friluftsmuseet/open-air-museum.html

---

## SPAIN

---

 **DREAM HUNT**

---

## Hunting the Mountains of Spain

BOB KEAGY*

For my wife Pam and myself, this was our fourth Spanish hunt, and it was purchased at the Greater Bay Area SCI Fundraiser two years ago. It was our third hunt with Giuseppe Carrizosa, whom I very highly recommend (Giuseppe@giuseppecarrizosa.com), and we were going to hunt Beceite ibex, Cantabrian chamois, and free-range mouflon.

Spain is a unique destination for hunters. Hunted for over 4,000 years, Spain has managed its game populations well, and for the last 20 years, King Juan Carlos (an active sheep hunter—he recently shot a monster Marco Polo!) has insured that the Spanish game management programs are very professionally run and well funded.

Spain boasts that it now has more game animals than Alaska! (True? Maybe!) There is, however, no other country in the world, to my knowledge, with an active mountain hunter as king!

Anyway, we landed in Madrid and transferred to the five-star Palace hotel, which, oddly enough, looks a good deal like the Palace in San Francisco, with even a "garden court." When checking in, the Palace will keep your rifle in safe keeping, issuing you a receipt.

(For this trip, I took a .257 Weatherby Crown Grade, with a Schmidt U Bender 3-12 Illuminated scope, but I popped off the fancy Crown Grade stock and used a Weatherby camo/fiberglass stock. I used .257 Weatherby 115-grain Barnes factory ammo.)

I always find it annoying when I read those "I-came-I-saw-I-shot-I-left" articles in the hunting magazines. Spain/Madrid has wonderful museums, great historical sites, fabulous, fabulous restaurants, superb wines, and friendly people. Anyone who doesn't sample these charms to enhance the overall experience of the hunt/trip is simply shorting themselves.

After four days of sightseeing, we were picked up by our guide, Giuseppe, and we drove to Huesca to begin our hunt for Beceite ibex, arriving at one of Spain's "paradors," or castles, restored by the Spanish government and run as luxury hotels.

It was still dark and starry when we left the next morning for the Beceite National Reserve, winding up a circuitous mountain road. We were met by two game wardens who had been spotting the Beceite ibex. (Imagine a U.S. game warden helping to spot! Ha!)

We drove up and up a narrow winding road, passing through multiple locked gates as we approached the high pastures where the big ibex were. We passed several pretty decent ibex as we chugged up the mountain. Coming to a wooded area just under the peak, the game wardens pulled over, and we stopped. Opening the doors quietly and "shushing" each other, we gathered our gear and began to walk. We went about 300 yards off the road, through to the edge of the woods. There we could overlook a broad alpine meadow.

As the morning mists rose, we could see about 20 ibex, busily grazing in the rich grass. Lying on our stomachs, and sliding forward, I was told that the big one wasn't there—and to wait.

Soon more ibex magically drifted out of the woods and began grazing in the mists. When the big one came out, he was with two other big male ibex, but he was noticeably bigger.

It used to be that there weren't medal fees on Giuseppe's hunts, but recently he's had to pass along a surcharge on ibex over approximately silver-medal class, and I knew I was looking at a fair amount of surcharges in that particular Beceite ibex.

Nevertheless, it was a stunner, and I didn't hesitate. Unfortunately, I then proceeded to miss! #!@%&%!!!! This was embarrassing, but I shot it on the second shot. The ibex was huge and will make a truly beautiful trophy.

Giuseppe was a bit reticent about taking meat from the ibex, but I can report that the skilled Spanish cooks fixed superlative ibex backstraps that were flavorful, mild, and tender.

Leaving the lovely parador of Huesca, we drove northwest across Spain to the area known as the "Picos de Europa" in search of Cantabrian chamois. En route, Giuseppe left us, and his son Curro, an accomplished guide in his own right, became the leader of our little party.

We checked into an alpine hotel in a deep valley, with rapidly flowing creeks, dense areas of wildflowers, and blue valley shadows. The country looked more like Austria than Spain! The hotel lobby had several excellent trophies shot by the owner, who went out of his way to ensure that we hunters were made much more than welcome.

Again, we left our alpine hotel in the blue, crisp predawn, shivering at the mountain cold. Once again, we drove up and through daunting mountain peaks, meeting our local guides in a small alpine village. We drove into the Picos de Europa park and quickly were on dirt tracks.

We hadn't driven for 10 minutes before they spotted a nice chamois on the opposite valley side. We stopped the cars, climbed out and down into the small valley, forded a rushing stream, and began to climb in a mixture of snow and rock.

We were trying to keep a huge boulder between us and the chamois, and the climbing was moderately tough, because the snow had a hard crust, and if you went through the crust (and I did), then you often dropped to your waist.

Nevertheless, we scrambled up the snow slope 300 to 400 yards behind the boulder and came out on top. After a moment I located the chamois just below the ridgeline above me, and I lay down in the snow to get into firing position. At that moment, the sun came out over the ridgeline, and I lost my sight picture in the sun's glare. The chamois insouciantly ambled around a rock and over the ridge into the sun.

Disappointed, we decided to follow the stream up the mountain and kept a sharp eye that our chamois friend didn't amble back into view behind us.

Two or three hours later, we topped out in a broad alpine bowl, surrounded by snowy slopes, covered in wildflowers, and so very, very familiar to every sheep hunter. There were at least two chamois in sight, but the guides spotted a third chamois off to our hard right, really in the next drainage over.

We worked our way over to yet another large boulder and ranged the chamois at almost exactly 300 yards, lying contentedly in a snow field.

A 75-pound chamois lying half-buried in snow is not a big target at 300 yards, and Curro said to

The flatter, lower, and warmer areas around To-ledo were in their full April coat of Spanish poppies and purple vetch, painting the landscape in broad swaths of rich red and purple.

We drove through the 25,000-acre ranch that we were staying at—"El Castenar"—but saw nothing.

The next morning we drove to a neighboring ranch that was cattle, but not game, fenced to look for mouflons. Suffice it to say that they led us a merry chase through heavy cover, and we were certainly foot sore by late morning, hot and tired.

We came upon some of the elusive mouflons while still in the Land Cruiser and before our planned destination for yet another hike. I got down out of the Land Cruiser, sneaked around the end, and shot, hitting a big, lovely, full curl mouflon dead in the heart.

So our Spanish adventure ended, a pleasant land of fine hunting, abundant game, great history, friendly people, good wine, and sunny days.

Spain will always be one of my favorite desti-nations, and this trip was particularly enjoyable and successful, with three solid gold-medal trophies. It must be noted, however, that there is a 16% value-added tax (VAT) and that the exchange rate on the euro is not favorable, so this trip's costs were not for the budget minded.

*Bob Keagy is past president of the Golden Gate Chapter of Safari Club International.*

wait until he stood up. I had a dead rest, and told Curro I thought I could hit it lying down.

We waited about 10 minutes, and the chamois showed no sign of getting up from his cool bed, so I decided to take the shot at the grapefruit-sized vital area, against Curro's advice.

Well, folks, Curro was, as it turned out, right—I again missed my first shot, but hammered it as it stood up. Heaving a sigh of relief, the guides pulled the chamois down to "my" boulder for pictures and skinning. The chamois was a beaut, perhaps mak-ing "top 10."

Coming back down the mountain to the cars, our hike was considerably enlivened by coming upon a Spanish viper in the middle of the path, sun-ning himself.

After an afternoon of photography for Pam, we began our drive to the area south of Toledo for our third trophy, a mouflon.

# Northern Asia

The mountains, plains, and forests of Asia are the home of some of the oldest hunting cultures on earth. This is truly wild country, often with landscapes that are spectacular as well as potentially dangerous both from nature and from political forces and their conflicts. On the other hand, the local people can be some of the warmest and most hospitable. Hunting here is critical for the survival of species that can be targets of poachers.

## HINDU KUSH MOUNTAINS

 ## DREAM HUNT

### Hunting the Hindu Kush Mountains

JAMES SWAN

In his thirteenth-century travels, Marco Polo wrote in his journal as he ventured into the province of Vokhan (roughly northern Afghanistan): "In this plain there are wild animals in great numbers, particularly sheep of a large size, having horns three, four, five, even six palms of length." This species of argali sheep has since been named for Polo, *Ovis ammon polii*, Marco Polo sheep.

Our images of the Hindu Kush Mountains from television are of towering snowcapped mountains rising up nearly three miles high in elevation from stark, dusty, rugged, arid sweeping landscapes.

The land seems desolate, but actually at one time this rugged mountainous area of Asia had a wealth of wildlife including several species of wild sheep, ibex, brown bears, red deer, wolves, snow leopards, leopards, tigers, otters, marten, lynx, pheasant, grouse, and ptarmigan, in higher elevations, and gazelles, hyenas, jackals, hares, hedgehogs, and many gerbils and other rodents in the deserts. Wars, poaching, and neglect have had their impact here, but the massive wild sheep that live among the clouds are still here in good numbers.

Aside from the challenge of hunting in these remote, rugged lands, the mature Marco Polo ram has immense curling horns, which sometimes measure over five feet long and nearly a foot and a half in girth at the base.

According to Gretchen Stark of Safari Outfitters and Travel (www.safaril.com), which books hunting safaris in Asia, in November of each year, as the snows come to the high, arid mountains of central and northeastern Afghanistan, herds of the large Marco Polo sheep migrate out of Afghanistan and into Tajikistan.

Another expert on hunting in Asia is Dennis Campbell, the editor of *Ovis* magazine, which is about the wild sheep of Asia, and executive director of Grand Slam Club/Ovis (www.wildsheep.org), a nonprofit organization concerned with the conservation of wild sheep. Dennis describes the mountains of that part of the world as "a very high desert, with immense, broad, totally open valleys, ringed with snowcapped peaks, and very little vegetation, except beside rushing snow-fed rivers." Apparently there are even trout in some of those rivers.

Dennis hunts the Marco Polo sheep and books hunts for others as well. He described a typical Marco Polo sheep hunt in Tajikistan as the animals migrate out of Afghanistan. You begin by flying into an airport at about the 12,000-feet elevation. Then you proceed by car as far as you could go, climbing upward. When the roads end, you switch to horses and foot, climbing still higher. It is not uncommon for people to hunt the giant Marco Polo rams at elevations from 14,000- to almost 18,000-feet elevation.

Such a Marco Polo sheep hunt typically costs about $25,000. For perspective, a hunt for the Afghan argali sheep, a related species found at lower altitudes, costs about half that much. Another favorite game animal of the mountains of Asia is the ibex, a large goat with immense curving horns sometimes 50 inches long, which is relatively abundant and also quite prized. Ibex hunts in Tajikistan, Turkmenistan, Uzbekistan, and Kyrgyzstan typically cost $4,000 to $5,000.

Campbell said that big game hunting in the high mountains of Asia is at least a $5 million a year business for those countries.

Another hunter who has journeyed to the Hindu Kush Mountains in pursuit of huge-horned sheep is attorney John Jackson III, former president of Safari Club International, now executive director of the worldwide conservation group Conservation Force.

Jackson, who is one of the leading authorities on animal importation law, was asked on behalf of the Foundation for North American Wild Sheep (www.fnaws.org), the Gland Slam-Ovis Foundation (www.wildsheep.org), and Conservation Force (www.conservationforce.org) to handle a case about importing of argali sheep trophies. John had never before hunted for Marco Polo sheep, and so he wanted firsthand experience.

John flew from New Orleans to Kyrgyzstan. That was as close as he could get to the Hindu Kush Mountains of southern Tajikistan along the Afghanistan border, where the hunt was to be held. Going there in the fall is tied to the annual migrations of argali sheep, especially the Marco Polo variety, that come into Tajikistan from Afghanistan and China as winter arrives. The next step of the trip involved two 16-hour days traveling by car across Kyrgystan and Tajikistan. The roads are not exactly superhighways, he said, but what made the trip so long were the six planned checkpoints they had to pass through in each country, plus several other unplanned searches. The checkpoints are meant to look for terrorists and drug runners, as Afghanistan is the opium capital of the world.

John said that the outfitter had brought along "gifts" for the soldiers at each checkpoint to help expedite their passage. Some people had advised John, as an American, to "keep a low profile," but he said that the Russian border guards were quite friendly to Americans and openly expressed their dislike for the Taliban and Al Qaeda.

They finally arrived at a base camp at the 17,000-feet level in southern Tajikistan. They were above the tree line, surrounded by tall snowcapped mountains rising out of expansive valleys. While the country looks desolate with no trees or bushes, John said that actually there is a good deal of grass and other low green vegetation—enough to support not only sheep and ibex but many rabbits, foxes, eagles, and wolves.

The Marco Polo sheep is one of the argali species, distinguished by its extremely long curving horns. John reported that while they were hunting, he saw 400 to 500 wild sheep every day, most at a considerable distance.

They camped at 17,000 feet and hunted at 19,000 or higher. To accommodate to the altitude, John had to take Diomax to sleep at night, which helps your oxygen absorption to compensate for the thin air at that altitude. If you don't, respiration slows at night when you sleep, and you tend to wake up feeling anxious, like you can't breathe. He didn't take the pill one day and experienced those symptoms firsthand.

They hiked daily to 19,000 feet or more, walking slowly, taking six to eight steps, then pausing to catch their breaths. John said the temperature was about –20°F, but to appreciate the experience, factor in a brisk wind, making the wind chill astronomically low. A gust of wind or blast of snow, as well as being swept away in a rockslide, was an ever-present danger. The one unexpected feature of comfort was thermal springs, which enabled him to have a hot bath every day.

On the third day, with the threat of a big snowstorm coming in, the guide spotted four good-sized rams. They made a stalk, which was painstakingly slow at that altitude and with so little cover. The guide advised John that he had better shoot. The rams looked very tiny. Jackson pulled out his range finder. It said the distance was 585 yards. The guide insisted that this might be their only chance. Jackson was reluctant, but the guide said that it might be now or never. So John sighted in and shot three times, bringing down the biggest ram in the group. It died almost immediately, as he hit him with all three shots.

The Marco Polo rams are known for their immense curling horns. The world record is 67 inches long, on each side. John's ram measured 50 inches on a side, with a 17-inch base. Its estimated live weight was close to 400 pounds. As always happens, the storm did not materialize, and so the next day he went out for a walk and saw several rams that would go 60 inches or more.

John found many argali sheep streaming into Tajikistan, which is in keeping with biologists of that country who believe controlled hunting is no threat to the argali populations. The Tajikistan government surveys indicate there are 12,000 to 14,000 Marco Polo in Tajikistan in the hunting areas annually. They are more numerous than any longhorn sheep in North America. Jackson says, "I saw 400 to 500 Marco Polo a day. It was nothing to see 60 to 80 rams in one herd."

Jackson also pointed out that Tajikistan receives $13,000 in license fees alone for each sheep hunter, and there are about 80 hunters a year, about half of whom come from the United States. This money is the primary support for research and conservation of sheep populations. The local clans are stakeholders in the sheep management program. Thus to stop the hunting of argali sheep would essentially cut off all money for sheep conservation in that part of the world, which might very well result in the species becoming endangered as a result of increased poaching.

I asked him if he saw any signs of the war. He chuckled. He said that one day they were buzzed by some U.S. jet fighters. His guide then explained that the area they were hunting was once supposedly the site of one of Osama Bin Laden's tent training camps. John said they saw no sign of the camp and that the jets did not come back. That was his only contact with the war.

If Afghanistan could reclaim its place as a place to hunt trophy sheep and ibex, this would inject several million dollars a year into their economy, as well as provide essential revenues to help conserve the animals. This story needs to be told, Jackson said, because in the high mountains of Asia, as in most of the world, hunters shoulder the lion's share of funding wildlife conservation and, unfortunately, get far too little credit for it.

---

**DENNIS CAMPBELL AND GRAND SLAM CLUB/OVIS**
Post Office Box 310727
Birmingham, AL 35231
Phone: 205-674-0101; fax: 205-674-0190
www.wildsheep.org

John Jackson III booked his hunt through Bob Kern's

**HUNTING CONSORTIUM LTD.**
45 Spring House Lane
Berryville, VA 22611
Phone: 540-955-0090; fax: 540-955-0091
www.huntcon.com/rk.htm

# DREAM HUNT

---

## The King of Mountain Goats

WAYNE LAU*

*When people asked, "O Messenger of Allah, is there a reward in doing good to the animals?" He (peace be upon him) said, "There is a reward in doing good to every living thing." (Bukhari and Muslim Sharif)*

Steven, my 16-year-old nephew, looked confused: "You try to save a mountain goat by hunting it?!"

I was telling him why I went hunting on the volatile Afghanistan-Pakistan border. He thought I was crazy for going there . . . as well as for hunting a rare animal.

Steven, trophy sports hunting can be the best way (sometimes the only way) to conserve endangered species. That's because they mostly live where humans don't: the driest deserts, highest mountains, impenetrable swamps, and jungles. The people who do live there are usually very poor. How can you tell them not to clear forest for farming and firewood, or poach game for meat, when they have families to feed?

When trophy hunters arrive, they pay a fortune in local wages for a chance to hunt. The hunters typically only want one live mature, male animal. And each live mature male needs up to two dozen females and young. So when the locals see that the animals are that valuable, they help conserve the habitat and stop poaching. Animal populations usually recover very fast.

One highly endangered animal is the Kashmir markhor—the world's largest mountain goat with majestic spiraling horns. It lives in north Pakistan near the Afghanistan border. Few Westerners visit because of fighting over the past two decades, which often spills over the border. With so many guns and refugees, the markhors were being poached to extinction.

In a desperate stroke of inspiration, CITES (Convention on International Trade in Endangered Species) allowed the hunting of a small markhor called the Suleiman markhor. When locals saw how much overseas hunters valued the Suleimans, they protected it. Its population recovered from near extinction levels of a few hundred to a few thousand today. The Suleiman project was so successful that a similar hunting conservation program was started for the Kashmir markhor by respected conservation groups such as the World Wildlife Fund (WWF) and the International Union for Conservation of Nature and Natural Resources (IUCN).

We were going to hunt in the hidden valley of Chitral, which is nestled high in the Hindu Kush Mountains in the greater Himalayan range. Alexander the Great conquered Chitral on his way to India. Then it became the westernmost branch of China during the opulent Tang Dynasty. Later on, the Chitrali sport of polo was made world famous by British colonists—with one key change: it is said that instead of a ball, polo was traditionally played with the severed head of a defeated foe.

Chitral's broad history glows in the faces of its people. Though mainly Muslim, there is a mix of religions and cultures.

The hardest part of the hunt was trying to get to Chitral. It took two tries!

Isolated by towering mountains, it's tough to get into the valley during the cold months of markhor hunting season. The two main roads were snowed in. A third old road goes through Afghanistan and dodgy Taliban territory. So the only practical way in is by airplane from the ancient fortress city of Peshawar, a six-hour drive from Pakistan's capital Islamabad. But the planes could only fly during the best of weather, which is rare in winter. It's not uncommon to wait in Peshawar for over a week.

Lucky for me, my guide was Raja Ali Alamdar, and my outfitter was his nephew Anchan Ali Mizra. Alamdar's family once ruled a kingdom in the mountains near K-2, the world's second highest peak. When Pakistan became independent after World War II, his father was forced to renounce the kingdom, and their lands were taken away.

When I arrived in Peshawar in February, bad weather had already canceled flights for a few days. Through Anchan's efforts, Alamdar and I managed to get on the first plane to Chitral the following day. Flying in a propeller plane through the world's highest mountain range has a way of lifting worries from one's mind. As we cruised toward the all-important Lowari Pass, the ground suddenly rose menacingly beneath us. We floated just a 100 yards over the snowed-in pass. I could have thrown a stone and hit the slopes.

One breathless moment later, the Chitral valley opened below us. Sensing my giddy enthusiasm, the pilot invited me to the cockpit and gave me an exceptional bird's-eye tour: to the left was the valley of the Kalash; far ahead was the castle of Alexander the Great and the village of his soldiers' descendants; there was the thin Wahkan Corridor of Afghanistan with the famed Marco Polo sheep hunting country of Takijkistan just beyond it. All too soon, we landed in Chitral. After quick visits to register with the District Conservation Office and Police, we had just enough daylight left to visit a sightseeing lookout at the Tooshi reserve, one of the three Kashmir markhor hunting areas (the other two were Shasha and my hunting area, Gharet).

In the waning light, we along with the local villagers watched about two dozen markhor nannies and kids drift down a steep mountain chute to drink at a river. Some were climbing trees to feed on their leaves! Suddenly I heard a rock roll behind me. Unbelievably, a young male markhor popped up! The hunting conservation program worked so well that these young markhors had never been hunted. Truly a miracle for a species that had been nearly poached to extinction.

We spent the night at the modest but very comfortable Pakistan Tourist Development Corporation (PTDC) hostel before setting off for the two-hour drive south to the Gharet hunting reserve. All along our ride, children and teenagers were playing cricket, Pakistan's national sport. In every available road ditch, riverbed, or mountain cranny, homemade bats swatted cloth-wrapped rocks at goals made of sticks.

In Chitral, game is plentiful owing to the hunting program's success in reviving markhor populations. But I wanted to try hunting a markhor with my compound bow. This hadn't been done before and was going to be challenging. Bow hunting meant stalking to within 50 yards of these mountain goats who have the best long-distance eyesight among mammals; they can spot predators miles away. The markhors are also among the best climbers in the world. As the only hoofed animal that can climb trees, vertical cliffs are no problem for markhors.

When we arrived at Gharet, an earnest but overly large hunting party of 8 to 10 local guides greeted us—none of them with any experience with close stalking. Though Alamdar did speak Urdu, Pakistan's national language, it was clear that the guides preferred to talk in a local dialect that kept us a bit out of the loop. Challenges!

After hiking up a valley for two or three miles, we spotted some trophy markhors that had dropped down into a bowl just above the riverbed. Alamdar and I were discussing how we should approach the bowl from downwind when suddenly one of the guides pulled me by my coat and started rushing across the riverbed, straight to the bowl . . . and the wind at our backs! Alamdar and I tried to protest that the markhors would smell us. But to no avail. As we were shoved up to the rim of the bowl, we saw that the markhors had long gone up the side of the mountain.

That evening, Alamdar and I came up with a strategy. Alamdar suggested that we set up a spike camp in the valley rather than waste over four hours traveling daily. We could also leave most of our party at camp. It was a beautiful valley, the weather was dry, and I was more than up for adventure. So we gathered up the needed equipment and made camp next to the river at a well-known markhor crossing between two lofty cliffs.

The camp was perfect, probably too perfect. We may have camped so far in the valley that the markhors could see our fires. Four days and we had only spotted a handful on distant cliffs. This strategy wasn't working, so the local guides came up with a plan to drive the markhors to a crossing and up a mountain path where we would be waiting. I was less than enthusiastic with the idea of a driven hunt. But in these mountains, to "drive" meant more like showing oneself on foot, then hoping the markhors went where one planned. And as that old saying goes, "When in Rome, do what the Romans do."

We spent a lazy morning waiting up a mountain chute where the guides thought the markhors would go. Just as the sun warmed up, we heard the unmistakable rattle of falling rock from across the riverbed. A herd of markhors were racing single file down the mountain to the crossing! We watched as the largest markhor leading the herd paused for a brief moment at the edge of the crossing. He then hurdled across the riverbed at full tilt, followed by the rest. I took a mental note: if I had been at that edge, I probably would have had a chance for a single bow shot at that lead markhor.

Hearts were racing as we scanned the mountain side, listening for the slightest click of rock fall signaling that the markhors were coming. I nocked an arrow and waited. Then there was a click. Then another! Then we heard rocks cascading down, above us! The markhors had taken a different path. They were now climbing behind us too high, too far, and too fast for a bow shot.

It was both a thrilling and disappointing moment. As we limped back to camp, we had to think through our plans. There was also a long period of bad weather coming up that may trap us in Chitral. Frustration was growing.

The lead guide mentioned that most rifle hunters shot a markhor in late March, when the markhors came down from the high peaks to feed on newly sprouting grass. Alamdar nodded knowingly. The season of the "new grass" came later in April or May but was also known for good hunting. So we decided to break camp and return to Chitral town. Alamdar and I would fly out while the weather permitted and return a few weeks later in mid-March.

Sadly, our return trip started badly. Flights from Peshawar to Chitral had been canceled for days, and the wait-list was growing. Forecasts were for bad weather for over a week. We only had at best a two-week window before the new grass season would end. After that the markhors would rise up to peaks where we couldn't hunt them. Then Alamdar heard a rumor that the snow blocking the Lowari Pass had melted. Vehicles still could not get through. But men on foot might climb over the 10,500-foot trail. In desperation, we decided to make a two-day journey to the pass to see if we could climb over it, then hire vehicles to carry us and our equipment to Chitral.

We made good time driving over the rolling plains surrounding Peshawar. The gaily decorated trucks, buses, taxis, and donkey carts unique to the region provided needed distraction. But the long drive up became much longer as the temperature dropped, and we ran into several landslides. At last, we reached the town of Dir late at night. Alamdar spent the next day gathering the latest information and organizing a trip. I was ill with stomach flu, so spending the day in the hotel's lovely garden courtyard was fine with me. I ended up playing with some children, giving them small toys that I bring as gifts when hunting in far-off lands.

Alamdar returned in the evening with both good and bad news: we would only know whether we could cross the pass by going there, but he had found a vehicle, and we would try to cross the next morning.

As we rose in elevation, small patches of roadside snow gradually merged into full sheets. We managed to get within sight of the pass when all vehicles had to stop. A few men coming from Chitral who had climbed the pass warned that the other side was very steep, and there was still snow everywhere. Thwarted and dejected, we returned to Dir and prepared for the long drive back to Peshawar. Although physically I was fine (even with a touch of fever), mentally I began wondering if I was asking too much from this hunt?

Then our fate turned. When we got back to Peshawar, the weather had suddenly turned, and flights resumed. Anchan managed to get us on the second flight to Chitral. Time was getting short. As soon as we landed, we made arrangements for setting up spike camp the next day in the valley out of sight of any markhors. It was next to a noisy stone quarry and seemed almost industrial compared to the serene beauty of our first camp. But we hoped it would be better for hunting. Luckily, it was.

When we hiked back up the valley, we saw several trophy markhors bedded on cliffs or munching leaves calmly in trees. The local guides had been scouting the valley and identified places where the markhors tended to cross the riverbed daily. We patiently watched one of the crossings throughout the afternoon. Quietly a herd of four markhors meandered down to the riverbed, then raced across to our side just as the sun set!

We now had to think carefully. It would be harder for a markhor to spot a bow hunter, and there was good cover. The problem was: from the best spot, we couldn't see exactly where the markhors moved in the riverbed and where they would climb out.

The next day we hid near a likely climbing spot and waited. Tension built up slowly as the sun began to set. We could see the markhors on the mountainside all afternoon grazing, resting, and gradually moving down. Were they going to cross before dark? Suddenly we heard rock fall. The markhors were moving!

We watched them start their race across the riverbed. In the fading light, we tried to spot the markhors without being spotted ourselves. Suddenly a guide motioned that we should move. We bolted out of our hiding spot and climbed a small cliff. Just ahead of us, I saw the tops of markhor backs above the brush, marvelous spiral horns waving against a red evening sky. They were over 70 yards away and climbing fast, well beyond my range with no ethical shot opportunity. Again, if I had been positioned perhaps 40 yards up the mountain, I might have had a shot. Yet again, that's hunting!

Now I had to make a bigger decision. I had wanted to hunt the markhor with a bow. But soon they would be crossing when it would be too dark for a shot, and they could soon start rising to the high peaks and end the season. One reason I wanted to hunt the markhor was that I hoped to make an application to the U.S. authorities to allow the import of a markhor trophy into the United States. Un-

til now, few U.S. hunters have participated in the hunting conservation program because their trophies could not be brought back. Someone has to submit a "test" application to start the approval process. John Jackson III from Conservation Force (www.conservationforce.com) had already volunteered his time and expertise to help. If we managed to get an import permit, the U.S. hunters might then be encouraged to support Pakistan's hunting conservation programs.

There was something greater at stake than just my pride to be the first modern hunter to bow hunt a markhor. So I made a decision. I asked to borrow a rifle. I believe that it is very possible to bow hunt a markhor, but it will be another hunter that does it.

There was only one major hurdle left: I didn't know how to use a rifle. I had never purposefully gone hunting with one before. So when the rifle arrived the next day, everyone was a bit anxious to see how I shot—especially me. A rock target with a 2-inch chalk dot was set up 100 yards away. My first shot was about 12 inches high. My second shot hit right on the first shot, and everybody began smiling. They said that the rifle was set for mountain hunting at a range of 350 meters (1,150 feet). So my shooting was fine.

We rushed up the valley to get into position. As expected, the markhors took even longer to come down the mountain. It was getting very dark when they reached the riverbed. We were following a splendid huge billy. He walked through the rocks and brush, offering a clear shot. I put my eye to the scope then . . . then . . . I couldn't see anything!

With some coaching from Alamdar, I could sort of make out his body and maybe a leg or head. But I wasn't sure. I thought about shooting, but if I shot and missed, we would have to let the valley rest for at least three days. By that time, the markhors could have started moving away for the season. I just wasn't confident that I could make that shot. As we walked to camp, Alamdar consoled me that it was the right thing to do.

The next day, we set up and waited. The markhors appeared as expected. But it was getting dark fast. We tried to pick out a trophy. But fading light and rough slopes made that difficult. Alamdar spotted a mature markhor munching leaves in a tree. There was no clear shot yet. After a few minutes, he disappeared. Alamdar instructed me to look at the rocks below the tree. Then suddenly he walked clear of the brush and stopped side on!

I put the crosshairs on his shoulder and slowly squeezed the trigger. The rifle surprised with me with its kick. But the markhor didn't fall! He started climbing the mountain fast, and I quickly lost him in the rocks. Alamdar was screaming at me to shoot again—or at least I thought he was saying that. I was too focused on trying to reload. I saw the markhor pop out on the mountainside, shot, and missed again. This happened two more times as the markhor raced up the cliffs. He reached the top of the ridge and was about to go over. I only had two shells left. Alamdar had already given up and started walking back to camp.

I aimed at the markhor's rump as he leaped over the crest, and fired. Like all the other shots, I thought I had hit him. On this shot, he had already gone over the top, and I couldn't see him. Some rocks rolled near where I shot. Then the local guide screamed that I got him and started hugging me. Alamdar stopped and muttered that they were only rocks falling. Then suddenly he started screaming that the markhor was falling down the mountain face. After a few seconds, I saw him, too! My shot had broken his hip, and he slid down nearly 1,000 feet back to the riverbed.

Alamdar had been screaming that my shots were high. But I was so exited that I couldn't hear him. The markhor had to run up the mountain until it was several hundred yards away before a bullet

would hit at the crosshairs. I felt foolish even as I ran toward the trophy, anxious to touch the Kashmir markhor's wondrous spiraling horns. But any regrets were soon overwhelmed by thrill. This magnificent King of Mountain Goats would be with me in mind and body for eternity!

When we returned to Chitral, fate seemed to smile again. Alamdar popped into a tiny hole-in-the-wall shop that was packed with old guns. I noticed a funny-looking shotgun way back in the cupboard. It turned out to be an antique percussion shotgun made by a G. Bales from Ipswich, England.

Mr. Bales made custom guns in Ipswich around 1840. Ipswich was also the base of England's highly decorated Suffolk Regiment. Even more intriguing was that the gun had an inscription in Arabic roughly saying, "I died for this gun!"

The old white bearded shopkeeper said this shotgun was bought from one of the 30,000 Afghan refugees who fled to Chitral when Afghanistan was invaded in 2001. Could it be that the shotgun once belonged to an English officer from the Suffolk Regiment who was killed by an Afghan warrior who died from his wounds? This is all speculation. But whenever I look at it, the shotgun brings back wonderful memories of the markhor hunt.

John Jackson III and I have submitted the test import application. With a bit of luck, perhaps other U.S. hunters will also soon be encouraged to try hunting the King of Mountain Goats!

My teenage nephew Steven smiled. "So do you feel rewarded for trying to do the right thing?"

I like to think so, Steven.

*See Section D for a special recipe.*

To book a markhor hunt, contact:

**KARAKURUM TREKS & TOURS**

21-B, Hotel Metropolitan

G-9 Markaz

Post Office Box 2803

Islamabad, Pakistan

Phone: +92 51 2252475;

mobile: +92 333 5376366

Email: karakurm@isb.comsats.net.pk

www.karakurum.com

*\*Wayne Lau enjoys hunting for a hobby and conservation as a passion. He believes that on occasion the two can overlap with great benefit.*

## MONGOLIA

One indication of the strength of the centuries-old hunting traditions of Mongolia is when their Winter Olympic athletes march in the opening and closing ceremonies wearing hats and coats of wild fox and wolf skins.

Mongolia is located in the middle of Central Asia, between the two superpowers of China and Russia, with Tibet to the south and Siberia to the north. It has a population of 2.7 million people (97% literacy rate) living sparsely over a rugged topography (42.5% mountains, Gobi desert, etc.) of 604,829 square miles, or equal to half the size of Europe.

Like Montana, the "big sky country," the azure sky dominates the seemingly endless steppes. This is why in ancient times the Mongols referred to their country as "Blue Mongolia." Mongols have developed deep traditions of reverence to The Heavens that reside in those blue skies as their main protector. Even today, old women will splash a little freshly brewed tea with milk into the morning air as an offering to the Blue Sky and Mother Nature.

Modern society is making inroads into this ancient culture. But hunting, with firearms and eagles, remains a central part of

Mongolian culture. We have two stories that share the spirit of this touchstone of hunting.

## DREAM HUNT

### Riding with Eagles: In Wild Mongolia with the Kazakhs

STEPHEN BODIO*

The oldest ways of hunting are passing swiftly. A few Inuit still hunt their traditional ways on dogsled and with spears, but these days most use rifles or snowmobiles, and who would deny them such useful modern tools? Even Pygmies in the Congo and the !Kung San of South Africa have abandoned most of their ancient ways.

But at least one culture still preserves a style of hunting at least 6,000 years old, while accommodating the modern world in other ways. The Kazakhs of Mongolia and Kazakhstan may now have Internet connections in their yurts, but they still hunt foxes, hares, and even wolves with trained eagles, aided by horse and tazi hound.

I first saw pictures of the Kazakh eagles in old books when I was a child in Boston. Such images grabbed me then and made me long to be a part of such adventures. But during the time of the Soviet Union, Kazakhstan, home to atomic testing and the Soviet space program, was even less accessible than Russia, while Mongolia was run as a Stalinist fiefdom by apparatchiks who preserved Stalin's ways and a stifling bureaucracy long after even the Soviets' system began to thaw.

In February 1998, chasing rumors of eagle hunters and armed with a Kazakh contact through *National Geographic* photographer David Edwards, I touched down in Ulaan Bataar's airport on a

30-below-zero night to begin a series of trips that would culminate in my 2003 book *Eagle Dreams*. Over the next couple of years, I would hunt foxes with the Kazakh horsemen; hear tales of wolf and snow leopard; live for weeks on stewed mutton, buttered tea, and vodka; and make friends for life. I would eventually be allowed to bring a stock of Kazakh tazi dogs—ancestral Asian salukis that participate in the hunt with eagles, flushing the quarry and guarding the kill—from Kazakhstan. And we would form a bond with these tough, merry, stoical hunters—people who have preserved their ways through decades of real persecution—that I hope will last all through our lives.

If you go to Mongolia, where the traditions are strongest (Kazakhstan is now actively reviving them, as they are no longer as subject to Soviet restriction), you can expect to fly first into Ulaan Bataar. (You can make connections through Korea and China.) Ulaan Bataar is an acquired taste; I enjoy its anarchic bustle, but it is dusty and, in the winter "eagling" season, blue with coal smoke from the city's Simpsons-style cooling towers, which provide steam heat for the entire city. The town, perched on the edge of forest-covered hills to the north and vast steppes to the south, is an odd mix of triumphalist boulevards designed as though to show off massed armies, dingy Soviet-style apartment blocks in crumbling concrete, and vast "ger"—yurt—suburbs, bristling with satellite television antennas and guarded by surly Tibetan mastiffs. The restaurants and bars are surprisingly good and filled with cheerful young people speaking into cell phones. The winter cold, especially at night, can be daunting, but the steam heat is so effective that hotel rooms are almost too warm.

If you stay long, you will find that, once past the grimy lobbies, real hospitable Mongolian life hides in brightly furnished apartments that belie their drab facades. But most likely you are impatient to get to the country of the Kazakhs. Regular flights in MIAT, the Kazakh airline, service Bayaan Olgii Aimag, the Kazakh province that occupies Mongolia's westernmost point, several times a week. When I was last there, a couple of years ago, the prop jets still stopped for a refueling break in a grassy field about two-thirds through the 600-mile-plus flight.

Olgii City, the Aimag's (an Aimag is a top-level administrative division [province] in Mongolia) capital, is a busy little town of approximately 30,000 people. Its paved roads end at the town's edge; the 700-mile-plus "highway" to Ulaan Bataar is a dirt caravan track that sometimes widens to a half-mile-wide series of ruts, vehicle parts, and animal bones. It is accessible to wheeled traffic, but Lada Nivas, UAZ trucks, and sidecar-equipped motorcycles share the road with camel caravans and sturdy little horses. When you leave Olgii, with its cell phones and Internet cafés, you will have regressed in time to a mixture of the 1960s and the 1600s, depending on where you look.

(The time span of eagle falconry is longer than that. Central Asia's bare rock walls and canyons are covered with rock art, petroglyphs that start as long as 6,000 years ago and carry on until the 1700s.

Some of the earliest show long-legged dogs and what may be great birds swooping down on hoofed game animals. Realistic portraits of falconers carrying eagles date to before the time of Christ.)

If you want to actually hunt with the eaglers, be prepared for Spartan if warm surroundings. You will stay in the herder's "winter-spending houses," to quote a Kazakh guide friend: adobe and log structures with flat roofs, cast-iron stoves fueled by dried dung, and plank floors on which you will sleep surrounded by family and children and, if it is late in the season, newborn lambs and kids sheltering from the ubiquitous wolves that are the eagle's most challenging quarry. You will be served endless dishes of fat boiled mutton washed down with salty bowls of "milk tea"—better to think of it as soup. The vodka toasts can be endless, and no one has ever heard of the dangers of passive smoking.

And, in the morning, after more mutton and perhaps a bowl of kasha, you will ride out in the iron cold, and it will be worth all the minor hardships. The little horses will climb up fins of volcanic rock you might otherwise ascend using both hands. The great black eagles on your companions' right arms, gloved to above their elbows, swivel hooded heads as though they possess radar. The hunters' fox-fur hats and silver belts are out of another time, another world.

And then, to quote from my book *Eagle Dreams*:

Time ticks away. The only sounds are the click of the horses' hooves, the creak of their saddles, an occasional low word from Manai, and the sound of my breathing. Then, with no warning at all, the eagle is off the glove, stroking, climbing upward.

I cannot see the fox at first. The eagle hits the wind as she tops the ridge but, instead of falling back, she cuts into it and rises like a kite. Manai gallops forward at a speed that seems reckless on the loose rocks, shouting. Now the fox appears, fawn-colored and supple, cascading down the rocky steps like a furry waterfall. The eagle towers two hundred feet above, turns, and falls like a hammer. The fox dodges once, but somehow the eagle is now ahead of him, turning. The two arcs of movement converge in a cloud of dust, and all is still.

If you are even luckier (if you are the kind of person who would take this trip at all, I'd bet you would consider it luck), you may, as I have yet not, see a flight at a wolf rather than a fox. Experienced eagles can and do take full-grown wolves on occasion. Manai, one of the more accomplished eaglers I know, says, "If you want to let your eagle go after ten years [Kazakh eaglers release the long-lived birds after a decade or so to breed], DON'T HUNT WOLVES." It is only fair to note that on a second visit he had a fresh eagle-caught wolf hide hanging on the wall of his winter house.

(The late Jeff Cooper, grand guru of pistol craft and legendary curmudgeon, engaged in correspondence with me on the matter of eagles and wolves but refused to believe in the possibility—even after I showed him photos!)

So, should you go? The Mongols say: "If you are afraid, don't do it; if you do it, don't be afraid." Do you want to see some of the oldest and most splendid hunting on the planet? Do you love wild people and wild places? Does your taste in landscape tend toward the austere, the savage, and the sublime rather than the pretty? Are you unbothered by the utterly politically incorrect? If so, and you can stand the cold, are not bothered by frozen and very primitive toilet facilities and sleeping on hardwood floors, can eat mutton and at least decline politely on your fifth offer of vodka, you won't be disappointed.

I should add: The last person I sent there was an adventurous 17-year-old female falconer from Oklahoma. She went alone, in winter, for a month— and now wants to apprentice there for six months.

## Resources

For an excellent view of eagle-hunting culture, I recommend the brilliant film *Kiran over Mongolia* (www.kiranovermongolia.com). Filmed by New York documentarian Joseph Spaid over the course of a winter, it tells the story of a young urban Kazakh from Ulaan Bataar who travels to Olgii in pursuit of his dream of becoming a falconer.

Canat Cheryasda runs Sher Blue Wolf Tours/ Mongolia Altai Expeditions (www.mongoliaaltai-expeditions.com) and will design a trip to fit your requirements. He knows (and is related to) some of the best eaglers in Olgii, speaks excellent English, and is familiar with the vagaries of Western culture and Westerners' requirements.

*Stephen Bodio is an award-winning writer and editor, and a passionate falconer.*

# DREAM HUNT

## A Winter Hunt in Mongolia

DR. SRDJA DIMITRIJEVIC*

I've had the fortune (or a misfortune, depending on the point of view) to hunt polar bear in March, when it was −44°F, then to hunt bear in central Siberia in February when the temperatures went as low as −55°F. But Mongolia in wintertime is something that must be experienced.

So here I am, landing in Ulan Bator, capital of Mongolia, in the beginning of December. This is my seventh trip here. Pass through the airport routine and then comes the blow in the stomach as you walk out into a beautiful day, with the sun high above, winter colors of the yellow steppe, and it's −17°F at noon!

I have planned this hunt almost a month with my Mongolian partner and friend Buyan (Buyandelger Ulanbayar), president of the Mongolian Hunters Association and many other associations. He is a direct descendant of Ghengis Khan, a fact that in Mongolia certainly isn't that bad.

We agreed to spend two to three weeks in the new parts of Mongolia to travel into unexplored hunting territories and to collect specimens for the Mongolian Hunting Museum in Ulan Bator.

The trip started well. My luggage arrived, everything except the suitcase with my winter clothes! The airline assured me that the missing suitcase would arrive, but we decided to depart without further delay, so I borrowed some winter clothes from Buyan. Lucky indeed that we're both of the same build.

We departed early in the morning for Gobi.

About 12 hours later we were in total darkness with roads (if land strips can be called that) branching every now and then with no signs, but our driver never hesitated. Finally at midnight we reached three yurts that would be our base camp. We got into our sleeping bags (at least these arrived) and fell asleep in the company of a good old Mongolian square stove.

## THE UNFORGETTABLE GOBI

In the morning a local guide took us to a small mountain with strange rocks on top resembling a huge open hand. We situated ourselves among its "fingers" and started scanning with binoculars. I didn't feel the cold yet, but with the wind slashing, it's not long before I started to freeze.

All around us is a stark, rocky desert with small valleys and hills almost without vegetation, on the border with China. We stayed there a couple of hours, seeing herds of Gobi argali, one of the most-sought-after trophies in the world. The guide and Buyan, being expert hunters, do not want to move. On the contrary, we waited for the animals to move from their nocturnal grazing field and bed down for the day. It's a really good technique but not at temperatures of −22°F with terrible gales of wind.

Finally we moved, and I warmed up from walking and climbing the hills. Our goal is to approach a small mouflon herd with a male in the middle that appears to be a good trophy.

After a half an hour walk, we reached a small valley and came nose to nose with the herd. They stood up and started to move in our direction, watching us, more curious than afraid. At some 66 yards, heart in my throat and a swift gun on my shoulder, Buyan calmly says that it's a young animal, and we'll find better ones. To me it seems enormous with huge horns, with two females on the sides, a truly unforgettable scene in full sun and such pure and transparent air that seems to make them seem so close.

We needed to harvest a female trophy for the museum, and Buyan indicates a fair female at the end of the herd, but while we are deciding what animal to shoot, they disappear like phantoms among the hills.

We continued to search for another herd that we saw earlier, walking miles in the crisp, icy air as the hills get steeper and steeper. The herd was in the distance, moving along a ridge and disappearing from our sight. Being very tired, we sat down and started surveying with binoculars. We noticed a small ibex herd in the mountains at about three to four miles, but no male in it, so we decided not to waste out time with them.

## FIRST DISAPPOINTMENTS

We spotted a single large female argali in the distance, grazing calmly on top of a hill. She descended a ridge and lay down. We moved in the opposite direction until she lost sight of us, then we started approaching her, making a huge deviation through the valleys so as not to be seen.

Sticking to the valleys, we turned and turned so many times that I felt completely disoriented. But our Mongolian guide feels confident, and after a while there I am lying on a ridge to catch my breath. The guide took off his sheepskin coat and placed it on the ridge very slowly to make a support for my rifle. I moved on my belly, positioning the rifle to catch sight of the animal lying down at some 219 yards, calm, looking at some other direction. "It's done," I'm thinking. I am calm, too. It is a female. After all, there is no trophy fever in this case. I aim at her and shoot, convinced that we'll soon be in our warm comfortable yurts. But the female rises, jumps a couple of times, and disappears

behind the mountain. I am amazed at what's happened. I was so sure of myself that the possibility of missing didn't even cross my mind. But it's happened.

The guide and Buyan rebuke me, not expecting something like that from an expert hunter like me. Nothing is clear to me either, but I keep silent. I'm the only one to blame, so I promise myself to repair the error next time.

But soon there was another opportunity: a small herd of females came out from behind a hill. I shoot running. It was my specialty once. I miss again, but at least I can see where the bullet has gone: almost 6.5 feet high and 10 feet to the left at only 87.5 yards of distance. I get very angry and choose a white rock at 109 yards away from me. I shoot at the center of it, but the 2×2 yard rock wasn't even touched.

I look at my rifle. The rear scope attachment is completely detached from the rifle. I will have a talk with my rifle supplier when I come back! He considers himself the best in the field—but we won't do gossip here.

I have another rifle with me but few cartridges. I wouldn't want to make another error, so I fix it the best I can.

At the end of the day, we had three Dzeiran gazelles and one kulan, which was our goal. When we took our bag to the camp, from the general excitement I deduced that we had done a very good thing. Kulan meat is a true delicacy, and in the following days we ate it with pleasure, cutting the meat from the frozen carcass with an axe at −22°F.

## GOBI ARGALI

The following day we spotted a beautiful herd of argalis with three males and a dozen females on a single high peak. We approached them through various gullies in the car. Then we started to stalk them on foot, keeping ourselves behind a granite rock that ran up high like a mushroom. After climbing to the top, we peeked above the ridge, and I saw them all, calm, several of them lying down. The male that looked bigger than the rest was standing in the position that was perfect for shooting.

I caught my breath after running up the hill and measured the distance with the laser, 295 yards, not very close but an absolutely good distance for

## WILD MULES AND GAZELLES

The local dignitaries held a festive reception for Buyan, serving lots of tea with milk and vodka, and mutton long into the night. After that, we decided to do some light hunting the day after, searching for black-tailed gazelles and kulans, the only wild mules in the world. We need these animals for the museum.

my 7mm Remington CZ. I have set the rifle to approximately 109 yards. Having few cartridges, I decide to compensate, aiming high.

I very calmly pulled the trigger. The animals scattered everywhere, and I can't see what I shot. The herd starts running in my direction and stops abruptly on a granite plateau at only 87 yards. My male with massive horns, making a full circle, is in the middle of them, totally ungrazed. I swiftly reloaded the rifle and shoot almost at the same instant. The big male jumps up and after two steps falls into a precipice. Buyan told me that the first shot went somewhere above the back of the animal, so I corrected it and shot at the back level, raising the rifle a bit. I had only three cartridges left; I cannot risk another try—I needed to harvest three more animals and decide to shoot a little lower the following time.

We run toward the precipice and find the splendid animal dead, with one horn tip broken while he was falling down. I searched for the missing part for over an hour without success. We take lots of photographs, but electronic cameras are not very reliable in this icy cold weather. In fact, I have only two photos—all the rest was destroyed by the cold.

## ADVENTURE IN THE COLD

The following day we traveled on a seemingly endless road to reach a flat mountain in search of ibex. From a distance the mountain doesn't appear special to me, looking like a tilted coffee cup in the middle of a flat desert. The terrain where we hunted argalis was a landscape of small stone cones, not gentle slopes of only a few hundred yards of height. The guide declared that ibex live on this flat mountain. Well, we'll see, but I am a little doubtful.

We started to climb. The UAZ is jumping awfully on the stones, and finally we arrive on top of an almost flat surface with enormous granite scattered around and without a blade of grass or anything else. I have never seen such a stark lunar landscape in all my travels throughout the world.

I can't imagine that there could be any ibex here. Besides, we have arrived in this area to look for new places for argalis, and we are more than satisfied with the result. In only a few days we have seen over 200 animals.

We placed ourselves on a heap of stones and start surveying the area with binoculars. It is dead cold. The temperature had dropped during the previous night. Now it has warmed up to −22°F. And the wind, I will never forget the insidious, constant icy cold wind of Gobi. In the entire day, we only saw one ibex female, two horses, and a herd of domestic goats.

We left early in the morning to visit a place four hours away. We finally reached low lunar hills with black gravel. The guide started to climb with the UAZ on the hills. Finally we see a group of one young male with three females. These are the ones we actually want. They see us and start running. The guide starts to pursue them, performing impossible things with the old UAZ. We get closer and closer. I prepare to shoot in the run. We descend an umpteenth valley and . . . stop. The car has stopped suddenly. We get off to see what has happened, and with a straight face, the Mongolian says that we're out of petrol. But how could you go on a trip in such a remote area without first checking how much gas you've got left?

And now the beautiful part starts: I ask what we were supposed to do. He casts me an embarrassed look and says that he doesn't even know where we are. He has lost orientation racing among the valleys and mountains pursuing the argalis. It is midday; the sun is high, but the temperature is less than −22°F; and wind—don't even ask. After spending five minutes out of the car, I am completely frozen. I get in the UAZ, which feels a little better. At least there is no wind in it, but after only a quarter of an hour, it starts freezing inside, too.

And now comes the miracle. From a side valley there emerges a Mongolian on a camel. We can't tell who is more amazed—he or we. They start talking, and he departs with the camel toward the closest hilltop while we follow on foot. He explains where the first yurt is to be found. At the question of how far it is, he answers vaguely that it's an hour's distance.

Oh, well, we cannot ask for more. We depart against cold wind, and in a couple of hours (then they explain to me that you/he/she has said that it's one hour by camel) we reach an empty yurt in the middle of nothing. We enter inside and see that it's inhabited. There are fresh supplies of food, but the master, a revered man of about 70 years, is nowhere to be seen, so we press on.

We were walking against an icy cold wind, and after a couple of hours more, we found another yurt in the middle of nowhere and empty. Like all yurts, it was open, we went in, lit the fire, and saw some remains of a meal. Later we found that a 70-year-old woman was the owner.

Tired and frozen I fell asleep, and after a couple of hours the lady of the house arrived on a camel. She kindly offers us some tea and a bottle with about half a gallon of gasoline. She also tells us that it's 10 miles to the next yurt, where we might find more gasoline.

Marvellous, we have half a gallon of gasoline, our car is at several miles in the opposite direction of the next yurt, and it is pitch dark. The temperature for sure is less than −22°F. The only thing left to do is to try.

We set out in the cold night. At least now the wind is behind us. The guide decides to take a shortcut on the way back, and of course we get lost. We reach our poor, frozen UAZ after three hours of walking, and its battery is at its minimum. After making a strange noise, the engine starts . . . only to stop six-tenths of a mile from the next yurt.

We reach the next yurt on foot at almost midnight; we called the master, who came out in his underpants and gave us another bottle of gasoline. He told us that after some 12.5 miles we'd find a clandestine gas station where gasoline from China was being smuggled.

At the end of the dawn of the following day we drive into our camp. Sixteen hours of cold because of the accursed Mongolian who started off without gasoline! I don't even try to imagine what could have happened to us if we had had to spend the night in the open at polar temperatures, considering that in the desert of the Gobi there is nothing to make a fire with. We had just been spared death from frostbite.

## GOBI IBEX

After resting a little, we left in the afternoon to retry the ibex hunt in the same lunar landscape of the previous day. Luckily the wind has stopped, and from our usual place of observation a little over a mile away, we see a small herd of females, then a young male and a solitary male approaching slowly. I survey him with the long scope. He has large horns, and he's almost entirely white. From his way of walking one can deduce that he's an old animal. He lays down on a characteristic rock and looks like he's fallen asleep.

I depart with the guide, the same one I cursed all the preceding day and night. We pass through various gullies that hide us and reach the rock where the animal had lain down, but we can't find him. I am desolate. I think that we missed the right rock, but the guide insists that that's the one, and he tells me to keep calm. And in fact, after a few minutes, from one of the side gullies our old male emerges. I rush and shoot without support. He starts running, making me think that I missed him. But with great satisfaction, I see him fall in a canyon at some 200-plus yards.

What a joy! I have only one cartridge left. I was following him with my binoculars to try a last risked shot on the run at that distance, but there he is. It is a perfect shot, but he still had the strength to run for over 100 yards. We get to the place where he fell and see an enormous animal with horns of over 40 inches—for the Gobi that is really a lot. A 14-year-old animal, he has almost white thick skin. We start kissing and hugging, taking photos, and *working hard* to get him to the car.

With the last cartridge and a little fortune, I succeeded in shooting the female Gobi argali that we still needed, and then we were homeward bound. Amid a heavy snowfall, it took us 12 hours to get back to Ulan Bator, where we bought more cartridges. I took a warm bath and then caught a flight for the high Altai mountains.

Watching the majestic Altai mountains through the airplane window as we headed back to so-called civilization, I privately asked myself if I would ever again have an opportunity to hunt these magnificent animals in the wondrous Mongolian land. Considering my age, not to mention the really prohibitive costs, I am satisfied. At least once in my lifetime I've realized a dream of every hunter—to harvest Mongolian animals. I met some extraordinary people, with my friend Buyan in the lead,

whom I will never forget. I thank all of them from the bottom of my heart for this extraordinary adventure in the cold Mongolian lands.

*Dr. Srdja Dimitrijevic is a former research scientist who has created Safari International to facilitate hunting trips in Europe and Asia. To book a Mongolian hunt, contact him at www.safariinternational.com.*

## HERITAGE DESTINATIONS

### Reconstruction of the Hunting Museum in Mongolia

In Ulan Bator, the capital of Mongolia, there is a one-of-a-kind hunting museum, owned by the Hunting Association of Mongolia. The museum was built in the 1970s and displays a line of dioramas with full-mount animals, prepared according to then-existing Mongolian taxidermy technology. Besides this, the museum houses a collection of the largest world trophies and wildlife of Mongolia.

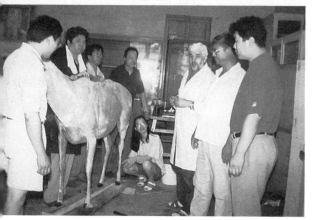

Around 50,000 visitors come to visit each year, mainly Mongolian children, so that it has a significant educational role. In the last years it has also been visited by a large number of foreign tourists.

The museum is presently in very bad condition, and the main preparations area is practically of no use. SCI life member, international director, and Serbia & Montenegro SCI Chapter president Dr. Srdja Dimitrijevic has donated brand-new mounts for all the Mongolian big game animals. He has hunted all the most important species with his own finances and has engaged very well known Italian taxidermist and sculptor Giorgio Bani to do the taxidermy preparations. Thus, the Museum will get new full-mount trophies of all the wild game species inhabiting Mongolia.

In order to fully renew the museum, it is necessary to build a 10,000-square-foot addition and to restore and rebuild new dioramas on 3,300 square feet. With these additions, the museum will again become the most important hunting museum in Asia.

Construction work will cost around $350,00. Contributions are sought for the reconstruction of this unique museum. All contributors will be listed at the entrance of the museum. For information on donating and supporting this very important effort, email Safari International (info@safariinternational.com) or Buyandelger Ulanbayar, president of the Hunting Association of Mongolia (monsafari@magicnet.mn).

## SIBERIA

 ## DREAM HUNT

### Hunting in the Shadow of the Tiger

JOHN BANOVICH*

Looking out the window of the Boeing 747, I was pleased to see the familiar ochre and sienna colors cloaked in a light blanket of snow. It was late November 2006, and I was a bit numb from the long overseas flight from Bozeman, Montana, to the Russian Far East city of Vladivostok.

This was my second trip to the Russian Far East; it is a stunningly beautiful place that lies between the Sea of Japan on the west, China on the east, North Korea on the south, and the Siberian coastal region to the north. This is home to the last wild population of one of the largest and greatest hunters on earth—the Amur tiger. Most commonly known as the Siberian tiger—or *Panthera tigris altaica*—it is one of only five subspecies or geographic races of the original eight subspecies of tigers that once roamed Asia.

Today perhaps less than 5,000 tigers exist in the wild, with only 450 of these being Amur. A primary reason for the loss is loss of habitat from human pressure and competition for resources. Others are the poaching of tigers and their prey, especially in the Russian Far East to make traditional Chinese medicine, and human-animal conflict with livestock and with man.

I was traveling with eight hunters from the United States and New Zealand. As the plane touched down, I could feel a great sense of pride: we were about to become the first group to ever legally bring firearms through customs and immigration through the former port of the Russian Pacific Fleet. At the Vladivostok airport, an important moment in conservation history was taking place: our efforts would represent the single hope to save the Siberian tiger.

It all started three years before when I was invited by my friend Mike Finley, former superintendent of Yellowstone National Park, to join him for a reception celebrating the merger and relocation of the Hornocker Wildlife Institute and the Wildlife Conservation Society (WCS) in Bozeman. We talked about saving tigers that evening, and within a few months, I was scheduled to join the WCS and Russian researchers for firsthand participation with the most comprehensive tiger study in the world.

I am an artist and a hunter. Growing up with the rich hunting area of Montana, I was constantly surrounded by the splendor of the animals of the West. Those early years of hunting instilled in me a great reverence for the forest and a deep understanding of its residents' anatomies seen so clearly in my first paintings. Having the privilege to paint animals from all over the world now, I have grown to be quite partial to big beasts with big teeth. Having the chance to look for Siberian tigers was really a dream come true.

It was on this first WCS trip that I learned what a precarious position the Amur tiger is in. With less than 20% of its current habitat protected, the remaining 80% is found outside of these areas—almost all of which is held in hunting leases, where tigers are viewed as being in direct conflict with the game hunters pursue for food in this very poor part of the world. After spending several weeks in the field with Dr. Dale Miquelle, director of the Russian Program for WCS, and lead biologist John Goodrich, and their Russian colleagues (including long conversations on history, politics, psychology, habitat, poaching, etc.), and discovering their passion, integrity, and long-term commitment to saving this highly endangered cat, I realized I had to help.

I have developed a history of working in partnership with conservation programs, but never one of this magnitude or significance. In a matter of hours, Dale and I penciled out a strategy to help create Tiger Friendly Certified (TFC) hunting leases and to engage the international hunting community to bring ungulate-hunting tourists into areas that have attained TFC status. This would link a community's economic well-being to the presence of tigers.

Given the mountain of problems leading up to this day, things went very smoothly for our group of international hunters, thanks to special assistance from a colonel in the police department and head

us to dinner at a favorite local restaurant located a short, but cold, walk from our hotel. Coming from the dry Montana climate, I found the moist sea air penetrated deep into my bones, especially when the wind blew, which seemed like all the time.

We began to get acquainted with our Russian hosts that first evening and talked of the adventure ahead. We called it our "test tour," as we were the first legal sport hunters ever in this part of the world, and our way of saying, "Be tolerant and patient, as shit does happen." With traditional Russian toasts washed down with rounds of vodka (just a small sip of what was yet to come), we were all excited about our journey ahead.

The next morning we were all scheduled to fly from Vladivostok to Plastun, a small city on the coast where logs are exported. This would leave only a short drive to the town of Terney on the edge of the Sikhote Alin Zapovednik (Biosphere Reserve), where we were to spend several days learning about the Siberian Tiger Project and tracking tigers in one of the most protected forests in the world. Because the Zapovediks are reserved for Russian and visiting scientists, we needed to get the thumbs-up from reserve director Anatole Anestov. Dale and I decided that at the close of our meeting we would donate $500 to the reserve. Since none of us spoke Russian, we relied heavily on interpretation. For our time in Terney, Luba Khobotnova, a former employee of Zapovednik, was our interpreter.

On our first day out, we hiked along a river drainage to one of my favorite places in the reserve, Khunta Mi Bay, a mile-wide, horseshoe-shaped sandy beach on the Sea of Japan. Overlooking this coastal paradise was a large distinct granite peak; "Khunta Mi" is a Chinese phrase that describes a "mountain that looks like a pagoda." This place has such magical characteristics and is such a favorite haunt of tigers that I adopted the name for our conservation initiative.

of weapons and tactics, Sergey. Because of my last-minute purchase of a new rifle (without enough time to get the proper documentation for importation), I asked to borrow a rifle for this hunt. Sergey was kind enough to allow me to use his personal weapon, the Russian version of the AK-47 equipped with a sniper scope. For me, I think this redefined the phrase "always use enough gun." It would be days before Sergey would feel comfortable enough to allow a pony-tailed American to be in possession of a police colonel–issued weapon on his own in Russia.

We overnighted in Vladivostok, the former base of the powerhouse Russian Pacific fleet, now a rusty bone yard for such weapons of war. Dale took

We spent a full day hiking, looking for tigers, but we only saw tracks. The feeling one gets from looking at fresh wild tiger tracks can be summed up by famed Bengal tiger expert Ullas Karanth: "When you see a tiger, it is always like a dream." Here we were in this ancient forest surrounded by "Amba" the Siberian tiger.

Each hunter was personally invited to be part of this test tour because of his ability to contribute to the scope of the project. The two hunting leases were chosen as they were both inhabited by tigers and had a strong prey base to support them.

I enjoyed the company of many colleagues on this trip: Ben Carter, past president of the Dallas Safari Club; Bill Robertson, a member of the Shikar Safari Club; Tee Faircloth, founder and owner of FM Allen; New Zealander Davey Hughes, owner of Swazi Wear; Patrick Meitin, former outfitter, bow hunter, and outdoor writer; Tyler Kaltrieder, filmmaker/writer, owner of Media Eleven; and Dr. Laurence Frank, founder of the Laikipia Predator Project and Kilmanjara Predator Project in Kenya, who has studied lions for nearly 35 years.

We split into two groups of four. My group was to travel southwest of Vladivostok to Neshinoe, a 250,000-acre lease located near the Borisovkoe Plateau Wildlife Refuge (Zakaznik), a protected area on the border of China. This is just one of four leases controlled by the 5,000 members of the Russian Military. Membership in these community hunting leases is the only legal way for Russians to own firearms; many own firearms but do not hunt. We drove the entire day with a short stop at the farm of Victor Yudin to photograph several captive tigers whose mother was shot nearly 15 years earlier. We passed through cities and villages but were surrounded most of the time by forest. Arriving after dark, we were shown our accommodations for the evening. I was most pleased to see the excellent accommodation, as we partially funded these buildings under our "Khunta Mi Initiative."

Following a great meal, we were all given our hunting licenses and membership into the hunting lease. Between enthusiastic toasts and free-flowing vodka, the new director, Ivan Ivanovich, presented me with a spectacular set of wild boar tusks mounted on a plaque. I was humbled, but acknowledged it was with only the help of the Dallas Safari Club, the Houston Safari Club, and my many friends and private donors that more than $70,000 was raised to usher in this historic moment—the first time international sport hunters were going to help save an animal they "Do Not Hunt."

We woke at 5:00 A.M. and were given a full breakfast. We then met the members of the lease that were going to conduct this first American drive hunt going for sika deer, the largest subspecies of this indigenous game animal. Since it was cold but without snow, the drive hunt was the way to go, collectively decided by a group of nearly 30 guys. Dale proceeded to tell me the large turnout

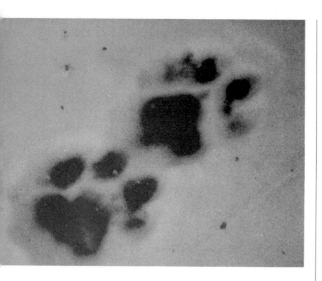

was part of the pomp and ceremony of hosting the first American hunters—an impressive gathering indeed.

The drive hunt works like this: five to seven men, the "beaters," are dropped off. The hunters are then taken several miles away and put in place 200 to 400 yards apart. The beaters then proceed to position themselves with enough distance apart to begin to flush forward all the ungulates in an area. The hunters are often stationed near a tree where they are to remain absolutely still for anywhere

from one to two and a half hours—no easy feat in freezing temperatures and holding a rifle in a position to fire accurately in seconds. Yelling and banging sticks together, announcing the beginning of their mountainside march with a gunshot (usually from two end beaters), the beaters begin to advance.

This technique seems a bit reminiscent of the bygone era of the maharajas' hunts for Bengal tigers in India. Before the tiger hunting ban in the mid-1960s, hundreds of men would gather in the forest on foot and on elephant back to beat the bush, driving frightened and enraged tigers through a small opening where the elite class of the day would bag tigers—often collecting many at the end of a successful hunt.

Sergey handed me his rifle, and though there was no interpreter with us, somehow I vaguely understood his detailed description of the finer points of handling such a weapon. A part of me was hoping I would not see anything, as there were still too many gray areas in his instruction session; my worries were to no avail, as there were no sightings.

After four drives that day, we saw nothing. Some of the beaters saw sika deer fleeing in front of them, but none of the hunters. I was always with Sergey, and it is hard enough for one person to remain quiet, let alone two. Finally, on the last drive of the day, Sergey let me take his gun into the forest alone. I could tell he had a great affinity for this rifle, and he said it was incredibly accurate. His trust was gained without ever understanding a word either of us was saying to each other. At the end of the day, this huge, stoic Russian policeman had a hint of a glimmer in his eye—a good day.

The second day, we started at daybreak once more, with the first drive taking place on the edge of a mountain overlooking a hillside. The second drive was in a beautiful river valley, and the third and last was in very dense cover. Except for a sighting by the last two guys to leave the lunch site, we came away empty again. But what I did come away with was the overwhelming sense of beauty in this forest. It was right out of a movie set with its massive Korean pine, fir, popular, aspen, birch, and oak. Never before have I seen such exquisite beauty in a northern forest.

On day three we decided to move to an area very close to the eastern border of China. Our host for this part of the trip was Alexander Kuguk. We met at his home, a large, beautifully constructed building, but like most Russian houses, in need of much TLC. As I went to shake his hand, I noticed his fit physique and very muscular forearm. I knew this guy was not your average Russian. He was a Cossack, one of the elite border military guards with reputations as very tough guys. They used to shoot Chinese crossing the border, but today they can only whip them back across. Judging from his character, I am sure any illegal he might encounter would prefer to be shot rather than the alternative.

When we first arrived at his farm, we still hadn't had a chance to sight in rifles, so we proceeded to the shooting range. Ben and Bill sighted in first, both hitting the target to the right of the bull's-eye. It was now my turn, and I was hoping to only hit the paper so as not to loose any ground I had made with my new friend Sergey. He spoke a few words in Russian and then handed me his rifle. Besides it being a completely foreign rifle and a sniper scope that had more dials than an airplane, it was also brutally cold and windy. I took off my gloves and immediately felt the bitter cold sink its fangs deep into my fingers.

As I knelt down and placed my elbow on the log used for stability, I glanced up at the Russian bystanders. Alexander was dressed in just a tee-shirt and a light, unbuttoned camouflage shirt rolled up at the sleeves—no gloves or hat. I was

dressed in every high-tech, cold-weather piece of gear available on the market today. As Alexander, Sergey, and several other Russians stood staring at me, I felt America's entire Cold War capacity was to be revealed on this one shot. I placed the fine crosshairs on the center of the bull's-eye and slowly squeezed. Its trigger was a free pull apart, then very stiff at the end. KABOOM!

Sergey pulled down the binoculars and looked right at me. He lifted his hand and gave me a smile and a thumbs-up. "Bull's-eye!" he said in English. America was safe.

That night we went after wild boars. The largest wild boars in the world are found here; they can weigh more than 600 pounds. We were all put in blinds overlooking soybean fields, with piles of carrots placed at strategic locations. The blinds were perched about 35 feet in the air, providing a perfect sightline to each bait. I quietly waited until there was barely enough light to make out if an animal had entered the field. Within 30 minutes, it was a very dark, moonless night, but we had used Russian Field technology to lengthen the shooting time— we taped a sure-fire flashlight to the stalk of my gun so I would have an extra 45 minutes.

Suddenly I could hear an animal coming through the leaves. A wild boar! When you cannot rely on your eyes, your ears become highly tuned. He was making his way out of the forest. But I also heard something else. The sound of a truck was fast approaching, and the beast beat a hasty retreat. Who could be coming down the road at this most inopportune time? As the guys pulled up, I asked why someone called on the radio for a pickup. They thought it was me. I checked my radio, which was dead, so even I didn't hear the call. A bad day for me—but a good day for the wild boar. We returned to the Cossack's house for a traditional Russian meal: meat, potatoes, bread, and vodka—which flowed even more than before.

The next day we drove—more like hobbled—two hours over roads a bulldozer could barely navigate. The first drive was on the edge of a large valley set among the most amazing forest of old-growth Korean pine. This is also known as a special place where the Amur leopard is found. One of the rarest cats in the world, maybe fewer than 50 animals are left.

We had three more drives today, and finally, on the last drive I heard five shots in rapid succession coming from the direction of the Cossack. Since he was at the far end of the drive, I thought maybe he was driving them toward me. Soon one of the beaters appeared, and we began to look for the Cossack. Suddenly there he was, standing over a young sika male. Sustaining five shots, there was not any meat left unaffected. I was very disappointed that he would do such a thing. He seemed to be very pleased and wondered why none of us shared his enthusiasm. In front of his clients, he shot an animal for his very own. This should never happen. If they want to get large trophies in this area, they must refrain from shooting everything they see, and let all the males grow older. It was at this moment I realized they are truly meat hunters. Trophies mean

nothing to them. On the way back to the main camp, Ivan Ivanovich and I discussed the concerns I had with the Cossack's behavior; he was left off of future itineraries.

The next morning we exchanged good-byes and departed for a three-hour drive to meet the other group. To our surprise, they did get three nice trophy roe deer and one huge Russian boar—in the photos, it looked like a huge grizzly. I believe the Russian wild boar will be the star species of the TFC hunting leases. We then ate lunch and drove four more hours to South Valley. The director of this lease has much experience as he is head of the Pacific Institute of Geography. He studies large carnivores and has been to many hunting areas in Montana. The lease is only eight years old, but it is composed of 410,000 acres with only 150 members. The survey has revealed six to eight resident Amur tigers and more than 2,500 sika deer. The only problem is that it is illegal to hunt sikas. Vladimir feels this may be changed in the near future, but for now we were setting our sites on wild boars and roe deer. The annual legal roe deer quota is only 20 in this area, making some very good trophies possible. With three villages located inside the lease, the local hunters are responsible for different sections and implementing antipoaching.

We were most looking forward to the heated outhouses with flush toilets (just add water) and a three-person *banya* (a Russian sauna for bathing). We had an excellent dinner, debriefing, and a good night's sleep.

We started the next morning with hunting regulations, getting licenses, meeting the professional hunters, and getting an overview of the hunting style at the lease. There was still no snow for tracking, so our best chance would again be driven hunts. We saw several roe deer and lots of sign of animals during the three drive hunts but no antlers. The roe deer drop their antlers around this time of year, so there could have been males, but no way to tell. Given all the sign and sightings, we were very encouraged for the next day.

We started the following day a bit late as a result of our conservations with Vladimir about the lease, budgets and salaries for guides and staff, and so on. We needed to remember we were there on a test tour of the Tiger Friendly Certified leases, and our first priority was to help them get this product on par with world sport hunting market expectations: to provide an incredible Russian hunting experience, to have the chance to obtain a large wild boar, red stag, sika deer (the largest of the 6 or 12 subspecies in the world and only found here), roe deer, Himalyan black bear, and possibly a grizzly. And all this would be done in part of the world never having been sport hunted before.

The tiger will only survive in its range if communities benefit from its presence. And as the first international hunters ever in this part of the Russian Far East, we hope to foster this idea.

On our first drive, we hiked up a beautiful river valley, then up a steep draw to the top of a ridge (about two miles away). The draw was dotted with Mongolian oak, which still retains most of its leaves even though they still turn rust color.

Three roes came by, one very nice buck and two does. I drew a bead on the buck but could not get a clear shot as he ran through a very thick treed area. And possessing a 10-round clip, I knew once I started to ring shots in the forest, it would be my only chance, as the Chechnian war would be quieter.

We had two more drives and no trophies. That evening, driving back, there was a very light snow on the road and tiger tracks—a female yearling and two cubs! She walked right down the center of the road for about two miles. This is really what we came to see, why we were here—the *Panthera tigris altaica*, the endangered Amur tiger!

As I gazed up at the darkening ridges, I somehow sighed a bit of relief. Somehow, through all the human screw-ups, this cat has survived. A most satisfying end to a great day.

Day three was our last day, and we spent much of it talking with more lease owners. Finally, we all decided that our late evening attempt would be for wild boar, and we drove where we would have a good chance to see some. As we came around a corner, suddenly seven large boars (three monsters) were running parallel to the road. As we scrambled for our rifles (unfortunately, mine was with Sergey in the car behind us), we drove quickly to try to get in front of them before they hit the timber. We could see several starting to disappear into a thicket, so we leaped out and ran quickly to attempt a shot. As Ben Carter was in the lead, he kicked the bolt, aimed, squeezed, and "click"—dry fired. In all the commotion, the shell never made it to the chamber, and the boars all disappeared into the forest. Our hearts were all racing, as this was as close as we were going to get to bagging a big boar on this trip.

Keeping our spirits high, we toured one of the villages on the way back. It was a most modern village, as it had electricity powered by two large semi–truck diesel engines mounted on cement blocks. Each one would alternate its time to provide one of the most basic utilities to all the village homes. Combine this with the fact that most residents still have no indoor plumbing and still fetch their water from surface sources and community wells, and you feel you have stepped into a land that is frozen in time. During the Soviet era prior to 1992, all Russian citizens had all their needs met by the government. Now people must go without many basic things, and jobs are few and far between. This is why, in the frozen Far East, they turn to the forest and harvesting animals to survive.

As we feasted the last night at camp on wild

boar, roe deer, potatoes, and vodka, we told stories from all of our hunting pasts. Each story took twice as long as all had to be interpreted twice. We felt a close bond to our new Russian friends. That is what a hunting experience is all about. The most memorable times come out of walking in the forest, admiring the solitude and silence, where your senses awaken after being dulled by the noise of a city. And then, as a counterpoint, an exchange of cultures you only get by traveling to these remote places where these animals live and by the bonding between each other as you share a camp with your band of brothers.

The Tiger Friendly Certified hunting idea is definitely not without its challenges. But if the Russian wildlife, lease, and community leaders continue to work hard with passion, commitment, and the desire to make this succeed, and we, the international sport hunter community, when looking for a species that TFC areas offer, choose to pursue our quarry in such a place, then it will work. As a result, we just might have tigers roaming wild in the Taiga Forests for a few more generations. For me, that is the ultimate trophy.

To participate in Tiger Friendly Hunting in Siberia, contact www.savingtigers.com or John Banovich.

*John Banovich is an internationally acclaimed wildlife artist and conservationist. Visit his Web site at www.johnbanovich.com.*

## TURKEY

 **DREAM HUNT**

### Hunting Ibex and Staying in "Luxury Caves"

JOE HOSMER*

It was a cold and snowy February along the Maine coast. The newness of a fresh blanket of snow had worn off weeks ago. I was looking for spring, for an adventure, for something alive and warm.

In the day's mail I found a Safari Club International–Maine Chapter flyer tucked in among the junk mail and the spring L. L. Bean catalogs. The papers were promptly stuffed into the woodstove, and the L. L. Bean catalogs were tossed aside to be savored later.

The SCI flyer was the preview list for the Annual Banquet and Fund Raiser. Definitely a *must-read-now* document. The event was coming up shortly and was a social tradition in our household, for more than a few years now.

As I read the flyer, I fell upon the phrase "Luxury Caves" and "Istanbul." Simply the word "Istanbul" excites me. It conjures up all sorts of visions of sultans, oriental carpets, belly dancers, jewel-handled daggers, espionage, narrow streets; and did I mention belly dancers? Adventure, alive, and warm—Istanbul was the answer to my winter doldrums! However, what did "Luxury Caves" mean? Perhaps this was a misprint or a joke tossed in to see who was and was not paying attention.

I started my homework immediately. Who from the Maine Chapter had gone on this trip before? Was it a reputable outfitter? The hunt was for an ibex. Now exactly what was an ibex, and how many different types of ibex are there, should I choose to peruse a SCI slam? It turned out that this hunt was for a bezoar ibex, a mountain goat that has beautiful long horns that curve back over its head in a huge arc.

Is it safe? Would/could/should my wife and daughter, Sandy and Brittany, go with me to Istanbul? What will the airfare cost be? Is this an excuse to get another rifle, or will the 30-06 be sufficient? Right then winter in Maine was not quite as cold.

The SCI–Maine Chapter event came. Yes, I was the high bidder on the ibex hunt in Turkey and was able to talk to several adventuresome types who had taken the trip already. They had nothing but praise for the outfitter, Orhan Konakci of Safari Tours, Inc. They believed that there was a connection between Orhan and Maine, but no one was very clear about it.

It was decided to make this a family trip and fly in to Istanbul for a few days of history and touring. We would then fly to Antalya and stay (as part of our package) at a luxury resort right on the Mediterranean Ocean. I would hunt the illusive ibex, while my wife and daughter toured southern Turkey. After my hunt, we would regroup and travel back to Istanbul by way of Ephesus and other amazing Turkish destinations. By now, spring had sprung, and it was as beautiful as ever. It is often said that you do not deserve a Maine summer unless you can endure its winters. This is probably true, but spring and fall in Maine are pretty special, too!

Istanbul was a real treat. The spice shops, the oldest bookstore in the world, history on top of more history. It was all I had imagined it would be, including the belly dancer who insisted I join her on stage for a few provocative moves. To the delight of Sandy and Brittany, I was then later pulled from the crowd to sing a duet of "New York, New York, it is a Hell of a Town" with a local vocalist. Knowing that I could always return to Istanbul and get a gig as an American comedian, we flew south to gorgeous Antalya, on the Mediterranean.

At the hotel several men were waiting for me. Before I could change my clothes, I was whisked away to a van of nice but rough-looking characters and one young Turkish man, probably in his early twenties. He identified himself as my official interpreter and explained how he had gone to the University of Alabama to study English. I mean no offense to anyone here, but Alabama should not be the first choice to learn English. Try to perceive the combination of a heavy Turkish accent with the more "casual" pronunciations and colloquialisms used in Alabama. The combination of "y-all" mixed into broken English, and it is a wonder I am here to write this story.

As the van puttered into the mountains, the countryside became more and more special: fields and terraces cultivated before Christ's day; everyone smiling and waving. Sometimes we would drop off a person, and later we would pick up someone else. It was all part of the adventure, and I loved it!

When we finally reached a small village, my entourage consisted of a Turkish government forest ranger/guide, an assistant government forest ranger/guide, two "packers," and of course my English-Turkish interpreter—*"Go Razor Backs."*

I had been told that my 30-06 would do me just fine on ibex. So that is what I brought, although when I looked up at the mountains, I was wishing for something with a little more "reach."

"Now we must make sure y-all's gun shoots

straight, sir" was my interpreter's request following a 15-minute huddle with the others They all smiled and nodded after he spoke, just as if they understood what he said. I agreed and figured that it would be a good idea to make sure that the rifle was sighted in properly.

"Can y-all hit the rock?" asked the interpreter.

It was only out about 100 yards and the size of a bathtub. I aimed, shot, and hit the rock. They were pleased.

The senior forest ranger/guide was named "Mustafa." As it turned out, the assistant forest ranger/guide and one of the packers were also named "Mustafa." They quickly became "Mustafa #1," the ranger; "Mustafa #2," the assistant; and "Mustafa #3," the packer.

Mustafa #1 went and placed a tin can in the middle of the rock that was my target. That was fine, except that he went and stood behind the rock—head, shoulders, and arms exposed outside the protection of the boulder. I had concerns and would not shoot the can with him just standing there. I was assured that my gun could not shoot through the rock, and Mustafa #1 would be totally unharmed! No way would I shoot with him standing there! Finally, Mustafa #1 agreed to kneel down behind the rock, with no extremities sticking out, so I would shoot the can. I shot the can, and a very disgusted Mustafa #1 emerged. Apparently I did not have enough faith in my gun to shoot with him exposed: If he had faith, why didn't I? This was an argument I was not going to win. I instinctively sprang back to my years of training as a husband—I kept my mouth shut and prayed that this would eventually blow over. Thankfully it did!

From here, we gathered up everything and started walking into the mountains. I was still in the clothes I put on this morning to fly out of Istanbul in. Street shoes, no camouflage—heck, I did not even have a jackknife in my pocket.

My interpreter said we would come out of the mountains in four or five days unless we had an accident or ran out of water. I began to think, "What have I gotten myself into?"

The more we walked, the steeper it got. The steeper it got, the hotter it got. Mustafa #1 and #2 stopped and conversed. Eventually they addressed my interpreter, who in turn told me they thought I was doing okay for someone who was fat and did not trust his rifle.

What seemed like forever found us on the precipice of a deep hole. We peered down into this hole, which was probably 100 yards across and 200 yards deep. As I was gawking over the edge, I looked back and found that my entourage had disappeared. A quick search found a narrow little path leading downward. I waited and eventually heard voices. Thankfully, it was my crew, and I caught up to them about the time we hit the bottom of this craterlike hole. Without saying a word, they all marched under a low overhanging ledge and into a fissure about 10 feet around. From this outlet came a wave of refreshingly cool air. Was this it—a luxury cave? Yes! Just one of several I would be residing in before this journey was through.

The cave had an uninviting dirt floor, but the porters soon cut pine bows and laid them into a little nest for me. On top of the pine bows they laid my sleeping bag. A fire was soon built at the entrance of the cave. The fire would be used for warmth as the night became cooler. Our cave entrance, at the bottom of this large rock silo, probably only saw the sun for a few minutes each day, around noon. The fire would also be used for cooking and keeping away any "beasties" that happened to wander by.

The back of the cave was blocked off, floor to ceiling, with stones. I have no idea why. This wall was probably 20 feet in from the entrance and stood 10 feet high and 20 feet wide. Through the stone flowed a steady stream of cool air. The air came up from the bowels of the cave through a catacomb of lava rock crevasses and fissures. My interpreter said that the mountains were called the "The Mountains of No Return." About then I remembered that I really disliked bats.

A feast of rice and goat's meat was cooked and served with great reverence. I was almost too exhausted to eat, but I did, and it was certainly well worth the effort! Using my jeans for a pillow, I soon forgot about bats and beasties and fell fast asleep.

The morning brought a chance to get into hunting clothes and hiking boots. This met with approval of the guides. Apparently they never understood why I was dressed the way I was the day before. After much chatter, Mustafa #1 and #2, my interpreter, and I departed the cave and began trekking up the steep wall of our silo, heading for the highest peak we could see.

A couple hours later found us on top of this world. My legs were throbbing, but my feet and ankles were grateful for the boots. The plan was to look for ibex from this vantage point, then stalk close enough to get a good shot. A problem seemed to be that it was unusually hot. The temperature was consistently over 100°F.

In such weather the ibex would stay under ledge overhangs or nestled out of sight between tall boulders for shade and the coolness. Our only hope was to find one that was out in the cool of the day, feeding. Eventually we spotted a pair of young ibex kids, but where was their dad? I watched the young goats play, seemingly unaffected by the temperatures of the day.

All of a sudden, I could only see one young ibex. Where did the other go? As I am scanning the terrain for the missing ibex, I see the remaining ibex bound from boulder to boulder, to a tree limb. The ibex was starting to climb up a huge pine tree! Soon I spot his missing sibling who is by now 50 or 60 feet up the same pine tree.

The two ibex climbed the tree, up and down, for well over an hour. Mustafa #1 said that it was unusual to see but not unheard of for the young ones to play in large trees. By now, it was midday. A large fire was built in the 100-degree heat, and hot soup and canned meat were on the lunch menu today.

I enjoyed my day of watching the young ibex play and climb, but that was a sideshow to what the guides were supposed to show me. We left our mountaintop vantage point at warp speed and bounded from boulder to boulder, not unlike the ibex I had watched earlier. My guides had decided to get me to see a good, shootable ibex trophy, even if it killed me!

We took a new route off the mountain and eventually came to a huge ledge outcrop with a fire pit and a rock-bounded bed of pine bows. Mustafa #1 went crazy! Apparently, another person was hunting in our territory, and this was his makeshift camp. Mustafa #1 being the senior man had never approved such an intervention.

An hour later, I saw our porters sitting around a fire, cooking our dinner, again at the mouth of another cave. Apparently, the porters had traveled the valley while we were climbing the peaks and jumping boulder to boulder. My pine bow bed was prepared, and my sleeping bag nicely laid out for me. I could tell that Mustafa #1 was still upset with the interloper.

The interpreter asked me if I wanted to go with Mustafa #1 to get water. I said, "Sure," and off the three of us went. We came to a small cave entrance that went down at about a 45-degree slant. I could walk down it, but I was hunched over all the way. Soon the cave opened up into a huge room. The entrance way was about 6 feet from the floor of the room. The room was maybe 50 feet high and twice as wide. I was cold for the first time. In the middle of the room's floor sat a great white and sparkling mound. I thought that Wilbur Smith could write an entire novel around this single moment.

The mound was snow. It sat in this natural refrigerator, unaware that the outside temperature was over 100 degrees. I was told that, in the winter, snow will fall in these mountains and blow into many of the caves. Who knows how long it will last or how old this snow really is. Certainly, the snow mound I am looking at did not fall in just one season.

We gathered up as much snow as we could. We filled the pans and containers we had brought, along with stuffing our pockets, hats, and anything else. I struggled with getting back up to the entranceway but eventually got a hand from my companions.

Once outside we set up a melting pot where we would place the snow. In minutes, the snow melted with just the outside temperature (80°F). Once melted, Mustafa #1 would pour the snow through his handkerchief, from one pot to another. I did not question his filtration system but prayed that our bounty would eventually be boiled. After dinner, I crashed exhausted onto my bed of pine bows and was asleep in seconds.

No, these were not my idea of "Luxury Caves"; but at the time, they sure felt like it. I was soon awakened by loud arguing and yelling. Apparently, the interloper, whose campsite we had discovered earlier, came for a visit. When the yelling had stopped, his guide/forest ranger had apologized and agreed to hunt in a different area over the next few days. He had not realized that he was encroaching on his boss's favorite hunting ground.

The next thing I knew, there was a tall man, wearing a big hat and puffing on a cigar, standing by my sleeping bag. I got up and slid into my jeans. Now, somewhat decent, I introduced myself. The stranger did the same. He spoke English. I asked if he, too, was from the States. He simply responded by saying, "Pennsylvania."

"Really?" I said. "I am from Maine, another Northeasterner!"

The man replied that he had a cousin who lives in Maine. Somewhere in the southern part of the state, south of Portland, actually Saco, Maine. I said that although I was from the Freeport area, north of Portland, I knew Saco fairly well. In fact, I had just dropped off my bird dogs at a kennel outside of Saco.

"Whereabouts?" he asked.

"Bar Mills," I replied. Well, as this conversation unfolded, the stranger's cousin worked his bird dogs at the same place I do. I know who his cousin is, by sight; and both the stranger and I own Gordon setters—arguably the best-kept hunting secret ever to be sneaked out of Scotland!

As we talked, we discovered that we both belong to and supported Safari Club International. This connection, of course, led us to several friends and acquaintances we had in common. What a small world! Sitting here in a cave, in the "Mountains of No Return," talking to another Gordon setter–owning American with several Maine and SCI connections in common. The stranger was Ed Yates, one of the most outstanding hunters in the world and, more important, someone who over the years has become someone I am proud to call a "friend."

Several more days and caves passed. The days were almost all like the movie *Groundhog Day*. We got up, trudged up a steep mountaintop, and watched for ibex. Seeing none, we moved to the next cave, ate rice and something, and started over. It was simply just too hot for the ibex to be out and about.

On our way out of the mountains on the last day, I heard a terrible screech, followed by noises I could not identify. Our entourage ran forward to where we could see what was happening. It was a giant golden eagle swooping down upon and trying to kill a goat. The goat was blatting, apparently hurt from the first hit. Soon the huge eagle came down upon and struck the goat again, and the mountains went silent. This was one hunter who had found his prey.

Upon my return to Antalya, I met Orhan Konakci, the owner of Safari Tours, Inc. Orhan had seen to it that both my wife Sandy and daughter Brittany had been taken care of like royalty. As Orhan and I talked, I asked him what his Maine connection was. Among many things, Orhan described how he had been an exchange student back in his high school days and had gone to Cape Elizabeth High School back in the 1960s. I asked if he was there in 1967, whereupon he responded positively! I asked if he had happened to play soccer. With a now-familiar smile, he assured me he was the star of the team and played center forward. As it turned out, I played soccer for a rival team—North Yarmouth Academy. Coincidently, I was the goalie Orhan was always trying to get around to score.

Orhan and I had been friendly high school rivals almost 30 years ago. We relived each game as though it was played only last week. It became apparent to me that Orhan was confused about some of the goals he made and did not make, but I forgave him, as he was a heck of a player nonetheless!

Although I came home emptyhanded, I will always recount this as one of my better hunting adventures—incomparable mountain climbing and hiking, the privilege to watch young ibex climb trees, and the awe of seeing a golden eagle kill a goat. Making a new friend, then finding an old one. Time to explore history and Turkey with my two girls. And Istanbul belly dancers! How lucky can I be?

To book your ibex hunt:

**SAFARI TOURS**
Post Office Box 199
07002 Antalya Turkey
Phone : +90 242 247 27 96 - 241 84 93;
fax : +90 242 243 56 86
Email : hunt@safaritours.us
www.safaritours.us/index.asp

*Joe Hosmer spends his winters and springs in Hunt, Texas, with his summers and falls in Durham, Maine. He is currently vice president of Safari Club International and chairs the Safari Club International Foundation Conservation Committee. Hosmer is the founder of MOUNTAIN, LTD., an international staffing and recruiting firm. He now works as a business consultant who specializes in coaching business owners on the principles of the fine art of growing their businesses.*

# Central and South America

 **DREAM HUNT**

## Robinson Crusoe's Goats

The wing shooting for ducks, geese, and doves in Argentina, Patagonia, and Chile is legendary—1,000 birds a day is not unreasonable.

That is certainly an extraordinary hunt, but even more unique and exotic is hunting Chile's offshore islands, which are just a few hundred miles north of Antarctica. And the most exotic huntable species has to be the dwarf goats of Robinson Crusoe Island of the Juan Fernandez archipelago in the South Pacific Ocean, some 400 miles offshore.

Dwarf goats in themselves are unusual game, but these goats are very special—the descendants of the goats that a stranded sailor lived on for four and a half years before being found—a real event that inspired the famous novel *Robinson Crusoe*.

In 1704 Scottish sailor Alexander Selkirk joined

a pirate expedition to the Pacific Ocean that was led by Capt. William Dampier. After numerous raids on the Spanish towns and shipping in the Pacific, in 1705 they were preparing to return to England with their booty. The ship had suffered considerable damage in battle, and Selkirk felt they needed to repair her before setting off around the Horn. The captain disagreed. After a heated argument and in a fit of anger, Selkirk refused to go any farther and demanded he be set ashore on the Island of Juan Fernandez, which is about 400 miles off the coast of Chile. This the captain was glad to do.

Once ashore, Selkirk realized what he had done. He thought others in the crew would join him, but none did. He changed his mind and tried to convince the captain to take him back. The captain refused, and Selkirk found he had marooned himself alone on an uninhabited island. Actually this was the smart thing to do since the ship later sank, killing most of those aboard.

After two years of isolation, a ship appeared, and Selkirk went down to meet it, only to find that it was a Spanish ship that fired on him as a pirate.

Selkirk was finally found in February 1709 by William Dampier, who was then pilot on a private expedition headed by Captain Woodes Rogers.

The archipelago where Selkirk was marooned, today known as the Juan Fernandez archipelago, is made up of three islands, Robinson Crusoe, Alejandro Selkirk, and Santa Clara. Only the first of these is populated, with 500 inhabitants who maintain a nineteenth-century serenity and indifference to the outside world.

Since 1977, the Juan Fernandez islands have been listed as World Biosphere Reserves; they are considered to be of maximum scientific importance because of the rare native species of flora and fauna. Some 101 of the 146 native species of plants are endemic. The red hummingbird is most famous for its needle-fine black beak and silken feather coverage. As one might imagine, hunting permits are very rarely approved. Only Huntingchile is allowed to bring hunters to this remote paradise.

Goats were introduced to these islands by sailors during the sixteenth and seventeenth centuries to create a food source for passing boats. After hundreds of years of inbreeding, the goats have changed their shape to a very small body with long horns, now known as the "dwarf goat."

There are even people on the Island of Tobago who claim to be descended from Robinson Crusoe. Also on the island is the cave where Selkirk spent part of his life and the dwarf goats he hunted.

You can see photos of the hunt and the island at http://new.photos.yahoo.com/huntingchilepics/album/576460762324791843.

Special Note. The landscape on Robinson Crusoe Island is very rugged—steep, rocky hills and thick vegetation in some places. Hunters must be in good physical condition and able to negotiate some tough terrain.

Travel. Hunters must fly to Santiago International Airport, where we will meet them and clear customs. A driver will take hunters to the Tobalaba local airport to catch a local flight to Robinson Crusoe Island.

Huntingchile specializes in unique hunts in what may be the last real wilderness on earth. In addition to dwarf goats, we also offer hunts for guanacos and a very remote population of whitetail deer in the southern Peruvian Andes. This is the most remote location for whitetail deer in the world. The animals live in high, rugged mountainous areas. Their antlers are small but nicely shaped.

We also offer hunts for Magellan goose at Cape Horn in a very remote and exclusive area.

And if you want privacy, you can also hunt beaver in the most remote human settlement worldwide, Isla Navarino, a Chilean island located between Isla Grande de Tierra del Fuego, to the north, and the Cape Horn, to the south. The island is the land base nearest to Antarctica.

Contact:

**HUNTINGCHILE, DIRECTOR CARLOS HERNANDEZ**
Maria Teresa 6248, Las Condes
Santiago, Chile
Phone: 56-2-2114130;
mobile: 56-9-94001223
www.huntingchile16.50megs.com

## MEXICO

In the Sonora region of Mexico, there are 8.5 million acres of outstanding hunting habitat that have been divided into 500 ranchero-owned Units of Management and Sustainable Use of Wildlife (UMAS), which are regulated and licensed by the state. It is one of the best hunting spots in Mexico.

# DREAM HUNT

## Sonora Coues Deer

JAMESON PARKER*

In *Meditations on Hunting*, the Spanish philosopher José Ortega y Gasset explains why men hunt: "When you are fed up with the troublesome present, with being 'very twentieth century,' you take your gun, whistle for your dog, go out to the mountain, and, without further ado, give yourself the pleasure during a few hours or a few days of being 'Paleolithic.'"

I'm not sure I want to go all the way back to the Paleolithic, but when I hunt I do want to get away from traffic jams and television and deadlines and 1040 forms from the IRS. I want above all to get away from the unrelenting noise of modern American life, and that is hard to do anywhere in America. Even in Alaska, airplanes overhead remind you how pervasive our civilization is.

Not so on the western slope of the Sierra Madre Occidental in Sonora, Mexico. In 1541, when Coronado passed through the village now known as Magdalena, it was not appreciably quieter than it is today. Traffic is scant. Small plots of land along the rivers are still farmed by horse- or donkey-drawn plow. And when you leave the hardtop, the only other travelers you may see are vaqueros covering great distances on small, tough, gaited horses. Hunting in these mountains is as close to going back in time as it is possible to get in this age of space stations and suicide bombers.

The Coues deer (it's supposed to be pronounced "cows," though no one does) is the smallest *huntable* subspecies of whitetail. (The smallest subspecies is the endangered Florida Key deer.) A product of geographic isolation, the Coues is found in mountainous areas of southern Arizona, southwestern New Mexico, possibly in a small part of extreme southeastern California, and above all in the Sierra Madre Mountains of Mexico. They have a reputation for being the most elusive of all whitetails, though I've never known any kind of whitetail to be careless or conspicuous during hunting season. It is more likely that they are extremely hard for most hunters to find because the deer are so small and the land they inhabit is so big. It just takes a while for your eyes to adjust. Not only is the land big; it is also extremely arid, so deer density is low. If you are used to midwestern whitetail hunting where deer density is high (15 per square mile or more in Missouri, for example), you are going to be disappointed the first time you hunt Coues deer.

By law, in Mexico, you must hunt with an outfitter. Unfortunately, just as in everything else in the world, there are plenty of crooks out there waiting to make a buck. Safari Club International has just (as of the start of 2007) issued a warning regarding unscrupulous outfitters who are breaking Mexican laws and sometimes encouraging their clients to do the same. Unless you want your hunt to end in a Mexican prison, make sure you find a good, reputable outfitter who is properly licensed and, if he is an American, legally documented to hunt in Mexico. You also want to make sure your outfitter is up to date on all the latest USFWS and USDA forms required at the border to bring a trophy into the United States. Otherwise, you risk having to spend a lot of additional money getting your trophy shipped to a licensed taxidermist or, worse, losing the trophy altogether.

After that, trust your guide.

The first time I hunted Coues deer in Mexico, my guide was a seventy-year-old man who spoke not a word of English, but he spoke deer fluently. Not only did he outwalk me; he could spot deer with his naked eye—he didn't even wear glasses—that I had trouble finding with 10-power binoculars. A good outfitter will have good guides, and these men know their stuff.

You also want to trust your guide when the time comes to make a shot. Coues deer are subject to both Bergman's rule (the farther away from the equator, the larger the body mass of any given species) and Allen's rule (the extremities of warm-blooded animals will be smaller in the colder, northern parts of their range and larger in the warmer, southern parts). What this means is that you will be looking at a deer not much larger than a German shepherd, but with larger-than-normal ears and tail, so good luck judging a rack. The first time I hunted Coues deer, I saw four or five bucks I thought were dandy, but my guide just shook his head. When he finally did find a deer that got him excited, I couldn't see the difference. It takes time and experience to get familiar with these diminutive deer, so listen to your guide when he tells you to shoot or not to shoot.

And your shot will probably be longer than you are used to, so you will need a highly accurate, flat-shooting rifle and first-rate optics. The *closest* shot I have ever made on a Coues deer was a touch over 300 yards. My guide spotted him (trust your guide) at the end of the day about 800 yards away up a long draw, and we scrambled, ran, and finally crawled, trying to beat the fading light, and we were incredibly lucky on two counts. The buck had fed down the draw as we came up the other side of the ridge and had come much closer than we could have hoped, only about 200 yards away. That was the good news. The bad news was that he knew we were there and took off running, but then he did something completely uncharacteristic of whitetails and stopped to look back at us at the 300-yard mark. Most shots will probably be longer than that.

Ten-power binoculars, or stronger, and a good spotting scope are a must, as is the finest rifle scope you can possibly afford. The most accurate rifle in the world won't get the job done if you scrimp on the optics. I would also recommend a laser range finder, because you will invariably misjudge the distance.

But don't forget you came to Mexico as much to get away from the twenty-first century as to hunt deer. Sonora is the second-largest state in Mexico, and the varieties of terrain are staggering, from tranquil beaches to arid desert to rugged mountains, and history is everywhere. In Magdalena, the mission dates to 1688. The town of Huatabampo is even older, dating back to 1614, while Alamos, founded in 1681, is considered one of the unspoiled jewels of Mexico. Everywhere, away from the big cities, the pace of life is slower and simpler and quieter.

You won't even hear an airplane overhead.

There are two American-based outfitters I can recommend. One is Kirk Kelso of Pusch Ridge Outfitters. Kirk and his wife Roxanne have years of experience and also guide for mule deer, antelope, elk, and desert bighorns. They can be reached at:

**PUSCH RIDGE OUTFITTERS**
11077 East Escalante Road
Tucson, AZ 85730
Phone: 520 544 0954
www.puschridgeoutfitters.com

The other is Patrick Holehan of Gone Huntin' Outfitters. Patrick guides for Coues deer, pronghorns, and Gould's turkeys. He is also a maker of fine custom rifles, so if you book with him, you have the advantage of being able to order one of his beautiful and highly accurate long guns. He can be reached at:

**GONE HUNTIN' OUTFITTERS**

5758 East 34th Street

Tucson, AZ 85711

Phone: 520-745-0622

Email: plholehan@theriver.com

www.plholehancustomrifles.com

*Jameson Parker is the author of* An Accidental Cowboy *(Thomas Dunne/St. Martin's Press) and the editor of the anthology* To Absent Friends *(Willow Creek Press). He writes the Sporting Life column in* Sporting Classics.

---

 **DREAM HUNT**

---

## Quest for the Ocellated Wild Turkey in the Yucatan

JEFF ENGEL

I took my first wild turkey many years ago. As thrilled as I was back on that cool spring morning in Wisconsin, I never dreamed that my interest in this challenging game bird would ultimately lead to an attempt to complete the World Slam of the wild turkey—one of each species: Rio Grande, Osceloa, Merriam's, eastern, ocellated, and Gould's.

A jungle hunt in the wilds of the Yucatan would be required to harvest my last bird for my World Slam, the ocellated.

The Yucatan Peninsula juts out into the Atlantic, forming the lower rim of the Gulf of Mexico outside of Merida, not far from the equator.

As you might guess, this is an area where the temperatures can get to be extreme. I experienced afternoon temperatures of well over 100 degrees with almost 100% humidity.

The camp that we stayed at was very remote,

complete with thatched roof lodges, open-aired windows, and mosquito netting surrounding our cots. Since there was no electricity, at night we would dine under the soft glow of a lantern. Our shower was also solar-powered with a 55-gallon drum resting safely on a wooden frame that you would walk into. It may sound primitive, but it was oh so refreshing.

This hunt began with a challenge: my luggage was lost. So I had to borrow someone else's old camouflage clothes and wear my deck shoes, not exactly the gear I had carefully packed for the hunt. The camouflage pants were extremely short; in fact, the cuff was well above my ankle. The only shirt I was able to borrow was a bit too small, and the sleeves ended well above my wrists. Never before have I hunted with such an interesting set of clothes, and I have to admit it felt very funny to walk in the jungle with a pair of deck shoes on my feet. Nevertheless, I had to make due with what I had borrowed. Hunting as we all know is about overcoming obstacles, and I was not going to let the loss of gear stand between me and the hunt I had prepared a year for.

The ocellated turkey is a distinct species from the other five turkeys that make up the World Slam. The eastern, Merriam's, Rio Grande, Osceola, and Gould's turkeys are all subspecies of *Meleagris gallopavo*. The ocellated is known among scientific circles as *Meleagris ocellata*. Unlike their northern cousins, it may be difficult to have them respond to a call. In addition, the thick jungle makes stalking them on the ground virtually impossible—this and the fact that males and females look very similar, with the exception that the males have long, sharp spurs.

When the birds are walking in the thick jungle, it is extremely difficult to tell a male from a female. The male will gobble on the roost, and the local people often call the gobble of the ocellated "singing." All of this means that taking a shot at a roosted turkey in the Yucatan is an accepted method by many people.

There are several techniques to choose from when hunting the ocellated turkey. One is to listen for a bird gobbling, or singing on the roost, just as it would start to get dark, and then find that spot again early in the morning in the dark and wait until light for a shot. If the hunter were to spook the bird off the tree and it would land on the jungle floor and walk off, it would be almost impossible to locate that bird again because of the extreme density of the jungle. Another technique that people are using with more success is being able to call the bird to them. A third technique would be to set up in an area where the birds are known to frequent and wait, like hunting for ducks or deer.

On our first day of hunting, we were up well before dawn as we walked through the thick jungle with the aid of a flashlight. Despite hours of creeping through the dense growth, we heard no gobbles and saw no birds. At times my guide paused and stood still and just listened, oftentimes making a call or whistle from his mouth to imitate a hen turkey in the hope of hearing or enticing a gobble.

After going back to camp at midday for the "mandatory siesta," which was welcome after getting up so early, we would head back into the jungle and try to listen for a gobbling bird on the roost. Again, that evening we didn't hear any gobbles.

The next morning we were up at 3:00 A.M. and again walking in the pitch-black jungle, hoping to hear a near or distant gobble. Like the day before, we didn't hear any turkeys. It's a challenge to walk with only a small flashlight in the dark, thick, dense jungle where poisonous snakes live, and I tried not to think about the fact that my knee-high snake boots were still missing from my feet. However, my deck shoes were getting a very good workout.

By midday, we headed back to camp and

rested for the afternoon hunt. Midafternoon, we were back in the jungle, listening for a gobble. As we walked through the jungle, I was acutely aware of the fact that poisonous snakes could be anywhere when we finally heard our first gobble. We quietly approached within about 150 yards of where the bird was and marked the spot.

The next morning we were again up at 3:00 A.M., this time with renewed enthusiasm. After driving down an old two-track road for about a half hour, we left the old army-style jeep and walked into the thick, dense jungle wall that was almost impossible to penetrate. Fortunately, my very competent Mayan guide had a machete and chopped a path through the impassable maize.

As we walked in the thick jungle, we would periodically hear the gobbler singing on the roost. After about half an hour of walking, we noticed the gobble getting louder and louder. Soon we were within about 30 yards of the roosted bird. We stood motionless, waiting for shooting light. I was very aware that the bird could pitch off the roost at any moment. When it was time to shoot, I slowly raised my shotgun and launched a jungle-penetrating load of #2 shot, and in a cloud of leaves and feathers falling, the bird came tumbling down. I had finally taken an ocellated turkey.

After years of hunting across the United States and Mexico, my World Slam quest was finally complete. I couldn't help but admire this unusually beautiful bird. The bird's feathers were iridescent, with a wide range of greens and blues throughout, with stunning unique tail feathers.

The ocellated turkey gets its name from the eyelike markings on his tail feathers. I was elated to have successfully taken such an astonishing game

bird, and I was humbled by the whole experience. As I looked at the turkey in my hand, I felt deep emotion realizing how fortunate I was to be able to hunt such an impressive game bird.

As we were walking along the edge of the jungle, going back to the truck, my Mayan guide who was walking in front of me suddenly came to a halt in midstep, turned back, and motioned for me to stop. I learned a long time ago that when language is a barrier, one must rely on hand signals and facial expressions—and his facial expression showed some form of terror. I instinctively froze in midstep. After about 30 seconds, I could hear the faint buzz of insects; and at that moment, just above us, at tree height, was a swarm of bees. The swarm was about the size of a Volkswagen. The bees flew directly over us and fortunately away. My Mayan guide had heard these bees a full 30 seconds before I had. I wondered if this had been a narrow escape.

Once our jeep rolled into camp, I shouted out in excitement "*pavo*," which means wild turkey, to our hunt organizer George Sansores, and he was elated that I had taken a tremendous bird. George helped me weigh the bird and measure the spurs. With a smile as broad as a slice of cantaloupe, he shook my hand and said, "Congratulations, you have just taken a truly world-class bird."

That night we enjoyed the meat from the turkey, and it was delicious.

I had a few days left on this hunt. With my quest completed, I enjoyed the opportunity to experience some other aspects of the Yucatan. We found some remote Mayan ruins and did some exploring in areas where there was no tourists. A trip to some of this region's intriguing ruins could not help but evoke images of the advanced culture that once inhabited this area.

If you are considering going on a hunt like this, there are several tips I would like to offer: It is a good idea to have a small, compact, portable battery-operated fan that you can use throughout the night, because no electricity means no air conditioning, and the extreme heat, along with the humidity, made sleeping rather warm. In addition, the outfitter provided the shotguns and shotgun shells, so there was no need to transport these with you. It is also a good idea to take along a pair of knee-high snake boots, just in case. I found the Mayan guides to be extremely competent. I found myself watching the guides very closely as to where to walk and where not to walk, and I would simply follow their lead as we walked through the jungle.

There is also a very good chance that you would be eating refried beans for breakfast, lunch, and dinner, and the main food type was Mexican. If your stomach does not tolerate this type of food, you may want to consider bringing along some of your own provisions. A very important item that should not be neglected is sunscreen, especially for your nose and the tips of your ears, as the sun here can be very intense. Also, make sure to check the most recent regulations as to the best way of importing your bird back into the United States.

Every turkey hunt is memorable, but hunting the ocellated turkey in the jungle of the Yucatan was truly an adventurous turkey hunt, one that I will never forget.

For hunting ocellated wild turkeys in Yucatan, contact:

**WINGSHOOTER SAFARIS**
Shane Smith
804 Busbey Avenue
Bridgeport, AL 35740
Phone: 256-495-2596
www.wingshootersafaris.com/ocellated_hunts.html

# Down Under

 **DREAM HUNT**

## Manuka Point Lodge, Rakaia Valley, Southern Alps—Live Like A King and Hunt the King's Stag

JAMES SWAN

The only mammals native to New Zealand are two species of bats. As European immigrants began to settle in New Zealand, the spectacular beauty of the islands' snowcapped mountains, lush forests, and rushing streams seemed ideal for many game species from other parts of the world, and so they began to import them—fallow deer, chamois, tahrs, wild sheep and goats, wild boars, wapiti, whitetail deer, and red stags.

On February 23, 1897, the steamer SS *Waikato* departed London with three stags and six hinds secure in crates on the foredeck. The lineage of these red stags can be traced back as far as 1066 to Stoke Park in Buckinghamshire, England, which has been owned and hunted by many members of the British royalty.

This small foundation herd of red deer was finally released into the wild Rakaia Valley west of Christchurch, South Island, at Manuka Point on October 21, 1897, and placed under protection. The first hunting licenses for them were issued to select persons in April 1907. Today, many trophy-class stags have come from these Southern Alps, and there are many more waiting for you when you hunt with Don Patterson, guide and owner of Manuka Point Lodge.

Manuka Point Lodge is in a spectacular alpine setting about two and a half hours' drive from Christchurch. You have to ford the Rakaia River to get there, which is why outfitter Don Patterson and his wife Julie convey hunters to the lodge in a vehicle with 32-inch tires and a snorkel exhaust.

There are 18,500 acres of private land, with both free-range and fenced estate hunting, and the snowcapped mountain setting is breathtaking.

Aside from the spectacular scenery and abundance of game animals, what makes this hunt especially interesting is that Don and Julie take only one

party at a time. You live in their gracious home, Julie cooks, and even does laundry.

Two private bedrooms, native timber furniture, original artwork on the walls, crystal glassware, leather suites, and New Zealand cuisine and fine wines.

Outfitter and guide Don Patterson has been awarded the New Zealand Best Trophy of all species. With Don's guidance, you can hunt record-book red stag, tahr, chamois, fallow deer, elk, wild boar, South Pacific goats, and South Pacific rams, plus ducks, geese, and more trout than you can imagine. See Section D for a special recipe.

Hunting season: March 1–August 31. Weather: temperate—lows around 30°; highs of 50° to 70°F.

**MANUKA POINT LODGE**

RD Methven, South Island, New Zealand
Phone: 64-3-318-5878; fax: 64-3-318-5879
www.manukapoint.com

# DREAM HUNT

## New Zealand Adventures

SHEROL ENGEL

Mountains rich with game rise from verdant valleys, laced with world-class trout streams. It seems spending time outdoors is important to everyone you meet in this beautiful island nation of 4 million people. The scenery could not be more beautiful. New Zealand is an outdoorsman's paradise.

Although turkey hunting and fishing figured prominently in our trip, one of the nice things about New Zealand is there is plenty to do for a nonhunter. For instance, a nonparticipating partner could accompany a hunter or fisherman to New Zealand and still have a tremendous trip. There are cultural aspects to enjoy, such as watching the entertaining Maori natives in concert. The Maori people are the natives of New Zealand who arrived from Hawaiki by voyaging canoes over 1,000 years ago. The Maori now make up over 14% of the population. Their language and culture have a major impact on all facets of New Zealand art, film, television, poetry, theater, and hip-hop.

After landing in Auckland, New Zealand's largest city, we sampled some tasty eats and took in some local sights. Water plays a big role in the recreation of New Zealanders. And so it is fitting that our New Zealand adventure began on Lake Taupo, trolling for rainbow trout.

Our guide Simon Jolly from Chris Jolly Outdoors promised us some fishing action, as well as our first good look at New Zealand's spectacular scenery, and he followed through on both admirably.

We were in the central part of the North Island of New Zealand on Lake Taupo, with snow-capped mountains as our backdrop. Lake Taupo is a world-renowned self-sustaining fishery. The trout weigh, on average, about 3 pounds. Some say they get as large as 20 pounds. The afternoon flew by, and as luck would have it, I caught my first rainbow trout.

As the sun dipped low and twilight fell upon us, we relaxed in the lower deck of the boat while Simon cleaned and prepared our fish for a delicious light supper, complete with some refreshing New Zealand brew. Jeff and I felt that if the rest of our trip was even half as nice as this fishing cruise, we would not be disappointed, and we certainly weren't!

One of the other unique nonhunting trips was our breathtaking aerial tour of the Milford Sound Mountain Range, known as the Southern Alps. From the heights of the mountains, we descended to the waters of the beautifully serene fjords, where we experienced awe-inspiring beauty at another level. For those who may not know what a fjord is, it is a long narrow arm of the sea that has invaded a valley that represents the seaward end of a deeply excavated glacial trough. The valley is partially submerged by the sea after the glacier, which created it, melts.

Abundant waterfalls, snowcapped mountains, and tranquil bays were stretched out as far as we could see. I'll be the first to admit that our camera had a hard time doing this indescribably spectacular scenery justice.

Now, let me take you on our turkey hunt adventure . . .

Virtually every culture on earth has a hunting tradition. And so perhaps it was not surprising that although I was as far from the United States as possible, I felt right at home here.

New Zealand is about two-thirds the size of

Wisconsin. But into that small space it packs a lot of diversity: a beautiful coastline, fertile valleys, rolling plains, and mountains, including what are rightfully called the Southern Alps.

Jeff and I elected mountain Merriam turkey hunting. Jeff would be the actual hunter; I would be filming for our show. For me, capturing a hunt on camera is as good as doing the hunting myself.

It was September, which is New Zealand's spring.

Wild turkeys were introduced to New Zealand around the 1890s. They have since flourished here. We wanted to see if hunting wild turkeys in New Zealand was as exciting and challenging as in the States, and we were about to be given that chance.

New Zealand is beautiful country to hunt. I was taken back by its rolling and, in places, even alpine landscape. It has a temperate climate with good rainfall, and everywhere we traveled was lush green foliage. We also soon realized that New Zealand is a turkey paradise. The flocks are large, and they roam unimpeded for miles over the rich countryside. It is also a turkey hunter's paradise. The season is open year-round, and there is no bag limit. For us, accustomed to bag limits of one or two bird per year per state, the opportunity to take several birds in one week was very unusual and made for some very exciting hunting.

While being driven to our hunting destination by Colin Jones, guide for Chris Jolly Outdoors, Colin briefed us on what to expect. He told us we would probably see 50 to 60 birds today. It was only seconds later when we saw 22 turkeys in one flock on a distant hillside. Jeff was anxious to get his hunting gear on. Once Colin stopped at our destination, Chris Jolly met us to also lend his guide expertise on our first hunt. Jeff walked to the hilltop and immediately saw 10 turkeys, five or six of them gobblers; one for sure had a long beard. Using a box call, Jeff began making some soft yelps, then changed to his

slate call and made some more soft yelps and a few purrs. Jeff excitedly whispered, "I see them. They are about 100 yards away and coming this way." He readied himself, with gun resting on his knees as he slowly and silently leaned against a large tree on

the edge of the field. Somewhere during his slow methodical movements, he set down his slate call and placed a reed call in his mouth. Maybe it had been there all along, as I never saw him move his hands.

The birds slowly approached, looking intently for the hen that had been calling them so seductively. At just the right moment, Jeff made a loud cluck with his mouth call; the turkeys raised their heads and stretched their long necks in a confused alert movement. Jeff took aim at the biggest gobbler that had moved far enough away from the flock and fired. Almost instantly, he was joined by Chris and Colin, who had been hiding in the woods, to share in Jeff's excitement. Colin pulled a weight hook from his pocket to see what size bird Jeff actually got. Mr. Tom turkey weighed in at exactly 19 pounds and sported a curly 7.5-inch beard. This is an average bird for this area.

Because there are no natural predators in New Zealand, the turkeys are comfortable roosting on fence posts, so we saw lots of turkey sign as we walked the hills and fields. There were about 20 turkeys over

the hill from where we were walking. Jeff was most interested in the gobblers he saw with the 8.5- to 9-inch beards. I was interested in getting the camera gear set up so I could film without being seen.

Now in position, Jeff alternated between using his mouth call and box call in an effort to draw these elusive birds within range. The flock slowly ascended the hillside and moved within range. Jeff, ever so slowly, raised his gun and waited for them to separate enough to give him a clear shot. Silently, he took off his safety—which can be a difficult thing to do with so many ears and eyes seeing and hearing the slightest sound or movement. Jeff aimed, shot, and hit his target. This guy had an 8.5-inch beard and had spurs three-fourths of an inch long, which was not a massive bird but still quite nice and plenty big for a nice turkey dinner. We could not have been luckier, as the chef of our hotel offered to make us a very special dinner using the very turkey Jeff had taken earlier. It was a feast we will always remember.

New Zealand is a remarkable place. We experienced some fantastic fly-fishing, bagged several great gobblers, and met some unexpected thrills. But I would have to say that what really impressed me was the scenery and the warmth and friendliness of this incredible place.

For information on New Zealand hunting, fishing, and adventure outings, contact:

**CHRIS JOLLY OUTDOORS**
Post Office Box 1020
Taupo 3351 New Zealand
Phone: 0800 252 628 (Within New Zealand)
or +647 378 0623 (From Abroad)
www.chrisjolly.co.nz

# Wild Game Recipes

# RECIPE CONTENTS

**AFRICAN WILD GAME**

## Bobotie—Mincemeat Pie
## South African Style

**SERVES 4–6**
**PREP: 40 min.**
**COOK: 1 hr. approx.**

**INGREDIENTS**

2 lb. chopped/minced beef (which
    means most any wild African game
    animal—kudu, impala, gemsbok,
    wildebeest, etc.)

2 fairly thick slices of crustless bread

1½ c. milk

2 Tbsp. oil

2 tsp. butter

2 onions, sliced

2 cloves garlic, crushed

2 Tbsp. curry powder

2 tsp. salt

1 Tbsp. apricot jam

2 Tbsp. fruit chutney

1 Tbsp. Worcestershire sauce

1 tsp. turmeric

2 Tbsp. brown vinegar

½ c. raisins

3 eggs

Pinch of salt and turmeric

Bay leaves

**DIRECTIONS**

Soak bread in milk.

Heat oil and butter in large frying pan.
Add onions and garlic, then fry.

When onions are soft, add curry powder,
salt, chutney, jam, Worcestershire sauce, turmeric, and vinegar. Mix well.

Drain and mash bread and reserve milk.

Add bread to pan, together with meat
and raisins. Cook over low heat, stirring.
When meat loses its pinkness, remove from
stove.

Add 1 beaten egg, mix well, and then
spoon into 9 × 13 greased pan. Beat remaining eggs with reserved milk and salt and turmeric. Pour over meat mixture and add a few
bay leaves on top.

Cook for 45 minutes at 325°F. Remove
bay leaves before serving.

    ■    ■    ■

## Cape Buffalo Oxtail Soup

BY KWEZI KENNEDY

**SERVES 8–10**
**PREP: 30 min.**
**COOK: 4 hr. 20 min. approx.**

**INGREDIENTS**

1 oxtail cut at each joint

1 onion, finely chopped

½ bunch celery, chopped

1 large carrot, chopped

1 15-oz. can tomatoes

4 c. beef stock

1 tsp. paprika

½ tsp. mixed herbs

Salt and pepper

1 Tbsp. vegetable oil

4 carrots cut into 2-inch pieces

1 15 oz. can haricot beans
    (white navy beans)

3 tsp. flour made into a paste with a
    little water, to thicken

**DIRECTIONS**

Brown oxtail pieces well in oil in large
heavy pot.

Remove oxtail, then sear all vegetables over high heat until just brown.

Then add stock and return meat to pot and reduce temperature. Simmer about 4 hours, keeping level of liquid up.

Then add canned tomato, carrots, white beans, and herbs. Cook approximately 20 minutes, then add flour mix and allow to thicken.

Season with salt and pepper.

The important step of this recipe is to brown the meat and vegetables. Cook meat long enough to get the meat really tender.

■   ■   ▦

## Kudu "Potjiekos"

**BY DOREA DUTOIT**

**SERVES 1 0**
**PREP: 10 min.**
**COOK: 6 hr.**

**INGREDIENTS**

9 lb. kudu shanks

1 lb. oxtail

8 c. dry red wine

17 oz. water

20 baby potatoes

5 large onions, whole

3 beef bullion cubes

1 packet brown onion soup

1 packet oxtail soup

4 Tbsp. mazina (or flour)

2 packages green and yellow baby squash

1 lb. baby carrots

2 tsp. crushed garlic

1 lb. washed mushrooms, chopped coarsely

1 pt. tin apricot jam

seasoning to taste—salt and oregano

4 c. rice

**DIRECTIONS**

In true South African style, we cook this entire meal in a big black iron pot over open flame—hence the name "Potjiekos."

Slowly cook kudu and oxtail meat in wine, water, soups, jam, and beef blocks over medium-temperature coals from the fire in a black iron pot with the lid on for 5 hours.

Ensure the meat is covered in liquids at all times; if necessary, add water to keep from drying out.

After 5 hours, add the potatoes, carrots, onions, and garlic to the meat. Stir thoroughly and replace lid. Cook for ½ hour longer.

Add the baby squash, mushrooms, seasoning, and mazina (mix mazina [or flour] with a little hot water to form a paste before stirring in). Stir and replace lid once more. Cook for another ½ hour.

Prepare rice while waiting.

Serve hot on a bed of white rice and enjoy true South African style!

# 🍁 ALLIGATOR

## Alligator Scallopini

BY DRAKE Q. DAWSON

SERVES 2–4
PREP: 20 min. + overnight marinate time
COOK: 15 min.

INGREDIENTS

8–16 oz. of gator meat
egg
milk
Cajun seasoning
steak sauce—few spoons of
  your favorite
seasoned bread crumbs
olive oil
onions
sweet peppers
1 lemon
¼ c. sweet red or white wine

DIRECTIONS

Cut thin 8–16 ounces of gator meat (use choice cuts of jaw or tenderloin) and lightly tenderize with a meat hammer.

Marinate in egg, milk, Cajun seasoning, and a few spoons of your favorite steak sauce (as little as 10 minutes; overnight is better).

Cut in silver dollar–sized pieces and dredge in seasoned bread crumbs.

Sauté in olive oil. Brown on both sides as you add in thin-sliced onions and multicolored sweet peppers. Add one lemon cut in 4 thick slices. Sprinkle all with generous amounts of Cajun seasoning.

When onion starts to glass, dash with ¼ cup of sweet red or white wine (be careful, as it may flame up). Cover for 5 minutes and serve. Total cooking time should be about 15 minutes.

According to Drake, alligator tastes like veal.

■   ■   ■

## Alligator Sauce Piquante (Spicy)

BY DRAKE Q. DAWSON

SERVES 10
PREP: 40 min.
COOK: 2 hr.

INGREDIENTS

1 c. oil
1 c. flour
1–2 large onions
1 large green pepper
3 stalks of celery
1 12-oz. can of tomato paste
2 14-oz. cans of whole tomatoes or
  equivalent fresh
4 c. water
6–7 lb. gator meat cut into silver
  dollar–sized pieces
garlic and pepper to taste
white rice
cold beer

DIRECTIONS

In a big black iron pot, add the oil and brown the gator nicely for 20–30 minutes. Add in flour to make a roux.

Add onion, celery, and green pepper. Stir frequently, adding water as it thickens.

Simmer for 30 minutes, adding water if needed.

Add tomato paste and tomatoes, more water, salt, garlic, and pepper to taste.

Simmer for an hour or longer, until gator meat is tender and flakes apart. Pour over hot white rice and serve with cold beer.

##  BEAR

### Braised Bear and Sweet Potatoes

SERVES 8
PREP: 50 min.
COOK: 1½ hr. approx.

INGREDIENTS

    4 lb. bear steak

    clove garlic, minced

    1 small onion, minced

    1 stalk celery, chopped

    5 sweet potatoes, peeled and cut
      lengthwise in quarters

    salt and pepper

    vegetable oil

DIRECTIONS

Cut meat into 2-inch cubes and brown in drippings or vegetable oil on top of stove.

Transfer to Dutch oven or roasting pan with lid. Add just enough water to prevent sticking, about ⅓ cup.

Add 1 minced clove garlic, 1 minced medium onion, and 1 chopped small stalk celery.

Cover tightly and place in preheated 350°F oven.

When meat begins to get tender, add sweet potatoes and add more water as necessary. Cover and continue cooking until meat and potatoes are done.

##  ELK

### Elk Swiss Steak

BY ROGER NITZSCHE

SERVES 4–6 per lb. of meat used
PREP: 40 min.
COOK: 2½ hr.

INGREDIENTS

    steak cuts of elk (recipe will also
      work with cuts of moose or venison)

    tomatoes

    celery

    carrots

    onions

    salt and pepper

DIRECTIONS

Pound flour into steak cuts, then brown, adding salt and pepper to taste.

Place browned steak in baking pan with cover.

Cover the steak with hunks of tomatoes, celery sticks, carrots (cut in half), and cut-up onions.

Cook at 350°F for 2½ hours.

■ ■ ■

### Elk Stroganoff

BY ROGER NITZSCHE

SERVES 4–6
PREP: 10 min.
COOK: 40 min.

INGREDIENTS

    1 lb. cubed meat (elk or venison)

    ½ c. minced onion

    1 clove garlic

¼ c. butter

1 lb. fresh or 8 oz. canned sliced
mushrooms

1 10½-oz. can cream of chicken soup

1 c. sour cream

2 Tbsp. minced parsley

**DIRECTIONS**

Sauté onion and garlic in butter over medium
heat.

Stir in meat and brown.

Stir in flour, salt and pepper, and mushrooms. Cook mixture for 5 minutes, then
stir in soup. Simmer uncovered for 10 minutes.

Stir in sour cream and heat through.
Sprinkle with parsley. Serve over noodles.
Garnish with additional parsley, if desired.

 **FISH**

## Sally's Salmon Dill Bake

BY NANCY FRANK

SERVES 2–3
PREP: 5 min.
COOK: 30 min.

**INGREDIENTS**

1 large salmon or trout filet, skin
removed

1 c. mayonnaise

1 tsp. dill weed

1 tsp. garlic powder

**DIRECTIONS**

Place filet on a jelly roll pan or in a shallow
baking dish.

Mix mayonnaise, dill weed, and garlic

powder, then spread evenly over filet, sealing
it to the pan.

Bake at 350°F for 30 minutes or until
mayonnaise is golden brown.

■   ■   ■

## Salmon Supreme

BY DAN SMALL

SERVES 4
PREP: 10 min.
COOK: 15 min.

**INGREDIENTS**

4 fresh salmon or trout fillets
(about 2 lb.) cut into serving
size pieces

4 Tbsp. oregano

1½ c. flour or breading mix

salt and pepper

2 Tbsp. butter

1 large onion, sliced

10–12 fresh mushrooms, sliced

juice of ½ lemon

½ c. sweet vermouth

**DIRECTIONS**

Mix oregano and flour or breading mix. Season with salt and pepper. Lightly flour each
fillet.

Sauté onions and mushrooms in butter
in a frying pan.

Move vegetables to the side while you
brown the fillets.

Sprinkle extra oregano and lemon juice
over fish.

When almost done, increase heat, add
vermouth, and sear all ingredients, turning
fish several times and stirring vegetables.
Serve on rice.

This recipe gives salmon a nutty taste. Even people who don't like fish love this one.

■    ■    ■

## Sweet Trout on the Trail

BY JIM FERGUSON

SERVES 2–4
PREP: 15 min.
COOK: 20 min. approx.

INGREDIENTS

1 trout 12–14 inches in length
2 Tbsp. brown sugar
2 Tbsp. honey
½ c. white wine
slivered almonds
¼ stick butter

DIRECTIONS

Filet trout from the inside, removing head, the ribs, and backbone. Leaving skin intact, rub flour on the flesh side and sauté until brown. Turn over.

Put brown sugar and honey on the brown side of the trout, then pour in the white wine. Cover until wine has nearly evaporated.

Remove trout from pan and cook down the butter, sugar, honey, and wine to a glaze. Pour over trout, then add slivered almonds.

Serve with tossed salad, garlic potatoes, and biscuits.

 **FOWL**

## Chukar with Wild Rice

SERVES 2–4
PREP: 25 min.
COOK: 1 hr.

INGREDIENTS

4 chukar
3 Tbsp. butter
1 Tbsp. chervil
1 tsp. marjoram
1 large onion, sliced
2 dashes Tabasco sauce
1 c. sour cream
wild rice

DIRECTIONS

Brown birds in hot butter on all sides in frying pan. Place them in a large Nesco oven or Dutch oven.

In remaining butter, sauté onions. Add the rest of the ingredients, except for the rice, to frying pan and heat until hot.

Pour mixture over birds and cover. Bake, basting periodically with pan juices, for about 1 hour. If using a Dutch oven, you can use the same recipe and cook using hot coals.

In the meantime, cook rice, then drain. Add butter and mix. Serve birds over hot buttered rice.

■    ■    ■

## Cornish Hens with Apple-Pecan Stuffing (good for grouse, chukar, quail)

BY DEANNA PICCHIOTTINO

SERVES 4
PREP: 20 min.
COOK: 2 hr.

INGREDIENTS

4 rock Cornish game hens
4 Tbsp. (½ stick) butter
6 small green onions with about 1-inch tops, sliced
1 can (3 oz.) chopped mushrooms, drained
½ c. chopped pecans
1 small unpeeled apple, chopped
6 slices bread, torn into small pieces
salt and pepper to taste
8 slices lean bacon, cut in halves
dry vermouth
cooking oil

DIRECTIONS

Melt butter. Add onions and mushrooms and sauté until onions are transparent.

Toss onion mixture with pecans, apple, bread, salt, and pepper. Add enough dry vermouth to hold mixture together.

Stuff each hen with mixture. Close cavities with skewers. Brush hens on all sides with cooking oil.

Place hens, breast sides up, on rack in roasting pan. Bake in 350°F oven for about 2 hours or until done. During last 45 minutes of cooking time, arrange bacon on top of hens.

## Flying Liver Duck

BY JOHN WAY

SERVES 4
PREP: 10 min. + two 8 hr. marinate times
COOK: 10 min.

INGREDIENTS

filet breast meat on 4 mallard ducks (no bones)
1 large bottle of Italian dressing
2 Tbsp. of chile powder
1 Tbsp. chopped garlic
1 tsp. pepper
¼ c. lemon juice
¼ c. soy sauce
1 c. used coffee grounds

DIRECTIONS

Filet out breast meat on ducks and clean.

Put fork holes in breast meat so marinade can get in. Place meat in marinade with Italian dressing, chile powder, garlic, lemon juice, soy, and pepper. Marinate meat for 8 hours or overnight.

In the morning after making coffee, dump used grounds into marinade. The acid in the grounds will soften the meat. Marinate in grounds for 8 more hours.

Remove meat from marinade, shake, and brush off.

Place meat on hot grill for approximately 10 minutes. Do not overcook. Meat must be red on the inside.

Slice thin and serve as an appetizer or for sandwiches.

## Mighty Layout Boys Duck Buffalo Wings

BY MARK RONGER

SERVES 6–8
PREP: 30 min. + 4 hr. marinate time
COOK: 4–5 min. approx.

### INGREDIENTS

Duck breasts sufficient to feed the size
   of the gathering
1 box of breading product, such as
   Shake 'n Bake or Shore Lunch
1 qt. milk
bottle of buffalo-style chicken wing sauce
cooking oil

### DIRECTIONS

Breast the ducks and cut into 1-inch-wide by
2-inch-long pieces, or thereabouts.

Place these pieces in a bowl deep enough
for the duck meat and for enough milk to
cover the meat. Put the bowl into a refrigerator for 4 hours.

Remove the bowl, drain the milk, and
add fresh milk.

In a separate bowl, pour 1 package of
any popular breading product that you
might prefer, such as Shore Lunch or Shake
'n Bake. An Italian version, or perhaps a
Cajun version, would be my recommendation.

On the stove top, pour ½ inch of cooking oil into a saucepan. Bring the oil to or
near 350° F.

Dredge the duck meat in the dry mix.
Place the duck pieces into the oil. Cook to
your liking, but I recommend leaving the
center of the meat pink.

Remove the cooked meat from the oil.
Place in a bowl. Cover the duck meat with
buffalo-style chicken wing sauce.

No need to bake—just serve! You'll be
very pleased with the results.

### Story behind Recipe

We were up at Port Rowan, Ontario, for the
10th Annual Mighty Layout Boys Convention/Hunt. A group of friends have been picking different places to hunt, some traveling a
good distance, all in the name of good fun.

We took several ducks, and as in years
past, we had a tailgater one evening. Brent
Mason, Ontario director of the Mighty Layout Boys, had been working on a new dish.
He instructed me: "Try this." He was curious
if I could identify the buffalo wing sauce.
I proceeded to bite into one of the tastiest
pieces of duck meat that I can recall eating.
You simply cannot go wrong with this recipe!

■  ■  ■

## Wild Duck on the Grill

SERVES 4–10
PREP: 20 min. + 1 hr. marinate time
COOK: 20 min. approx.

### INGREDIENTS

4–10 duck breasts
⅔ c. soy sauce
¼ c. not too sweet red wine
1 small onion
3 Tbsp. lemon juice
1 Tbsp. sugar
1 lb. bacon

### DIRECTIONS

Mix all ingredients above, except bacon, together in large bowl. Marinate duck breasts
in the mixture for up to 1 hour.

After marinated, wrap each breast in bacon and grill to no more than medium rare.

■   ■   ■

## Roast Wild Duck

SERVES 4–6
PREP: 45 min. + overnight soak time
COOK: 2½ hr. approx.

INGREDIENTS

ducks, 4–6

salt

baking soda

1 c. apple, chopped

1 c. onions, chopped

1 c. celery, chopped

1 c. carrots, chopped

DIRECTIONS

Skin and wash ducks thoroughly. Soak them 10 hours in water to which 2 tablespoons of salt and 1 tablespoon of soda have been added for each gallon of water. (This will draw out gamy taste.) Wash ducks in cold water after they have been removed from salt solution. Wipe dry with paper toweling.

Mix chopped apples, onions, celery, and carrots in desired proportions.

Lightly stuff ducks with apple mixture. It is not necessary to close the opening since the stuffing should be discarded before ducks are ready to serve. Stuffing's purpose is to absorb the strong flavor and add its own flavors to the meat.

Roast the ducks, covered, in 325°F oven about 2½ hours or until done.

Because there is wide variation in wild ducks, it is best to start testing for doneness after the first 1½ hours roasting time. Salt ducks when halfway done.

Ducks may be glazed with the following currant mixture, if desired.

Currant Glaze Ingredients

1 jar 8 oz. red currant jelly

2 Tbsp. lemon juice

½ tsp. dry mustard

¼ tsp. cloves

2 Tbsp. grated orange rind

METHOD

Heat jelly until melted, stirring until it is smooth. Stir in remaining ingredients, mixing well.

Spoon glaze over duck about 20 minutes before end of roasting time.

■   ■   ■

## Wild Goose Breast with Onions, Mushrooms, and Red Wine Sauce

BY BJORN BIRGISSON

SERVES 4
PREP: 10 min.
COOK: 20 min.

INGREDIENTS

deboned breasts from 2 geese

coarse sea salt and freshly ground black pepper

2 Tbsp. vegetable oil

2 oz. butter

Sauce Ingredients

10 oz. pearl onions

3 Tbsp. sugar

3 Tbsp. red wine vinegar

1 c. red wine

wild mushrooms

1 oz. butter

1 tsp. fresh timian (thyme)

1 c. water

1 c. cream

1 Tbsp. bouillon

**DIRECTIONS**

Heat the oven to 300°F. Put coarse salt and fresh ground pepper on the breasts.

Heat the vegetables.

Grease the frying pan with butter. Fry breasts on moderate heat for 7–8 minutes. Then move them to the oven for 10 minutes while preparing the sauce.

Increase the heat on the frying pan and put in the onions. Add butter if needed.

When the onions have been fried, spread the sugar on the pan and let it turn to caramel. Then add the wine and vinegar and boil until 50% is evaporated. Then pour into a bowl and keep warm.

Add more butter to the pan and fry the mushrooms. Then add the spices and let them become brownish. Then pour the onions and wine from the bowl into the pan, as well as the water, cream, and the bouillon.

Boil the sauce and add salt, pepper, and red wine according to taste.

Serve the goose breast sliced with the sauce and the onions.

■    ■    ■

## Snow Goose/Eider Recipe

*Dr. Michael Billig of Vermont, one of the most ardent waterfowl hunters in the Northeast, makes an annual pilgrimage to hunt snow geese along the St. Lawrence River. He suggests the following recipe for both snow geese and eiders.*

SERVES 1–2 per breast
PREP: 20 min. + overnight marinate time
COOK: 10 min.

**INGREDIENTS**

goose or duck breasts,
   desired quantity

spring water

1 Tbsp. baking soda

1 Tbsp. vinegar

butter or olive oil

honey teriyaki sauce

cornmeal (optional)

**DIRECTIONS**

Breast out each bird. Take breasts and let them soak overnight in spring water with 1 tablespoon of baking soda and 1 tablespoon of vinegar. This removes all wild taste. (Billig swears this will work for mergansers and even coots.)

Half an hour before your meal, heat up some butter or olive oil in a frying pan. Slice up the breasts in bite-size pieces and drop them in honey teriyaki sauce.

Then drop them in the hot frying pan and cook about 10 minutes. (Some people will add in a step of dropping the pieces of breast meat covered with honey teriyaki sauce into cornmeal before frying.)

※　※　※

## Sautéed Grouse

BY AL ARNDT

SERVES 1 person per breast
PREP: 5 min.
COOK: 6 min.

INGREDIENTS

grouse breasts, desired quantity

1 clove minced garlic

3 Tbsp. virgin olive oil

½ small onion, chopped fine (optional)

DIRECTIONS

Sauté garlic, onion, and oil until browning. Add grouse breasts and fry uncovered about 2½–3 minutes per side. Cut open and check to see if done. Do not overcook.

This recipe works great for venison steaks as well.

※　※　※

## Grouse à la Pressure Cooker

BY AL ARNDT

SERVES 4–6
PREP: 5 min.
COOK: 45 min.

INGREDIENTS

4–6 grouse breasts

2 c. chicken broth

1 c. water

salt and pepper to taste

DIRECTIONS

Add all to pressure cooker. Set at 10 pounds of pressure. Once pressure cooker starts to jiggle, cook for 45 minutes. It doesn't get any easier than this.

※　※　※

## Governor Knowles Pheasant

*This dish has always been a favorite in my family. My father, Roger Nitzsche, an avid hunter and outdoorsman, always prepares this meal. It has now become one of my children's favorites as well. We enjoy it now when we are all together "Up North" at our family's lake home.— The Fuller Family*

SERVES 1–2—can be multiplied
PREP: 20 min.
COOK: 1½–2 hr.

INGREDIENTS

1 pheasant breast, boned
 and filleted

1 Tbsp. butter

1 can cream of mushroom soup

½ soup can sherry wine

DIRECTIONS

Preheat oven to 325°F.

In frying pan, brown pheasant breast in butter. When brown on all sides, put in roasting pan. Season pheasant with salt and pepper, to taste.

Save pan drippings and combine with cream of chicken soup and sherry wine in saucepan. Bring all ingredients to a rolling boil. Pour over pheasant in roaster. Bake for 1½–2 hours. Poke with fork to test doneness.

This recipe can be doubled, tripled, and

so on. Use soup and sherry accordingly. Rule of thumb: 1 can soup and ½ soup can sherry per pheasant breast.

Goes well with mashed potatoes, using the sauce as a great gravy. Enjoy!

■   ■   ■

## Patti's Easy Crockpot Pheasant Tacos

BY PATTI KENNEDY

SERVES 4–6
PREP: 10 min.
COOK: 6–9 hr.

INGREDIENTS

2–3 boneless pheasant breasts or 2- to 3-pound venison roast

2 jars of Pace (or other brand) picante sauce (or enough to cover)

soft flour tortillas

sour cream

shredded cheddar cheese

diced tomatoes

lettuce

guacamole

DIRECTIONS

Place meat in crockpot with enough picante sauce to cover.

Simmer over low heat for 6 to 9 hours.

Use two forks to pull meat apart.

Place meat into tortillas and top with favorite toppings.

■   ■   ■

## Paul Nelson Farm Pheasant Recipe

SERVES 6–8
PREP: 20 min.
COOK: 1–1½ hr.

INGREDIENTS

4–6 pheasant breasts, tenderized (or pounded)

flour

1 can (10 oz.) cream of mushroom soup

1 can (10 oz.) cream of chicken soup

¼ c. Parmesan cheese, grated

4 oz. can mushrooms, drained

1 c. sour cream

½ c. whipping cream or heavy cream

½ c. onion, chopped

Kitchen Bouquet (optional, for brown color)

DIRECTIONS

Roll each pheasant breast in flour. Salt and pepper.

Fry in hot oil on both sides until brown.

In a bowl, combine soups, cheese, mushrooms, sour cream, whipping cream, onion, and Kitchen Bouquet.

In bottom of casserole dish, layer sauce, pheasant, and then top with another layer of sauce until completely covered.

Put lid on casserole and bake at 300°F for about 1–1½ hours or until tender.

Could also put in crockpot for 6 hours on low setting.

■   ■   ■

## Pheasant à la Orange

SERVES 4
PREP: 40 min.
COOK: 2 hr. approx.

INGREDIENTS

2 large pheasant or 4 small ones
bacon
2 Tbsp. butter or margarine
3 green onions, minced
¾ tsp. dried tarragon leaves
1½ c. orange juice
3 Tbsp. finely shredded orange rind
6 Tbsp. currant jelly
¼ tsp. dry mustard
¼ tsp. salt
1½ c. orange sections, well drained
cooked rice

DIRECTIONS

Sprinkle pheasant inside and out with salt and pepper.

Put pheasant, breast side up, in roasting pan. Cover breast with slices of bacon.

Roast, uncovered, in 350°F oven until tender, allowing about 30 minutes per pound.

Melt butter; add onion and tarragon and sauté about 3 minutes. Add orange juice, rind, jelly, mustard, and salt. Bring mixture to a boil, stirring.

About 20 minutes before pheasant are done, remove from oven and place them in the orange sauce. Bring to boil, reduce heat, and simmer, covered, about 20 minutes.

Remove pheasant to serving platter.

Blend orange sections into sauce. Heat sauce quickly and serve with pheasant and rice.

## Patti's Pheasant Chop Suey

BY PATTI KENNEDY

SERVES 4
PREP: 35 min.
COOK: 35 min.

INGREDIENTS

2 pheasant breasts
1 Tbsp. vegetable oil
½ lb. celery, chopped
1 lb. fresh bean sprouts
4 oz. fresh sliced mushrooms
½ onion, sliced
salt to taste
1 c. water
1 tsp. sugar
1 tsp. soy sauce
1 tsp. cornstarch mixed with 1 Tbsp.
  water

DIRECTIONS

In large sauté pan, cook pheasant in 1 table-spoon oil. When it is browned, add celery, onion, and mushrooms and cook until tender. Add salt if desired.

Add water; cover and cook until water begins to boil.

While mixture cooks, in a small dish combine sugar and soy sauce.

When water begins to boil, gradually add cornstarch and water mixture, stirring to combine well. Reduce heat to low and add soy sauce mixture and bean sprouts. Heat through, then remove from heat and serve over hot cooked rice.

## Pheasant Chili Crockpot Style

SERVES 4–6
PREP: 40 min.
COOK: 6 hr.

INGREDIENTS

1½–2 lb. of meat of choice (pheasant or shredded venison preferred using small roast or chuck steaks)

2 cans of chili beans (Chili Magic brand: Traditional, Texas, or Mexican style)

2 cans of diced tomatoes with green chili (any Mexican brand can)

2 cans of Italian-style diced tomatoes

2 cans of Italian-style stewed tomatoes

5 cloves of sliced or chopped garlic (add to taste)

½ onion, chopped

2 stalks of celery, chopped

chili powder to taste (some chili taste already built in with beans)

DIRECTIONS

In a crockpot, cook the meat with the 2 cans of diced tomatoes/green chili on high for 5 hours or until meat is fully cooked and falls part easily.

Remove meat, let cool, then shred.

Strain off excess liquid from crockpot and return tomato/green chili mixture to the pot along with the meat. Add the remaining cans of diced tomatoes, stewed tomatoes, and chili beans.

Or pan fry the meat slowly and add the remaining ingredients. Combine in crockpot and simmer for several hours.

In a frying pan with olive oil, over medium heat, sauté the sliced garlic, onions, and celery until onions become soft, then add to crockpot.

Mix all ingredients well, then let cook on low for an additional hour or until hot. Add chili powder as needed.

Serve or freeze for later use.

■    ■    ■

## Pheasant en Crème

BY JEANNE TROTTER

SERVES 4
PREP: 10 min.
COOK: 2 hr. approx.

INGREDIENTS

1 pheasant, quartered

1 can (10½ oz.) condensed cream of chicken soup

½ c. apple cider

1 Tbsp. plus 1 tsp. Worcestershire sauce

¾ tsp. salt

⅓ c. chopped onion

1 clove garlic, minced

1 can (3 oz.) sliced mushrooms, drained

paprika

DIRECTIONS

Heat oven to 350°F. Place pheasant in ungreased baking dish, 9×9×2 inches. Mix soup, cider, Worcestershire sauce, salt, onion, garlic, and mushrooms; pour over pheasant. Sprinkle generously with paprika.

Basting pheasant occasionally with sauce, bake uncovered 1½–2 hours or until fork-tender. After baking pheasant 1 hour, generously sprinkle again with paprika.

Note: For two pheasant, place pheasant in 13½×9×2-inch baking dish and double all ingredients.

## Pheasant Enchilada Casserole via Crockpot

BY SHEROL ENGEL

SERVES 6
PREP: 55 min.
COOK: 7 hr.

INGREDIENTS

6 boneless, skinless pheasant breasts, cooked (sautéed lightly) and chopped

2 small onions, chopped

2 cloves garlic, pressed

2 tsp. cumin

12 corn tortillas

1 (28 oz.) can green enchilada sauce (El Torito's brand)

12 oz. low-fat cheddar cheese

DIRECTIONS

In a skillet, sauté ½ the onion in about a tablespoon of oil. Cook for 2 minutes and add garlic. Cook another 2 minutes and add cooked and chopped pheasant and cumin. Mix well; set aside.

In a blender, add the rest of the onion and the can of enchilada sauce. Blend well.

In a crockpot, pour about ½ cup sauce on the bottom of the pan and begin building your casserole. Start with sauce (already said that), tortillas, pheasant mixture, and a little cheese and repeat this pattern till finished. Pour the rest of the sauce evenly over the top and cook on low for 7 hours (but check it often—newer crockpots sometimes cook faster).

Reserve a little cheese to sprinkle on the top just before serving.

## Pheasant Poppers

BY DON HOLT

SERVES 8–10
PREP: 1 hr. 30 min.
COOK: 20 min.

INGREDIENTS

several pheasant breasts

½ stick of real butter

1 15-oz. bottle of Worcestershire sauce

¼ c. balsamic vinegar

whole milk

onion

jalapeño peppers

cream cheese

toothpicks

bacon

DIRECTIONS

Preprep birds before marinading: Filet breast meat. Slice pieces off back to bottom of breast meat, making thin pieces about 2×4×¼ inch or thereabouts. Place breast pieces in whole milk in a fridge overnight (not necessary but best way).

Next day, rinse the meat and place in it a wedge of onion, jalapeño pepper, and a bit of cream cheese. Roll the breast meat over the ingredients, wrapping the bird with bacon, and hold together with a toothpick (one strip of bacon—quarter it so there is not too much bacon on the meat; it is to hold it together and to keep the meat from drying out).

Prepare the marinade: large bottle of Worcestershire sauce, ½ stick of real butter, and ¼ cup of balsamic vinegar. Put all ingredients in a pot to melt and blend. While warm (not hot!), place poppers into marinade for a minimum of 1 hour—better to marinate poppers for 3 hours. Warming the marinade aids in penetrating the meat better.

Remove poppers from marinade and place on hot grill for approximately 20 minutes (depending on how hot the grill is). Important: Do not overcook.

Use this recipe for white meat. For dark meat (ducks, geese, and doves), use zesty Italian dressing for your marinade; just remember to warm.

## Rocko's Cheesy Mozzarella Pheasant

BY LISA GORSKI

SERVES 10–12
PREP: 10 min.
COOK: 35 min.

INGREDIENTS

½ stick butter
6 to 8 boneless pheasant breasts
2 c. baby carrots, fresh (or frozen for faster prep)
6 c. cut potatoes, fresh (or frozen for faster prep)
2 c. shredded mozzarella cheese
salt and black pepper, to taste

DIRECTIONS

Use an electric fry pan or stove top large skillet.

Melt butter and brown pheasant on medium heat. Season with salt and pepper to taste. Turn over pheasant to brown other side.

When the pheasant is browned, place the carrots and potatoes on top of the pheasant, cover, and cook until the vegetables are tender. Add a little water if needed to steam vegetables. When done, place shredded mozzarella cheese on top until melted, then serve.

## Parmesan Honey Dijon Pheasant

BY RICK AND JAE DEAN BERTONI

SERVES 4–6
PREP: 25 min.
COOK: 18 min.

INGREDIENTS

¾ c. dry seasoned bread crumbs
¼ c. grated parmesan cheese
¼ c. butter (½ stick)
4 Tbsp. Dijon mustard
4 Tbsp. pure honey
4 skinless, boneless pheasant breast halves

DIRECTIONS

Heat oven to 375°F. Mix seasoned bread crumbs and parmesan cheese in large bowl.

Combine Dijon mustard and pure honey in separate bowl.

Dip pheasant in honey Dijon mixture, then coat with crumb mixture.

Melt butter in a nonstick pan. Brown breaded pheasant on both sides.

Place pheasant on a baking sheet and bake for 15 to 18 minutes.

■   ■   ■

## Pigeon Stew

SERVES 4
PREP: 30 min.
COOK: 1½–3 hr.

INGREDIENTS

8 pigeons (or band-tailed doves)
1 qt. water
4 chicken bouillon cubes
2 onions, chopped
4–6 carrots, cut in small pieces
4–6 potatoes, cut in small pieces
salt and pepper to taste
1 tsp. thyme
flour, for thickening

DIRECTIONS

Place birds, water, bouillon cubes, and onions in large stew pot. Cover and simmer until birds just become tender.

Add carrots, potatoes, and thyme and cook another 30 minutes.

Add salt and pepper to taste and thicken with flour (put flour and a little bit of cold water in bowl or shaker and mix until smooth; add to hot stew to thicken).

■   ■   ■

## Engel's Quail with Cream Sauce

BY ROSS ALLEN

SERVES 4
PREP: 30 min. + 30 min. marinate time
COOK: 10 min.

INGREDIENTS

8 quail, cleaned and dressed
2 c. whole milk
2 c. flour
salt, pepper, and garlic powder to taste
2–3 c. vegetable oil in deep pot or
   electric deep fryer

Sauce

1 can low-sodium chicken
   broth (1¾ c.)
3 oz. almond paste
½ tsp. white pepper
⅛ tsp. cayenne pepper
¼ tsp. garlic powder
1 Tbsp. butter
½ c. heavy cream
½ c. sliced almonds for garnish

DIRECTIONS

Remove backbone from quail with poultry shears. Rinse quail with cold water and drain on paper towels.

Season the quail with salt, pepper, and garlic powder. Cover with plastic wrap and return to refrigerator for 30 minutes.

Remove quail from the refrigerator and preheat the oil. Once the oil has reached 325°–350°F, dip each quail in milk, then dredge in flour. Please in the hot oil and fry until golden brown, 8–10 minutes. Drain on paper towels and keep warm in the oven set to 200°F.

For almond cream sauce: Pour broth into saucepan and heat over medium heat. Add all ingredients to broth except the heavy cream and almonds. Bring just to a simmer, then reduce the heat to medium-low. Continue to simmer and stir until the sauce is reduced by ⅓. (Sauce will be thick and yield 1 cup.) Slowly stir in heavy cream and continue to stir for 5 minutes.

Serve over quail and garnish with sliced almonds.

■   ■   ■

## Grilled Woodcock

SERVES 4
PREP: 15 min.
COOK: 30 min.

INGREDIENTS

8 woodcocks
salt and pepper
8 slices of bacon
butter, melted

DIRECTIONS

Salt and pepper birds. Wrap each bird in a slice of bacon and fasten with a toothpick.

Basting with butter, grill for 8–10 minutes per side.

Meat should be a little pink. Best if not overcooked.

## MOOSE

### Moose Steak Cowboy Style

SERVES 1–2
PREP: 10 min.
COOK: 14 min.

INGREDIENTS

thick steak from the rump of a young moose
shredded horseradish
cooking oil
fried onions

DIRECTIONS

With a sharp knife, make an incision in the shape of a cross in the steak and fill it with shredded horseradish.

Dip steak in oil and fry or broil quickly, turning twice.

Serve with fried onions.

■   ■   ■

### Spaghetti with Vegetables and Ground Moose

SERVES 4
PREP: 15 min.
COOK: 30 min.

INGREDIENTS

1 lb. spaghetti (cooked)
1 lb. ground moose
2 Tbsp. salt
½ c. extra virgin olive oil
4 garlic cloves, finely chopped
1 Tbsp. minced Italian parsley
1 Tbsp. crushed hot pepper
¼ Tbsp. dried oregano

2 Tbsp. grated cheese (Romano or
  Parmesan)
1 small bunch broccoli, chopped
¼ lb. sliced mushrooms
½ c. sliced zucchini

### DIRECTIONS

Brown ground wild meat and set aside.

Place broccoli in microwave dish. Add ¼ cup water and microwave on high until tender. Drain off water.

Cook the spaghetti in water salted with the 2 tablespoons of salt. Drain well.

Heat the olive oil in a heavy skillet, along with the garlic and hot pepper.

Add broccoli, zucchini, and the sliced mushrooms. Sauté on medium. Add drained ground wild meat.

When the garlic starts to change color, toss in the spaghetti. Let the spaghetti sit in the mixture for 2–3 minutes to absorb the flavor. Then stir or "toss" the spaghetti in the mixture.

When the pasta is thoroughly coated in the olive oil, toss in the parsley, oregano, and cheese of your choice. Serve warm.

■  ■  ■

## Herb's Moose Burgers

**BY HERB ENGEL**

**SERVES 6–8**
**PREP: 10 min.**
**COOK: 10 min.**

### INGREDIENTS

1 large onion, diced
1 potato, peeled and grated
1 carrot, peeled and grated

2 eggs
salt and pepper to taste
1 beer (optional)
2 lb. ground moose (this will also work
  with ground elk and venison)
8 rolls

### DIRECTIONS

In a large bowl, mix eggs, diced onion, grated potatoes, carrots, and a small amount of beer together. Season with salt and pepper.

Preheat the grill to medium-high.

Shape the ground meat into 8 patties, about ½-inch thick. Season the patties with salt and pepper.

Grill the patties on both sides until pink is gone, about 5 minutes per side.

Toast the rolls on the grill.

Serve the burgers on the toasted rolls.

■  ■  ■

## Yukon Trappers & Hunters Stew

**BY BRUCE GILBERT**

**SERVES 6–8**
**PREP: 30 min.**
**COOK: 2 hr.**

### INGREDIENTS

1 lb. chopped bull moose meat
1 lb. chopped ram sheep meat
1 lb. chopped bull caribou meat*
1 package dry French onion soup mix
potatoes
onions

### DIRECTIONS

Put all ingredients into large pot and cover with water. Cook at a slow boil 2 hours or until meat is tender. Stir often. Last hour add potatoes and onions. Serve and enjoy.

It may be unusual to have all three of these meats to be fresh at the same time. When we did, we made this stew. The caribou tasted the best. In the Yukon, by a crackling fire, we have enjoyed this stew, sitting in the snow under the stars.

*Caribou bull must not be in rut.

##  RABBIT

### Rabbit Fricassee

SERVES 4–6
PREP: 15 min.
COOK: 1½ hr.

INGREDIENTS

Minced or ground meat from the
  forequarters of a rabbit
2 lb. ground pork
3 oz. minced bacon (optional)
6 oz. sliced bacon
3 slices of bread (2 soaked in wine and
  squeezed dry, and 1 slice grated)
1 or 2 eggs
dash of salt and pepper
½ c. sour cream

DIRECTIONS

Mince or grind the meat from the forequarters of a rabbit with 2 pounds of pork. If the pork is lean, add 3 ounce of minced bacon.

Add 2 slices of bread, soaked in wine and squeezed dry, and 1 slice grated. Add 1 or 2 eggs, a dash of salt and pepper, and ½ cup sour cream.

Mix together well, form into a loaf, cover

with sliced bacon, and bake with vegetable oil and onions, basting frequently.

Bake at 350°F for 1½ hours or until done.

■ ■ ■

### Rabbit in Cream

SERVES 1
PREP: 20 min.
COOK: 1½–2 hr.

INGREDIENTS

¼ lb. leg of rabbit
½ c. cold water
2 Tbsp. cream
salt
pepper

DIRECTIONS

Clean rabbit, debone, and cut into small pieces.

Place in 2-quart saucepan with water and salt. Cover partially and steam slowly 1 to 1½ hours.

Remove meat to cutting board and pound well.

Put pounded meat into a frying pan, add the cream, and season with salt and pepper to taste.

Serve on toast.

## SQUIRREL

### Squirrel in the Slow Cooker

BY AL ARNDT

SERVES 4–6
PREP: 10 min.
COOK: 6 hr.

INGREDIENTS

4–6 squirrels, quartered
1 package Lipton onion soup mix
1 c. water
1 can cream of mushroom soup
¼ c. soy sauce
1 Tbsp. Worcestershire sauce

DIRECTIONS

Mix all ingredients. Place in slow cooker for 2 hours on high and 4 hours on low.

■   ■   ■

### Boneless Tree Rat (Squirrel) Wings

BY DOUG LOOSE

SERVES 4–6
PREP: 30 min. + 2 days to marinate
COOK: 25 min.

INGREDIENTS

squirrel fillets, 4–6 (see directions)
2 eggs
¼ c. milk
½ c. flour
¼ c. cornmeal
¼ lb. butter
3–4 c. peanut oil
1 pinch red pepper
1 pinch garlic salt
1 pinch ground cumin
¼ c. of your favorite dry rub
1 c. of your favorite hot sauce (I use Frank's Red Hot)

DIRECTIONS

After skinning and washing thoroughly, remove the legs (and back straps). Remove the bone from the meat. Make a slice the length of the bone and fillet it out. For the birds, use a pair of pliers to remove the pin bones.

Combine the meat with the dry rub and place in the fridge over night (2 days for best results).

In a bowl combine eggs and milk and whisk thoroughly.

Combine all the dry ingredients in a dredge pan and stir thoroughly (for a little extra crisp, add ¼ cup cornmeal).

Place the individual pieces of meat first in the egg wash and then in the flour mixture (dredge).

Add the peanut oil to a 1- to 2-quart saucepan and heat on high or to about 400°F.

Place the pieces in the oil carefully, a few at a time. Allow to cook until they float. Remove and place in a large mixing bowl.

*The Sauce.* Place the butter in a small saucepan and melt. Stir in your favorite hot sauce. Experiment with small splashes of the real hot stuff.

*The Final Step.* Once the butter and hot sauce are thoroughly blended, pour over the precooked meat.

Shake or stir the meat to ensure that each piece is thoroughly coated.

Place the pieces on a cookie sheet and into a preheated 300°F oven. Cook the meat for about 20 minutes or until the coating is glazy.

## Story behind Recipe

As a young boy living in rural Michigan, my friends and I spent our afternoons and weekends stomping the brush. We carried our trusty Ruger 10-22s into the woods every chance we got. We hunted for partridge, rabbits, and the incredibly smart Tree Rat (squirrel to the common folk). Our bag was rarely, if ever, empty. The Tree Rat was extra special to us boys. While the thrill of the hunt and the taste of the meat, cooked in cream of mushroom soup, were great, Tree Rats carried a much higher value than the other game we pursued. The tails could be either sold outright for cash or traded to Mep's Spinner Company for spinners. We were trout fisherman as well, and the "free" spinners were a huge plus.

Until recent years, I, along with most of my generation, had basically given up the pasttime of chasing squirrels in the fall. I used to love it. Now in my late thirties I have started spending much more time in the woods. A couple of years ago, I noticed that there were hundreds of squirrels . . . everywhere. They have invaded the cities, the suburbs, and every rural wood lot has evidence of nests towering above the ground. I once again started putting my trusty 10–22 to work. It is/was very easy to get a bag limit in no time. My daughter, now seven, accompanies me at times and has a blast pointing out the Tree Rats jumping high above us. But with the harvesting comes the responsibility to consume what you take.

This recipe was tried out on a few of my closest friends—some are hunters, others are not, but they all join me in the fall for what I call my "Harvest Dinner." The dinner is a compilation of wild harvest from all over the United States including venison (elk and whitetail), pheasant, turkey, partridge, salmon, halibut, crab, abalone, scallops, rabbit, and Tree Rat. I do not reveal the content of the meal until well into the eating. Anyhow, I worked on this recipe for about four years. I have used it on pheasant legs, rabbit, and squirrel, as well as goose and duck legs.

##  TURKEY

### Pork-Stuffed Wild Turkey

BY DAN SMALL

SERVES 6–8
PREP: 15 min.
COOK: 4 hr. (for 12 lb. turkey)

INGREDIENTS

1 10–12 lb. wild turkey
salt and pepper

**Stuffing Ingredients**

1 onion, chopped
1 lb. pork sausage
6 c. soft bread crumbs
2 tsp. salt
1/4 tsp. pepper
3 Tbsp. parsley, chopped
4 slices bacon

DIRECTIONS

Pluck and dress turkey and let it age in refrigerator for 4–5 days. If frozen, allow to thaw in refrigerator. Wash turkey under cold running water and pat dry with paper towels.

Sprinkle turkey inside and out with salt and pepper.

Cook onion and sausage over medium heat in a heavy skillet for 5 minutes or until onion is tender.

Combine bread crumbs, salt, and pepper in a large bowl. Add onions and sausage; mix well. Mix in a little hot water if stuffing mixture is too dry. Lightly stuff and close both cavities of the turkey and place breast-side down in a roasting pan.

Roast uncovered at 325°F for 10 minutes per pound of turkey (weight before stuffing).

Turn turkey breast-side up and place bacon slices on breast. Continue cooking uncovered for 10 to 12 minutes more per pound. Turkey is done when juices run clear when a fork is pushed into the thickest part of the thigh.

■　　■　　■

## Wild Turkey Appetizers

BY JEFF ENGEL

SERVES 10
PREP: 20 min.
COOK: 3–5 min.

INGREDIENTS
   1-inch strips of turkey meat from one
     breast
   3 eggs
   bacon grease or cooking oil and
     margarine or butter
   cooking sherry (optional)

Breading Ingredients
   1 c. crushed soda crackers
   1 c. flour

2 Tbsp. lemon pepper
1 Tbsp. seasoned salt

DIRECTIONS
Dip turkey strips into beaten eggs and then into breading. Fry in hot bacon grease until golden brown.

You may substitute bacon grease with ½ cooking oil and ½ margarine (or butter) that is ¼-inch deep in pan.

Add cooking sherry to liquid if desired.

■　　■　　■

## Wild Turkey Chipped and Creamy

BY SHEROL ENGEL

SERVES 6
PREP: 20 min.
COOK: 30 min.

INGREDIENTS

3 c. cooked cubed turkey

2 c. sweet cream

2 Tbsp. flour

½ c. chicken broth, plus some extra

1 c. thinly sliced mushrooms

½ thinly sliced green pepper

¼ c. butter

2 egg yolks

2 tsp. lemon juice

½ tsp. paprika

3 Tbsp. sherry

¼ c. minced pimento

salt and pepper (white pepper preferred)

buttered toast

DIRECTIONS

Sauté green pepper in butter briefly; add chicken broth and let simmer for a short time.

Add mushrooms and simmer a bit longer; then mix flour with enough chicken stock so it will pour. Turn down heat and add flour mixture slowly, stirring briskly to prevent lumping.

Simmer a bit longer. Turn off heat and add cream, turkey, and egg yolks, continuing to stir. Add all other ingredients.

Heat but do not boil. Serve on buttered toast.

Green vegetables or salad makes for a nice garnish/side dish.

##  VENISON

## Canning Venison

BY AL ARNDT

SERVES 4 per jar
PREP: 15 min.
COOK: 75–90 min.

INGREDIENTS

venison

½ tsp. canning salt

DIRECTIONS

Remove venison meat from the bones; remove any membranes or fat. Chop into ½- to 1-inch pieces. Pack into pint jars approximately 1 inch from top.

Sprinkle ½ teaspoon canning salt on top.

Put lid on tightly. Place jars in pressure cooker and fill pressure cooker halfway with water. Pressure cook for 75 minutes at 10–15 pounds of pressure.

If you use quart jars, increase salt to 1 teaspoon and cook for 90 minutes.

Cool. Store in your pantry.

■   ■   ■

## Venison Stroganoff

BY AL ARNDT

SERVES 6–8
PREP: 5 min.
COOK: 15 min.

INGREDIENTS

16 oz. of medium egg noodles

1 medium onion, chopped (optional)

1 pt. canned venison

1 clove minced garlic

1 lb. fresh or two 6½-oz. cans sliced mushrooms

2 10½-oz. cans cream of mushroom soup

1 can French onion with beef stock soup (Campbell's)

2 c. (16 oz.) sour cream

½ tsp. salt

¼ tsp. pepper or to taste

## DIRECTIONS

Boil noodles. Drain, rinse, and set aside.

In large pot, heat soups, onion, garlic, mushrooms, sour cream, salt, and pepper and stir until hot (all ingredients except noodles). When hot, mix in noodles and serve!

■   ■   ■

## Chris's Miracle Venison Meatloaf—If You Can Tell It's Venison, It's a Miracle!

BY CHRIS CALIENDO

SERVES 4–6
PREP: 20 min.
COOK: 2 hr.

## INGREDIENTS

2 lb. ground venison (or ground elk, etc.)

1 small onion, chopped fine

2 cloves garlic, minced

2 eggs

1–1½ c. bread crumbs

1 can tomato soup, split

¾ c. sour cream

2 Tbsp. fresh parsley, chopped

1 tsp. dried oregano

1 tsp. dried basil

2 Tbsp. olive oil

1 Tbsp. butter (to grease standard loaf pan)

## DIRECTIONS

Preheat oven to 350°F.

Sauté onion and garlic in olive oil until soft (3–4 minutes) and set aside to cool.

Mix venison with eggs, sour cream, ½ can of tomato soup, parsley, oregano, and basil.

Add onion and garlic and bread crumbs. Add bread crumbs until mixture is moldable into loaf.

Add loaf to buttered loaf pan. Bake at 350°F for 1½ hours.

After 1 hour, spread remaining tomato soup to cover top of loaf and bake remaining 30 minutes.

Recipe may be spiced up by substituting barbecue sauce for tomato soup!

■   ■   ■

## Creamed Venison with Wild Rice and Biscuits

BY JIM FERGUSON

SERVES 8
PREP: 10 min.
COOK: 20 min. approx.

## INGREDIENTS

5–6 lb. venison cut into 1-inch cubes (beef, buffalo, pheasant, or quail can be substituted for venison)

1 stick of butter

1 can chopped green chilies

1 bunch of green onions, chopped

1½ c. cilantro

1 c. white wine

1 qt. heavy whipping cream

1 package wild rice

4 c. flour

4 tsp. baking powder

½ tsp. salt

½ c. sugar

2 c. milk, warmed

4 Tbsp. Butter-flavored Crisco

## DIRECTIONS

Sauté the venison cubes in the butter until brown. Take off heat and drain.

Add chilies, green onions, and cilantro. sauté until tender.

Pour in white wine and reduce by ½. Add heavy whipping cream and let venison simmer until cream thickens.

Serve over wild rice with a tossed salad and biscuits.

For biscuits, preheat oven to 400°F.

Put flour, baking powder, salt, and sugar in a bowl. Mix dry ingredients. Add Butter-flavored Crisco, cutting in with a fork.

Pour in warmed milk, mixing completely. If the mixture is sticky, sprinkle more flour on the ball until you can pick it up with your hands.

Put on flat surface and, using a biscuit cutter, cut biscuits and put them on a cookie sheet. Depending on the size, can make up to 2 dozen. I like mine larger, so this recipe will make about 16 biscuits.

Place in oven until tops turn brown, 7–15 minutes.

Serve with sausage gravy, butter, and jam.

■   ■   ■

# Doc Coffman's Deer Roast

*This hearty and homey recipe is great for a hunting camp or having friends over for venison, even if they think they don't like it. It is designed for cooking in a smoker. —Martin Coffman*

SERVES 6
PREP: 20 min.
COOK: 5 hr. + 45 min. sitting time

## INGREDIENTS

1 medium onion, cut in chunks

1 Tbsp. good old yellow mustard

1 Tbsp. Worcestershire sauce

1 Tbsp. brown sugar

4 garlic cloves, minced a bit

1 tsp. salt

1 tsp. black pepper

¼ c. corn oil or canola oil

1 14½-oz. can of whole tomatoes with juice

3–4 lb. venison roast

## DIRECTIONS

The night before you are going to cook the roast, mix the paste up in a blender until the onion is finely chopped and you have a thick puree. Slather the paste over the roast; put it in a large zip-loc bag, then refrigerate over night.

Take the roast out of the refrigerator about 45 minutes before you are going to start cooking.

Get your smoker up to about 220°F. Put the roast in the smoker and cook it for 3 hours. If you are using a real wood-smoker, you might need to baste it with some barbeque sauce periodically, but if you are using a water-type smoker, this is not necessary.

After 3 hours, take the roast out of the

smoker; place it on some heavy-duty aluminum foil and pour the tomatoes and juice over the roast; seal up the foil and cook it for about 2 more hours.

■    ■    ■

## Grace's Ground Venison Meatloaf

BY GRACE ENGEL

SERVES 4–6
PREP: 10 min.
COOK: 1½ hr.

INGREDIENTS

2 lb. ground venison or other ground meat

1½ c. diced Swiss cheese

2 eggs, beaten

½ c. (or more) chopped onion

1 tsp. salt

½ tsp. pepper

½ tsp. paprika

⅓ tsp. celery salt

1 c. milk

1 c. bread crumbs

DIRECTIONS

In a large bowl, mix all ingredients together. Put in a greased 9×5×3-inch pan or two 7⅜ × 3⅝ × 2¼-inch pans.

Bake at 350°F for 1½ hours or until done. (You can add ketchup on top of loaves before baking, as a variation.)

■    ■    ■

## Stalkers' Red Stag Venison Casserole with Field Mushrooms

*A special recipe from Jule Patterson at Manuka Point Lodge*

SERVES 6
PREP: 30 min.
COOK: 3 hr. 30 min.

INGREDIENTS

5 rashers bacon, chopped

2 medium-sized onions, sliced

4 gloves garlic, crushed (optional)

2 oz. butter

3 lb. prime red stag venison cut into chunky pieces

2 Tbsp. flour

1 c. red wine

1 c. beef stock, or 1 tsp. beef stock powder dissolved in 1 c. water

2 Tbsp. tomato paste or puree

1 tsp. rosemary, thyme, and sage or 1 Tbsp. chopped fresh herbs

1 stick celery, sliced

6–8 small carrots, scrubbed

8 oz. field mushrooms, sliced

chopped parsley

salt and freshly ground black pepper to taste

chopped fresh parsley to garnish

DIRECTIONS

Fry chopped bacon slowly in a large fry pan, extracting as much fat as possible. Remove bacon to a large ovenware casserole, leaving fat in fry pan.

Fry onion and garlic in bacon fat for 5–6 minutes, then remove to casserole dish. Add butter to frying pan.

Dust venison pieces in flour and brown in butter. Add meat to casserole dish.

Swill out pan with red wine, beef stock, or water and stock. Add tomato paste and stir to include all the meat juices and pan scrapings. Pour into casserole. Add herbs, celery and carrots, sliced mushrooms, and salt and pepper to taste.

Place lid on casserole and cook in a slow oven, 300°F, for 3 hours or until meat is really tender. Stir every now and then. To serve, garnish with extra chopped parsley.

Serve with baked potatoes, a side of fresh salads, and lots of crusty bread to mop up all the delicious gravy.

■  ■  ■

## So Good You Can't Stand It Marinated Stuffed Venison

*This is a recipe my dad and I used to prepare after a successful day in the woods, and if not successful, we just hunted the freezer! —Deb Raschella*

SERVES 2–4
PREP: 45 min. + 3 hr. marinate time
COOK: 45 min.–1 hr.

INGREDIENTS
venison (probably a couple of
   tenderloins, more or less!)
6 slices of lean bacon

Ingredients for Marinade
¾ c. vegetable oil
¼ c. honey
2 Tbsp. finely chopped green onions
   + ⅓ c. finely chopped green onions

¼ c. soy sauce
2 Tbsp. vinegar
1 large clove garlic, finely chopped
salt and pepper

DIRECTIONS
Combine all ingredients for marinade and mix well. Cut venison in ¾–1-inch slices. Put in shallow pan and marinade, turning frequently for 3 hours.

Drain marinade from meat. Cook bacon and save the grease for later use.

Cut a pocket in the side of each slice of venison. Mix ⅓ cup green onions with crumbled bacon and stuff in each pocket.

Brown the steaks in the reserved bacon grease. Season to taste with salt and pepper.

Cover and simmer over low heat about 45–60 minutes. If needed, add small amounts of water to keep moisture in.

■  ■  ■

## Speedy Venison Loin Loaf

BY DOUG LOOSE JR.

SERVES 4–6
PREP: 45 min. + 1 hr. or overnight marinate time
COOK: 45 min.

INGREDIENTS
venison loin about 12 inches long
1 bunch green onion (or chives)
1 lb. of your favorite mushrooms
   (I prefer shitake or portabella)
1 lb. smoked bacon
1 16-oz. bottle of your favorite BBQ
   sauce (I make my own)
your favorite dry rub
a box of toothpicks

## DIRECTIONS

Using a very sharp fillet knife, you need to do what I call "unrolling the loin." Start by slicing into the loin lengthwise, about ¼ inch. Turn the knife 90 degrees and continue to slice, rolling the loin away from the blade as you cut. You should end up with a piece of meat that is about ¼–½-inch thick, 12 inches wide, and 18 inches long.

Shake a very thin coating of dry rub on both surfaces of the meat. Roll it back up and place in the fridge, for about an hour or so (over night is best if you plan ahead).

Open the package of bacon. On an 11 × 13-inch cookie sheet, lay the strips crossways on the pan, side by side, until the pan is completely covered. Set aside.

Slice the green onion lengthways into quarters; no need to slice chives if you choose to use them. Slice the mushrooms into 1/8-inch slices.

Take your loin out of the fridge and, on a clean surface, unroll it left to right. It is okay if it comes apart a little; just place the pieces in their correct spot.

Without covering the first or last 2 inches, cover the entire surface with a layer of mushrooms, then a layer of onions.

Roll it back up and place the "loaf" on the bacon-layered cookie sheet lengthways.

One at a time, wrap the bacon strips over the top in sort of a scarf overlap, until all of the strips are wrapped over the loaf. Place a toothpick through each strip of bacon, where it crosses, to hold everything together.

Place in a 400°F preheated oven for 15 minutes.

Turn the oven down to 250°F for an additional 20–25 minutes, depending on the size.

Remove the loaf—or pan of minirolls—and pour the BBQ sauce over the entire loaf.

Return to the oven for about 10–15 minutes or until the sauce starts to caramelize.

Remove and slice into ¾-inch slices and serve.

## Story behind Recipe

The venison tenderloin has long been abused by the traditional hunter. All of us remember going to deer camp, and with any luck, the opening day dinner revolved around the tenderloin of the first deer harvested. The menu was pretty much the same everywhere, with a few local variations. Thinly sliced tenderloin steaks dredged in flour, seasoned, and fried in butter and onions until it was absolutely, without question . . . dead. For a side dish, some sliced potatoes laced with lots of onions, salt, and pepper. A real meat-and-potatoes meal for the men of the woods. While I would not trade those meals for anything, as I grew in age and culture, I soon discovered the similarity between venison loin and the fillet mignon. As a teenager I worked at the local country club, learning how the finest steaks and seafood were prepared. The hunting season of 1986 I embarked on what turned out to be the best, and worst, mistake of my cooking creativity. After bagging a deer late on opening morning, the only deer in camp, I decided to add some culture to the family hunting camp. Not real popular with my father. After at least an hour of intense argument, we agreed that I would cook one loin my way, and he would cook one the right way. I cooked the loin Divan style, with lots of onions and bell peppers and deglazed with burgundy wine. He cooked the traditional shoe-leather butterfly steak. While he refused to taste my creation, at least not while I was there, the entire camp raved about the meal. I was informed 15 years later by my uncle that my dad did indeed try my style and loved it. He still hasn't brought it up, now going on 20 years.

The recipe is a direct result of that experiment, and many more that were tried over the years. Treat venison like beef or pork or chicken, and you will greatly expand the number of friends that truly enjoy eating venison at your gatherings.

■   ■   ■

## Sun-Dried Tomato Venison Burgers with Basil Mayonnaise

BY SHEROL ENGEL

SERVES 4
PREP: 15 min.
COOK: 10 min.

### INGREDIENTS

¼ c. light mayonnaise
1 Tbsp. fresh basil, chopped
½ tsp. finely minced garlic (optional)
salt to taste and freshly ground black
  pepper
1 lb. ground venison
4 dehydrated sun-dried tomatoes, finely
  chopped
4 hamburger rolls
lettuce leaves, for garnish

### DIRECTIONS

Preheat grill to medium-high heat.

In a small mixing bowl, combine the mayonnaise, basil, garlic, salt, and pepper. (The mayonnaise mixture can be made in advance and stored in the refrigerator for up to 2 days.)

In a large bowl, combine the ground venison, sun-dried tomatoes, salt, and pepper. Mix well. Using your hands, lightly shape into four ½-inch thick patties. (Try to leave some air in the burger and avoid packing them too densely.)

Cook the burgers on both sides over the hot grill for about 5–6 minutes per side for medium burgers.

Lightly toast the buns on the grill.

Serve the burgers on toasted buns with basil-mayonnaise and lettuce leaves.

■   ■   ■

## Terrific Taco Pie with Ground Venison

BY THE FULLER FAMILY

SERVES 4–6
PREP: 15 min.
COOK: 50 min.

### INGREDIENTS

1 lb. ground venison
½ onion, chopped
1 package taco seasoning
⅓ c. ripe olives, sliced
1 8-oz. can tomato sauce
1 package crescent rolls or buttermilk
  biscuits
1 c. sour cream
1 c. shredded cheddar cheese
tomato, lettuce, corn chips

## DIRECTIONS

Brown venison with onion. Drain off grease. Stir in taco seasoning, olives, and tomato sauce. Simmer for 15–20 minutes.

Press rolls into greased pie pan (9 inches or larger), covering bottom and sides. Add meat sauce and spread sour cream over top. Cover with shredded cheese.

Bake 20–25 minutes in 400°F oven. May sprinkle crushed corn chips on top for last 5 minutes of baking.

Serve with shredded lettuce and tomato pieces. *Enjoy!*

■   ■   ■

## Venison Burritos

BY SHEROL ENGEL

SERVES 6
PREP: 15 min.
COOK: 20 min.

### INGREDIENTS

For Salsa:

1 small onion, chopped
15 oz. diced canned tomatoes, drained
1½ cloves garlic, peeled
⅔ jalapeño chili pepper, stemmed and seeded
2 Tbsp. chopped, fresh cilantro
1 c. water
salt, to taste
freshly ground black pepper, to taste
sugar—a pinch

For Burritos:

6 large flour tortillas
1 lb. ground venison
salt and pepper, to taste

2 c. cooked white rice
¾ c. sour cream (fat-free or light)
¼ c. fresh cilantro leaves

### DIRECTIONS

*For Salsa.* Combine all the salsa ingredients in a small saucepan. Bring to a boil, adjust the heat so that the mixture simmers, and cook until half of the liquid evaporates, about 15 minutes.

Turn off the heat and let cool.

Pour the cooled mixture into a blender and puree. Chill.

(Salsa can be made in advance and stored in the refrigerator for up to 1 week.)

*For Burritos.* Preheat the oven to 350°F. Wrap the tortillas in foil and warm them in the oven for about 10 minutes.

Brown the ground venison in a large skillet over a medium heat until cooked through.

Break the venison into small pieces as it browns. Drain off any fat and season with salt and pepper.

Meanwhile, reheat the cooked rice in the microwave.

Create your own burritos with venison, rice, salsa, and sour cream. Garnish with extra salsa, sour cream, and cilantro leaves, if desired.

■   ■   ■

## Venison Sauerbraten

SERVES 6
PREP: 45 min. + 3 days marinate time
COOK: 3½ hr.

### INGREDIENTS

3–3½ lb. venison chuck roast
2 onions, sliced

2 bay leaves

12 peppercorns

6 whole cloves

2 tsp. salt

1½ c. red wine vinegar

1 c. boiling water

2 Tbsp. shortening

¾ c. crushed gingersnaps, approx. 12

2 tsp. sugar

## DIRECTIONS

Place venison in glass or ceramic bowl or baking dish with onions, bay leaves, peppercorns, cloves, salt, vinegar, and boiling water.

Cover tightly; refrigerate at least 3 days, turning meat twice a day. Throughout the marinading process, *avoid* piercing the meat!

Drain meat, reserving the marinade. In heavy skillet, brown meat on all sides in shortening. Add marinade mixture. Cover tightly; simmer 3–3½ hours or until meat is tender. Remove meat and onions from skillet and keep warm.

Strain and measure remaining marinade. Add water if needed to measure 2½ cup liquid. Pour liquid into skillet, cover, and simmer 10 minutes.

Stir gingersnaps and sugar into liquid. Cover and simmer for 3 minutes more.

Serve meat and onions on platter with gingersnap gravy.

■   ■   ■

# Easy Venison Stew

BY AL ARNDT

SERVES 4–6
PREP: 25 min.
COOK: 7 hr.

## INGREDIENTS

1 lb. venison, cut up

7 large carrots, peeled and cut into small pieces

5 large potatoes, peeled and quartered

1 tsp. salt

½ tsp. black pepper

1 tsp. garlic powder

2 cans of beefy mushroom soup

1 can of French onion with beef stock

2 4-oz. cans mushrooms—do not drain

¼ c. soy sauce

¼ c. cornstarch

## DIRECTIONS

Mix all ingredients together (except cornstarch) and cook in slow cooker on high for 3 hours and then on low for 4–5 hours more.

Thicken with cornstarch (mix ¼ cup cornstarch and ½ cup cold water until creamy—slowly add to stew).

■   ■   ■

# Wine Marinade for Venison Roast

**SERVES 4–6**
**PREP: 15 min. + overnight marinate time**
**COOK: 2–3 hr.**

## INGREDIENTS

1½ c. burgundy or other red
  dinner wine

1½ tsp. ginger

2 tsp. salt

½ tsp. pepper

¾ tsp. garlic powder

1 Tbsp. instant minced
  onion

1 venison roast, 3–4 lb.

6 strips bacon

½ c. currant jelly (optional)

## DIRECTIONS

Combine ingredients except venison, bacon, and jelly. Pour wine mixture over roast.

Cover and marinate in refrigerator overnight or longer, turning several times.

Drain meat well, reserving marinade. Arrange strips of bacon across meat. Pour ½ cup water in bottom of roasting pan. Roast meat at 450°F until brown, approximately 10 minutes.

Reduce temperature to 325°F; pour part of marinade over meat. Continue roasting until meat reaches desired degree of doneness. Baste with remaining marinade during cooking time, approximately 2–3 hours.

Skim excess fat from pan juices. Melt currant jelly and blend into juices; serve as gravy with meat.

# Bringing 'Em Back

# DREAM HUNT

## Taking Care of Trophies across State Lines or International Date Lines

JOHN JANELLI*

Imagine going back to a time when an average safari would yield anywhere from 30 to 100 separate trophies from just one client. Luminaries such as Ernest Hemmingway kept many foreign and local taxidermists extremely busy in preparing the shipment and mounting of his coveted safari trophies.

By today's prices, Hemingway saved a bundle when you consider that back in 1935, according to Carlos Baker in his book *Ernest Hemmingway: A Life Story*, it cost him just $368.50 to mount an open-mouth lion and leopard skin rug, a roan and sable antelope, and oryx and impala shoulder mounts—and all by one of the nation's premier taxidermists, Jonas Brothers of New York. Those pieces were just several dozens more of what he brought back from this single hunt.

Surely those days are gone forever. In today's world, an overseas hunt requires only a calend ar to set the dates and a credit card to pay for everything in between that time frame. With so many reputable booking agents who have been there and done that for you, most every single risk factor is eliminated, you would think. Yet no amount of planning and customer service can prevent an otherwise great trip from being eroded into a nightmare of red tape or, worse, lost or ruined trophies.

To begin with, decide before you leave, well in advance of departure, just who will mount your prized collection. Not just who the taxidermist will be but where the taxidermist is as well.

The reason for this is that so many outfitters these days seem to take total control of where a client has his or her animals sent either for processing, documentation, or full-scale taxidermy services from crate to wall. For all intended purposes, it becomes just one less thing the client needs to be concerned with. However, with that sentiment comes an extraordinary risk factor as to how well you will enjoy the investment you have made in your hunt.

So to give you, the prospective traveling big game hunter, an inside scoop on the logistics required, none other than the National Taxidermists Association (www.nationaltaxidermists.com) was asked to provide this information with the hopes of obtaining maximum enjoyment from your sporting adventures.

In all probability, you have already seen some kind of animal being processed from field to freezer. If you haven't, make it your business to visit a taxidermist before you embark on your hunt. Remember to be courteous enough to phone in advance for an appointment. This should almost be mandatory before an overseas trip is made and for any hunting trip where a trophy may be harvested.

With the ongoing CWD crisis within our own states these days, there also are more restrictions on transportation of game in the United States. For example, in Pennsylvania a resident deer hunter can no longer just drive home from an out-of-state hunt with his harvested game to be hung and cooled in the backyard. The animal must be processed or, at the very least, skinned, deboned, and all spinal material properly disposed of before the meat can cross state lines. Antlers must now be sawed free from the skull and cleaned from all remaining tissue and flesh.

Once you become familiarized with these essential steps of field care, you will at least know what to look for when you see your guides or skinners at work on your own trophies in the field. These "skinners" are literally worth their weight in gold, as they are not only the ones who have the ability to use an extremely skillful knife, but they know all the adverse effects that stains, dirt, humidity, and most of all, negligence—coupled with improper care— can have on a once-in-a-lifetime trophy.

Too often, once an animal is taken, it's only seen for a relatively short period of time during picture taking and being unloaded after the hunt. That is of course, unless the animal is miles away from camp and inaccessible from roads or waterways. In which case, you become the apprentice on location.

While your guide is making ready the proce-

dures for transportation, take a moment and note any abnormalities of your animal. Perhaps there is some unique feature that you would like accentuated in the finished mount—a torn ear from a previous embattlement, a deeply scarred muzzle, or maybe even some gnarled and broken teeth worthy of reproduction by the taxidermist's art.

Any professional taxidermist can tell you that you must have at your disposal a set of skinning tools containing, at the very minimum, a knife, an ax, or a bone saw. Preferably all three should be designed for no other purpose but field preparation of trophies.

Assuming that your guide knows what he's doing—and in all probability he does—you will still be faced with what to do with the raw materials— that is, cape, skin, skull, antlers—once they are safely secured back at camp. Prepare yourself to hear any number of reasons why you will be asked to leave your trophies behind. The most common is: "It's best you leave your bear and moose with us because it's illegal now to transport them back to the U.S. like this." Interpret this to mean: "There's too much red tape to deal with when we get back into town, so why not just leave everything here with us and we'll let 'our taxidermist' deal with it for you."

Let me state here and now that this in no way reflects upon the quality or standards of foreign taxidermy anywhere but the States. It simply implies that you need to explore and investigate every regulation and law that could allow you, not prohibit you, from taking your skins and skulls home with you, barring, of course, overseas locations.

For example, if you're hunting for fall moose and bears in British Columbia, different regulations apply as opposed to making a plains game hunt in South Africa. While you are entitled to every ounce of wild harvested meat from Canada, the USDA and U.S. Customs prohibit any meat whatsoever to be brought in from your plains game hunt in South Africa.

The knowledge and the laws are easy to obtain

with a simple click of your computer mouse. Keep in mind that this shouldn't be done the night before you leave for the hunt. Rather, it needs to be done months ahead of time, keeping notes on people's names, contact phone numbers, and email addresses. More effective are letters of inquiry and phone calls with key names of the department heads you had dialogue with about your queries.

There are certain states, such as California, that do not allow the importation of mountain lions from any state or country whatsoever. This would mean that a California hunter traveling to Argentina for a red stag should think long and hard about taking a puma as a second trophy, simply because he is restricted from importing the trophy back into his home state where the lion/puma is fully protected.

The same thing holds true for CITES (www .cites.org) animals as well. CITES, which stands for Convention on International Trade in Endangered Species, was conceived in 1963 to regulate the trade in wild animals and plants crossing borders between countries to safeguard certain species from overexploitation.

CITES today accords varying degrees of protection to more than 30,000 species of animals and plants, whether they are traded as trophies, live specimens, fur coats, or dried plants and herbs.

Many an unsuspecting hunter thinks that a CITES animal is only referred to when regarding spotted and striped cats, pachyderms, or marine mammals. While CITES regulations indeed pertain to those species and subspecies as well, they also govern, but are not limited to, many common big game like the North American black bear and the highly sought after bontebok from South Africa.

Therefore, it is imperative to secure all information and permits from both country of export and import pertaining to CITES animals prior to your departure. In addition, don't hesitate to keep in constant contact with your booking agent and

outfitter. Insist on knowing every regulation that can ultimately assist in the expedient release of your trophies or, worst-case scenario, the confiscation of said trophies.

Recently I took clients on a moose and bear hunt in British Columbia where the taking of an elk trophy was equally promising. We were successful. Much communication about elk tag costs and meat shipment was discussed, but as the field taxidermist, I was never told by anyone that a compulsory inspection was mandatory before any elk parts were allowed to leave British Columbia. We found that out only hours before we left for the long drive to the airport and did not arrive to the prescribed inspection station until an hour before midnight. Had we not stopped at the local provincial wildlife office for a friendly visit to be sure we were in compliance with all export laws, we might have had a genuine trophy lost to negligence of the law.

Having trophies shipped in from overseas requires compliance with a whole other set of governmental regulations from the U.S. Department of Agriculture in juncture with the U.S. Fish and Wildlife Service and U.S. Customs.

Of all the safaris I have made over the past 30 years, I have never had one mishap with my clients' trophies with the taxidermists, shipping, and brokerage firms that were employed to get the job done. That was because each time I used a reputable booking agent and a seasoned outfitter who knew what it took not only to keep clients happy but to keep happy clients returning time and time and again.

To import trophies, you must identify every foreseeable problem or concern ahead of time. If hunting for a spotted cat or other species that requires a CITES permit, for example, obtain the permit from the USFWS months before your anticipated travel plans go into effect. Call the brokerage firm of your choice or that of the outfitter's suggestions to get ballpark prices for expediting your trophies home. Decide as soon as possible if you will leave your trophies abroad or if you will have them sent home only in the salt.

Keep in mind that when you have the capes, horns, and skins sent home, you can have one piece mounted at a time or several, depending on your financial situation. Salted and dried skins, when kept in a relatively dry environment, can last almost indefinitely. Those same skins when tanned by a professional tannery will only have a shelf life of about 6 to 12 months before they lose their stretch and subtleness.

In addition, when you have your trophies mounted at home, you control the time factor with regard to delivery and quality control. It's a lot easier taking a short drive to the studio of your choice than to deal with time zone differences and overseas exchange rates.

Very briefly, make sure your outfitter has all bases covered on what you intend to bring home from your hunt by way of trophies or raw materials. Know the laws governing your intended utilization of the wild life resources that you are planning to enjoy. Get yourself acquainted with the mechanics of skinning and disarticulating mammals of the size you might be encountering on your hunt. Involve yourself with the people and the process by which your trophies are made ready for that special trip home. Know that for every regulation there is an interpretation that should only satisfy you coming from those who enforce the law. Why take the word of a crossing guard about a motor vehicle regulation when you should be asking a police officer?

The most important item in a hunting camp in almost unlimited quantities is *salt*. It is virtually impossible to use too much salt on a skin, yet all the salt in the world will not penetrate a folded skin or pounds of flesh and tissue adhering to the hide. Better to have a ton of unused salt and no trophies than one trophy without a pound of salt.

Finally, take care of the people who take care of your trophies. Oprah Winfrey once said that "TIPS" means "Taking Interest in Personal Service." When you are convinced that someone has in fact done just that for you, by all means let it be known by way of some sort of gratuity, either financial or tangible.

While on an African bow hunt for cape buffalo, I found myself on the last day tipping the staff and skinners. I gave every person who made my safari all the more enjoyable some kind of cash appreciation. My personal skinner did the most for me, enabling me to spend more time hunting and less time "working." He spoke no English at all, and when I handed him an American hundred-dollar bill, he gazed upon it in a most perplexing way. Minutes afterward, an elderly woman approached me, handing the money back to me. In perfect English she told me that the skinner had no use for cash but instead would very much like to have some of my buffalo meat for his family and my scalpel handle, along with a few extra blades for it.

After giving him every scalpel handle and about 1,000 extra blades for them that I had, I made arrangements for all my buffalo meat to go to the entire staff and their families. This was done not just from sheer appreciation but also in hopes that the next hunter coming into that camp will be treated even better than I was—if that was at all possible.

Whether it's spike elk from a drop camp across the state line or an Asiatic banteng across the International Date Line, taking care of your trophies is taking care of business that should always be an enjoyable experience. Long after we are gone, our trophies will leave behind a legacy of ourselves that other sport can begin to emulate.

*\*John Janelli works at the National Taxidermists Association.*

# Appendix

# HUNTERS AND SHOOTERS OF THE WORLD

| | COUNTRY | HUNTERS | | | SHOOTERS | | | TOTAL USERS | USERS = 1 INHAB ON : | POPULATION (1992) |
|---|---|---|---|---|---|---|---|---|---|---|
| | | YEAR | NUMBER | SOURCE | YEAR | NUMBER | SOURCE | | | |
| | **FRANCE\*** | 98 | 1479562 | ONC | 99 | 139389 | FFT | **1618951** | 35 | 56700000 |
| | BELGIUM | 97 | 28947 | RSHCB | 98 | 15400 | UNACT | 44347 | 223 | 9900000 |
| | LUXEMBG | 99 | 2141 | Min. Environ. | 87 | 1000 | AFTSC | 3141 | 121 | 380000 |
| E | HOLLAND | 98 | 29752 | KNJV | 2000 | 36000 | KNSA | 65752 | 228 | 15000000 |
| | **RFA\*** | 98 | 339160 | VHJSM | 99 | 1585562 | DSB | **1924722** | 41 | 79500000 |
| | **ITALY\*** | 2000 | 730000 | ANPAM | 99 | 134687 | ANPAM | **864687** | 67 | 57700000 |
| | **U.K.\*** | 97 | 719000 | BSSC | 97 | 225000 | BSSC | **944000** | 61 | 57500000 |
| U | IRELAND | 95 | 120000 | FACE | | | | 120000 | 29 | 3500000 |
| | **DENMARK\*** | 2000 | 175000 | DSSA | 96 | 180000 | DSSA | **355000** | 14 | 5100000 |
| | **SPAIN\*** | 98 | 1200000 | A.Armera | 96 | 58953 | Stat. Sport | **1258953** | 31 | 39000000 |
| | **PORTUGAL\*** | 98 | 231246 | Ambas-sade | 95 | 13500 | AFTSC | **244746** | 42 | 10400000 |
| R | GREECE | 95 | 293000 | Stat. Agri | 95 | 7000 | AFTSC | 300000 | 34 | 10100000 |
| | TOTAL U.E.(12) | | 5347808 | | | 2396491 | | 7744299 | 45 | 344780000 |
| | **AUSTRIA** | 97 | 110000 | Stat. Agri | 97 | 10000 | Steyr | **120000** | 64 | 7700000 |
| | SWEDEN | 97 | 310000 | FACE | 97 | 200000 | AFEMS | 510000 | 17 | 8600000 |
| O | FINLAND | 97 | 291738 | Stat. Agri | 97 | 200000 | AECAC | 491738 | 10 | 5000000 |
| | **TOTAL UE (15)** | | **6059546** | | | **2806491** | | **8866037** | **41** | **366080000** |
| | NORWAY | 98 | 180000 | AFEMS | 98 | 170000 | AFEMS | 350000 | 12 | 4300000 |
| P | SWITZERLAND | 98 | 32000 | AFEMS | 98 | 250000 | AFEMS | 282000 | 24 | 6800000 |
| | HUNGARY | 98 | 48000 | AFEMS | 98 | 5000 | AFEMS | 53000 | 196 | 10400000 |
| | REP. CZECH | 99 | 233700 | Czmanu-fact. | 96 | 16300 | IEACS | 250000 | 63 | 15700000 |
| | POLAND | 94 | 98747 | FACE | ? | 2000 | AFEMS | 100747 | 379 | 38200000 |
| E | RUSSIA | 99 | 2454000 | Baïkal | 99 | 2618 | Baïkal | 2456618 | 61 | 150000000 |
| | UKRAINE | 99 | 346000 | Baïkal | 99 | 3050 | Baïkal | 349050 | 148 | 51700000 |
| | SLOVENIA | 94 | 22734 | FACE | ? | 3000 | AFEMS | 25734 | 74 | 1914000 |
| | BULGARY | 94 | 3846 | Stat.Sport | | | | 3846 | 1820 | 7000000 |
| | MALTA | 95 | 12000 | FACE | | | | 12000 | 33 | 400000 |
| | TOTAL EUR. OTH. | | 3431027 | | | 451968 | | 3882995 | 74 | 286414000 |
| | **EUROPE total** | | **9490573** | | | **3258459** | | **12749032** | **51** | **652494000** |
| A | **BRAZIL \*** | | | | | | | **0** | | 153000000 |
| M | **CANADA\*** | 98 | 2500000 | CILA | 98 | 6000000 | CILA | **8500000** | 3 | 26800000 |
| E | **USA\*** | 98 | **19000000** | NSSF | 98 | **18500000** | NSSF | **37500000** | 7 | 252800000 |
| R | | | | | | | | | | |
| I | | | | | | | | | | |
| C | | | | | | | | | | |
| A | | | | | | | | | | |
| | **AMERICA total** | | **21500000** | | | **24500000** | | **46000000** | **9** | **432600000** |

| | COUNTRY | YEAR | HUNTERS NUMBER | SOURCE | YEAR | SHOOTERS NUMBER | SOURCE | TOTAL USERS | | USERS = 1 INHAB ON : | POPULATION (1992) |
|---|---|---|---|---|---|---|---|---|---|---|---|
| A | **STH AFRICA*** | 98 | 100000 | SAGA | 98 | 30000 | SAGA | **130000** | | 312 | 40600000 |
| F | MAROC | ? | 20000 | Chas.Fr. | | | | 20000 | | 1310 | 26200000 |
| R | SENEGAL | ? | 2000 | Chas.Fr. | | | | 2000 | | 3750 | 7500000 |
| I | BURKINA-FASO | ? | 6000 | Chas.Fr. | | | | 6000 | | 1567 | 9400000 |
| C | TCHAD | ? | 4500 | Chas.Fr. | | | | 4500 | | 1133 | 5100000 |
| A | | | | | | | | | | | |
| | **AFRICA total** | | **132500** | | | **30000** | | **162500** | | 546 | **88800000** |
| A | JAPAN | 99 | 191282 | A.Armera | 99 | 30000 | A.Armera | 221282 | 11/00 | 559 | 123800000 |
| S | KOREA STH | 99 | 40000 | ELEY | 99 | 6000 | ELEY | 46000 | | 939 | 43200000 |
| I | THAILAND | | | | 99 | 5000 | ELEY | 5000 | | 11760 | 58800000 |
| A | | | | | | | | | | | |
| | **ASIA total** | | **231282** | | | **41000** | | **272282** | | 829 | **225800000** |
| O | **AUSTRALIA*** | 98 | 600000 | SSAA | 98 | 177000 | SSAA | **777000** | | 23 | 17500000 |
| C | **N ZEALAND*** | 97 | 113700 | NZSSA | 97 | 10500 | NZSSA | **124200** | | 28 | 3500000 |
| E | | | | | | | | | | | |
| A | | | | | | | | | | | |
| N | | | | | | | | | | | |
| I | | | | | | | | | | | |
| A | | | | | | | | | | | |
| | **OCEANIA total** | | **713700** | | | **187500** | | **901200** | | 23 | **21000000** |

| | | | | | | | | | | |
|---|---|---|---|---|---|---|---|---|---|---|
| **WORLD known** | 32068055 | 53% | 28016959 | 47% | 60085014 | 86% | | 1420694000 |
| **WFSA MEMB.** | 27297668 | 50% | 27064591 | 50% | 54362259 | 78% | | 800100000 |
| | | | | | | | | |
| Unknown | 5291741 | 53% | 4623245 | 47% | 9914986 | 14% | | 3939517477 |
| **Est. WORLD tot.** | 37359796 | 53% | 32640204 | 47% | 70000000 | 100% | | 5360211477 |

Source: Chart courtesy of World forum on the Future of Sport Shooting Activities.

# Resources

## GENERAL READING

*In Defense of Hunting*, by James Swan (HarperCollins, 1994).

Designed to help hunters understand their passion and better communicate why they hunt, it is a comprehensive psychology of hunting. "One of the best books in print"—*New York Review of Books*.

*Know Hunting: Truths, Lies and Myths*, by Dr. David E. Samuel (Know Hunting Publications, 1999).

An excellent presentation of the biology, sociology, and politics of hunting by a noted former professor of wildlife management.

*Meditations on Hunting*, by José Ortega y Gasset (Scribners, 1986).

The Spanish philosopher Ortega y Gasset has captured the spirit of the hunt in his poetic prose.

*The Sacred Art of Hunting*, by James Swan (Willow Creek Press, 1999).

Examines mythology, folklore, and religious traditions all around the world, showing how at every step of the hunt guidance leads the ethical hunter to make hunting profoundly spiritual.

*A Sand County Almanac*, by Aldo Leopold (Oxford University Press, 1949).

If you are going to read one book about the guiding spirit of conservation, read this one.

## RESOURCE READING

*Black's Wing and* Clay, (Masters Press, annual).

An annual guide to wing shooting that provides the latest information on equipment, instruction, and destinations for clay shooting and wing shooting.

*The Hunter's Guide*, by National Rifle Association (NRA, 1998).

All the basics you need to know to become an ethical hunter.

## RESOURCE VIDEOS AND DVDS

*Conquering Buck Fever: With Sports Psychology Techniques*, by James Swan, Ph.D. (Snow Goose Productions, 56 min.)

Draws on modern sports psychology to give hunters a number of practical techniques to manage the natural excitement of hunting and turn buck fever into shooting in "the zone." Includes appearances by Ted Nugent, Dave Watson, Jeff and Sherol Engel, Kim Rhode, and Lily Sieu. Available from Snow Goose Productions at www.jamesswan.com/snowgoosecp.html.

*A Question of Balance* (Snow Goose Productions, 56 min.).

On May 1–2, 2003, the World Forum on the Future of Sport Shooting Activities (www.wfsa.net) hosted an international firearms scholars' symposium titled "The Legal, Economic and Human Rights Implications of Civilian Firearms Ownership and Regulation" at the Tower of London in London, England. Over eight hours of presentations have been distilled from that program to become a 56-minutes-long DVD that includes numerous graphics, video footage, and photos, plus a special 13-minute overview of major topics covered. Available from Snow Goose Productions at www.jamesswan.com/snowgoosecp.html.

## GOOD HUNTING MOVIES

No better way to keep the hunting instinct fired up between seasons than to go down to the video store, rent a video or two, and enjoy it with the family and a bucket of popcorn. Don't just enjoy these films, folks—support them and tell others about them. The more successful such films are, the more people who fund films will want to make more.

*Atanarjuat: The Fast Runner* (2001).

Winner of six Genie Awards (Canadian Oscar) and numerous other awards, this Inuit story is Canada's first feature-length film written, directed, and acted by Inuit.

*The Clan of the Cave Bear* (1985).

Based on the best-selling book by Jean Auel, *The Clan* shows a strong woman, Ayala, who is banned from her clan because she wants to hunt. The story is set in Paleolithic times, but the immense popularity of the book and the movie show that when hunting is woven into a good story, many people will enjoy it even if they have no experience with hunting.

*Dances with Wolves* (1990).

Winner of seven Academy Awards, including Best Picture and Best Director. The heart of Kevin Costner's masterpiece saga about a soldier's desire to see the Old West is an Indian buffalo hunt. Ethical hunters are very definitely the heroes here, and we get a taste of the awful carnage caused by market hunting.

*Davy Crockett: King of the Wild Frontier* (1955).

Walt Disney may have given us *Bambi*, but he balanced things with his Davy Crockett series (*The River Pirates*, *Indian Scout*), starring Fess Parker, with a hunter hero that the world fell in love with.

*Dersu Uzala* (1975).

Akira Kurosawa gave us one of the most touching stories of hunting ever told on the screen. A native hunter rescues a Russian army explorer in the Siberian wilderness. When the hunter follows the explorer back to modern civilization, he discovers his woods lore is of little value, which shows how alienated modern society is from nature and human nature. It won an Oscar for Best Foreign Language Picture.

*The Edge* (1997).

Written by David Mamet, this tale begins with a billionaire bookaholic (Anthony Hopkins) and his trophy wife model who go to a resort in Canada for a photo shoot. The wife and the photographer are having an affair. When the husband and photographer go off on a plane ride to scout a location, the plane crashes, and they are lost. In the long journey back, they are pursued by a huge bear who steals the show.

*Escanaba in Da Moonlight* (2001).

An uproarious, slapstick comedy set in a northern Michigan deer hunting camp, written, directed, produced, and starring Jeff Daniels. See www.escanabathemovie.com.

*The Ghost and the Darkness* (1996).

Inspired by the book *The Man-Eaters of Tsavo*. Some lions become serial killers, preying on construction crews who are building an East African railroad, and must be stopped. Winner of one Academy Award and starring Val Kilmer and Michael Douglas, the wildlife photography and sound track are as outstanding as the story.

*Gosford Park* (2001).

An award-winning story of a weekend pheasant shoot in the British countryside that is a social commentary, with hunting being the "McGuffin," or reason, for the story to take place.

*In the Blood* (1989).

George Butler's *In the Blood* is a superb docudrama about a group of modern hunters who follow in the footsteps of Teddy Roosevelt's 1909 African safari to seek out the spirit of the hunt in modern life. You can rent this through some video stores, or buy copies for $19.95 by calling 1-800-626-4277.

*Jeremiah Johnson* (1972).

Robert Redford stars in this nineteenth-century tale by John Milius of a man who turns his back on civilization and learns to survive in the wilds.

*King Solomon's Mines* (1937).

An epic saga of a safari in search of the fabled diamond mines of Africa. As the party treks across the Dark Continent, they must face unruly natives, sandstorms, and many wild animals. The old wildlife footage captures the golden age of African hunting safaris, and the animals killed are for real.

*Kiran over Mongolia* (2006).

An extraordinary coming-of-age story in Mongolia of a teenage boy who wants to become an eagle hunter. We see him catch his bird, train his eagle, and make his first kill on a fox. Mongolian music and spectacular scenes make this unforgettable.

*The Last Safari* (1967).

Stewart Granger stars as an ethical African professional hunter who retires from being a guide but decides to go on a last hunt to track down a rogue elephant that killed his partner.

*Out of Africa* (1985).

Robert Redford and Meryl Streep star in this turn-of-the-century romantic tale about a European woman moving to Africa and falling in love with a big game hunter. Don't forget your handkerchief.

*Pathfinder* (1987).

The reindeer herding Saami, or Lapps, of northern Scandinavia are dependent on hunting, fishing, and reindeer herding for survival, living off the land in *lavuu*, which are like teepees. Beautifully shot, written, and directed by Nils Gaup, a Saami. If you love wild places and native people, see this northern Scandinavian epic based on a Saami legend.

*The Snow Walker* (2003).

Set in northern Canada in 1953, "Charlie Halliday" (Barry Pepper), is a cocky bush pilot sent on an assignment to drop off people and fuel in a remote tundra area. When he lands, a group of Inuit appear and persuade him to take an Inuit woman with TB to get medical care in Yellowknife. On the way back, the plane crashes, and they have to try to survive. The caribou hunting scenes are fabulous.

*Tembo* (1951).

   *Tembo* is a feature film documentary describing Howard Hill's African safari to kill an elephant with a long bow. Funded in part by Hill's hunting buddy Errol Flynn, it was an immensely successful picture. Copies of "Tembo" are available from Hill's nephew Jerry. The cost is $20.00, plus shipping. Order by calling 1-205-669-6134 or Jerry Hill Longbow Co., 515 McGowan Rd., Wilsonville, AL 35186.

*Will Penny* (1968).

   Charleton Heston plays a range-wandering loner who escapes from a family of outlaws by re-treating to the wilderness to become a hunter-trapper. Outstanding cinematography. Heston considers this his personal best work.

*The Wind and the Lion* (l975).

   Based on a turn-of-the-century true story about an American woman (Candace Bergen) and her two children who are kidnapped by a Moroc-can rebel (Sean Connery) and Teddy Roosevelt's (Brian Keith) strategy to get her free. The picture gives us some real quality time with TR, including when he hunts and kills a monster grizzly, which he then has stuffed and displayed in the White House.

# RESOURCES

## ONLINE DIRECTORIES OF PLACES TO HUNT

Hunting and fishing guides for North America: www.hunting-fishing-guides.com

Hunting directory for southern Africa: www.hunt ingfinder.com

Hunting Trips R-Us: Directory of hunting guides and outfitters for North America at www.hun tingtripsrus.com/index.html

National directory of upland bird hunting clubs in all States, Canada, and the United Kingdom: www.gamebirdhunts.com

Online shooting-hunting directory (worldwide): www.shooting-hunting.com

Web site with many links to shooting ranges and places to hunt throughout the United States: www.huntandshoot.org

WingshootingUSA.org: www.wingshootingusa.org is a free online directory of places to hunt birds

## INTERNET RESOURCES

African hunting information newsletters: see www.africanindaba.co.za/news.htm and http://africanhuntinginfo.com/register.php

The Bowsite: The premier Web site for bow hunt-ers; see www.bowsite.com

Dr. Dave Samuel's Web site: Dr. Samuel spent 30 years as a professor of wildlife management at West Virginia University; a bowhunter for over 50 years, he has been the conservation editor of *Bowhunter* magazine since 1971; see www .knowhunting.com

HuntersPro.com: International Web site seeking to support sustainable hunting around the world; see www.hunterspro.com

HuntInfo.com: Access to all 50 official wildlife agency Web sites—find state-specific hunting information on season dates, application dead-lines, license fees, hunter education classes, and more at www.huntinfo.org

*The Hunting Report*: A subscription-based news-letter for international travelers where hunters from around the world write reviews of their hunts, outfitters, and guides; see www.huntin greport.com/current_issue.cfm?id=120

Jim Powlesland's Hunting Page: A treasure chest of information and links, especially in Canada but including a good deal in the United States, with a number of quotes about philosophy and ethics;

see www.ucalgary.ca/~powlesla/personal/hunting/hunting.html.

## LIST OF HUNTING AND WILDLIFE CONSERVATION ORGANIZATIONS

### Europe

**CIC—INTERNATIONAL COUNCIL FOR GAME AND WILDLIFE CONSERVATION H-2092 BUDAKESZI**
Post Office Box 82
Hungary
Phone: +36 23 453 830; fax: +36 23 453 832
www.cic-wildlife.org

**COUNTRYSIDE ALLIANCE**
The Old Town Hall
367 Kennington Road
London SE11 4PT England
Phone: 020 7840 9200 or 020 7793 8484
www.countryside-alliance.org

**FACE—FEDERATION ASSOCIATION DE CHASSEURS DE EUROPE**
rue F. Pelletier
82-1030 Brussels, Belgium
Phone: +32.2.732 69 00;
fax: +32.2.732 70 72
www.face-europe.org/fs-home.htm

### United States— National/International

**CONSERVATION FORCE**
3240 South I-10 Service Road West, Suite 200
Metairie, LA 70001-6911
Phone: 504-837-1233
www.conservationforce.org

**IWMC—WORLD CONSERVATION TRUST**
*U.S. Office:*
1470 Heather Ridge Boulevard, Unit 104
Dunedin, FL 34698
Phone/fax: 727-734-4949
www.iwmc.org

**SAFARI CLUB INTERNATIONAL**
4800 West Gates Pass Road
Tucson, AZ 85745-9490
Phone: 520-620-1220; fax: 520-622-1205
www.scifirstforhunters.org

### United States—National

**DELTA WATERFOWL**
*U.S. Office:*
Post Office Box 3128
Bismarck, ND 58502
Phone: 888-987-3695
www.deltawaterfowl.org
*Canada Office:*
Unit 22-62 Scurfield Boulevard.
Winnipeg, MB R3Y 1M5
Phone: 877-667-5656

**DUCKS UNLIMITED**
One Waterfowl Way
Memphis, TN 38120
Phone: 800-45DUCKS or 901-758-3825
www.ducks.org

**FARMERS AND HUNTERS FEEDING THE HUNGRY**
Post Office Box 323
Williamsport, MD 21795
Phone: 866-GET-FHFH;
fax: 301-745-6337
www.fhfh.org

**FOUNDATION FOR NORTH AMERICAN
WILD SHEEP**
720 Allen Avenue
Cody, WY 82414-3402
Phone: 307-527-6261; fax: 307-527-7117
www.fnaws.org

**NATIONAL SHOOTING
SPORTS FOUNDATION**
Flintlock Ridge Office Center
11 Mile Hill Road
Newtown, CT 06470-2359
Phone: 203-426-1320; fax: 203-426-1087
www.nssf.org

**NATIONAL RIFLE ASSOCIATION**
11250 Waples Mill Road
Fairfax, VA 22030
Phone: 800-423-6894; fax: 703-267-3985
www.nra.org

**NATIONAL WILD TURKEY FEDERATION**
770 Augusta Road
Post Office Box 530
Edgefield, SC 29824-0530
Phone: 800-THE-NWTF; fax: 803-637-0034
www.nwtf.com

**NORTH AMERICAN HUNTING CLUB**
12301 Whitewater Doctor
Minnetonka, MN 55343
Phone: 952-936-9333
www.huntingclub.com

**PHEASANTS FOREVER AND
QUAIL FOREVER**
1783 Buerkle Circle
St. Paul, MN 55110
Phone: 651-773-2000 or 877-773-2070;
fax: 651-773-5500
www.pheasantsforever.org

**QUAIL UNLIMITED**
Post Office Box 610
Edgefield, SC 29824
Phone: 803-637-5731
www.qu.org

**ROCKY MOUNTAIN ELK FOUNDATION**
5705 Grant Creek Road
Missoula, MT 59808
Phone: 800-CALL ELK (800-225-5355)
or 406-523-4500; fax: 406-523-4550
www.rmef.org

**TED NUGENT UNITED SPORTSMEN
OF AMERICA**
4008 West Michigan Avenue
Jackson, MI 49202
Phone: 517-750-9060; fax: 517-750-3640
www.tnugent.com/about_tnusa/index.shtml

**U.S. SPORTSMEN'S ALLIANCE**
801 Kingsmill Parkway
Columbus, OH 43229
Phone: 614-888-4868
www.ussportsmen.org

# Index

*"And remember, every time you go into the field, you want to take out something with you. It doesn't always have to be something in your game bag—it could simply be coming out with the Outdoor Experience."*